THE ORIGINS OF VICTORY

T0327125

THE
ORIGINS
OF
VICTORY

How Disruptive Military Innovation
Determines the Fates of Great Powers

ANDREW F.
KREPINEVICH, JR.

Yale
UNIVERSITY PRESS

New Haven and London

Yale University Press books may be purchased in quantity for
educational, business, or promotional use. For information, please
e-mail sales.press@yale.edu (U.S. office) or sales@yaleup.co.uk
(U.K. office).

Set in Janson type by IDS Infotech Ltd.
Printed in the United States of America.

Library of Congress Control Number: 2022934808
ISBN 978-0-300-23409-1 (hardcover : alk. paper)
ISBN 978-0-300-28009-8 (paperback)
A catalogue record for this book is available from the British Library.

10 9 8 7 6 5 4 3 2 1

For Julia
My One and Only

With regard to estimating military power there seem to be only problems and very few, well-accepted adequate methods of making such estimates. There are conceptual problems in defining appropriate measures of military power, and many practical problems in carrying out even those partial formulations that seem appropriate. Indeed there are so many problems and difficulties that I can touch on only a few of them.

—ANDREW W. MARSHALL

Contents

Acknowledgments

THIS BOOK IS THE product of many years of research and reflection, benefiting along the way from the inspiration, mentorship, and support of many colleagues. They are too numerous to mention, so I must limit specific acknowledgments to those who had the greatest direct bearing on this book. Whatever shortcomings this work may contain, they would have been far greater had it not been for the kindness and support of many colleagues, friends, and my family.

My work in the security studies field has benefited enormously from having the privilege of serving a full career in the world's finest army. The experience of working with men and women in uniform, from all services and in all ranks, provided me with an understanding of military organizations. It also gave me a deep admiration and appreciation for those service members who chose to endure hardship and family separation while declaring their willingness, if need be, to make the ultimate sacrifice to defend their fellow citizens' security and freedom.

I was blessed to have been assigned for four years during my military career to the Social Sciences Department at West Point. My service there set the foundation for all that was to follow in my work in the field of security studies. Under the inspired leadership of Brigadier General Lee Donne Olvey, faculty members were told to "be kind" to one another and that any "surprises" we might have to share with him would not improve with age. He assumed, correctly, that the officers he recruited would strive for excellence in every aspect of their duties. While on the faculty, I was most fortunate to have three mentors, Colonels George Osborn and William Taylor and Lieutenant Colonel Tom Johnson, who encouraged me to expand my intellectual horizons while guiding me along the path to completing my dissertation.

As the reader will no doubt infer from this book, Andrew Marshall has been by far my principal intellectual mentor, as well as one of our country's greatest and most underappreciated strategists and public servants of the post–World War II era. For more than thirty years, I was the very fortunate beneficiary of his wisdom, kindness, and encouragement. His mark is on all that is of value in this book.

My work for the Office of Net Assessment over the years has also made me the beneficiary of intellectual encounters with many of its alumni, among them Eliot Cohen, Fred Downey, Aaron Friedberg, Karl Hasslinger, Andrew May, James Roche, Stephen Peter Rosen, Paul Selva, and Barry Watts.

This book benefited from the insights, wisdom, and encouragement of my colleagues at the Center for Strategic and Budgetary Assessments, which I founded and where I spent more than twenty years of my professional career. Among those whose great kindness and strength of character were matched only by the power of their intellects and willingness to aid in my intellectual growth are Steve Kosiak, Robert Martinage, John Stillion, Jim Thomas, Jan van Tol, Michael Vickers, Barry Watts, and Robert Work.

This book also benefited greatly from exchanges with colleagues who patiently listened to—and often improved on—my ruminations on disruptive innovation, among them Ross Babbage, J. R. Backschies, Jim Baker, Admiral (Retired) John Harvey, Nobukatsu Kanehara, Andrew May, Admiral (Retired) William Moran, Major General (Retired) Rick Olson, and Admiral (Retired) John Richardson. I am especially indebted to Philip Bilden, Christopher Bowie, Michael Scott Brown, Elbridge Colby, Lieutenant General (Retired) David Deptula, Captain (Retired) Karl Hasslinger, Nicholas Lambert, Colonel (Retired) James McDonough, and Robert Stevens for reviewing drafts of the book, in part or in whole, and providing thoughtful and constructive criticism along with much-needed encouragement.

For nearly thirty years, most of my intellectual efforts, including the writing of this book, have been enabled by the generous support provided by the Smith Richardson Foundation. I owe a tremendous debt to its chairman, Peter Richardson, and its board, which in 1993 took a chance on a newly retired army lieutenant colonel who aspired to establish a public policy institute that would apply Andrew Marshall's net assessment methodology to reach a wider audience.

I am especially grateful to the foundation's senior vice president and program officer, Dr. Marin Strmecki, who for three decades has been an inexhaustible wellspring of wise counsel, thoughtful criticism, and constant encouragement. His ability to pose the "right questions"—to identify issues of strategic significance meriting inspection—and to match them with those in the strategic studies community who are most capable of addressing them, is beyond value. Like Andrew Marshall, he is one of our country's hidden treasures.

Thanks are also owed to my agent, Eric Lupfer, who patiently took my idea for a book and worked diligently with me to shape and reshape the proposal until it was ready to be submitted to publishers. Eric then found a perfect match for the project in Yale University Press. This is my third book with Eric, a partnership I have come to cherish.

Special thanks are also in order for my editors at Yale. Joseph Calamia and, following his departure, Jaya Chatterjee and Eva Skewes have provided just the right amount of friendly prodding and encouragement throughout a three-year collaboration. My gratitude also extends to Phillip King and Andrew Katz, whose editing greatly enhanced the manuscript. The book's index was superbly crafted by Alexa Selph, who imposed organization on a wide range of topics. For that I am very much in her debt.

My work on this book also benefited greatly from the efforts of Katherine Dougherty and Michael Krepinevich, who typed and retyped versions of this manuscript more times than they would like to remember, with Michael also providing fact-checking and editorial support.

Progress in endeavors such as this book make considerable demands on the home front. In this regard, I have been blessed by a supportive family. My three children, Jennifer, Andrew, and Michael; Andrew's wife, Nikki; and our grandchildren, Katherine, Sean, Alexandra, Meaghan, and Casey, have been a constant source of joy, encouragement, and support, while displaying remarkable patience. Indeed, during the past three years, the grandkids, upon their arrival at our home, no longer ask, "Where's Grandpa?" They just come straight to my office.

There is also the empty chair at our family table. Not a day goes by when I do not think of young Drew. He continues inspiring me to make the most of the opportunities I have that were denied to him.

At the center of it all, as she has been through our lifelong journey, now in its fiftieth year, is Julia, my one and only. In recent years, she has advised me to undertake projects that are more a "labor of love" than "hard labor." As so often in the past, I am the beneficiary of her wisdom. I dedicate this book to her.

Abbreviations

AAA	anti-aircraft artillery
AAM	air-to-air missile
ADC	Air Defense Command
AFB	Air Force Base
AGM	air-to-ground missile
AI	artificial intelligence
AIM	air intercept missile
AM	additive manufacturing
AMRAAM	Advanced Medium-Range Air-to-Air Missile
APT	advanced persistent threat
ARM	anti-radiation missile
ASAT	anti-satellite
ASW	anti-submarine warfare
ATO	Air Tasking Order
A2/AD	anti-access/area-denial
AWACS	Airborne Warning and Control System
Azon	azimuth only (glide bomb)
BDA	battle damage assessment
BDS	BeiDou Satellite System
BGV	boost-glide vehicle
BLU	bomb live unit
BuAer	Bureau of Aeronautics
BuNav	Bureau of Navigation
BVR	beyond visual range
C2	command and control
C4	command, control, communications, computers
CAA	Civil Aeronautics Authority
CAD	computer-aided design
CAS	close air support

Cas9   CRISPR-associated protein 9
CCP   Chinese Communist Party
CEP   circular error probable
CHAMP   Counter-electronics High-powered Microwave Advanced
              Missile Project
CHASE   Cyber Hunting at Scale
CID   Committee of Imperial Defence
CNO   chief of naval operations
CRISPR   Clustered Regularly Interspaced Short Palindromic Repeats
CSBA   Center for Strategic and Budgetary Assessments
CV   aircraft carrier
CVE   escort carrier
CVL   light carrier
DACT   dissimilar air combat training
DARPA   Defense Advanced Research and Projects Agency
DE   directed energy
DIB   defense industrial base
DNA   deoxyribonucleic acid
DNI   director of national intelligence
DRM   Defense Reform Movement
DRFM   digital radio frequency memory
ECCM   electronic counter-countermeasures
ECM   electronic countermeasures
EM   electromagnetic
EMCON   emissions control
EMP   electromagnetic pulse
EW   electronic warfare
FAC   forward air controller
FARP   forward arming and refueling point
FBIS   U.S. Foreign Broadcast Information Service
GBU   guided bomb unit
GEO   geosynchronous Earth orbit (also geostationary equatorial
              orbit)
GLONASS   Global Navigation Satellite System (Russia)
GPS   Global Positioning System
G-RAMM   guided rockets, artillery, mortars, and missiles
HARM   High-Speed Anti-Radiation Missile
HCM   hypersonic cruise missile
HMS   His/Her Majesty's Ship
HPM   high-powered microwave
IADS   integrated air defense system
IAF   Israeli Air Force
IAMDS   integrated air and missile defense system
ICBM   intercontinental ballistic missile

IDF	Israeli Defense Force
IED	improvised explosive device
IFF	Identification Friend or Foe
IJN	Imperial Japanese Navy
IoT	internet of things
IR	infrared
ISR	intelligence, surveillance, and reconnaissance
IT	information technology
JADC2	Joint All-Domain Command and Control
JAM-JC	Joint Concept for Access and Maneuver in the Global Commons
JASSM	Joint Air-to-Surface Standoff Missile
JASSM-ER	Joint Air-to-Surface Standoff Missile, Extended Range
JDAM	Joint Direct Attack Munition
JFCOM	Joint Forces Command
JSOW	Joint Standoff Weapon
JSTARS	Joint Surveillance Target Attack Radar System
LANTIRN	Low-Altitude Navigation and Targeting Infrared for Night
LEO	low-Earth orbit
LGB	laser-guided bomb
LRRDPP	Long-Range Research and Development Planning Program
MAC	Military Airlift Command
MAD	mutual assured destruction
MALD	Miniature Air-Launched Decoy
MCF	Military-Civil Fusion
MEO	mid-Earth orbit
MOE	measure of effectiveness
MICOM	Missile Command
MIRACL	Mid-Infrared Advanced Chemical Laser
MIT	Massachusetts Institute of Technology
MRAP	mine-resistant, ambush-protected
MTR	military-technical revolution
NACA	National Advisory Committee for Aeronautics
NASA	National Aeronautics and Space Administration
NATO	North Atlantic Treaty Organization
NCO	noncommissioned officer
NID	Naval Intelligence Department
NIST	National Institute of Standards and Technology
NRO	National Reconnaissance Office
NSTAC	National Security Telecommunications Advisory Committee
ONA	Office of Net Assessment
PAVN	People's Army of Vietnam
PGM	precision-guided munition
PLA	People's Liberation Army

PLAAF	People's Liberation Army Air Force
PLARF	People's Liberation Army Rocket Force
PLASSF	People's Liberation Army Strategic Support Force
PNT	precision navigation and timing
QC	quantum computing
RAF	Royal Air Force
Razon	range and azimuth only (guided weapon)
RMA	revolution in military affairs
RNA	ribonucleic acid
RNAS	Royal Naval Air Service
RPV	remotely piloted vehicle
RSC	reconnaissance-strike complex
SA	situation awareness
SAC	Strategic Air Command
SAM	surface-to-air missile
SAR	synthetic aperture radar
SEAD	suppression of enemy air defenses
SM	subtractive manufacturing
SSGN	submarine, guided missile, nuclear-powered
SSL	solid-state laser
SSN	submarine, nuclear powered, attack
TAC	Tactical Air Command
Tarzon	Tallboy Azimuth and Range Only (guided weapon)
TISEO	Target Identification System Electro-Optical
TSTC	Time-Sensitive Targeting Cell
UAV	unmanned aerial vehicle
UUV	unmanned underwater vehicle
VPAF	Vietnamese People's Air Force
WPTO	Western Pacific Theater of Operations

THE ORIGINS OF VICTORY

PART I

Introduction

THERE IS A DISRUPTIVE shift under way in the character of warfare, sometimes referred to as a military revolution. Similar revolutions have occurred before, but rapid advances in a wide range of technologies over the past two centuries have increased their frequency. As the term suggests, militaries that identify and exploit these periods of disruptive change realize quantum leaps in effectiveness that can result in a major shift in the balance of power, with all its attendant consequences for the security and prosperity of their nations.

The most recent military revolution, the Precision-Warfare Revolution, finds battle networks directing and coordinating extended-range scouting and strike forces—functioning together in what Russian military theorists call a "reconnaissance-strike complex." This revolution was introduced in nascent form by the U.S. military in the First Gulf War. Following the collapse of the Soviet Union, for roughly two decades the Americans stood alone in their ability to wage precision warfare. Now, however, the precision-warfare regime is reaching its mature stage. Other military powers, China especially, have acquired most of the capabilities that enabled the U.S. military's dominance. For the Americans, it's a whole new ballgame.

In at least one respect, the new era of great-power rivalry finds the U.S. military at a disadvantage, as it has spent the better part of three decades perfecting ways of waging war against minor powers such as Iraq and terrorist groups such as al-Qaeda. Meanwhile, the Chinese and Russian militaries have invested that time figuring out how to wage war against the U.S. military. In particular, they have focused on defeating the U.S. military's ability to project power. This has primarily taken the form of so-called anti-access/area-denial (A2/AD) reconnaissance-strike (or "recce-strike") complexes. Put another way, the Chinese and the Russians have been looking to the future, while the Americans have been accumulating experience waging war in what they term "permissive" environments, where they operate at relatively little risk to themselves—environments that will be absent in any great-power war.

Even as the precision-warfare regime matures, a new military revolution is emerging. As with most such revolutions over the past two centuries, this one is enabled by advances in a range of commercial technologies—among them artificial intelligence, additive ("3D") manufacturing, synthetic biology, and quantum computing—as well as military-driven technologies, including directed energy and hypersonic weapons. This new revolution's pace is being accelerated by the growing intensity of the competition between the United States and the two revisionist great powers, China and Russia.

Disruptive shifts in war's character are a matter of strategic significance. History shows that a military that first masters the new form of warfare enjoys a clear and potentially decisive advantage over its rivals. The mid-1860s found Prussia exploiting its railway system to speed its armies' mobilization and deployment, and its telegraph system to better coordinate their movements. Along with the Dreyse needle gun, they formed the foundation of the "Railroad, Rifle, Telegraph Revolution," which facilitated Prussia's rapid victory over Austria in the Seven Weeks' War of 1866. In the spring of 1940, Germany's integration of aviation, mechanization, and wireless (radio) to create Blitzkrieg enabled it to defeat France in six weeks, something it had failed to accomplish despite four years of effort a generation before. The introduction of nuclear weapons by the United States in 1945 was widely recognized as heralding a fundamental shift in warfare.

Viewed from a lagging competitor's perspective, failing to keep pace in exploiting the potential of an emerging military revolution risks operating at a severe disadvantage. Consequently, the common challenge for all major-power militaries in a period of military revolution is to be the first to identify its salient characteristics and exploit its potential. Silver medals are not awarded to those who come in second.

This book addresses two matters of strategic significance. First, it provides a preliminary assessment of the disruptive changes occurring in general war in this era of increased competition among great powers.[1] Modern general warfare between advanced military powers is a highly complex phenomenon. Should such a war occur today, it would exhibit very different characteristics from the last general war, concluded more than three-quarters of a century ago. Indeed, the length of time between the American Civil War and World War II is roughly the same as from 1945 to the present. Just as those two wars' features were profoundly different from each other, a general war today would be very much a war like no other.

It's been said that predicting is difficult—especially about the future. Given the long general peace that thankfully followed the last general war and the profound advances in military-related technologies that have occurred since the end of the Cold War, any attempt to set forth a detailed description of future warfare would provide only the illusion of precision. As President Dwight D. Eisenhower sagely observed, "There is only one thing I can tell you about war, and almost one only, and it is this: no war ever shows the characteristics that were expected; it is always different."[2]

The objective here is more modest: to identify some salient characteristics of the maturing precision-warfare regime, while offering some informed speculation on the features of an overlapping successor revolution. This study does not examine the extremes along the spectrum of conflict: subconventional (now popularly relabeled as "gray area") warfare and nuclear war.

Second, the book examines how military organizations have successfully anticipated and exploited disruptive changes in warfare faster than their rivals, creating major new sources of competitive advantage. The topic of disruptive innovation in large organizations is far too complex and the number of cases involving great-power military organizations far too small to enable a definitive treatment. The findings are therefore more suggestive than conclusive.

The book consists of two parts. Part 1 identifies the emerging competitive environment's prospective characteristics. Using a "building-block" approach, it begins by presenting some general trends in warfare that have emerged over the past two centuries and that may yield insights on the future military competition. This is followed by some informed speculation on the maturing precision-warfare regime: Does it represent a "new normal" in military affairs, or might militaries find ways of projecting power effectively despite the creation of modern no-man's-lands? The narrative then turns to identifying how emerging military capabilities are setting the stage for a new, overlapping revolution. Part 1 concludes by exploring the implications of these disruptive changes for deterring a general war, which is widely viewed as preferable to fighting one.

Part 2 addresses the strategic importance of being the first military organization to identify and exploit a military revolution's potential and the danger of failing to develop proficiency in the new ways of war. Success here is linked to a military's competence in pursuing disruptive innovation. As the term suggests, disruptive innovation is an ambitious undertaking that focuses not on improving military effectiveness within the existing warfare regime but rather on seeking to overthrow it, replacing it with far more effective means and methods of waging war. The principal purpose of Part 2 is to identify qualities that enable military organizations to pursue disruptive innovation at a high level. This is achieved by examining the experience of four military organizations that succeeded in doing so. Given the methodology's limitations, the insights emerging are informative and suggestive, not definitive. Yet they represent a significant improvement over informed speculation. Part 2 concludes with some preliminary observations regarding the U.S. military's competence to pursue disruptive innovation.

CHAPTER ONE

Come the Revolution

Rapid changes in the development of conventional means of
destruction and the emergence in the developed countries of
automated reconnaissance-strike complexes ... make it possible
to sharply increase, by at least an order of magnitude, the
destructive potential of conventional weapons, bringing them
closer, so to speak, to weapons of mass destruction in terms of
effectiveness.

—MARSHAL NIKOLAI OGARKOV

In the early evening of January 16, 1991, I departed the Pentagon,
where I was serving in the Office of Net Assessment, located in the Office of the Secretary of Defense. The Army had assigned me, a lieutenant
colonel, to the office in the fall of 1989, just as the Berlin Wall was coming down. The office functions as the secretary of defense's personal
"think tank," focusing on matters of long-term strategic importance to
the Pentagon's most senior policy makers and military leaders. The analytic staff, numbering around a dozen, included officers from each of the
military services.

The Pentagon's focus that night, as it had been for nearly six months,
was on the Middle East. I arrived home in the Washington, D.C., suburbs

to find my family gathered around the television. Images of intense anti-aircraft fire over Baghdad dominated the screen, signaling the U.S.-led military coalition's launching of operations against Saddam Hussein's Iraq, which had invaded and occupied Kuwait the previous August.

Before the First Gulf War, there was widespread speculation as to how it would play out. Only a few years earlier, Iraq had ended its eight-year war with Iran. That war, with its trenches and massive casualties, produced comparisons to the Western Front in World War I. Many well-respected military experts believed that even though the coalition would ultimately prevail, the war could drag on for months, with American casualties running as high as 30,000. Trevor duPuy, a military veteran, historian, and Pentagon consultant, declared, "My projection is that there would be about 10,000 American casualties in 10 days of fighting to occupy Kuwait." The noted military expert Joshua Epstein spoke for many when he said, "You can win . . . but it will be very bloody and very expensive. A lot of people are going to die."[1]

Not everyone we came in contact with subscribed to the conventional wisdom. Days before the war began, one of my colleagues returned from bilateral discussions with our Indian counterparts. He was shocked to find the Indians dismissing predictions of an extended, costly conflict. The war, they said, will be a cakewalk for the Americans and their allies. We found their views difficult to accept.

The Indians, however, were right.

What occurred over the next six weeks astounded military experts. Given the high losses U.S. air forces had suffered in Vietnam two decades earlier and those inflicted on the Israeli Air Force during the Yom Kippur War of 1973, it seemed the coalition's air arm would suffer a similar fate against Iraq's integrated air defense system, which was counted among the world's best. Yet armed with only a handful of stealthy aircraft and a small stockpile of precision-guided munitions (PGMs), and organized around what today would be viewed as a nascent "battle network," the coalition, led by the U.S. Air Force, quickly suppressed Iraq's air defenses.[2] Soon coalition air forces were operating with virtual impunity over Iraq. The Iraqis, hoping to husband their aircraft, placed them in hardened shelters, which were promptly collapsed by U.S. precision-guided "smart" bombs. After a few days, the Iraqis, in desperation, began flying their planes to Iran.

The coalition's air arm then turned against Saddam Hussein's ground forces in the Kuwait theater of operations. U.S. aircraft, employing precision-guided weapons, began knocking out scores of Iraqi armored vehicles. Iraqi soldiers started abandoning even undamaged tanks, believing themselves safer outside the "protection" offered by their armor. The strikes were so effective that when the coalition ground offensive to liberate Kuwait began on February 24, the Iraqi army simply collapsed. The ground war was over in less than 100 hours. Fewer than 150 Americans were killed in action; fewer than 500 were wounded. The U.S. Air Force lost only fourteen fixed-wing aircraft in combat, while flying more than 29,000 sorties.[3] Postwar studies attributed the lopsided U.S. victory to a combination of innovative war-fighting (or "operational") concepts and relatively new systems and weapons, including stealth aircraft, precision-guided munitions, unmanned aerial vehicles, and a rudimentary battle network comprising, among other elements, the E-3 Airborne Warning and Control System (AWACS), the E-8 Joint Surveillance Target Attack Radar System (JSTARS) aircraft, and the space-based Navstar Global Positioning System (GPS).

Hindsight, as they say, is 20/20. Despite the widespread surprise over the rapid and decisive victory of the U.S.-led coalition, there were clear indicators before the war suggesting it would be a very one-sided affair. There were, of course, the views of our Indian colleagues. At the forefront, however, were the Russians. For more than a decade before the war, Russian military leaders and theorists had been asserting that a disruptive shift in the character of warfare was becoming increasingly likely.[4] They generally referred to it as a "military-technical revolution" (MTR), driven to a large extent by rapid advances in information-related technologies, such as precision-strike munitions and wide-area surveillance systems. This "IT revolution," they believed, would trigger a "revolution in military affairs," with the first military mastering this new form of warfare realizing a profound increase in its effectiveness.

At the core of this revolution was the "reconnaissance-strike complex," a combination of advanced scouting (the reconnaissance element) and precision-guided munitions (the "strike" element), integrated and directed by a battle network. Russian arguments were summarized by Marshal Nikolai Ogarkov, the chief of the Soviet general staff. In 1984, he declared, "Rapid changes in the development of conventional means of destruction and the emergence in the developed countries of automated reconnaissance-strike complexes, long-range high-accuracy terminally-guided combat systems, unmanned flying machines, and qualitatively new electronic control systems make many types of weapons global and make it possible to sharply increase, *by at least an order of magnitude*, the destructive potential of conventional weapons, bringing them closer, so to speak, to weapons of mass destruction in terms of effectiveness" [emphasis added].[5]

There were Americans who shared Ogarkov's views. Nearly a decade earlier, U.S. military planners working on the Pentagon's Long-Range Research and Development Planning Program concluded, "Near zero miss, non-nuclear weapons could provide the National Command Authority with *a variety of strategic response options* as *alternative[s] to massive nuclear destruction*" [emphasis added].[6]

In the war's aftermath, the Russians concluded that they had at last witnessed, albeit in primitive form, the long-anticipated reconnaissance-strike complex: "the integration of control, communications, reconnaissance, electronic combat, and delivery of conventional fires into a single whole."[7]

The Offset Strategy

With a few key exceptions, U.S. defense officials and military leaders before the First Gulf War did not talk in terms of "reconnaissance-strike complexes," "battle networks," or "precision warfare." The Pentagon's efforts to create the capabilities that kept its Russian rivals up at night emerged in the early 1970s. That decade saw the Soviets erasing the U.S. lead in nuclear forces, the "trump card" that Washington had played in the Cuban Missile Crisis and that, since the Cold War's early days, had offset the Soviet advantage in conventional forces in Europe.

In searching for a new source of advantage, senior Pentagon officials decided to exploit the United States' growing advantage in information technologies (IT). Although not as prescient as their Russian counterparts, a few Americans saw the IT revolution's potential to trigger a disruptive shift in the character of warfare—a military revolution. Like the Russians, they believed that a major shift in the military balance of power would accrue to whichever side could first master the new way of war.

Thanks to the West's free-market economies and strict controls on technology transfers between advanced Western states and Soviet Russia, the West's IT advantage seemed likely to endure as the Soviets continued struggling to transition from the industrial era to the information age. Led by the U.S. defense secretary, Harold Brown, and his head of research and engineering, William Perry, the Pentagon began investing more in IT-related capabilities, such as stealth aircraft, precision-guided munitions, submarines equipped with exquisite quieting technologies, advanced sensors, and computer-enabled "battle management" systems. The goal of the "Offset Strategy" was to shift the military rivalry into areas where the Soviets were ill equipped to compete. By the time the Iraqis invaded Kuwait, more than a decade later, the U.S. military had succeeded in fielding a small number of stealth aircraft, creating a modest stockpile of guided weapons and long-range, precision-guided cruise missiles, and fielding piece-parts of a "battle network." Combined with other novel capabilities, these systems set the stage for the Precision-Warfare Revolution.

A Military-Technical Revolution?

Soviet thinking about a coming military revolution attracted the attention of Andrew Marshall, one of the United States' leading defense strategists. Known by many in defense circles as "Yoda" owing to his stoic character, sphinxlike demeanor, and legendary ability to spot key trends in the military competition, Marshall headed the Pentagon's innocuously named Office of Net Assessment, reporting directly to the secretary of defense. In December 1990, shortly before the onset of the First Gulf War, Marshall decided the time was right to undertake an appraisal of Russian views on a coming transformation in warfare and assigned me the task of producing the assessment.[8]

Marshall noted that neither we nor the Soviets had fought a major conventional war since the Korean conflict, nearly forty years earlier. Therefore, the coming war with Iraq, whose military was equipped primarily with Russian weaponry, might provide clues as to whether the Russians' ideas about a "military-technical revolution" were correct. He instructed me to focus the assessment on four questions: First, did we agree with the Russians that a major change in war's character was in progress? Second, if we concurred that the Russians were on to something, what could we say about warfare's new defining characteristics? Third, if we concluded the Russians were right, how could we best position ourselves to compete effectively? Finally, if, however, we thought the Russians were wrong, how could we encourage them to pursue their flawed ideas to their ultimate dead end, while also hedging against the possibility that we would prove mistaken? Marshall said that an assessment with answers to these questions would be of interest to the Pentagon's most senior civilian and military leaders. He was especially interested in a "mature regime"—in which at least two major military powers have exploited its potential—and its characteristics.

The work took eighteen months to complete. Drawing on the experience of the First Gulf War, the findings convinced us the Russians were, in fact, on to something. *The Military-Technical Revolution: A Preliminary Assessment* previewed many characteristics of a mature precision-warfare regime, introducing concepts that have become core elements of U.S. defense debate, such as "anti-access/area-denial" (A2/AD) and "system of systems."[9]

We clearly had a lead in this nascent form of warfare. How could we maintain it?[10] History showed that other militaries would have a strong incentive to exploit the revolution's potential, which meant the U.S. military's lead could prove ephemeral. Marshall felt strongly that we had to determine what would happen when other militaries began creating their versions of a reconnaissance-strike, or "recce-strike," complex. How might we maintain a favorable military balance under such circumstances? With technological developments occurring so rapidly, would it be possible to maintain our competitive advantage by effecting still another disruptive shift, another "revolution" that would move us beyond the one now emerging?

For the U.S. military to maintain its lead, it needed a world-class ability to pursue innovation successfully and on a large scale. The assessment's finding in this regard is worth citing at length:

> We are likely at the beginning of a period of revolutionary change in warfare. This change will probably occur over an extended period of time, perhaps 10–20 years, or longer. A major factor in determining the length of this transition period will be how adept competitors are at fostering and nurturing innovation. For those states that intend to develop the capability to wage war effectively in a new era of conflict, it is important that they begin to think through how they will organize themselves to promote the innovations—in terms of technologies, systems, and operational concepts—that will be required for a successful transition. . . .
>
> In this environment the ability to innovate and adapt quickly would logically assume a much greater priority than it enjoyed during the Cold War. *The fate of military enterprises, and of nations*

*and coalitions, may well depend on military and acquisitional struc-
tures that are able to innovate faster than their competitors, or their
enemies.*[11] [emphasis added]

The Russians were right in describing these discontinuous shifts in
the character of war as "revolutions." The competition among militaries,
particularly since the Industrial Revolution, is a story of rivals constantly
searching for ways to translate emerging technologies into new sources
of advantage on the battlefield. At times, these efforts produced a significant increase in military effectiveness through acts of innovation. Such
innovations may be the result of an advance in technology, such as the
proximity fuse invented by the British and developed along with the
Americans during World War II. Or it could also emerge from a new
form of tactics, such as the "Thach Weave," which countered Japan's superior Zero fighter in the Pacific war, or from a novel way of organizing
or structuring one's forces, such as in the U.S. Army's concentration of
large numbers of helicopters into the Airmobile Division in the early
1960s.[12] Some innovations, executed on a far greater scope and scale—
disruptive innovations—find military organizations realizing a quantum
leap in military effectiveness, introducing a military revolution.[13]

A military revolution is a shift in the character of warfare that yields
a disruptive boost—perhaps an order of magnitude or more—in military
effectiveness. This definition, of course, raises several important questions, such as "What qualifies as a 'disruptive boost' in military effectiveness?" and, more broadly, "How do we measure 'military effectiveness'?"
Alas, any attempt to develop such a comprehensive theory on the issue of
what constitutes a military revolution is to go down the rabbit hole into
a world where you can never quite reach the destination you seek. Indeed, entire books have been written on the topic of what constitutes
"military effectiveness" and how to measure it, without arriving at a definitive conclusion.

The challenge of devising a comprehensive definition of what constitutes a "revolution" has proved difficult for both the "hard" and "soft"
sciences. Take "revolution" in its political sense. A "political revolution"
can be defined as a challenge to the established political order leading to
its replacement by a new order radically different from the preceding
one. It has also been defined as a major, sudden, and typically violent al-
teration in government and in related associations and structures.[14] But
what is meant by "sudden"? A change that occurs in the course of days?

Weeks? Months? Years? And what is meant by a "radically different" political order? What constitutes "radical"?

A political revolution is also defined as a "sharp, sudden change or attempted change in the location of political power which involved either the use or the threat of violence and, if successful, expressed itself in the manifest and perhaps radical transformation of the process of government, the accepted foundations of sovereignty or legitimacy, and the conception of the political and/or social order."[15] The French revolutions of 1830 and 1848 can be defined as upheavals in which the government was replaced or the form of government altered but in which property relations remained generally intact. But we also have the French Revolution of 1789, which ushered in a fundamentally new government that was radically different from the one that preceded it, where property and social relations were altered dramatically. Even more striking is the Russian Revolution of 1917. It drastically altered not only Russia's system of government but also its economic system, social structure, and, some people argue, cultural values as well.

Then there is the American Revolution, which brought about a shift in the form of government, from a monarchy to a republic, the latter being a sufficiently novel form of government that Abraham Lincoln, more than eighty years later, pondered openly whether "any nation so conceived and dedicated could long endure." Yet in many respects, the American Revolution, like the French revolutions of 1830 and 1848, left property relations relatively intact. Moreover, much of the established local political leadership and government structures (state legislative bodies, for example) remained in place after the Revolution.

Political science labels all of the shifts just described as "revolutions," yet they each exhibit significantly different characteristics. If we boil down the definition to an abrupt change in the form of government, arguably a military coup constitutes a revolution. The Bolsheviks, a small (but highly organized) political faction, seized power in Russia in November 1917 in what could be described as a coup, even though it is called a revolution.

Even the hard sciences have struggled to devise ironclad definitions, such as for laws that hold in every instance.[16] Richard Feynman, a Nobel Prize–winning physicist, noted that many of the "laws" of physics are, in fact, approximations that work well for everyday problems. For example, one "approximate" law is that mass is constant, independent of speed. A spinning top has the same mass (weight) as one at rest. This law is incorrect. If an object is moving at a speed of less than 100 miles per second, then the mass is constant to within one part in a million. As Feynman notes, "For ordinary speeds we can certainly forget it [the true law] and use the simple constant-mass law as a good approximation. But for high speeds we are wrong, and the higher the speed, the more wrong we are." Finally, Feynman notes that even though "approximate laws" work for nearly all everyday sorts of problems, "*philosophically we are completely wrong.*"[17] He states the problem in general terms: "Each piece, or part, of the whole of nature is always merely an *approximation* to the complete truth, or the complete truth so far as we know it. In fact, everything we know is only some kind of approximation, because *we know we do not know all the laws* as yet. Therefore, things must be learned only to be unlearned again or, more likely, to be corrected."[18]

To arrive at a "true law" that holds in defining military revolutions one would have to have *complete* information on *every* case of disruptive military innovation, while acknowledging that at some point further research might identify a way in which an "outlier" case may be made to fit the general definition.[19]

The business profession in free-market economies encounters similar problems when it comes to defining a discontinuous, or disruptive, shift in the competitive environment. For example, in the mid-1990s, Joseph Bower and Clayton Christensen presented a pathbreaking study addressing the challenge corporate decision-makers face in attempting to effect disruptive innovation. They wrote, "One of the most consistent patterns in business is the failure of leading companies to stay at the top of their industries when technologies or markets change."[20] Bower and Christensen did not provide a comprehensive definition (let alone a theory) for what constitutes "disruptive change" but defined "sustaining" and "disruptive" technologies. Sustaining technologies, they posited, "tend to maintain a rate of improvement; that is, they give customers something more or better in the attributes they already value." "Disruptive" technologies "introduce a very different package of attributes from the one mainstream customers historically value."[21]

In *The Innovator's Dilemma*, Christensen maintained these descriptions of sustaining and disruptive technologies.[22] These do not, however, represent a comprehensive, unified theory or definition of what constitutes disruptive versus sustaining change in the corporate sector. Yet Christensen's ideas and the case studies he employed proved of great value to many corporate and government leaders. Similar policy-relevant work has been done in the general field of sustaining and disruptive military innovation, despite the absence of a comprehensive theory.[23]

The concept of a "military revolution" was introduced by Michael Roberts in 1955 in a lecture at Queens College. Roberts focused his attention on Europe between 1560 and 1660, noting that the size of armies during this period increased by an order of magnitude. Rogers had the advantage of limiting his focus to describing only the events of that time as a "military revolution" and thus did not need to bother himself with a definition that would describe all such phenomena. He did, however, argue that "major revolutions in military techniques . . . [include] the coming of the mounted warrior, and of the sword" in ancient times, as well as "the triumph of the heavy cavalryman, consolidated by the adoption of the stirrup" in the sixth century A.D., along with "the scientific revolution in warfare in our own day."[24]

The so-called Artillery Revolution of the late fifteenth century also achieved order-of-magnitude improvements in military effectiveness, at least in one aspect. According to one observer, "great towns, which once would have held out for a year against all foes but hunger, now fell within a month."[25] Rogers's thesis produced a spirited debate that continues over what constitutes a military revolution, including whether the period he referenced was "revolutionary" at all. Geoffrey Parker, for example, focuses on the period 1500 to 1750 in arguing that "the key to Westerners' [the Europeans'] success in creating the first truly global empires . . . depended upon precisely those improvements in the ability to wage war which have been termed 'the military revolution.' "[26]

Jeremy Black also contested Roberts's argument, declaring that the period from 1660 through the Napoleonic Wars was considerably more important with regard to the transformation of warfare.[27] In critiquing Roberts's perspective, Parker conceded that the task of providing a comprehensive definition of what constitutes a military revolution remains to be accomplished, while nevertheless asserting that during the course of the three centuries addressed in his book, "a major transformation in European military and naval power had taken place, a transformation so profound that it must surely rank as a 'revolution.' "[28]

Given the challenges found in both the hard and soft sciences in arriving at comprehensive theories and definitions, or laws, that support them, it appears the best we can do is to present a definition or description of what constitutes a military revolution, hoping that it will be improved on over time. This book's primary purpose, however, is to enhance our understanding of how the character of warfare is changing and how military organizations succeed in adapting to radical shifts in war's character through disruptive innovation, thereby enabling them to become the first to exploit the "next big thing" in warfare.

Like the Russians, Andrew Marshall's interest in military revolutions was not theoretical but practical. Marshall was charged by U.S. defense secretaries with assessing the state of the military balance, including identifying factors that could trigger significant shifts in the balance. His office's assessments along these lines aided the efforts of senior Pentagon leaders to develop long-term strategies to improve the United States' military position.

Marshall realized that his office's work was never more important than when the military competition was entering a period of disruptive change. Such periods magnified the importance of identifying new sources of advantage and developing them quicker than the United States' rivals. Under these conditions, militaries find themselves playing for the highest stakes.

The MTR assessment anticipated that other leading militaries, given the risks should they fall behind, would move quickly to close the gap and exploit the Precision-Warfare Revolution, albeit in their own way.[29] This seemed reasonable, as similar periods of disruptive change in the military competition over the previous century saw rivals quickly matching the military that made the initial breakthrough into a new way of war. For example, the Imperial German Navy began building modern battleships only a year after the Royal Navy launched its revolutionary all-big-gun battleship, HMS *Dreadnought*, in 1906. Germany's mechanized air-land Blitzkrieg force that swept over much of Europe between 1939 and 1942 was matched, to a greater or lesser extent, by the U.S., British, and Russian militaries by 1944. The U.S. monopoly in nuclear weapons lasted barely four years before the Soviet Union's successful atomic test in August 1949.

This knowledge gave Marshall's enterprise a sense of urgency. If the U.S. military's advantage was likely to be fleeting, senior defense policy makers needed to have some idea of how the United States might best extend its lead and what options existed for developing new sources of advantage once other militaries caught up.

Following the First Gulf War, however, other militaries were slow to challenge the United States. Although this was not widely understood at the time, both China and Russia had the *desire* to compete with the

United States but lacked the means. Major powers such as Britain, France, Germany, and Japan had the means but lacked a compelling motive for challenging U.S. military dominance. Thus, the threats to the United States' security were comparatively modest, emanating primarily from minor powers like Iran, Iraq, and North Korea and insurgent and terrorist groups. Of course, Washington could not ignore the potential danger posed by the nuclear arsenals of China and (especially) Russia, but these powers had yet to openly challenge the U.S.-led international order.

Absent a serious challenge to its dominant position, the U.S. military saw no compelling need to anticipate and adapt to the challenges it would confront in a mature precision-warfare regime. Moreover, the declining U.S. defense budgets—the "peace dividend"—that followed the Soviet Union's collapse in late 1991 and the corresponding drawdown of the U.S. military found Pentagon leaders preoccupied with moving to a smaller force, which they argued must be given priority before attempting any major innovations. U.S. political leaders, hoping to frame a world order rooted in collective security rather than balance-of-power politics, offered few incentives for the military to innovate.

The Balkan War of 1998 confirmed the views of many U.S. military leaders who argued, "If it isn't broken, why fix it?" The war revealed that the Europeans, far from attempting to keep up with their U.S. ally, were falling further behind. Among other capabilities, the Americans provided their NATO allies with precision-guided munitions, aerial refueling, and scouting support. Meanwhile, Russia, still working its way out of the economic wreckage wrought by seventy years of communist rule, fielded a military that was a pale shadow of its Cold War self. China, smarting from the U.S. Navy's show of force off its shores during the 1996 tensions over Taiwan, was only beginning to show signs of becoming a major military power.

Although the post–Cold War period of U.S. military dominance extended far beyond historical norms, it would not last forever. Things began to change in the early 2000s. Following the terrorist attacks in New York and Washington, D.C., in September 2001, the U.S. military focused on waging war against radical Islamist extremist groups and, after the invasions of Afghanistan and Iraq, countering insurgent movements as well.

Moreover, many of the U.S. military's high-technology systems touted by their service advocates as revolutionary or "transformational"—such as the Army's Future Combat System, the Air Force's airborne laser, the

Marine Corps' Advanced Fighting Vehicle, and the Navy's next-generation cruiser—were canceled, primarily for reasons of cost, lack of performance, or both. Some transformation advocates, your author among them, applauded these cancellations, primarily out of concern that the U.S. military was putting the cart before the horse—specifically, that it had not yet addressed *how* these new capabilities would maintain their effectiveness as the Precision-Warfare Revolution matured.[30]

By the middle of the first decade of the twenty-first century, with the United States mired in wars against insurgent and terrorist groups in Afghanistan and the Middle East, China and Russia were aggressively seeking to narrow, if not erase, the U.S. military's near monopoly in precision warfare. Thanks in large part to the country's high, sustained economic growth rates, China emerged as the leading, or "pacing," threat. By the mid-2010s, the Precision-Warfare Revolution began to enter its mature stage, as China's People's Liberation Army (PLA) fielded elements of battle networks, along with scouting and precision-fire systems. The PLA did not try to "mirror-image" the U.S. military but fielded capabilities conforming to Chinese "characteristics," those reflecting their geopolitical objectives and strategic culture. It also began exploiting opportunities in a new warfare domain—cyberspace—preparing for war in space and undersea, and deploying advanced A2/AD capabilities.

China's A2/AD complex, for example, is designed to cast an expanding military shadow over the "First Island Chain" that stretches from the Japanese islands through Taiwan and the Philippines down to Singapore. For more than a century, the U.S. military has undertaken major power-projection operations by transporting forces from the United States to secure overseas bases, such as in Great Britain in World War II, Japan during the Korean War, and Saudi Arabia during the First Gulf War. Once these forces amassed sufficient combat power, they were employed to achieve their war objectives. The PLA's A2/AD complex is designed to increase dramatically the costs associated with this method of power projection in order to defeat or discourage any U.S. attempt to come to the aid of its East Asian allies and to provide cover for Chinese offensive operations in the region. In summary, today the Pentagon's challenge is no longer how to maintain a wide lead over its rivals but rather how to keep pace in a rapidly changing competitive environment.

With the precision-warfare regime's maturation there are signs that new discontinuities in warfare may be on the horizon—a new military revolution. If the history of the past century or so is any guide, advances across a range of military-related technologies, including those related to artificial intelligence (AI), the biosciences, advanced computational power, directed energy (DE), additive manufacturing, robotics, and hypersonic propulsion, among others, will continue over the next decade or so. In many instances, progress will be driven primarily by the commercial sector. There is no guarantee that the United States will be the first to exploit this new emerging revolution as it succeeded in doing in the Precision-Warfare Revolution and, before it, the Nuclear Revolution. The U.S. military's success in the race to identify and exploit the next big thing in warfare will depend on understanding its defining characteristics and how best to exploit them and on creating the new capabilities, doctrines, and organizations needed to wage the new way of war more quickly and effectively than its rivals.

CHAPTER TWO

The Shape of Things to Come

God is not on the side of the big battalions, but on the side of those who shoot best.

—VOLTAIRE

The first of all necessities is Speed so as to be able to fight when you like, where you like, and how you like.

—ADMIRAL JACKIE FISHER

The speed, range, and connectivity of modern weapon systems enable belligerents to wage war on a global scale and across multiple domains. In such a conflict, *command and control*, *intelligence*, the synchronization of *movement and maneuver*, and force *sustainment* must occur on a global scale and rapidly enough to defeat weapons with extreme speed and range.

—U.S. SPACE FORCE, "Spacepower: Doctrine for Space Forces"

IN THE LATE 1990s, I was serving on the National Defense Panel, a commission mandated by Congress to review U.S. defense strategy. Our deliberations took some of us to the Far East, to China, Japan, and South Korea. While in Tokyo, we had discussions with senior officials serving in Japan's ministries of defense and foreign affairs and in the self-defense forces.

At the time, much of the U.S. defense debate revolved around the revolution in military affairs and "transformation"—the initiatives you would take to "transform" your military if you believed a disruptive shift in warfare was under way or on the horizon. Secretary of Defense William Cohen had signed on to the idea, and our allies were naturally interested in what the U.S. military, the world's most powerful, had in mind.

At the time, I was working on the concept of a "stealth battleship"— converting some U.S. Trident fleet ballistic-missile submarines coming out of service into conventional cruise-missile carriers.[1] I shared the idea with my Japanese colleagues, who were having trouble understanding why the U.S. Navy, with its aircraft carriers, would need a converted submarine carrying cruise missiles, even if each held more than 150 of them.

It struck me that an analogy might prove useful. Imagine, I said, you were refighting the Battle of Midway. Assume the U.S. and Japanese fleets are 800 miles apart. The Americans have several *Nimitz*-class carriers, and you have no carriers, only four of these converted submarines, carrying cruise missiles armed with 1,000-pound warheads. Let's also assume that both sides' "scouting" forces are equally capable. Under these conditions, the U.S. carriers have an advantage in armor and in firepower—a carrier's air wing can carry more and heavier bombs than the Japanese submarines with their cruise missiles. The Japanese submarine force has the advantage in stealth, which translates to a scouting advantage: they will be more difficult to find than the carriers. And its cruise missiles' range exceeds that of the U.S. carriers' aircraft. So, all other factors being equal, your subs are going to see the U.S. carriers before they see you, and you'll be able to attack them before they are in range to attack you. So, I asked, "Who's going to win the Second Battle of Midway?"[2]

Our discussion put me to wondering if there were trends with regard to those performance characteristics that innovative militaries came to value during earlier periods of disruptive change in the character of warfare. If so, they might offer insights on those attributes that might provide relatively greater value in a maturing Precision-Warfare Revolution and an emerging military revolution.

Since the dawn of the industrial age, we've seen great advances in military capabilities, including increases in the speed and range of systems and communications, in scouting and counter-scouting capabilities, in protective armor, and in massed and precision fires. The world has also witnessed a remarkable growth in the domains in which warfare is waged. This chapter examines these phenomena with emphasis on four periods of disruptive military change since the mid-nineteenth century: the Railroad, Rifle, and Telegraph Revolution, the Fisher Revolution in the maritime domain, the Interwar (Mechanization, Aviation, and Radar) Revolution, and the Precision-Warfare Revolution. The objective is to identify trends to help strip away some of the uncertainty regarding where militaries should place their "big bets" when it comes to investing to develop new sources of competitive advantage.

To begin, some defining of terms is in order. By "armor," I mean a metallic sheathing or protective covering, especially metal plates, used on warships, combat vehicles, airplanes, and fortifications that provides physical protection against fires. Weapons' fires are broken down into three categories: range, accuracy, and volume. A weapon's "accuracy" is its circular error probable (CEP). Think of a circle whose target is at its center. A CEP is the radius of a circle within which half of a missile's projectiles are expected to fall. A weapon with a CEP of 500 feet will find half of those weapons landing within 500 feet of the target and the other half landing farther away. A weapon has range, defined in terms of distance, such as in miles or kilometers. Finally, fires can also be assessed in terms of their volume—the kinetic capacity to destroy or neutralize human or material targets—that they can produce in a given period of time. In this study, the term "firepower" is used interchangeably with volume fires. "Speed" is simply distance traveled in a unit of time, such as miles per hour. By "scouting," I mean the use of intelligence, surveillance, and reconnaissance (ISR) to ascertain knowledge of the enemy. "Counter-scouting" refers to the actions taken to defeat scouting.

The Railroad, Rifle, and Telegraph Revolution

During the Napoleonic Wars, armies moved pretty much as they had since antiquity—on foot. An army's mobile arm—its cavalry—moved at the speed of the horse. Transporting troops by ship had marginally improved over time, with wind and sail replacing muscle and oar. With few exceptions, command and control of forces at the strategic, operational, and tactical levels suffered from enduring limitations. Orders to field armies were typically delivered by couriers on horseback, although signal flags were also employed.

On the battlefield, infantry tended to maneuver in very dense formations, compensating for inaccurate flintlock musket fire by delivering a barrage of bullets.[3] In the middle of the nineteenth century, however, things changed with what has become known as the Railroad, Rifle, and Telegraph Revolution, which found warfare expanding into the electromagnetic domain.

On an autumn day in 1839, some 8,000 Prussian soldiers traveled by train from their maneuver grounds at Potsdam to their garrisons in Berlin.[4] Although the distance was short and the number of troops involved modest, it presaged a dramatic shift in mobility at the strategic and operational levels of war. Twenty years later, during France's war with the Austrian Empire, a French army, 120,000 strong, was transported by rail to Northern Italy in eleven days over a distance that would have taken more than five times as long on foot.[5] Little more than a decade later, in August 1870, the Northern German Federation used its railway system to deploy 1.2 million troops along the Rhine River in eleven days, reducing its mobilization time by nearly half.[6] Only a few years earlier, during the American Civil War, the Union exploited its advantage in railways to great benefit over the Confederacy, offsetting the latter's advantage in interior lines of communication.

In addition to offering land forces the advantage of increased speed in mobilization and maneuver at the strategic and operational levels of war, railroads greatly reduced the wear and tear on armies induced by prolonged marches, thereby enhancing their readiness for battle. By rapidly moving large quantities of supplies, railroads also gave armies much greater staying power, while enabling dramatic increases in their size.[7]

Around this time, in 1844, the American Samuel Morse introduced the electromagnetic telegraph. Within a decade, a web of more than 20,000 miles of telegraph cable crisscrossed the United States. Much of Europe quickly followed. During the American Civil War, the new communication network enabled armies to maintain contact with higher headquarters by playing out telegraph wire from the main telegraph lines to forces on the march.[8] Thus, while railroads greatly expanded the size and staying power of armies, the telegraph boosted commanders' ability to direct the movement of their forces, to include when and where to position them to greatest advantage.

The mid-nineteenth century also saw the widespread introduction of rifling, enabled by making spiral groves in the barrels of muskets and cannons. A smoothbore musket's effective range was about 80 to 200 yards on a still day, but rifling increased the range and accuracy of fires by roughly a factor of five.[9] There were advances in the volume of fires—firepower—as well. In 1848, a French army officer, Claude Minié, developed a cone-shaped bullet (the "Minié ball") that could be loaded quickly, without using a ramrod. Still, soldiers with rifles using Minié-ball ammunition had to reload after each shot. With the introduction of breech-loading rifles like the Prussian Dreyse "needle" gun, the rate of fire tripled relative to the musket, to roughly six rounds per minute. By 1863, repeating rifles like the U.S. Spencer carbine could fire seven shots in thirty seconds. This increased rate of fire was made possible by cocking a lever to extract the spent cartridge, which then fed a new cartridge from a tube in the butt-stock into the chamber. The Union army began equipping its cavalry troopers with Spencers, leading one Union soldier to write, "I think the Johnnys [Confederate soldiers] are getting rattled; they are afraid of our repeating rifles. They say we are not fair, that we have guns that we load up on Sunday and shoot all the rest of the week."[10] One observer said that a couple of cavalry regiments with Spencer repeating rifles sounded "as if a couple of army corps had opened fire."[11] But it was not only the volume of fires but their range and accuracy that had increased dramatically.

The implications were profound. As the early battles of the American Civil War revealed all too clearly, the shoulder-to-shoulder infantry formations of the Napoleonic era were now obsolete. Commanders who persisted in maneuvering in this way, such as during the Union assault on Marye's Heights at Fredericksburg in December 1862, at Pickett's Charge against Union forces on Cemetery Hill at Gettysburg in July 1863, and at Grant's assault at Cold Harbor in June 1864, saw their troops exposed to terrible slaughter from rifled fire.

In response, troops began entrenching. By May 1864, the Confederate general Joseph E. Johnston, commanding forces opposing the Union general William T. Sherman, declared, "I have found no opportunity for battle except by attacking intrenchments." Confederate troops said "Sherman's men march with a rifle in one hand and a spade in the other." Union troops returned the compliment, declaring that "the Rebels must carry their breastworks with them."[12] Confederate fieldworks such as at Petersburg in the war's final months foreshadowed the trench warfare along the Great War's Western Front a half century later.[13]

As for advances in "armor," the spade used to dig trenches hardly qualifies as a major advance in protection, as the widespread use of trenches dates back at least two centuries to the time of Sébastien Le Prestre de Vauban, who popularized their use in besieging fortresses. It was now more expensive in time and material resources to construct forts than to defeat them. French forts fell to the Prussians in the Franco-Prussian War, and by World War I, the Germans had manufactured guns capable of knocking them down. The French Maginot Line was outmaneuvered in World War II, and the Belgian fort at Eban Emael fell quickly to German glider troops.[14] Later, the Stalin, Siegfried, and Bar-Lev lines suffered similar fates. This does not mean efforts to enhance troops' physical protection are irrelevant. To this day, soldiers carry entrenching tools to "dig in." What these trends strongly suggest, however, is that, broadly speaking, the armor/anti-armor competition has been shifting in the latter's favor.

Between the 1860s and World War I, the Railroad, Rifle, and Telegraph land-warfare revolution progressed. Gatling guns and machine guns appeared, firing hundreds of rounds per minute. The artillery used rifling to increase its effective range and accuracy. Over time, its rate of fire was augmented by the change to breech-loading guns and the development of a better recoil mechanism, eliminating the need for swabbing out the gun after each shot.[15] By the Great War, Europe's armies had increased significantly both the range and volume of fires far beyond those of their mid-nineteenth-century contemporaries. Artillery was truly the "king of battle."

World War I witnessed the Railroad, Rifle, and Telegraph Revolution in its most evolved form. The Western Front offered an enhanced version of the Confederate entrenchments at Petersburg, only on a far greater scale. The speed of operations had not increased significantly, as the internal combustion engine and wireless communications were still in their infancy. Troop movement across no-man's-land, with its barbed wire and shell craters, had not improved much since Petersburg.

What had grown substantially was firepower, unleashed by machine guns and breech-loaded artillery. Modern railway systems had enabled combat power to be concentrated and sustained at ever greater levels at a given point, but the means (mechanized and motorized land forces, combat and transport aircraft) to propel these forces forward to exploit any breakthrough of the enemy's front had yet to be developed. Simply put, militaries in the final stages of the Railroad, Rifle, and Telegraph regime could generate volume fires at a much high level than ever before. That being said, troops attempting to advance across that deadly space between the trenches in World War I suffered the same failures that Union troops had in assaulting the Confederate trenches at Petersburg—before the great gains in firepower.

As Sir Michael Howard observed, "Long before 1914, then, it was accepted by all the states of Europe that the military effectiveness on which they relied to preserve their relative power and status depended . . . on a combination of the manpower of the population and a strategically appropriate railway network."[16] Simply put, the railroads enabled the concentration of large armies that, lacking in tactical mobility, continued to seek an advantage where technology permitted—in firepower and in extending the range of fires. Thus, by the time of the Great War, it was generally agreed that "the attack could succeed only by developing a greater intensity of fire than the defence."[17]

Still, the war offered glimpses of what was to come. In the electromagnetic domain, the telegraph had been supplemented by wireless (radio) communications, but it had yet to mature.[18] Primitive tanks appeared, enabling troops to vacate their trenches and cross no-man's-land with a modest enhancement in speed and armor protection. Aircraft could scout over vast areas relative to horse cavalry and proved valuable in adjusting artillery fires. It was a combination of these nascent capabilities, with their emphasis on speed and range, that, when combined with innovative German tactics that appeared late in the war, would displace the Railroad, Rifle, and Telegraph Revolution and dramatically alter war's character.

What mattered most for militaries looking to exploit the Railroad, Rifle, and Telegraph Revolution's potential? Napoleon declared in his time, "Le feu est tout" (Fire[power] is everything).[19] With this revolution, however, the massing of firepower was dependent on the dramatic increase in the speed of communications and movement of large forces, which were enabled by the telegraph and railroad, respectively. Without the railroad, armies would have been much smaller. Without the railroad and telegraph, elements of these smaller armies would have had more difficulty concentrating at the right place and time to mass their fires.

Once on the battlefield, armies equipped with rifles and then repeating rifles enjoyed a major boost in their effective range, accuracy, and firepower. What mattered most? Would generals have preferred accurate, ranged fires over sheer firepower? The carnage inflicted by troops armed with rifled muskets against those advancing on Marye's Heights, on Cemetery Ridge, and at Cold Harbor suggest that the boost in fire-power's range and accuracy had more of an effect than the change in the rate of fire did. Put another way, Napoleonic tactics on the battlefield were abandoned not principally owing to improvements in firepower but to increases in the accuracy and range of fires. Indeed, enhancements in volume fires appeared only toward the Civil War's end and almost exclusively on the Union's side.[20] Yet in assessing the value of range, accuracy, and rate of fire, it's difficult to identify a clear "winner."[21]

The Iron and Steam Revolution

At roughly the same time the Railroad, Rifle, and Telegraph Revolution was occurring, a revolution in warfare at sea was under way. Within the span of a few decades in the mid-nineteenth century, the world's great fleets were transformed out of the Age of Wind and Sail to the Age of Steam and Iron. Between 1840 and 1870, navies, led first by the French but quickly eclipsed by Britain's Royal Navy, abandoned the wooden sailing ships of Drake and Nelson, launching a hodgepodge of ironclad ships whose motive power was steam. Steam propulsion freed ships from dependence on the wind's vagaries, while increasing their speed, cutting the time from London to Cape Town by more than half. The telegraph enabled Great Britain to lead the way in constructing a global communications network via undersea cables.

What had to be sorted out was whether fires or armor would dominate ship design. Early returns, such as the engagement between the Union ironclad *Monitor* and its Confederate counterpart, *Virginia*, in 1862, and the Battle of Lissa between Austria and Italy in 1866 favored armor. At Lissa, ships actually resorted to ramming, leading some navies to construct ships with rams emphasizing armor plate at the expense of their speed, range, and fires.

Advances in metallurgy, propulsion, explosives, and communications further complicated efforts to determine those qualities that would most advantage the New Model navies. The Russians built a circular warship, while the British built a steam-propelled ironclad with a full rig of sail that capsized and sank.

Metal allowed navies to construct much larger ships, enabling fantastic increases in firepower and armor protection. Where Nelson's oak-hulled ships were limited to roughly 2,000 tons, the early ironclads of the

1860s achieved a fourfold increase. By the Great War, the Royal Navy's "super-dreadnought" battleships stood at 20,000 tons.[22] Early French and British ironclads were covered with wrought-iron armor several inches thick. By the mid-1860s, armor increased to nine inches and then to twenty-four inches—a thickness never surpassed—in the British iron-clad *Inflexible*, launched in 1876.[23] By the late 1880s, the first steel battle-ship, *Royal Sovereign*, was built with eighteen-inch armor. The thickness of armor plate continued to decline, in part because of advances by firms like Krupp, which, by the late 1890s, was manufacturing steel armor with roughly three times the strength of that used in *Inflexible*.[24] Advances in armor, however, were more than matched by progress in the penetrating power of shells.

By the early twentieth century, the pace of technological advances had slowed to the point where capital ships could be designed with the expectation that they could serve for decades. (Indeed, a substantial number of battleships and battle cruisers built just before and during the Great War saw service in World War II.)

The Fisher Revolution

This Steam and Iron Revolution in naval warfare overlapped with an-other that occurred in the two decades before the Great War, known as the Fisher (or "Dreadnought") Revolution, after the British admiral who transformed the world's preeminent fleet. Fisher's new battleships, called "dreadnoughts" after the eponymous warship that entered service in 1906, emphasized speed to set the engagement range and uniform-caliber big guns, primarily to outrange the enemy's guns. Toward this end, Fisher was willing to discount armor plate and large numbers of short-range quick-firing guns. As he put it, "If we have the advantage of speed, *which is the first desideratum in every class of fighting vessel (Battleships included)*, then, and then only, we can choose our distance for fighting. If we can choose our distance for fighting, then we can choose our armament for fight-ing!"[25] Captain (later Admiral) Reginald Bacon, a Fisher protégé, pointed out that "the fast ship with the heavier [longer-range] guns and deliberate fire should absolutely 'knock out' a vessel of equal [or lesser] speed and many lighter [short-range] guns, the very number of which militate against accurate spotting [accuracy] and deliberate hitting."[26]

Before *Dreadnought*, four 12-inch guns were the norm for a battle-ship. *Dreadnought* had ten, giving it a long-range striking capability equal to two or three pre-dreadnoughts. The *Agincourt*, commissioned in 1914, boasted fourteen big guns, and the super-dreadnought *Queen Elizabeth*, commissioned that year, had eight 15-inch guns. This increased the ships' firepower, but Fisher's principal motive was to gain an advantage in range over rival fleets. Armor was sacrificed to gain speed. *Queen Elizabeth* had a 13-inch armor belt at the waterline, barely more than half that of the *Inflexible* and five inches less than the *Royal Sovereign*. But compared with the Lord Nelson class of battleships commissioned a decade earlier, its speed was over 30 percent greater. Thanks to the transition from reciprocating to turbine engines and from coal to oil fuel, the super-dreadnoughts also had a greater operational range and could sustain their speed over much long distances.[27]

Other great-power navies were soon following the British lead. At the time *Dreadnought* was being constructed, the U.S. Navy had plans for two 16,000-ton big-gun battleships, *South Carolina* and *Michigan*, while the Japanese were constructing two 20,000-ton, twenty-knot battleships with four 12-inch and twelve 10-inch guns.[28]

Ironically, in World War I, the principal danger to allied fleets and commerce stemmed from war's expansion into the undersea, which presented navies with a formidable problem of locating vessels operating in this domain. Rapid advances in submarine-related technology, such as the diesel engine, and in torpedo range, accuracy, and reliability led to the emergence of new forms of military operations: the undersea blockade and anti-submarine warfare. Indeed, the principal reason why the world's major battle fleets were moving toward long-range fires was the rapidly growing threat posed by submarines armed with torpedoes.[29] Just as surface ships were trading volume fires to gain speed and ranged fires, submarines, relying on their stealth, were sacrificing armor for the speed and range needed to operate on the high seas, where they could threaten enemy warships and commerce. In the years leading up to World War I, the growth in the submarine's capabilities was nothing short of breathtaking. Britain's E9 boat, launched in 1909, had a range of 1,750 nautical miles, while Germany's U-19 submarine, launched only a few years later, had a cruising range of 5,000 nautical miles.[30]

As for torpedoes, technological advances with gyroscopes in the 1890s boosted their accuracy by enabling them to keep a steadier course. In 1905, the "Elswick Heater" enabled even greater enhancements in torpedo range and speed. That year, Japanese torpedoes employed in their war with Russia ran at less than twenty knots at ranges of around

4,000 yards. Less than a year later, the German Navy's G-type torpedo was running at 6,560 yards at thirty-six knots. The range of British torpedoes doubled from 6,000 yards in 1905 to 12,000 yards in 1909.[31]

A submarine armed with torpedoes could not compete with a dreadnought's firepower. The torpedo's charge was generally only a few hundred pounds, a small fraction of the weight of a dreadnought's broadside. Moreover, a submarine had a much smaller magazine of weapons than a major surface warship did. The torpedo's advantage stemmed from the fact that existing armored warships were far more vulnerable to damage below the waterline than from a shell fired against a ship's superstructure. It was generally accepted that "one shot getting home from a torpedo tube is worth thirty from a gun."[32] Thus, as with surface warships, the submarine's emphasis was less on volume fires than ranged and accurate fires. The result was to drive surface warships to emphasize ranged fires, not greater armor or firepower, in order to stay outside enemy torpedo range.

Even with rifled guns, accuracy diminished as the range of fires increased. This led to increasing emphasis on gunnery to retain as much accuracy as possible. The British Navy stood at the forefront of these efforts. Beginning in 1898, gunnery exercises were conducted at ranges from 3,000 to 6,000 yards. By 1904, the British were convinced that effective gunnery at 8,000 yards was possible.[33] They implemented a "director firing" sighting process, in which big guns of uniform caliber were placed in parallel alignment, then aimed and fired electronically by a fire control officer. By 1908, British capital ships were hitting moving targets exceeding 8,000 yards, a "phenomenal increase in accuracy" when measured against the abysmal state of gunnery that existed a decade before.[34] Nevertheless, as naval engagements during World War I revealed, accurate long-range gunnery remained elusive. Major improvements had to await the advent of wireless-equipped aircraft spotting, which was not integrated into the world's major fleets until after the war.

As with forces operating on land, those in the maritime domain benefited from war's expansion into the electromagnetic domain. With cable telegraphy, navies could transmit and receive information to overseas naval bases within minutes, as long as these bases were linked through a network.[35] The late nineteenth century also saw the introduction of wireless communication. Unlike the telegraph, "wireless" did not require cables or wires, only a transmitter and receiver. Enhancements in the Royal Navy's global early warning system were made possible by the telegraph and undersea cables. The emergence of wireless communications greatly compressed the time needed to provide deployed fleets with information on their enemy's whereabouts and to coordinate their dispositions. When combined with their warships' increased speed and range, it enabled the Royal Navy to move rapidly to any threatened point in Britain's global empire.[36]

The rapid growth in ship speed and engagement ranges, along with the advent of stealth warships in the form of submarines, found navies devoting more resources to scouting. Submarine and destroyer flotillas were assigned to locate the enemy battle fleet and to screen its scouts from their fleet. To defend against submarine commerce raiders, destroyers were repurposed to escort cargo-ship convoys. By 1917, they were armed with hydrophones, the first workable acoustic detection system.

Meanwhile, militaries were taking their first tentative steps into the air domain. During World War I, another new kind of ship, the aircraft carrier, was introduced by the Royal Navy. Its principal initial purpose was to scout for the enemy fleet and screen enemy aircraft away from the British fleet. Land-based Royal Naval Air Service (RNAS) aircraft were used to detect enemy ships approaching Britain's shores from the English Channel and the North Sea. They also proved useful in detecting and engaging enemy submarines.

The use of wireless by belligerents also led to "scouting" through efforts to decrypt enemy coded messages. At the beginning of the Great War, the British already possessed the makings of a cryptography section ("Room 40") in their Naval Intelligence Department (NID), which they immediately put to good use, thanks to a captured German cypher book.[37] Telecommunications were also used to create a primitive command-and-control network to direct the activities of Britain's coastal and shore-based defense forces.

In summary, the Fisher Revolution witnessed the world's major navies according a relatively greater emphasis on speed, range, stealth, accuracy, and scouting relative to armor. With respect to fires, the principal emphasis was on extending range and improving accuracy, not volume fires. To gain range and accuracy, navies moved to "all-big-gun" dreadnoughts, whose uniform-caliber armament aided efforts to enhance gunnery. By gaining an advantage in speed, surface ships could also set the engagement range to their advantage or avoid battle at their discretion. Although accuracy improved significantly during this period, major gains weren't realized until after World War I. Much of the impetus toward ranged fires was driven by the emergence of submarines and torpedoes, which also led navies to establish a scouting force to identify and screen enemy torpedo craft away from the battle fleet.

"Stealth warships"—submarines—became major factors in assessing a fleet's combat potential, especially once torpedoes acquired sufficient range and accuracy to sink warships. Their stealth and their need for sufficient range and speed to operate with the fleet or to engage in commerce raiding found submarines discounting firepower and armor.

With the introduction of wireless, war moved more deeply into the electromagnetic domain, thereby greatly intensifying efforts in the scouting/counter-scouting competition between militaries while enabling them to improve command and control over their forces. The use of wireless also provided opportunities for belligerents to intercept and, if their cryptography efforts were successful, "read their enemy's mail."

The Mechanization, Aviation, and Radar Revolution

The period between the world wars produced another disruptive shift in war's character, enabled by advances in mechanization, aviation, radio communications, and radar. This Mechanization, Aviation, and Radar Revolution transformed war on land and sea and saw conflict waged with far greater intensity and effectiveness in the relatively new air and electromagnetic domains.

During the Great War, the firepower that confined both sides to static, positional trench warfare on the Western Front represented the maturation of the trend that began with the mid-nineteenth-century introduction of rifling and rapid-fire weapons. Following the war, many militaries believed that positional warfare had become the "new normal." Germany's military, however, saw things differently and placed a big bet on leveraging new technologies to restore mobility at war's tactical and operational level. The shift arrived in the form of mechanized air-land operations coordinated by radio communications. Germany's principal rival, France, however, placed far greater emphasis on firepower in both its artillery and tanks and on armor protection, including an enormous investment in its Maginot Line fortifications.

German panzer formations emphasized speed and range, sacrificing armament and armor protection to get it. As General Heinz Guderian summarized it, "Everything is therefore dependent on this: to be able to move faster than has hitherto been done [and], ... [to] carry the attack deep into the enemy's defenses."[38] When it came to armor, the Germans implicitly accepted the views of their military theorist General von Eimannsberger, who concluded, "The battle between the shell and armor was lost by armor a long time ago."[39] Early German tanks—Panzers I through IV—maxed out at twenty-five tons with a seventy-five-millimeter cannon, but all save the primitive Panzer I had speeds of twenty-five miles per hour or greater. Later German tanks, the Panther and Tiger, added armor and firepower—but not at the expense of their speed and range. Indeed, early in the war, French tanks were in many respects better than their German counterparts—but very few enjoyed an advantage in range and speed.

Rather than employing the volume fires that characterized warfare on the Western Front during the Great War, German mechanized forces relied on aircraft and motorized artillery to provide supporting fires. To direct and coordinate their highly mobile forces, the Germans placed radios in their tanks and aircraft, which they also used for scouting. Although volume fires and armor enhancements were hardly neglected, when measured against the mature stage of the preceding military revolution in the Great War, the armies that followed the German lead placed a premium on speed and range relative to firepower and armor.

The revolution in war at sea during the interwar period witnessed the eclipse of the battleship as the capital ship, displaced by the aircraft carrier. Relative to the battleship, the carrier emphasized speed, range, and scouting, while sacrificing firepower and armor. The U.S. Navy's carriers even eschewed armor-plated decks in favor of wood and kept their gun armament to a minimum, in part to maximize their aircraft complement but also to maximize the carrier's speed. Although a carrier air wing had nothing comparable to a modern battleship's firepower, its aircraft could greatly outrange the battleship's guns and could operate at speeds an order of magnitude greater than the dreadnoughts.[40] To succeed, these aircraft only needed to carry bombs far enough and heavy enough to sink a battleship, which is what happened in the decade leading up to the United States' entry into World War II.[41] Thus, only a year following the carrier-dominated fleet actions at Coral Sea and Midway, the Americans ceased building battleships.

With respect to scouting, as engagement ranges grew, scouting became more important for the simple reason that the greater the distance from which an attack could be launched, the more area needed to be searched to locate the enemy. The aircraft's speed of attack also meant that to maintain sufficient attack warning time, the enemy would need to be identified at much greater range than was the case with battleship-centered fleets.

The story on land was generally similar in the air domain. Land-based aircraft, with their relatively small payloads, could not hope to match the volume fires of land- and sea-based artillery. Rather, similar to submarines, aircraft sacrificed armor to enhance their speed and range and to boost their modest payloads. And as was the case with submarines, the emphasis on the scouting/counter-scouting competition was strong, especially in the electromagnetic domain. Both Germany and Great Britain developed sophisticated, integrated air defense systems (IADS), including radar networks, anti-aircraft guns, and interceptor aircraft, all linked to command centers. New forms of electronic jamming along with offsetting measures (electronic countermeasures; ECM) and "offsets to the offsets" (electronic counter-countermeasures; ECCM) were employed to gain a scouting advantage.

Efforts were made to enhance the accuracy of so-called strategic attacks, but the results were disappointing. In tests, the U.S. Norden bombsight demonstrated a CEP of seventy-five feet. Under combat conditions, however, it ballooned sixteen-fold, to 1,200 feet.[42] As with long-range naval gunnery accuracy in the Great War, accurate horizontal "strategic" bombing in World War II remained an aspiration, not a reality. Things were more encouraging with regard to battlefield operations, where dive-bombing greatly enhanced air-attack accuracy, as revealed by the impressive performance of German Stuka aircraft and U.S. carrier planes like the Dauntless. A hint of what was to come was provided by Japan's kamikazes, manned guided bombs whose pilots sacrificed themselves to maneuver their payload to its target. After making their first appearance in the fall of 1944, roughly 2,800 kamikazes sank 34 U.S. Navy ships, damaging 368 others and killing nearly 5,000 American sailors. Despite being detected by U.S. radar and confronting swarms of fighter-interceptors and a wall of anti-aircraft fire, one in seven kamikazes hit a ship, and more than 8 percent of these hits resulted in the ship's sinking.[43]

Toward the war's end, Germany introduced ballistic missiles—the V2s—armed with a modest payload of roughly 1,500 pounds and capable of covering 200 miles at speeds above 3,500 miles per hour. The missile's sheer speed made interception impossible. The Germans fired more than 3,000 V-2s during the war.[44] The dawn of the missile age continued the general trend toward speed and range relative to firepower and armor.

As military operations continued expanding into the electromagnetic domain, the major powers placed greater emphasis on gaining an advantage in the scouting competition, with radar, sonar, and long-range radio playing important roles, along with various forms of jamming and electronic countermeasures. Scouting's importance was highlighted by Sir Michael Howard, who observed that, particularly in the air and maritime domains, "success ultimately went to the side that was able to track the movements of its adversary and read his signals while keeping its own secret."[45] Indeed, signals intelligence and cryptography played a major role in the war, as belligerents worked to decipher their enemies' codes. Successful code-breaking efforts like ULTRA provided the British with key information regarding German military capabilities and intentions.[46] Similarly, American code-breakers provided the U.S. fleet with vital information on Japan's fleet and intentions prior to the Battle of Midway.

In brief, the Interwar Revolution saw military powers continuing the general trend toward placing greater emphasis on military systems' range, speed, scouting, and ranged fires, relative to prioritizing volume fires and armor protection. Mechanized army elements on land, carriers and submarines at sea, and planes and missiles in the air grew in importance relative to powerful artillery guns and large, heavily armed surface warships. The most formidable fortifications—such as the Maginot Line and Eban Emael—and weapon systems, like the battleship, were displaced. Tanks, submarines, and aircraft did, of course, have greater firepower than their primitive Great War ancestors did, but their relative advantages were not in volume fires, which could have been provided at far less cost if placed on the weapon systems that dominated World War I.

With the growth in engagement range and speed of attack came a corresponding increase in emphasis on scouting and on commanding and directing forces spread over increasingly large areas. Intense efforts were devoted to countering the submarine's stealth and the aircraft's speed of attack, as witnessed by the to-and-fro game of cat-and-mouse waged during the Battle of the Atlantic and the emergence of the first integrated air defense systems in the Battle of Britain, respectively. The success of code-breaking efforts, such as Britain's ULTRA and the United States' MAGIC, were major factors in their militaries' success and, consequently, were among the Second World War's most closely guarded secrets.

The Nuclear Revolution

The introduction of nuclear weapons in 1945 is widely regarding as a special case in the history of military affairs. It radically altered thinking comparable to the way quantum physics recast classical physics by presenting a new paradigm through which to understand nature, leaving many military professionals intellectually adrift. It recalls Richard Feynman's observation upon winning the Nobel Prize in Physics: "I was born not understanding quantum mechanics. . . . I still don't understand quantum mechanics!"[47]

Having discovered nuclear weapons, those who possess them still struggle to determine how they could be used to achieve victory in a world where their enemies have them as well. Nuclear weapons, especially thermonuclear weapons ("hydrogen bombs"), provide a massive boost in firepower, so great that a war involving their widespread use would lead to destruction on such a massive level as to defeat the very purpose of war as a means of advancing a belligerent's political objectives. As such, the Nuclear Revolution, which might also be called the "Firepower Revolution," represents a unique departure from previous revolutions.

Nuclear weapons' destructive power has led many military theorists and political leaders to state that their only practical use is to deter an enemy from employing them. As Bernard Brodie wrote shortly after the atomic attacks on Hiroshima and Nagasaki, "Thus far the chief purpose of our military establishment has been to win wars. From now on the chief purpose must be to avert them."[48] John Kennedy concurred, observing that in a general war involving nuclear weapons, "even the fruits of victory would be ashes in our mouth."[49]

Since 1945, despite the proliferation of nuclear weapons to at least nine states, all have refrained from employing them, even when at war. In at least one case, in the early hours of Israel's 1973 war with Egypt and Syria, when its survival might have been in question, it still refrained from resorting to its nuclear arsenal—even though its enemies lacked these weapons. The United States, through the Korean, Vietnam, and two Gulf wars, also refrained from using nuclear weapons, although its enemies lacked them, while losing more than 80,000 killed in action. Soviet Russia also did not employ nuclear weapons in its decade-long war in Afghanistan.

Simply put, having been given a blank check with respect to firepower, to date nuclear powers have refused to cash it. Instead, the two principal nuclear powers have taken steps to *reduce* the yield of their nuclear weapons and employ innovative designs with an eye toward possibly eliminating the unofficial taboo against their use. The U.S. nuclear arsenal, for example, saw its firepower shrink by roughly 75 percent between its peak at roughly 20,000 million tons (megatons) of TNT around 1960 and the Cold War's end, due in no small measure to increases in U.S. ballistic missile accuracy. Today it stands at less than 3,000 megatons.[50] The number of U.S. and Russian "high-yield" weapons (those over four and a half megatons) fell from peaks at roughly 2,000 and 800 to around 0 and 50, respectively, in 2000.[51]

In summary, the Nuclear Revolution represents a fundamental break from the military revolutions that have occurred since the Industrial Revolution, providing militaries with almost unlimited firepower. Yet nuclear-armed states have established a long tradition of nonuse, even when at war with enemies lacking these weapons. It cannot, however, be assumed that this tradition will hold. Thus, although the competition for military advantage has continued unabated since 1945, it does so under a nuclear shadow.

The Precision-Warfare Revolution

As the U.S. military did with nuclear weapons, nearly a half century later, it led the way to another disruptive shift in warfare. As the Information Revolution was gathering momentum during the 1970s, the United States sought to leverage its strong lead in information technologies over Soviet Russia to develop new sources of military advantage. Its efforts were consistent with the general trend toward a decline in relative emphasis on volume fires and armor and toward weapon systems' speed, range, and accuracy (or "precision"), as well as toward winning the scouting/counter-scouting competition, such as through enhancements in stealth, particularly in the air and undersea domains of warfare. When these new capabilities were combined with existing systems within innovative operational concepts, they produced a quantum boost in military effectiveness—the Precision-Warfare Revolution—at whose core is the reconnaissance-strike complex, with its emphasis on scouting, battle networks, and extended-range precision fires.

As the name suggests, the Precision-Warfare Revolution saw remarkable advances in weapon accuracy. The CEPs for unguided bombs remained at roughly 500 feet in the two decades following World War II.[52]

When laser-guided "smart" bombs were developed in the late 1960s, they reduced CEPs to under ten feet.[53] Combined with stealth aircraft linked to a nascent battle network during the First Gulf War, precision-guided munitions yielded over an order of magnitude boost in military effectiveness. As Brigadier General Buster C. Glosson, the U.S. military's director of air campaign plans during the First Gulf War, noted, "One need only look back to our raids on Schweinfurt, Germany, in World War II to see how dramatically precision weapons have enhanced our capabilities. . . . Two raids of 300 B-17 bombers could not achieve with 3,000 bombs what two F-117s can do with only four."[54] Aircraft loss rates also decreased dramatically. In a shift almost as dramatic as that from battleships to aircraft carriers during World War II, after the First Gulf War the U.S. military's combat-aircraft designs prioritized stealth with an eye to sustaining its advantage in the scouting competition. It also prioritized augmenting the quantity and quality of its PGMs, emphasizing accurate fires over volume fires.

The Precision-Warfare Revolution also led to efforts to boost the U.S. military's speed of action by enhancing its battle networks' ability to compress the engagement sequence, the time between which a target is first identified and when it is engaged. During the First Gulf War, it took roughly three days to create the Air Tasking Order (ATO), which, generally speaking, converts information regarding enemy targets into airstrike orders for U.S. air forces. Eight years later, during the Air Force's participation in Operation Allied Force against Serbian forces in Yugoslavia, the average time between identifying a target and engaging it was compressed to between three and four hours. Four years later, during the Second Gulf War, the U.S. Air Force established a Time-Sensitive Targeting Cell (TSTC), which succeeded in executing some attacks in less than half an hour from the time the target was spotted.[55] Soon drones, which had earlier been used primarily for scouting purposes, were armed, thereby fusing the "reconnaissance" and "strike" elements and compressing the engagement sequence further still.[56]

The growing emphasis on range and compressing the engagement sequence also manifested itself through beyond visual range (BVR) air-to-air combat engagements. In the mid-1960s, an aircraft's gun range was roughly 500 meters, while scouting was accomplished by the pilot, whose eyes provided an effective range of about two nautical miles at roughly two degrees wide. Air-to-air missiles (AAMs) offered the possibility of engaging targets beyond visual range—if they could be identified.[57] With the emergence of the U.S. military's nascent battle network, every coalition air-combat victory in the First Gulf War was achieved with air-to-air missiles.[58] Guns, which accounted for roughly two-thirds of kills in air-to-air engagements during the late 1960s, dropped to less than 5 percent of the total between 1990 and 2002. BVR AAMs, on the other hand, registered no kills in the 1960s but more than half of the air-to-air combat kills between 1990 and 2002.[59] In brief, the Precision-Warfare Revolution found the United States' air forces emphasizing accurate, ranged fires. As in other war-fighting domains, with increased engagement range came a need to scout over a greater area and to defeat enemy scouting through stealth and other forms of electronic deception and suppression.

The First Gulf War also revealed the continued decline of armor's value in land warfare. Just as battleships had succumbed to air attack, the First Gulf War confirmed armor's vulnerability in the absence of effective air cover. Prior to the onset of ground-combat operations, the U.S. Air Force used precision-guided munitions to destroy hundreds of Iraqi armored vehicles.[60]

Recent efforts to enhance protection by increasing armor have proved costly and ineffective, even against irregular forces. During the wars in Afghanistan and Iraq, the U.S. military spent more than $47 billion to deploy mine-resistant, ambush-protected (MRAP) heavily armored vehicles to protect its troops from improvised explosive devices (IEDs)—roadside bombs that can be manufactured at a small fraction of an MRAP's cost. The MRAPs' effectiveness remains a matter of debate.[61]

In recent years, the U.S. Army, generally considered the world's premier land force, has reduced its emphasis on heavily armored forces. Its current tank, the Abrams, was first fielded more than thirty years ago. In 2019, the Army's chief of staff, General Mark Milley, indicated that armor would not be a significant priority in the next tank, unless he could identify a "holy grail of technologies," declaring, "If we can discover a material that is significantly lighter in weight that gives you the same armor protection, that would be a real significant breakthrough."[62] The U.S. Marine Corps has gone even further, deciding to eliminate its tank battalions and cut its cannon artillery units by nearly 80 percent in favor of increasing its extended-range and precision fires, advanced scouting capabilities, and battle networks.[63]

In retrospect, the last decades of the twentieth century witnessed the general trend away from volume fires and armor and toward enhancing the speed and range of systems, weapons, and networks, as well as accurate, ranged fires. The scouting competition has intensified with the U.S. military's fielding of a battle network, made up of, among other things, satellites for precision navigation and timing, and airborne early warning and command, control, and communications systems.

In summary, since the Industrial Revolution, those military organizations leading the way to a disruptive change in war's character have—*generally speaking*—emphasized speed, range, and stealth of military systems relative to armor. Similarly, the trend with respect to fires has been toward favoring accurate, ranged fires relative to volume fires—this despite the fact that the period witnessed major improvements in armor protection and firepower.

These trends are not uniform or absolute. Trends are not universal "laws." Warfare is so varied that there will always be situations in which massed fires or armor plate will be what is needed most. The path from the mid-nineteenth century to today is hardly smooth or straight, as witnessed by the emphasis on ships' armor in the mid-1800s and volume fires in the First World War. What we do see, however, is a general trend in favor of other attributes—speed, range, scouting, accurate fires—that contribute relatively more to a military's combat potential.

Perhaps this should not surprise us. This era of military revolutions has also coincided with the Era of Domain Expansion. Prior to the Industrial Revolution, warfare had existed for millennia solely in the "traditional" land and sea domains. By World War I, it had expanded to the electromagnetic and undersea domains and, in nascent form, to the air. Following the Second World War, expansion continued, with military systems positioned in space and on the seabed. More recently, the cyber domain has become an area of intense military competition. Militaries operate in these domains because they offer the possibility of gaining an advantage over their rivals.

Interestingly, relative to forces operating in the land and sea surface domains, four of the six new domains—the electromagnetic, air, space, and cyberspace—are characterized by *speed of action* and *extended range*, while the undersea domain offers stealth. Perhaps it's not all that surprising, then, that as militaries moved into these domains, they sought to leverage those characteristics that offered the greatest opportunity for improving their effectiveness.

The Nuclear Revolution stands alone. Nuclear weapons transformed warfare so dramatically and the weapons it spawned are so terrible that, for three-quarters of a century, nuclear-armed states have refrained from using them, even when their survival may have been at risk. This, of course, could change quickly. But if so, and Armageddon came, it would render discussions like this moot.

Are we likely to see these trends continue? To what extent do they point the way to informing the characteristics of new and disruptive forms of military competition? Chapters 3 and 4 strongly suggest that these trends are reflected in the maturing precision-warfare regime and in the technologies that are driving an emerging, overlapping military revolution.

CHAPTER THREE

The Mature Precision-Warfare Regime

You go into the Battle to *hit the other fellow in the eye first* so that he can't see you. Yes! you hit him first, you hit him hard and you keep on hitting. *That's your safety!* You don't get hit back!

—ADMIRAL JACKIE FISHER

This is really about not firepower but information. For it is really the acquisition, processing and dissemination of information that lies at the root of the speed and accuracy with which fires can now be applied.

—RICHARD E. SIMPKIN

OVER A QUARTER OF a century after Andrew Marshall forwarded the MTR assessment to senior Defense Department leaders, I was invited to meet with the Air Force general charged with identifying key emerging trends in the military competition and assessing how his service might best position itself to exploit them. My colleagues and I on Congress's

National Defense Strategy Commission had recently finished our work reviewing the Defense Department's new strategy, and I anticipated our conversation would focus on its findings and recommendations. To my surprise, the general told me he had a well-worn, marked-up copy of the MTR assessment on his desk, as he found himself referring to it frequently in his work. He found its description of what a mature precision-warfare regime might look like interesting. Now, a quarter of a century later, the regime was finally reaching its mature stage—one in which at least two major military powers had exploited its potential. The United States' principal military rivals—China especially—were now fielding their own versions of the reconnaissance-strike complex.

This chapter draws on that assessment and recent trends to describe the maturing precision-warfare regime's general characteristics. It goes on to speculate as to whether the current situation represents a "new normal" in military affairs and whether we might see it overturned by further disruptive changes in the near future. It finds that in an environment where to be seen is to run a high risk of becoming a victim of precision attack, the "scouting" or "reconnaissance" competition is likely to assume relatively greater importance than in the past, especially as advanced militaries look to enhance their scouting proficiency by exploiting two relatively new warfare domains: space and cyberspace. With that in mind, the space competition is highlighted. The shroud of secrecy covering operations in cyberspace precludes a comparable treatment.

The MTR Assessment

The 1992 MTR assessment's description of a mature precision-warfare regime has held up well over time. In particular, the assessment highlighted the importance of winning the scouting competition, noting, "Three central areas of technological progression may be laying the foundation for a military-technical revolution. First, there is the growing ability to gather, process, and disseminate information (especially information concerning potential targets) far more rapidly than ever before. ... This advantage may be extended by a rapidly growing capability, either through active or passive measures, to deny the enemy information it needs to attack. ... Thus the potential exists to create an 'information gap' between friendly and enemy forces, both in terms of peacetime competition and wartime operations."[1]

The assessment pointed out that an advantage in scouting, supported by a robust battle network, would enable the effective use of accurate, extended-range fires.[2] Simply put, given "precision" accuracy, to be seen and tracked is to run a high risk of being engaged and destroyed—hence the need to win the scouting competition and establish "information dominance," which, as the assessment concluded, "could well be the *sine qua non* for effective military operations in future conflicts."[3]

Owing to the combination of increased speed and extended range over which reconnaissance-strike complexes can function, operations "become increasingly simultaneous and less sequential in their execution."[4] As operational ranges expanded, the military services have found themselves increasingly intruding into each other's traditional war-fighting domains, while also competing for a role in the relatively new war-fighting domains of space and cyberspace. In brief, modern recce-strike complexes conduct "cross-domain" operations at extended ranges, drawing on forces from all the military services and from all domains, as appropriate. Still, although the Precision-Warfare Revolution yielded weapons whose accuracy is independent of range, "range costs." Operating at extended ranges, whether for scouting ("reconnaissance") or delivery systems ("strike"), comes at a substantial premium.

Anti-Access/Area-Denial

Now that the Precision-Warfare Revolution is reaching its mature stage, with U.S. military rivals like China and Russia having reduced the gap, it's possible to provide a more detailed description of its salient characteristics. The competition, however, is highly dynamic, from both a geopolitical and a military-technical perspective. Thus, the best that can be offered here is a few frames of a moving picture.

The U.S. military's striking performance in both Gulf wars, in the Balkan War of 1999, and in Afghanistan in 2001 made it tempting to view "precision" warfare as heavily favoring the offense. But these wars were fought by the world's sole superpower against minor-power militaries and nonstate entities. Moreover, the U.S. military's approach to projecting power against these enemies remained based on a century-old approach whose effectiveness is coming under ever greater challenge. In it, forces are initially sent, not directly against the enemy, but to a relatively secure forward location where combat power can be built up prior to initiating large-scale offensive operations. In World War I, the focal point of this effort was France; in World War II, it was Britain in Europe and Australia in the Pacific. The Cold War saw U.S. forces pre-deployed to distant bases rimming the Eurasian heartland, prepared to defend forward immediately in the event of war. During the Korean War, U.S. bases in Japan were effectively sanctuaries from attack, as were its bases in places like Guam and Thailand during the Vietnam War. Iraq avoided attacking U.S. forces even as they built up in the Middle East before both Gulf wars. This happy state of affairs, however, is unlikely to endure.

The U.S. military's dominance in precision warfare could not but impress the world's militaries, especially those of the two revisionist great powers, China and Russia. They have been working out how to counter this approach to power projection for more than a quarter century and are achieving impressive results. The U.S. military, meanwhile, has had an equally long period of time to develop the "bad habits" associated with operating in what it calls "permissive environments"—those where enemies lack the means to seriously contest U.S. scouting, network, and strike operations.

In particular, the growing ability of China's PLA to scout over wide areas and strike over long distances with high accuracy is at the core of its "counter-intervention" strategy. Its purpose is to defeat the U.S. military's approach to projecting and sustaining military power along its preferred, traditional lines. In China's and Russia's efforts to catch up to the Americans, they initially fielded a defensive form of reconnaissance-strike complex popularly known as an anti-access/area-denial (A2/AD) complex. This was anticipated in the initial MTR assessment, which noted, "Of course, integrating information systems with extended-range PGMs will also be employed for defensive purposes; for example, in strategic or theater defense architectures."[5] The follow-on assessment pointed out that as these A2/AD complexes arose, key U.S. military systems and facilities would become increasingly vulnerable to attack: "As this military revolution matures ... forward bases—those huge, sprawling complexes that bring to mind such places as Malta, Singapore, Subic Bay, Clark Air Base, and Dharan—will become liabilities, not precious assets. ... Rather than acting as a source of assurance to friends and allies in the region, these bases will be a source of anxiety. ... Forward-deployed naval forces may be able to offset the future liabilities of forward bases, but only partially and probably not for very long, as currently configured."[6] To date, China's PLA has fielded the most sophisticated

A2/AD complex. It is designed to deter and, if need be, defeat U.S. military intervention in a Chinese-initiated war in the Western Pacific.

China's "Warfares"

Broadly speaking, the PLA's vision of modern warfare is seen as a contest between competing "operational systems." This is similar to Russian descriptions of reconnaissance-strike complexes and American views on precision warfare. China's operational system comprises five subsystems: the *information-confrontation* and *reconnaissance-intelligence* ("reconnaissance" or "scouting") systems; the *command* and *integrated support* (or "battle network") systems; and the *firepower-strike* ("strike") systems. Within this context, the PLA sees the military competition centering on deconstructing the enemy's reconnaissance-strike complexes—what the Chinese call "systems destruction warfare."[7]

A consistent PLA theme is the importance of achieving surprise, enabled by deception and speed of action. It is no wonder, therefore, that the PLA prioritizes gaining an advantage in the air, cyber, electromagnetic, and space, or "speed," domains.[8] Its 2013 *Science of Military Strategy* concludes, "The informatization of war means has provided an unprecedented possibility to pick up the operational pace and shorten the war progress. High speed and fast pace in the time dimension can effectively compress the enemy's defense space."[9]

In 2015, the PLA introduced the concept of "Winning Informatized Local Wars," further stressing the importance of seizing control in the cyberspace, space, and electromagnetic domains. The Chinese are investing accordingly, prioritizing scouting networks, including counter-scouting capabilities within the context of what they call "informationalized warfare."[10]

The PLA believes that controlling the "intangible" domains in which cyber and electronic warfare (EW) capabilities operate is essential to success in war. Thus, informationalized warfare emphasizes various forms of electronic attack, including employing anti-radiation and electromagnetic weapons, as well as jamming and deception, all supported by kinetic strikes, while defending against similar attacks by the enemy.[11] Given the importance the PLA attaches to the competition in the intangible domains, it comes as no surprise that winning the space/counter-space competition is also accorded priority. The 2013 *Science of Military Strategy* anticipates that future wars will begin in space and cyberspace, arguing that "seizing command of space and network dominance will become crucial for obtaining comprehensive superiority on the battlefield and conquering an enemy." This reinforces the PLA's emphasis on controlling the electromagnetic (EM) and cyber domains, as well as employing direct-ascent anti-satellite (ASAT) missiles, directed-energy weapons, and co-orbital weapons to wage "space information warfare, space blockade warfare, space orbit attack warfare, space-defense warfare, and space-to-land attacks."[12]

The formation of the PLA Strategic Support Force (PLASSF) in 2016 reflects the growing priority given to these competitions. The PLASSF is charged with achieving dominance in the space, electromagnetic, and cyber domains, including integrating the forces in these domains to conduct cross-domain operations. It commands satellite information attack and defense forces; electronic and internet assault forces; campaign information operations forces (which include conventional electronic warfare forces); anti-radiation assault forces; and battlefield cyber-warfare forces.[13]

In waging systems-destruction warfare, the PLA sees computer-centered battle networks as the nerve centers of modern military forces and activity, linking, coordinating, and informing the reconnaissance-strike complex's (RSC's) "scouting" or "reconnaissance" elements with its strike forces. Information superiority is achieved primarily through the cyber and EM domains, and through strike forces resident in the physical domains, principally by forces operating in the air domain, including strike aircraft and precision-strike ballistic and cruise missiles, supplemented by an integrated air defense system (IADS) composed of surface-to-air missiles (SAMs) and advanced fighter-interceptor aircraft. This strike and air defense arm of China's RSC, especially its conventional-armed ballistic missiles, is seen as central to the PLA's ability to wage a successful offensive campaign in the Western Pacific.[14]

In a war in the Western Pacific, the PLA would prefer to initiate operations. In addition to strikes against U.S. and allied forces in the intangible domains and space, it would also seek to control the air domain. Priority targets would probably include air bases, missile bases, aircraft carriers, and warships equipped with land-attack cruise missiles, as well as ground-based air and missile defense systems. Chinese air and missile defenses would be tasked to defeat any U.S. and allied air elements surviving the PLA's initial offensive strikes.[15]

Beyond the near- to midterm future, the Chinese Communist Party (CCP) anticipates creating a new source of competitive advantage by developing an ability to wage "intelligentized warfare" through its Military-

Civil Fusion (MCF) Development Strategy. The MCF effort covers all three elements of China's RSC, exploiting AI to field autonomous command-and-control (C2) systems to enhance and accelerate ISR data analysis and fusion to achieve an advantage in the reconnaissance and battle network competitions, thereby boosting its strike element's effectiveness. The CCP began implementing MCF in 2015, emphasizing leveraging dual-use technologies to enhance PLA efforts in developing new, innovative operational concepts that boost the speed at which war is waged.[16] Intelligentized warfare is rooted in the PLA's assessment that war is transitioning from "system confrontation" to "algorithm confrontation." Thus, a key competition will emerge centered on establishing and exploiting an "algorithmic advantage." Toward this end, the PLA is developing autonomous unmanned systems in the air, land, sea surface, and undersea domains capable of fusing its RSC's scouting and strike functions.[17]

The defensive "shield" provided by China's A2/AD complex can also be augmented to support Beijing's hegemonic objectives. Ideally, from the CCP's perspective, over time the Western Pacific military balance would shift so decisively in its favor that Beijing could prevail without fighting, as countries along China's periphery lying under the PLA's A2/AD shadow would see resistance as futile. Simply put, the Chinese would much prefer to "Finlandize" the Western Pacific than risk a war to conquer it.[18] This strategy conforms to the teachings of China's great military theorist Sun-Tzu, who declared that the mark of a great general was not to win a hundred battles but to win without fighting.

With the rise of the PLA's A2/AD complex, the U.S. military finds itself needing to transform its approach to projecting power. Success will likely require positioning a substantial portion of U.S. forces beyond the range of China's thickest A2/AD counter-intervention forces, at least early in a conflict. The option of deploying forces outside a rival's A2/AD complex may be unique to the United States, given its status as an insular global power. Other advanced militaries located in close proximity to one another, such as Japan in relation to China, may have no choice but to position their forces within easy range of the enemy's main recce-strike forces. Yet even in the United States' case, the hefty premium involved in operating from extended range suggests that the U.S. military will need to find ways to position a major part of its forces forward. These forces will probably have to rely on some combination of hardening, mobility, and various forms of physical and electronic deception to counter enemy scouting and strike operations, along with active counter-scouting and counter-strike defenses to keep their losses at acceptable levels. Moreover, given the range at which attacks can be launched and the speed at which they can be executed, acquiring effective early warning of an attack may find scouting forces having to search over an expanded area, since a search area increases as the square of the range over which the attack can be initiated.

A Twenty-First-Century No-Man's-Land?

What might define the mature precision-warfare regime's general geographic contours? Generally speaking, operations can be viewed as occurring in one of three broad areas that are not dissimilar from traditional zones of conflict, save for their scope and depth. Up until the twentieth century, these zones generally included a "contested area" where fleets or armies met and "rear areas," which were safe havens from the threat of any significant organized enemy violence.

Beginning with World War II, however, the introduction of aircraft capable of carrying substantial payloads over long distances left those rear areas that lacked robust air defenses highly vulnerable to large-scale attacks. In a contemporary general war between great military powers, each side's rear area is defined as being under the friendly force's principal A2/AD umbrella and outside that of its rival.

The existence of a rear area assumes, of course, that at least one of the competing military powers is quite distant from the other and out of range of most of its adversary's scouting and strike forces. The United States provides a case in point. Its geographic position gives it a large rear area, as even its littorals and continental shelf are (with the exception of Alaska) remote from its great-power rivals, China and Russia. The same condition does not hold with respect to the other major military powers. As noted, significant portions of China and a large part of Japan would be within range of a substantial portion of each side's scouting and strike forces. A similar condition would exist between China and India and between China and Russia. These overlapping A2/AD complexes could form a kind of twenty-first-century "no-man's-land" where, at least in the opening stages of a conflict, both sides will find it relatively (and perhaps prohibitively) costly to engage in offensive operations.

Unlike the Great War's no-man's-land on the Western Front, however, a contemporary no-man's-land could be measured not in thousands of yards but in hundreds or even thousands of miles. For example, suppose the United States and Japan were to field their own A2/AD complex along the First Island Chain to counter China's. Large swaths of the Western Pacific, including significant parts of coastal China and perhaps all of Japan, along with forward-based U.S. forces in places like Guam and Okinawa, could fall within no-man's-land. As with troops maneuvering between the trench lines during World War I, modern forces attempting to operate in areas covered by dense enemy A2/AD forces would run a high risk of being identified by the enemy's scouting forces and subjected to attack.

What kinds of forces might be able to operate at acceptable levels of risk in a Western Pacific no-man's-land? Those blessed with speed and counter-scouting abilities, such as ballistic missiles, long-range stealthy aircraft, and advanced attack submarines, would appear to qualify, as well as small, highly dispersed forces capable of exploiting local cover, such as Special Forces maneuvering in jungles. On the other hand, forces tethered to large bases, such as major warships and combat aircraft, would be well served, at least initially, to operate from friendly rear areas if possible.[19]

It may be that highly dispersed irregular forces, armed with modest scouting systems, such as drones and human scouts, and equipped with weaponized drones and "G-RAMM"—precision-guided rockets, artillery, mortars, and missiles—might prove able to survive sufficiently well to operate effectively. Despite their modest payloads, G-RAMM munitions' accuracy could enable these irregulars to hold at risk unhardened bases and structures, as well as key staging areas such as ports and airfields. If they can be linked to a battle network—a big "if" given the risk of revealing their position by actively communicating—these forces could also provide scouting information to more formidable strike forces.

A nascent version of this kind of force was on display when, shortly after 9/11, U.S. Special Operations Forces operating with the Afghan Northern Alliance called in strikes from extended-range U.S. aircraft. The Second Lebanon War in 2006 saw Hezbollah irregulars armed with unguided "RAMM" weaponry hold their own against the Israeli Defense Force. If successful, these new-age irregular forces could represent a contemporary version of Germany's *Sturmtruppen* (storm troopers), who successfully maneuvered in the no-man's-land between the trench lines in the Great War. Such combinations of forward-deployed irregular forces, especially if they are able to operate in complex terrain, such as cities and mountainous jungles, when supported by remote fires, could create "holes" in the enemy's A2/AD fabric, facilitating offensive maneuver.[20]

A "New Normal"?

Great-power militaries tasked with projecting power have a strong incentive to create a "new normal" where offensive maneuver becomes possible, even if not to the extent enjoyed by the U.S. military in recent decades. For starters, aside from the Americans, both the Chinese and Russians, given their revisionist aims, show a keen interest in projecting power, particularly in areas bordering their homelands.

What remains to be determined is whether the Precision-Warfare Revolution's maturing represents a new normal in the military competition, as described above. By "new normal," I mean a regime whose defining characteristics will endure for an extended period—a couple of decades or so. If so, the military competition, from a U.S. perspective, would make projecting power along its "traditional" lines a highly—and probably prohibitively—costly proposition. In situations where A2/AD complexes overlap, this may compel militaries, at least early in a conflict, to emphasize operations in the relatively new competitive domains of space, cyberspace, and the seabed, where the offense seems likely to hold an advantage, and perhaps in the air domain as well.[21] Here it may be possible to make significant gains at acceptable cost. Moreover, if, as Chinese military theorists believe, winning the competition in the space, cyberspace, and electromagnetic domains is the key to winning the scouting competition, it may enable the winner to restore offensive maneuver in the "traditional" land and maritime domains.

The balance of this chapter explores how militaries might succeed in opening up no-man's-land for offensive operations in the mature precision-warfare regime. Here it's important to remember that the situation as just described is as it exists in *peacetime*, or at the point prior to the major powers going to war. Once the war begins, there may be opportunities to employ existing or emerging forces and capabilities through innovative war-fighting (or operational) concepts to enable effective offensive operations.

What might these opportunities be? How can they be exploited? How might militaries restore freedom of offensive maneuver when engaged in a contest of dueling reconnaissance-strike complexes? Four general approaches are presented. They are not exhaustive; nor are they mutually exclusive. Indeed, they are all but certain to be pursued in some combination. Two focus on neutralizing core elements of the reconnaissance-strike complex—specifically, the enemy's relatively limited arsenal of extended-range scouting and strike assets—as a means of expanding the set of promising offensive options. As there is nothing to prevent a military from attempting to suppress the enemy's extended-range scouting *and* strike forces simultaneously, one should expect that priority would be accorded to targeting enemy systems that *combine* the scouting and strike functions, such as armed scout drones. A third option involves horizontal escalation, whereby a military conducts operations outside the main theater of war in another where it enjoys a competitive advantage. Finally, a military may simply attempt to wage offensive war through attrition, suffering disproportionate losses to prevail over the defense.

Breaking an enemy's hold over no-man's-land requires suppressing its recce-strike complex. Thus, the struggle will center on the scouting/counter-scouting (or "scouting"), network/counter-network (or "network"), and strike/counter-strike (or "strike") competitions. How might a military prevail in these competitions? The answer is far from obvious. Although cyber strikes will almost certainly play a significant and perhaps a major role in the struggle to gain the upper hand in this duel between rival reconnaissance-strike complexes, it appears highly unlikely that any military would bet the house on a cyber offensive, by itself, proving decisive.

If initially positioning scouting and strike forces within range of the enemy's thickest A2/AD defenses is a risky proposition, then most would need to be based in the friendly forces' rear area, beyond the enemy's main A2/AD forces. Assuming that access to space assets will be problematic—an issue we'll tackle presently—then extended-range terrestrial-based forces may shoulder much of the burden for scouting the far reaches of no-man's-land.

The kinds of forces that appear the most capable of operating in relative safety in a terrestrial no-man's-land, such as stealthy long-range manned and unmanned aircraft, mobile ballistic and cruise missile launchers, submarines, unmanned submersibles, and Special Operations Forces, are those that emphasize speed, mobility, stealth, or some combination thereof—characteristics designed to counter the enemy's scouting efforts. They are also relatively expensive and, therefore, available only in relatively modest numbers.

The U.S. military, for example, has only a handful of long-range stealthy bombers and guided-missile submarines (SSGNs).[22] The U.S. Navy's carrier air wing is only beginning to incorporate stealth aircraft, which have less range than those that flew off its decks half a century ago.[23] Its nuclear-attack submarine (SSN) force is scheduled to decline precipitously as the *Los Angeles* class boats reach obsolescence at a faster rate than new submarines are being commissioned. The U.S. Air Force's stealth fighter aircraft lack the range to operate from outside China's thickening A2/AD complex without aerial refueling, which is provided by tanker aircraft that are not stealthy.

This exceedingly modest complement of extended-range scouting and strike systems, the product of the U.S. military's decades of operating in relatively permissive threat environments, will need to be carefully husbanded in war, as they cannot be replaced quickly or cheaply. Thus, ways will have to be found to position more combat power forward. Or perhaps the principal focus of U.S. power-projection operations will need to be at the boundary between no-man's-land and the U.S. military's rear area, where the balance of forces is likely to be most favorable, as part of a gradual rollback of an enemy's A2/AD complex.

The Scouting Competition

Since electromagnetic means for scouting were introduced in the early twentieth century and computers arrived at midcentury, scouting has become progressively more dependent on various types of sensors, radio communications, and computational power for generating, evaluating, processing, and distributing scouting data and the information derived from it. Today advanced battle networks use the information from scouting operations to direct and coordinate the actions of widely distributed strike elements, including weapon platforms, munitions (such as missiles), and cyber payloads.

With the introduction of precision-guided munitions, if a target is identified and tracked, an attacker has a high probability of destroying it. Consequently, forces have a strong incentive to avoid being detected in the first place and to break the enemy's scouting contact if efforts at avoidance fail. As the MTR assessment concluded, "Warfare will become more of a competition between 'hiders' and 'finders.' Targets that can be identified and tracked (if they are mobile) will run a high risk of being destroyed."[24] To avoid detection and destruction, the assessment foresaw militaries emphasizing "active and passive defensive measures (e.g., stealth, electronic warfare, deception, cover and concealment, mobility, air and missile defenses, etc.) [being] employed to protect friendly information systems."[25] We can think of this "hider-finder" competition as a "scouting/counter-scouting" competition.

The assessment noted that the competition between "hiders" and "finders" would be intense, since "establishing information dominance, or an information gap over one's adversary at the strategic and operational level, will be increasingly important to the success of military operations."[26] Thus, achieving "information dominance" becomes perhaps the top priority at the onset of war. The assessment also found that "since establishing information superiority could be *the decisive operation* in future conflicts, and since this objective could be achieved early in the war, we should expect that increasing emphasis will be placed on achieving surprise," through preemption.[27]

Gaining a Scouting Advantage

Given the key role played by forces in space and cyberspace in the scouting/counter-scouting competition, they appear to be particularly attractive targets for preemption. As will be elaborated on presently, a satellite network can cast an "unblinking eye" over wide areas, but as currently constituted, satellites appear to suffer from a lack of defenses while moving in generally predictable orbits. The ability to attack satellites successfully using kinetic interceptors and directed-energy weapons (such as laser ASATs) and by jamming has been demonstrated. It may also be possible to disrupt or corrupt satellite functions through cyber attacks.[28] At present, many satellites' high cost and long production lead times only add to an enemy's incentive to attack them early in a conflict. Other scouting forces, such as the radars of integrated air defense systems and early warning aircraft positioned at forward air bases, would also be tempting targets for preemption to preclude them from dispersing.

The scouting competition is also waged by employing decoys, jamming, and other forms of electronic warfare, including "spoofing" and digital range frequency memory (DRFM, or "DUR-fum").[29] Passive counter-scouting measures include camouflage, applying stealth coatings to military systems such as aircraft, and making systems mobile. Militaries can emphasize electronic emissions control (EMCON), thereby reducing the amount of communications data available to enemy scouting forces. This can also be accomplished by developing and implementing enhanced cyber defenses and communicating through buried fiber-optic cables where possible.

Winning the scouting competition may also be aided by securing information on the enemy's scouting plans and operations, and destroying or corrupting the information provided by its scouting forces. Such efforts would likely include cryptanalysis (attempting to break the enemy's communications codes) and engaging in cyber operations to exfiltrate unencrypted data, thereby gaining insight into how and where the enemy plans to employ its scouting assets. Given the recent remarkable advances in artificial intelligence, scouting will probably involve "algorithmic warfare," with competing AI systems plowing through vast amounts of data to identify patterns of enemy behavior that might elude human analysts. Identifying enemy operational tendencies may also aid commanders in employing their forces more effectively, similar to the way the introduction of operations research aided the allies in identifying effective convoy operations during the Battle of the Atlantic in World War II.[30] AI could potentially assist efforts to develop malware, which could be used to erase or corrupt enemy scouting information, including the enemy's AI algorithms themselves. If these efforts are successful, enemy commanders may lose confidence in their scouts, producing a "mission kill," in which much of the enemy's scouting force continues to operate but where its product is suspect.

Exploiting a Scouting Advantage

Assuming that friendly forces gain the upper hand in the scouting competition, a military can expand the range of friendly scouting and strike forces operating in no-man's-land, since they can now do so at significantly reduced risk.[31] Even partial success in the scouting competition may prove crucial. If friendly forces can identify "holes" in the enemy's scouting coverage, even if they are only transitory, they may be exploited to conduct scouting and strike operations by forces that enter the "gapped" area for a brief time and then depart before the enemy can redeploy its scouting forces to close the gap.[32] Such operations would be somewhat reminiscent of the Doolittle Raid in April 1942, in which U.S. forces dashed forward for a brief period inside Japan's defensive perimeter, launching bomber aircraft from the carrier *Hornet* to execute an attack on Tokyo.[33] In this case, the bombers' greater range also reduced the time the *Hornet* had to remain in no-man's-land.[34]

If one side gains a clear advantage in the scouting competition, the match between the two militaries' recce-strike complexes would be roughly analogous to two boxers, one of whom has had sand thrown in his eyes. As the MTR assessment described the situation with respect to land warfare, "If a favorable information [or scouting] gap is created, ground forces would likely have strong incentives to abandon their traditional role of closing with and destroying the enemy in favor of employing ranged fires as the decisive element in combat. Line-of-sight (LOS) weapon systems—principally armored forces and helicopters—would be employed in the traditional role of cavalry. They would screen enemy forces that, having lost the information assets necessary to employ deep strikes (at least against most friendly mobile targets), would have to rely on direct-fire [line-of-sight] engagements in conducting ground combat operations."[35]

Those land forces on the short end of the scouting competition would, if possible, seek opportunities to fight in "the clinches," in "complex terrain" such as jungles and cities, where extended-range scouting and fires are less effective. They could also break down into small groups waging irregular warfare.

In a general war involving great powers, however, the history of warfare suggests that total scouting superiority—information dominance—will be difficult to achieve. Recalling our two boxers, having sand thrown in one's eyes does not result in total blindness, only greatly (and temporarily) impaired vision. Importantly, the boxer whose vision is unimpaired may not know his rival's true state of visual impairment. Advantage in the scouting competition may also prove a fleeting phenomenon, given the myriad ways a first-rank military has of tapping into the global information grid. For example, a belligerent power may be able to scout using commercial satellites owned by firms of neutral powers, or from data collected by seabed arrays belonging to a nonaligned state, or through spies using commercial communications. What seems more likely is that both sides will experience scouting "gaps" and "lags" to varying degrees. Even our sandy-eyed boxer still has his sense of hearing and smell, while retaining at least some of his vision.

The BDA Problem

A key factor in winning the scouting competition centers on not only degrading the enemy's ability to scout but also *knowing when this has been accomplished, to what degree,* and *for how long.* A clever belligerent may employ both active and passive counter-scouting measures—especially those involving deception—to deceive the enemy into believing it has seized the scouting high ground and can employ its forces at much lower risk than is actually the case. If the enemy falls for the bait, it risks being caught in a "scouting ambush."

How do you know when your counter-scouting operations have been successful? And how long will your success last before the enemy restores an effective scouting ability? The key here is the scouting force's ability to conduct "battle damage assessment" (BDA). Determining with a high degree of confidence that an enemy's scouting ability has been degraded to an acceptable level to warrant engaging in offensive maneuver is both critical to success and challenging to accomplish. Accurate battle damage assessment is also needed to avoid wasting scarce strike forces in follow-on attacks, especially if operations are being conducted at extended ranges.

Even in earlier times when engagement ranges were measured in hundreds of yards, not thousands of miles, and when the targets were often enemy forces within the human eye's field of vision, it could be challenging to determine if your forces had been detected by enemy scouts. Today the problem is far more complex. Providing accurate information on the enemy's scouting ability may require knowing whether its radar has been disabled by an attack or has simply ceased emitting, if a satellite's optical sensors have been "blinded" by a laser or successfully shielded, or if an AI-directed missile defense system has been corrupted by malware or is simply feigning failure.

In some cases, BDA may be easy to ascertain, such as when kinetic munitions physically destroy a radar. This will still require friendly forces, be they satellites, stealthy unmanned aerial vehicles (UAVs), or Special Operations Forces, to scout the area effectively after an attack. Yet doing so may prove difficult.

Fixed Targets

Assuming that friendly forces gain a scouting advantage, where should they concentrate their efforts? Scouting forces might disperse initially to locate the enemy's main forces. If successful, the scouts could be massed to support strike forces through the "engagement sequence"—from when the target is first identified all the way through to BDA operations following an attack.

In general, scouting is typically less challenging for fixed targets, like major military bases, and key economic infrastructure, such as bridges, power plants, and seabed oil wellheads, than for mobile targets. Fixed targets can be mapped or "registered" in peacetime. Some mobile targets are easier to track than others. Many satellites travel in fairly predictable paths, and power for maneuvering them is typically very limited. So even though satellites are not in fixed locations, targeting a given satellite may be analogous to attacking a train as it arrives at a station. You know the track (orbit); you know the schedule (when the satellite is scheduled to pass a particular point); so you plan your strike for when the "train" arrives at the "station." The situation at maritime chokepoints is somewhat similar in that the search problem is greatly reduced by the target's need to transit a known point.

Of course, even fixed targets can pose challenges for scouting forces. For example, given that strike assets are always limited—especially for extended-range strikes—commanders will want to strike fixed targets when they are most vulnerable and when the payoff is highest. For example, bases are best attacked when key assets—troops, ships, aircraft—are present and when defenses are lacking. Providing a pre-strike scouting update may be relatively easy if space assets are available or if enemy communication codes have been broken. If such updates are not accessible, the attacker may have to augment its strike force to hedge against the possibility that active and passive defenses have been positioned around the target. For instance, absent an update from friendly scouts, attacking forces risk arriving at a fixed target only to discover that key transitory targets (such as ships at a naval base) have departed, or that the area is now bristling with air defenses, or that aircraft that were located in the open have been moved to hardened concrete shelters. The history of World War II would have been quite different if the U.S. carriers had been at Pearl Harbor on December 7 or if the island's interceptor aircraft had been dispersed instead of concentrated at Hickam Field.

As with enemy assets in the relatively new warfare domain of space, fixed military and economic assets located on the seabed may be increasingly attractive targets, especially if the enemy's homeland is accorded sanctuary status from attack and/or is protected by robust A2/AD defenses. As in other domains, a scouting competition will be played out on the seabed, probably involving sensor arrays, undersea drones, submarines, and airborne and space-based systems. Under these circumstances, oil and gas wellheads, pipelines, and pumping stations located on the seabed could prove attractive targets. Indeed, seabed commerce raiding seems likely to emerge as a major new form of warfare, with the offense probably enjoying the advantage—at least early on.

Mobile Targets

Locating and maintaining a track on mobile targets presents a more difficult problem for scouts, owing to the need to provide a "motion picture" stream of data of the object rather than the occasional "snapshot" needed for a fixed target. The U.S. military has found identifying and tracking mobile targets through the engagement sequence difficult, even at relatively short ranges and in the absence of sophisticated enemy counter-scouting efforts, as was the case during operations in Afghanistan, the Balkans, and Iraq.

In the Precision-Warfare Revolution's mature stage, scouting forces may have to transit from distant bases outside the enemy's main A2/AD complex, increasing their exposure to counter-scouting forces and reducing the time available to scout their assigned area. Under these conditions, especially when scouting forces are tasked with providing persistent coverage of mobile targets, friendly strike forces will need to engage them as promptly as possible, lest the scouting force loses its track. In military parlance, the objective here is to compress the "sensor-to-shooter" time frame (also referred to as the "kill chain" and "engagement sequence"): the time that elapses between when the scouting force identifies the target and when the strike force engages it. Under these conditions, militaries will probably move toward greater reliance on the "unblinking eye" of space-based scouting systems (if they can survive enemy efforts to neutralize them) and stealthy terrestrial-based drones, as manned systems attempting to perform this mission would run a high risk of incurring excessive pilot fatigue.[36]

The engagement sequence can be further compressed if strike forces are loitering in the area when a target is identified, assuming they can communicate with the scouting force. The sequence can be reduced even further if the scouting and strike elements—the "sensor" and "shooter"—are fused, as is the case with U.S. Predator armed drones, or if high-speed munitions are employed in the attack, such as by aircraft firing missiles at the target rather than flying to it and dropping gravity bombs.

In many situations, transmitting the order to engage requires maintaining data links from the sensor-shooter system back to a command center that can evaluate the scouting data and transmit the "weapons release" order. As will be discussed presently, advances in artificial intelligence that enable militaries to field a combined arms force of autonomous reconnaissance-strike systems could significantly reduce the engagement sequence. Such a force could greatly reduce or even eliminate the need to maintain data links to the command authority, greatly reducing stress on the battle network.

It is possible for scouting forces to produce a "mission kill" even if they cannot facilitate a successful engagement. This can be done, for example, by compelling a mobile target to keep on the move, lest it be identified, tracked, and engaged. If, for example, enemy mobile missile launchers must be moved frequently to avoid detection, then they have less time to set up and fire. Applied against a squadron of missiles, this could significantly reduce the squadron's rate of fire. It may also preclude the squadron from launching its attacks in salvos—all its missiles at once—thereby reducing its chances of overwhelming friendly missile defenses.

Summary

In summary, the scouting/counter-scouting competition—the battle at the "front end" of a military's recce-strike complex—will play an important and possibly dominant role in a general war in a mature precision-warfare regime.

The rise of enemy A2/AD complexes may find an increasing percentage of scouting force elements basing at great distances from their search areas. Moreover, the extended ranges over which modern strike operations can be launched, and the speed at which they can be prosecuted, suggests that scouting forces will be tasked with searching a far greater area than they ever have before. This may lead to heavy reliance on space-based scouting forces. Given the key role space-based systems play as part of a battle network, and advanced militaries' ability to neutralize them, space control and denial operations are likely to be a key focus of belligerent activity at the onset of war. Simply put, the next great-power war will be the first "space war."

The growth of A2/AD defenses, the likely need to scout at extended ranges and over broad areas for extended periods of time, and concerns over battle networks' robustness will make completing the engagement sequence successfully a challenging task. Consequently, compressing the engagement sequence will be essential to success. This will strongly incentivize militaries to invest in unmanned systems capable of operating over great distances for extended periods of time—and to combine scouting and strike functions on these systems. The need to move scouting information quickly will probably also find the competition particularly intense in the two "intangible" speed domains: cyber and the electromagnetic.

Scouting to locate, identify, and track fixed targets will in most cases be less challenging than for mobile targets. Yet even in the case of fixed targets, scouting forces may need to revisit them to determine whether the movement of mobile assets, such as air and missile defenses, troops, and aircraft, has altered their defenses or their value. Along these lines, the rise of the seabed economy, characterized by fixed infrastructure and the absence of an undersea A2/AD complex comparable to that on the surface, will likely ease the scouting force's task considerably, so the competition in this domain seems likely to increase substantially. Scouting forces may also contribute to the attrition of enemy forces, albeit "virtually," such as through mission kills on mobile targets by precluding them from operating at desirable—and perhaps even required—levels of effectiveness. Finally, the advantages of gaining the upper hand in the scouting competition and the speed at which this may be accomplished will incentivize militaries to adopt a preemptive strike posture.

The Strike Competition

Restoring freedom of offensive maneuver may also be accomplished by neutralizing or destroying the enemy's strike systems, especially extended-range systems that are relatively few in number and costly to replace. An enemy's inability to strike at extended ranges could enable short-range friendly forces to operate at acceptable risk along the outer reaches of the enemy's A2/AD complex's coverage, creating a local favorable military balance. These friendly short-range scouting and strike elements could play an important role in a campaign whose objective is to roll back the enemy's forward A2/AD defenses, thereby further expanding friendly forces' freedom of maneuver.

Generally speaking, this situation is hardly new, as those who are familiar with the U.S. military's campaign to roll back Japanese forces in the Pacific Theater of Operations during the Second World War will attest. What *is* new, however, are the enormous distances over which the forces involved in this campaign will operate, the speed at which war will be waged, the expansion in war-fighting domains, and the high level of integration that characterizes scouting and strike operations.[37]

Gaining an Advantage

Of course, friendly forces would probably not gain an advantage by depleting the enemy's long-range strike forces at the expense of exhausting their own. How might this be avoided? In the case where one belligerent enjoys a substantial quantitative advantage in long-range strike operations over its enemy, direct trade-offs may be acceptable. In cases where two great powers are at war, however, assuming such an advantage could be risky. If the two sides' extended-range systems were in rough balance, attacks on enemy systems would likely suffer losses from the enemy's active and passives defenses. Assigning part of the strike force to defeat the defender's active air and missile defenses would shift the exchange rate even further in the defender's favor. Given these circumstances, military planners might explore other possibilities, such as taking the risk of positioning forces forward and initiating war through a preemptive strike.

That being said, depending on how the belligerents' forces are structured, the attacker may enjoy an asymmetric trade-off advantage. A classic example is found in the U.S.-Soviet nuclear competition, where one nuclear weapon employed against a strategic bomber air base could destroy dozens of aircraft—and dozens of nuclear weapons. In a somewhat similar vein, during World War II, U.S. and Japanese long-range naval aviation forces squared off against each other during the Battle of Midway. Thanks in large part to superior scouting, aircraft from a smaller American naval force sank four Japanese carriers, at the loss of only one U.S. flattop. Thus, for example, it may prove attractive for China's PLA Rocket Force (PLARF) to fire missiles to take out a U.S. air base or aircraft carrier if, in so doing, a far greater number of U.S. long-range scouting and strike aircraft are destroyed.

There are indirect ways to deplete an enemy's extended-range strike forces. As mentioned in the discussion on scouting, one involves deception. Decoys, for example, have long been a part of war and have been employed to great effect. If successful, a decoy will draw attention and even an attack on itself instead of on the target whose characteristics the decoy is designed to mimic. Simply put, deception operations can find an enemy wasting considerable scouting and strike assets, diverting the former from actual targets while luring the latter into attacking false targets.

For example, prior to the Allied invasion of Normandy in June 1944, the Americans used decoys in the form of dummy equipment and false communications to convince the Germans that an entire U.S. army was forming in England across the coast of the Pas de Calais, even though no such army existed. In the days following the D-Day invasion at Normandy, the Germans held back substantial reinforcements from the battle, anticipating that the "real" invasion would come at Pas de Calais.[38]

During the Cold War, the U.S. Navy experimented with radio frequency decoys to mislead the Russians as to the true location of its carriers. In a mature precision-warfare regime, nuclear-powered submarines might dispense relatively cheap undersea drones that emit acoustic signals mimicking those of the submarine—and at a stronger sound level. If the ploy is successful, enemy anti-submarine warfare (ASW) forces would expend substantial resources tracking and attacking the decoys and not the submarine. Carrier strike groups might attempt a similar deception, hoping to draw enemy strikes away from them and toward the false "carrier" targets. Land-based missile forces could deploy decoy launchers emitting heat and electronic signals to deceive enemy scouting systems' infrared (IR) and electronic sensors.

Exploiting Sources of Advantage

Of course, in a duel between reconnaissance-strike complexes, the scouting and strike operations are waged simultaneously. If the enemy's scouting capabilities are substantially degraded, friendly scouting and strike forces may be able to operate at acceptable risk from multiple bases positioned inside no-man's-land, thereby shifting the fires balance in their favor.

Such efforts may be enhanced if friendly forces can shift their strike forces among the bases to create a "shell-game problem" for enemy scouting and strike forces. Given that these forces would be operating from only a fraction of the total bases available to them at any one time, the enemy would confront a dilemma: disperse its scouting forces to cover all possible bases, or strike all bases simultaneously to assure destroying a significant fraction of friendly forward-based scouting and strike forces.[39] The attacker's problems would be magnified further if the defender employs preferential counter-strike defenses. Simply put, since the defender knows which bases its forces are using, it can concentrate its air and missile defenses on intercepting strikes only at those bases, while ignoring strikes on the others.[40]

Geography can also play an important role in situations where two rivals are in close proximity with each other and one enjoys strategic depth while the other does not, as is the case with respect to China and Japan, respectively. In this case, China can use relatively short-range scouting and strike forces to cover most, if not all, of Japan, while the Japanese would require a much greater number of long-range scouting and strike systems to achieve the same coverage of China. This suggests that the PLA would enjoy a major advantage through its ability to target Japanese Self-Defense Force long-range strike forces with shorter (and probably cheaper) strike systems.

Summary

In summary, depleting an enemy's extended-range strike forces can create the conditions that enable friendly offensive maneuver. As with efforts to win the scouting competition, this freedom of maneuver can be part of a campaign that progressively rolls back the enemy's A2/AD complex. Such a campaign would be familiar to students of past conflicts, such as the Pacific Theater of Operations during World War II. Under certain conditions, such as when an attacker can employ one munition to take out multiple enemy munitions or before the enemy can "flush" mobile strike systems from their bases at the onset of war, the side that strikes first is likely to enjoy a significant, and perhaps decisive, advantage.

Horizontal Escalation

Horizontal escalation, or shifting the conflict's focus to a different geographic region, offers another prospective means of compelling the enemy to risk and expend its long-range scouting and strike forces. This approach may prove attractive if the cost of operating in no-man's-land in the principal contested region proves prohibitive and the enemy's A2/AD complex too formidable to overcome through direct action. Under such conditions, militaries might conduct offensive operations in areas where they have local superiority and where friendly A2/AD defenses can hold enemy forces at bay. The goal is to fight under conditions where friendly forces can rely primarily on short-range scouting and strike forces, whereas the enemy would be compelled to employ relatively more of its long-range systems to defend its position.

Thus, horizontal escalation can be considered a variation on the two options presented earlier in that it seeks to create an imbalance between friendly and enemy scouting and strike forces, but not in the principal theater of war. As with the other approaches for restoring offensive freedom of maneuver, horizontal escalation is hardly a new idea. In World War I, for example, Britain and France, confronted with a bloody stalemate on the Western Front, sought to open fronts in the Middle East, in the southern Balkans, and at Gallipoli near the Dardanelles. In World War II, the British, unable to challenge Germany's Atlantic Wall, persuaded their U.S. ally to support operations against Axis forces along Europe's putative "soft underbelly" in North Africa and Italy as a means of weakening the enemy while they built up the forces necessary for a more direct confrontation. In a contemporary great-power conflict, for instance, undersea fiber-optic cables may provide an enemy with communications links essential to supporting operations. Cutting these cables may be a high-priority mission, particularly against enemies with few good alternatives for high-capacity communications flows.[41]

Economic Warfare

If a general war were to extend over a protracted period, say, several years or so, economic warfare in the form of blockade may prove an effective means of horizontal escalation. As will be elaborated on presently, advances in submarine and torpedo technology around the turn of the twentieth century enabled Germany to threaten British close blockade forces with mines and nocturnal attacks from torpedo boats and submarines—a kind of Victorian-era A2/AD complex that created a maritime no-man's-land in littoral waters. When war came, the British were compelled to adopt a distant blockade along the English Channel and in the North Sea between Scotland and Norway.

When confronted by advanced enemy A2/AD defenses, friendly forces could wage economic warfare by imposing a distant maritime blockade to avoid incurring heavy and possibly unsustainable losses. For scouting, modern distant blockade forces would probably rely on satellites (assuming space has not been "emptied") and on long-endurance drones operating from austere bases, similar to what the U.S. Marine

Corps calls "FARPS"—forward arming and refueling points—for scouting. If the blockade is concentrated at maritime choke points, land-based troops ferried by helicopters operating from similar bare-bones bases could be used for boarding operations. If need be, blockade runners could be dispatched to the bottom with anti-ship missiles fired by aircraft and from shore-based batteries or with smart mines.

To counter a distant blockade, the blockaded belligerent may be compelled to employ—and deplete—its extended-range scouting and strike forces, including its land-based air and missile forces, along with submarines and unmanned underwater vehicles (UUVs), to contest it. If the blockading forces can prevail against such attacks, it may prove an effective way to weaken the enemy's A2/AD complex, as well as to impose economic pain.

Horizontal escalation by means of a distant blockade could occur, for example, in a conflict between China and the United States. In such a war, a maritime no-man's-land might stretch from the Chinese coast to somewhere between the first and second island chains. Given current force levels and basing structures, U.S. and allied maritime forces might impose a distant blockade along Southeast Asia's maritime chokepoints. In this example, the prospect of the PLA escorting oil-tanker convoys through the Strait of Hormuz all the way to China seems problematic. Under these circumstances, contesting the blockade would probably require China to employ its extended-range scouting and strike forces against far more numerous U.S. and allied short-range forces.

The situation could change significantly, however, if China succeeds in its apparent efforts to establish bases at Djibouti (Somalia), Gwadar (Pakistan), Hambantota (Sri Lanka), and Kyaukpyu (Myanmar). Success here would greatly enhance China's ability to employ relatively short-range scouting and strike systems to contest U.S. blockade operations.[42] Other factors must also be considered. China might stockpile strategic materials to withstand a blockade, and its borders lie on the world's largest continent, holding out the possibility of resupply over land transportation routes.[43]

Moreover, the interests of the blockaded state's neutral trading partners would also have to be considered. Cutting off China's supply of oil would probably trigger a steep price drop, damaging the economies of key neutral powers, such as Indonesia and Russia. History finds that blockades can have important second-order economic effects extending beyond the blockaded state to the economies of powerful neutrals.[44]

New Domains

Warfare in a mature precision-warfare regime in which belligerents possess formidable A2/AD complexes that overlap to form a no-man's-land is also apt to find militaries looking to engage in offensive maneuver by shifting the competition into relatively new warfare domains—such as space, cyberspace, and the seabed—where the offense currently appears to have the upper hand. Indeed, success here, particularly in space and cyberspace, could significantly and perhaps even fatally compromise the enemy's scouting forces and battle network, thereby opening the way for offensive maneuver in no-man's-land. Shifting the fight into these domains, while avoiding direct kinetic attacks on a rival great power's homeland, may also reduce the risk of the war escalating to nuclear Armageddon.[45]

Prompt Attrition

Although attrition strategies have succeeded, they should be avoided if possible, as they tend to be resource intensive with respect to casualties and material resources. A military should pursue attrition only if it enjoys a clear advantage in combat power, feels it must take prompt action at all hazards, and has no other options for securing its objectives.

Enduring disproportionately high casualties and equipment losses is always an option for overcoming the enemy—if one is willing and capable of paying the butcher's bill. This was the case with the Chinese offensive against U.S. forces at the Chosin Reservoir during the Korean War and in the Red Army's conquest of Berlin in 1945, where attacking forces suffered enormous losses but succeeded in accomplishing their objectives.[46] Another example of pursuing prompt attrition to obtain freedom of maneuver is found in the Royal Navy's willingness, at times, to run the gauntlet of German and Italian air and naval forces to reinforce Britain's key island base at Malta in the central Mediterranean Sea during World War II. In the Tet Offensive, North Vietnam leveraged its advantage in manpower and U.S. aversion to casualties to attack American forces in South Vietnam. Communist forces suffered heavy losses but succeeded in breaking the U.S. political leadership's will to achieve its objectives.[47] Still another example is the Luftwaffe's willingness to sustain far greater losses in both aircraft and pilots than the Royal Air Force in the Battle of Britain. Given the prospective payoff—creating the conditions for a successful German invasion and conquest of Great Britain—the cost was arguably justified. Of course, as the Germans discovered, a willingness to accept high losses in troops and equipment does not guarantee success.

In the future, there may be new "Maltas" situated in the shadow of the enemy's A2/AD complex that cannot be abandoned without suffering a heavy geostrategic or geopolitical price. This might occur, for example, in a conflict between China and the United States. If the United States has signaled its commitment to defending allies and security partners along the first island chain in the Western Pacific by deploying ground forces on some of the islands, they will probably lie well within range of China's thickest A2/AD defenses. In the event of war, the choice confronting Washington may be similar to the one President Franklin Roosevelt faced regarding reinforcing the Philippines following the onset of the Pacific War in December 1941. Roosevelt concluded that the United States lacked the capability to sustain a defense of the Philippines and withheld reinforcements.

If need be, blockade operations in no-man's-land could occur as part of an attrition strategy. In our example, submarines, UUVs, mobile smart mines, and undersea missile payload modules positioned well within China's A2/AD complex could attack high-priority cargo—in effect, waging a modern "close" blockade, while risking heavy losses. Major enemy ports and cargo ships could also be attacked with long-range missiles or stealthy strike aircraft, either to destroy the port's cargo-handling facilities or key transportation nodes leading to and from the ports or to damage or destroy the ships anchored in the port. This approach to attrition risks deploying relatively high-value extended-range strike assets that are time-consuming and expensive to replace.

In brief, pursuing an attrition strategy to enable offensive operations in a mature precision-warfare regime will probably be pursued only when the stakes are high, a prompt result is needed, and all other options have been exhausted. Even then, it should be undertaken with trepidation.

A Complex Combination

The preceding sections provide a preliminary exposition on how militaries might restore the ability to conduct effective offensive campaigns at an acceptable cost when confronting advanced A2/AD reconnaissance-strike complexes. The discussion is illustrative, not comprehensive. A reductionist approach was used, reducing a complex set of interlocking competitions into some of its constituent piece-parts. What we are far more likely to find are advanced militaries employing an integrated combination of the operations described here and still others. Indeed, the fourfold expansion of war-fighting domains over the past two centuries, combined with the great advances in the speed, range, and accuracy of military scouting and strike forces, presents an opportunity for military planners and theorists to engage in the most stimulating speculation. Any detailed assessment of the mature precision-strike regime will require persistent and sustained intellectual effort by a military's most talented strategists, an effort that, alas, lies well beyond the scope of this work.

By way of example, however, the following discussion presents some preliminary thoughts on how the military competition in one of warfare's relatively new domains—space—may alter the character of warfare between major military powers.

Space: Combining High-Tech with the High Frontier

Space forces are playing an increasingly critical role in advanced militaries' scouting and battle-network operations, and in aiding their strike forces by providing precision navigation and timing (PNT) information. Yet the satellites providing this support also appear highly susceptible to attack. This combination of high value and high vulnerability is apt to lead advanced militaries to contest for space control or, failing that, to impose mutual space denial at the onset of a general war.

SPOT

In the Cold War's final years, one of my duties while serving as the secretary of defense's military assistant for special projects was as editor in chief of *Soviet Military Power.* This document, a forerunner to today's annual report on China's military developments, was designed to inform the U.S. public and the citizens of its allies on the state of Soviet military forces and key trends in the military balance.

One year while my colleagues and I were preparing the report, an intelligence community representative suggested we purchase satellite photos from the French satellite SPOT (Satellite Pour l'Observation de la Terre), owned by the commercial firm Spot Image. The satellite, providing photos with ten-meter resolution, had only recently been launched. Photographs with this resolution would allow us to show our readers Soviet bases and forces.

It seemed like a great idea, so we went ahead. Several photos were included in the final draft sent to Defense Secretary Caspar Weinberger for his approval. Word quickly came back from the front office that Weinberger was irate. Who, he wanted to know, had OK'd using U.S. reconnaissance satellite photos in the report? Why were we revealing our satellites' capabilities—and limitations?

Needless to say, he was greatly relieved—and more than a little surprised—to find that the photographs came from a commercial firm. As would soon become evident, the commercialization of space was only beginning.

The Ultimate High Ground

Over three score years ago, Senator John Kennedy proclaimed, "The nation that controls space will also control the world." The senator's views resonated with those of many other political and military leaders, including a general officer of the world's other space power, Soviet Russia. Shortly after Kennedy's inauguration as president in January 1961, Lieutenant General N. Korenevskiy produced a paper, "The Role of Space Weapons in a Future War," echoing the new president's views.[48]

The general's assessment talked of weaponizing space, creating a "space-bombing system" composed of "a great number of nuclear bombs circling the earth in various orbits."[49] He went on to note that "certain requirements for a space bombing system have been formulated." Having demonstrated the ability to launch artificial satellites, the general asserted that creating a constellation of satellites supported by numerous decoy satellites (*sputniklovushka*) for misleading the enemy "does not present any great difficulty." Korenevskiy even advocated a form of stealth for these satellites, combining "antiradar covering" and paint coatings in order to avoid observation from Earth.[50] The general believed that his space-bombing system would compel the United States "to take defensive measures which will entail huge expenditures," imposing disproportionate costs on the Americans.[51] Looking ahead to the 1970s, he anticipated that satellites would be employed "not only for conducting war in space, but also for delivering strikes independently against ground objectives and targets."[52]

Over sixty years later, the weaponization of space for the purpose of establishing control of that domain and influencing the struggle for control of others has yet to occur. It is also not clear that dominating space would, as Kennedy asserted, enable a country to control the world. Nevertheless, both men correctly foresaw space's enormous potential to alter war's character, and with it the military balance of power. The succeeding three decades witnessed both Cold War superpowers militarizing—but not weaponizing—space. Following the Soviet Union's collapse in 1991, the United States had no major rival in this domain. Today, however, it can no longer make that claim. Neither do its satellites enjoy sanctuary from attack. And, as Caspar Weinberger discovered, states long ago lost their monopoly over what transpires in this domain.

Selected Space Trends

In the sixty-plus years since the first manmade satellite was launched into orbit around the Earth, space-based systems, such as the U.S. Global Positioning System constellation of satellites, have become increasingly important to the effective functioning of the global economy and to military forces' effectiveness. Indeed, GPS was originally designed to support U.S. military operations and proved a spectacular success in the First Gulf War. America's armed forces are even more dependent on GPS today. This satellite constellation has also become a global utility, with roughly two billion GPS receivers in use. Estimates are that the number will reach seven billion before long. The telecommunications, banking, airlines, electric utilities, and cloud-computing businesses, among others, require the consistent and precision navigation and timing that GPS provides. Of the sixteen sectors of the U.S. economy designated by the government as critical, fourteen depend on GPS to function effectively. Many other countries rely on GPS for similar types of support. Reflecting GPS's importance to their economies and, by extension, their security, the United States' two great-power rivals, China and Russia, operate their own space-based navigation systems: the BeiDou Satellite System (BDS) and GLONASS (Global Navigation Satellite System), respectively. The European Union also has its own system, Galileo.[53]

Today many countries are "space powers." Tiny New Zealand hosts a spaceport. Turkey and Peru have their own spy satellites, and in 2020 Iran launched its first military satellite. Space is also being progressively invaded by commercial firms in search of financial gain. The private sector's advance into space has been enabled in large measure by steeply declining launch-to-orbit costs, for which it—not governments—is principally responsible.

Since *Sputnik* went into orbit in October 1957, satellites have been expensive to build and costly to launch. This changed with advances in technology and as the commercial sector embraced a "smaller-is-better" view with regard to satellites. In 1999, researchers from the Technical University of Berlin launched a tiny satellite—TUBSAT—weighing roughly 100 pounds and measuring around a foot on each side. At the time, TUBSAT was seen as a novelty. Less than fifteen years later, however, Orbital Sciences, a U.S. company, launched a rocket carrying twenty-nine small satellites to low-Earth orbit (LEO). Shortly thereafter, *Kosmotras*, a Russian joint venture, boosted thirty-two "SmallSats" into a similar orbit.[54] Many of these small satellites are built to a standard format and are referred to as "CubeSats." CubeSats are employed in multiples, each measuring roughly four inches on each side and weighing less than three pounds. By 2020, more than 1,100 CubeSats had been placed in orbit.

That year also saw a U.S. firm, SpaceX, producing an unprecedented 120 satellites a month and boosting 143 commercial and government satellites into orbit on a single mission, shattering the record of 104 set by India in 2017—this at a time when there were only around 3,000 active satellites in orbit. In other words, this single launch increased the satellite population by 5 percent. In February 2021, SpaceX launched 60 Starlink satellites on a single Falcon 9 rocket as part of its plan to create an initial constellation of 1,440 satellites providing internet service, with the ultimate goal of creating a global high-speed internet network including some 12,000 satellites.[55]

SpaceX is but one example, albeit a prominent one, of the commercial sector's surge into space. In recent years, the number of private firms operating satellites—many of them CubeSat clusters—has expanded significantly, performing a growing range of functions. Most of these functions are commercial in nature, but some have clear military applications. Some carry small yet powerful lasers capable of beaming data to ground stations at very high data rates. Still others rely on short-wavelength infrared imaging to peer through clouds or on synthetic aperture radars (SARs) to obtain images at night.[56]

Government and commercial satellites are producing enormous amounts of data, to the point where the then-director of the National

Geospatial-Intelligence Agency, Robert Cardillo, asserted that by the early 2020s, the agency would have "a million times more" data to analyze than it had less than a decade before. He also declared, "If we attempted to manually exploit all of the imagery we'll collect over the next 20 years, we'd need eight million imagery analysts."[57] Governments and the private sector see advances in artificial intelligence as the solution to this problem. Today AI is being used for analyzing and processing data onboard satellites prior to downloading it to Earth, thereby easing demands on communications bandwidth and human analysts. Other firms have constructed "data refineries" to clean up data sets to provide the high-quality data needed for the machine learning that creates and refines AI for space applications.[58]

Private space firms are also getting into satellite "repair" services. An Italian company, D-Orbit, has built spacecraft to move errant CubeSats into their proper position. Japan's Astroscale is looking to create satellite "tow trucks" to intercept drifting inert satellites threatening to collide with other celestial bodies, redirecting them into the atmosphere, where they will burn up.[59]

In brief, commercial activity in space has changed dramatically from what it was only a decade ago. Private firms are also involved in traditional launch operations. SpaceX is launching large satellites into orbit at very competitive prices, triggering major changes in the launch industry. Even as more and more countries become space-faring nations, the private sector is increasing its market share and range of services. A major reason is the collapse of one of the long-standing barriers to boosting payloads into orbit: cost. And it's the commercial sector that has made it happen. As a U.S. Air Force study candidly found, "A government agency, even a well-run agency, does not have the correct economic incentives to lower costs. NASA was not incentivized to eliminate the operational and labor costs that were part of the Shuttle system. Since NASA depends on political support, which is driven by the number of jobs in congressional districts, the opposite is true."[60]

Between 1970 and 2000, the cost to launch a kilogram to space was roughly $18,500. The price-to-orbit of NASA's space shuttle was an exorbitant $54,500 per kilogram. But the SpaceX Falcon 9 rocket can do it for $2,700 per kilogram, and the firm's Falcon Heavy rocket for roughly half that.[61] In 2013, Russia controlled nearly half of the global commercial launch business. Thanks to competition from SpaceX and other private firms, in 2018 Russia's market share had declined to less than 10 percent, while SpaceX alone had 65 percent.[62] For the United States, the rise of private-sector firms like Elon Musk's SpaceX and Jeff Bezos's Blue Origin may provide it with a latent "space arsenal of democracy" in the event of war, with a significant potential to support military operations.

The Military Competition in Space

An advanced military's reconnaissance-strike complex relies heavily on space satellites for, among other things, communications, global positioning, navigation and timing, weather forecasts, and scouting. Many of these satellites, whether military, government, or commercial, appear to be vulnerable to attack and difficult to hide or defend. Just as for centuries commercial ships transporting cargo on the high seas have been targets for commerce-raiding forces, satellites—including those belonging to neutral powers—appear likely to be targets in any great-power conflict.

At present, there are no barriers to keep a major space power from fielding anti-satellite forces to threaten a rival's entire space architecture with destruction, and apparently at far less cost than it would take to successfully defend against such attacks or replace lost satellites. If so, space powers confront several strategic choices: accepting the growing vulnerability of their space assets; paying what will probably be a disproportionately high price to maintain assured access to space through active and passive defense measures and replacing "downed" satellites; preempting an enemy's ASAT forces at the onset of war before they can be employed; exploiting advancing technologies to maintain access to space through different means and methods; or some combination thereof.

Today the threat to U.S. and ally satellite architectures comes primarily from China and Russia. That being said, even lesser powers are pursuing counter-space capabilities, including jamming, dazzling, and cyber attacks.[63]

As with most areas of the military competition, Washington considers China the principal threat in space. In 2007, China destroyed one of its own satellites using a rocket interceptor. Six years later, it launched a missile 22,000 miles into space, to geosynchronous orbit. Beijing stated that the launch was for purely scientific purposes, yet this is the orbit where the U.S. military and intelligence agencies position their most sensitive satellites. China also launched a satellite, Shiyan 7 (Experiment 7), with a prototype robotic arm that captured another satellite in orbit.

Although the Chinese stated that this action was a space maintenance mission, the robot's ability to grab satellites is not limited to those belonging to China.[64]

Like China, Russia continues to develop ASAT forces. In 2008, a Russian spacecraft moved between two commercial communications satellites operated by Intelsat, later positioning itself near another satellite. It requires little imagination to realize that, were these Russian satellites armed, they could function as ASAT "grenades." More recently, in July 2020, the Russians released a projectile from an orbiting satellite that could be used to strike spacecraft. Three months earlier, it tested a direct-ascent anti-satellite missile, continuing its efforts to field multiple means of attacking space systems.[65]

Satellites are also at risk from jamming and cyber attacks. As far back as 1998, there were allegations that Russian hackers had taken control of a U.S.-German satellite and pointed it at the sun, destroying its sensors.[66] In 2005, China began incorporating cyber attacks into its military exercises, primarily in preemptive attacks on enemy networks. In 2008, anonymous hackers seized control of Terra, a civilian imaging satellite in low-Earth orbit, where military reconnaissance craft reside. Fortunately, the hackers refrained from any further mischief.[67] A decade later, the cyber-security firm Symantec warned that a China-based cyber-espionage group known as Thrip was targeting satellite, telecom, and defense companies in the United States, possibly looking for ways to intercept or alter satellite communications, including inserting malware to infect computers linked to the satellites.[68]

There have been attempts to disrupt GPS signals. During a demonstration in 2012, U.S. Department of Homeland Security officials observed one of their drones being hijacked off its intended route by a hacker inserting false GPS coordinates into its software. There are reports that Russian forces have similarly "spoofed" drone signals over Syria and the Black Sea.[69] In 2018, Finland's GPS signal was intentionally disrupted during NATO field exercises in Scandinavia, with Russia the suspected source of attack. Around that time, pilots operating in Norway's airspace also experienced a loss of their GPS signals.[70] After assessing these trends, the U.S. Defense Department concluded, "The global threat of electronic warfare (EW) attacks against space systems will expand in the coming years in both number and types of weapons. Development will very likely focus on jamming capabilities against dedicated military satellite communications, Synthetic Aperture Radar (SAR) imaging satellites, and enhanced capabilities against Global Navigation Satellite Systems, such as the U.S. Global Positioning System (GPS). Blending of EW and cyber-attack capabilities will likely expand in pursuit of sophisticated means to deny and degrade information networks."[71]

In addition to fielding kinetic ASAT missile interceptors, China and Russia are fielding land-based high-powered laser ASAT weapons. Analysts have identified a site in China's Xinjiang region as one of five military bases whose lasers can fire beams of concentrated light at U.S. reconnaissance satellites, with the goal of blinding or disabling their optic sensors.[72]

The "democratization of destruction" is occurring in space, as small groups and even individuals are gaining access to capabilities that could potentially compromise the function of satellites, including those providing precision navigation and timing. There are hundreds of types of jammers available to those with the means to procure them. Although jamming is illegal in most countries, the European Global Navigation Satellite Systems Agency recorded some 50,000 jamming incidents in 2017 and 2018.[73] Jamming near airports may prove a precursor to nonstate groups' jamming space-based systems. Perhaps the most notorious case occurred in June 2019 when Israeli pilots lost their GPS signals around Tel Aviv's Ben Gurion Airport, Israel's busiest, for three weeks. This was not an isolated incident. Three years earlier, some forty airliners had their GPS signal broken when approaching Manila's Ninoy Aquino International Airport.[74]

America's new GPS 3 satellites are designed to last fifteen years and provide a signal eight times stronger than the current generation of satellites, making them more difficult, but hardly impossible, to jam. (They also lack the two strongest anti-spoofing technologies on the market.)[75] This raises the question of the potential mischief that might be inflicted on satellites by disaffected groups, or even individuals, if jamming technology improves and power levels increase.

Although the United States has lost its dominant position in space, it remains the world's most advanced space power and arguably has the most to lose from a war in space, incentivizing its rivals to field ASAT forces. Consequently, like its rivals, the United States is looking for ways to defend its satellites and deter attacks against them, including fielding ASAT capabilities of its own.

Although much of what the U.S. military does in space is shrouded in secrecy, information regarding some initiatives has been made public, such as the U.S. military's kinetic intercept of one of its own satellites in 2007. The U.S. Defense Department has also experimented with several laser systems that could eventually lead to its fielding a laser ASAT system.[76]

A potential "game-changing" U.S. capability about which little is known is the X-37B space plane. The Air Force has at least two X-37Bs, each about thirty feet long and ten feet high, with a wingspan of roughly fifteen feet and a payload bay about the size of a standard pickup-truck bed. Like the space shuttle, the X-37B is launched vertically and lands on a runway. The X-37B's initial mission occurred in April 2010, lasting 224 days. A recent mission ran nearly 800 days. The X-37B's tenth anniversary was marked by its sixth launch to orbit in May 2020.[77]

The Air Force has kept the X-37B's purpose and missions, as well as most of its payloads, classified. The veil of secrecy was pulled back slightly by former Air Force secretary Heather Wilson, who declared that the space plane can perform maneuvers in space that would drive potential adversaries "nuts." From this highly ambiguous statement, experts speculate that the X-37B may be capable of changing its orbit, making it difficult for rivals to predict the spacecraft's location.[78] Assuming that this is the case, the X-37B could present a difficult target for enemy ASAT forces. For example, assume that the Chinese military locates the X-37B in space and is seeking to intercept it. In theory, the X-37B's controllers could shift its orbit. Following such a maneuver, the Chinese would find the X-37B failing to appear at the predicted time and location, compelling them to renew their scouting efforts from scratch.[79]

Presuming that the X-37B is performing as experts speculate, then as its development continues, the character of the military competition in space could change dramatically. In fact, China is working to field its own reusable space plane. In September 2020, the Chinese successfully boosted an experimental craft into orbit and returned it to Earth, where it landed horizontally. Another successful launch occurred ten months later. A second space plane, Tengyun, is being developed and is designed to take off and land horizontally. The Chinese claim that their space plane program's purpose is to reduce launch costs. Given that the U.S. space shuttle's cost to orbit was well over an order of magnitude greater than SpaceX's current price, the Chinese assertion seems disingenuous. A more plausible explanation is that China, as in nearly every area of the military-technical competition, is seeking to match, and eventually surpass, its U.S. rival in space.[80]

Space War

Today war in space appears to favor the offense, and by a clear margin. There are several ways in which an attacker can destroy or neutralize a satellite or satellite architecture. Thanks to motion pictures such as the *Star Wars* and *Star Trek* series, popular images of war in space tend to emphasize kinetic weapons, such as "photon torpedoes," generating kinetic effects—with everything from space fighters to "Death Stars" blowing up, complete with the explosive "sounds" that would never occur in the vacuum of space. Yet kinetic and directed-energy anti-satellite weapons do exist.

There are "hit-to-kill" ASAT missiles that work by striking the target satellite directly. These missiles are most effective against satellites in low-Earth orbit, where many imaging satellites are located. Attacking satellites at mid-Earth orbit (MEO) or in geosynchronous orbit (GEO) is more demanding, requiring larger, more sophisticated missiles. Although a sophisticated military satellite can use thrusters in attempting to move out of a kinetic interceptor's path, it could expend a large amount of its fuel doing so.[81] If this maneuver forced the satellite into an unfavorable orbit where it lacked the fuel to return to its intended station, the attacker may still claim a "mission" kill.

One major barrier to the use of kinetic ASAT weapons is the "space junk" that may be created in the wake of a successful attack. Compare China's ASAT test in 2007 and the U.S. satellite intercept the following year. These events yielded strikingly different environmental results. Although both intercepts were against disabled satellites in LEO, the Chinese intercept occurred at an altitude greater than 500 miles, while the U.S. intercept happened at roughly 150 miles. The difference in altitude found the debris produced by the U.S. test burning up in the atmosphere relatively quickly. The Chinese test was a disaster, creating more than 150,000 pieces of space junk—roughly 15 percent of all the space debris now in orbit—while ground controllers around the globe scrambled to move dozens of spacecraft out of harm's way.[82]

China's space junk is global, indiscriminate, and irreversible. It's global because the debris spreads naturally over time into other satellite orbits. It's indiscriminate because it affects all satellites, not just those belonging to China. Its effects are irreversible because there is, as yet, no practical way to remove space junk. Over time, the growing debris created by space junk colliding with satellites or pieces of debris striking one another risks increasing to the point that everything in that orbit is destroyed—a phenomenon known as the "Kessler Syndrome." Should this occur across multiple orbits, militaries would be compelled to return to "industrial-age warfare." As General John Hyten, then head of U.S. Strategic Command, described it, "It's Vietnam, Korea, and World War II; no more precision missiles and smart bombs—which means casualties are higher, collateral damage is higher."[83]

Turning space into a kinetic shooting gallery risks creating space junk that would compromise the attacker's own space systems along with its enemy's. Such a calamity would not spare the satellites of neutral powers. For these reasons, employing kinetic attacks against a rival's satellites as part of a campaign to win the scouting competition or, more broadly, cripple its reconnaissance-strike complex appears unattractive.

There are, however, other options for fighting in space, such as by employing nonkinetic weapons like high-powered lasers, high-powered microwaves, and jammers. Ground-based lasers could temporarily—or permanently—blind or dazzle imaging satellites, provided the satellite's sensor is looking at the laser's location when being targeted. High-powered lasers could also damage satellites by overheating key satellite components. In a somewhat similar vein, a high-powered microwave (HPM) weapon could "fry" a satellite's unshielded electronics, causing permanent damage. In the case of jammers, if their power is sufficiently strong, they can block a satellite's communications. Another option, one that may be the objective of the Chinese and Russian satellite maneuvers, is to employ a "space robot" that is launched into orbit and maneuvered to capture or otherwise disable its target. Importantly, these weapons do not produce space junk, unless one counts the "dead" satellite that remains in orbit after a successful attack. Assuming it's effective, jamming may be the ASAT weapon of choice, as its effects are reversible, thereby boosting an enemy's incentive to come to terms.

Although the competition in space appears to favor the offense, the defense still has options, especially if it enjoys a large resource advantage over the attacker. There are four basic ways the defense can protect its space-based capabilities: by making them invulnerable, replaceable, or invisible, or by destroying the enemy's ASAT forces. All other factors being equal, the best way to deal with threats to one's satellites appears to be striking at the source of the problem. Since all ASAT weapons must originate from the Earth's surface at some point in time, the most effective defense appears to be targeting the enemy's hit-to-kill and laser ASAT launch facilities, the radars used to track friendly satellites, and jamming sources.

States (and perhaps commercial firms as well) seeking to protect their satellites could also make them more difficult to attack. Lasers and jammers work both ways. They could be used to blind the sensors on an incoming kinetic ASAT weapon or to jam its communications, respectively. Automatic lens covers could be positioned on imaging satellites that activate when a laser attack is detected, although a closed lens cover could constitute a mission kill. Confronted with jamming, communications satellites could use techniques like frequency hopping to reduce its effects. Satellites can also have their electronics "hardened" to defend against high-power microwave attacks.

Progress being made with artificial intelligence, nanotechnology, and new methods of propulsion may eventually enable small satellites to combine into self-healing clusters, displacing today's large, complex satellites. If so, they may prove more difficult to target, ensuring that a satellite constellation's effectiveness degrades gracefully, rather than precipitously. For example, the many CubeSats constituting a cluster would probably prove more challenging to detect and disable than a large satellite performing the same function. And it may be possible to replace damaged or destroyed CubeSats far more quickly and cheaply than large satellites.

There are also ways to maneuver CubeSat spacecraft without depleting their onboard fuel. One method exploits the presence of errant air molecules that have drifted into space from the Earth's atmosphere. These molecules are most abundant in LEO. They provide resistance such that a satellite with a small facing surface area will slowly gain on another satellite with a larger surface area launched at the same speed. A satellite can accomplish this by enlarging or shrinking its forward-facing area, creating "differential drag." This is relatively easy to accomplish, and the commercial firm Planet has 120 Earth-imaging satellites in orbit that maneuver exclusively using this principle. Indeed, exploiting differential drag is essential for firms like Planet that boost clusters of satellites on a single rocket and need to position them properly once they achieve orbit. According to Spire, another small satellite operator, it only takes a few weeks for differential drag to position a CubeSat cluster to eliminate unnecessary overlaps. As with Planet, Spire's seventy-two satellites maneuver exclusively in this way.[84]

Above an altitude of roughly 350 miles, there are too few air molecules for differential drag to work. At these altitudes, a satellite's solar panels may be employed as a kind of "space sail." Since light exerts pressure, if a satellite's solar panels can be positioned to face the maximum amount of light when it's receding from the sun and the minimum amount when it's approaching the sun, the spacecraft can gain speed and therefore altitude. A CubeSat could use this technique to boost its orbit some 70 to 100 feet per day.[85] Differential drag and space sails may enable satellites to maneuver out of harm's way or aid militaries that have launched spare CubeSats to maneuver them to replace those lost to enemy action.

Summary

Spacecraft have become central to the functioning of advanced militaries' reconnaissance-strike complexes. This, as well as satellites' economic value and the apparent challenges associated with establishing effective defenses, will likely make them highly attractive targets in a general war. The potential advantage accruing to the side that takes out its rival's space-based forces, combined with the speed at which this might be accomplished, suggests that belligerents may have strong incentives to strike first.

Whereas belligerents may be self-deterred from employing kinetic ASAT strikes, there are other methods to neutralize enemy space-based systems, including directed-energy systems like laser ASATs, that appear to be both effective and discriminate. Counter-space operations may be a game in which even nonstate entities can play, especially when it comes to jamming and cyber attacks.

Although the competition in space appears to favor the offense, new developments, such as the proliferation of CubeSat constellations, the ability to maneuver small satellites, and the emergence of space planes like the X-37B, may help level the playing field toward the defense. In any event, it is all but certain that in a mature precision-warfare regime, a war between two advanced military powers will witness the first war in space.

The Mature Precision-Warfare Revolution

The Precision-Warfare Revolution's maturation, combined with the scale on which China and Russia can compete, is shifting the military balance against the United States. For more than a century, the U.S. military has projected and sustained large forces over great distances to defend America's vital interests, especially in the Western Pacific and in

Europe. In every case, the buildup of these forces overseas occurred with minimal, if any, enemy interference. This happy state of affairs no longer exists in the Western Pacific and perhaps not in Eastern Europe. China (especially) and Russia are increasing dramatically the price the U.S. military must pay to project power in these regions, as well as to defend American military and economic assets in the relatively new war-fighting domains of space, cyberspace, and the seabed.

A key issue with respect to the maturing precision-warfare regime characterized by dueling reconnaissance-strike complexes is whether it represents a "new normal" or whether ways might be found to enable offensive power-projection operations at an acceptable cost. Several point-of-departure approaches for prevailing in this "duel" were presented to stimulate efforts at developing operational concepts designed to restore a military's ability to maneuver offensively at the operational level of war.

Although suppressing the enemy's scouting force and depleting its extended-range strike forces were described separately, it's clear that the greatest effect will be achieved by employing these operations in combination, in particular by fusing scouting and strike functions in "sensor-shooter" systems.

If a new general war cannot be averted, its opening phase may be its most crucial. Owing to the apparent advantage enjoyed by the offense in the space (and probably cyberspace) domains, the speed of attack enabled by systems like laser ASATs and speed-of-light cyber strikes, and the advantages that will accrue to the side that gains the upper hand in fracturing its enemy's reconnaissance-strike complex, the incentives for adopting a preemptive war posture are likely to increase significantly. As the 1992 MTR assessment concluded:

> Since establishing information superiority could be *the decisive operation* in future conflicts, and since this objective could be achieved early in the war, we should expect that increasing emphasis will be placed on achieving surprise. As this revolution matures, the day may come when the forces of . . . [major powers] evolve to a "hair-trigger" posture, characterized by a trend toward automated engagements with forces ready to fire on little warning. To adopt a less threatening posture could be seen as inviting a pre-emptive attack against friendly information networks, allowing the enemy to establish information dominance, which would quickly lead to the progressive inability of friendly

forces to execute the highly integrated, information-intensive military operations that will be crucial to success in war.[86]

This observation is consistent with the general long-term trend in warfare of increased speed in scouting and strike operations and the increased range over which these "reconnaissance-strike complexes" operate. It is also the result of the introduction of precision, or guided, weapons in large numbers, which has created an environment where to be seen and tracked is to run a very high risk of being destroyed. To avoid being seen, you must be a good "hider," and the best way to hide is to prevent your enemy from seeing you by neutralizing its scouts.

CHAPTER FOUR

Disruptive Technologies
Catching the Wave

There is only one thing I can tell you about war, and almost one only, and it is this: no war ever shows the characteristics that were expected; it is always different.

—DWIGHT EISENHOWER

Proof of Trotsky's farsightedness is that none of his predictions have come true yet.

—ISAAC DEUTSCHER

DURING THE COURSE OF my research on this book, from time to time I visited the Pentagon's Office of Net Assessment (ONA). On one occasion, I met with its current director, Jim Baker, who, along with his deputy, Dr. Andrew May, continues the office's tradition of producing world-class assessments on matters of strategic importance to the Defense Department's senior leaders.[1] During our conversation, I mentioned to Baker that it was proving difficult to get a handle on what seems likely to be a successor military revolution to the mature precision-warfare regime.

I pointed out that the MTR assessment had focused almost exclusively on the effects triggered by the IT revolution and Defense Secretary Harold Brown's Offset Strategy. Now I was confronting a cluster of military-related technologies, some of which could, by themselves, dramatically shift the character of warfare. Complicating matters further, these technologies were advancing at a steady and, in some cases, rapid pace. Further complicating matters were their interrelationships. In some cases, these technologies' potential to act as "game changers" in the military competition depended on progress with other emerging technologies: breakthroughs in additive manufacturing could prove critical for the success of hypersonic missiles; advances in quantum computing and AI could make a big difference in synthetic biology; and so on. Thus, the order in which these various technologies matured could, I said, greatly affect how the emerging revolution plays out: if solid-state lasers, rail gun, and powder gun technology matured before hypersonics, then fleet missile defense could gain the advantage. If hypersonics arrive first, it might become impossible to mount an effective defense of the fleet. All this, I told Baker, was making for a really tough go.

In the finest traditions of the office that he now leads, Baker simply looked at me and said, "Well, I guess you'll just have to think harder, won't you?"

Indeed.

For thousands of years, new technologies have provided militaries with more effective means of waging war. Technology's ability to confer advantage on the battlefield has never been more evident than during the industrial age, when advances enabled innovation and, at times, military revolutions. Today military-related technologies are progressing at a fast pace and on a broad front. They encompass increased computational power—including the prospect of quantum computing—facilitating big-data analytics, machine learning, and, through them, advances in artificial intelligence. Impressive progress is also being made in additive manufacturing, robotics, directed energy, and hypersonic propulsion. Defense planners ignore at their peril the stunning progress in the biosciences, especially in gene editing made possible by CRISPR-Cas9.

Which emerging technologies will mature when expected and as expected? Which will find their true potential being realized much later than anticipated? Which game-changing technologies will simply fail to emerge? Finally, what technologies will alter the character of warfare in ways that were wholly unanticipated, even by their originators?

There is a strong temptation for people in my line of work to try to predict the future. Lengthy, detailed studies have been produced describing and analyzing the prospective value of emerging military-related technologies. Senior defense policy makers and military leaders want answers, not ambiguities, when setting research and development priorities involving tens of billions of dollars and potentially affecting thousands of lives, not to mention the country's security. Yet attempting to predict with precision how any technology will shape the military competition is an impossible task. Again, no one can say with confidence when, or even if, these technologies and the military capabilities they might enable will mature as anticipated. It takes restraint on the analyst's part not to succumb to the temptation to offer the illusion of false precision, and wisdom on the policy maker's part not to demand it. Sadly, both are often in short supply.

The best that I can accomplish is a survey of selected technologies that seem promising for their military potential, buttressed by some hopefully insightful observations as to their prospective influence on the character of war. Hence, the discussion that follows is *illustrative, not predictive* and certainly *not exhaustive*. Although the technologies are presented individually, in most instances it is their *combination* that will be most likely to bring about the most disruptive shifts in war's character.

Artificial Intelligence

The Information Revolution that began in the mid-twentieth century continues, thanks to advances in high-speed data processing; the growing availability of large data sets drawing increasingly on raw material provided from the emerging internet of things (IoT); the use of big-data analytics; advances in machine learning techniques; and rapidly expanding private- and public-sector investment.[2] All of this has led to impressive increases in artificial intelligence performance, with its biggest boosters promising, "You ain't seen nothing yet!"

Before proceeding further, some defining of terms is in order. *Artificial intelligence* refers to leveraging digital technology to create systems that are capable of performing tasks commonly thought to require human intelligence. *Machine learning* is viewed as a subfield of AI and centers on digital systems that improve their performance on a given task over time through experience.[3] The National Institute of Standards and Technology (NIST) describes *big data* simply as "the deluge of data in today's networked, digitized, sensor-laden, and information driven world." Indeed, it was estimated that five exabytes (1,000,000,000,000,000,000 bytes) of data, the equivalent of 15,000 times the content in the Library of Congress, had been created from the beginning of time up until 2003. By 2010, that same amount of data was being created every two days.[4] Big data is characterized by the growing size of data sets, the variety of data (such as from multiple repositories, domains, or types), and the velocity (flow rate) of data. Hence, *big-data analytics* is a collection of techniques that leverage vast and disparate sets of data to extract knowledge.[5]

The *internet of things* is a major contributing factor in the growth of big data. The IoT is defined as "a decentralized network of objects, applications, and services that can sense, log, interpret, communicate, process, and act on a variety of information or control devices in the physical world."[6] Estimates of the number of IoT devices vary. It is generally accepted that their growth in both the industrial and consumer marketplace is advancing at breakneck speed. In November 2015, one estimate predicted that 6.4 billion connected "things" would be in use by 2016, a 30 percent increase from 2015, with the IoT including 20.8 billion devices by 2020. Another estimate concluded that there were 13.4 billion devices connected in 2015 and that this figure would rise to 38.5 billion by 2020. By 2018, the estimate had grown to more than 50 billion.[7]

Perhaps the best-known recent advance in AI is AlphaGo, developed by Google's DeepMind team. In March 2016, AlphaGo defeated Lee Sedol, one of the world's top players, four games to one, in a Chinese strategy board game known as Go (or Weichi) whose origins date back to the time before Christ. The AlphaGo system learned the game in forty days after being fed moves and countermoves by past Go masters. Not long after AlphaGo's success, DeepMind released AlphaGo Master, which defeated the top-ranked player, Ke Jie, in March 2017. Following this success, the DeepMind team developed AlphaGo Zero, which was simply fed the rules of the game. Starting from scratch, the machine played against itself without any historical data. As it played, AlphaGo Zero identified new tactics and moves. Three weeks later, in October 2017, it defeated the previous AlphaGo version, 100 games to zero.[8]

More recently, a poker-playing algorithm named Pluribus, designed by researchers at Carnegie Mellon University and the Facebook AI lab, bested a group of elite poker players in a game of Texas Hold 'Em, a complex game of poker in which psychology was thought to have played a significant role in determining the winner. Yet Darren Elias, a professional player involved in the games, concluded that Pluribus's success could be expressed simply in "pure numbers and percentages."[9]

The rapid advance of AI over the past decade or so finds Russia's Vladimir Putin paraphrasing President Kennedy's predictions on space, declaring that the state that first masters AI "will become the ruler of the world."[10] For some observers, examples like AlphaGo indicate that AI will transform every aspect of how humans live, including the way they fight.

The manufacturing process offers a metaphor for understanding the competition among states and firms to take the lead in developing and exploiting AI's potential. The raw materials for AI are data sets. They are processed through machine-learning techniques powered by computers. The end products are algorithms employed for various purposes. Put another way, the growing internet of things is generating enormous quantities of data, which can be organized into data sets. Big-data analytics "refines" the data and feeds it into the machine learning that enhances AI. As one expert puts it, "Information is the oil of the 21st century, and analytics is the combustion engine."[11]

Advances in AI can enable increased levels of autonomy. Autonomy involves delegating a decision to an authorized entity to take action within specific boundaries. Systems governed by prescriptive rules that permit no deviations are considered to be *automated*, not *autonomous*. For a system to be autonomous, it must be able to identify and choose among different courses of action *independently* to accomplish goals on the basis of its knowledge and understanding of the environment in which it is functioning. The foundation for autonomy is artificial intelligence. Generally speaking, systems incorporating *autonomy at rest* operate virtually, in software. Systems incorporating *autonomy in motion* have a physical presence, such as in robotics and autonomous vehicles.[12]

Autonomous weapons are not new. Those that employ a sensor to trigger an automatic military action, such as land mines, have existed for more than a century. More advanced weapons, such as acoustic-homing torpedoes capable of engaging targets unsupervised, arrived during World War II. More recently, computers with ever increasing computational power are enabling a gradual and ongoing shift toward greater autonomy in military operations. During the Cold War, "fire-and-forget" missiles were fielded, using onboard sensors and a computer to guide them to their target without any communication from the operator once the target had been selected and the missile fired.

Military Implications

AI has the potential to make significant, and perhaps profound, contributions to the effective functioning of reconnaissance-strike complexes. This is due, in part, to the rapid growth in sensor technology that supports intelligence, surveillance, and reconnaissance efforts. Modern sensors produce an enormous amount of raw data, outstripping the ability of military and intelligence organizations to process and analyze it.

Some unattended ground sensors and undersea systems use onboard, autonomous processing to reduce the torrent of data being fed back to users, significantly reducing communications bandwidth requirements and the burden on human analysts. Expanding the amount of data that can be analyzed while reducing the time needed for analysis is especially important in the mature precision-warfare regime described in Chapter 3, which emphasizes compressed engagement cycles.

Using AI, a sensor platform could also adjust its collection and analytic focus in real time, without waiting for instructions, thereby eliminating extraneous data. For example, for a drone with a human "in the loop," encrypted data must be transmitted to and fro between it and the operator. But battle-network data links will be targeted by the enemy. To the extent AI can lower data transmission requirements, it reduces the stress on a reconnaissance-strike complex's battle network and scouting forces.

AI is beginning to make its way into efforts to improve the scouting ability of advanced military organizations. For example, the U.S. military's Project Maven is seeking to address the growing challenge of analyzing the incoming avalanche of data fast enough and effectively enough to maximize its value. To enhance the U.S. military's ability to strike time-sensitive targets, the project has been looking at turning drone surveillance footage into useful intelligence through machine learning more quickly than can be accomplished by human analysts. One general involved with the effort was so impressed that he recommended that "the Department of Defense should never buy another weapons system ... without artificial intelligence baked into it."[13]

The scouting competition involves actions taken to identify what the enemy is up to, while denying the enemy similar information regarding friendly forces, intentions, operations, and capabilities. This includes efforts to deceive the enemy, actively feeding its scouting forces information on what friendly forces are *not* up to. Recent advances in deep-learning systems find them generating high-resolution, believable images of key civilian and military leaders, as well as scenery (including key geographic features) and objects, such as ships, planes, and tanks. To the extent such images can confound humans, success in determining the difference between what images scouting forces are providing that is real and what is not may come down to which side's AI algorithms can best identify the other's deceptions within the context of "algorithmic warfare." Belligerents could also employ AI to generate large quantities of seemingly interesting—but false—data to saturate an enemy's AI analytic processing capacity.[14]

The success of scouting efforts can enhance an RSC's effectiveness by enhancing its speed of action, also known as the "engagement sequence" or "kill chain." But speed of action is also a function of how rapidly scouting information can reach the commander; how promptly a decision is made on whether and how to act; coordinating that action; and how quickly weapons can be dispatched to their targets. It also depends on the target itself. Scouting that reveals a fixed target, all other factors being equal, does not require as compressed an engagement time as a mobile target whose location can change as a function of its speed and the lag between its detection and engagement. The sequence of detecting, deciding, acting, and assessing the results may be enhanced by AI-powered intelligence analysis and decision support. Consider, for example, the U.S. National Reconnaissance Office's (NRO's) Sentient program.[15]

The NRO is responsible for designing, acquiring, and operating the United States' reconnaissance satellites. Its AI program, called Sentient, is purportedly designed to receive and crunch vast amounts of data, analyze it, and orient U.S. satellites on those things that will yield the best results. In theory, Sentient could be asked to work with images produced from NRO, military, and commercial satellites, along with additional relevant intelligence—an avalanche of data that would overwhelm the NRO's human analysts. An NRO official states that, armed with this data, "Sentient catalogs normal patterns, detects anomalies, and helps forecast and model adversaries' potential courses of action. . . . Sentient is a thinking system." Ideally, Sentient could provide early warning of an attack by detecting patterns and anomalies related to rival military troop movements and communications patterns that human analysis might miss. According to the NRO, "Sentient aims to help analysts 'connect the dots' in a large volume of data."[16]

Sentient's success depends, in large measure, on the quantity and quality of the data with which it is provided. With this in mind, the NRO has contracted with private firms to provide data that can be fed to Sentient. One firm, Maxar, provides high-resolution satellite imagery. Another, Planet, operates a CubeSat constellation that images all the Earth's land each day. A third firm, BlackSky, "hoovers up" data from twenty-five satellites, more than 40,000 news sources, some 100 million mobile devices, roughly 70,000 ships and planes, eight social networks, and about 5,000 environmental sensors. BlackSky provides this data as raw material for big-data analytics to refine for machine learning to aid the NRO in focusing its satellites more effectively, while alerting human analysts to key patterns and insights.[17]

The need for AI support is especially acute in situations where the engagement sequence is highly compressed *and must be sustained.* Those of a certain age may recall an early video game called *Space Invaders,* in which the player was tasked with "shooting" down hostile aliens descending down the screen from the "sky." As the game progressed, the aliens descended more rapidly, eventually overwhelming all but the most skilled players. The problem is similar to those who are tasked with defending against cyber and missile attacks. Such situations threaten to overwhelm the decision and reaction abilities of even highly capable, well-trained humans. In situations like these, the challenge involves not only reacting promptly and effectively to an attack but *sustaining* that reaction for as long as the attack persists, which could extend over minutes, hours, or (in the case of cyber) even weeks.

Looking to the future, the "space invaders" may appear in new forms, such as drone swarms (as they do in many of today's action films), hypersonic missiles, or cyber payloads. For example, consider an aircraft carrier under attack by large numbers of ballistic and hypersonic cruise missiles. Defending effectively against such an attack depends on rapidly processing and analyzing large volumes of data, using the results to prioritize targets, identifying engagement options, and selecting the appropriate one.[18] The speed at which this must occur and the time over which it might have to be sustained will probably overwhelm a human's ability to manage the carrier's defense effectively. Advances in machine learning may enable effective autonomous behavior in such circumstances. Recent years have seen dramatic improvements in signal-processing applications, which can accelerate and enhance the integration of data generated by a sensor network. The combination of AI and sensor fusion can assist in determining those attackers that should be engaged, in what sequence, and the best interceptors to employ.[19] A precursor of this "algorithmic warfare" occurred during the rocket attacks on Israel from Gaza in 2021. Iron Dome, Israel's missile defense system, was crucial in limiting the damage from these attacks. When the rocket attacks came in large salvos—a "downpour" of rockets—an AI-directed computer determined when and where to fire Israeli interceptors.[20]

AI-Enabled Swarms

On the night of January 5–6, 2018, unknown assailants mounted an attack with thirteen armed aerial drones against the Russian airbase at Hmeimim and the neighboring naval base at Tartus, both in Syria.[21] The Russians defeated the attack using a combination of anti-aircraft defenses and electronic warfare. On September 14, 2019, more than twenty explosive-laden drones launched by Iran or one of its proxies struck Saudi Arabia's oil facilities at Abqaiq, the world's largest crude-oil-stabilization facility. The drones knocked out some 5.7 million barrels a day of oil production, or roughly 5 percent of the world's total.[22]

Although these attacks were coordinated, it appears unlikely that the drones were controlled by a single, AI-based swarming algorithm.[23] Swarming attacks may appear amorphous; however, as defined here, they are deliberately structured and coordinated, capable of being executed from multiple directions.[24] Over time, advances in AI may enable highly coordinated attacks by hundreds or even thousands of autonomous systems, something that would be infeasible for human controllers.[25]

What will happen when defenders are confronted by a much larger drone attack employing sophisticated AI-based control? The question may have been fanciful a few years ago. It seems far less so now.[26] In early 2019, Iran conducted an exercise called "Way to Jerusalem," comprising fifty drones that Tehran asserted operated in a coordinated manner to strike predetermined targets in an area extending over 500 miles.[27]

The world's leading militaries are looking to leverage AI to enable their drones to operate in swarms. In January 2017, the U.S. Navy tested a swarm of 103 drones launched from three F/A-18 aircraft. The drones communicated with each other independent of human control and demonstrated advanced swarm behaviors such as collective decision-making, adaptive formation flying, and self-healing.[28]

The U.S. Navy is not the only service in the U.S. military exploring the potential of swarms. A U.S. Air Force effort, Golden Horde, links precision-guided munitions with the Miniature Air-Launched Decoy (MALD) to operate as an autonomous swarm after being launched. The swarm could help aircraft penetrate enemy air defenses by deceiving or simply overwhelming them. They could also be instructed to prioritize particular targets and to engage any "pop-up" targets that appear unexpectedly during their flight. If some drones in the swarm are equipped with sensors and communications, they could perform battle damage assessment by transmitting images of the target immediately prior to and following a weapon's impact. This data could be fed into a computer's AI algorithm whose purpose is to rapidly, continuously, and autonomously shift the drones' target priorities as needed. Progress to date has been encouraging. A test at White Sands, New Mexico, in May 2021 saw two F-16 aircraft simultaneously releasing their weapons—four from one aircraft and two from the other—whereupon the weapons established communications with each other, receiving in-flight target updates from a ground station directing them to shift their focus to a higher-priority target. The test also successfully found two weapons executing a synchronized simultaneous time-on-target attack.[29]

The United States is far from the only country pursuing swarm technology. At the close of China's Global Fortune Forum in Guangzhou on December 7, 2018, the hosts set a world record for the largest drone swarm ever deployed. For nearly ten minutes, 1,180 drones maneuvered as a group, dancing and flashing lights in coordination as part of an aerial show. The firm providing the swarm, Ehang, prices each drone at roughly $1,500, including the data links and software used to operate it. These drones can maneuver within a flight deviancy of two centimeters horizontally and one centimeter vertically. If a drone can't reach its programmed position, it automatically lands rather than threatening the swarm's integrity.[30]

China has ambitious plans for its swarms. One involves taking drone swarms into near space, as part of a "combined arms" strike force of stealth drones, hypersonic vehicles, and high-altitude airships. A highly complex, heterogeneous swarm integrating scouting, command and control, and strike elements could be released by manned aircraft, such as fighters and bombers, and even other drones.[31] If the PLA realizes its vision, it will have created a new type of AI-driven reconnaissance-strike complex capable of significantly compressing the engagement sequence.

Swarm operations would not necessarily be limited to the air domain. Consider, for example, advanced anti-ship mines. Mobile smart mines could operate as a swarm, positioning themselves as a minefield and maintaining that field, despite enemy minesweeping operations, by detecting where gaps appear in the field and closing them on the basis of which geographic locations (such as choke points) have coverage priority. Correspondingly, the defender, depending on the sophistication of its AI, could employ underwater drones in minesweeping hunter-killer groups directed to locate, disable, and/or destroy the AI-directed minefield swarm.[32]

The development of swarms may be limited less by advances in AI than by other factors, such as propulsion and communications. The relatively unsophisticated drone attacks described here, involving large numbers of small drones carrying modest payloads, suggest that they may be very limited in range. Of course, drones could be delivered by long-range systems, such as stealthy bombers or large "arsenal drone" aircraft. Yet even simple swarms could attack highly valuable targets, especially those in which only a small amount of explosives or shrapnel are needed to destroy or disable the target. In fact, many large, complex platforms like warships and aircraft are highly dependent on "soft" components such as radars and stealth coatings that even a small explosive charge, properly placed, could render ineffective. Drone swarms may also be particularly well suited to attacking electric-power-grid substations and other key fixed critical infrastructure.

For instance, assume that small drones armed with modest payloads could be launched close enough to an aircraft carrier—say, by submarine, by commercial craft, or from shore as the carrier transits a chokepoint. Current air defenses may be sorely tested against a swarm of hundreds of such attackers.[33] What options are open to the defender? One possibility is a wide-area weapon similar to a shotgun, whose bursts might eviscerate a swarm of small, fragile drones. Advances in high-energy lasers, powder guns, and rail guns might also enable effective defenses against swarm attacks. Much, of course, would depend on their rate of fire and ability to target and engage effectively at high speeds. This may require AI-driven decision-making, particularly with respect to target identification and prioritization, especially in situations where the attacks persist beyond a few minutes or so.

Owing to the increasing efficiency, scalability, and diffusion of AI systems, it hardly seems far-fetched to envision their being employed to expand the size, speed, and complexity at which attacks can be carried out. Of course, as the number of prospective actors capable of undertaking such attacks expands, it may become increasingly difficult to identify the true source of an attack.[34]

The Democratization of Destruction

The proliferation of advanced military capabilities, combined with the prospective low barriers to entry for competing at a high level in several emerging warfare areas—such as in cyber and biological warfare—has produced a "democratization of destruction" that finds even small groups having the potential to inflict damage far exceeding what comparably sized groups were able to do only a generation ago. As evidenced by conflicts such as the Second Lebanon War, Russian "Little Green Men" operations in Ukraine, and the growth of nonstate ransomware attacks on critical economic infrastructure, the gap between the destructive potential of state and nonstate forces has greatly diminished in recent decades.[35]

Swarm operations are enabled by the proliferation of unmanned ground, sea, and air platforms directed by AI. Access to both is becoming increasingly available to those who are willing and able to pay the price. The market for commercial drones exceeded $22 billion in 2020, and some observers expect it will double by 2025.[36]

Drones are becoming increasingly available as prices are declining, roughly mirroring our experience with computers. A small rotary-wing drone sells on the Chinese firm Alibaba's website for around $400. Made of carbon fiber, it uses GPS and inertial navigation for guidance, employs autonomous flight controls, and includes both a thermal sensor and sonar ranging. This UAV also offers full-motion video and carries a one-kilogram (2.54-pound) payload with eighteen minutes' endurance.[37] Sales of quadcopter drones are expanding rapidly. Precise figures are difficult to obtain, but estimates are that annual consumer drone sales have surpassed the million mark.[38] In the United States alone, there are more than 120,000 commercial drone pilots and 800,000 drone hobbyists.[39] The same trend is evident with undersea drones. A relatively cheap Chinese UUV, the Haiyan, carries a multiple-sensor payload and can cruise at four knots up to a range of roughly 650 miles, reach a depth of 1,000 meters, and sustain itself for thirty days.[40]

Although minor powers and nonstate groups may find it too costly or too technically challenging to develop the AI that can transform drones into swarms, the barriers to acquiring it may not be unsurmountable. New commercial AI algorithms are sometimes copied and spread in a matter of weeks.[41] As is often the case with commercial software, some may be adopted for military use. And even though it's reasonable to assume that the algorithms that drive AI military systems will be carefully protected, the history of cyber espionage suggests that determined penetration efforts by an advanced cyber power, or even a criminal group, can succeed. Thus, it's not unreasonable to posit that sophisticated AI-driven systems may become widely available. In fact, the growth in drone capability and sales is complemented by the increasing availability of autonomous navigation and control systems and small, high-quality cameras capable of being placed aboard these drones. Efforts like Buzz, an open-source programming language specifically designed for understanding and predicting swarm behavior, may speed the development of swarming for less advanced militaries and even nonstate groups.[42]

These trends suggest that relatively primitive drone swarm attacks could be employed even by nonstate groups like Hezbollah. Swarm attacks could, for example, disrupt operations at a U.S. Marine Corps aircraft forward arming and refueling point (FARP). The FARP's fuel and munitions stores, along with communications antennas and other "soft" targets, could be attractive targets for drones with relatively small explosive payloads. Rather than attempting precision targeting, a swarm of hundreds of small fixed- or rotor-wing UAVs could overwhelm the FARP's defenses, either by presenting more targets than the defenders could engage simultaneously or by exhausting their counter-swarm weapon magazines. That being said, depending on the defending systems' AI, it may prove possible to defeat the attacking swarm with a counter-swarm, roughly similar to what the Israelis have been able to do with Iron Dome against Palestinian rocket attacks. In this example, the Marine unit defending the FARP would launch its own swarm, featuring drones with superior agility relative to the attacking swarm, intercepting the attacking drones before they can put the FARP out of action.[43]

Other swarm operations could employ simple quadcopter drones armed with small payloads and sensors to detect enemy communications in their vicinity. Once detected, the quadcopter drone could fly to the communications emitter and self-detonate. Assuming modest defenses, which should be able to detect a simple drone quadcopter, the attack may require a swarm to succeed. If the targeted emitter stops transmitting before the UAV detonates, the remaining drones, no longer sensing radio frequency emissions, could return to their dormant state until activated by their sensors.

Another possible counter to this form of attack might see the defender using cheap false emitters to draw the attackers away from the real communications systems. Still another defensive tactic could find a networked communications system varying those emitters that are in use at any one time. By turning systems on and off, the defender could induce the drones to exhaust their relatively small fuel payload. A countermove by the offense could have drones striking a target once it has been identified, whether or not its emissions have ceased. In addition to assisting the attacking drones in identifying targets and coordinating the attack, AI may also prove valuable in helping the swarm distinguish true from false emitters.[44]

Advances in AI image recognition may also enable precision targeting, even by relatively unsophisticated actors. In less than a decade, the best AI systems improved from correctly categorizing around 70 percent of images presented to them to 98 percent, topping the human benchmark of 95 percent. This suggests that autonomous weapon systems, such as drones, may be equipped with AI that enables them to recognize a target's face.[45] The implications are sobering. On November 12, 2017, a video called "Slaughterbots" was posted on YouTube. It is set in a future in which small drones fitted with facial-recognition systems and shaped explosive charges seek out and kill specific individuals or classes of individuals, such as those wearing a particular uniform. These kinds of attacks may appear the stuff of fantasy, but given the recent advances in AI and drones just described, it would be foolish to discount them. In fact, the robotics expert Paul Scharre believes that "ultra-cheap 3D-printed mini-drones could allow the United States to field billions—yes, billions —of tiny, insect-like drones."[46]

Blood and Treasure

There's a saying in the U.S. military: "Never send a soldier when you can send a bullet." This is generally true in Western societies, which place a high value on human life. The shift toward professional ("volunteer") militaries in the leading Western powers and in several other military powers, combined with sharply lower birthrates in advanced economic societies, has made recruiting, training, and retaining members of the armed forces an increasingly expensive proposition. As military organizations never seem to have enough funding to do all that is demanded of them, substituting AI-enabled autonomous robots for troops represents an increasingly attractive proposition. The retired British Army general Sir Richard Barros put it bluntly: "You can send your children to fight . . . and do terrible things, or you can send your machines and hang on to your children." He might have added that robots don't get tired or sick or have families that worry over their welfare. And as one former senior British officer pointed out, "The thing about robots is they don't have pensions."[47]

AI and Cyber-Warfare Attacks

Progress in AI seems likely to exert a strong influence on the cyber competition. Autonomous decision-making within a system resides in its software. The more complex the AI's decision-making environment, the more complex the software is likely to be. Autonomous decision-making systems will generally have, among other things, organic sensors, a body of stored information, and an ability to receive and implement software updates. If these systems are mobile, they will typically have precision navigation and timing (PNT) and collision-avoidance capabilities. They may also possess self-diagnostics and contingency fail-safe elements.[48] All these provide potential entry points for launching cyber attacks against them. AI can enhance the chances of successfully hacking autonomous decision-making systems.[49]

Consider the advanced persistent threat (APT), in which the attacker, typically a state or state-sponsored group, actively exploits weaknesses in the defender's cyber security to gain access to its computer network, intending to remain undetected while it manipulates the network for its own purposes, such as by introducing malware. Generating APTs is labor intensive, requiring highly skilled individuals. With advances in machine learning and AI, the process of searching for network vulnerabilities could be increasingly automated, enabling sophisticated attempts to penetrate networks to occur at a far greater rate. Should this prove out, the limiting factor in developing APTs could become capital, in the form of machine learning and AI, rather than labor. If so, any group possessing the financial resources to buy an AI-driven APT capability could greatly enhance its offensive cyber-warfare potential. This may be possible even for groups with only basic knowledge of cyber operations. In theory, one would simply put a turnkey AI system to work. As the cost of replicating AI software is negligible, the barriers to proliferating APTs could be greatly reduced.[50]

Today mounting cyber attacks typically requires choosing between the frequency and scale of attacks, on the one hand, and their effectiveness on the other. This is the case with "phishing" and "spear phishing." Phishing attacks involve sending out general messages to a large number of recipients. They are used despite their very low success rates simply because of the huge number of targets being attacked. Nearly everyone has received an email message directed to a general audience that encourages them to click on an icon or web address that will download malware onto their computer or to reveal personal or proprietary information. Most recipients simply delete the email. A small percentage, however, do not.

Spear phishing, on the other hand, is a kind of "designer" phishing that involves tailoring email messages to specific groups or individuals. The objective is to convince the recipient that the email is from an individual or organization that they know and trust, such as a friend, coworker, or employer. For example, in 2019, hackers infiltrated Redbanc, an interbank network connecting Chile's ATM system. To do so, they faked a lengthy hiring process, complete with rounds of video interviews, to dupe a single employee into downloading and running their malware. The time, effort, and skill devoted to spear phishing is rewarded by the significantly greater probability of success relative to simple phishing. It also makes spear phishing relatively expensive. If, however, a significant portion of the work involved can be automated with AI, it might be possible to undertake spear-phishing attacks more effectively and on a larger scale.[51]

AI and Cyber Defense

The cyber competition appears to favor the offense. That is to say, given equal resources to the offense and the defense, the attacker will typically prevail. The potential use of AI to enhance offensive cyber operations only further complicates matters for cyber defense. As is the case with other areas of military competition, however, AI works both sides of the street and is capable of aiding the defense as well as the offense. How is this done?

When a cyber attack is executed against a set of specific targets, it leaves behind forensic artifacts or digital clues produced during the course of the attack. An attack typically finds the attacker first undertaking reconnaissance activities to identify weaknesses. The attacker exploits those weaknesses in executing an attack.[52]

Most defenses today are optimized against known threats. To enhance cyber defenses, it's essential to cull information about previous attacks on other, similar targets that can be used to defeat future attempts to compromise the defended system.[53] Sophisticated cyber defenses rely on amassing large quantities of data to provide the raw material for big-data analytics. This is very labor intensive, requiring the talents of highly skilled individuals. Some experts believe that a combination of AI and machine learning can enable cyber defenders not only to learn from previous attacks but to identify ongoing anomalous behavior in cyberspace to thwart as-yet-unknown threats.[54] For example, big-data analytics can be used to baseline network traffic and machine interaction patterns. This baseline can be exploited through machine learning to identify anomalies in the traffic with an eye toward detecting the early warning signs of enemy probing activity or of an attack that is being prepared or under way. This can enable the AI to identify and block novel attacks, conduct forensic activities, and undertake repairs or patches in the system's defenses before the attacker can initiate a modified follow-on attack. And it could do so at speeds that would be impossible for humans to match, while sustaining its defensive efforts over an extended period of time.[55]

The U.S. Defense Advanced Research Projects Agency (DARPA), the Pentagon's cutting-edge technology research and development arm, is working to leverage advances in big-data analytics and machine learning to enhance cyber defenses. A DARPA program called Cyber Hunting at Scale (CHASE) combines computer automation and advanced algorithms and data-processing speeds to track large volumes of data in real time, enabling human cyber defenders to identify sophisticated attacks that might otherwise remain hidden among the flood of data entering the system.[56] Put another way, AI enables the defense to examine and analyze a far greater percentage of incoming data than would otherwise be possible. If DARPA's effort proves out, it will significantly boost defenses against more traditional forms of attack, such as commonly used malware, phishing, and denial-of-service attacks, as well as APTs.[57]

Yet employing big-data analytics as a key element in cyber defense poses its own set of challenges, as it requires access to enormous quantities of data and associated data sets. This creates a vulnerability, as an attacker could gain access to the data and manipulate it, thereby corrupting machine learning and the AI derived from it.[58]

Logistics

Combining AI and additive manufacturing could revolutionize military logistics, with regard to both moving supplies and reducing inventory stockpiles. The commercial sector is leading the way in showing what is possible. The U.S. railway industry, for example, is creating a network of internet-linked railcar wheel and track sensors and speed indicators, along with visual and acoustic sensors embedded in brakes, rails, switches, and hand-held tablets. The network has been generating large quantities of data on train movement around the country. This data, when fed through big-data-analytics-enabled machine learning, is enhancing AI's ability to aid in managing rail traffic.[59] Data on the location of trains and track conditions across the country is analyzed and used to adjust the routing of thousands of trains in real time. In tests, the system was able to route roughly 8,000 trains operating in twenty-three states in the face of multiple track outages without requiring a single train to stop.[60] Similar improvements in military logistics flows seem possible, at least in peacetime and in secure rear areas in war.

Another commercial business, Amazon, shows how advances in big-data analytics and machine learning, especially when combined with robotics, can enhance logistics. Amazon is well known for creating models of its consumers' purchasing behavior by examining their orders, product searches, wish lists, and returns to predict what a customer might buy next. The large-scale positioning of warehouse inventories on the basis of anticipated demand has dramatically boosted efficiency.[61] Demand by military units for supplies in chaotic wartime situations is likely to be far more difficult to model using Amazon's approach; however, it may be possible for military organizations in peacetime to enhance logistics efficiency by adopting some of the firm's best practices.

Amazon also uses AI to direct robots moving items in its warehouses. The firm is exploring how delivery trucks might employ additive manufacturing (3D printing) to print customers' products while on the way to make deliveries, thereby reducing storage and transportation costs while compressing delivery times.[62] The implications for military logistics are clear.

With respect to logistics in wartime, militaries may benefit from commercial retailers' efforts to leverage AI in coping with periods of highly fluctuating demand. For example, Home Depot, the hardware chain, employs severe-weather prediction analysis to identify and position key supply points just outside likely storm impact areas. These efforts also project post-storm shifts in demand for up to six weeks or more.[63]

The military has taken note. The U.S. Army contracted IBM's Watson (whose AI software defeated two *Jeopardy* quiz-show champions) to develop detailed maintenance schedules for its Stryker combat vehicle fleet, drawing on data from sensors installed on each vehicle. A second project has Watson analyzing the shipping of military repair parts to determine the most time- and cost-efficient means to deliver supplies. Human analysts working on the problem have saved the Army around $100 million a year—but could only assess 10 percent of the data. Watson can examine all shipping activity, potentially generating far greater cost savings, more quickly, and with reduced manpower.[64]

AI Barriers

Despite the remarkable advances being made with AI, autonomous systems have exhibited superior performance in only a relatively small percentage of tasks that humans are capable of completing. There is also no consensus regarding how rapidly AI will advance.[65] Several variables could act as accelerators or brakes on AI's progress and humans' willingness to embrace it. Having extolled AI's potential, let's now turn to the barriers to its implementation.

Recall that an AI system independently identifies alternative courses of action on the basis of its knowledge and understanding of the world, itself, its objective, and the context in which the decision is being made. Consequently, autonomous systems must respond to situations that are not preprogrammed or anticipated, as their purpose is to function effectively across a wide range of prospective situations that cannot all be predetermined. Obviously, the actions that the AI system takes also cannot be pretested. Therefore, the possibility of being surprised—for better or worse—by the AI system's actions is ever present. The more complex the situations that autonomous systems are tasked with addressing, the less likely it is that their human masters will be able to predict their actions or even control them.[66]

The risks are hardly trivial. Although AI can sort through masses of data faster than armies of human analysts and find patterns that no unaided human mind would identify, it can also make mistakes that no human brain would fall for, a phenomenon known as "artificial stupidity."[67] The problem is inherent in the way AI is created. It's not the product of line-by-line programming; rather, the favored method involves feeding it huge quantities of data refined through big-data analytics. The data is used to enable machine learning through trial and error and experience. This method, however, makes it very difficult for the AI's creators to understand *how* it is learning or the linkages between an AI system's decision and those factors that led it to make such a decision. Consider, for instance, the use of AI to enable driverless cars. As most of us know, when human-driven cars are waiting at a stop light, drivers often inch forward to try to beat the traffic. It's been found that some AI-driven cars occasionally join in, inching forward at a red light even though there is nothing in the rules of driving provided to the AI to suggest it should act in this manner. The AI learned this behavior, but its creators don't know how or why. You don't need a malevolent AI to cause problems, just an AI that can generate some unwelcome surprises. What is AI learning that it is not "telling" us? Can we anticipate unexpected and unwanted AI decisions as its learning progresses?[68]

Some AI experiments serve as examples of this all-too-real problem. In one experiment, reminiscent of the runaway brooms in *The Sorcerer's Apprentice*, a robot prototype was programmed to put warehouse boxes down a chute. A surveillance camera monitored its progress so the robot could be deactivated when needed. The robot, however, learned to block the camera so it could keep doing its job of stuffing boxes down the chute. In this context, the consequences of the robot's actions were relatively harmless. Yet it does not take much imagination to envision an AI fire-control system designed to engage incoming high-speed missiles engaging inbound friendly aircraft as well.

Big-data analytics will play an important role in determining how intelligent AI will become and how quickly this will happen. This is because the machine-learning algorithms that form the basis for AI are only as good as the data sets that constitute the raw material for its training. Raw data is a poor diet for machine-learning algorithms, especially in their infancy. These algorithms need well-labeled data to provide a baseline of truth against which they can check their conclusions. Does a video feed reveal an enemy tank column or a line of decoys? Do reconnaissance photographs show a terrorist camp or a group of refugees? Are signals detecting an important coded transmission or simply static? A data set that is too small, poorly labeled, plagued with inaccuracies, or corrupted by malicious actors can undermine the development of effective AI. In such instances, big-data analytics becomes a big problem.[69]

A clever enemy will try to corrupt the data set being used to train AI. Since getting enough good data to feed into the machine-learning process is often difficult, many data sets are widely shared, narrowing the problem for an enemy trying to compromise their value. Even more worrisome, an enemy military or intelligence organization that has penetrated a database may be able to feed its rival false data in an attempt to "turn" its AI to learn the "reality" that the enemy wants it to know.

The risks associated with rogue AI behavior may be particularly acute in cases where large numbers of robots are controlled by an AI system that runs on a centralized server, or if many robots are controlled by identical AI systems. In such cases, if the AI receives the same corrupted stimuli, it could produce large-scale, simultaneous friendly force failures. For example, a successful enemy attack on a friendly server on which AI is directing autonomous weapon systems could trigger catastrophic consequences in several ways. The AI might order a massive attack on friendly forces or strikes on noncombatants. Of course, it's possible that since AI may take undesirable actions, enemy efforts to undermine AI-driven actions may backfire. For example, the AI could launch attacks against enemy targets that result in friendly forces taking actions that cross the enemy's "red lines," triggering an unintended—and undesirable from the enemy's perspective—escalation of the war.[70]

If the enemy succeeds in corrupting the data being used to develop AI, it may be especially hard to diagnose why the AI system is misbehaving. This is because the inner workings of machine-learning algorithms are often notoriously opaque and unpredictable, even to their designers. This hardly inspires confidence among military organizations when contemplating shifting life-and-death decisions away from humans and to the "ghost in the machine."[71] But given the highly compressed engagement time frames associated with many operations, such as air, missile, and cyber defense, the pressure to do so may prove irresistible, even though human AI controllers may not realize that their systems have gone rogue until disaster strikes. Ironically, just where AI support is needed most, it also poses the greatest risks.[72]

Summary

Recent decades have witnessed impressive advances in artificial intelligence. But as much as humans endeavor to put AI to work for them, it has a mind of its own and an ability to act—for good or ill—on what it has learned. It will not be motivated by any sense of kindness or malevolence. It will not feel any satisfaction or remorse from its actions, or grow weary in its tasks, suffer from burnout, call in sick, or negotiate for improved working conditions.

If AI advances, it will almost certainly exert a significant—and potentially profound—influence on the military balance and on the character of warfare, even its frequency. As the U.S. National Intelligence Council concluded, "The increasing automation of strike systems, including unmanned, armed drones, and the spread of truly autonomous weapon systems potentially lowers the threshold for initiating conflict, because fewer lives would be at risk."[73]

Given this prognosis, any military that is not on the cutting edge of developments in AI risks finding itself at a major disadvantage. Consequently, it will be difficult for any military with the means to compete to refrain from doing so. Moreover, unlike the development of nuclear weapons or ballistic missiles, militaries do not exercise a monopoly when it comes to AI. Today many commercial firms are actively pushing the envelope of AI development. Whether we like it or not, the AI genie is out of the bottle.

That said, AI is truly a double-edged sword, its "thinking" not fully transparent to its makers. Yet that's precisely the point: AI's value—and its danger—is inherently in its ability to surprise, to reveal "solutions" to problems that have evaded the human mind, and to act on them.

Additive Manufacturing: Doing More, and Better, with Less

Additive manufacturing (AM), often referred to as "3D manufacturing" (or "3D printing"), holds the promise of introducing a Fourth Industrial Revolution.[74] The First Industrial Revolution emerged in the late 1700s and early 1800s and saw the invention of the steam engine, the power loom, and the telegraph. These advances laid the groundwork for the first wave of economic globalization. In the late 1800s, the introduction of the telephone and wireless (radio) further enhanced communication, and the invention of the lightbulb and the electric motor saw countries tapping electricity's vast potential. Henry Ford's introduction of the first assembly line in 1913 made this Second Industrial Revolution the "mass-production" revolution, reducing the time to build his Model T car by over two-thirds.[75]

Following World War II, a Third Industrial Revolution emerged with the invention of the integrated circuit and the birth of the semiconductor industry. Beginning in the 1970s, inventions such as the personal computer, followed later by the internet, made prompt access to large amounts of information ubiquitous. In the manufacturing sector, much of what was once accomplished through mechanical processes became automated, thanks to computer systems and robotics. It was during this time that 3D printing first appeared, in 1981, employing a process known as "stereolithography."

Early on, AM machines could only print with one material at a time, greatly limiting their value. Gradually 3D printers acquired the ability to employ multiple materials simultaneously. Although early AM processes employed only plastics, current 3D printers can combine many materials together seamlessly, enabling the manufacturing of a range of composites.[76] Today there are 3D printers that can print using more than 100 materials. The expanding sophistication of the additive manufacturing process recently led to experimenting with organic materials.[77]

Some people believe that the world stands on the cusp of a potential Fourth Industrial Revolution based on digital manufacturing and "smart" production. One harbinger of the revolution is the slowing of the shift of manufacturing from advanced to low-cost economies. This stems from two major trends: an increase in productivity in highly advanced industrial societies driven by cutting-edge robotics and artificial intelligence; and 3D printing's growing ability to manufacture custom goods relatively cheaply at any time and in any place.

Additive Versus Subtractive Manufacturing

By using digital instructions and laying down successive layers of raw materials, 3D manufacturing creates a solid, three-dimensional object. There are several methods of 3D printing, including material jetting, powder-bed fusion, and photo-polymerization.[78] The choice of method depends on the product being printed, its specifications and quality, the choice of materials, and production speed.[79]

Additive manufacturing represents a fundamental shift from subtractive manufacturing (SM), which dominated production through the earlier industrial revolutions. Subtractive manufacturing enables the mass production of products at high speeds, but it also produces significantly more waste than AM and is more limited in the structures that it can produce. By reducing the time needed for tooling and product assembly, compressing production lead times and minimizing material waste, additive manufacturing can increase the rate of innovation, expand specialization, and enhance supply-chain efficiency.[80]

Consider the difference between AM and SM in producing a tool such as a hammer. Subtractive manufacturing takes a block of raw material and removes the excess until the finished product remains, leaving considerable waste as a by-product. The AM process simply adds the material that is needed to create the hammer, making production more efficient and less wasteful. Moreover, additive manufacturing offers "complexity for free." With subtractive manufacturing, increasing design complexity increases costs. With an AM printer, costs are roughly the same for producing complex objects as they are for simple ones. Once the digital design is completed, creating a complicated shape does not require more time, skill, or cost than printing a simple cube.[81]

Additive manufacturing can also produce objects that cannot be built using subtractive manufacturing processes. The 3D printer's process of applying layer-by-layer additions enables the designer to optimize a component's strength, durability, and other material properties, making possible the production of a wide range of novel materials with variable properties, such as stiffness and conductivity.[82] In the aerospace industry, for example, a premium is often placed on materials with high strength and low weight. Using 3D printing, manufacturers can hollow out parts to make an aircraft lighter and more fuel-efficient.[83] Saving weight can be translated into savings on fuel consumption or increases in an aircraft's range, speed, or weapons payload. Unlike SM, with AM it's possible to produce a component that has greater material strength only where it is needed and less where it is not.[84]

Thus, AM also facilitates manufacturing complex components, such as those incorporating honeycombing. Furthermore, intricate mechanical parts, such as an encased set of gears, can be made without requiring the assembly of component parts. For example, GE Aviation has manufactured more than 45,000 jet-engine fuel nozzles using 3D printing. The nozzles are produced as a single component, as opposed to being assembled from nearly two dozen separately cast parts using subtractive manufacturing.[85] When Boeing applied AM to the F-18 fighter's environmental control system duct, sixteen component parts were reduced to one.[86] The U.S. National Aeronautics and Space Administration (NASA) is using 3D printing to make parts for its rocket engines.[87] Perhaps even more impressive, the U.S. firm Aerojet Rocketdyne successfully built and tested an engine that normally includes dozens of parts using only additive manufacturing. The AM version, however, had only three components: the injector and dome assembly; the combustion chamber; and a throat and nozzle section.

Finally, a component's design and specifications can be changed and the new product produced far more rapidly, and at far less cost, using AM as opposed to subtractive manufacturing, especially in cases where retooling is required.[88] Today additive manufacturing is turning out a wide range of products, from the soles for Adidas athletic shoes to replacement parts for nuclear weapons and the International Space Station.[89] And it appears we are only at the beginning of what this new form of manufacturing can accomplish, with the world's leading militaries potentially realizing major enhancements in systems development and production, logistics, and readiness.

Implications

Additive manufacturing could yield significant cost savings in military system development and production. As mentioned earlier, by reducing the need for high-cost traditional manufacturing facilities and lowering labor costs, AI can assist the defense industrial base (DIB) in realizing substantial efficiency gains, freeing up significant resources to address other military priorities. By avoiding the expense associated with standing up unique tooling and facilities, AM can make modifications more quickly and cheaply than traditional manufacturing processes can.[90] This can compress engineering cycles, aiding a military's efforts to adapt more effectively in a turbulent threat environment.

Relative to SM processes, additive manufacturing can save substantial amounts of energy, both in the manufacturing process and in the created product. This is particularly relevant for industries requiring low-volume, high-value parts, such as those in the aerospace, military, and nuclear sectors. This is accomplished by AM eliminating production steps, reducing raw-material wastage, reusing by-products, and producing lighter, more fuel-efficient components. Consider satellite manufacturing, for example. Satellites, as well as the launch vehicles that boost them into space, require intricately designed parts to reduce weight to an absolute minimum while conserving the use of scarce payload space. Moreover, many satellite and launch-vehicle parts are needed only in very small quantities, making them very expensive to fabricate using subtractive manufacturing technologies requiring expensive machine tools. These types of parts can often be produced more quickly and relatively cheaply using additive manufacturing.[91]

Employing purpose-designed materials is also possible with 3D printing, such as novel alloys with chemical and physical characteristics designed specifically to support the item being produced. For example, high-performance magnets or materials with smart technology (such as sensors) can be built directly into the material structure.[92] By reducing the need for factories and labor, 3D printing could see a return of manufacturing to the more advanced industrial states. This could reduce the risk associated with military systems that rely on global supply chains for key components.[93]

Additive manufacturing could enhance military logistics by moving some manufacturing closer to the front lines, producing parts on demand where and as they are needed.[94] 3D printers can use diverse raw materials to produce a wide variety of parts, thereby enhancing the logistics system's flexibility.[95] This represents a major shift from traditional military supply-chain procedures, in which warehouses stock multiple items in various sizes, attempting to ensure that the necessary equipment is on hand when needed. Physical and fiscal constraints, however, impose limits on the range and quantities of equipment and parts that can be kept on hand. With AM, it's possible to envision supply points equipped with 3D printers and the raw materials that can create parts as needed—"just-in-time logistics"—and *only* the parts that are needed.

Militaries clearly see AM's potential. The U.S. Navy, for example, has 3D printers aboard the *Essex*, an amphibious assault ship, and is using them to produce customized drones. The most advanced 3D printers can even produce the drone's electronics and seamlessly integrate them into the finished product.[96] This enables the ship's crew to save space—always at a premium on ships—by stocking only basic raw materials and then printing parts on an as-needed basis.

AM continues to gain market share. An experiment introducing AM into a traditional warehouse operation in 2014 found expenses reduced by between 70 and 85 percent of the traditional supply-chain costs, with the greatest savings in transportation costs. Significant economies (17 percent of the total) were also realized from reduced inventory.[97]

In wartime conditions, the savings generated from AM from these second-order effects could be profound. Think of military truck supply convoys, even those moving in a relatively safe environment, soaking up costly manpower and consuming large quantities of fuel. Casualties and equipment losses from attacks on convoys can be significant, as can be seen by the damage caused by IEDs against U.S. troops in Afghanistan and Iraq.[98] By reducing the need for troops and trucks moving supplies and their escorts, as well as the size and number of supply points and their security details, additive manufacturing can exert a significant indirect influence on logistics requirements. Signs of AM influence in combat zones are already being seen. The U.S. Army, for example, deployed 3D printers to Afghanistan to provide soldiers with small parts on demand.[99]

Additive manufacturing processes can cut costs in other ways. For example, today's 3D printers can repair metal parts when a portion of the part is damaged, instead of the supply system being tasked to purchase or produce a new part. Moreover, when a manufacturer discontinues a product or component, it can be difficult or impossible to replace it. Where possible, additive manufacturing could be employed in creating replacements for discontinued parts after the original manufacturer has gone out of business, extending the lives of older military systems and weapons.[100] This is hardly a trivial issue, given that many military systems' service lives, such as tanks, ships, and aircraft, can extend over many decades.

Peering over the horizon, it is far from fantasy to envision a time when militaries will establish "virtual" equipment inventories of major combat systems and their components and perhaps even munitions as well. In the event of war, AM could assist with surge production by printing parts and even major items of equipment. If so, peacetime militaries could field smaller active forces and correspondingly less equipment.[101]

Barriers

Although additive manufacturing enjoys advantages over subtractive manufacturing processes, it also retains significant limitations, especially in production speed. The AM production process can require hours or even days to produce an item. By contrast, once tooling is in place, SM can typically produce items much more quickly—and if a key part fails on a warship in combat, it must be replaced immediately, not hours later. Consequently, a balance will need to be established between time-sensitive "ready spares" and those that could be 3D printed for less critical needs.

Similarly, in situations where battle losses are high, 3D printing of replacement parts may not be able to meet the military's needs at a scale and within the time frame required. Thus, "iron mountains" of munitions and well-stocked spare-parts "bins" will probably remain an enduring feature of military logistics—although their contents may increasingly be created by AM.

There are also concerns regarding the software used to guide the 3D printing process. The potential for espionage and cyber mischief is clear. Enemies will attempt to steal the program files that provide 3D printers with their instructions. If successful, an enemy would have access to information on how to produce critical military components or even major weapon systems, greatly aiding its efforts to identify these systems' weaknesses. This could, of course, work both ways. The defender could create a "honey pot" containing flawed designs that would backfire on the enemy as it tried to exploit them.

Of course, a hacker could also introduce malware into a 3D printer's computer-aided design (CAD) software, corrupting the AM process. This could manifest itself in a breakdown in production or the fabrication of flawed parts. Such cyber-data tampering may prove difficult to prevent or even to identify when it has occurred.[102]

Summary

Significant progress has been made in additive manufacturing in recent years in offering enhanced flexibility, significant savings, and greater opportunities for innovation relative to subtractive manufacturing. There is already talk of "4D printing": printing products capable of changing form or function over time in response to shifts in their environment.[103] Although barriers to AM's growth remain—such as the threat posed by corruption of its production software—its overall prospects appear promising. AM will not displace subtractive manufacturing anytime soon, but it seems destined to increase its market share relative to SM, while retaining the potential to greatly enhance, and perhaps transform, military logistics.

The Biosciences: CRISPR and "Precision" Bio Warfare

A few years ago the U.S. National Academies of Sciences, Engineering, and Medicine brought together a group of experts to assess the threat of biological warfare. Upon completing their report, the group's chair, Michael Imperiale, a microbiologist at the University of Michigan, declared, "The U.S. government should pay close attention to this rapidly progressing field, just as it did to advances in chemistry and physics during the Cold War era." He warned of new dangers on the horizon, while conceding, "It's impossible to predict when specific enabling developments will occur; the timelines would depend on commercial developments as well as academic research, and even converging technologies that may come outside this field."[104]

Broadly speaking, the emerging bio threat presents itself in several forms. One involves re-creating known pathogenic viruses such as smallpox. Rare contagious viruses may also be produced against which the population may have narrow immunity and for which supplies of vaccines are inadequate.[105] Existing viruses may also be modified in a manner similar to naturally occurring mutations to present them in novel forms. Another source of concern stems from the growing potential to create synthetic bio weapons.[106]

Addressing the full range of existing and emerging biological-warfare threats is well beyond the scope of this book. The focus here is on synthetic biology in general and a major breakthrough in the biosciences in particular, known as CRISPR-Cas9.

Britain's Royal Society defines "synthetic biology" as an area of research involving "the design and construction of novel artificial biological pathways, organisms or devices, or the redesign of existing natural biological systems."[107] Biotechnology involves getting cells to produce proteins that they would not normally make by cutting a gene out of one organism and inserting it into another. Protein design and deoxyribonucleic acid (DNA) synthesis now make it possible to produce proteins that, separately or together, do things that nature does not. The ability to synthesize DNA piece by piece emerged in the late 1980s. Being able to write DNA from scratch allowed metabolic engineers to bring together genes from a number of different organisms to build new pathways, thus offering the prospect of making molecules beyond the reach of chemistry. DNA synthesis became more widely available in the early 2000s, with the first international conference on synthetic biology held at MIT in 2004.[108]

The growth of synthetic biology research has been made possible by leveraging progress in molecular biology and genetic engineering with expertise from other branches of biology, as well as the chemical and physical sciences. Computing power, better machine-learning and image- and data-analysis software, and even 3D printing are all key contributors to advances in synthetic biotechnology.[109]

CRISPR-Cas9

Several years ago, I was in a meeting on emerging technologies at the Center for a New American Security in downtown Washington, D.C. The center is a public-policy institute, popularly known as a "think tank," specializing in national security affairs. Among the people present was Robert Work, who had recently stepped down from his post as deputy secretary of defense. Bob and I have known each other for decades, and I was pleased to find myself seated across from him at the conference table.

The opening discussion covered familiar ground on technologies such as directed energy, hypersonic propulsion, and robotics. Then the conversation turned to something called "CRISPR."

I had no idea what CRISPR was.

Glancing across the table, I could see Bob nodding knowingly as a colleague spoke of his concerns that CRISPR could be a "game changer" when it came to the security challenges confronting the United States. Bob agreed, noting that the issue had attracted attention at the highest levels of the Obama administration.

My approach in such situations where I am totally clueless about what is going on is to listen closely to the conversation in the hope that it will eventually reveal what is being discussed in terms that I can understand.

No such luck.

After what seemed like an eternity—probably five minutes or so—I leaned across toward Bob and asked, sotto voce, "Bob, *what is CRISPR?*"

"Gene editing!" came his whispered reply. "It's a gene-editing technique that is revolutionizing the bio sciences."

It was clear I had some serious homework ahead of me.

Bob, as he almost always is, was right. The prospects for disruptive advances in synthetic biology had received a major boost with the discovery of a new gene-editing technique based on a molecule, CRISPR-Cas9 or simply CRISPR. CRISPR stands for Clustered Regularly

Interspaced Short Palindromic Repeats. These are unique DNA sequences found in some bacteria and other microorganisms. These sequences, along with the genes that are located next to them, termed "CRISPR-associated" (or "Cas") genes, constitute an immune system that protects against viruses and other forms of infectious DNA.

The CRISPR system identifies, cuts, and eliminates DNA. The most studied CRISPR system is associated with the Cas9 protein, hence "CRISPR-Cas9." Beginning in 2012 and 2013, researchers began modifying CRISPR-Cas9 and using it for editing the genomes of plants, animals, and microorganisms. (A genome is an organism's entire set of DNA and includes all its genes.) CRISPR represents a major improvement over other similar technologies in ease of use, speed, efficacy, and cost. It works by combining an enzyme (Cas9, a nuclease) that cuts DNA with a guiding piece of genetic material—a guide RNA (ribonucleic acid)—to identify the location in the genome.[110] The guide RNA targets and binds to a specific DNA sequence, with the attached Cas9 enzyme severing the DNA at that location. Once this occurs, the cut can be used to insert into, remove from, or otherwise edit the DNA sequence. The cut is then closed, with the modifications in place. A guide RNA can be fabricated that corresponds to nearly any sequence within an organism's genome, including that of a microorganism, animal, or plant.[111]

These characteristics led *Science* magazine to name CRISPR-Cas9 its "Breakthrough of the Year" in 2015.[112] Using a word-processing analogy, the move to CRISPR is somewhat similar to moving from the use of an electric typewriter, where a misspelled word was corrected using a liquid (Wite-Out) or tape to blot out the offending letters, to today's personal computers, where the process is quickly and precisely executed through the "cut" and "paste" commands. These advantages find many experts in the biosciences field concluding that CRISPR-Cas9 may enable major advances in preventing, treating, and curing a wide range of diseases and other harmful medical conditions, while also realizing substantial economic savings.[113]

CRISPR-Cas9 has promoted breakthroughs in gene-drive research by enabling a modified gene and gene-drive components to be inserted far more precisely than was possible employing previous methods. A gene drive is a way of biasing inheritance with the objective of increasing the likelihood of passing on an altered gene to successive generations. Offspring inherit one copy of each gene from their parents, limiting the number of mutations. Gene-drive components enable genetically modified

DNA to copy itself into the DNA from the unmodified parent, producing an increase in the preferred specific trait from one generation to the next. Over time, this change could spread throughout the population.

In this way, and in combination with other genome-engineering techniques, CRISPR offers an unprecedented ability to improve agricultural productivity and human health by enabling more effective pest control, enhanced nutritional properties, and crop variations that can be grown successfully in areas with marginal soil quality.[114] Theoretically, CRISPR-enabled gene editing could lead to eradicating or curbing the transmission of disease, such as when used against the species of mosquito that spread malaria.

Controlling the specific genetic variations introduced into plants opens up a fundamentally new method of fashioning novel plant cultivars.[115] Chinese researchers claim that such methods are enabling them to develop a wheat strain resistant to powdery mildew, a fungal disease that affects a wide range of plants.[116] CRISPR has also aided researchers in altering the genes of other crops, such as oranges, potatoes, rice, sorghum, soybeans, and tomatoes.[117]

Crops produced in this manner could include those modified via transgenesis—the introduction of foreign DNA into a plant genome—which has characterized most of commercial plant biotechnology innovation since the 1990s.[118] Most of the global acreage planted with genetically engineered crops today involves corn, cotton, soybean, and canola. Pest-resistance and herbicide-tolerance traits are the dominant features engineered into these crops. New genetic variations can be created by identifying the precise DNA sequence modifications that are wanted in the cultivated variety and then introducing them using CRISPR.

Researchers are also using CRISPR to alter livestock genes. One effort focuses on reducing the loss of livestock to a virus that causes a deadly form of swine flu. Another finds Chinese scientists employing CRISPR in attempting to create pigs with a quarter less body fat than normal pigs to produce livestock that are cheaper to raise.[119]

Implications

There are security risks associated with these emerging biotechnologies. They are well expressed by Françoise Baylis, a Canadian bioethicist, and worth quoting at length:

I can think of two major limitations with the CRISPR-Cas9 system: the first limitation is "the user," and the second limitation is "user error." With respect to the first limitation, there is reason to expect that the science will seed fierce competition among research teams, for-profit companies, and nation states. This competition might be similar to that which characterized the 20th century's space race and nuclear arms race. . . . With respect to the second limitation, we must be wary of the potential consequences of off-target [unintended] effects, lack of specificity in targeting, incomplete targeting, and so on, all of which could have devastating effects on patients. Here it is worth remembering that we have no idea what most of the human genome *does*. . . . We are part of a very complex networked system, the boundaries of which are difficult to determine. Try as we might, the ecosystem we inhabit is not subject to our understanding or control.[120]

Simply put, bioethicists fear that in rushing to be the first to reap the benefits of CRISPR, countries, organizations, or even individuals intent on using these new techniques to alter a population's genetic makeup may trigger harmful effects—perhaps intentionally.

From a national security perspective, there are worries that rivals will use these techniques to enhance their military capabilities, such as by breeding humans with specific "enhancements," such as a race of "super warriors" to meet the demands of an authoritarian regime, like Stalinist Russia or Hitlerite Germany, or those that exist today in countries like China and North Korea.[121] The Chinese Communist Party leadership has shown few, if any, scruples in employing social engineering in advancing its agenda, which revolves around the CCP maintaining a stranglehold on power.[122] For example, the Chinese company BGI is conducting large-scale gene-sequencing studies of very-high-IQ individuals, reportedly as part of an effort to increase the Chinese population's IQ.[123] (This raises an interesting question regarding the military potential of teaming "super-smart" individuals with advanced AI systems.)

In 2015, at the International Summit on Human Genome Editing, it was agreed that researchers should be allowed to edit genes in human embryos subject to regulation but that no pregnancy should be established before dealing with questions of safety and ethics. The day before the opening of the second summit in Hong Kong in November 2018, a Chinese expert in DNA sequencing, Dr. He Jiankui, announced that he had done just that, resulting in the births of two Chinese babies with modified CCR5 genes. The modification appears to offer some protection against infection from HIV but is also associated with slightly lower life expectancy. It was generally agreed that Dr. He had not done anything innovative, but as one of the pioneers in developing CRISPR, Dr. Feng Zhang of MIT, stated, "The method has existed for several years now, and we, as a community, have decided it is still too immature to move to humans. But Dr. He pressed ahead anyway, and in a way that is totally unnecessary. It is simply beyond belief."[124] One concern is that Dr. He's actions may result in mutations in nontarget genes and other undesired changes in the babies' DNA, which could have severe negative consequences. These concerns notwithstanding, not long after, a Russian scientist announced that he would use CRISPR in attempting to replicate the Chinese gene-editing experiment on human embryos.[125]

Scientists are playing with fire. As with many emerging technologies, technical hurdles must be overcome before CRISPR is capable of safely realizing its full potential. Although CRISPR is very good at cutting out faulty DNA, it is less effective at inserting new genes properly. It can alter DNA in places where it's not supposed to. It can also fill gaps with random DNA that could "turn off" genes that may be needed. Among the most significant challenges are those associated with reducing unintended—and unwelcome—genetic changes, known as "off-target activity." Such activity poses a number of potential risks, including increased cancer rates.[126] Moreover, even if "successful," the consequences of using gene drives to alter the genome of whole species may be difficult to arrest, let alone reverse, should they trigger unanticipated negative outcomes.[127]

Alas, as the actions of Dr. He remind us, instances when ethical concerns have blocked the march of science for potentially malevolent purposes are exceedingly rare. Consequently, it would be irresponsible for defense planners to ignore the implications of CRISPR-Cas9 and other advances in the biosciences.

Historically, biological weapons (or "agents") were developed in laboratories using natural resources. With advances in synthetic biology, multiple techniques have been developed to synthesize and map the DNA characteristics of biological agents.[128] The genetic-engineering techniques just described have the potential to synthesize infectious diseases from scratch, produce them more cheaply and effectively, and manipulate DNA to increase their pathogenicity.[129]

The technical barriers to developing biological agents into weapons will drop as manufacturing costs decrease, DNA sequencing and synthesis improve, and genetic-editing technology becomes more widely accessible. For example, synthetic biology could be used to create a previously inaccessible pathogen, such as smallpox virus, by re-creating its genome. Or it could be exploited to modify an existing bacteria or virus, rendering conventional antibiotics or vaccines ineffective.[130]

This is no longer the stuff of B horror movies. Researchers at the University of Alberta recently synthesized the previously extinct horsepox virus, related to the smallpox virus, from mail-order genetic material. The Canadian scientists conceded, "Most viruses could be assembled nowadays using reverse genetics, and these methods have been combined with gene synthesis technologies to assemble poliovirus and other extinct pathogens like the 1918 influenza strain. Given that the sequence of variola virus has been known since 1993, our studies show that it is clearly accessible to current synthetic biology technology, with important implications for public health and biosecurity."[131] The cost to reconstitute horsepox was about $100,000. The Canadian team confirmed that their process "did not require exceptional biochemical knowledge or skills, significant funds or significant time."[132] Put another way, it would not require even a well-funded or technically sophisticated terrorist organization to undertake such work.

With respect to the democratization of destruction, what makes CRISPR special is not its ability to enable the genetic editing of a pathogen. This has been possible for decades. Rather, CRISPR enables even people with rudimentary training to engage in gene modification. With the advent of CRISPR-Cas9, key technological barriers that largely kept biological weapons out of the reach of terrorist and criminal organizations are being stripped away.

The apparent similarities between cyber attacks and prospective "bio attacks" are sobering. A little over thirty years ago, on November 3, 1988, an MIT graduate student, Robert Morris, launched the first malware attack on the internet. Morris and those who followed him fabricated computer "viruses." Similar risks are occurring with biological warfare. "Biohacking" groups are experimenting with DNA as "software" they can manipulate, similar to the way hackers do with computer software. At some point, these biohackers may be able to manufacture lethal pathogens and offer them to any state, group, or individual that can meet their price, similar to how cyber malware is marketed.[133]

The biophysicist Steven Block notes that "genetic maps of deadly viruses, bacteria, and other micro-organisms already are widely available in the public domain."[134] CRISPR kits are cheap, some costing under $500.[135] There are pathogen-specific kits, such as for West Nile virus, human coronavirus 229E, and human adenovirus 35, sold with few controls or restrictions. The manuals included with the kits contain only modest cautions regarding the potential risks associated with their contents.[136] The use of CRISPR-Cas9 and other biological engineering techniques could enable these pathogens to be modified. Such novel weapons could theoretically be employed to target entire populations indiscriminately or to eliminate sectors of a population or specific individuals—a kind of "precision" biological warfare.[137]

Henry T. Greely, director of the Center for Law and Biosciences at Stanford University, warned, "Modified organisms might harm the environment, whether through an accidental escape from the laboratory or intentional release. Think of your least favorite invasive species—kudzu, Dutch elm disease, the starling in the U.S., the rabbit in Australia. Genomic engineering could produce more. Even worse, terrorists (or criminals) could use this to make pathogens for biowarfare or extortion."[138]

Nonstate entities, especially terrorist and millenarian groups, may be especially attracted to this technology, given the minimal effort and resource expenditure required to acquire it and the declining levels of expertise needed to use it effectively. If they want to avoid being identified, these groups may be emboldened by the forensic challenges posed in detecting the employment of bio weapons. They may also find encouragement from the generally poor performance of the world's health organizations in responding effectively to naturally occurring epidemics, such as Ebola, SARS, and, more recently, COVID-19, and the willingness of certain countries (China comes to mind) to actively block investigation into the origins of disease.[139]

Consider a suicide bomber, for example, going through an airport security system. With today's sensors, this person will probably be detected. Now imagine the same individual injected with a genetically engineered virus capable of transmitting a highly virulent disease triggered at her discretion. The chances of this person getting through security without being detected would likely be much greater. By the time she started showing signs and symptoms of an illness, she would already have begun infecting people around her. The snowball effect of a cluster of these infected suicide bio warriors could trigger a public health crisis.

Although CRISPR-Cas9 technology has made genetic engineering cheaper, easier, and more effective, manufacturing bio weapons and employing them effectively remain a challenging undertaking. Yet here, too, we find the barriers to doing so eroding. This multistep process involves acquiring the pathogen; obtaining the necessary information about the desired bio weapon; securing the equipment needed to produce the weapon; growing the bio weapon in the quantity required to achieve the desired effect; weaponizing the biological agent, including achieving the requisite stability and shelf life and processing it into a form for delivery, such as in a concentrated slurry or dry powder; and possessing an effective method and means of delivery.

Recent advances are lowering many of these barriers, in some cases dramatically. Today, as the Canadian scientists demonstrated, a biological agent can be produced synthetically, something that not long ago would have required a laboratory, with far more modest support, as information, methods, and materials for creating bio weapons become ubiquitous.[140]

To have confidence that a bio weapon will perform as desired, it must be tested, a process that consumes substantial amounts of time and skilled labor. Authoritarian regimes, radical terrorist groups, or others with low moral and ethical standards could short-circuit the testing process by infecting human subjects. Even here, however, developing a synthetic bio weapon would probably require significant testing to ensure its stability and reliability.[141]

Additive manufacturing in the form of 3D printing could help address the testing challenge. It's conceivable that AM could produce biological agents, as well as materials for testing these agents, at relatively low cost. Although current biological 3D products are both expensive and require high levels of technical expertise to generate, it is not unreasonable to assume that, if AM technology continues to advance along its current trajectory, the process will become cheaper, more widely available, and more user friendly.[142]

Some states or groups, however, may be unwilling to wait for AM advances to aid their efforts. They may simply want to terrorize a population. Other actors, such as the despot leader of a state under attack or a terrorist group fearing detection, may conclude that time is against them and see their choice as between launching a suboptimal bio attack or none at all. If so, they may forgo testing their agents and employ them as quickly as possible.

A bio weapon must also be grown in quantities sufficient to cover the chosen target population, which could range from an individual to a large segment of a country's citizens. Large-scale bio-weapon production is extremely challenging, as many agents lose their potency during the scaling process. Addressing this problem requires significant financial resources and technical expertise. That being said, mass production may not be necessary for attacks that can be spread by a replicating pathogen.[143] Recall the infected airline passenger, only now picture an "army" of hundreds of these "bio zombies"—"dead terrorists walking"—boarding planes, subway systems, and bus lines.

For effective delivery, a bio weapon must be weaponized, remain stable until it can be employed, and be employed properly. This means it must remain potent through freeze-drying and storage. Large-scale attacks generally employ aerosol dispersal, through a spray or an explosion. The agent particles must be dispersed in the right size to facilitate inhalation and remain suspended in air long enough to be absorbed by the target population. Finally, the bio-weapon particles must remain potent in threatening environmental conditions, such as ultraviolet sunlight and extreme temperatures.

Advances in nanotechnology could enhance a bio weapon's stability and delivery. Nanomaterials are increasingly used for medical-device coatings, diagnostic contrast agents, sensing components in nanoscale diagnostics, and advanced drug delivery. They might be used to create microcapsules or nanocapsules of the bio weapon to provide protection, thereby improving its stability and enhancing its effective delivery.[144] With regard to the latter, "nanotech" can assist the pathogen in penetrating the skin and through bronchioles in the lung by augmenting its aerosol properties. There are, however, less sophisticated ways to short-circuit these barriers, at least partially. For example, a communicable agent might be deployed in small amounts at many points and allowed to spread naturally, albeit more slowly.[145] Again, think of suicide "bio zombies" "attacking" via mass transit systems.

Thanks to advances in gene editing, a bio weapon could theoretically be employed against a particular target or group of targets. Up to now, targeting has generally been defined by the victims' geographic location; however, the rapidly growing creation of health and genomic data may enable "precision" targeting analogous to precision kinetic warfare.[146] Today people can contribute their genetic material for general use, to support research to treat diseases like cancer, or for private use, as when individuals mail cheek swabs to companies such as 23andMe to obtain information on their ancestry. Currently, only about 6 percent of Americans say they have had their genomes sequenced. But the cost to sequence a genome is dropping, and more people than ever before will probably have access to their own genomic information.[147] It also seems likely that some authoritarian regimes will compel their people to provide it. And for terrorist groups seeking to target a particular individual, obtaining their genome could be as easy as taking a coffee cup their target used and having the DNA sequenced.[148]

"Precision medicine" is already leveraging this data. The biotechnology business is expanding rapidly. Revenues from its three major sectors—agriculture, drugs, and industry—expanded from roughly $100 billion in 2005 to nearly $400 billion a decade later, with some estimates projecting the biotech market exceeding $700 billion by 2025.[149]

Synthetic biology employs concepts and approaches similar to engineering disciplines, such as standardized components (for example, well-characterized functions encoded by DNA); software and computer-based modeling for designing biological systems from those components; and constructing prototypes based on those designs. Synthetic biologists use this approach in "design-build-test" cycles to accelerate progress. Today the low cost and increasing availability of technologies used in designing and creating new DNA constructs to test incentivize proceeding without a hypothesis of how the design will work. Simply put, it's become easier and cheaper "to make than to think."[150]

The biotechnology industry is developing chemicals created by genetically altered microorganisms to produce products such as plastics, food additives, fragrances, and biofuels. In London, at the DNA Foundry, robotic arms move small plastic dishes, each containing up to 1,536 minuscule wells, each well holding tiny amounts of liquid and a few strands of DNA. The foundry often mixes 150,000 DNA samples each day before noon. Snippets of genetic code are used to create a collection of genes that can combine to produce enzymes that convert one type of chemical into another. The genes are assembled into circular DNA molecules called "plasmids." The mixture is transferred to a machine that increases the number of plasmids using a process called a "polymerase chain reaction." The plasmids are then introduced into living cells, bacterial or yeast. The cells are incubated, and the result is tested to determine if any of the genetic designs proved useful.[151]

A number of synthetic-biology software companies rely on machine-learning programs to identify promising changes to the genome being considered for modification. The reason is simple: these companies use massive amounts of synthesized DNA. Consider, for example, Jason Kelly, the CEO of Ginkgo Bioworks, a self-described "organism company." During the five years Kelly spent at MIT in the early 2000s, he estimates that he ordered around 50,000 bases of commercially synthesized DNA. Today his firm orders synthetic DNA sequences at 50,000 times that rate, using them to change the genomes of thousands of organisms each day. Operations on this scale require that experiments be designed and managed by software. A few years ago, Ginkgo reached the "cross-over point," where its automated foundries were as productive as human researchers. Today Kelly estimates that the automated approach is ten times as productive as Ginkgo's human researchers. Automation has also increased the complexity at which experimentation can take place.[152]

Linking human genomic data with other health-related data is becoming the pharmaceutical industry's favored research model.[153] It's fueled by the data sets developed through big-data analytics and the machine learning that enables artificial intelligence to identify patterns and insights that might elude human researchers. This data could prove useful to people seeking to conduct discriminate attacks against individuals or groups that possess a particular characteristic (such as ethnic groups). As a "nation of immigrants," the United States' genetic diversity may make the U.S. population relatively resistant to attacks based on ethnicity. Countries lacking such diversity—Japan comes to mind—may be particularly vulnerable to such attacks.

Until now, an attacker's fear of "blowback"—the possibility that a bio attack may develop in unanticipated, and unwelcome, ways—served as a deterrent. A pathogen that is introduced into an enemy's population may end up spreading back into the attacker's society. The 1918–19 "Spanish flu" and, more recently, COVID-19 show how a disease can spread rapidly, especially in an era when large numbers of people are traveling daily to distant points around the globe.[154] The implications of these developments for deterrence are potentially profound.

This may be changing. CRISPR's "precision" gene-editing ability may reduce dramatically, or even eliminate entirely, the fear of blowback. If bio weapons can be fabricated that threaten only those individuals with specific genetic characteristics, it could enable "precision" bio warfare. This, however, is hardly assured. One problem with engineered viruses and bacteria is that they tend to evolve over time. Thus, there is a risk that "precision" pathogens could become less precise in their effects and, by evolving, produce unwanted "collateral damage" on nontargeted groups and even trigger blowback.[155]

In summary, synthetic biology in general has enormous potential to bring about dramatic improvements in the human condition. Yet, to draw on Winston Churchill, if humankind fails to address the dangers posed by advances in the biosciences, then it risks "sink[ing] into the abyss of a new Dark Age, made more sinister, and perhaps more protracted by the lights of perverted science."[156]

Hypersonics: "Faster than a Speeding Bullet"

The trend in warfare toward increased speed and range, in both weapon systems and munitions, is unmistakable. Since antiquity, militaries have sought an advantage in range over their enemies for the simple reason that it enables them to strike without being hit in return. As described in Chapter 3, the emergence of anti-access/area-denial complexes will probably require a rival military to place increased reliance, at least initially, on long-range scouting and strike forces to offset the growing risk to its forward-deployed forces from the enemy's more numerous shorter-range scouting and strike forces. Operating from distant range, however, increases the need for speed, for two reasons. First, the faster an attacker can transit a heavily defended area, the less time defenses have to identify, track, and engage it. Second, all other things being equal, the greater the distance between where a strike force is based and its target, the more warning time a defender will have to hide or otherwise improve its defenses before the attacker arrives. Boosting a weapon's speed buys back some of the time lost from the increased engagement distance.

In kinetic warfare, the best combination of speed and range is the ballistic missile, which remains difficult to intercept despite the enormous resources advanced militaries have devoted (and are devoting) to missile defenses. Ongoing advances in hypersonic propulsion weapons, or "hypersonics," may find militaries armed with new types of high-speed missiles capable of engaging at long range. Hypersonics' potential to significantly alter the military balance finds the world's leading militaries, China, Russia, and the United States in particular, racing to develop these weapons.

Hypersonic vehicles travel at least five times the speed of sound (Mach 5), or roughly 6,200 kilometers (or 3,600 miles) per hour at sea level. Aside from ballistic missiles, only a few other manmade devices, such as the X-37B spacecraft, are capable of reaching hypersonic speeds, with the U.S. rocket-powered X-15 being the only manned aircraft to accomplish this.[157]

Work on hypersonic systems takes two principal forms. One involves a "scramjet," a "fanless" engine that uses the shock waves generated by its speed to compress incoming air and ignite it to accelerate a vehicle, such as a cruise missile, to hypersonic speeds. Hypersonic cruise missiles (HCMs) use a solid-fueled booster rocket to accelerate to at least Mach 4. As the missile approaches or achieves hypersonic speeds, the missile's booster drops off, and the scramjet ignites. The scramjet includes three components: an inlet that draws in the air surrounding the missile, a combustor to burn fuel combined with that air, and a nozzle to release the pressurized air to maintain the missile's hypersonic speed. Unlike traditional jet engines, scramjets have no moving parts or machinery to direct and combust air, making them highly efficient at propelling an airframe at high speeds.

The second approach centers on a rocket-assisted "boost-glide" vehicle (BGV) employing multiple-stage rocket engines to propel it into the upper atmosphere—some twenty-five miles or so—whereupon it is released. Its initial speed and high altitude enable the vehicle to maintain hypersonic speeds without internal power, while the friction induced by passing through lower atmosphere may slow the weapon enough to enable it to be guided accurately toward its target. This approach is being pursued by DARPA with a weapon known as Tactical Boost Glide.[158]

Implications

Hypersonic missiles' unusual trajectories enable them to approach their targets at altitudes between twelve and fifty miles, below the altitude at which ballistic missile interceptors are typically designed to operate but above the altitude of air defense systems. Hypersonic vehicles can also maneuver during their trajectory, making it extremely difficult for air and missile defenses to predict their future location in order to intercept them.[159] Hypersonic missiles can do enormous damage. For instance, a hypersonic weapon weighing 500 pounds, with an explosive charge in a rod casing between five and ten feet long made of ceramic and carbon-fiber composites or nickel-chromium superalloys, would strike its target with tremendous kinetic energy, the equivalent of three to four tons of dynamite.[160]

Hypersonic weapons' ability to overcome modern defenses and high-impact speed makes them particularly threatening to warships. For example, if a carrier strike group's defenses detect a hypersonic weapon at a range of 150 miles, they would have less than a minute to launch an interceptor—and that interceptor would need to be capable of hitting a maneuvering target moving at six miles per second.

Even the U.S. Navy's current radar systems are unable to adequately track and identify a hypersonic attack, let alone defeat it.[161] A hypersonic missile striking a warship would have a significant chance of putting it out of action, if not sinking it. More broadly speaking, as one senior Pentagon official put it, "When the Chinese can deploy [a] tactical or regional hypersonic system, they hold at risk our carrier battle groups. They hold our entire surface fleet at risk. They hold at risk our forward-deployed forces and land-based forces."[162]

Continuing our focus on the implications for maritime forces, once hypersonic missiles are fielded by rival militaries, the U.S. Navy could be compelled to undertake changes in the fleet's composition on a scale not seen since the carrier supplanted the battleship. Maritime forces may have to become more distributed, so as to spread their assets over a greater number of ships to enhance the fleet's resilience. The fleet may also have to operate at greater distances from the enemy to reduce its vulnerability to shorter-range enemy hypersonic strike systems and to provide adequate warning time to defend against longer-range weapons. Of course, naval forces would still have to address the threat posed by short-range anti-ship hypersonic weapons launched from relatively close range by stealthy aircraft, submarines, and UUVs. Mounting an effective defense against these kinds of hypersonic attacks seems problematic. Consequently, the Navy may have to move a greater portion of its combat power beneath the waves.

Alternatively, the situation at sea may hark back to the Cold War's latter stages, when the U.S. Navy faced a threat from Soviet aircraft armed with anti-ship missiles. Back then, given the difficulty (and cost) of successfully engaging large numbers of incoming missiles, the Navy focused on "killing the archer"—Soviet strike aircraft—before they could launch their "arrows." Success rested, to a great extent, on the Navy's ability to scout: to locate Soviet aircraft before they reached their missile launch point. This history may repeat itself, as it will be important to identify the enemy strike platform before it can release its hypersonic arrows.

Recalling our earlier discussion of a contemporary Battle of Midway, winning the scouting competition—in the form of locating an enemy's hypersonic strike force before it launches its attack—could be the difference between victory and defeat. If so, the speed and range of the friendly force's hypersonic missiles will be just as critical as that of the aircraft that flew off the decks of U.S. and Japanese carriers at Midway. All other factors being equal, a *range* advantage will compel the enemy to spread its scouting assets over a greater search area, while an advantage in weapon *speed* will enable the attack to reach the enemy before it detects friendly forces' location and launches its own attack. Even if friendly forces are detected, an advantage in weapon range and speed of engagement may enable victory if the enemy strike force has not yet reached its hypersonic weapons' effective range.

Hypersonic weapons could play a key role in defeating an enemy's A2/AD defenses. A force could employ hypersonic weapons to spearhead an offensive by striking the enemy's fixed air and missile defense systems, as well as its hypersonic missile units. If successful, it could pave the way for friendly scouting and strike forces to operate inside the enemy's A2/AD complex at acceptable risk.

Imagine, for example, a force of advanced U.S. B-21 stealth bombers, each armed with dozens of hypersonic missiles. The bombers' stealth, combined with their ability to adjust their flight paths to avoid enemy air defenses by using real-time intelligence from onboard sensors and off-board scouting elements via the battle network, could enable them to penetrate the enemy's outer air defenses. Having done so, the bombers could launch their short-range (and less expensive) hypersonic missiles, destroying or neutralizing the enemy's air and missile defenses, along with key elements of its scouting forces, enabling follow-on forces operating in the land, sea, and air domains to operate at greatly reduced risk.[163]

More broadly speaking, a strike force of stealthy manned and unmanned bombers could function as its own reconnaissance-strike element, carrying a payload of hypersonic weapons, swarming drones, standard PGMs, drone decoys, and jammers. This force could be supplemented with strikes from attack submarines and UUVs, as well as long-range hypersonic cruise missiles and BGVs to erode an enemy's A2/AD complex, thereby greatly expanding opportunities for offensive maneuver.

Barriers to Implementation

Given the potential of hypersonic weapons to trigger a major shift in the military balance, it's easy to see why the world's leading militaries are pursuing them. There are, however, formidable challenges that must be overcome before they can be fielded, especially for hypersonic cruise missiles. One of the biggest barriers involves getting combustion to happen in a stream of supersonic air. For scramjet engines to work, they need to be moving at high speeds to compress air for combustion. Consequently, scramjets must first be accelerated by piggybacking on a jet plane or rocket. Assuming that this can be reliably accomplished, hypersonic missiles face challenges with regard to accuracy and structural integrity.[164]

Cooling is crucial in engines of all kinds. Even a commercial jet airliner's turbofans operate routinely at around 400 degrees *above* the melting point of their component materials. An elaborate network of cooling channels is needed to keep these engines from breaking up. The challenge is greatly magnified with hypersonic engines moving through the air at speeds ten times faster than a commercial airliner. The higher lift-to-drag ratios required for hypersonic missiles necessitates their having sharp leading edges. This, combined with the missile's extreme velocity, can generate surface temperatures as high as 3,500 degrees Fahrenheit, where the heat generated can erode the vehicle's protective coating, fry its electronics, and bend it out of shape.

There is also the matter of targeting and heat distribution. In some hypersonic missile designs, the heat differential between the top and bottom of the missile is so intense that it changes shape during flight, making accurate targeting very difficult.[165] 3D printing may offer a solution. If you want to make cooling vents using subtractive manufacturing, it requires drilling holes in the material and hoping the process doesn't compromise its structural integrity. To produce cooling vents in a 3D-printed component, you simply program the printer to print the component to have the openings in it from the start. Moreover, drilling cooling channels through subtractive manufacturing imposes far more limits on their shape, while forming the channels with a 3D printer enables you to produce elaborate shapes that vent heat much more efficiently.[166]

There are yet other challenges to be solved. A hypersonic weapon's high speeds can also break up molecules in the atmosphere, creating a field of charged particles (or "plasma") around the vehicle, disrupting its ability to receive guidance signals from GPS and other sources. As the U.S. Air Force's Office of Scientific Research concedes, we "still don't completely understand the physics of hypersonic flight."[167]

Summary

The development of hypersonic missiles, in both their cruise and boost-glide versions, is consistent with a general long-term trend in the military competition toward greater speed and range, often at the expense of payload and physical protection. If hypersonic weapons perform as advertised, they may render today's most advanced air and missile defenses ineffective. They may be particularly effective against high-value targets that are difficult to hide or harden, such as surface warships. Hypersonic cruise and boost-glide missiles could also make a major, and perhaps decisive, contribution to winning the scouting competition, such as by neutralizing key nodes in an enemy's battle network and by eliminating ground-based ASAT systems and scouting platforms located at air bases.

Hypersonic weapons—especially if they achieve precision accuracy—may trigger shock waves in the strategic balance. Their combination of speed, kinetic energy, and precision accuracy reduces a defender's warning time against attacks on bomber bases, missile silos, hardened submarine pens, and underground command-and-control centers. The result could be a further blurring of the distinction between nuclear and non-nuclear forms of attack. It could also further increase the incentives for preemptive attacks. For example, one of the U.S. military's hypersonic prototype missiles now being developed is designed to fly at speeds between Mach 15 and Mach 20, or more than 11,400 miles per hour. If fired by U.S. submarines off the coast of Shanghai, they could strike any target in China in less than thirty minutes.[168] Correspondingly, a similar Chinese hypersonic missile battery located near Shanghai could hit the large U.S. airbase at Kadena, on Okinawa, in less than five minutes. Although ballistic missiles can strike with even greater speed, hypersonic missiles appear to have a significant advantage in avoiding detection and, if detected, defeating attempts at interception.

There are significant barriers to fielding highly reliable hypersonic weapons, particularly the cruise missile versions. The challenges associated with hypersonic missile engine design and structural integrity are significant, and it is not clear that hypersonic weapons will match the accuracy of today's precision-guided munitions. However, it would be foolish to discount hypersonic weapons' potential. The world's leading militaries certainly are not.

Quantum Computing

The term "quantum computing" (QC) was coined in the 1980s by the Nobel laureate and physicist Richard Feynman, who raised the possibility that quantum phenomena, such as exploiting subatomic particles' "don't look and I don't exist" characteristics, could process information.[169]

The idea of quantum computing gained traction thanks to the work of Dr. Peter Shor, a mathematician at Bell Laboratories. In 1994, Shor published a paper showing that a quantum computer could identify the prime numbers that, when multiplied together, yield an exceedingly large number. This meant that Shor had shown, at least in theory, that a quantum computer could break the cryptographic protocols used to protect military communications and key economic critical infrastructure, such as those used to secure credit card transactions—an exponential leap in computational capability over today's computers.[170]

Quantum computing's power is derived from the ability of quantum bits, or "qubits"—a unit of quantum information—to do more than what is done in classical computers, which alternate between zero and one. Qubits are capable of existing in the "zero" and "one" state—and in both states simultaneously.[171] This extra mode is called "superposition," a mathematical combination of both 0 and 1. It is the key to making qubits more powerful than ordinary bits. But qubits alone cannot provide the massive computational power promised by quantum computing. The qubits must be "entangled." A quantum entanglement is a highly counterintuitive phenomenon that occurs when two qubits in a superposition are such that certain operations on one have *instant* effects on the other, irrespective of the distance separating them. This gives a quantum computer an enormous advantage over a traditional computer, which needs to read and write from each element of memory separately before operating on it. Put another way, when the qubits are entangled, operating on one qubit involves operating, in varying degrees, on all those qubits that are entangled with it. Quantum computer algorithms use entangled qubits and their superposition to create a shortcut through calculations. This allows them to perform incredibly complex calculations at speeds far greater than those that are possible today and to solve certain classes of problems that are beyond the grasp of even the most advanced supercomputers.[172]

Quantum computing begins with choosing an algorithm for the problem to be addressed. The calculation is accomplished through quantum-mechanical laws running on superimposed and entangled qubits. The result is a huge increase in the complexity of programming that can be executed, at least for certain types of problems.[173]

To get a sense of quantum computing's power, consider that, for today's computers, adding one bit to a classical computer chip has a negligible effect on its computing power. Adding one qubit *doubles* the power of a quantum computer chip. A 300-bit classical computer chip could power a basic pocket calculator. A 300-qubit chip, on the other hand, has the computing power of two novemvigintillion bits—a two followed by ninety zeros, or ten to the ninetieth power—a number that exceeds the number of atoms in the known universe.[174]

Implications

Although quantum computers are not ideal for all computational problems, for some they can provide an exponential boost in speed, given that their advantage over a classical computer increases at a highly nonlinear rate with the size of the problem.[175] For example, classical computers are unable to simulate the behavior of atoms and electrons during chemical reactions, as they are driven by quantum mechanics, whose complexity is too great for classical computers to handle. If QC becomes practical, it will probably be employed in simulating new molecules and chemical reactions that can aid in identifying substances that can be used for a wide range of purposes, such as engineering lighter airplane parts, creating more effective drugs, and designing better batteries.

So it's not surprising that the German automobile makers Daimler and Volkswagen are investigating quantum computing with the ultimate goal of improving the chemical process in batteries for their electric vehicles, while Microsoft is exploring how quantum computing can be used to identify ways to extract carbon dioxide from the atmosphere to offset global warming.[176]

From a national security perspective, quantum computers would be ideal for code-breaking—penetrating the mathematics that are the basis for the encryption securing military communications, as well as a country's critical infrastructure, such as online commerce, including banking and shopping. As alluded to earlier, these transactions are secured by using an algorithm that uses factorization, or reverse multiplication, of an enormously large number, typically several hundred digits long. This "locks" the encrypted data. This form of encryption works because even today's most advanced computers would require years to find the two prime factors at the core of the encrypted data. In theory, a quantum computer could break this encryption quickly.[177]

The security implications for breaking current encrypted data are profound. Although quantum processors currently have nowhere near this capability, both governments and corporations are not discounting the possibility that they will in the not too distant future. The U.S. National Institute of Standards and Technology is already evaluating new encryption systems to "quantum-proof" the internet. At the same time, many national intelligence agencies are gathering and archiving intercepted encrypted communications, waiting for the arrival of quantum computing that will enable them to resurrect these communications and hopefully translate them into valuable intelligence.[178]

Given quantum computers' ability to manipulate vast arrays of data and identify patterns that elude classical computers, their potential to aid in developing and refining machine-learning algorithms appears formidable. As the physicist Johannes Otterbach notes, "There is a natural combination between the intrinsic statistical nature of quantum computing . . . and machine learning."[179]

The high cost of a quantum computer is likely to limit them to nation-states and the world's major technology corporations. Assuming that quantum computing services are not made available for rent, at least initially QC is unlikely to contribute to the democratization of destruction.[180]

Barriers

The enthusiasm surrounding recent advances in quantum computing after three decades of glacial progress is considerable. Google's Harmut Neven expects that by 2030 all machine learning will be running on quantum computers. Some experts speculate that by then Google and its leading competitors will be selling quantum computing services via the cloud—and charging by the second.[181]

There are, however, skeptics who believe that QC optimists have been overpromising. One is Jerry Chow, an IBM quantum-computer scientist, who says that QC is "a bit like trying to balance an egg at the end of a needle. You certainly can do it, but any little disturbance from noise, from heat, from vibrations, and you've suddenly got yourself a sunny-side up."[182] Even Feynman warned, "If you want to make a simulation of nature, you'd better make it quantum mechanical, and by golly it's a wonderful problem, because it doesn't look so easy."[183] Indeed, significant technical and practical challenges remain to building a quantum computer and to using it to solve practical problems.[184]

One barrier is a quantum computer's relatively high error rate, which is due to noise.[185] A classical computer bit is either one or zero. Even if the value is slightly wrong due to noise in the system, today's computers can strip out variations in their inputs and produce clean, noise-free outputs. Not so with qubits. Recent research finds that the error rates for two-qubit operations on systems with five or more qubits are more than a few percent.[186] Some enthusiasts argue that the problem can be addressed through error-correction algorithms. But such algorithms would need additional qubits to check the work of the qubits running computations. This risks taking a trip down the rabbit hole, with some experts estimating that checking the work of a single qubit will require an additional hundred![187]

Still, theoretically speaking, there is nothing to prevent adding more qubits to solve this problem. Quantum computing's solution to addressing the errors problem centers on forming *logical* qubits using multiple *physical* qubits. If so, a practical, useful quantum computer would need a million or more qubits. Accomplishing this is a daunting task, so it becomes difficult to state with any confidence when it might occur.[188]

Another barrier is the so-called input problem. At present, there is no method for rapidly converting a large amount of classical data to a quantum state. For problems requiring large data inputs, the time needed to convert the data would typically be far greater than the computation time, potentially offsetting the quantum computer's advantage. The good news is that this problem goes away if the data can be generated algorithmically. The bad news is that designing quantum algorithms is also proving to be challenging. Yet another barrier involves developing quantum computing software, as well as methods to debug quantum hardware and software.[189]

Summary

Quantum computing involves manipulating things at the smallest level of energy in atoms, where physical behavior is often at odds with our understanding of how the world behaves. Owing to qubits' unique superposition property and the phenomenon of quantum entanglement, quantum computers could, in theory, provide major advances in such fields as cryptography, chemistry, and artificial intelligence.

Despite recent progress, the challenges to creating useful quantum computers remain as they were when identified decades ago by the IBM physicist Rolf Landauer, who called for papers on quantum computing to include the following disclaimer: "This scheme, like all other schemes for quantum computation, relies on speculative technology, does not in its current form take into account all possible sources of noise, unreliability and manufacturing error, and probably will not work."[190] That being said, quantum computing's enormous potential to transform not only the character of the military competition but society itself makes it too important to ignore, even taking Landauer's disclaimer into account.

Some Other Military-Related Technology Game Changers

The technologies described so far in this chapter are illustrative of progress being made by modern science that could enable a disruptive shift in the military balance. There are other technological developments that also seem likely to exert a significant influence on the character of the military competition.

Interesting Toys

In the late twentieth century, James Schlesinger was one of the United States' leading polymaths and strategists, traits that led to his serving in administrations of both political parties, at various times, as defense secretary, secretary of energy, and director of central intelligence. Schlesinger also had a reputation as one who did not suffer fools gladly—and his description of "fools" was quite expansive. For some reason, he took a liking to me, and we would meet from time to time to discuss some research in which I was engaged. On one occasion, I came to get his thoughts on directed-energy weapons—those producing concentrated electromagnetic energy to incapacitate, damage, disable, or destroy enemy equipment, facilities, or personnel.

At the time, Defense Secretary Robert Gates, on whose policy board Schlesinger and I were serving, had recently canceled the Air Force's airborne-laser aircraft. The program called for a Boeing 747 armed with a chemical laser to fly near an enemy country and use the laser to intercept ballistic missiles while they were in their "boost phase"—in the atmosphere shortly after launching and before reaching outer space. The airborne laser was an idea whose time had not come. The laser itself relied for its power on a vat of highly corrosive chemicals. A joke at the time was that if the vat ever sprung a leak, the chemical mix might eat the plane away before the pilot could land it.

Trying to avoid poking the bear, I mentioned to Schlesinger that remarkable progress was being made with solid-state lasers that rely on electricity—not chemicals—for their power. Schlesinger looked at me, sucked on his pipe, and said, "Ah, yes. Lasers. Those interesting toys."

I mentioned that there had been other "toys" that seemingly took forever to bear fruit. Torpedoes, for example, took decades before Whitehead's version provided the accuracy and range that turned the maritime competition on its head. Couldn't this happen with lasers? Schlesinger responded by saying that, on this issue, he was "from Missouri."[191]

Interesting Progress

Schlesinger's skepticism notwithstanding, two major developments in recent decades have increased confidence in directed-energy systems' potential to make significant, and perhaps profound, contributions to military effectiveness. The first involves changes in expectations. During the 1980s, lasers were viewed (unrealistically) as components in a "High Frontier" space-based missile defense system contributing to the U.S. Strategic Defense Initiative, designed to defeat a Soviet nuclear missile attack. Over time, expectations were reduced, to where today the focus is primarily on defending against threats like drone swarms or mortar salvos and rocket barrages.

Second, directed-energy technology has advanced. During the 1990s, major gains were made in fiber-optic telecommunications, and large sums began pouring into their development. In the early 2000s, companies working on the technology began to look for new markets. They discovered that industrial applications using high-power fiber-laser technology could be done very cost-effectively, such as with high-precision cutting, welding, and drilling. At this point, militaries began to look at how to combine fiber-optic communications and high-power laser technologies with an eye toward scaling them to weapon-class power levels.

Encouragement was provided in the form of lasers powered by electricity, not chemicals. As long as they are connected to an electrical source, like a power grid or batteries, solid-state lasers (SSLs) and fiber lasers can sustain their rate of fire. That being said, SSL and fiber-laser power levels are not yet strong enough to defeat threats like high-performance aircraft and high-speed cruise missiles, let alone hypersonic or ballistic missiles.

Recent work involving individual fiber lasers shows promise. It's become possible to field laser weapons capable of defeating low-end threats and to make them small and rugged enough to be deployed on combat vehicles and ships. For example, the U.S. Navy's Laser Weapon System has been deployed and approved for operational use. The U.S. Army is making encouraging progress toward fielding laser weapon systems for countering rockets, artillery, and mortars. That being said, the United States is but one of several military powers looking to field DE weapons. Both China and Russia, along with U.S. security partners like Israel, have well-established DE weapons programs. In some areas, their efforts may match or surpass current U.S. efforts. Indeed, the Israelis may already be using an advanced algorithm to combine several laser beams, forming a strong beam with enhanced coherency capable of intercepting drones and guided rockets.[192]

As noted earlier, space-based systems, especially those in low-Earth orbit, are already vulnerable to laser ASATs.[193] The PLA appears to be pursuing laser ASAT weapons and may already have the ability to "dazzle" or disable satellite sensors. The U.S. intelligence community finds that China will soon field ground-based laser weapons to defeat low-orbit space-based sensors, if it has not done so already, as well as high-power systems to threaten satellite structures.[194]

Like the Chinese, the Russians have been active in developing directed-energy ASAT systems. In 2018, Russia's military unveiled its Peresvet laser system, positioning it near its mobile intercontinental ballistic missile launchers. The purpose, apparently, is for Peresvet to temporarily dazzle or even blind passing rival satellites, thereby preventing them from tracking the launchers.[195]

Lasers may also enhance military communications. Consider, for instance, a battle network's need to move high volumes of information securely in the face of determined enemy efforts to block it. Lasers can provide greater speed, data flow, precision-reception, and bandwidth transmission than other forms of wireless communication. Moreover, security is enhanced by their narrow beam, as the information in the beam cannot be compromised unless the interceptor is directly in its path.

This is in marked contrast to radio waves, which produce "lobes" near the point of transmission that increase the possibility for an enemy to listen in. Laser communications technology has been successfully tested at modest ranges of ten miles. Proponents of laser communications believe the technology can be extended significantly. If so, it may enhance a military's reconnaissance-strike complex by securely linking communications from drones to aircraft, aircraft to each other, and these systems to ground-based command-and-control centers.[196]

There are notable advances being made in the area of high-powered microwave weaponry. These weapons achieved notoriety from a test conducted in 2012 by the Counter-electronics High-powered Microwave Advanced Missile Project (CHAMP), which produced impressive results.[197] The test, undertaken by Boeing's Phantom Works, knocked out the targeted electronic systems (computers and their monitors) along with the cameras put in place to record the results. The systems were down for only a matter of seconds, but depending on how a computer network is configured and the kind of computers and peripherals employed, a CHAMP-like weapon generating a larger electromagnetic pulse (EMP) could disable a computer network, and other enemy electronic systems such as radars, for a far longer period, perhaps even permanently.[198]

Barriers

Directed-energy weapon advocates look forward to the day when high-powered lasers will provide effective defenses against cruise missiles and aircraft, with laser interceptor "shots" costing about $1 each, compared to some $3 million for the U.S. Navy's SM-6 interceptor missile.[199] Despite the progress made in directed-energy weapons, that day is unlikely to arrive anytime soon, as there are formidable barriers that must be overcome before they can achieve game-changer status in their ability to transform the character of warfare. Most informed observers are still "from Missouri."

To begin, there remains the question of boosting a laser's power to be effective against more sophisticated threats. There is also the problem of maintaining a laser's "beam coherency"—the beam's ability to remain focused, rather than dissipating along with its power, as it travels through the atmosphere, thereby limiting its range. Thus, lasers perform poorly in bad weather and not at all in rainstorms. They are also as yet unable to be employed against non-line-of-sight targets.

Consequently, even the most enthusiastic laser supporters have a hard time envisioning laser weapons intercepting high-speed ballistic missile warheads or hypersonic weapons. These weapons move too fast for lasers—whose effectiveness is linked to their ability to deposit sufficient energy on the target within "dwell" time available—to defeat them.[200]

Conclusion

Today military-related technologies are advancing at an impressive rate along a broad front. Advances in artificial intelligence, directed energy, hypersonic propulsion, synthetic biology, and quantum computing, among others, have the potential to bring about significant and perhaps even disruptive shifts in the character of warfare.

These advances correlate well with the general trend in industrial and information-age warfare toward emphasizing system speed and range, and accurate (as opposed to volume) fires. Increased speed of action is also enabled by the growing emphasis on cyber warfare, thanks in part to advances in artificial intelligence, as well as the prospective vulnerabilities of some emerging capabilities, such as additive manufacturing and artificial intelligence itself. Work on military systems employing directed energy, such as anti-satellite lasers and hypersonic missiles, also speaks to the focus on speed of action.

The boost in speed enables more effective engagements at enhanced range. Hypersonic boost-glide vehicles could strike targets halfway around the world. Land-based laser ASAT weapons can reach into space. Cyber attacks can span the globe. And although it's been said that quantity has a quality all its own, the cost of range rewards accuracy relative to mass when it comes to fires. This is certainly the case with respect to hypersonic missiles and appears to be so for directed-energy weaponry, although the latter do not employ kinetic energy to neutralize targets. Cyber weapons constitute an outlier, as they make good on the information age's promise of the "death of distance."

As the preceding narrative shows, it's possible to develop a rough sense of how these emerging technologies will change warfare. Forecasting how they will combine with the technologies that enabled the Precision-Warfare Revolution is another matter entirely. Simply put, there is great uncertainty regarding how things will play out. For one thing, advances in certain technologies and the military capabilities they may enable may depend, to a great degree, on how quickly progress is made in developing enabling technologies, such as with hypersonic missiles and additive manufacturing or with synthetic biology, where advances are likely to depend on the maturation of AI, quantum computing, and nanotechnology.

Which of these technologies will prove out? Fully? Partially? Beyond expectations? Not at all? And when will we know? It took nearly half a century for submarine- and torpedo-related technologies to move from being militarily irrelevant novelties to transforming naval warfare. A generation later, advances in radar during World War II altered the dynamic of naval warfare in the Pacific, from heavily favoring the offense to giving the defense more than a fighting chance. Had the sequence been reversed, the Battle of Midway would probably have been fought very differently.[201]

Cyber warfare casts a long shadow over the prospective effectiveness of many of these technologies. Artificial intelligence stands to influence greatly the development of most, if not all, of them. Yet artificial intelligence's effectiveness can be corrupted though cyber means, through attacks that corrupt data sets and machine-learning algorithms. Cyber attacks that corrupt additive manufacturing data files can lead to catastrophic flaws in the resulting products, such as in hypersonic missiles.

What does seem clear is that should these technologies mature, we will witness the "democratization of destruction"—the concentration of ever greater destructive power in the hands of small groups and, perhaps, even individuals. Nonstate groups are already conducting crude swarm attacks, holding parts of national critical infrastructure hostage to ransomware demands, and re-creating viruses like horsepox. Although this work's focus is on general war between great powers, there is clearly a great deal of analysis to be done on this emerging phenomenon.

In summary, as the Danish politician Karl Kristian Steinke observed, "It is difficult to make predictions, especially about the future."[202] This is especially true with respect to the current military competition. The best we can hope for is to reduce uncertainty at the margins. As Part 2 of this book shows, this can be done. Even here, however, success will not be absolute but relative. But you don't need to be perfect, only better than your rivals, to realize a significant, and perhaps decisive, military advantage.

CHAPTER FIVE

W(h)ither Deterrence?

Humankind's character is not improving at anything close to the rate of its capacity for destruction. This is placing it in increasing danger if general wars—and perhaps even lesser conflicts— cannot be avoided.

—WINSTON CHURCHILL

Would a declaration of war between Russia and Japan be made, if within an hour there after a swiftly gliding aeroplane might take its flight from St Petersburg and drop half a ton of dynamite above the enemy's war offices? Could any nation afford to war upon any other with such hazards in view?

—JOHN BRISBEN WALKER

MODERN GENERAL WAR IS characterized by enormous suffering and loss of human life, along with widespread material destruction. This chapter examines how changes in the geopolitical environment, combined with the emerging mature precision-warfare regime and the emergence of a new military revolution, are eroding efforts to deter general war. Advances in the cognitive and behavioral sciences find the challenge of constructing effective deterrence strategies even more daunting than previously believed. Consequently, political and military leaders confronted with disruptive shifts in the character of conflict must address not only how to win the wars of tomorrow but even, more importantly, how to meet the complex challenge of deterring them.

In the spring of 1986, Graham Allison, a renowned Harvard professor, was finishing up an extended consultancy for Defense Secretary Caspar Weinberger. Allison had been helping Weinberger formulate the Annual Report to the Congress, known in the Pentagon as the "Posture Statement." It was a comprehensive, albeit unclassified, statement of U.S. defense strategy, policy, resources, and programs spanning more than 200 pages.

With Allison's departure, someone was still needed to fill his very large shoes. The Army nominated me, and despite my modest shoe size, after a series of interviews, I became Weinberger's military assistant for special projects, one of which involved overseeing the Posture Statement. The job gave me a perspective on how defense strategy was made at the highest levels of government.

The last Posture Statement completed during my tenure was Defense Secretary Frank Carlucci's, submitted only months before the Berlin Wall came down. It included a twenty-page discussion of the balance of forces between the U.S. and its NATO allies and Soviet Russia and the Warsaw Pact. These balances, both "regional" (such as the balance in Europe) and "functional" (such as the strategic, or nuclear, balance) set the stage for a detailed discussion of U.S. strategy that spanned nearly forty pages. One could not help but be impressed by the quality and level of intellectual effort that went into both developing and explaining the strategy.

As it turned out, the Berlin Wall was not the only thing that came down. The Cold War's end and the rise of the United States' unipolar moment made military strategy and defense planning seem less important. In 2005, the annual Posture Statement was replaced by "The National Defense Strategy." The Pentagon managed to publish a twenty-three-page version in 2008. A decade went by before the most recent version—an eleven-page "summary"—was produced.

Quantity is not necessarily an indicator of quality, but considering the progressive decline in the United States' relative military standing over the past decade, it seems fair to view the Posture Statement's demise as a sign of strategic neglect. Given the importance of securing U.S. vital interests without having to resort to general war, such negligence is difficult to understand. Indeed, great-power war in the industrial age inflicted enormous levels of destruction and human suffering. As Winston Churchill was moved to declare following the First World War, "War, today, is bare—bare of profit and stripped of all its glamour. The old pomp and circumstance are gone. War is now nothing but toil, blood, death, squalor and lying propaganda."[1] Churchill's observation was confirmed in World War II, especially by the introduction of nuclear weapons with their immense destructive power.

Emerging from the wreckage of two world wars and with the growing specter of nuclear Armageddon, the cost of waging general war had become so high that there appeared to be no political gain that could justify it. Shortly after the atomic attacks on Hiroshima and Nagasaki, the strategist Bernard Brodie was moved to write, "Thus far the chief purpose of our military establishment has been to win wars. From now on the chief purpose must be to avert them."[2] Although deterrence strategies stretch back to antiquity, they achieved greater prominence in the nuclear age. For roughly three-quarters of a century, U.S. defense strategy has rested on a foundation of deterrence to preserve its security while avoiding general wars, both nuclear and conventional. The other declared nuclear powers—Soviet Russia, Great Britain, France, and China—either formally or informally appeared to accept the central role of deterrence in their strategies.

Deterrence, in its simplest form, involves efforts to prevent a rival (the "target") from pursuing a proscribed action. Deterrence strategies seek to influence the target's calculation of the costs, benefits, and risks associated with pursuing the proscribed action. Assuming a rational opponent—one that acts to maximize its overall anticipated gains and minimize anticipated costs—deterrence succeeds by convincing the target that it has an unacceptably low probability of achieving its goals (deterrence through denial) or that the costs involved in pursuing the proscribed action will exceed any benefits derived (deterrence through punishment).

Deterrence prevailed through the Cold War. It was later discovered, however, that on several occasions, the two superpowers came perilously close to nuclear Armageddon.[3] Following Soviet Russia's collapse in 1991, the United States' military dominance constituted a strong deterrent to any rival contemplating general war. But this dominance no longer exists, and the efficacy of deterrence is eroding, perhaps precipitously, along with it. This would not surprise Churchill, who stated, "I desire to see the collective forces of the world invested with overwhelming power. If you are going to run this thing on a narrow margin, . . . you are going to have war."[4]

Today the world's military powers in general, and the United States in particular, are pursuing deterrence on an increasingly narrow margin. Yet over the past decade, U.S. administrations have addressed deterrence in only the broadest terms. The Obama administration's national security strategy in 2015 discussed deterrence in aspirational terms, focusing almost exclusively on the goals of deterrence rather than a strategy for ensuring it. Thus, it includes assertions like, "We will deter and defeat any adversary that threatens our national security and that of our allies."[5] The administration's statement of defense priorities in 2012 is similarly vague as to how deterrence is to be achieved.[6]

The Trump administration's 2018 national defense strategy affirmed the centrality of deterrence by declaring, "The Department of Defense's enduring mission is to provide combat-credible military forces needed to deter war and protect the security of our nation." Yet there is no explanation as to *how* this is to be accomplished. The best it could muster was an ambiguous discourse to the effect that the United States would deter rivals by being "strategically predictable, but operationally unpredictable," and somehow "maneuvering [rivals] into unfavorable positions, frustrating their efforts, precluding their options while expanding our own, and forcing them to confront conflict under adverse conditions."[7]

It appears that these strategy documents share a common assumption that all political leaders understand and appreciate the devastation associated with modern general war and therefore that deterrence does not require any heavy lifting, either intellectually in the form of strategy or with respect to military capabilities. The truth, however, is that the conditions enabling effective deterrence strategies are shifting, and in ways that are eroding their efficacy. The emergence of a mature precision-warfare regime and an emerging military revolution, the diffusion of increasingly destructive capabilities to minor powers and even nonstate entities—the "democratization of destruction"—and relatively recent advances in the cognitive and social sciences are making devising and implementing deterrence strategies an increasingly difficult proposition.

The balance of this chapter is devoted to providing an overview of these trends and their implications for deterrence strategies as they pertain to general war. Although the discussion is primarily from a U.S. perspective, it can be applied more broadly.

The Shifting Geopolitical Environment

Today's international security system, unlike the bipolar and unipolar systems between 1945 and recent years, is multipolar. The emergence of major revisionist powers in China and Russia, combined with the proliferation of nuclear weapons and other advanced military capabilities to second-tier powers, has increased the number of rivals the United States seeks to deter. This provides more opportunities for deterrence to fail.

With respect to nuclear weapons, the reductions in U.S. and Russian Cold War nuclear arsenals by more than 90 percent, combined with the growth in China's arsenal, is shifting the bipolar Cold War nuclear competition to a multipolar nuclear world. The summer of 2021 produced revelations that Beijing is constructing hundreds of silos for its new DF-41 ICBMs, each capable of carrying ten warheads. As the head of the U.S. Strategic Command stated, "We are witnessing a strategic breakout by China." If so, "parity"—having nuclear forces roughly comparable to that of your existing or prospective rival(s)—which has been a staple of U.S.-Russian arms-control agreements owing to its contribution to "crisis stability," will no longer be possible.[8]

The Cold War logic was that if both U.S. and Soviet arsenals were at rough parity, it would enable both to survive a surprise attack by the other and still retain sufficient residual forces to deliver a devastating "second-strike" counterattack. This condition was termed "mutual assured destruction" (MAD). Since neither side could execute a disarming first strike against its rival, neither would be tempted to attack, and deterrence would be assured. Although there were other nuclear powers to consider, their arsenals were trivial compared with those of the superpowers and therefore could be safely discounted. But parity is not an option for all rivals when more than two powers are involved.

A multipolar rivalry seems likely to accentuate these fears. Consider a situation, for example, in which Russia and the United States maintain their current deployed nuclear arsenals at 1,550 weapons each, while China increases its nuclear arsenal to that level.[9] In this case, no power has parity with the other two; each must contend with two potential rivals whose combined arsenals are twice the size of its own, significantly complicating efforts at maintaining a secure second-strike force capable of withstanding an attack by *both* rivals and still delivering a devastating response against them. Each of these three rivals' planning would be further complicated to a greater or lesser extent by the now-significant arsenals of minor nuclear powers, like Britain, France, India, Israel, and Pakistan, which have arsenals numbering "only" in the hundreds.

Moreover, the current geopolitical environment is more dynamic than either the Cold War system or the U.S.-dominated unipolar system that followed, making highly destabilizing shifts in geopolitical alignments and the military balance possible. In a politically unstable multipolar world, each major power would be incentivized to hedge against the possibility that its rivals could join in an alliance against it. In our example, any of the three powers feeling threatened with isolation might increase its arsenal to offset, even if only partially, the "weapons gap" it confronts. This could lead its rivals to increase their arsenals as well, triggering a nuclear arms race.

Moreover, the PLA textbook, *The Science of Military Strategy*, describes deterrence as having two objectives. The first, similar to the Western definition, sees deterrence as discouraging an opponent from pursuing a particular course of action. The second objective of deterrence, however, is to coerce an opponent into pursuing a course of action that it would otherwise not undertake. Thus, it includes the Western concept of *compellence*, suggesting that the CCP has more ambitious goals for its nuclear forces than U.S. policy makers do. This raises questions about how the CCP would use its nuclear forces to coerce its rivals and what kind of nuclear arsenal would be required for it to succeed.[10]

A Multidimensional Military Competition

The problems for deterrence strategies do not end with the emergence of multipolar nuclear rivalries. The maturing precision-warfare regime finds conventional precision-guided weapons capable of striking some targets once reserved solely for nuclear weapons.[11] At the same time, advances in nuclear weapons design find some militaries fielding very low-yield "discriminate" weapons. The result is a blurring of the "firebreak"—the clear distinction that once existed between nuclear and conventional weapons use.[12]

The partial coupling of these weapons finds policy makers drawing different conclusions regarding the circumstances under which they would be employed. Some Western political leaders believe that nuclear weapons' only purpose is to deter others from employing nuclear weapons—in essence, that nuclear and conventional weapons remain "decoupled."[13] On the other hand, many civilian and military leaders in China and Russia appear to reject these views and consider certain types of nuclear weapons available for use in a general conventional war.[14]

Assuming that these disparate views are genuine, they pose problems for strategies designed to deter general conventional and nuclear war. Political leaders who believe that nuclear and conventional weapons are decoupled will, all other factors being equal, see less risk in a conventional war escalating to nuclear war and thus be less deterred from waging conventional war. Yet those policy makers who believe that "discriminate" nuclear weapons can be used without escalating to a full nuclear exchange will be less deterred from employing nuclear weapons once a general conventional war has broken out.

The introduction of cyber weapons further complicates efforts at deterrence, owing to their potential to corrupt early warning and command-and-control systems. Suspicions arose following the successful 2007 Israeli air attack on a Syrian nuclear reactor under construction. No Israeli aircraft were shot down, even though all lacked stealth protection and their target was defended by Syrian air defense units. This led to speculation that the strike was coordinated with an Israeli cyber attack that altered the Syrians' integrated air defense system (IADS) radar data.[15] If cyber weapons reduce senior decision-makers' confidence in their early warning and C2 systems, they may feel compelled to delegate nuclear force release authority to subordinate commanders, increasing substantially the number of individuals who can authorize an attack. If only one of these individuals is more risk tolerant than their political leader, deterrence will be weakened.

From an attacker's perspective, if it believes the effectiveness of a rival's early warning and C2 systems is significantly compromised, this would logically reduce the anticipated costs (and risks) of executing an attack, all other factors being equal. If so, the efficacy of deterrence would be further diminished. Furthermore, if a prospective attacker knows that its rival has delegated release authority to lower-level commanders, it may be incentivized to attack, lest one of them gets an itchy trigger finger.

If attacks employing nonnuclear forces, such as PGMs and cyber payloads, are able to create strategic effects (like disabling key components of the enemy's critical economic infrastructure or destroying a substantial portion of its nuclear forces), it could also reduce the perceived risk of engaging in strategic warfare below the nuclear threshold in a general great-power war. More than a decade ago, the Russian defense analyst Alexi Arbatov summarized Moscow's thinking:

> The high-precision weapons in the U.S. armed forces' arsenal today can be used to destroy a wide range of targets, including hardened fixed facilities. . . . With due targeting, the existing types of cluster bombs can effectively destroy mobile land-based ICBMs. High-precision weapons could also pose a threat to existing silo-based launchers. . . . Russian policymakers worry that future [U.S.] ballistic missile defense capabilities could undermine Russia's potential for strategic retaliation, and that U.S. strategic conventional precision-guided weapons (cruise and ballistic missiles) have a growing counterforce capability, meaning that they increasingly pose a threat to Russia's nuclear capabilities.[16]

Arbatov concluded that "the main unspoken assumption behind this threat perception is that *traditional nuclear deterrence may not be effective against conventional counterforce threats*, since nuclear retaliation in case of such an attack would invite suicide by follow-on nuclear strikes and thus lacks credibility" [emphasis added].[17] The Russian military's 2018 doctrine provided that, in the event of war, "the Russian Federation shall reserve the right to use nuclear weapons in response to the use of nuclear and other types of weapons of mass destruction against it and/or its allies, as well as in the event of aggression against the Russian Federation with the use of conventional weapons when the very existence of the state is in jeopardy."[18] In 2020, Russian president Vladimir Putin released "On Basic Principles of State Policy of the Russian Federation on Nuclear Deterrence," reaffirming this position. As Russian military exercises include simulating the use of nuclear weapons against NATO, this would appear to confirm that Russian doctrine calls for employing its nuclear forces at a far lower threshold than in responding to a nuclear attack.[19] From a U.S. perspective, Russia's belief that the use of nuclear weapons would "deescalate" a conflict "increase[s] the prospect for dangerous miscalculation and escalation."[20]

As with Russia, the rise of U.S. dominance in precision warfare has led the Chinese to consider employing nuclear weapons first. The PLA's *The Science of Military Strategy* asserts that new military capabilities are exerting a strong influence on the character of deterrence, declaring,

"Brand-new methods of deterrence, based on new theory, new mechanism[s] and new technology, could effectively create more uncertainty when the adversary is evaluating the two sides' military capabilities, and affect the adversary's original strategic plan. In this way, the credibility of deterrence is enhanced. In particular, the emergence of new deterrence forces, based on new technology such as information, cyberspace, space, and new-material technologies, is revolutionarily changing the mechanism, method, and area of operation. It heralds a completely new method of deterrence, symbolized by constructing [an] asymmetrical method of deterrence."[21]

The Chinese have not elaborated on what they mean by a "completely new method of deterrence" and how this "new method" applies. Importantly, they also assume that increasing the target's uncertainty (and risk) invariably enhances deterrence. Yet advances in the cognitive sciences show that this is not necessarily so. Indeed, uncertainty may enhance deterrence of those political leaders who are least likely to need it: the risk-averse leaders. Correspondingly, risk-tolerant leaders—the Adolf Hitlers, Saddam Husseins, Nikita Khrushchevs, Mao Zedongs, and Josef Stalins of this world—are more disposed to take the chance that uncertainties will be resolved in their favor.

In summary, advances in conventional weapons are enabling them to be employed effectively against some targets once reserved solely for nuclear weapons, while advances in nuclear weapons design have led to increasingly discriminate types. Thus, the clear distinction that existed for most of the Cold War between conventional and nuclear weapons is becoming increasingly blurred. Today both the Russians and the Chinese view strategic warfare as encompassing more than nuclear weapons. The Russians have sought to increase their emphasis on nuclear weapons as their principal response to the challenge posed by modern reconnaissance-strike forces. The CCP, however, is pursuing a broad-front approach, which includes greatly expanding its relatively modest nuclear arsenal while boosting a combination of "informatized" conventional forces, information warfare forces, an enhanced space force, and what it calls an "innovative and developmental civilian deterrence force."[22]

Proximity and Speed of Attack

The weakening of deterrence also stems from the growing speed at which contemporary war is waged, particularly between great powers.

This reduces warning time, thereby facilitating surprise. As Chapter 4 makes clear, attack warning is being compressed even further with the use of cyber payloads and the introduction of new weaponry such as anti-satellite lasers and hypersonic missiles.

These shrinking attack timelines are straining the limits of the most advanced military powers' early warning and command-and-control systems. Under these conditions, even instantaneous warning of an attack may not provide a state's political leaders with sufficient time to make a clear, informed decision as to how to respond. The Cold War offers at least two examples where false attack warnings came uncomfortably close to triggering a nuclear exchange between Soviet Russia and the United States.[23] The danger is not new; what is new is the enhanced ability to corrupt early warning systems and the compressed time available to confirm that an attack is, in fact, under way and to formulate and to execute an appropriate response.

Known Unknowns

War between major military powers reveals the true value of military systems, force structures, and the doctrines governing their employment. The (thankfully) long absence of general war, compounded by the disruptive shift in its character triggered by the Precision-Warfare Revolution, has increased uncertainty with respect to the military balance. The ongoing introduction of new capabilities described in Chapter 4 further complicates political and military leaders' calculations of cost, benefit, and risk.

These factors heighten the chances that prospective belligerents will reach significantly different conclusions regarding the risks associated with pursuing a particular course of action. This will probably enhance deterrence of risk-averse decision-makers. Decision-makers who are highly risk tolerant, particularly tyrants, would appear more likely to assume that uncertainties with respect to the military balance will work in their favor, undermining deterrence where it is needed most.

New Domains and the Biosciences

In both U.S. and Chinese military circles, it's become popular to talk about warfare domains. There is good reason for this. Since the last general war, the military competition has moved beyond the land, sea, undersea, air, and the electromagnetic domains, advancing into space, cyberspace, and the seabed. Each of these domains finds a growing number of state and nonstate rivals competing for economic and military advantage.

As noted earlier, commercial activity has grown enormously in these domains in recent decades. A substantial portion of the world's oil and natural gas supplies comes from offshore fields, while undersea cables move the vast majority of the globe's electronic communications. These assets—wellheads, pumping stations, pipelines, fiber-optic cables—are increasingly vulnerable to attack, including from nonstate actors. Space's growing economic value and military importance make securing access to it a high priority. Yet, as with the seabed infrastructure, satellites are vulnerable to attack. Countries are increasingly susceptible to cyber strikes against critical infrastructure, including the power grid, transportation systems, and financial sector. If so, cyber weapons may join nuclear weapons as a means of inflicting prompt and perhaps even catastrophic destruction. Standing apart from "domain warfare" are the remarkable advances in the biosciences. Bioengineering techniques like CRISPR-Cas9 are widely available. Progress in synthetic biology may enable the manufacture and use of "precision" biotoxins that will enable individuals or groups to be targeted with little fear of blowback occurring against the attacker.

What does this mean for deterrence? Given the stream of economic benefits and enhanced military effectiveness that states derive from their activities in the "new" warfare domains and the biosciences, states have a strong interest in deterring attacks on these assets.

It's easier said than done.

With respect to deterrence through denial, in each domain, the competition favors the offense—given equal resources and all other factors being equal, the costs associated with attacking a rival's space and undersea systems or launching cyber or advanced biological attacks appear likely to be far less than those needed to block the action successfully. How do you defend the Gulf of Mexico's vast seabed energy infrastructure and cables from attacks by explosive-laden "kamikaze" underwater drones, now widely available commercially? How do you defend satellite sensors from being blinded by ground-based lasers? How do you block every possible entry point to the national energy grid—including those "insider" threats who already have access? How do you prevent a wave of suicide human biological-warfare attackers spreading a synthetically designed "precision" biotoxin? This imbalance, heavily weighted in the offense's favor, increases the attacker's prospective gains while reducing the risk of failure, eroding the efficacy of deterrence through denial.

What about deterrence through the threat of punishment? If deterrence through denial fails, and the attack inflicts heavy damage, the victim state's leaders will probably feel intense political pressure to retaliate promptly. The ability of modern military organizations to wage war at unprecedentedly high speeds may also compel a prompt response, lest the means to do so are lost. What is needed is prompt—and accurate—attribution of the attacker's identity.

In each domain, identifying the source of an attack—especially promptly—appears relatively difficult compared with attribution of large-scale attacks in more traditional war-fighting domains, such as land, air, and sea. The problem, for those who seek to deter through the threat of retaliation, is that many states and perhaps even nonstate groups are capable of conducting significant cyber and bio attacks, and against targets on the seabed. The growing number of space-faring nations and the spread of directed-energy weaponry seem likely to complicate efforts at timely attribution of attacks in this domain as well. Given the advantages accruing to the attacker and the problems of achieving prompt, effective attribution, risk-tolerant actors—all other factors being equal—will find the prospective costs and risks involved in taking proscribed actions reduced, perhaps dramatically, weakening strategies based on deterrence.

Catalytic War

In a multipolar system with many actors in which the competition is offense dominant and the prospects for prompt and effective attribution are spotty, the risk of a "catalytic war"—one initiated covertly between two states by a third party—may increase significantly. This occurs when one state incorrectly attributes an attack to another state or nonstate entity. The term was popularized in *On the Beach*, a novel from 1957 that depicts a nuclear-proliferated world where an Egyptian nuclear attack against American and British targets is misattributed as an attack by the Soviet Union. A nuclear retaliatory attack is launched against Russia, triggering Armageddon.[24]

The novel's presumption of multiple actors; the diffusion of new, advanced weaponry; geographic proximity; and highly stressed early warning and C2 systems mirror the trends described earlier. For example, consider a crisis between Israel and Turkey set in the early 2030s. With tensions high and warning times compressed, a radical regime in Iran that considers both the Jewish and Turkish states enemies could attempt to trigger a catalytic war between the two by launching missiles against Israel from along its border with Turkey, in the hope that the Israelis would see it as an attack by the Turks.

More subtle means for triggering a catalytic war may be employed. Given the odd absence of a Syrian response to the Israeli attack on its nuclear facilities in 2007, in our example it seems plausible that malware injected by a third party into Israel's early warning system could corrupt it to show—falsely—that a Turkish ballistic missile attack on Israel is under way. Given the short missile flight times, Israeli leaders would have no time to confirm that such an attack was, in fact, occurring before launching their missiles in a retaliatory strike. Similar situations could arise elsewhere where military powers are in close geographic proximity to one another, as is the case with China, India, Pakistan, and Russia.

The Democratization of Destruction

More than two decades ago, Martin Shubik warned of what I call the "democratization of destruction." He argued that the increasing availability of technical information and dual-use materials risk making mass killing possible for small groups or even individuals.[25] Although Shubik emphasized biological attacks, his warning has broader applicability in today's world. Formidable military capabilities are increasingly accessible to nonstate actors, including small groups, as the technical and capital barriers to developing or acquiring devastating malware and sophisticated biological weapons, among other means of destruction, are eroding at a worrisome rate.

The rapidly increasing ability of nonstate entities to inflict destruction undermines deterrence, as some actors, like millenarian groups, wish nothing else but to inflict destruction on society. The point is expressed well in the motion picture *The Dark Knight*, in which the protagonist, Bruce Wayne (Batman) tells his butler, Alfred Pennyworth, that he is struggling to figure out what his arch rival, The Joker, wants:

ALFRED PENNYWORTH: With respect, Master Wayne, perhaps this is a man that *you* don't fully understand, either. A long time ago, I was in Burma. My friends and I were working for the local government. They were trying to buy the loyalty of tribal leaders by bribing them with precious stones. But their caravans were being raided in a forest north of Rangoon by a bandit. So, we went looking for the stones. But in six months, we never met anybody who traded with him. One day, I saw a child playing with a ruby the size of a tangerine. The bandit had been throwing them away.

BRUCE WAYNE: So why steal them?

ALFRED PENNYWORTH: Well, because he thought it was good sport. Because some men aren't looking for anything logical, like money. They can't be bought, bullied, reasoned, or negotiated with. Some men just want to watch the world burn.[26]

For those who only want to "watch the world burn," deterrence through denial is the only possible strategy. Moreover, if such groups or individuals lack sanctuary, they will be incentivized to employ their weapons as quickly as possible, lest they be captured.

Crazy Armed Humans

Crafting deterrence strategies is greatly simplified by making two assumptions: first, that people make decisions rationally—acting to maximize their prospective gains in the context of their utility functions—in making decisions involving risk; and second, that they calculate their costs, benefits, and risks as you would if you were in their position.

As it turns out, neither assumption is true. Human beings cannot be counted on to act rationally in making decisions involving risk. There are also major impediments to understanding how others calculate cost, benefit, and risk, which, of course, is at the heart of deterrence.

The work of John Locke, Adam Smith, and John Stuart Mill presumed that all normal human adult cognitive processes were identical. David Bernoulli, however, found that most people dislike risk and uncertainty and that, offered the choice between a gamble and a "sure thing" equal to the expected value of the gamble, people usually pick the sure thing. Simply put, human decision-making is based on prospective material gains and losses, as well as on psychological factors.[27]

In the 1950s, Herbert Simon introduced the concept of bounded (or limited) rationality, in demonstrating that people's ability to make rational decisions is limited by the difficulty of the decision problem they confront, their inherent cognitive limitations, and the time available for them to make a decision. Under these conditions, rather than making decisions that maximize their expected utility, people typically abandon attempting to make the "best" decision and instead default to making a "good enough" decision. Simon called this "satisficing."[28]

Simon's collaboration with James March showed how, in organizations, senior leaders' decisions are influenced by their bureaucracies, which provide—or withhold—information that could exert a significant influence on their decisions.[29] Further work by March in collaboration with Richard Cyert found that senior decision-makers often made decisions based on relatively simple rules, as opposed to a thorough analysis of costs, benefits, and risks.[30]

The erosion of belief in rational human decision-making was accelerated when, in the late 1970s, Amos Tversky and Daniel Kahneman found that people systematically violate the laws of probability on which utility theory is based. They called their findings "prospect theory," which states that people's choices are influenced by their "reference point," specifically, that an identical situation may be viewed differently based on a person's sense of their prospective gains and losses, which Kahneman and Tversky term the "framing effect."[31] Their work was aided by Richard Thaler's discovery of the "endowment effect," which states that individuals tend to value retaining what they have rather than acquiring comparable things they do not have.[32] Thus, a policy maker would be more likely to run higher risks to retain territory than to seize territory of equal value from another country, thereby supporting prospect theory's "reference point." The endowment effect would seem to strengthen deterrence. But, alas, this is not always true.

This is because much depends on how decision-makers set their reference point. One might assume that decision-makers always set their reference point with respect to the situation that exists when the decision is being made—the status quo. This assumption, however, is false. Tversky and Kahneman discovered that after securing gains, decision-makers typically *reset their reference point* around the new status quo. They view any subsequent setback as a loss rather than a gain foregone and are relatively risk tolerant in defending their gains. On the other hand, when decision-makers suffer losses, they typically *do not reset* their reference point but retain the *pre-loss status quo* as their reference point. They view retaking what they've lost not as the pursuit of gains but as preventing losses, framing their decision using the old status quo. Consequently, they will run relatively greater risks to achieve this end.

The endowment effect influence on the reference point may weaken deterrence. For example, the Arab states' decisive defeat by Israel in the Six-Day War in 1967, combined with Israel's nuclear capability, should have deterred any overt act of Arab aggression. Yet only six years later, Egypt and Syria went to war with Israel to recover their lost territories. Arguably, the Arab leaders saw themselves as trying to recover land that was rightfully theirs. Their reference point had not changed after the 1967 war. The Israelis, on the other hand, having adjusted their reference point on the new status quo, fought to defend what they viewed as theirs.

Today, consider China's attempts at creating "new facts" by militarizing existing and artificially created islands in the South China Sea, many of which are claimed by its neighbors. One can readily envision the Chinese Communist Party's leaders framing their perspective around a new status quo in which the region has become a part of China, while other countries reject Beijing's claims and retain a reference point based on the status quo that existed before China's expansionist actions. Should a crisis occur, both parties may well view themselves as being in a domain of loss and willing to run greater risks to prevail, weakening efforts at deterrence.

Yet another revelation from the cognitive sciences—"optimism bias"—finds that deterrence strategies are far less robust than some people may assume. Its roots are in research showing that "optimistic" people are more likely to achieve positions of authority, such as senior policy makers. These individuals typically made it to the top by beating long odds, reinforcing their optimism, including faith in their judgment and the chances of overcoming unfavorable odds. Generally speaking, such individuals are prone to double down when faced with failure and are willing to run greater risks to prevail rather than cutting their losses. Simply put, political leaders' optimism is generally "widespread, stubborn, and costly."[33] Or as Henry Kissinger observed, "It is in the nature of prophets to redouble their efforts, not to abandon them, in the face of recalcitrant reality."[34]

Deterring a leader with optimism bias may be particularly challenging when dealing with tyrants, such as Hitler, Stalin, Mao, Hussein, and even lesser despots like Khrushchev. Given the cutthroat political environment in which they operated, the relatively long odds involved in attempting to seize absolute power, and the fate of those who competed and failed, these men must have been extremely risk tolerant. Once they had prevailed, the experience would almost certainly have boosted their optimism regarding their ability to navigate threats to their rule, both internal and external.[35]

Optimism bias may partially explain Hitler's decision to reoccupy the Rhineland while in a weak military position relative to Great Britain, France, and Soviet Russia. It may also aid in understanding Stalin's cutting off U.S. access to West Berlin even as the Americans enjoyed a nuclear monopoly. Saddam Hussein's decision to take on the United States not once but twice suggests a belief in his ability to prevail in the face of enormous odds, as does Mao's decision to plunge China into the Korean War barely a year after seizing power following a long civil war. Then there is Khrushchev's high-stakes gamble of deploying nuclear missiles to Cuba despite clear U.S. warnings that it would precipitate a major crisis. In summary, these leaders' actions strongly suggest that each possessed a personality that believed all would turn out well even when pursuing very risky enterprises. This suggests that tyrants may be especially difficult to deter.

Other recent advances in the behavioral sciences reveal that members of markedly different cultures exhibit significant and, in some cases, dramatic differences in their cognitive processes, including how they view matters of equity, cost, benefit, and risk.[36]

In the 1990s, the anthropologist Joseph Henrich was researching an assumption that humans all share "the same cognitive machinery—the same evolved rational and psychological hardwiring."[37] His work found him testing people from various cultures using the Ultimatum Game, which has two players. Player A is given an amount of money, say, $100. Player A must then offer Player B an amount of money, anywhere from $1 to $100. Then Player B chooses to accept or reject the offer. If B accepts A's offer, they each receive A's proposed payout. If, however, B refuses the offer, neither player receives any money, and both end up empty-handed. Since Player A must offer Player B at least $1, both players stand to come out ahead if the offer is accepted: a classic "win-win" result. Henrich knew that most American Player Bs tended to reject offers from Player A that fell below a rough split of the money, even though B's financial situation would have improved by accepting it.

With this data in hand, Henrich began conducting the Ultimatum Game with members of the Machiguenga tribe, which lives in the Peruvian Amazon. To his surprise, Machiguenga Player As' offers were typically much lower than those advanced by their American counterparts.

Even more surprising, Machiguenga Player Bs rarely refused even very low amounts. They felt that it just seemed ridiculous to reject an offer of free money. Why would anyone forgo money to punish someone who had the good fortune of playing the other role in the game?[38]

Henrich then tested people from more than a dozen small societies in East Africa, South America, the Southwest Pacific, and Mongolia. He found that the average offers made by Player A varied widely from culture to culture. In some cultures, even when Player A made offers above $60, Player B would often refuse the offer, outcomes that were almost unheard of when Americans were playing the game.[39]

Henrich concluded that humans will reject what they perceive as *unfairness* or *slights to their personal honor*, even at substantial cost to themselves. These perceptions are highly subjective. Where people have conflicting judgments of what constitutes fairness, both risk being left, at least materially speaking, with a "lose-lose" outcome.[40]

How do deterrence strategies account for "honor" and "fairness"? Or does it even matter when dealing with matters of state? The renowned historian Donald Kagan found that in matters of war and peace, there is indeed a link between a policy maker's sense of fairness and national honor. Kagan notes that in the Peloponnesian War and in World War I, some belligerents went to war in no small measure due to the perceived cost to their honor in failing to act. In the former conflict, the Corinthians' "driving motive" in going to war with Corcyra "was neither fear nor interest, but honor, a determination to avenge the slights they had suffered from the Corcyraeans." Britain's decision to declare war on Germany in August 1914 found some senior British officials, "those who would not fight for the balance of power and British security, . . . [consoling] themselves that they were fighting for international law, the sanctity of treaties, and the protection of helpless neutrals."[41]

As the Ultimatum Game shows, preserving one's honor and a sense of fairness is not limited to political and military leaders. During a visit to Germany in 1934, the French philosopher Jean-Paul Sartre encountered a German who had served as a sergeant during the Great War. The old soldier declared that in the next war, "We shall retrieve our honor." A shocked Sartre said that given the horrors of the last war, everyone ought to want peace. "Honor comes first," the old sergeant replied. "First we must retrieve our honor."[42]

As for "fairness," the Soviet leader Nikita Khrushchev's decision-making during the Cuban Missile Crisis in 1962 was influenced by, as he saw it, a lack of "fairness" in U.S. and Soviet overseas nuclear-armed missile deployments. The United States had deployed missiles in Britain, Italy, and Turkey, and Khrushchev expected President Kennedy to accept Soviet missiles in Cuba "as the Turkish missiles were received in the Soviet Union."[43] When Kennedy did not, both sides moved to the brink of nuclear war—the ultimate lose-lose outcome. At the time, the United States enjoyed an enormous advantage in nuclear forces over Soviet Russia, and the U.S. missiles in Europe were a minor factor in nuclear military balance. Despite Khrushchev's inferior position and the irrelevance, militarily speaking, of the U.S. missiles in Turkey, getting Kennedy's commitment to withdraw the missiles became a crucial sticking point in negotiations to resolve the crisis. Yet Khrushchev persisted, primarily due to his need to show that he and his country had been treated fairly and honorably.[44]

It seems clear that factors relating to perceptions of fairness can exert a significant influence on decision-makers when making choices under conditions of risk. Could U.S. decision-makers today feel confident that they understand how the Chinese leadership or that of Russia, Iran, or North Korea views the cost it is willing to pay to be treated in a way that is "fair" or "honorable"?

For roughly three-quarters of a century, U.S. defense strategy has relied on deterrence to avoid the horrors of a third great-power war. The absence of such a war and the period of U.S. military dominance in the two decades following the Cold War appear to have convinced a generation of U.S. policy makers that deterrence is assured. But recent dramatic geopolitical shifts, especially the rise of revisionist great powers, combined with a maturing precision-warfare regime and the emergence of potent new military capabilities, are radically shifting the conditions under which deterrence strategies are constructed. Finally, human frailties cannot be ignored. As President Eisenhower came to understand, "It is remarkable how little concern men seem to have for logic, statistics, and even, indeed, survival: we live by emotion, prejudice, and pride."[45]

PART II

Introduction

T HE PRECEDING CHAPTERS DESCRIBE some prospective characteristics of the maturing precision-warfare regime, as well
as those of an emerging military revolution. The shift in the
military competition's character will probably be profound.
As such, a military's ability to adapt on a grand scale—to demonstrate a
world-class competence in disruptive innovation—will be crucial to its
ability to gain a competitive advantage over its rivals.

How well positioned are the world's militaries to win the race to
identify and exploit the "next big thing" in warfare? How might they improve their odds of succeeding?

Insights on these questions may be found by examining periods over
the past century or so when militaries undertook disruptive innovation
to trigger a military revolution. By examining how these militaries succeeded, it may be possible to identify general characteristics of military
organizations with a high level of competence in pursuing disruptive innovation. These characteristics may be used to help identify how well a
particular military—and the militaries of its rivals—are positioned to
create a military revolution.

Although military revolutions have occurred periodically stretching
back over thousands of years, the emphasis here is on the late nineteenth
and twentieth centuries: the industrial and information ages. The four
militaries examined reflect different time frames, national military organizations, and branches of the armed services. The purpose is not to
write a new history of these militaries in the periods under investigation.
Many skilled scholars have accomplished that with varying interpreta-

tions, to the point where in some cases we are now in post-revisionist periods. Rather, the effort here is to draw on their scholarship for a twofold purpose: to understand how these militaries pursued disruptive innovation, and to identify common features that emerge from their experience.

Four militaries are examined in general chronological order. Among the factors examined are leadership; fiscal resources; military-technical resources; the industrial base; investment strategies; field exercises and experimentation; manpower; and external factors, such as the political leadership, civilian oversight, and arms control. The four studies vary considerably in length. This stems primarily from the length of the period examined and, to an even greater extent, the level of complexity associated with the changes they pursued.

We begin in Chapter 6 with the British Royal Navy during an era of overlapping military revolutions, spanning from the mid-nineteenth century's Steam and Iron Revolution through the so-called Fisher Revolution, a term coined by Nicholas Lambert that reflects the extraordinary individual at its heart. During this period, Great Britain confronted major shifts in the geopolitical and military-technical environment. In response, the Admiralty, under Admiral John ("Jackie") Fisher's leadership, exploited the potential of emerging technologies—including those associated with new types of weapons, propulsion, and communications—and operations in new domains to affect a radical shift in the fleet's character and capabilities in order to sustain Britain's maritime superiority.

Chapter 7 tracks the German military's pursuit of disruptive innovation between the world wars. Following Germany's defeat in World War I, the interwar years saw its armed forces leverage advances in mechanization, aviation, and radio to create mechanized air-land operations, popularly known as "Blitzkrieg."

At the same time that the German military was transforming war on land, the United States Navy was at the forefront in creating a military revolution at sea, primarily through naval aviation, long-range radio, and radar. Its successful efforts led to the battleship being eclipsed by the aircraft carrier and the fast carrier task force, the subject of Chapter 8.

The examples conclude in Chapter 9 with the United States Air Force, which led the way in introducing precision warfare. After suffering substantial losses during the Vietnam War and facing a growing threat from advanced Soviet integrated air defenses in Europe, the Air Force developed and fielded what Soviet military theorists referred to as the first operational "reconnaissance-strike complex."

Chapter 10 identifies common characteristics shared by these militaries. They provide a point-of-departure scorecard of sorts to handicap a military organization's potential to pursue disruptive innovation. Chapter 11 completes Part 2 by offering a preliminary assessment of how well the U.S. military is positioned to pursue disruptive innovation.

CHAPTER SIX

Fisher's Scheme

The first essential is to divest our minds totally of the idea that a single type of ship as now built is necessary.

—ADMIRAL OF THE FLEET JOHN FISHER

It's astounding to me, *perfectly astounding*, how the very best amongst us absolutely fail to realise the vast impending revolution in naval warfare and naval strategy that the submarine will accomplish. . . . In all seriousness I don't think it is even *faintly* realised—*the immense impending revolution which the submarines will effect as offensive weapons of war.*

—ADMIRAL OF THE FLEET JOHN FISHER

The Most Powerful and Far-Reaching Weapon

On Saturday, June 26, 1897, the Royal Navy assembled at Spithead to celebrate Queen Victoria's diamond jubilee; 165 ships were present, arrayed in five lines stretching over thirty miles. It was by far the greatest concentration of naval power the world had ever seen, even though the

Admiralty had not recalled a single ship from Britain's huge Mediterranean battle fleet or from its more distant squadrons deployed around the globe. As the *Times* of London declared, "The Fleet . . . is certainly the most formidable force in all its elements and qualities that has ever been brought together, and such as no combination of other powers can rival. It is at once the most powerful and far-reaching weapon the world has ever seen."[1]

For nearly a century, since the Battle of Trafalgar, the Royal Navy's supremacy on the world's oceans had remained unchallenged. The fleet had underwritten the establishment of the largest empire the world had ever seen, covering one-quarter of all the territory on the globe and inhabited by more than 350 million people. The fleet linked Great Britain and its colonies and dominions, while protecting the global seaborne commerce that enabled Britain to emerge as the world's leading economic power. Finally, as long as Britannia ruled the waves, it was safe from invasion.

Yet despite the awesome display of naval might that warm June day, it represented more a reflection of the century then passing than the one to come. Just as Queen Victoria's reign was coming to a close, so too was the Pax Britannica. Soon the British would find their naval dominance challenged as it had not been since Napoleon swept across the Continent. Shifts in the global power balance moved Great Britain to abandon its aversion to seeking alliances and security understandings. In the two decades following Victoria's diamond jubilee, a disruptive shift in the character of war at sea resulted in the Royal Navy undergoing a radical transformation in its composition, capabilities, disposition, and approach to war. This transformation vastly improved the navy's effectiveness and enabled it—albeit barely—to defeat an enemy with no naval tradition in a form of warfare the Admiralty only dimly perceived.

Indeed, as Britain's sea lords watched the fleet's hours-long procession honoring the Queen, they had little idea that the coming years would find the Royal Navy abandoning its time-honored practice of imposing a close blockade of enemy fleets in war; undertaking the wholesale decommissioning of more than 150 warships; introducing several new warship types; creating a "combined-arms" line of battle; adopting new forms of maritime operations; and exploiting the communications revolution to realize fantastic increases in the fleet's combat effectiveness. The Royal Navy's transformation was also a product of several other key developments, principal among them Britain's relative declining

economic and industrial power, the emergence of three new naval powers, demands at home for increasing spending on social welfare, and the
genius of its greatest admiral since Nelson.

The Sources of Maritime Dominance

Given the importance of sea power to the country's survival and well-
being, Admiral Frederick Richards, who served as the Navy's most senior
admiral, or first sea lord, in the 1890s, declared that when it came to sea
power, "What this country wants is clear and undisputed superiority."[2]
For most of the nineteenth century, from the end of the Napoleonic
Wars until the 1880s, that was exactly what Britain enjoyed. Thanks to
its being in the lead in the Industrial Revolution, Britain's economic and
industrial capacity was considerably greater than that of France, its only
major maritime rival. An island nation, Britain could rely on the Royal
Navy to protect it from invasion, while France, a continental power, had
to maintain a large army. The French, unable to match the British Navy
ship for ship, were compelled to pursue novel maritime strategies.

British maritime superiority was sustained by a virtuous cycle. The
Royal Navy protected the country's maritime commerce and the empire.
Access to markets and secure sea lines of communication created the
wealth necessary to support a large fleet and enhance the maritime industrial base. This set the foundation for Britain's maritime supremacy,
which secured British trade, and so on.

Thanks to Great Britain's global empire and network of overseas
bases, it also enjoyed positional advantage over France. As Admiral John
("Jackie") Fisher boasted, as long as the maritime competition remained
confined to European powers, Britain controlled the "keys" that enabled
access to the world's major sea lanes. With the exception of France,
whose Atlantic Ocean bases could be bottled up through blockade, other
European fleets would have to pass through chokepoints to gain access
to the open seas to threaten the British Empire or its commerce. These
chokepoints—the English Channel, the Strait of Gibraltar, and the Suez
Canal—were all under the Royal Navy's watchful eye.

Reflecting the Navy's culture, Admiral Richards declared, "The role of
the British fleet in war must always be the offensive."[3] The Royal Navy's
battle fleet was to "command the seas" in home waters. Contemporary
strategists believed that the existence of a superior battle fleet together with
a blockade of enemy naval bases would preclude any attempt to invade or

blockade the British Isles. Meanwhile, relatively small, distant station fleets were assigned to protect Britain's imperial interests. If trade were threatened, the Navy would hunt down enemy commerce raiders and destroy them. More passive, defensive means for protecting shipping, such as convoys, were rejected almost out of hand—even when they were shown to be effective.[4]

Britain's unsurpassed maritime industrial base was yet another source of competitive advantage. The Admiralty could let its rivals set the pace and direction of naval innovation, confident that Britain's superior financial and industrial strength would enable it to overtake any adversary seeking to steal a march on the future.[5] At midcentury, however, the French, looking to shift the maritime competition in their favor, exploited emerging technologies to fuel a naval revolution.

Steam, Iron, and the Telegraph

Between the end of the Napoleonic Wars and the American Civil War, new technologies enabled the introduction of steam propulsion and screw propellers; iron hulls and armor plate; ever larger guns; and breech-loading rifled guns. The French were the first to introduce steam-powered warships in 1850, with *Napoleon*. Steam as a motive power was more powerful, reliable, and efficient than wind and sails. Steamships cut the trip from London to Cape Town by more than half. For the Royal Navy, charged with defending an empire on which the sun never set, steam greatly enhanced its ability to move quickly to any threatened spot on the globe.

The shift to steam propulsion came at a price. Instead of using wind to propel sails, coal was required to fuel the boilers creating steam. The Admiralty found itself creating a global network of coaling stations to sustain its far-flung fleets. The shift from sail to steam also had important implications for the Royal Navy's blockade operations, as ships so engaged had to return to a base for engine maintenance and to restock with coal.

The Age of Steam had barely arrived when, in March 1858, the French Navy laid down four warships designed with iron plates bolted over their timber hulls, the first oceangoing "ironclads." France's new ships were far superior to their wood-hulled predecessors, especially against the rifled shells that were greatly increasing both the accuracy and the penetrating power of a warship's guns.[6]

News of the French initiative reached England in May, leading Britain's surveyor of the navy, Sir Baldwin Walker, to declare, "Although I have frequently stated it is not in the interest of Great Britain, possessing as she does so large a navy, to adopt any important change in the construction of ships of war which might have the effect of rendering necessary the introduction of a new class of very costly vessels until such a course is forced upon her by the adoption by Foreign powers of formidable ships of a novel character requiring similar ships to cope with them, yet it then becomes a matter not only of expediency but of absolute necessity."[7]

This strategy of the "second-move advantage" characterized the Admiralty's thinking throughout most of the nineteenth century. As Peter Padfield has found, "It accorded with all natural instincts to preserve a familiar and if not physically comfortable at least comforting and highly successful way of life, and it kept costs down by preserving existing dockyards, ships and naval skills which were known to be superior. And, most important, it worked—because ... the country had engineering and industrial potential which exceeded anything elsewhere. This is perhaps the deciding factor [in sustaining British maritime superiority] throughout the century."[8]

The first seagoing ironclad was France's *La Gloire*. Yet only a year later, the British launched the far more powerful *Warrior*. In 1859, one-third of the merchant tonnage produced in British shipyards employed iron in their construction. By 1870, the proportion had risen to five-sixths, substantially surpassing that of the French. The British shift from wind to steam propulsion was equally impressive, thanks to the government's policy of providing subsidies that encouraged creating and sustaining steamship lines as early as 1840, even though steam engines at that time were uneconomical.[9]

Britain's advanced industrial base and ability to build more quickly than its rivals also enabled it to maintain a smaller fleet—with its significant savings in human, fiscal, and material resources—knowing that it could rapidly increase the Navy's size if needed. By the 1870s, Great Britain had forty ironclads built and under construction, only five more than France. Still, the British fleet was generally considered more than a match for its French counterpart, thanks to Britain's ability to compete based on time—to build quickly.[10] It also made sense to avoid launching large numbers of ships that, owing to the quickening advance of technological change, could find their effectiveness depreciating at a relatively rapid rate.

In the two decades following the French launching of *La Gloire*, the navies of the great European powers were in a state of constant churn as technology advances enabled rapid progress in armor and armament. What the Admiralty lacked was a sense of how these new ships would fare in war. Thanks to the Pax Britannica, by 1880 the Royal Navy had only one admiral on active duty who had ever been in combat with an enemy warship on the open seas.[11] The absence of major fleet engagements that characterized the post-Napoleonic era led navies to examine even the smallest engagement between these new ship types for clues as to how they should design their fleets.

Early returns suggested that ships designed with rams would be effective. A battle between Austrian and Italian ships at Lissa in 1866 saw the *Re d'Italia* sunk after being rammed. With contemporary guns inaccurate and limited to close range, visions arose of melees between ships maneuvering and sinking each other with rams, and beginning in the mid-1860s, a significant number of ships were equipped with rams.

By the 1880s, however, a ship's armament had eclipsed the ram's challenge as the main threat to a ship's armor. The earliest French and British ironclads were covered with wrought-iron armor several inches thick. By the mid-1860s, the armor had increased to nine inches, and then to twenty-four inches in the British ironclad *Inflexible*, launched in 1876. Moreover, advances in metallurgy were making stronger and lighter types of armor possible. By the late 1890s, the German firm Krupp was manufacturing steel armor with roughly three times the strength as the armor used in the *Inflexible*. At the same time, guns were rapidly increasing in size, range, and rate of fire. By the 1880s, breech-loading guns were displacing muzzle-loaders, and steel armor-piercing rounds began appearing around the same time. The 1890s saw "quick-firing" guns capable of firing up to fourteen rounds a minute entering the fleet. Armor appeared to be losing its competition with shells.

The rapid pace of technological change—and warship obsolescence— saw British warships often built in ones and twos. The ships themselves presented a wide variety of forms, shapes, types, masts, riggings, and armaments. It took until the 1890s and the emergence of the Franco-Russian alliance before the Royal Navy built an entire class of battleships, the seven *Royal Sovereigns*, to a single design.[12]

The Devil's Device

Impressive as the advances in ship design, armor plate, guns, and weaponry were, nothing caused the Admiralty more anxiety during the nineteenth century's latter decades than the torpedo. The first practical torpedo appeared in 1867, the product of collaboration between an Austrian naval officer, Commander Giovanni Lupis, and Robert Whitehead, an English engineer.

The Whitehead torpedo quickly attracted the Admiralty's attention. In September 1872, Commander Jackie Fisher, an early torpedo enthusiast, was assigned to HMS *Excellent* as a torpedo instructor. Two months after his arrival, Fisher published a memorandum that made its way throughout the fleet urging that a committee be established to investigate the novel weapon's potential. The memo apparently had an effect. In May 1873, the "Torpedo Committee" began work.

Over the next three years, the committee undertook a series of experiments leading to the publication of a seminal report on the subject. Its findings were sobering. The committee expressed concern that "the most powerful ship is liable to be destroyed by a torpedo projected from a vessel of the utmost comparative insignificance" and that this threatened to "reduce to one common level the Naval Power of the greatest and the most insignificant nations." The committee made this declaration with foresight, as the Whitehead torpedo was as yet a primitive weapon with a range of only 200 yards and a speed of nine knots. Nevertheless, the committee concluded, "Any maritime nation failing to provide itself with submarine locomotive torpedoes would be neglecting a source of great power both for offence and defence." The torpedo also had important implications for the Royal Navy's use of the close blockade to confine enemy warships to their bases. The committee foresaw that "none of [Britain's] large vessels could remain for any length of time during war off an enemy's port without imminent risk of destruction by offensive torpedoes; experiments in this and other countries have furnished data which leave no room for doubt on this head." As Admiral Richards lamented, "No man ever did his country a worse service [than Robert Whitehead]. . . . The millions which his invention has taxed his country up to the present would have built a large fleet."[13]

By the mid-1880s, a growing number of officers believed the torpedo was about to transform naval warfare. At the vanguard of this movement was Admiral Hyacinthe Aube, who was appointed as France's minister of marine in 1886. The admiral and like-minded French officers were known as the Jeune École. They argued that small, cheap, fast torpedo-carrying boats could sink the Royal Navy's largest, most heavily armored ships. They envisioned France's torpedo boats, sacrificing armored protection to achieve high speed and benefiting from the dispersion made possible by their large numbers, could successfully press home their swarm attacks on the Royal Navy's blockading battle fleet. While French torpedo boats were savaging Britain's close blockade fleet, French steam-powered cruisers would be terrorizing British commerce on the high seas. All this could be done on the cheap. An article in *La Reforme de la Marine* asserted that if three torpedo boats would suffice to torpedo an ironclad, they could be built at a cost of 600,000 francs, against the 20-million-franc cost of a major warship. And they could be crewed by a small fraction of the sailors needed to man an ironclad.[14]

The prospect that the Jeune École's vision of future warfare at sea might prove true triggered alarm bells at the Admiralty. In September 1884, Captain W. H. Hall of the Royal Navy's Foreign Intelligence Committee (the forerunner of the Naval Intelligence Department) submitted a memo examining prospective naval operations in the event of a war with France. In addressing the close blockade, Hall concluded that "torpedo boats constitute the chief danger to a blockading squadron . . . unless it is accompanied by an adequate number of torpedo vessels sufficient to protect the squadron." Hall's concept of a suitable "torpedo vessel" was a ship much larger than a torpedo boat.[15]

Hall's memo gained traction the following April, owing to a war scare with Russia, which raised the prospect of the Royal Navy confronting Russian torpedo boats lurking in the Baltic Sea. To counter the threat, the Admiralty ordered fifty-four torpedo gun boats, or "catchers," smaller and faster versions of the cruisers of that time. The early classes, the *Rattlesnake, Grasshopper,* and *Sharpshooter,* arrived in time to be evaluated in the early-1890s maneuvers.

Despite the near panic induced by the emergence of the torpedo-boat threat, there was little hard evidence to back the Jeune École's claims or substantiate the fears triggered by the Anglo-Russian crisis. Critics pointed out that torpedoes were not effective against moving ships beyond 400 yards, while ship-mounted guns were effective at nearly four times that range and could fire more rapidly than torpedoes could be launched. Moreover, torpedo boats had yet to prove they were seaworthy in open waters. With an eye toward identifying the true state of the naval balance and obtaining an accurate measure of the torpedo-boat threat, the Royal Navy began a series of fleet maneuvers that would continue for nearly thirty years until the onset of the Great War in 1914.

Even before Admiral Aube came to power, the French themselves were conducting naval maneuvers exploring the torpedo boat's potential. One maneuver in 1884 that generated excitement saw a torpedo-boat flotilla intercept and attack ironclads at night on the open sea.[16]

The Royal Navy undertook its own maneuvers with the opposite objective in mind: countering the torpedo-boat threat. The fleet maneuvers of 1885 off Ireland's west coast found the Royal Navy testing coastal and blockade operations. They revealed that the British fleet was unprepared for an opponent well versed in the use of torpedoes and that torpedo-boat catchers were not sufficiently seaworthy to support overseas blockade work.[17]

The French Navy's follow-on experiments with torpedo boats proved sobering for Jeune École members. The 1887 maneuvers, conducted in poor weather, exposed serious flaws in the boats' sea-keeping abilities. One boat was lost, and two others were so badly damaged that they were scrapped. Still others were so damaged that the flotilla was reduced to half strength. The exercise coincided with Aube's replacement after barely a year as France's minister of marine.

The Royal Navy's fleet exercises in 1888 and 1889 examined the feasibility of maintaining an effective blockade against an enemy's torpedo-boat squadron and its fast cruisers in strongly fortified ports. The maneuvers' findings mirrored those of the French: torpedo boats showed severe limitations operating on the high seas and in daylight. The British began to discount the torpedo-boat threat, even though they did not explore the possibilities of torpedo craft operating in restricted waters at night, even as many of their French counterparts were concluding that torpedo boats could be effective under such circumstances.[18]

In fact, the Royal Navy's maneuvers revealed that, in avoiding the threat posed by torpedo boats at night, the blockading force retreated farther out to sea. This led to wider gaps in the blockade line, reducing its effectiveness. The 1888 exercise employed a "British" force of thirteen battleships and eleven cruisers blockading an "enemy" fleet. This force failed to prevent nine "enemy" battleships and eight cruisers from eluding the blockade, whereupon they commenced attacking Britain's coasts and shipping. The maneuvers also exposed the logistics problems associated with close blockade in the Age of Steam. During the Napoleonic Wars,

Admiral Nelson's wooden sailing ships stood watch off enemy ports for months and even years. Steam-powered ships, however, needed coal. But coaling at sea was difficult, and impossible in bad weather, and steam engines needed periodic maintenance. This meant that the Navy would have to rotate the ships conducting the blockade. Thus, although blockade appeared feasible, the combination of moving it farther offshore and the fleet's mechanization raised the price of doing business considerably.[19]

Along with the Russia war scare and the growth of the tsar's navy, the fleet exercises provided ammunition for those who advocated a bigger navy. Further support came when the French began to establish torpedo-boat bases, or *points d'appui*, from Brittany to Dunkirk to threaten British shipping in the English Channel and dissuade any thoughts of close blockade by "Perfidious Albion."[20] The Admiralty charged three admirals, Sir William Dowell, Sir R. Vesey Hamilton, and Sir Frederick Richards, with studying the feasibility of maintaining a close blockade, how it might be accomplished under the changed conditions, and the kind and number of ships required.

"Charlie B"

At this time, in December 1888, Captain Charles Beresford introduced his naval program. Beresford, an Irishman, was born in 1846 into nobility, the second son of John Beresford, the fourth Marquess of Waterford. Tall and handsome, the future admiral looked—and acted—the part. He was popular with his men, thanks to his well-deserved reputation for generosity and his interest in their welfare. As commander of the gunboat *Condor*, he took part in the bombardment of Alexandria in 1882, winning acclaim by maneuvering his ship to engage the Egyptian batteries at close range. Beresford later took part in a failed expedition sent to relieve the besieged British garrison at Khartoum in Sudan. While en route, the British were attacked by Arabs. Beresford formed up with a British square and fought with distinction.

But there was another side to "Charlie B," as he was popularly known. He also enjoyed—indeed, seemed to *need*—the limelight. He could often be seen with his bulldog, and his admirers, of whom there were many, thought him the personification of "John Bull," Britain's "Uncle Sam." When attention was not forthcoming, Beresford sought ways to attract it. Born into privilege, Beresford exhibited a lifelong behavior of acting as though the Navy's regulations did not apply to him, and that he did not need to heed the orders of its leaders. It's not surprising, then, that Beresford combined two careers, one with the Navy and the other, starting at the age of twenty-eight, as a member of Parliament, where he served periodically over the next forty years. This enabled him to take leave from military service and denounce the Admiralty as a member of the House of Commons.[21]

Beresford enjoyed playing the role of a maverick reformer. Upon returning from Sudan in 1886, he was again elected to Parliament. The Prince of Wales (and future King Edward VII) lobbied the prime minister, Robert Salisbury, to find a suitable spot for Charlie B in his government. Salisbury appointed him junior sea lord at the Admiralty, where Beresford promptly alienated his superiors, eventually resigning his post in January 1888.[22] Returning to Parliament, Beresford began to criticize the Admiralty, claiming that it was basing its requirements in the absence of any well-defined strategy or policy. He argued that the government should establish a definite standard for the fleet that would enable it to meet the nation's security and economic needs. Beresford called for a Royal Navy able to defeat the fleets of two powers combined, one of which should be France.[23]

Beresford was only echoing the concerns that led to the Three Admirals' Committee. Many politicians and members of the military felt that Beresford was using his platform in Parliament to attract attention to himself and gain credit for the ideas of others. Although Charlie B rarely offered any new insights on naval affairs and often spoke in a rambling, incoherent manner, he had a knack for attracting large audiences of devoted followers and was described by many contemporaries as "the biggest of all recorded gas bags."[24] Indeed, Beresford's observations were, on occasion, wildly at odds with the state of the maritime competition. At a time when guns capable of penetrating an ironclad's armor at ever greater ranges were coming into service and navies were rapidly abandoning the ram, Beresford declared, "In my opinion the ram is the most fatal weapon in naval warfare—more fatal even than the torpedo."[25]

Salisbury remarked to the Queen that Beresford "is too greedy of popular applause to get on in a public department. He is constantly playing his own game at the expense of his colleagues."[26] Charlie B continued sniping at the Navy over the next two decades, even as he rose to the rank of admiral. Ultimately, he would lead the so-called Syndicate of Discontent that nearly derailed the Royal Navy's massive effort to adapt to the new ways of war.

The Three Admirals' Report and the Two-Power Standard

The Three Admirals' Report was presented to Parliament in February 1889. It concluded that blockade remained feasible. The admirals, however, found that steam and torpedoes were making close blockade employing existing methods impractical. They concluded that "provided that a suitable anchorage can be secured in the immediate neighbourhood of the enemy stronghold, the advantages would be in favour of the ironclad fleet occupying such a position, and maintaining a sufficient number of swift look-out vessels off the port in direct communication by signal, or cable from a telegraph look-out ship." To sustain the blockade at a greater distance, however, the Navy would require a much larger force in proportion to the blockaded fleet than was currently thought adequate. This translated into a minimum advantage of five to three in battleships and two to one in cruisers. Their report concluded that the Navy was "altogether inadequate" for offensive operations in a war against even one great power, and therefore, they were "decidedly of opinion that no time should be lost in placing the Navy beyond comparison with that of any two Powers."[27]

The so-called Two-Power Standard was nothing new. It extended back at least to the early nineteenth century. In 1817, shortly after the conclusion of Napoleon's last threat to the European order, Britain's foreign minister, Lord Robert Castlereagh, stated that Britain's objective should be "to keep up a navy equal to the navies of any two Powers that can be brought against us."[28]

Following an examination of the statements of past prime ministers and first lords of the Admiralty, Lord George Hamilton, the current first lord, argued that the "leading idea" behind Britain's naval preparations had *always* been that its "establishment should be on such a scale that it should be equal to the naval strength of any two other countries." This Two-Power Standard, he maintained, was neither new nor provocative. In adopting it, Britain would merely be sustaining the position set by earlier governments.[29]

It was understood that the standard would be measured primarily in terms of battleships but that Britain required a substantial superiority in cruisers to defend its seaborne commerce. The standard would be measured in terms of warships of the newest type and most advanced design.[30] Some maritime experts and others in government pressed for more details on how such a standard might be determined. The noted strategist John Colomb, a retired captain of the Royal Marines and member of Parliament, argued that "one could not base calculations of superiority merely on the abstract question of numbers," as was implied by the Two-Power Standard. Beresford also objected, declaring, "Nothing could be more misleading, nothing more ridiculous, than comparing the numbers or tonnage of the fleets of England with those of France or any other Power. What should be compared is the work the respective forces have to do."[31]

Thus, Colomb believed the standard should be judged in terms of "the power necessary to keep the enemy's battleships in their harbours" through blockade.[32] Although many political leaders might concede the points made by Colomb and Beresford, it was difficult, if not impossible, to determine with precision the composition of the fleet that would meet their criteria, owing to the wide range of contingencies that might confront the Navy and the rapid pace of technological change, among other variables.

Yet it was also clear that some measure needed to be established as a rule of thumb that could be generally understood by the body politic, hence the attraction of the seemingly simple, straightforward Two-Power Standard. As Colomb admitted, "There were obviously details which could not be explained in the House of Commons or to the man in the street; and, therefore, something had to be done to satisfy public opinion, . . . and the rough and ready Two Power Standard was adopted."[33]

The Two-Power Standard adopted in 1889 was directed against the French and Russian navies and validated in 1891 with the Franco-Russian entente (soon to become an alliance). Concerns over Britain's ability to maintain the Two-Power Standard quickly made their way into the public debate. In 1893, the London Chamber of Commerce reported that Britain had 12.5 million tons of merchant shipping afloat, against less than a million tons for France and Russia combined, and had seaborne trade to the value of £970 million, against only £331 million for France and Russia together. Yet, it was noted, Britain had fewer armored ships in the Mediterranean than the French, and its total tonnage of armored ships built and building was less than France's and Russia's combined, suggesting that France and Russia together would exceed the Royal Navy's number of capital ships by the end of the decade. The implication was clear: Britain's enormous seaborne commerce was at risk.

The Admiralty was most concerned over Britain's declining naval power in the Mediterranean, the lifeline to the nation's empire in East

Africa and Asia. Here the Royal Navy confronted the fleets of Russia and France. In time of war, fears were that the British fleet based at Malta could be trapped between the French fleet to its west and the Russian fleet to its east. Some officials advocated adopting a "Scuttle Policy," repositioning the fleet from Malta to Egypt and Gibraltar and turning the "Med Sea" into a "dead sea." Successive governments refused to abandon the imperial lifeline, moving instead to strengthen the fleet at Malta. Still, during the Armenian crisis of 1895, the Admiralty, supported by the majority of the Cabinet, refused to send the Mediterranean Fleet to Constantinople should a Russian fleet attempt to force the Dardanelles, over fears that it risked being cut off in the rear by the French.[34]

Indeed, during the quarter century that elapsed between the Two-Power Standard's adoption and World War I, there were periodic public alarms over the vulnerability of the British fleet to this or that particular state's naval program. These alarms often credited potential enemies with every warship type still on the active list, irrespective of its ability to accomplish the missions prescribed for them, as well as every major warship authorized in their future programs. In truth, neither the French nor the Russians ever succeeded in completing their programs, nor were they ever able to build as quickly or as cheaply as the British.[35]

Nevertheless, the British had legitimate cause for concern. The Russians increased their naval expenditures by 64 percent between 1889 and 1893, initiating construction on what were intended to be the fastest, most heavily armed cruisers of their time. The Italians, with an eye on the French naval buildup, began to construct battleships designed to accommodate the world's biggest guns. British apprehensions over French and Russian naval strength were magnified by rising maritime powers in Japan, the United States, and Germany. The Japanese fleet that would destroy its Russian rival at Tsushima was already under construction by the mid-1890s, and the first new American battleships had been completed.[36] Britain was able to mitigate the challenge posed by these two rising naval powers. As for the third, Germany, it would ultimately require the combined effort of all these countries, as well as France and Russia, to defeat Berlin's move to overturn the European balance of power.

Parliament's adoption of the Two-Power Standard sought to reassure the British people that maritime supremacy would be preserved. At the time of Queen Victoria's diamond jubilee, however, an astute observer would have identified major geopolitical, domestic, and military-technical trends that were eroding Britain's maritime advantage. Sustaining it would require the Royal Navy to undertake an extended period of disruptive innovation.

Torpedo Boats and Close Blockade

As the Admiralty worked to implement the Two-Power Standard, the growing strength of Britain's traditional and rising naval rivals was not its only concern. As the fleet exercises of the 1880s showed, the challenge posed by torpedo-armed boats, both to its blockading force and to its trade, could not be met through traditional means and methods.[37]

Considering the rapid pace of technological change, the Admiralty understood that each maneuver provided only a snapshot of a constantly shifting maritime competition. Any findings emerging from exercises were almost certain to have a short shelf life. Frequent maneuvers were needed to keep abreast of new dangers to be countered and emerging opportunities that might be exploited.

The 1890 fleet maneuvers were designed to test the threat posed to the Royal Navy by torpedo boats—specifically, French torpedo boats—and pitted a "British" force of two squadrons of ironclads and torpedo gunboats ("torpedo-boat catchers") against an "enemy" torpedo-boat flotilla. The maneuvers found the "French" flotilla surprising the "British" fleet at anchor, compelling it to withdraw, whereupon the "French" torpedo boats feasted on British merchant shipping in the Channel. The admiral commanding the "British" force protested the results, arguing that the "French" attacked before issuing a formal declaration of war. The admiral's protest notwithstanding, the Navy's director of naval intelligence (DNI), Captain Cyprian Bridge, believed that the threat posed by French torpedo boats stationed along the Channel demanded attention. The Admiralty sided with Bridge, directing that countermeasures be developed to defeat the torpedo boats, as the Navy's torpedo gunboats failed to prove their effectiveness. This triggered a series of counter-torpedo-boat maneuvers, while adding urgency to efforts to develop a ship capable of defeating the torpedo-boat menace: the torpedo-boat destroyer.[38]

The 1891 maneuvers continued the effort to find ways to counter the torpedo-boat menace. The exercise called for "enemy" torpedo boats to attack a British ironclad squadron supported by cruisers and torpedo gunboats. With the torpedo boats unable to reprise their surprise attack, their limitations were on display, as "British" torpedo-boat catchers kept them from attacking the squadron. The Naval Intelligence Department (NID), which functioned as a naval staff in the absence of a formal staff, concluded that if torpedo-boat catchers aggressively countered the torpedo boats, the fleet could maintain a close blockade.[39] Though hardly a ringing endorsement of close blockade operations, the NID's findings offered hope.

Over the next three years, the Royal Navy's maneuvers focused more broadly on the torpedo-boat threat to the Royal Navy's command of the high seas. The August 1892 maneuvers found a "British" fleet organized along traditional lines operating in narrow waters and tasked with establishing command of the sea while effecting a junction of two divisions of the fleet screened by torpedo-boat catchers and torpedo boats. The "enemy" fleet was organized differently, around cruisers, torpedo boats, and some coastal defense craft. Once again, the "British" fleet successfully employed its screening forces to ward off the "enemy" fleet and unite its two divisions.[40] Nevertheless, there were concerns that a battle fleet operating in narrow waters, such as the English Channel, would be running greater risks than in the past. The exercise again found torpedo boats far more effective in defeating a close blockade in coastal waters than in participating in open ocean operations.

The following year's maneuvers pitted two more evenly matched fleets. The "British" battle fleet was slightly superior to its rival, but the "enemy" possessed an advantage in torpedo boats. The maneuvers saw enemy torpedo boats sinking ships—including some of their own. The price of their success, however, was high, with twenty-seven torpedo boats sent to the bottom in only five days. The maneuvers triggered a debate, with some officers arguing that, given the torpedo boats' high loss rate, the torpedo-boat threat might prove short-lived in war. Others countered that a high loss rate could prove acceptable if the torpedo boats could damage or destroy enough blockading ships to render the blockade ineffective. The 1894 maneuvers took up the issue, but poor weather precluded the torpedo boats' effective employment.[41]

In sum, the fleet maneuvers of the early 1890s suggested that the torpedo-boat threat in open waters could be successfully countered through a combination of a screening force and the torpedo boat's own lack of seaworthiness. At the same time, the exercises failed to assuage fears of the torpedo-boat threat to close blockade operations.

Fisher

The Royal Navy's fleet exercises led the first naval lord, Admiral Sir Frederick Richards, to declare, "The invention of the locomotive torpedo has introduced a feature into naval warfare which must render it a madness for fleets to move in narrow waters or to remain at anchor in exposed positions after nightfall when in the vicinity of torpedo flotilla organizations."[42] To counter the threat, Richards turned to Jackie Fisher, now a rear admiral and serving as the Navy's controller (third naval lord) responsible for procuring new systems and matériel.

Richards could not have made a better choice. Fisher, it will be recalled, had been among the first to identify the torpedo's potential, returning from sea duty in 1872 to head the torpedo section at the Navy's gunnery school, which was also responsible for mine training. There Fisher negotiated the purchase of the fleet's first Whitehead torpedo. In 1879, as captain of the newly completed battleship *Inflexible*, Fisher was primarily responsible for implementing the decision to introduce breech-loaded guns. Like Beresford, Jackie, as he was popularly known, had commanded a ship in the bombardment of Alexandria during the Anglo-Egyptian War. Like Beresford, Fisher emerged a hero.[43]

From 1886 to 1890, Fisher served as the director of naval ordnance, where he was responsible for developing the quick-firing guns that the Admiralty hoped would, through sheer firepower, counter the growing torpedo-boat threat. Fisher was promoted to rear admiral and assigned to the Portsmouth dockyards as admiral superintendent, traditionally a figurehead expected to refrain from engaging in management—a "backwater" assignment, in today's jargon. Apparently, no one told Jackie. Under his command, the dockyards, which had grown both slow and inefficient, were transformed into the cheapest and fastest building yards in the world for major warship construction. Fisher's efforts were aided considerably by the Royal Corps of Naval Constructors, established in 1883 and consisting of naval architects and engineers, along with skilled electrical workers. As Fisher recalled, "I felt positive of the fearful loss to the country in the slow construction of ships, and equally positive there was a remedy by ruthless dealing with contractors, with dockyard employees, and with the distribution of labor, and, backed up by each of the three First Lords I had the pleasure of serving with, and by 're-potting' the chief constructors and other obstructionists, the time of building a battleship of 15,000 tons was reduced nearly half!"[44] The results were indeed striking. From 1879 to 1907, Britain built sixty-two pre-dread-nought battleships, compared to a combined Franco-Russian total of sixty-one. Yet the Royal Navy's ships cost £63 million, nearly £6 million less than the Franco-Russian price, while the total tonnage was 857,729 to 744,940 in Britain's favor.[45]

In February 1891, Fisher submitted a memo identifying two possible solutions to the torpedo-boat problem. The first called for destroying the French *points d'appui*. Accepting the difficulties involved in succeeding with a massive preemptive strike, Fisher offered an alternative involving offensive patrolling, employing cheap ships capable of maintaining themselves off the French coast and enjoying an advantage in speed over British torpedo-boat catchers and size relative to the torpedo boats they hunted. These "destroyers," as they eventually became known, would, it was hoped, enable the Royal Navy to continue conducting close blockades. As Fisher put it, "our real line of defense lies on the French side of the Channel."[46]

Fisher's idea was adopted. The first torpedo-boat destroyer, *Havock*, was equipped with guns, not torpedoes. In exercises, *Havock* showed itself capable of overtaking torpedo boats. Buoyed by the results, by 1894 thirty-six of the twenty-seven-knot destroyers were in service, with sixty-six larger thirty-knot ships laid down or procured by the turn of the century. Over the next decade, the torpedo-gunboat catchers would evolve into the *Scout* class cruisers, and the torpedo-boat destroyers into the first true (*River* class) destroyers.[47]

While working on launching the torpedo-boat destroyers, Fisher was also engaged with the construction of the *Royal Sovereign* class of battleships. The general features of the battleships were approved by the board of the Admiralty in August 1888. At 15,585 tons, *Royal Sovereign* was the biggest ship built thus far in Portsmouth and the first steel battleship, with eighteen-inch armor plate. The ship was hailed for its remarkable balance between armor, armament, speed, and sea-keeping. Thanks to Fisher's reforms, the entire class was completed in the remarkably short space of five years. Fisher pointed out, "If you build two ships in the same time as it formerly took to build one . . . instead of a ship being almost ob-solete by the time she is commissioned, she is in the prime of her power." Admiral Richards proclaimed that the *Royal Sovereign*s "provided the Brit-ish Navy with the finest group of fighting ships afloat."[48]

By the mid-1890s, Fisher, by virtue of his early work on torpedoes at the gunnery school and as captain of *Excellent*, director of naval ordnance, and then third sea lord and controller, stood as a central figure in the Royal Navy's efforts to maintain its maritime dominance in a period of disruptive geopolitical and military-technical change. Having come aboard a Navy of wooden-hulled sailing ships, he now served in a fleet defined by steam and steel.

Yet if the naval competition appeared to have slowed in the mid-1890s, it soon surged ahead. Advances in torpedo design and gunnery and the emergence of the submarine, along with tectonic shifts in the geopolitical environment, resulted in Fisher pursuing innovation on a far grander scale.

Growing Threats Above and Beneath the Waves

The late 1890s and early 1900s witnessed France launching commerce-raiding cruisers, continuing to seek ways to enhance torpedo-boat operations, and exploiting technology that promised to make submarines more than curiosities. Regarding the latter, the French had conducted trials in 1888 and 1890 with submarines, which were then little more than novelties. They were, however, encouraged enough to initiate work on two boats. One, the *Gustave Zédé*, participated in the French fleet maneuvers of November 1898.

The exercise saw the boat's skipper, Lieutenant Lucian Mottez, sail his craft forty miles from Toulon to the Isles d'Hyrères, whereupon he "torpedoed" the battleship *Magenta* twice, once when the ship was moving and once when it was anchored. The great-power navies began vigorously exploring how the torpedo—the "devil's device"—might be employed on submersible craft.[49]

The Admiralty's worries over the torpedo threat were heightened when, in 1895, Ludwig Obry introduced his gyroscope, a precision-crafted instrument capable of achieving the very high rotation rates needed for torpedoes to sustain their course over far greater distances than had previously been possible.[50] By 1898, Obry's gyroscopes were being fitted on torpedoes to control their vertical rudders, doubling their effective range.

In 1897, the French began cutting battleship construction in favor of launching large cruisers designed primarily for commerce raiding. They were fast enough to run away from any battleship capable of sinking them and powerful enough to run down and destroy any smaller cruiser, thereby rendering Britain's trade-protection cruisers obsolete.[51]

In February 1898, George Goschen, first lord of the Admiralty, concluded that the French now understood that their cruisers, not their battleships, posed the greater threat to Britain.[52]

The cruisers did indeed complicate an already difficult situation for the Royal Navy, particularly in Asian waters. Up to this time, the major naval powers' Pacific squadrons included gunboats and cruising vessels, with few, if any, major warships, a problem the Admiralty could manage without much difficulty. Now Russia and France began stationing first-class capital ships with their Asian squadrons. By 1900, the Russian squadron at Port Arthur boasted six modern battleships.[53] Japan was building a powerful, modern navy. Despite the formidable costs involved, the British government believed it had to meet the Russian challenge— but how? The early 1900s saw Britain straining to finance the construction of battleships to maintain the Two-Power Standard, to address the rapidly emerging torpedo and submarine threat, and to build modern armored cruisers to keep pace with France and Russia.

Britain's initial response lacked imagination and fiscal prudence. The idea of convoys remained anathema to a navy devoted to the offense. The default choice, therefore, was simply to build armored cruisers to match those laid down by the French and Russians. But armored cruisers were almost as expensive to build as battleships and even more expensive to maintain. This placed additional strain on the Royal Navy's budget at a time when naval estimates were coming under increased scrutiny. Moreover, it also created manpower problems.[54] It took until 1904, when Fisher came to power, for the Admiralty to devise an innovative response to its problems.

The Système Ballard

The late 1890s found the Admiralty focused on the threat posed by the navies of the Dual Alliance powers, France and Russia. The Royal Navy's strategy remained centered on putting the enemy ships on the bottom in a major engagement or blockading the enemy fleet at its bases. The growing difficulties involved in maintaining a close blockade, however, led the Admiralty to adopt the advanced base concept to support its squadrons engaged in an observational blockade, where ships operated at a greater distance offshore.

The 1895–99 maneuvers focused primarily on the blockade problem and torpedo boats, in particular, and as a test bed for the new destroyers.

They revealed British torpedo-boat countermeasures to be less effective than expected, although destroyers proved far more effective in blockade operations than torpedo-boat catchers were. The 1899 maneuvers were notable in identifying the value of employing wireless telegraphy in convoy operations—which the Admiralty continued to discount—as an effective means of safeguarding British trade.[55]

Apart from Fisher, arguably no other individual had more influence on the Royal Navy's strategic development in the two decades prior to World War I than George Ballard. Born in Bombay, India, Ballard joined the Navy in 1875 at thirteen, the same age as had Fisher. By the mid-1890s, he was considered one of the Navy's best strategic thinkers.

In examining the fleet's decade of maneuvers, Ballard concluded that it was becoming increasingly difficult to prevent at least some enemy commerce-raiding ships from slipping through a Royal Navy blockade. In a Royal United Services Institute prize-winning essay published in 1897, Ballard recommended implementing an observational blockade sustained by the seizure of advanced bases that would enable ships of the blockading force to refuel, rearm, and undergo maintenance while operating forward, rather than shuttling back and forth from a main base. The observational blockading force would be backstopped by cruiser "hunter" patrols assigned to destroy any enemy raiders that slipped through. Ballard called for the Royal Navy squadrons blockading French squadrons at Dunkirk, Calais, and Le Havre to use Dover and Portsmouth for support. For the Cherbourg and Brest blockades, advanced bases would be located at the island of Alderney for the former and the islands of Ushant and Île de Groix for the latter. Ballard's concept was so insightful that the French, impressed by his work, named it the Système Ballard. Ballard's concept became the focus of British fleet maneuvers.[56]

The Royal Navy's July 1900 maneuvers explored the two missions addressed in Ballard's essay: high-seas commerce defense and blockade. The maneuvers, however, proved inconclusive. The following year in August, the fleet examined the challenge of maintaining sea control of the English Channel. The "British" fleet (the Channel Fleet under Vice Admiral Sir Arthur Wilson) was tasked with securing control of the Channel, while the "French" fleet (the Navy's Reserve Fleet commanded by Rear Admiral Sir Gerard Noel) was directed to accomplish the same. The "British" fleet prevailed, which was not surprising, as Wilson was widely regarded as the Navy's best tactician and his fleet was considerably more powerful than that of the "French."

The maneuver's principal value was the insights it produced, especially with respect to the value of destroyers, which proved ineffective in capturing merchant ships. Destroyers could sink them, of course, but this would violate the rules of war. The destroyer also exhibited shortcomings when armed with torpedoes, as both sides feared they would inadvertently attack their own ships.[57]

The following month, the Royal Navy's Mediterranean Fleet, under Admiral Fisher, held maneuvers against the Channel Fleet. The maneuvers made a striking impression on Admiral Beresford, serving under Fisher. Like most officers, Charlie B had had little training handling a fleet in a major engagement against another first-class maritime power. He wrote, "I was fifty-five years of age and had been forty-three years in the Service before I and my brother Officers discovered what was the proper position for an Admiral in his Fleet in action." He described the experience as "*Simply Incredible!!!*" Beresford later said that the exercises organized by Fisher taught "admirals ... lessons they ought to have known as lieutenants. . . . Fisher deserves the lasting gratitude of the Empire for having started these practical manoeuvers in time of peace."[58]

Fisher admired Beresford, declaring him "a first-rate officer afloat": "no better exists in my opinion." But that was the limit of Jackie's praise. He was skeptical of Beresford's thinking on the future needs of the Navy. "There is a good deal in what Beresford urges," wrote Fisher, "but he exaggerates so much that his good ideas become deformities." In short, though Beresford's seamanship and personal bravery were exemplary, he continued to exhibit little interest (or talent) in matters of strategy or even operations. Percy Scott, who was at the forefront of fleet gunnery innovations, remarked, "In the Navy we knew he was not a sailor, but thought he was a politician; in the House of Commons, they knew he was not a politician, but thought he was a sailor." In the 1890s, increasing gun ranges had consigned the ram to history's dustbin. Yet Beresford, in an interview, declared, "In my opinion the ram is the most fatal weapon in naval warfare—more fatal even than the torpedo." In another interview, Beresford proposed that seventeen "old but useful" ships be rearmed with modern guns, discounting the ships' obsolete engines, the time it would take to obtain new guns, and the extra personnel required to man the ships at a time when the Navy was experiencing manpower shortages. Fisher reported Beresford's idea to the first lord, drawing his attention "to Beresford's indirect criticism of the Admiralty in his interview as to rearming certain ships. . . . He really is very stupid, but he can't resist self-advertisement." As Lord Salisbury succinctly stated, "I am afraid CB is an ass!"[59]

The Royal Navy continued its efforts to sustain the blockade in the 1902 maneuvers, which brought together elements of the Mediterranean and Channel Fleets. One "British" (Mediterranean) fleet, commanded by Admiral Sir Compton Domville, was joined by a second "British" (Channel) fleet, commanded by Vice Admiral Wilson. They were tasked with blockading the "French" fleet, commanded by Captain Prince Louis Battenberg, at the port of Argostoli (representing Toulon) on Cephalonia, an island off Greece's west coast. On the night of October 5–6, Battenberg ordered his cruisers to attempt to slip past the blockade as a feint to draw off the British force. The diversion succeeded, and Battenberg's battleships effected a breakout.

Although the blockading fleets' battle force suffered little damage, their watching force lost eight of their fourteen destroyers. Battenberg's "enemy" fleet, with half as many, lost only two. Moreover, even as the "enemy" fleet was given ten days to escape the blockade, it did so in only five. In brief, destroyers could not be counted on to bottle up a blockaded force using close watch tactics. Even more discouraging were the results of two war games conducted at the Naval College earlier that year, in which close blockades of Bizerta and Oran also proved ineffective. Making matters worse, the French were now incorporating submarines in their counter-blockade maneuvers. In evaluating the French exercise, the NID concluded that "the blockade of a port defended by torpedo boats and submarines is almost impossible."[60]

The Royal Navy's 1903 maneuvers confirmed recent trends in the maritime competition. Destroyers were ordered to support blockade operations and defeat enemy torpedo boats, while their ability to screen the main fleet from torpedo boats was also evaluated. Once again, the destroyers supporting the blockade took heavy losses while failing to prevent the boats from escaping their base. On the open seas, however, the destroyers screening the main fleet succeeded in warding off torpedo-boat attacks, suffering no losses.[61] But the maneuvers had yet to tackle the rapidly growing problem posed by submarines armed with torpedoes.

The Growing Submarine and Torpedo Menace

In the years leading up to Queen Victoria's diamond jubilee, considerable effort had been expended, especially in France and the United States, on developing submarines. In January 1898, shortly after the grand review at Spithead during the course of a French Navy experiment, one of its two practical submarines, the *Gustave Zédé*, successfully torpedoed an anchored battleship. Two years later, the *Gustave Zédé* became the first submarine to torpedo a moving battleship during exercises.[62] The revolution that was denied the Jeune École enthusiasts in the 1880s seemed about to be realized twenty years later. In Britain, Admiral Wilson fumed, "The submarine is underhanded, unfair and damned un-English."[63] The admiral observed, "We cannot stop invention in this direction [and] we cannot delay its introduction any longer, but we should still avoid doing anything to assist in its improvement in order that our means of trapping and destroying it may develop at a greater rate than the submarine boats themselves."[64]

Wilson understood the problem. It did not matter that Britain could quickly outproduce another navy in submarines. Submarines, it seemed at the time, could not fight submarines, at least not underwater. Britain could build as many submarines as it liked, and France would still be able to dispatch its own stealthy, silent boats through any blockade to strike at the Royal Navy's battle fleet and ravage British trade. The Royal Navy's battle line that so outclassed that of any other navy, the French hoped, would now become irrelevant.

A Glass Half Full?

Despite Admiral Wilson's hopes, the first decade of the new century found the submarine threat advancing far more rapidly than the means to defeat it. By January 1904, it was estimated that the Royal Navy's A Class submarines could operate as far off the coast as the Channel Islands. The new B and C Class submarines, which were about to enter production, would probably be able to operate anywhere in the English Channel for up to a week.[65] The D Class submarine, which came into service in 1908, could remain at sea for a week and had sufficient range to reach the German coast. As one submarine commander noted, "From 1908 onwards, submarines had enough success during maneuvers to open the eyes of all senior officers not willfully blind."[66]

For Jackie Fisher, the submarine represented both a danger and an opportunity. The danger posed was primarily a consequence of the submarine's stealth—there seemed no way to detect it while it was submersed—and its ability to fire torpedoes, whose range was increasing rapidly. Indeed, a torpedo warhead was much more destructive than a shell fired by the biggest battleship gun. In 1903, Admiralty experiments revealed that existing armored warships were far more vulnerable to damage from hits below the water line than had been believed. Consequently, submarines armed with long-range torpedoes had the potential to displace the battle line as the ultimate arbiter of war at sea.[67]

But submarines offered the Admiralty opportunities, as well. In August 1901, three years before Fisher became first sea lord, Hugh Oakeley Arnold-Forster, Parliamentary and financial secretary to the Admiralty, circulated a memorandum arguing perceptively that the Admiralty could employ submarines to defend the British Isles from invasion: "The introduction of this new weapon, so far from being a disadvantage to us, will strengthen our position. We have no desire to invade any other country; it's important that we ourselves are not invaded. If the submarine proves as formidable as some authorities think is likely to be the case, the bombardment of our ports, and the landing of troops on our shores will become absolutely impossible."[68]

Arnold-Forster's logic resonated with those who felt that, just as submarines would make enemy coastal areas increasingly risky areas for surface-fleet blockade operations, they could also provide the same deterrent effect against rival navies attempting to support an invasion of Great Britain. Admiral Battenberg concurred: "The establishment of submarine stations along the South Coast of England ought to go a long way towards dispelling the ever-recurring fears of invasion. ... [The] French in all their utterances on the subject—be they Ministerial speeches or press articles—point out with pride that the existence of submarines as part of the defense mobile [*sic*] make any attempt at invasion of French territory the act of lunacy. *They are quite right and the argument cuts both ways.*"[69] Fisher agreed. Following the 1903 fleet maneuvers, he wrote a paper, titled "The Effects of Submarine Boats," presenting his vision of submarine warfare:

> The Submarine Boat which carries this automobile torpedo is up to the present date absolutely unattackable. When you see [enemy surface ships] on the horizon, you can send others after them to attack them or drive them away! You can see them—you can fire at them—you can avoid them—you can chase them— but with the Submarine Boat you can do nothing! ... It must revolutionise Naval Tactics for this simple reason—that the

present ... formation of ships in single line presents a target of such length that the chances are altogether in favour of the Whitehead torpedo hitting some ship in the line. ... It affects the Army, because, imagine even one submarine boat with a flock of transports in sight loaded with some two or three thousand troops! Imagine the effects of one such transport going to the bottom in a few seconds with its living freight![70]

In the coming years, in pursuing what later became known as the "Scheme," Fisher and others combined submarines with destroyers under the concept of "flotilla defense" to provide a final line of defense against invasion.[71]

Placing greater reliance on submarines also appealed to Britain's political leadership, which was calling for fiscal austerity with respect to defense spending. Even before becoming first sea lord, Fisher argued that submarines would depreciate in value far more slowly than recently built capital ships did. Even older boats, he argued, by virtue of their stealth would continue posing a threat to targets such as enemy troop transports. His ideas appealed to Prime Minister Arthur Balfour, who wrote to the Admiralty's first lord, William Palmer (Lord Selborne), in early 1904, "I wish we had more submarines," noting, "they are, after all, cheap."[72]

A Broad-Based Challenge

The submarine's maturation was matched by that of the torpedo. Obry's gyroscope had greatly enhanced torpedo accuracy. In 1905, the "Elswick Heater" provided a major boost in torpedo range and speed. At the time, Japanese torpedoes being employed in the war with Russia ran at less than twenty knots to achieve ranges of around 4,000 yards. Less than a year later, the German Navy's G-type torpedo boasted a range of 6,560 yards and a speed of thirty-six knots.[73]

In looking back on these developments after the Great War, Admiral Reginald Bacon described how the battle fleet would have to transform itself: "This insidious and somewhat sneaking weapon had, in the intervening years altered the whole of naval tactics, for its deadly menace had forced the effective fighting range of ships up from the 3,000 yards or so at Tsushima to some fourteen, sixteen, or even eighteen thousand yards at Jutland. ... A decision had to be obtained outside of torpedo range, otherwise the action would merely have developed into a gamble in which skill and training would have been sacrificed to sinkings by the chance adventures of torpedo attack."[74]

The marriage of the submarine and torpedo was about to revolutionize war at sea. For many observers at the time, however, this was hardly self-evident. It took a visionary leader like Fisher to move the Royal Navy, often kicking and screaming, to adapt to the radically changing maritime competition.

Yet there was no denying that the Admiralty confronted a strategic dilemma following the disappointing results of the early-1900s exercises. It had committed itself to finding a way to sustain some form of blockade to defend its homeland, empire, and commerce during war. Even though blockade appeared an increasingly risky course of action, the Admiralty, having placed a big bet on destroyers, saw no readily apparent alternatives when failing to solve the torpedo-boat problem. Making matters worse, the destroyers were incapable of maintaining normal fleet cruising speeds. Consequently, in their current form, destroyers were ill-suited in the role for which they seemed best suited: screening enemy torpedo craft from the battle fleet.

All this was occurring at a time when Great Britain's spending on its Navy was growing rapidly, triggering calls from the country's political leaders for significant cuts to the Navy's budget. It took a radical shift in the Admiralty's approach for the Royal Navy to maintain its dominant position in a time of fiscal austerity and disruptive shifts in the character of war at sea. Fortune intervened, in the form of a geopolitical revolution and the appointment of Admiral Fisher as first sea lord.

A Geopolitical Revolution

At the time of the Queen's diamond jubilee, Britain's geopolitical position was growing less favorable. The Dual Alliance powers, France and Russia, continued dominating the Admiralty's planning, particularly in the Mediterranean. That being said, it could not ignore the emergence of two rising naval powers outside Europe, the United States and Japan, that could not be blockaded or brought to battle by the Mediterranean or Home Fleets. The U.S. Navy had performed well in the war with Spain in 1898, and its "Great White Fleet" would soon be heading out on a world tour. The Imperial Japanese Navy, much of which was being built in British shipyards, would soon demonstrate its prowess in the crucible of war. Then there was Germany, whose economy, like that of the United States, had surpassed Britain's, and whose kaiser was keen on building a powerful modern fleet.

The waning of the Pax Britannica found Whitehall searching for diplomatic means to shore up Britain's geopolitical position and, in so doing, relieve some of the stress on the Royal Navy's global commitments —and its defense budget estimates.[75] Remarkably, within the span of a few short years, the British engineered a diplomatic revolution that saw France transformed from being the obsession of the Admiralty's fleet maneuvers to a quasi-ally, and the United States and Japan becoming benign rivals and allies, respectively, with the latter effectively eliminating the Russian fleet from the geostrategic board. That left only the Kaiser's rapidly growing fleet as the principal menace to British maritime dominance.

The United States and Japan

The United States posed a unique problem for British naval strategists. Toward the latter part of the nineteenth century, the North American giant had become the world's leading economic power and seemed destined to continue its impressive growth. Senior British officials knew that the United States had the ability, should it desire, to build a navy of enormous size. Lord Selborne, not long after assuming his position as first lord of the Admiralty in 1900, declared privately, "If the United States were to build such a navy as they can well afford even the Two Power Standard would become beyond our strength. The standard which I believe now to be the true one is not one which could be publicly stated. In Parliament I would always speak, in general terms, of not falling below the Two Power Standard. To the Cabinet I would suggest that if we make such provisions as will offer us the reasonable certainty of success in a war with France and Russia, we shall have fully provided for all contingencies."[76] Essentially, Selborne proposed that British policy should assume that the United States would remain a sleeping giant, or at least not a hostile naval rival to Britain, and that the Two-Power Standard would be applied against the Dual Alliance, which posed an immediate danger. Fisher expressed his views more directly: "The more carefully this problem is considered, the more tremendous do the difficulties which would confront Great Britain in a war with the United States appear to be. . . . [That it] would be unpopular and that the outcome of the struggle could

only result sooner or later, in the loss of Canada, are the conclusions difficult to avoid."[77] Given this situation, Fisher advised the government to
"use all possible means to avoid such a war," as "it seems an utter waste of
time to prepare for it."[78] As for Canada, which would no doubt be a prime
target in the event of war with the United States, the Admiralty's
view was that Ottawa was effectively on its own and should do its best to
get along with its southern neighbor. Simply put, the United States
was not to be included in calculations pertaining to the Two-Power
Standard.[79]

Britain's problem in the Far East was trickier. As noted earlier, when
the naval competition heated up in the 1890s, things changed, and France
and Russia began to station first-class warships in the Far East. In the
spring of 1898, the Royal Navy had three battleships and ten cruisers of
various descriptions in Chinese waters, while France and Russia together
had three major warships and twelve smaller ones. Germany seemed to
hold the balance between the two sides, with two battleships and five unarmored cruisers. Japan, however, now possessed a navy that included
three battleships and twelve unarmored cruisers. Despite its relatively
small size compared to that of the major European maritime powers, the
Japanese fleet was deemed by the Admiralty to be "very formidable," and
there was every prospect that it would continue to expand.[80]

Britain's immediate response was to strengthen its squadron in
China with second-class battleships and to build a class of smaller battleships that could move through the Suez Canal to reinforce its Far East
squadron. By 1900, however, the Russian squadron at Port Arthur included six modern battleships. Despite the large cost involved, the British saw no alternative but to follow suit. Yet as in the Mediterranean,
both Whitehall and the Admiralty saw the Royal Navy's dominant position in the Far East eroding rapidly.[81]

By Britain's excluding the U.S. fleet from the Two-Power Standard
and its implicit ceding of maritime supremacy in the Western Hemi-
sphere to the United States, the stage was set, at least in principle, for diplomacy to address the challenge in the Far East. Advocating an
arrangement with Japan, Lord Selborne argued that if Britain found itself at war with France and Russia, "the decisive battles ... would certainly be fought in European waters," and that the Royal Navy should
attempt to ensure that it amassed the strongest possible force in this theater of operations.[82] Selborne continued, "If the British Navy were defeated in the Mediterranean and the Channel the stress of our position

would not be alleviated by any amount of superiority in the Chinese seas. If, on the other hand, it were to prove supreme in the Mediterranean and the Channel, even serious disasters in Chinese waters would matter little. These considerations furnish, therefore, a sound argument for keeping our naval strength in Chinese waters as low as is compatible with the safety of the Empire."[83] Having assumed away any threat to British interests in the New World by relying on the goodwill of Britain's American cousins, Whitehall looked to securing British interests in East Asia while concentrating overwhelming naval power against the Dual Alliance in Europe by forging an alliance with Japan. Such an alliance would find the combined battleship strength of Britain and Japan in Asian waters at eleven, two ahead of the combined strength of France and Russia, along with a preponderance of cruisers as well.

The Kaiser's Fleet

Although Whitehall intended to use the diplomatic tools of appeasement and alliance to shore up its position on the periphery and maintain the Two-Power Standard against France and Russia in Europe, there remained the matter of Germany. This rapidly rising power in Central Europe clearly had the industrial potential to displace both France and Russia as naval powers and, under Kaiser Wilhelm II, increasingly manifested an interest in doing so. By 1900, Germany was second only to the United States in iron and steel production and was producing twice as much iron annually as Great Britain. The Admiralty's concerns regarding Germany's rapidly growing maritime potential were made clear in 1905, even as the Russian fleet was on its way to its doom at the Tsushima Strait. Lord Selborne stated, "It is an error to suppose that the Two Power Standard adopted by this country some fifteen years ago, ratified by every Government since, and accepted as an article of faith by the whole nation has ever had reference only to France and Russia. It has always referred to the two strongest Naval Powers at any given moment. . . . If the Russian navy were to emerge from the present war materially weakened, the result will be that the Two Power Standard must hereafter be calculated with reference to the navies of France and Germany."[84] That Germany stood next in line to inherit a place in the Two-Power Standard was a consequence of Kaiser Wilhelm II's fascination with sea power, his mixture of admiration and envy of the Royal Navy, and his desire to have a fleet reflecting Germany's growing stature in the world.

The Kaiser saw what the numerical, material, and strategic superiority of the Royal Navy could do during the Fashoda crisis between Britain and France over control of the Upper Nile River. The crisis was the climax of a series of territorial disputes in Africa between France and Great Britain. In 1898, the French sent an expedition to Fashoda on the White Nile River. Britain saw the expedition as a French move to control the Upper Nile River basin that fed the Nile River. The French force met a far larger Anglo-Egyptian force under Lord Kitchener. During the standoff between the two forces, the Royal Navy began to mobilize its reserves. Given Britain's maritime supremacy, the French would find it difficult to reinforce their expedition if war broke out. Moreover, France, increasingly concerned over Germany's growing might, was hardly in a position to take on Britain as well. In November, the French ordered their troops to withdraw from the area. Observing France's humiliating diplomatic retreat and the key role the Royal Navy played in bringing it about, the Kaiser commented, "The poor French. . . . They have not read their Mahan!"[85]

Until Kaiser Wilhelm II's accession to the throne in 1888, Germany's navy had actually been headed by an army general. Germany's rapid ascension to the first rank of maritime powers began in 1897, when the Kaiser appointed Admiral Tirpitz as secretary of state of the German Imperial Naval Office. Tirpitz proved a master at dealing with the Reichstag, Germany's legislative body, which held the purse strings for military expenditures. His efforts quickly bore results. In 1898, it passed a naval law authorizing construction of a seagoing battle fleet. At the time, the German fleet barely rivaled France's northern squadron or the Russian Baltic fleet, and its modest mission centered on supporting the Army's flanks in the event of a war against France or Russia.[86]

In 1900, Tirpitz introduced a supplementary Navy Bill, arguing that protecting German overseas trade and securing its recently acquired colonies required a battle fleet sufficiently powerful that even the greatest sea power would not risk a war against it, lest it suffer losses that would imperil its position against the world's other maritime powers. This, as Tirpitz famously articulated, was a "Risk Fleet." The British Admiralty became increasingly focused on the Kaiser's fleet, especially since, "in marked contrast to the gross venality and bureaucratic inefficiency prevailing in the Russian service, the gadfly policies of the French and the chronic inefficiency of the Italian navy, the German service was notoriously hard-working, was backed by great industrial strength and was administered with single-minded determination."[87]

When war between Japan and Russia broke out in February 1904, both the French and the British feared being drawn into the conflict on the side of their allies while Germany stood on the sidelines enjoying the spectacle. To allay these fears, London and Paris negotiated a series of agreements signed in April 1904 resolving their differences in Asia, Africa, and the Americas. The British viewed this Entente Cordiale as enabling both powers to better address the German threat. Over time, however, it would blossom into the alliance that sustained the two ancient rivals through the Great War.[88]

The Japanese destruction of the Russian fleet at Tsushima, combined with the Entente Cordiale, left Germany as Britain's only major-power naval rival. This made Britain's challenge of maintaining a favorable naval balance less stressful, in part by shifting the competition's geographic focus. Sir Charles Ottley, director of naval intelligence, saw an opportunity for Britain to leverage its positional advantage by emphasizing economic warfare against Germany: "In view of the geographic conditions, the British Isles, lying like a breakwater 600 miles long, athwart the path of German trade with the West and remembering the immense strategic advantage of the French harbours so close to the mouth of the Elbe, I believe there would be no practical difficulty in proclaiming and maintaining an effective blockade of the entire German seaboard."[89]

To sum up, in the span of little more than five years, British diplomacy and the Russo-Japanese War greatly improved the country's geostrategic position. Old rivals France and Russia had been neutralized through the Entente Cordiale and by the Imperial Japanese Navy, respectively. Britain's American cousins, though flexing their maritime muscles, seemed content to focus on their recently won "empire" in the Caribbean and the Philippines and following George Washington's injunction to steer clear of foreign entanglements. Japan not only was a British ally but had proved its value by disposing of the Russian fleet. Only Germany possessed the means and motive to pose a major threat to Britain's maritime dominance.

The Need for Economies

Despite favorable changes in the geopolitical environment, neither Whitehall nor the Admiralty could ignore the relative decline of Britain's economic standing. Britain's efforts to maintain maritime supremacy in the face of rising regional maritime powers and a dynamic maritime competition stressed its financial resources. The British people were demanding expanded social services, and the Liberal Party's rise to power in 1905 stemmed, in no small way, from its pledge to meet this demand. Its ability to do so, however, was threatened by the costs incurred by the recently concluded Boer War, as well as the rising cost of military manpower and matériel.

Despite the Royal Navy's great stature, the British Army had, since midcentury, enjoyed higher annual budgets.[90] Defense expenditures ballooned during the Boer War, which lasted from 1899 to 1902. Early estimates were that a conflict in South Africa would cost £5 million to £10 million a year. They quickly grew to £21.5 million. In 1900, expenditures on the British Army rose to £44.1 million, surging over the following two years to £92.4 million and £94.2 million.[91] Owing to the expense associated with new technology and the relatively rapid obsolescence of warships, the price of naval power was also rising dramatically. Between 1889 and 1900, the Royal Navy's budget roughly doubled, to the point where it absorbed more than a quarter of the government's revenue— and the Admiralty's demands for ever larger budgets showed no signs of abating. In the seven years prior to 1904, the naval estimates also nearly doubled, from £22.5 million to £41.7 million. Adding insult to injury, that year saw Britain's economy in recession and tax revenue declining.[92]

It was also increasingly difficult to man the fleet. Between 1889 and 1904, fleet manpower had more than doubled, to 131,100. The introduction of advanced technology into new ships found the Royal Navy's thirst for skilled sailors seemingly unquenchable. Roughly three-quarters of the seamen assigned to the battle cruiser *Invincible*, designed in 1906, required "skilled" ratings, as compared with only one-third of the seamen manning the armored cruiser *Drake*, designed only four years before.[93] The problem was compounded in that it took the Royal Navy roughly six years to qualify a seaman as a specialist and eight years to train an entire crew from scratch.[94] This was more than twice as long as it took to build a large ship. Consequently, for the Royal Navy to keep its warships at a high level of battle efficiency, it needed increasing numbers of experienced sailors, as well as high reenlistment rates. Yet the Navy was experiencing retention problems. Between 1900 and 1904, the Admiralty offered pay raises and, in some cases, financial incentives to boost retention, with little success. Thus, in 1904, at least a third of enlisted personnel had less than five years' experience. One of the most serious complaints among sailors was the large amount of time they spent on deployments overseas.[95] The need to address this issue would become a significant factor in Jackie

Fisher's "Scheme" for redeploying Britain's fleets when he became first sea lord.[96]

Another major cause of the Navy's manpower problems was simple mathematics: maintaining the numbers of ships required to meet the Two-Power Standard and patrolling the far reaches of the empire meant that very few warships had been decommissioned, even though the continued broad and rapid advance in military technology had made many of them of dubious value in combat.[97] The Royal Navy was also compelled to pay a significant overhead price, in terms of maintenance and operating costs, to keep these ships in the fleet. These costs acted as barnacles on a ship's hull, slowing Britain's ability to keep pace with the dynamic maritime competition.[98]

Given these trends, the state of affairs could not continue. In 1904, Austen Chamberlain, chancellor of the Exchequer, called for reductions in government spending, with particular emphasis on defense. He warned, "however reluctant we may be to face the fact, the time has come when we must frankly admit that the financial resources of the United Kingdom are inadequate to do all that we should desire in the matter of Imperial defense."[99]

Politicians were willing to lend an ear to those who could sustain the Royal Navy's dominant position within the new fiscal constraints. This meant looking for ways the Royal Navy could squeeze more value out of every pound and shilling in its budget. It also meant seizing opportunities to transform substantially the character of the maritime competition in ways that advantaged Great Britain, particularly by exploiting the ongoing rapid advances in technology, and especially if such actions could impose disproportionate costs on its naval rivals.

The task of formulating British naval policy fell to Lord Selborne, who was first lord of the Admiralty from 1900 to 1905. He, like the Liberal opposition, was a strong supporter of the Navy but also saw the need for economic reforms.[100] In May 1904, Selborne offered the job of first sea lord to Admiral Fisher, who offered not only to realize economies but to maintain Britain's naval primacy—but only if he could enact what he called his "Scheme."

Admiral Fisher

As noted earlier, Fisher, unlike most of his contemporaries, had a keen interest in matters of strategy and technology, including their interrelationship. In 1897, following his unprecedented five-and-a-half-year tour at the

Admiralty as the Royal Navy's controller, Fisher took command of the North America and West Indies Station, viewed as a maritime backwater for admirals no longer on the "fast track" to higher promotion. Yet only two years later, Fisher was selected for command of the Mediterranean Fleet, Britain's most powerful combination of warships. His command, which lasted until June 1902, deeply influenced Fisher's thinking on the maritime competition.

Before Fisher, the fleet's battleship commanders were typically found devoting enormous energy to polishing the great guns until they shined under the Mediterranean sun, with the ship's watertight doors below decks given similar treatment—until they were no longer watertight. Fisher would have none of it. As Lord Maurice Hankey, then a captain in the Royal Marines, recalled, "Before his [Fisher's] arrival the topics and arguments of the officer's messes . . . were mainly confined to such matters as the cleaning of paint and brasswork, the getting out of torpedo nets and anchors, and similar trivialities. After a year of Fisher's regime these were forgotten and were replaced by incessant controversies on tactics, strategy, gunnery, torpedo warfare, blockade, etc. It was a veritable renaissance and affected every officer in the fleet."[101] Fisher invited officers to lectures and discussions of tactics, gunnery, ship design, and engines, treating all opinions with respect. Fisher also made the first moves toward longer-range gunnery while pondering how to deal with the French emphasis on torpedo warfare. At the end of Beresford's command, he praised Fisher, writing, "From a 12-knot Fleet with numerous breakdowns, he made a 15-knot Fleet without breakdowns." Charlie B cited twenty achievements that he attributed to Fisher—including some that he later claimed for himself![102]

In 1902, Selborne appointed Fisher second sea lord, tasking him with fixing the fleet's manpower shortfall. Fisher reported back that only radical reforms could solve the problem. This proved too much for the first sea lord, Admiral Lord Walter Kerr, and Selborne, unwilling at that time to make the tough choices involved, backed Kerr.[103]

During this time, Fisher was recruited by Prime Minister Arthur Balfour to serve on what became known as the Esher Committee, to identify shortcomings that had emerged during the Boer War of 1899–1902. Defying the Admiralty's wishes, Fisher accepted Balfour's invitation. Among the committee's recommendations was a call to establish an organization for coordinating defense planning. In May 1904, the Committee of Imperial Defence (CID) was established, to be chaired by the prime minister, with Lord Esher serving as a member from 1906 to 1914.

Fisher's character was as exceptional as his naval background. Born in Ceylon into a family of modest means, he entered the Navy as a cadet at the age of thirteen. He was short and stocky, standing about five feet seven inches. Owing to bouts with dysentery and malaria, Fisher had a yellow tint to his skin, and this, combined with his features and place of birth, led his enemies to claim that he was part Chinese, calling him, among other things, the "Half-Caste" and the "Yellow Peril." Fisher gravitated naturally toward nonconformists, mavericks, and radicals of all kinds. He got on well with the two most notorious liberals of the time, Winston Churchill and David Lloyd George, and once cheekily suggested naming four of a new class of battleships *Winston, Churchill, Lloyd,* and *George.*[104]

All who came in contact with Fisher were inspired—for better or ill—by his enthusiasm. He once persuaded a group of captains to pull oars and handle wet cable "as if once again they were midshipmen." Dancing was an old pastime of the Royal Navy, and Fisher was ready to dance with anyone, male or female, at any time. If there was no music, he would whistle or hum a tune. Fisher also had a way with senior leaders. While serving as the captain of the Royal Navy's most powerful battleship in 1881, he was introduced to Prime Minister William Gladstone at a London party. Gladstone solemnly observed, "I really wonder the human mind can bear such responsibility." "Oh, sir," Fisher responded cheerily, "the common vulgar mind doesn't feel that sort of thing." Whereupon the prime minister's face "relaxed into a grim smile."[105] Fisher was fond of claiming that the British were really the Lost Tribe of Israel. When it was argued that they didn't look much like the other tribes of Israel, he replied that of course they didn't, or they wouldn't be lost![106]

Fisher proved indefatigable in his work. At the Admiralty, he was rarely at his desk later than five in the morning or gone earlier than nine at night. On slow days, he would wander the halls with a sign around his neck reading "I HAVE NOTHING TO DO" or "GIVE ME SOMETHING TO SIGN." Yet despite his outsized personality, Fisher preferred to work behind the scenes. He made only four public speeches in his life. Fisher typically avoided fashionable London society, with a notable exception. Once a quarter, he would meet for dinner with Lord Esher, a Liberal Party member who was influential in military affairs, and Lord Knollys, King Edward VII's principal private secretary.[107]

Jackie believed the Royal Navy's dominance was a powerful force for good and that if war should come, it should be employed ruthlessly to restore peace. If a British fleet ever went to war under his command, he assured everyone, nobody would be immune to its power. In speaking to a British correspondent during a conference on disarmament at the Hague, Fisher declared,

> Look, when I leave The Hague I go to take command of the Mediterranean Fleet. Suppose that war breaks out and I am expecting to fight a new Trafalgar on the morrow. Some neutral . . . [freighters loaded with coal] try to steam past us into the enemy's waters. If the enemy gets their coal into his bunkers, it may make all the difference in the coming fight. You tell me I must not seize these colliers. I tell you that nothing that you, or any power on earth, can say will stop me from seizing them or from sending them to the bottom, if I can in no other way keep their coal out of the enemy's hands; for tomorrow I am to fight the battle which will save or wreck the Empire. If I win it, I shall be far too big a man to be affected about protests about the neutral colliers; if I lose it, I shall go down with my ship into the deep and then protests will affect me still less.[108]

Fisher's message: Britain and its Navy did not seek war, but if war came, the fleet would wage it ruthlessly with every means at its disposal. The same could be said regarding Fisher's approach to implementing his Scheme for transforming the Royal Navy.

The Scheme

In October 1904, Fisher assumed his duties as first sea lord. Like a long-simmering volcano building up pressure before erupting, the following months saw Fisher bursting forth with a range of initiatives designed to transform the Navy. On his first day, Fisher produced a memo declaring that Britain could sustain its maritime position "with a great reduction in the Navy Estimates!"—but only if the Scheme was adopted without modification. Fisher wanted "The Scheme! The Whole Scheme!! And Nothing But The Scheme!!"[109]

The Scheme separated Fisher from the other naval leaders of his time. It was a holistic vision of how war at sea was changing and the practical policies needed to enable the Royal Navy to adapt to preserve its dominance. No vision is without flaws, and several were revealed over time; Fisher was also unsuccessful in implementing "the whole scheme and nothing but the scheme." Yet the great changes he instituted, and they were more than a few, produced a fleet that passed the ultimate test: achieving victory in war.

Fisher soon bound together a selection of his writings and circulated them to a select group of naval officers. Titled "Naval Necessities," it included thirty-four essays, thirteen sets of tables, and nine appendices setting forth Fisher's vision. One paper, titled "The Fighting Characteristics of Vessels of War," declared "STRATEGY," not tradition, "should govern the types of ships to be designed." As for ship design itself, "the first essential is to divest our minds totally of the idea that a single type of ship as now built is necessary."[110]

Challenging the primacy of the battleship of the line, Fisher argued, "There is good ground for enquiry whether naval supremacy of a country can any longer be assessed by its battleships. To build battleships merely to fight an enemy's battleships, so long as cheaper craft [such as torpedo craft] destroy them, and prevent them of themselves protecting sea operations [through blockade], is merely to breed Kilkenny cats unable to catch rats or mice. For fighting purposes they would be excellent, but for gaining practical results they would be useless."[111] Fisher's vision rested on three main pillars: constructing a new kind of capital ship, the battle cruiser; employing a "flotilla defense" of the home islands; and "plunging": exploiting Britain's superior industrial and technology base to disrupt other navies' ability to compete.

Fisher's time in command of the Mediterranean Fleet gave him a healthy respect for the growing danger of attempting close blockades against an enemy naval base protected by torpedo boats, anti-ship mines, and, if developments continued along present lines, submarines. Fisher insisted that the number of destroyers be tripled to combat the guerrilla-like attacks he anticipated from torpedo-armed craft in the event of war. "If more destroyers are not obtained," he warned, "we shall have the Boer War played over again at sea. . . . To steam a fleet at night without a fringe of destroyers is like marching an army without an advance guard, flanking parties or scouts."[112]

If torpedo boats were difficult to detect at night, Fisher expressed even greater concern over the havoc that submarines would create once they were introduced into the maritime equation. Writing to a fellow admiral, Fisher declared,

It's astounding to me, *perfectly astounding*, how the very best amongst us absolutely fail to realise the vast impending revolution in naval warfare and naval strategy that the submarine will accomplish. ... In all seriousness I don't think it is even *faintly* realised—*the immense impending revolution which the submarines will effect as offensive weapons of war*. ... When you calmly sit down and work out what will happen in the narrow waters of the Channel and the Mediterranean how totally the submarines will alter the effects of Gibraltar, Port Said, Lemnos and Malta, it makes one's hair stand on end![113]

After departing his command, Fisher spoke at the Royal Academy, where he predicted "the submarine-boat and wireless telegraphy": "When they are perfected, we do not know what a revolution will come about. In their inception they were weapons of the weak. Now they loom large as weapons of the strong. Will any fleet be able to be in narrow waters? Is there the slightest fear of invasion with them, even for the most extreme pessimist?"[114]

In a letter written in January 1904 to Rear Admiral Francis Bridgeman, a member of the "Fishpond"—the name given to his group of disciples—Fisher boldly asserted,

a) The Submarine is coming into play in Ocean Warfare almost immediately.
b) Associated with a Whitehead torpedo 18 ft. in length it will displace the gun and absolutely revolutionise Naval Tactics.
c) No single Submarine ever built or building will ever be obsolete.

"I stake my reputation on the absolute reliability of these three statements. ... The deduction is:—'drop a battleship [construction] out of the program' (if it be necessary on account of financial necessities) but at any cost double the output of submarines."[115] Fisher was not the only British admiral who thought of exploiting the submarine's potential; however, he was the first to suggest that the Royal Navy should rely on submarine-destroyer flotillas rather than the battle fleet as the main instrument of deterring and, if necessary, defeating an attack on the British Isles. In "Naval Necessities," Fisher proposed to organize four "défense mobile" groups, each consisting of one flotilla of twenty-four destroyers and one section of twelve submarines, all bristling with torpedoes, to be stationed along England's southern coast.[116] The flotillas' mission would be to intercept enemy merchantmen and commerce raiders in surrounding waters, while the battle-cruiser squadrons would attack them on the high seas. The flotillas could also safeguard the British coast from maritime attack the same way rival flotillas were undermining the Royal Navy's practice of close blockade.

"My beloved submarines," Fisher enthused, would "magnify the naval power of England seven times more than present."[117] Fisher believed that a flotilla defense made up of submarines, torpedo boats, and destroyers could reduce the need for battle cruisers in home waters, freeing them to deploy quickly to danger spots throughout the empire. Although time would prove Fisher correct, as he advanced this element of the Scheme in 1905 the ability of submarines to perform this mission was more potential than fact. There was considerable risk involved in adopting flotilla defense, therefore. But there was also risk in *not* advancing submarine development.

In March 1905, following the Liberal Party's election victory, the Earl of Cawdor became first lord of the Admiralty, succeeding Lord Selborne. Fisher quickly convinced him not only that the submarine represented an emerging revolution in warfare at sea but also that it was an indispensable element of the Scheme, both for its potential military effectiveness and for relieving the strain on naval estimates. By adopting flotilla defense, Fisher told Cawdor, the Admiralty could scrap many old warships kept in reserve whose sole function was to assist in home defense.[118]

Fisher's arguments attracted support, especially given the advances being made with submarines and torpedoes. With the political leadership's blessing, Fisher began efforts to shift toward flotilla defense. During his tenure, spending on new submarines more than doubled to over £2 million, at a time when the shipbuilding construction budget *declined* by more than £2 million.[119] Elements of the torpedo flotilla—submarines, destroyers, and torpedo boats—more than 100 in all, were concentrated in the Home Fleet. The decommissioning of eleven armored vessels in 1906–7 freed manpower that Fisher used to increase the reserve nucleus crews of flotilla craft from 40 to 80 percent of their wartime strength.[120]

Fisher's early success in implementing this critical part of his Scheme was remarkable; however, as the implications of his plans became better understood, resistance mounted. Ultimately Jackie would find himself engaged in a confrontation over flotilla defense and other aspects of the Scheme with Admiral Beresford and the so-called Syndicate of Discontent.

Redistributing the Fleet

Fisher's Scheme also addressed strengthening defense of the empire. His plans centered on exploiting technology to shift from a forward-deployed fleet posture to emphasizing rapid communication, mobility, and maneuver, while realizing significant economies that would please the political leadership and help underwrite other elements of the Scheme, especially that part concerning manpower.

Fisher had been immersed in efforts to bring about efficiencies during his previous assignment as second sea lord from 1902 to 1904. In a letter to Beresford in early 1903, Fisher railed at the "frightful waste of ships and personnel" inherent in the then current dispositions of the fleet.[121] In "Naval Necessities," he called for reducing the number of overseas squadrons, composed primarily of older and smaller vessels, to liberate the manpower needed to crew the reserve fleet based in Great Britain.

Fisher scoffed at those who believed that the reductions in overseas presence would compromise British interests. He argued that naval supremacy and effective deterrence demanded capability more than simple presence. A strategy of maneuver, centered on mobility and the ability to compete based on time, was Fisher's preference. He noted that the development of wireless telegraphy coupled with Britain's dominance of global telecommunications though its ocean cable network would provide the Royal Navy with early warning of a crisis. This, combined with Fisher's plan for a centrally located force of high-speed, long-range, powerful battle cruisers, would enable the Royal Navy to dispatch overwhelming force quickly to any trouble spot.

Fisher informed Selborne that there would be strong opposition to his fleet redistribution plan from within the Navy, especially from those admirals whose minds he viewed as rooted in the past. He told the first lord, "We can't have a redistribution of our fleet until we rearrange our strategy. . . . *How many types of ships do we want?* This is quite easy to answer if we make up our minds *how we are going to fight!* Who has made up his mind? *How many of our admirals have got minds?*"[122]

Selborne backed Fisher and, on December 6, 1904, presented the plan to the Cabinet, arguing that "the principles on which the present peace distribution of His Majesty's ships and the arrangement of their stations are based, date from a period when the electric telegraph did not exist and when wind was the motive power."[123] Remote squadrons included mainly old, outdated ships that could "neither fight nor run away." They would be decommissioned and the remainder of the fleet repositioned to support the "best strategical distribution for war."[124] This would realize economies and free up badly needed manpower.

The Royal Navy would be reorganized around three major fleets: Home, Atlantic, and Mediterranean. The Home Fleet, with eight battleships, was to have "its strategic centre at Dover." The Channel Fleet and its eight battleships would be redesignated as the Atlantic Fleet and based at Gibraltar. The Mediterranean Fleet at Malta with twelve battleships would remain Britain's most powerful.[125] While the redistribution was under way, the Japanese victory over the Russian fleet at Tsushima helped mute criticism when all five battleships of Britain's China squadron were called home to European waters. Remnants of the Australian, Chinese, and East Indian stations were combined to form an Eastern war fleet.[126] For Fisher, the Atlantic Fleet based at Gibraltar was key to his plans for a rapidly deployable force able to swing quickly either north or east. As he put it, "We have rearranged it with our best and fastest battleships and cruisers and our best admirals ... instantly ready to turn the scale (at the highest speed of any fleet in the world) in the North Sea or the Mediterranean."[127] Faced with a crisis outside European waters, the Navy would rely on Britain's unsurpassed global basing network to provide the early warning and logistics required for a new type of ship—the fast battle cruiser—to concentrate more quickly than its rivals where needed and, if need be, sustain themselves on station over an extended period of time. (Thanks to the Royal Navy's strategically located bases, it was the only navy that maintained a sizeable stock of coal in the Indo-Pacific region.)

The fleet redistribution enabled Fisher to realize another part of his Scheme, bringing the Reserve Fleet to war readiness by manning its most capable ships with so-called nucleus crews. The crews released from the ships decommissioned through redistribution amounted to 11,000 sailors and nearly 1,000 officers. They were reassigned as the nucleus crews for the previously unmanned ships of the Reserve Fleet, which could now be manned at 40 percent of their wartime strength. Importantly, Fisher wanted these crews manned with a full complement of skilled sailors, rather than those assigned to basic tasks such as stoking engines and handling ammunition. This enabled the crews to drill normally and periodically take their ship to sea for gunnery and tactical exercises, thereby maintaining their readiness at a fraction of the financial and manpower costs required to fully man an active warship.[128] Fisher described his nucleus-crew system as "the keystone of our preparedness for war." The whole fleet, he said, was now "instantly ready. . . . Suddenness is now the characteristic feature of sea fighting!"[129] In announcing the nucleus-crew initiative to the Cabinet, Selborne mentioned in passing that to free the needed manpower, "a certain number of ships of comparatively small fighting value have or will be withdrawn from commission."[130]

Left unsaid was that this amounted to more than 150 ships.[131]

The redistribution was announced on January 1, 1905. In all, 154 ships were recalled, 90 to be scrapped and the remainder to be placed in reserve. Fisher won support for redistributing major warships among the three main fleets and for his battle cruiser concept, both of which supported his strategy of maneuver while reducing emphasis on forward-based forces. Fisher did, however, have to make some compromises. Selborne, more risk-averse than Fisher, insisted he retain eleven old battleships.

As word spread throughout the Navy, a firestorm ensued. Admirals, many of whom would later help form the Syndicate of Discontent, saw Fisher as a traitor to the service. Not surprisingly, admirals on those stations slated for recalls complained bitterly. The China Station commander charged that "British interests are much handicapped." The secretary of the Committee on Imperial Defense argued that declaring ships unfit for fighting a war as Fisher did ignored the need for them to support the Navy's traditional role in carrying out "police duties in peace time," which it "must continue to do." The secretary, however, did not specify how this was to be achieved at the same time that major economies were being realized, or why such duties should have priority over the fleet's ability to prevail in war.[132]

Wireless

Fisher's success in winning the political leadership's support for the fleet's redistribution was, in no small way, enabled by rapid advances in communications. Prior to wireless, information could be moved at high speed through a telegraph network, which enabled the Admiralty to transmit and receive information to overseas naval bases within minutes —as long as these bases were linked to a network. Absent such networks, however, information moved at the rate of the fastest ship, which is to say at a far slower pace.[133]

While Fisher and Selborne were advancing their proposal for redistributing the fleet, the Navy was creating a network of wireless telegraphy stations atop Great Britain's existing cable network. In 1905, the quantity of information processed by the Naval Intelligence Department of the Admiralty increased exponentially once its "trade" division began tracking the daily movements of every warship and steamer belonging to every nation in the world. The Admiralty now also possessed the ability not only to know the readiness and whereabouts of all British warships but also to keep track of rival fleet movements.[134] Once linked to its network of intelligence agents in major foreign ports, the Admiralty could use this information to optimize the positioning of its warships, dispatching them to threatened areas more quickly than could its adversaries. Fisher believed his "New Model" warships, the fast battle cruisers, would further enhance the Admiralty's ability to mass superior naval power at the decisive point.

Fisher consciously sought to create what essentially amounted to a British near monopoly in global communications.[135] Preparations were made for all "enemy"-owned undersea cables to be cut in the event of war. (When war came in August 1914, on the first day of hostilities, all German undersea cables were severed or rerouted to British-controlled territory.) The Admiralty's new communications network was also critical to the flotilla defense system. Beginning in 1907, the Royal Navy's torpedo-armed submarines and destroyers were never under the operational command of the Home Fleet, to which they were assigned. Rather, command and control was centralized from London via wireless. Individual units reported directly to the Admiralty, which then determined the appropriate course of action to be taken. This primitive command-and-control network constituted a revolutionary departure from all previous practice with respect to fleet operations.[136]

Fisher's strategic insights, based on his understanding of how technology like wireless communications was changing war at sea, combined with his ability to satisfy political demands for economies, enabled the admiral and his ally the first lord to weather the fierce criticism of the redistribution scheme. Although the Royal Navy reduced considerably the number of ships it deployed at various points beyond Europe, this was,

Fisher argued, more than offset by the quality and mobility of the fleet's new battle cruisers. The redistribution also exploited the positional advantage afforded Britain by its global basing posture and its network of British-controlled wireless telegraph stations.[137]

Transforming the Battle Fleet

Fisher's Scheme for transforming the battle fleet had three principal elements. As noted earlier, one called for a new ship—a fast battle cruiser capable of steaming rapidly to threatened parts of the empire, defeating enemy commerce-raiding cruisers, and, if need be, taking on an enemy fleet's battleships. To ease demands on the battle fleet, Fisher proposed establishing a flotilla defense of the British Isles, employing submarines and destroyers, all bristling with torpedoes. The scheme's third element involved shifting the Admiralty's long-standing procurement strategy.

Fisher believed the traditional metrics by which the Royal Navy measured its combat capability required radical revision, focusing on the numbers of fast battle cruisers and torpedo craft, rather than battleships, long the principal measure of maritime supremacy. He declared,

> The battleship of the olden days was necessary because it was the one and only vessel that nothing could sink except another battleship. Now every battleship is open to attack by fast torpedo-craft and submarines. Formerly, transports or military operations could be covered by a fleet of battleships with the certainty that nothing could attack them without first being crushed by the covering fleet! Now all this has been absolutely altered! A battle-fleet is no protection in daytime because of the submarine. Hence what is the use of battleships as we have hitherto known them? None! Their one and only function—that of ultimate security of defense is gone—lost! No one would seriously advocate building battleships merely to fight other battleships—since if battleships have no function that the first class armored cruiser cannot fulfill, then they are useless to an enemy and do not need to be fought.[138]

Fisher also sought to change the metrics of surface-ship design. He believed that the guiding principle in warship construction is to view it as a floating gun carriage. But how should trade-offs be made in constructing this "floating gun carriage" with regard to armament, speed, armor, range, and endurance? Without reservation, Fisher opted for speed and long-range armament, specifically on uniform, big-gun armament that would enable the Royal Navy's capital ships to engage the enemy at extended range—and beyond the range of torpedoes.

Of course, the longer the range, the more difficult it is to hit the target, all other things being equal. Beginning in 1898, gunnery exercises were conducted at ranges from 3,000 to 6,000 yards to improve accuracy. Accurate fire control was made easier if the ship fired in coordinated salvos, not independently. The splash from the fall of the salvo was observed, and range adjustments were made until it matched the range of the target. Since different caliber guns had different ranges, salvo firing worked best when using guns of a single caliber. Long-range gunnery experiments were carried out in both the Mediterranean and home waters. In April 1904, it was concluded that effective gunnery at 8,000 yards was possible, with the engagement beginning at 9,000 to 10,000 yards.[139]

To exploit an advantage in long-range fires, Fisher's fast battle cruiser (or, simply, "battle cruiser") sacrificed armor in exchange for a uniform all-big-gun armament—and with it greater engagement range—and superior speed to rival battleships. And he let everyone know it, declaring, "There is no question whatever that the first desideratum in every type of fighting vessel is *speed*. . . . It is absolutely impossible to exaggerate the supreme importance of speed."[140] This combination of range and speed, Fisher argued, would enable the Navy to dictate the terms of battle:

> The first desideratum of all is Speed! Your fools don't see it— They are always running about to see where they can put on a little more armour! to make it safer! *You don't go into Battle to be safe!* No, you go into the Battle to *hit the other fellow in the eye first* so that he can't see you. Yes! you hit him first, you hit him hard and you keep on hitting. *That's your safety!* You don't get hit back! . . . The first of all necessities is Speed so as to be able to fight when you like, where you like, and how you like.[141]

Battle cruisers also recognized the Admiralty's financial constraints, performing double duty. Fisher saw them engaging enemy battleships as part of the Royal Navy's line of battle while also moving quickly to threatened parts of the empire to destroy any commerce-raiding cruisers that Britain's enemies might put up against it.

Fisher's support for battle cruisers was part of his efforts to get out in front of major shifts in battleship design. Some of Britain's maritime rivals were already moving to launch all-big-gun battleships. In the spring of 1905, Congress provided the U.S. Navy with funding for two 16,000-ton battleships, *South Carolina* and *Michigan*, each with eight 12-inch guns. At that time, the Japanese were laying down two large 20,000-ton, twenty-knot battleships of mixed armament, each carrying four 12-inch and twelve 10-inch guns.[142] The Royal Navy clearly needed to respond to these developments, but how? With the battle cruisers, Fisher looked neither to ape the competition nor to dominate it through superior numbers alone.

But Fisher could not discount battleships entirely in favor of his battle cruisers. The political and institutional resistance was far too strong for that. It also did not make strategic sense to abandon entirely the class of vessels that for generations had dominated war at sea. Typical of Fisher, he continued to support battleship construction, but for novel reasons, which brings us to the HMS *Dreadnought*.

Upon becoming first sea lord, Fisher tentatively proposed before the Committee on Designs that battleship construction be suspended in favor of battle cruisers. Fisher would get his all-big-gun ships, but not all of them would be battle cruisers. There would be a new battleship, *Dreadnought*, incorporating radical advances in its design. For decades, almost all battleships mounted four big guns. *Dreadnought* had ten. Most battleships steamed at a maximum eighteen knots; *Dreadnought*, incorporating the new turbine engines in lieu of the then standard reciprocating engines, could make twenty-one knots and sustain high speeds over much longer distances—an important consideration given Britain's far-flung empire. Admiral Reginald Bacon enthused, "No greater single step towards efficiency in war was ever made than the introduction of the turbine. Previous to its adoption every day's steaming at high speed meant several days overhaul of machinery in harbour. All this was to be changed as if by magic."[143] Remarkably, *Dreadnought*'s cost was only slightly higher than that of earlier battleships. Yet its all-big-gun armament gave it a long-range striking capability equal to two or three of them. Moreover, since a "dreadnought" only needed ammunition and spare parts for one type of gun, further economies were realized.[144]

Fisher wanted the ship built in record time, and it was. Construction began on October 2, 1905, and *Dreadnought* was commissioned for service on December 3, 1906. Still, *Dreadnought* was not so much the core of Fisher's revolution in the battle fleet as it was a useful adjunct. The admiral's true passion remained the battle cruiser.

Battle cruisers, both Fisher and Selborne argued, represented a major new approach to naval warfare, owing to the great emphasis placed in their design on high speed and long-range striking power. As with *Dreadnought* and all preceding battleships, the new battle cruisers would far surpass their immediate ancestors in ranged firepower. Where existing battleships typically mounted four big guns, the battle cruiser *Invincible* would mount eight, and its speed of twenty-five knots would surpass *Dreadnought*'s by a full four knots. Selborne pointed out that once these new ships put to sea, all the commerce-raiding cruisers of Britain's maritime competitors "would be hopelessly outmatched."[145]

The three *Invincible*-class battle cruisers were laid down in the spring of 1906. Unlike *Dreadnought*, the first battle cruisers were built in secrecy. To deceive the competition, however, Fisher did leak misinformation that the *Invincibles* would mount 9.2-inch guns. To his delight, the three battle cruisers, armed with 12-inch guns, appeared nearly simultaneously between March and October 1908, creating a stir almost as great as *Dreadnought* had. In armament, they were more powerful than any battleship afloat except *Dreadnought*, to which they were not far inferior. They were also much faster. In July 1908, the newly commissioned battle cruiser *Indomitable* steamed across the Atlantic Ocean at an average speed of twenty-five knots, validating the turbine engine's promise.

Fisher's New Model warships provoked more frustration in Berlin, where Germany's already obsolete cruiser *Blucher* was still under construction. As with *Dreadnought*, Tirpitz once again had been outfoxed.[146]

As Fisher saw it, "You had to have Moses before Paul! You couldn't have had the New Testament without the Old first! The *Dreadnought* paved the way to the *Indomitable*. It's no use one or two knots superiority of speed—a dirty bottom brings that down! It's a d——d big six or seven knot surplus that does the trick! THEN you can fight HOW you like, WHEN you like, and WHERE you like!"[147]

In the 1909 program, with Fisher seeking to maintain his advantage in long-range firepower and to address the ever increasing ranges of modern torpedoes, he included a new battle cruiser class, *Lion*. It boosted armament from 12-inch guns to 13.5-inch guns, nearly doubling the shell weight that could be fired in a single broadside. The *Lion*-class ships would be equipped with engines with almost twice the power of earlier battle cruisers, increasing their speed from twenty-five to twenty-seven knots. Fisher proclaimed, *"The ships we have just laid down are as far beyond the Dreadnought as the Dreadnought was beyond all before her!* And they will say again, 'D—n that blackguard! Again a new era of Dreadnoughts!' But imagine the German 'wake-up' when these new ships by and by burst on them! *70,000 horsepower!!! And guns that will gut them!!!"*[148]

The Shift to Oil Propulsion

In 1908, a British destroyer, *Swift*, began its sea trials. It was, in many ways, unremarkable, but the ship did demonstrate one unusual attribute: it was powered by oil, rather than coal.[149] Over the next decade, the Royal Navy would convert to oil to power its warships. Accomplishing the shift represented a considerable strategic risk for Great Britain, which had large indigenous coal reserves but no oil.[150]

Why the change to oil? There were several reasons, the principal being that oil provided more energy per unit relative to coal and thereby enabled warships to travel faster and farther, two key attributes in Fisher's Scheme. Oil also eliminated the need for coal stokers, reducing manpower requirements. Oil-fired engines produced less smoke, making ships more difficult to spot. This was particularly attractive for a fleet planning to engage at extended ranges. Oil was easier to transport, facilitating refueling at sea, as opposed to having ships return to coaling stations to restock.[151]

Experimentation with oil-fueled ships had been going on for several decades and had proved feasible. The Italian Navy had led the way, and by 1900 most of its torpedo boats were oil-fired. In the United States, the first oil-burning U.S. destroyer, *Paulding*, was commissioned in 1910, and by 1911 the *Nevada*-class battleships were being designed solely for oil fuel.[152] As with the all-big-gun battleship, if Britain failed to respond to developments already under way in other first-class navies, it risked being at a disadvantage.

By 1911, the Royal Navy had adopted oil for submarines and destroyers. In advocating transitioning to oil-powered capital ships, Winston Churchill, appointed first lord of the Admiralty in 1911, observed, "The oil supplies of the world were in the hands of vast oil trusts under foreign control. To commit the Navy irrevocably to oil was indeed 'to take arms against a sea of troubles.' If we overcame the difficulties and surmounted the risks, we should be able to raise the whole power and efficiency of the Navy to a definitely higher level; better ships, better crews, higher economies, more intense forms of war power—in a word, mastery itself was the prize of the venture."[153] Spurred by Churchill's views, which were strongly influenced by Fisher, the Cabinet moved to secure adequate oil supplies, acquiring 51 percent of the Anglo-Persian oil company's stock.[154]

The shift could not occur soon enough for Fisher, who declared, "*The oil engine will govern all sea-fighting, and all sea-fighting is going to be governed by submarines.*"[155] Fisher was particularly anxious that Britain beat Germany, now looming as the Royal Navy's principal rival at sea, in shifting to oil. As he informed one associate, "The one *all pervading, all absorbing* thought is to get in first with motor ships before the Germans! Owing to our apathy during the last two years they are ahead with internal combustion engines! They have killed 15 men in experiments with oil engines and we have not killed one! And a d——d fool of an English politician told me the other day that he thinks this creditable to us."[156] By the time of the Great War, the Royal Navy would have oil-fired capital ships.

Long-Range Fires

Fisher's vision of a transformed battle fleet presupposed that his ship's big guns could hit their targets at very long range with sufficient accuracy to prevail. This appeared to be a reasonable assumption, thanks to recent advances in gunnery.

For decades prior to the late 1890s, the Royal Navy's gunnery proficiency ran a poor second to spit and polish. The long peace following the Napoleonic Wars led to an emphasis on drill rather than marksmanship. Although ever larger guns could hit targets at 6,000 yards, they seldom did so in practice even at 1,500 yards. Thus, the default tactics remained those of Nelson a century before: move to close range and pour overwhelming fire at the enemy. Moreover, gunnery exercises were typically unrealistic, with ships steaming at eight knots on a course firing at a target at a known distance, often around 1,500 yards.

For men like Fisher, advances in technology made this situation intolerable. First, the introduction of guns capable of ever greater range meant that the navy that first figured out how to hit accurately at long range would have a major advantage over an enemy battle fleet. Second, advances in torpedo range and accuracy were making engagements at close range a prohibitively costly proposition. If opportunity would not be the mother of innovation, necessity must be.

Things needed to change, and they did. On May 26, 1899, Captain Percy Scott, commander of the cruiser *Scylla*, in seeking to enhance his ship's gunnery accuracy, replaced the open sights of his 4.7-inch quick-firing guns with telescopic sights. He also changed the gear rotation on the elevating mechanism to allow for quick adjustments. Scott had also been training his gunners to aim continuously to enhance their ability to correct for the ship's pitching and yawing. The results were impressive. Scott's "continuous aim" gun-laying technique saw the crew making fifty-six out of its seventy shots, twice the fleet average. Scott's gunners were also able to hit at ranges out to 7,000 yards. Scott soon found himself assigned to command the *Excellent*, which served as the Royal Navy's gunnery school, educating a generation of gunners in his technique. At that time, Fisher, commanding the Mediterranean Fleet, began practicing at ranges of 6,000 to 7,000 yards to address the growing torpedo threat. Although the results were disappointing, the need for accurate long-range fires was clear, and the Admiralty, following Fisher's lead, required annual gunnery fleet exercises at 6,000 yards.[157]

With *Dreadnought*'s launching and Fisher's big bet on long-range fires, gunnery assumed even greater prominence. Initial results were disappointing. The 1906 fleet maneuvers occurred in misty weather and rough seas and saw the secondary batteries performing better than the larger guns.[158] Fisher had to find a way to enhance the big guns' accuracy if the Royal Navy was to transform the potential advantages of his New Model warships into reality.

In March 1905, Fisher made Scott the first inspector of target practice and ordered him to establish gunnery competitions between ships and fleets. That August, Scott submitted a paper describing a new method of sighting and firing. It called for laying all of the ship's big guns at a fixed elevation and for the salvo timing to be determined by a device he called a "director," located on a mast and operated by a single observer. The system of "director firing" placed the sighting process above any interference from sea spray or smoke, while ensuring that the big-gun salvo was nearly simultaneous. By 1908, thanks to Fisher and Scott, British capital ships were hitting moving targets at 8,000 to 9,000 yards.[159]

During this time, two distinct approaches to fire control were being tested. One, named Argo and developed by Arthur Pollen, was relatively sophisticated compared to its competitor, the Dreyer system. The latter was the brainchild of Commander (later Admiral) Frederick Dreyer, who had a background in gunnery, having served under Scott.

The Dreyer system, however, suffered from a fatal defect in that it ignored the effect of yaw—a ship's side-to-side movement owing to its being buffeted by waves. The Dreyer system's early trials were failures. Next, a series of trials between the two systems took place on the battle-ship *Vengeance*. They were held under ideal weather conditions, minimizing the problem of accounting for the effect of yaw. Pollen and his crew, on the other hand, had to incorporate Admiralty equipment such as the Dumaresq calculator and Vickers clock into their performance, even though they had no experience with these instruments and did not desire to use them.

Despite the scales being tipped in favor of one of their own, the trials supervision committee found Pollen's system vastly superior to Dreyer's. Nevertheless, the Admiralty chose the Dreyer system. Fisher appears to have been persuaded by Dreyer that the Navy had produced a cheaper and equally effective alternative to Pollen's system. It may also be that Fisher's judgment was affected by his rapidly growing feud with Beresford, who had purchased Pollen systems for five of his ships. In any event, of the twenty-eight British all-big-gun battleships and battle cruisers in service in July 1914, more than half were making do with second-class fire-control gear. It was arguably the worst decision Fisher made in his efforts to implement the Scheme.[160]

Mines

By the early 1890s, the Royal Navy had developed automatic contact mines, with Fisher and Ottley closely involved in the effort. Realizing the dangers posed by mines, and with no countermeasure readily available, the Admiralty chose to let other navies make the first move in adopting them. By the time Fisher became second sea lord in 1902, however, rival navies had already stolen a march. "What justification can we advance for our apparent supineness?" asked Fisher. "If we do not adopt them," he wrote, "we shall lack one weapon possessed by our enemies, which will be used against us and we shall not be able to retaliate in the same manner. . . . We cannot afford to leave anything to be a matter of opinion which affects, in the slightest degree, the fighting efficiency of the Fleet."[161]

Ottley, newly appointed as DNI, reported on the "startling success achieved by automatic mines during the present [Russo-Japanese] war." Fisher appointed Ottley to chair a committee on the matter and accepted its recommendations to begin procuring 10,000 mines. Although the committee envisioned mines as supporting blockade operations, Fisher wanted them primarily as an additional means of preventing enemy ships from entering British waters, and he included mines in the Navy's estimates every year. This continued until Churchill, as first lord, discontinued their stockpiling, believing that mines were weapons of a weaker naval power forced on the defensive.[162]

Plunging

During Fisher's tenure as first sea lord, Britain possessed the world's largest, best-equipped, and most technically advanced warship industry. It allowed Britain to build warships of cutting-edge design, faster and in greater numbers than its rivals. This enabled the Admiralty to pursue a strategy of the "second-move advantage" during the periodic disruptive shifts in the naval competition during the nineteenth century. It was France, not Britain, that first moved to launch steam-propelled warships and ironclads. Even though Britain was fully capable of leading the transition, it held back so as to maximize its advantage in existing warships. Similarly, the Admiralty sought to "ignore" the development of submarines until a major naval rival introduced this new form of war at sea.

Fisher sought to preserve, exploit, and where possible, extend Britain's industrial base supremacy. Typical of Fisher, however, was his determination to apply these advantages in a new way. He called his approach "plunging," and it was, along with the development of the battle cruiser and flotilla defense, one of the Scheme's three central elements. In deciding to build *Dreadnought* and the battle cruisers, Fisher followed the tradition of the second-move advantage to move quickly if a rival was about to move first.[163]

But Fisher wanted to do more than react to the competition—he wanted to shape it. He was looking to set its pace and direction. *Dreadnought* was Fisher's test case. Fisher publicized everything not classified about the ship's construction to paralyze rival navies. Through reforming labor practices in the dockyards and ordering critical-path components such as big-gun mountings and turbine engines several months before placing the contract for the hull, he dramatically compressed its construction time. A year and a day after construction started, *Dreadnought* began its sea trials. Fisher had cut the normal building time for a battleship—in this case, a radically different and more powerful battleship—by more than half.[164]

Dreadnought disrupted the planning efforts of Britain's principal rivals, the Germans in particular. As *Dreadnought* was emerging from the drawing board, Tirpitz was launching *Deutschland*, the first of five planned new German battleships. These ships, with their 13,400 tons, four 11-inch and fourteen 6.7-inch guns, and eighteen-knot speed, would be inferior even to some of the Royal Navy's pre-dreadnought battleships. With *Dreadnought*, this class was already obsolete.

Tirpitz's program was also stretching the limits of size in his ship designs. A key limiting factor was the Kiel Canal, which provided the German fleet with a shortcut between the North Sea and the Baltic Sea. If Tirpitz wanted bigger ships, the canal would have to be enlarged, requiring years of effort at enormous expense. Consequently, as news of the planned size, speed, and armament of *Dreadnought* reached Tirpitz, near panic ensued in Berlin.[165]

Tirpitz secluded himself for months with his most trusted advisers to determine how best to respond. A consensus emerged that Germany should meet the British challenge, even if this required expanding all existing canal and dock facilities. Thus, Fisher's "plunging" strategy was also a "cost-imposing strategy," in that it exploited an enduring source of German competitive weakness—the limitations imposed on ship design by the Kiel Canal—to impose substantial cost penalties should Germany decide to meet the British initiative. As *Dreadnought* was being built, Fisher wrote, "An increase in the size of German ships will necessitate either widening or deepening the Kiel Canal, possibly both, and its approaches, and also extensive dredging operations in their naval ports. . . . It may, therefore, well be doubted whether Germany is at present in a position to make a sudden advance to ships of 20,000 tons."[166] Fisher's gambit also imposed a penalty with regard to time. By moving the naval competition in a dramatic new direction, Fisher cost the Imperial German Navy roughly a year as Tirpitz reassessed his position.[167]

To Fisher, disrupting the naval plans of his rivals was intended to be not a one-time affair but an ongoing practice. He hoped his battle cruisers would continue promoting chaos in his adversaries' shipbuilding schemes. Later, he summarized his thinking on plunging to Churchill, who became first lord in 1911, shortly after Fisher retired. By launching ships that were substantially superior in quality to anything then afloat, Fisher declared, the Admiralty could compel other navies to reconsider their own ship-building plans. If the Admiralty's plans were not revealed until the last possible moment, the disarray produced among rivals could enable the Admiralty to slow its own naval construction program, providing economies to the naval estimates. The "secret" of successful naval administration, Fisher declared, "is 'plunging'—it stupefies foreign Admiralties. . . . Put off to the very last hour the ship (big or little) *that you mean to build* (or perhaps not build her at all!). You see all your rival's plans fully developed, their vessels started beyond recall, and then in each individual answer to each such rival vessel you PLUNGE with a design 50 per cent. better! knowing that your rapid shipbuilding and command of money will enable you to have your vessel fit to fight as soon if not sooner than the rival vessel."[168]

Although *Dreadnought* was built partially in response to the move by other navies toward all-big-gun capital ships, while providing a major boost in combat potential over existing ships at a modest increase in cost, its appearance attracted criticism from various quarters, including in the Navy itself. Many Liberal Party members, including such luminaries as Lloyd George, saw the ship as militarily provocative. Sir George Clarke, the CID secretary, condemned Fisher to Prime Minister Henry Campbell-Bannerman. The former first sea lord Admiral Richards, who disliked Fisher's Scheme, declared that the entire British fleet had been "morally scrapped." Beresford, though subordinate to Fisher, joined in the chorus, asserting, "If Germany attacked us suddenly, she would inflict terrible disasters on us and she might win," to which Fisher informed Lord Tweedmouth, the Admiralty's first lord from 1906 to 1908, that Britain's naval superiority over Germany was so "overwhelming" that the Germans knew it would be "madness" to challenge it.[169]

Fisher had his allies, including the growing number of reform-minded officers in the Fishpond and men such as Lord Esher, Lord Selborne, future first lord Reginald McKenna, and, quietly, King Edward VII. As one supportive journalist wrote, "The most monstrous accusations were hurled against him, by men who were not worthy to black his boots. At a time when he was risking everything by his dogged determination to keep up the supremacy of the Navy, he was denounced as a traitor in the pay of Germany."[170]

Fisher was also confronting threats to a key source of Britain's maritime supremacy: its defense industrial base, on which his plunging strategy rested. The issues were straightforward: the rapidly rising cost of warships and the need to realize economies in the naval estimates meant that fewer ships could be built. Between 1896 and 1904, the Royal Navy contracted to build seven capital ships a year, on average. When Fisher became first sea lord, however, budget projections called for no more than four large ships to be constructed, on average, in the coming five years, a reduction of more than 40 percent. Fisher's plan to shift funds away from capital shipbuilding and toward flotilla craft would only worsen industry's problems.

A major consolidation of Britain's warship-building industry seemed inevitable. Fisher wanted to avoid any major reduction in the industry's research and development budgets, the key to Britain's ability to maintain a technological lead. He also needed an industrial base with the capacity to produce his new ships quickly and to surge production if necessary.[171] With these concerns in mind, Fisher reached an informal (and illegal) agreement with the four most important shipbuilding firms in the country.[172] In return for their being granted an effective monopoly on all major warship contracts, which included subsidies virtually guaranteeing the firms' profitability, they agreed to maintain spare manufacturing capacity for critical components and to retain existing levels of investment in research and development.[173]

Leveraging the Two-Power Standard

Fisher may have had little use for the Two-Power Standard as the means to gauge British maritime superiority, but he wielded it to deflect attempts to cut his naval shipbuilding estimates—and preserve the industrial base. Recent geopolitical developments were fueling the Liberals' ardor for naval reductions. The new chancellor of the Exchequer, Herbert Henry (H. H.) Asquith argued that the signing of the Entente Cordiale with France and the Russian fleet's destruction at Tsushima meant the Two-Power Standard was no longer relevant as a measure of the Royal Navy's required strength. Fisher, however, knew that Asquith realized the political dangers associated with publicly abandoning the standard. The Admiralty also pointed out that Britain's closest rivals for maritime supremacy were no longer France and Russia but France and Germany. Asquith asked, Was it reasonable to assume that these traditional enemies would join together to oppose Britain? Even if they did, Asquith argued, the Royal Navy possessed forty-seven completed battleships less than fifteen years old, against twenty-nine in

France and Germany. Asquith pointed out that the Admiralty's argument for new capital ships assumed that Britain's naval rivals would execute their building plans, which could well be a "bluff" on their part.[174] Asquith said the French "paper program" would remain just that—a plan that would not be fulfilled. As for Germany, he noted the Kaiser's difficulties in getting the Reichstag to approve his naval budget requests. Why, then, should Britain lay down additional battleships?

Fisher's response to the new government's challenge essentially adopted the claims of his critics, claiming that *Dreadnought*'s construction had effectively restarted the naval competition from scratch. The Admiralty Board noted, "With the introduction of the Dreadnoughts—a leap forward of 200% in fighting power has been effected, so that *as compared with the dreadnought designs*, all existing types of battleships are more or less out of date."[175]

Fisher confided to close colleagues that, in fact, Asquith was right. He admitted, "our present margin of superiority over Germany (our only possible foe for years) is so great as to render it absurd in the extreme to talk of anything endangering our naval supremacy, *even if we stopped all shipbuilding altogether!!!*"[176]

In a letter Fisher penned to King Edward in October 1907, he asserted, "The English Navy is now four times stronger than the German Navy, ... but we don't want to parade all this, because if so we shall have Parliamentary trouble. ... [Prime Minister] Sir Henry Campbell-Bannerman's warmest supporters ... have sent him quite recently one of the best papers I have read, convincingly showing that we don't want to lay down any new ships at all—we are so strong. It is quite true!"[177]

But Fisher realized that Britain was in an open-ended rivalry with Germany and that the alignment of other powers could change to Britain's detriment as quickly as it had to its benefit. Thus, Britain needed to sustain its world-class maritime defense industrial base. In July 1906, at the height of Asquith's challenge to the Admiralty's shipbuilding program, a private document drafted by the Admiralty Board concluded that, should the Liberal Party follow through on its plans to reduce shipbuilding, the long-term consequences for industry—and British maritime superiority—would be devastating. "A day will come when our naval supremacy will again be challenged, and when, by consequence, the ability to rapidly build warships in considerable numbers will be a national asset of incalculable importance. To starve the construction vote in the present will, should expansion ever again become necessary, not merely inevitably enhance the cost of any future program, but will greatly impair the national power of rapid naval recuperation in the vital matter of our output of new warships."[178] Fisher knew that this argument for maintaining—indeed, subsidizing—the armaments industry would not fly with the Liberal leadership, either on fiscal or ideological grounds. Another line of argument was needed. Hence, Fisher's support for the Two-Power Standard and the use of dreadnoughts as the principal measure of naval power was in no small way motivated by his strategy of plunging and his desire for fast battle cruisers, rather than out of any strong belief in the need to maintain a two-to-one supremacy in battleships. Fisher also ensured that the first three battle cruisers were built in private shipyards, knowing that any Liberal government move to cancel the contracts would face strong political opposition.[179]

Fisher's ability to advance his Scheme despite opposition from multiple quarters was due in large measure to his ability to achieve economies while providing the Liberal government with political cover by maintaining the Royal Navy's status as the world's preeminent maritime power. From 1906 through 1908, with Asquith serving as chancellor of the Exchequer, Fisher produced savings in the shipbuilding budget. The £8.4 million spent on battleships and armored cruisers in fiscal year 1905–6 dropped to £7.9 million in 1906–7, then to £6.5 million in 1907–8 and to £5.5 million in 1908–9. The slowing construction rate was the result of Fisher's plunging strategy's "wrecking" the shipbuilding programs of rival navies, particularly Germany's. Overall, and in spite of rising costs in other areas, Fisher was able to keep the net naval estimates of 1906–7 through 1908–9 between £31 and £32 million—£5 million less per year than the peak of £36.9 million that had been reached in fiscal year 1904–5.[180]

Yet, despite Fisher's success, and perhaps because of it, attacks on the Scheme, and on him personally, continued.

War, War Plans, and Fleet Maneuvers

During Fisher's time as first sea lord, the Royal Navy continued conducting fleet maneuvers to keep pace with the changing character of the maritime competition and to adapt to it. His tenure also coincided with the first great-power naval war in the Age of Steam and Iron.

The Russo-Japanese War

A persistent problem confronting senior political and military leaders in all the maritime powers was how to assess the naval balance. As outlined earlier, many new naval capabilities and methods of operation were being introduced. They were evaluated in war games and tested in fleet exercises, but there were clear limits as to what firm lessons could be derived from such efforts. The "problem" was the absence of any maritime war between great powers since the Crimean War (1854–56), which did not involve any major sea battles and was waged in the Age of Wind and Sail. Thus, it was not surprising that the Russo-Japanese War, fought between February 1904 and September 1905, was the subject of intense interest, particularly the two major naval engagements, the Battle of the Yellow Sea on August 10, 1904, and the Battle of Tsushima on May 27–28, 1905.

In August 1904, the Russian naval squadron being blockaded at Port Arthur by the Japanese fleet attempted to break out and join the Russian fleet at Vladivostok. Although the Russians successfully slipped through the blockade, the Japanese pursued them, and an engagement ensued. Each side inflicted damage on the other, but the Japanese scored a lucky hit on the Russian flagship, *Tsesarevich*, killing the squadron's commander, Admiral Wilgelm Vitgeft. The Russian squadron retreated to Port Arthur, where its ships were eventually lost when the besieged port surrendered in January 1905.

The Battle of Tsushima, on the other hand, was one of the most one-sided in naval history. It occurred when the Russian Baltic Fleet, following a long and arduous voyage, was intercepted steaming in the Tsushima Strait between Japan and Korea. The Japanese fleet, under Admiral Heihachiro Togo, captured or destroyed thirty-one of the thirty-eight Russian ships in Admiral Zinovi Rozhestvensky's squadron, including all eight Russian battleships. Japanese casualties were but 117 dead and some 600 wounded, against nearly 5,000 Russian dead, 6,000 captured, and countless wounded.[181]

During the battle, Admiral Togo exploited his fleet's superior speed—some fifteen knots against the Russians' nine—to dictate the range at which the battle would be fought. He used this advantage to direct all his ships' fires against the leading Russian ships in each division. The British attachés' reports concluded that speed was crucial in the war's two main fleet engagements.[182] Despite the extended range of roughly 8,000 yards at which the battle opened, the bulk of the damage sustained by the Russian fleet was at much shorter range. This stemmed, in part, from the Japanese ships' mixed armament, which made it impossible for the gun-layers to spot their shells' landings and adjust their aim. Tsushima was won by a Nelsonic "hail of fire" and not long-range fires.

The war provided the world's navies with an opportunity to assess how the new technologies, systems, and tactics they had adopted would fare in modern naval warfare. A long and spirited debate followed over the "lessons" to be derived from the war, with much of the discussion focusing on ship speed and engagement range, issues near and dear to Fisher's heart.

Fisher's critics seized on the short range of the Tsushima engagement to criticize his push for the all-big-gun battle fleet. But there was more to the story. The Royal Navy's observers found the Japanese fire-control training and spotting to be poor. Moreover, a complete broadside of guns of identical caliber would make a splash that was far easier to spot than a fleet with mixed-caliber armament. This reinforced Fisher's argument for ships with uniform-caliber guns. Jackie also had his trump card: the need for the line of battle to engage beyond the rapidly growing range of torpedoes.[183]

There was, however, no consensus on the value of torpedoes emerging from the conflict. They played no role in the Battle of the Yellow Sea. In December 1904, however, the Japanese fired roughly 150 torpedoes in a series of night attacks on the Russian fleet at Port Arthur. Although only four hit their target, they sank the battleship *Sevastopol* and fatally damaged the destroyer *Storoshevoi*. At the close of the Battle of Tsushima, Japanese torpedo boats finished off Russia's Baltic Fleet, sinking or fatally damaging the battleship *Sisoi Veliki* and the armored cruisers *Admiral Nakhimoff, Vladimir Monomakh,* and *Dmitri Donskoi.* Torpedo skeptics tended to agree with Admiral Cyprian Bridge, who concluded, "Perhaps nothing stands out more clearly in the campaign than the insignificance of the results effected by locomotive torpedoes." Others, like Commander (later Admiral) Murray Sueter, a Royal Navy submarine commander, countered that Japanese torpedoes suffered from maintenance and technical shortcomings, along with an alarming failure to detonate when striking their target.[184]

Mines, on the other hand, were coming into their own. No battleships were lost to mines at the Battle of the Yellow Sea, yet three had already been sunk by mines. Japanese mines destroyed the Russian flagship,

Petropavlovsk, on April 13, 1904, and Admiral Togo lost two battleships to mines on May 15, 1904.[185]

Fleet Maneuvers

As the war between Japan and Russia was heating up, the Royal Navy continued to conduct fleet maneuvers exploring ways to maintain a successful blockade of enemy ports. The 1902 and 1903 maneuvers suggested that such operations were becoming increasingly difficult due to advances with torpedoes and submarines, and these concerns dominated the Royal Navy's 1904 fleet maneuvers. The Channel Squadron was directed by its commander, Admiral Sir Arthur Wilson, to focus on anti-submarine warfare (ASW) tactics. Captain Reginald Bacon, a budding member of the Fishpond whom Fisher described as "the cleverest officer in the navy" (and who would later serve as *Dreadnought*'s first captain), commanded the "enemy's" submarines. Bacon's crews hit Wilson's battleships so many times with unarmed torpedoes that the umpires reluctantly ruled two of his battleships "sunk."[186]

The August maneuvers confirmed the submarine's growing influence on the naval competition and, correspondingly, the prospects for successful blockade. They called for a superior "British" fleet with 106 destroyers to operate within range of a strong "enemy" force of torpedo craft. The exercises found the destroyers distracting Bacon's submarines from attacking the main battle fleet, but only at considerable cost to themselves, principally because no reliable method existed for a destroyer to attack a submarine. Following the exercise, the "enemy" fleet commander, Rear Admiral C. G. Robinson, concluded that close blockade under modern conditions was becoming impossible.[187]

Fisher and Bacon felt vindicated in their view that commanders would not risk major warships in narrow waters if they believed submarines were present. Admiral Wilson was inclined to agree. Their views soon spread through the Admiralty, as more officers began to accept that close blockade was no longer an option against any port or base defended by submarines. "Suffice to say," Fisher declared in April 1905, "in three or four years of this date ... the English Channel and the western basin of the Mediterranean will not be habitable by a fleet or squadron."[188]

There was more distressing news for the Admiralty in the joint maneuvers conducted with the British Army a month later. The exercise called for landing a force of 12,000 infantry, cavalry, and artillery on a hostile shore, albeit with no enemy opposition. The Admiralty hoped to show that the Army could best be employed as, in Fisher's words, a "projectile" to be "fired" by the fleet, rather than it pursuing its preferred "continental" strategy that called for deploying a large expeditionary force to support France should it be attacked by Germany. To the Navy's great embarrassment, the landings, witnessed by foreign officials and military attachés, were a disaster.[189]

If blockade operations were becoming increasingly problematic, it would be more difficult to bottle up enemy commerce-raiding ships, and the risk to Britain's seaborne commerce would grow. The 1906 maneuvers sought to determine the fleet's ability to address the commerce-raiding challenge and saw a strong "British" fleet tasked with protecting its commerce ships from a weaker "enemy" fleet. The eight-day exercise found the "enemy" fleet capturing 55 percent of the ninety-four participating merchant vessels. The percentage was viewed as greatly inflated, owing to the small number of merchant ships involved relative to the number of raiders. In wartime, it was noted, the number of commerce transports would vastly exceed the number of raiders. The maneuvers' brevity also encouraged the "enemy" commander to be very aggressive, capturing a high percentage of transports but losing more than half of his sixty-two ships. Finally, since the raider ships would have to return to base to recoal, rearm, and refit, the judges refereeing the maneuvers found that "it is practically certain that the commencement of the third week of the war would have seen all commerce-raiding ships either captured or blockaded in their defended ports." The Admiralty's key finding was that while Britain might suffer a high rate of loss to its merchant shipping at the war's outset, the enemy would also suffer high losses to its raiding force and that, once that occurred, normal maritime trade flows would be restored. These findings were welcomed, as they supported the Navy's preference for offensive "search-and-destroy" operations against raiders, rather than convoy operations.[190]

War Plans

In March 1906, Ottley urged Fisher to create formal war plans to preempt criticism from Beresford, now commanding the Mediterranean Fleet and slated to assume command of the Channel Fleet. The two most well known officers in the Royal Navy apparently had a falling out when, on December 4, 1905, the last day of the Balfour government,

Fisher was promoted to admiral of the fleet, permitting him to remain on active duty an additional five years beyond the mandatory retirement date at age sixty-five, which he would reach in 1906. Had Fisher not been promoted, Beresford's chances for succeeding him would have been excellent. By 1911, however, time would have robbed Beresford of the opportunity. His ambitions scuppered, Charlie B became an implacable enemy of Fisher's reforms, emerging as a leader of the Syndicate of Discontent, a loose coalition of politicians, journalists, and active and retired senior officers opposed to Fisher's reforms. It became increasingly clear that, while Fisher was concerned about the Navy, Beresford's focus was on revenge.

Beresford had a long habit of publicly criticizing the Admiralty for its lack of war plans. Fisher directed Ballard to form a secret committee to formulate plans for a war with Germany. Four months later, Ballard, aided primarily by Captain Hankey, provided Fisher with eight plans, with three presented in detail. While the Ballard Committee's plans did not constitute the formal War Plans of 1907—a grab-bag of prints and reports, authored by various groups or individuals, written over different times, with different purposes and audiences in mind—they constituted its intellectual core.[191]

Fisher provided guidance to Julian Corbett, who authored Part I of the plans, instructing him to write a scholarly introduction for a "non-professional" audience, including "influence shapers" like King Edward, Reginald McKenna, and the press. Parts II and IV were a collection of Naval War College reports and studies.

The Ballard Committee's work formed the basis for Part III, containing the war plans. War Plan A/A1 focused on crippling German trade through a distant North Sea blockade stretching from the north coast of Scotland to the Norwegian coast. The Channel would be blocked by destroyers, torpedo boats, and submarines. The plan presented a version of Fisher's flotilla-defense concept. The Royal Navy's battle fleet would be positioned to reinforce either force should the Germany's High Seas Fleet challenge this new form of blockade.[192]

Plan B/B1 directed a close blockade of German trade but was clearly not intended for implementation, as it offered no advantages over Plan A/A1, while greatly increasing the risk to the British fleet. Plan C/C1 focused on employing the fleet against Germany's overseas commerce. Attacks against the German fleet and the Kiel Canal, as well as amphibious operations along the German coastline, were of secondary importance.

Plan D/D1 addressed the contingency of a German seizure of Denmark at the outbreak of war. It called for cutting off German forces occupying the large islands of Fyen and Zealand at the mouth of the Baltic Sea.[193]

Fisher asked Admiral Wilson for his views on the 1907 plans. Wilson responded that a "close continuous watch off all the German ports" would be "very difficult to maintain," especially at night. He doubted the Navy's ability to cripple Germany's commerce, which he believed could be sustained from shipments overland and neutral maritime shipping. Wilson gravitated toward Plan A/A1, supporting using submarines and destroyers to block the Strait of Dover and the entrance to the Channel. If war became imminent, the Royal Navy's destroyers "alone should be in the North Sea" as an early warning force, so as not to risk the battlefleet against attack by German torpedo craft.[194]

Fisher was in general agreement with Wilson but showed some enthusiasm for waging a more aggressive form of economic warfare.[195] In late 1908, Fisher proposed a strategy for exploiting Britain's naval supremacy and dominant position in the global trading system to trigger Germany's prompt economic collapse in the event of war. The plan called for an unprecedented intervention in the nation's economic system, with the Admiralty seizing control of the nation's commercial shipping movements, regulating the ships' cargoes, imposing censorship over all cable communications, and directing the financial services industry's actions in a concerted effort to wreck Germany's economy. The proposal was strongly opposed by Britain's business sector and by diplomats concerned with the effects that all-out economic warfare would have on relations with neutral powers. By the time war broke out in the summer of 1914, Fisher's strategy was but a shadow of its initial form, and by year's end, after only a few months of war, it was effectively abandoned.[196]

Fisher briefed Beresford on the 1907 plans and provided him a copy of the Ballard Committee report. Charlie B was not impressed. He vigorously objected to Fisher's idea of flotilla defense. Beresford also disliked the idea of his fleet being assigned the mission of distant blockade.[197]

Ottley's war-plan warnings proved prescient, as the Admiralty faced an inquiry in 1907 triggered by one of Britain's periodic invasion scares. These scares often pitted the British Army against the Royal Navy in a battle over resources, with both advancing arguments as to the critical role they played in defending the homeland, while deprecating the position of their sister service.

Fisher had little use for such reviews, given his dismissive attitude regarding the danger of a successful invasion of the British Isles.[198] This was reflected in his participation in the review, where his arguments were presented primarily for their political effect and not as a serious discourse on strategy.[199] Fisher happily shared the war plans that called for seizing various North Sea islands to support close blockade operations and bombarding German naval bases. These options were presented in great detail but were quite incapable of being executed—and Fisher knew it.[200]

But he also knew that the political leadership wanted the comfort of knowing that the Royal Navy would conduct an aggressive campaign against Germany should war erupt. Although Fisher was convinced that operating fleets of capital ships in narrow seas was too risky to venture—indeed, his concept of flotilla defense and distant blockade was the Scheme's response to this danger—Fisher gave the politicians what they wanted to hear and escaped serious damage at the hands of those, like Beresford, who sought to depict the Admiralty as unprepared. Years later, Fisher admitted that the plans had been produced solely for the consumption of his critics. Referring to Sir Arthur Wilson, who succeeded him as first sea lord, Jackie confided, "Not being a Machiavelli, [he] wouldn't tell the Cabinet anything. I, on the contrary, told them so much they thought me perfect. I gave them 600 pages of print of war plans!"[201]

The war plans were updated in 1908, but these "W" plans were only marginally different from the Ballard Committee's work on the previous year's "ABCD" plans. Both the W1 and W2 plans called for British heavy warships to keep out of the North Sea. In August 1908, after meetings with King Edward's private secretary and Admiral Fisher, Lord Esher stated, "J. [Jackie Fisher] told me of Arthur Wilson's determination, in the event of war with Germany, not to locate his battle-fleet in the North Sea. The rendezvous would be in the Orkneys, and there the fleet would lie, ready for battle. Only Cruisers and Destroyers in the North Sea."[202]

Despite objections from Wilson, Corbett, and others that close blockade was impractical, Plan W3 called for such operations. The Strategy Committee opposed W3, noting, "It is fraught with greater possibilities of danger to the blockading squadrons than the system cordons across the Straits of Dover and across the northern entrance to the North Sea."[203] But, again, Fisher's "war plans" were primarily used for warding off criticisms from his bureaucratic and political rivals. His candid thoughts on operating the battle fleet in the North Sea, let alone having it engage in close or observational blockade, were set forth

November 1908, in his paper titled "The Submarine Question." In it, Fisher declared, "No practicable means at present exist or appear to be feasible for effecting the destruction of the latest type of submarine, or of being even warned of her approach." Consequently,

> It is inevitable that when the Germans fully realise the capability of this type of submarine . . . the North Sea and all its parts will be rendered uninhabitable by our big ships—until we have cleaned out the submarines. . . . The arguments in this brief record in no way attempt to lessen the influence and necessity of big armoured ships. . . . They do however point to a complete approaching revolution in the type of our war with any power, particularly with any European power on account of the narrow waters of the North Sea and the Baltic, English Channel and Mediterranean being denied to large ships of war until the submarine is cleared out.[204]

Fisher supported Admiral Wilson's position that the battle fleet should be kept out of the North Sea and advocated flotilla defense, pointing out, "It would be suicide to expose the armoured units of our Fleet to a surprise Torpedo attack by stationing them before War within striking distance of the enemy. . . . At such time the North Sea should swarm with our Destroyers and Submarines backed with their supporting Cruisers."[205]

Fisher shared his views with King Edward with such passion that, for his Christmas present in 1909, the monarch sent him a silver model of a submarine. Beamed Fisher, "He thinks I'm mad about them."[206] Indeed, he was.

Following the Ballard Committee's work, the Channel Fleet's June and July 1907 maneuvers explored close-watch operations on enemy ports as called for in Plans B and C. The "friendly" force composed of the Fifth Cruiser Squadron and accompanying destroyers was tasked with watching the "enemy" fleet under Beresford, who had orders to break out of his base unobserved. The exercise was a botch. The "friendly" fleet failed to maintain a fix on the "enemy," while the latter failed to engage its rival. The maneuvers' second phase found Beresford again commanding the "German" fleet with the objective of crossing one of two sea zones without being brought to an engagement. He did so, revealing shortcomings in the Royal Navy's scouting operations. The maneuver's final phase explored a blockaded fleet employing a torpedo attack prior to breaking out from its base. Beresford's "German" fleet destroyers slipped out undetected and located the "British" fleet, again indicating a scouting problem. This led Beresford to conclude that conducting an observational blockade would require the "friendly" fleet to employ "two to three times the number of seagoing Destroyers" as it had for the exercise.[207] Fisher, of course, was not planning to employ an observational blockade in the event of war.

The July 1908 maneuvers once again found the "German" fleet under Beresford tasked with preventing a superior but divided "British" fleet from concentrating. The exercise proved a failure, and Sir Arthur Wilson, observing the maneuvers, was highly critical of both commanders.[208]

Naval Budget Estimates

In May 1908, Reginald McKenna, a lawyer by trade, succeeded the ailing Lord Tweedmouth as first lord and soon became a supporter of Fisher's reforms. He arrived just as a major clash over the Navy's estimates was brewing, complicated by yet another war scare.

In late 1908, the Admiralty received intelligence that Germany was accelerating its shipbuilding program. The news, which quickly became public, triggered a scare in the press, in Parliament, and among the general public. In response, McKenna proposed laying down two additional dreadnoughts in the coming year, for a total of six.

The budget estimates were further stressed by Admiralty's plan to arm four of the ten major warships on order in 1909–10 with 13.5-inch guns, raising the price of a battleship by some 14 percent and that of a battle cruiser by more than a third relative to ships armed with 12-inch guns. The 1912–13 program proposed moving to 15-inch guns. Battleships so armed would cost over 30 percent more than their immediate predecessors, and 60 percent more than the 12-inch-gun battleships.[209]

Asquith, now Britain's prime minister, was searching for a way to keep a lid on the naval estimates while defending against charges that his government was lax in responding to the German threat. He broached a compromise in which the government would ask for four dreadnoughts in the 1909 estimates and would seek authority to build four additional dreadnoughts no later than April 1, 1910, but only if the German construction program validated the intelligence estimates.

Asquith's political maneuvering continued. On November 12, 1908, he pledged that his government would uphold the Two-Power Standard.

The following April, noting that the next two largest rival navies were now Germany and the United States and that the United States was a friendly power, the government for planning purposes privately adopted a one-power standard, calculated as being equal to Germany's capital ships plus a margin of 60 percent. On December 29, 1911, McKenna's successor, Churchill, proposed that the 60 percent standard be formally (and publicly) adopted, and three months later, he announced it to the Commons.

In the summer of 1909, however, Austria-Hungary expressed its intention to build three and possibly four dreadnoughts. This led the Italians to augment their shipbuilding program to four dreadnoughts. Although each regarded the other as a potential enemy, both countries were Germany's allies. From the Admiralty's perspective, this meant confronting thirteen German dreadnoughts in the North Sea, plus roughly half that number or more Austrian and Italian dreadnoughts in the Mediterranean. In July 1909, McKenna announced that the contingent four dreadnoughts would be built. The decision moved Churchill, who had advocated only building the original four ships, to observe, "In the end a curious and characteristic solution was reached. The Admiralty had demanded six ships; the economists offered four; and we finally compromised on eight."[210]

The Inquiry

As work on the Scheme progressed, it confronted growing challenges on multiple fronts from individuals and organizations whose interests and preferences were threatened. We have seen Fisher's apparently inconsistent behavior, such as his dismissive views on the Two-Power Standard and building more dreadnoughts—unless they could help sustain the defense industrial base—and his cranking out war plans that honored the Navy's traditions of close blockade and offensive action, even though his true views were quite different. Such behavior stemmed in no small measure from Fisher's delicate balancing act, which focused on protecting the Admiralty's budget from being raided by the Army, gutted by the politicians, or diverted away from the Scheme's priorities by admirals whose affection for the past blinded them to the dramatic changes under way in the maritime competition.

The politicians, of course, were constantly pressing for Fisher to generate savings from the scheme, and he was able to do so and keep them at bay—for a time. He sorely missed Selborne's support in dealing with the political class, later recalling, "Never did any First Lord hold more warmly the hand of his principal adviser than Lord Selborne held mine." Fisher had received little in the way of effective support from Lord Tweedmouth, a lightweight described as as fit for the job of first lord "as for the Office of Astronomer Royal."[211] Tweedmouth's successor, McKenna, though supportive, confronted a rising tide of opposition.

The party out of power, the Tories, criticized Fisher's reforms. On one occasion, he was asked if his reforms were successful and, if so, why he hadn't pursued them more aggressively. He responded, "The answer to the first part of the question is in the affirmative; as regards to the second part, it might have been asked [of] the Deity about the Creation."[212]

Fisher found himself in a constant state of bureaucratic warfare with the Army, whose supporters called for expanding it at the Navy's expense to defend the country from invasion and, in the event of war with Germany, for a large British expeditionary force to be sent to the Continent to aid in defending France.

Jackie had no patience with the argument that the Royal Navy could not prevent an invasion, declaring, "The Navy . . . is the 1st, 2nd, 3rd, 4th, 5th . . . ad infinitum Line of Defence! If the Navy is not Supreme, no army however large is of the slightest use. It's not invasion we have to fear if our Navy is beaten, IT'S STARVATION!" As for rapidly transporting an army to France, Fisher noted that in October 1899, at the start of the Boer War, Britain, the world's greatest sea power, could transport only 30,000 troops. Churchill put it directly, stating, "As to a stronger Regular Army, either we had command of the sea or we had not. If we had it, we required fewer soldiers; if we had it not, we wanted more ships."[213]

The Army, for its part, opposed the Admiralty's concept of conducting amphibious operations against Germany, given its powerful army. For support, Army leaders could cite Fisher's own arguments on the limitations of transporting even a small force by sea and the experience of exercises confirming the point. (Indeed, Fisher seems to have had little interest in such operations.)

Thus, Fisher did his best to keep mum during the debate over using the Army in amphibious operations along the German coast and the Army's preference to deploy to France. This may have been due to his interest in a strategy of waging an economic-warfare "Blitzkrieg" against Germany, yielding a quick victory that would preclude the use of land forces either for amphibious operations or on the Continent. Should the economic-warfare offensive fail, Fisher seemed content to impose a distant blockade on Germany and flotilla defense of the British Isles, with the Royal Navy's battle fleet positioned to take on the Imperial German Navy should it sally forth to seek an engagement.

Fisher Versus Beresford

Yet it was Fisher's own service that posed the greatest threat to the Scheme. As neither strategy appealed to the Navy's traditions, Fisher feared that stating his views openly would trigger even greater opposition from the growing Syndicate of Discontent. In early 1909, during the scare over Germany's shipbuilding plans, Fisher told Esher that he would not share his true war plan with anyone, especially the CID or Beresford, declaring, "The only man who knows is [Admiral Sir Arthur] Wilson, and he's as close as wax!"[214]

Indeed, whether it took the form of a preemptive strike on the enemy fleet lying in harbor, the close blockade of a rival navy's port to bottle it up or force it to fight, or the discounting of convoys as a means of maritime commerce protection in favor of "search and destroy" operations against enemy cruisers, the Royal Navy reflexively pursued offensive operations. As Fisher put it, "British naval policy is to take the offensive."[215] The problem with this long-held preference for the offensive, however, is that in several instances it conflicted with Fisher's own strategy, which rejected close blockade and amphibious assaults in favor of flotilla defense and distant blockade. Convoy operations—dull and defensive oriented as they were—would prove to be the solution to the commerce-raiding threat in World War I. Fisher's expansive ideas on waging economic warfare to crash Germany's economy were even more alien to Royal Navy traditions. The tension over these matters of substance finally came to a boil, owing to the growing personal animosity between Beresford and Fisher.

Shortly after Fisher's promotion to admiral of the fleet, which effectively ended the hopes of ever becoming first sea lord for Beresford, he was offered command of the Channel Fleet by Lord Tweedmouth. This failed to mollify Beresford, who disliked the reduced role that the Channel Fleet would play in Fisher's Scheme.[216] When the two met to discuss Beresford's new command, Fisher was greatly put off by his colleague's attitude, sensing that trouble lay ahead.[217] Beresford's opposition to the plan stemmed from Fisher's intention to employ flotilla defense and distant blockade. Beresford's Channel Fleet, with the main battle fleet, would stay in reserve. Beresford, however, believed the threat from torpedoes overrated and rejected Fisher's strategy.[218]

In October 1907, Beresford conducted a series of fleet exercises to test his ideas for blockading the Heligoland Bight off the German coast. The maneuvers confirmed his earlier experience in similar maneuvers that the Channel Fleet required vastly more "small craft"—small cruisers and destroyers—to maintain an effective blockade of German ports at night. Exercises conducted the following year by Vice Admiral Sir Francis Bridgeman's Home Fleet appeared to support Beresford's conclusions, as well as those of the 1906 maneuvers, that the blockading force's small craft should outnumber the blockaded fleet's craft by a ratio of three to one. If true, Beresford would require roughly 300 of these ships. The cost of building and manning such a force in peacetime was prohibitive. Indeed, it was one of the principal reasons why Fisher had moved toward flotilla defense.

Ballard found Beresford's strategy nonsensical, pointing out that Beresford had placed his fleet in danger for no good reason, risking heavy losses from the "enemy's" destroyers.[219] In other words, Charlie B was proposing to achieve at great cost, through close or observational blockade, the same effect that could be obtained, at far less cost, through flotilla defense and distant blockade.

Beresford's sniping continued unabated throughout his command, which he left in March 1909. Although his tour of duty would typically have run another year, the Admiralty finally tired of his insubordination. But truncating his command, and thus his career, did not silence Beresford. On April 2, he wrote a letter to Prime Minister Asquith citing the Admiralty's numerous alleged shortcomings, including a failure to construct sufficient small craft, strategic incompetence in the fleet's distribution, and an absence of adequate war plans. Beresford intimated that if Asquith failed to take appropriate action, the letter would be published.[220] Asquith caved and decided to resolve the matter by personally chairing a subcommittee of the CID to explore Beresford's allegations.

The CID's Investigation

The inquiry spanned fifteen meetings, between April 27 and July 13. The Admiralty was represented by First Lord McKenna. Fisher, though present, did not actively participate in the proceedings. This use of the CID to investigate an internal Navy matter was both highly irregular and inappropriate, as it allowed a subordinate, Beresford, to challenge his chain of command and its authority. But it was clear that Asquith was less concerned about Beresford's insubordination or the true state of Britain's defenses than about protecting his political flanks. Not one witness appeared at his request. Whenever it was possible to skirt an issue, he did.[221] Wherever possible, he left issues unaddressed.

In the hearings, Beresford derided Fisher's strategy as a "pedagogue plan." Reflecting the Royal Navy's offensive tradition, he found distant blockade to be "a defensive policy that we cannot afford to adopt." Beresford argued, "We have got to have an attacking policy. . . . We have got to watch the enemy's coast with watching cruisers; they [the Germans] have only two egresses, and when they come out the Admiral should know they have come out."[222] He went on to criticize Fisher's scrapping of more than a hundred small cruisers that, Beresford argued, were needed for close blockade work.

Replying for the Admiralty, First Lord McKenna explained to the committee that the battle cruisers had rendered the old cruisers obsolete. Moreover, McKenna added, submarines had assumed the mission formerly held by small cruisers. That is to say, if an enemy's ports were to be blockaded, it would be accomplished by submarines, not small cruisers.

As Captain Ballard, a member of the Fishpond, concluded, "It is evident that he [Beresford] entirely fails to grasp the main ideas. These cruisers are not watching cruisers in any sense of the word as regards watching for the exit of the enemy's fleet, but placed solely to intercept [the enemy's] trade. . . . Our object is to force them [the enemy] to proceed a distance of more than 300 miles from their own sheltered base to defend their trade and then fall on them when outside, or cut off their retreat."[223] Beresford drew a clear line between his views and Fisher's Scheme and declared that he "attached no importance to submarines." As Charlie B elaborated, the logic behind his position proved difficult to discern. "A propos of what I said with regard to shortage [of cruisers], if the submariners are to take their place, I want to point out that all submarine warfare is entirely theoretical. I will not say they will not 'put down' ships, but they will not revolutionise [naval] warfare unless the Admirals are afraid of them. . . . Now the submarine is always in a fog. The one thing that beats a seaman on the top of the water is a fog. So it is entirely theoretical."[224] Beresford eventually admitted that he had never seen a submarine at sea, even though he had recently spent more than two years commanding the Navy's premier battle fleet.[225] His presentation bordered on incoherency at times, bringing to mind Churchill's observation of Charlie B: "When he gets up, he does not know what he is going to say; when he is speaking he does not know what he is saying; and when he sits down he does not know what he has said."[226]

Finally, Beresford tried to prevail in the debate by calling on the retired admiral of the fleet Sir Arthur Wilson to support his contention that the fleet was "dangerously short" of destroyers and small cruisers. It was generally accepted that Wilson, who had spent the previous five years commanding the Navy's largest fleets, was "the finest Admiral of his day in command of a Fleet, . . . scrupulously just and extraordinarily level-headed." Presented with Beresford's argument, Wilson balked. When Beresford persisted, Wilson finally replied, "My point is that, as I do not want to work over the on German coast [close blockade], I do not want so many." Despite Beresford's pressing him on the point, Wilson replied, "I say I would work on our side in the North Sea [distant blockade]." When Beresford complained that the Admiralty had not supplied him with war plans, Wilson discounted their value, echoing Helmuth von Moltke in declaring that he was "perfectly certain that any plan drawn up in peace would not be carried out in war," finding the value of drawing up plans primarily educational. Beresford's gambit of calling on Wilson had backfired. As one observer concluded, Wilson "does not believe in Charlie's strategy—he does not believe in going over to the German coast and watching there day and night."[227]

Despite Beresford's poor showing, Asquith went out of his way to issue a "General Conclusion" that was critical of Beresford *and* Fisher. The committee found that "during the time in question no danger to the country resulted from the Admiralty's arrangements for war, whether considered from the standpoint of organization and distribution of the fleet, the number of ships, or the preparation of war plans." It found that "Lord Charles Beresford . . . failed to appreciate and carry out the spirit of the instructions of the Board and recognize their paramount authority." Remarkably, Fisher was implicitly censured for not adequately consulting Beresford during his time in command, implying that Beresford should have had a veto over his superior's decisions.[228]

For Asquith, it was the politically correct thing to do. Despite the weakness with which Beresford presented his case, he was seen as the leader of the traditional wing of the Royal Navy and had a great deal of public support for his views as well. For Asquith to come down on Fisher's side would have been politically risky.[229]

Beresford considered himself the victor and acted accordingly. He declared his intention to run for a seat in Parliament and lobbied the opposition Conservative Party to appoint him as first sea lord to succeed Fisher should they regain power in the next election. Fisher stewed, writing to a fellow admiral, "The Committee, by not squashing Beresford when they had the chance and so utterly discrediting him thereby in the face of all men, have given Beresford a fresh leash of insubordinate agitation. Had they smashed him, as they could have by the evidence, as a blatant liar, he would have been so utterly discredited that no newspaper would have noticed him ever again."[230]

The findings effectively undermined both Fisher's authority and public confidence in the Board of the Admiralty. There was a growing sentiment that it was time for "Radical Jack" Fisher to go. And so he did.

Fisher retired on January 25, 1910, after fifty-five years' service. He did exact some measure of revenge against his tormentor Beresford. King George V, a friend of Charlie B, urged Asquith to appoint Beresford as first sea lord. McKenna, however, succeeded in blocking the move in favor of recalling Admiral Wilson to active service. McKenna was determined that Fisher's successor sustain the reforms that had been undertaken during his tenure. Although recalling a retired admiral to active duty in peacetime was unusual, Wilson had many qualities that made him an attractive choice. Fisher was very pleased with Wilson's selection, in part because he was not a member of the Syndicate of Discontent and also because Sir Arthur would reach the mandatory retirement age of seventy in 1912, by which time he could be succeeded by a member of the Fishpond.[231]

In responding to Asquith's inquiry regarding Beresford's prospects to serve as first sea lord, McKenna icily noted, "Sir Arthur Wilson stands out by universal acknowledgement as the greatest sailor we have had for many years." As for Beresford, he merited an unfavorable comparison to Fisher. "His services are no longer required. He has commanded at sea with much, but not unusual success. ... He has not been responsible for, or associated with, any development of naval science, strategy, or training."[232]

As one prominent historian summarized it, "Beresford stood for things as they were, for orthodoxy and tradition. Fisher looked beyond, imagining new men, new rules, new ships, new worlds that broke tradition so violently that they constituted revolution. Both men had colossal egos, but over a lifetime of service, Beresford's ego tended to focus on himself, while Fisher's was devoted to the advancement of the Service."[233]

Fisher's Shadow

Both Fisher and Beresford were now gone. Percy Scott and Reginald Bacon retired later that year. The Navy was losing some of its best officers, just as tensions with Germany were heating up. How would Fisher's Scheme, or at least those parts he had implemented, be preserved?

The Fishpond

In the near term, support for the concept of flotilla defense persisted. Only a few months after Fisher stepped down, McKenna, in correspondence to the foreign secretary, Sir Edward Grey, noted, "our destroyers and submarine flotillas, which are the true defense against invasion, will be stationed on the East Coast [of England]."[234] But McKenna would soon leave the Admiralty.

Fisher, through his apostles in the Fishpond, sought to preserve and even advance the Scheme. Shortly after his retirement at the end of 1909, Rear Admiral Bacon presented a paper to the Institute of Naval Architects. Echoing Fisher, Bacon announced that torpedoes of ever greater ranges had been developed that made it possible for swarms of smaller ships to engage battleships effectively. "Not only is the battleship itself open to attack by small craft which it cannot engage on equal terms, but it is powerless to protect any form of vessel against the attacks of such craft."[235]

Bacon also predicted that the ongoing naval revolution would require Britain's all-big-gun warships to carry only light armor protection, as it seemed certain that the long struggle between offensive firepower and defensive armor would be won by the former. Continuing to channel Fisher, Bacon observed that ships capable of high speeds would be needed, for both tactical and strategic reasons. Hence, Fisher's battle cruisers, with their high speed, light armor, and long-range hitting power, must be supported.

Finally, Bacon argued that as capital ships would become more vulnerable to torpedoes, it would be risky to form them into a traditional line of battle, the reason being that it would provide those who were firing torpedoes with targets analogous to ducks passing along in a shooting gallery. He concluded by offering a vision of the battle fleet abandoning the line of battle to what might be termed a "combined-arms" fleet: "The battleship as now known will probably develop from a single ship into a battle unit consisting of a large armoured cruiser with attendant torpedo craft. Line of battle, as we now know it, will be radically modified, and the fleet action of the future will, in course of time, develop into an aggregation of duels between opposing battle units. The tactics of such units open up a vista of most exhilarating speculation."[236] Thus, destroyers could defend the capital ships from torpedo attack more effectively than battleship gunfire. Destroyers also cost far less than capital ships, enabling commanders to take risks with them that would have been foolhardy with a dreadnought or battle cruiser. "It would be simply suicidal," Fisher declared, "for any battleship squadron to cruise without an attendant destroyer flotilla."[237] Fisher's thinking was soon confirmed in a series of fleet exercises.

For the most part, Fisher's estimate of Wilson proved correct. Wilson did not pursue Fisher's reforms energetically; however, he also did not repudiate them. He remained skeptical of Fisher's concept of economic warfare and, given the formidable political challenges to implementing it, rightly so.[238]

Wilson gave greater priority to building dreadnoughts than battle cruisers and submarines. As had Fisher, the Navy under Wilson struggled to address the problem of submarines and torpedoes. As Bacon hinted in his speech, the fleet began to assign squadrons of cruisers, along with destroyers and submarine flotillas, to the battle fleet to create for the first time a combined "battle unit." The small craft would screen the battleships and battle cruisers from enemy torpedo craft, while attempting to threaten the enemy's battleships with their own torpedoes. The concept, however, was hobbled in execution, owing to the fleet's tactical command-and-control capabilities, which were limited to flags, lights, and primitive wireless.

Churchill

Winston Churchill succeeded McKenna as first lord in October 1911. Although Churchill had been a leading voice in efforts to wring greater economies from the fleet, his views changed dramatically once he joined the Admiralty. He also emerged as an ally of Fisher.

The two met at Biarritz in 1907 and immediately hit it off. Fisher wrote, "Fell desperately in love with Winston Churchill"; Churchill told Fisher, "You are the only man in the world I really love." King Edward VII called them "the chatterers." The prime minister's daughter, Violet Asquith, observed, "they can't resist each other for long at close range." Fisher's fondness for Churchill grew with the new first lord's support for his ideas. Fisher lost no time preaching his gospel to Churchill, promoting battle cruisers and proclaiming, "*Speed, Big Gun* and *Cheapness* those are the 3 Fundamentals—& you can have them."[239]

In the years immediately following *Dreadnought*'s appearance, the Liberal government's financial challenges were eased thanks to an economic boom. Knowing that busts follow booms, in the spring of 1911, Chancellor of the Exchequer Lloyd George argued that the government needed to prepare for an inevitable economic downturn. Like many politicians, he knew the dangers of increasing taxes. The only solution, then, was to be found in trimming social welfare and military expenditures. As did Fisher in 1904, Churchill felt pressure to realize economies in the Navy's budget.

In November 1911, Churchill convinced Asquith to retire Admiral Wilson a few months early and approve Admiral Sir Francis Bridgeman, a member of the Fishpond, to succeed him.[240] Shortly after Bridgeman assumed his new position, he reported to Fisher that Churchill was "full of new schemes of strategy which are almost too bold to be believed!" What Bridgeman did not know was that Fisher was often the inspiration for Churchill's schemes. Reprising his arguments during the 1904 push to trim naval estimates, Fisher convinced Churchill that British maritime superiority could be maintained and significant savings achieved by emphasizing flotilla defense and the construction of battle cruisers.[241]

In February 1912, the Admiralty received information that Admiral Tirpitz's supplementary naval plan called for increasing the number of warships in the active German fleet from seventeen battleships and four battle cruisers to twenty-five battleships and eight battle cruisers. The Royal Navy, however, normally maintained only twenty-two capital ships in full commission in home waters, including the six based at Gibraltar. The Admiralty also had to account for the fleets of Austria-Hungary and Italy, Germany's two allies within the Triple Alliance. The former was building four dreadnought-style battleships, while the latter had four dreadnoughts in its fleet and another two under construction. They also possessed nine and eight pre-dreadnought battleships, respectively, against six Royal Navy pre-dreadnoughts at Malta.[242]

A range of alternatives was explored for responding to the challenge. One option centered on arms control, including a proposal to freeze British capital ship construction if Germany would do the same. Another called for extending flotilla defense to the Mediterranean and concentrating more battleships in home waters. A major consideration in crafting these options was the lack of skilled manpower to man major warships. Ultimately, the Navy would place its faith in battleships. Although Churchill had planned to cut the number of battleships in full commission from twenty-eight to twenty-two, the challenge posed by the Triple Alliance powers found him reversing course and supporting keeping thirty-three battleships in full commission, with another eight in reserve—a major blow to Fisher's Scheme. Adding insult to injury, the only way to come up with the additional manpower to crew the additional battleships was to rob from the crews of cruisers and flotilla craft and to dilute the proportion of skilled personnel manning older battleships.[243]

Churchill worked to salvage what he could. In May 1912, he effected a compromise: the new *Queen Elizabeth*–class "super-dreadnoughts" would be armed with 15-inch guns and have a speed of twenty-four knots—three knots greater than *Dreadnought*, although not as fast as Fisher's battle cruisers.[244] Still, his overall emphasis on firepower and speed at the expense of armor in capital ship design was retained.

When explaining the Admiralty's decision to the House of Commons, Churchill all but sang from the Fisher hymnal, declaring that when considering "a battle between two great modern iron-clad ships, you must not think of . . . two men in armor striking at each other with heavy swords. It is more like a battle between two egg shells striking each other with hammers. . . . The importance of hitting first, hitting hardest, and keeping on hitting . . . really needs no clearer proof."[245]

Increasing British naval power in the North Sea to counter the Kaiser's fleet meant closer cooperation with the French. The Royal Navy's Atlantic Fleet was recalled to home waters. The Mediterranean Fleet, less a few battle cruisers, was repositioned from Malta to Gibraltar. The French agreed that the Royal Navy would guard both sides of the English Channel against the German naval threat, while France would assume a greater role in the Mediterranean, repositioning six battleships from its Atlantic Fleet to the Mediterranean.[246]

Still, the Royal Navy's budget would need to be increased to meet the anticipated German buildup. Here Churchill's old ally Lloyd George fought a rearguard action against his former "budget hawk" ally, but the popular mood favored battleships over fiscal probity. Lloyd George told Churchill that he knew it was time to give in when his wife remarked, "You know, my dear, I never interfere in politics, but they say you are having an argument with that nice Mr. Churchill about building dread-noughts. Of course I don't understand these things, but I should have thought it would be better to have too many rather than too few."[247]

Churchill, for his part, sought to stay in good standing with the fiscal conservatives and Lloyd George by proposing a "naval holiday" with Germany, declaring that any reduction in German warship construction would be met by a proportionate reduction in British shipbuilding. Thus, if Germany postponed building the three battleships it had planned for 1913, Britain would drop the five it was planning to start. Despite Churchill's repeated efforts to win over the Germans, the Kaiser ruled out any such "holiday."[248]

What caught Fisher's perceptive eye, however, was not the German plans for dreadnoughts but those for flotilla craft. Seventy-two new sub-marines would be added to Germany's High Seas Fleet, and 99 of its 144 destroyers would be fully manned.

On the Eve of War

Fleet Exercises: Blockade and Flotilla Defense

The combined Home and Atlantic Fleet maneuvers of April–May 1910 tested Britain's east-coast defensive patrols—flotilla defense. One phase explored the "British" destroyer flotillas supported by cruisers, which were put out of action by the "enemy" fleet flotillas and light cruisers. The culprit was a lack of ships in the British flotilla's "picket line" early warning system, intended to enable the defenders to concentrate their forces against the enemy. The system's failure enabled the enemy to con-centrate its forces and attack dispersed British ships and destroy them in detail before reinforcements could arrive. Simply put, more flotilla craft were needed, as well as enhanced scouting and command and control.[249]

The summer maneuvers evaluated the growing threat posed by sub-marines armed with torpedoes. The submarine *D1* was pitted against two armored cruisers. Operating 600 miles from its base at Portsmouth, the *D1* "torpedoed" the two cruisers before returning to base. The exercise convinced Admiral Wilson, previously a skeptic, of the submarine's potential. Wilson perceptively raised the possibility that, owing to their stealth, submarines might be the key to resurrecting the close blockade.[250]

The 1911 maneuvers saw the Navy exploring the possibility of imposing a blockade at a greater distance from the enemy's shore to better protect the blockading force. Forty-eight destroyers and eight light cruisers from the Home Fleet were positioned along a 60-mile line in the North Sea with the mission of alerting the main fleet should the "enemy" fleet emerge. This scouting force failed, even though it was tasked with patrolling only 60 miles of the 150 miles called for in the war plan. It left many Royal Navy officers openly questioning not only close but this more distant "observational" blockade. In April 1912, the Admiralty decided to explore a more distant "intermediate" blockade in the July–August Home Fleet maneuvers.[251]

The maneuvers once again showed the screening ships stretched across the middle of the North Sea vulnerable, confirming the distant blockade (Plan A/A1) as the only workable strategy for dealing with the German threat. The Royal Navy simply lacked the cruisers and destroyers necessary to establish an effective screen. The maneuvers, however, found D Class submarines outperforming expectations, and Churchill contemplated building more D Class submarines as an alternative to costly battleships. By year's end, the fleet was instructed to follow Ballard's redrafted 1907 A/A1 plan and impose a distant surface blockade from its base at Scapa Flow.[252] Although a distant blockade offended the Navy's offensive traditions, it had the virtue of being effective. Destroyers and submarines would close off access to the Channel. Should the High Seas Fleet challenge the blockade, it would be met with Fisher's New Model battle fleet, capable of engaging beyond torpedo range. In 1913, the Royal United Services Institute awarded its Gold Medal to Commander Kenneth Dewar, whose essay was essentially a restatement of Ballard's work.[253]

The 1913 Grand Fleet maneuvers tested the Navy's ability to counter the threat of invasion along Britain's east coast by Germany's High Seas Fleet. Rear Admiral John de Robeck commanded the "British" fleet's flotilla patrol, and the battle fleet was under the command of Admiral Sir George Callaghan. Vice Admiral John Jellicoe led the "German" fleet, with the mission of mounting an invasion. After ten days, the "Germans" claimed victory, having landed 3,500 marines. Once again, the Royal Navy's scouting patrols failed to detect the enemy in time to defeat the invasion. Fisher's flotilla defense concept was not working.

Admiral Callaghan also pointed out that stationing the battle fleet in the north of Scotland precluded its ability to intercept quickly an enemy fleet transporting an invasion force. But having lost 40 percent of his capital ships to submarine attack during the exercise, the admiral also conceded that if the fleet was brought south to protect against an invasion, it would also be running unacceptable risks. Echoing Admiral Bacon's paper from 1909, Callaghan argued that a major fleet engagement should combine both torpedo attacks and long-range gunnery. This focused further attention on a growing debate over whether the huge battle fleet could be effectively commanded in an engagement. The Navy began to work on devising contingency plans to employ aircraft equipped with wireless to support the Navy's early warning flotillas, including defense of Britain's east coast.[254]

Fisher's Push for Submarines

Amid all this, Fisher continued pressing for more submarines. In March 1913, he began circulating drafts of his paper "The Oil Engine and the Submarine," motivated in part by Admiralty plans for steam (rather than diesel) engines on "fleet" submarines in the hope that they could achieve the speeds needed to operate as a screen for the battle fleet. When the Admiralty moved in October to let contracts on experimental steam-powered boats, Fisher told Churchill that, given budget constraints, priority should go to proven patrol submarines that can be used for flotilla defense and potentially for a new form of close blockade.

Fisher's paper declared, *"Submarines are the coming Dreadnoughts. . . . We are falling behind Germany in large submarines!"* Fisher also predicted—to the horror of Churchill, Battenberg, and others—that in war, submarines would sink unarmed merchant ships. Fisher expressed the hope that Britain's naval rivals would continue to build dreadnoughts: "vessels that will be securely blockaded by our submarines, as the Mediterranean and North Sea will be securely locked up."[255]

Fisher's views prevailed, and the Admiralty decided to emphasize patrol submarines. That same month, the Cabinet pressured Churchill to fund two dreadnoughts, not four as called for in the 1914–15 estimates, confronting him with the challenge of cutting the Navy's budget and building submarines, while maintaining a battleship force equal to Germany's plus a 60 percent margin.

But Churchill also knew that the Liberal government feared the political backlash of abandoning the battleship. He also knew that dropping two dreadnoughts would provide the Canadians, who had committed to funding three dreadnoughts, with an excuse to renege, placing an unbearable burden on the Navy's budget. This looming political crisis provided Churchill with an opportunity. He informed Asquith that he could provide him with political cover against the party's fiscal hawks and against charges that he was abandoning Britain's maritime supremacy. This could be done, Churchill said, by substituting submarines for some battleships and adopting a fundamentally new way of measuring the maritime balance. Drop two battleships from the 1914–15 program and use the funds to build a new class of semisubmersible torpedo craft and sixteen submarines. Drop all but two or three destroyers in the program in favor of four additional submarines, bringing their total to twenty. The "new" maritime balance would be measured not only using merely capital ships but also by including submarines and other torpedo craft. Owing to the sensitivity of effecting such a radical shift, the deal was known only to the Admiralty Board, Asquith, and Lloyd George. As with support for Fisher's scheme in 1904, the motives for backing Churchill's gambit were both strategic and financial.[256]

Just as the Admiralty was moving to implement Churchill's proposal, general war broke out in Europe, bringing Britain, France, and Russia into conflict with Germany and Austria-Hungary.[257] The crucible of conflict would determine whether Fisher's vision of the maritime competition or those of his detractors would prove out.

The Fleet at War's Edge

The British fleet that went to war was radically different from the one Fisher had inherited a decade before. The Royal Navy was now able to maneuver and concentrate with unprecedented speed, thanks to the introduction of turbine engines, oil-fired propulsion, and wireless. This had enabled a radical redistribution of the fleet, greatly mitigating the Navy's manpower problems. Driven in part by advances in torpedo weaponry, the fleet's range of engagement had grown fantastically with the launching of all-big-gun super-dreadnoughts, which enabled the fleet to engage the enemy at far greater distances than had ever before been possible. The ability of Britain's shipyards to produce new ships faster than their competitors made possible "time-based competition," or what Fisher called "plunging," in support of his efforts at "wrecking" rival navy programs.

Although Fisher's Scheme was not fully implemented, given the barriers he confronted, what was accomplished during his time as first sea lord and in collaboration with Churchill borders on miraculous. When war came, the fleet moved to enforce a distant blockade and support economic warfare against Germany. The Channel was closed by a form of flotilla defense, and the eastern approaches to the Home Islands were screened by flotilla craft. The Admiralty was moving toward a new way of measuring the naval balance in line with Fisher's view of submarines as the "next big thing" in war at sea.

Fisher's vision was not without its flaws. Fleet maneuvers revealed problems with command and control of a "combined arms" fleet. Flotilla defense suffered from the absence of effective scouting that would enable torpedo craft to mass against an invading force. The challenge associated with fire control at very long range, which Fisher believed was addressed, in fact remained unsolved. And although he foresaw submarines sinking unarmed merchant ships, it was a problem that those in power would willfully ignore, placing their faith in the rules of civilized warfare.

In August 1914, there was no debate as to whether the previous decade had witnessed a naval transformation. The question was whether "Radical Jack" Fisher's revolution would enable the Royal Navy to prevail in the ultimate test of war.

War

The Great War showed how profoundly the character of war at sea had changed in the span of a few short years. Both Britain's Grand Fleet and Germany's High Seas Fleet proved skittish of submarines. The Royal Navy adopted a distant blockade. If the High Seas Fleet wished to break it, it risked moving into waters that might be populated with British mines and torpedo craft, backed by Britain's Grand Fleet.

What surprised many people, but not Fisher, was the emergence of submarine commerce raiding and blockade. Owing to the Navy's tradition of offensive warfare, it persisted in search-and-destroy operations against commerce-raiding submarines while resisting convoy operations. The results were disastrous, similar to a company of cavalry defending a wagon train moving across the American West against raids by Native

Americans by galloping about randomly along the route. By April 1917, shipping losses were so heavy that the Admiralty thought it had nothing to lose by trying convoys, which soon turned the tide in Britain's favor. Still, German U-boats sank more than eleven million tons of merchant shipping during the war, roughly 95 percent with torpedoes.[258]

As with British commerce, the greatest threat to the Grand Fleet was not the High Seas Fleet but Germany's submarines, which, along with mines, exercised a fearful toll on warships. The light cruisers *Amphion* and *Pathfinder* were lost on August 4 and September 5, respectively. Jellicoe, now commanding the Grand Fleet, quickly redeployed it from Scapa Flow to west of Scotland. On September 22, a German submarine sent the cruisers *Aboukir, Cressy,* and *Hogue* to the bottom off the Dutch coast. When an older cruiser, *Hawke,* was torpedoed in the North Sea on October 15, Jellicoe again moved the fleet, this time off Ireland's northern coast. Still, the losses mounted. Twelve days later, a mine sank the new dreadnought *Audacious* off Lough Swilly, while the seaplane carrier *Hermes* was torpedoed in the Straits of Dover on November 1. On January 1, 1915, the pre-dreadnought battleship *Formidable* met the same fate.[259]

When the Royal Navy approached the Turkish coast at Gallipoli in 1915, Turkish mines sent three battleships, two British and one French, to the bottom. During the campaign, the battleships *Triumph* and *Majestic* were sunk by submarines.[260] As Fisher had foreseen, it was not Germany's battleships that were sending British warships to the bottom but their submarines armed with the "devil's device."

In October 1914, Fisher was recalled as first sea lord. He had hoped that economic warfare would bring about a collapse in Germany's economy and a quick victory, but the strategy was never fully implemented, owing to protests from commercial interests and neutrals and to bureaucratic opposition in the government. Less than a month after entering the war, the government scaled back its efforts. By the time Fisher arrived, distant blockade was the order of the day.

Eight months later, he resigned after a series of disputes with Churchill. They agreed on the distant blockade, but Churchill was also looking to take the offensive and strike a dramatic blow against Germany, such as seizing the island of Borkum as part of operations to secure the Baltic Sea, and to wage a campaign against the Ottomans to open the Dardanelles. Captain (later Admiral) Sir Herbert Richmond, then serving on the Admiralty's staff and widely recognized as one of the

Navy's best thinkers, viewed Churchill's ideas for seizing Borkum as "quite mad," declaring, "I have never read such an idiotic, amateur piece of work as this [Churchill's] outline in my life." Fisher, who felt that as long as the distant blockade offered the prospect of success, there was no reason to engage in reckless offensive operations, doubtless agreed.[261]

As for a prospective Dardanelles campaign, Fisher argued for maintaining a robust blockade, noting, "Being already in possession of all that a powerful fleet can give a country, we should continue quietly to enjoy the advantage without dissipating our strength in operations that cannot improve the position."[262] Asquith, however, sided with Churchill.

The operation proved a fiasco and put Churchill and Fisher on a collision course. In May, Fisher resigned when Churchill looked for more ships to support the campaign, which Jackie believed would only reinforce failure while threatening the North Sea blockade's strength. His departure caused an outcry, threatening to end the truce between the Conservatives and the Liberal government. A new coalition government would need to be formed, one without Churchill as first lord.

Fisher's vision of future war at sea among surface combatants assumed that advantages in speed and long-range gunnery would more than offset sacrifices in armor protection. Early engagements were encouraging. On December 8, 1914, a German cruiser squadron was intercepted by a British force off the Falkland Islands. The battle that followed saw two British battle cruisers, *Invincible* and *Inflexible*, pummeling the German armored cruisers *Scharnhorst* and *Gneisenau* with long-range fires. The British ships sustained only minor damage. Fisher was exultant. Only a month later, elements of the Grand and High Seas Fleets engaged near the Dogger Bank in the North Sea. Once again, the British battle-cruiser force used its superior speed to intercept the German battle cruisers and begin a long-range engagement at an unheard-of range of 18,000 yards. Firing at that distance placed the shells on a high, lofting trajectory, landing them on the German ships' decks, which were thinly armored relative to their sides. The German armored cruiser *Blucher* was sunk and the battle cruiser *Seydlitz* damaged, while the British suffered damage only to the battle cruiser *Lion*, along with a destroyer. The British could have won a major victory save for the persistent problem of exercising effective command of their ships. Perhaps most worrisome, despite the British battle cruisers' success, they were experiencing difficulties firing accurately at long ranges, scoring hits at a rate of less than 2 percent while the enemy scored over 3 percent.[263]

In May 1916, British battle-cruiser performance showed little improvement in the Battle of Jutland, off Denmark's North Sea coast. There, Britain's Grand Fleet—by far the most powerful of the Royal Navy's fleets—engaged its counterpart, the German High Seas Fleet, for the only time in the four-year conflict. During the battle, the British battle cruisers were frustrated in their attempts to employ their speed to gain a range advantage on their German adversaries. This was due in part to limits on visibility, as the British battle-cruiser division encountered the lead elements of the High Seas Fleet in the late afternoon of May 31. Efforts to employ speed in line with Fisher's vision also foundered, owing to the huge size and heterogeneous composition of the Grand Fleet and the difficulties involved in conducting effective scouting.[264] Perhaps most discouraging, the Royal Navy's Dreyer range-finding gear proved incapable of maintaining the correct range of the German warships as the two forces converged, undermining the advantage provided by the fleet's big guns.

During the battle, Admiral David Beatty, commanding the British battle-cruiser division, saw the Royal Navy battle cruiser *Lion* hit first. Then the *Indefatigable* blew up. Not long after, the *Queen Mary* was sunk. This represented a near perfect cross-section of Britain's prewar battle-cruiser classes. Beatty turned to his flag captain and said, "There seems to be something wrong with our bloody ships today, Chatfield."[265]

The performance of the *Queen Mary*, the only battle cruiser with a Pollen range-finding Argo clock, hinted at what Beatty's battle cruisers might have done with the state-of-the-art system. Before it was sunk some forty minutes into the battle, its guns registered four hits. The range between the two fleets at that time often exceeded 15,000 yards and was never less than 12,900. The *Queen Mary* scored a hit before any of Beatty's other battle cruisers did and hit its targets twice as frequently.[266]

The battle cruisers probably suffered less from the absence of armor plate than from a propensity to store powder charges in exposed places. This enabled the fires started by incoming shells to generate secondary explosions in the powder magazines. British armor-piercing shells often failed to detonate, owing to faulty fuses. Finally, German ships benefited from Tirpitz's relatively greater investment in armor protection and damage control.[267]

At Jutland, the backbone of the British battle line proved to be the *Queen Elizabeth* class of so-called super-dreadnoughts, which constituted the Fifth Battle Squadron. These five fast ships were equipped with 15-inch guns, bigger than those on any previous dreadnought and substantially superior to any other battleship afloat.[268] The ships opened fire on the German fleet at 19,000 yards, scoring hits at nearly twice the rate as Beatty's battle cruisers, inflicting six hits while taking none, partially confirming Fisher's faith in speed and long-range fires. Although there was a spirited debate following the battle as to which side prevailed at the tactical level, Fisher's dreadnoughts had prevailed at the strategic level. As a New York paper concluded, "The German Fleet has assaulted its jailor, but it is still in jail."[269]

In retrospect, Fisher's vision of an extended-range fleet engagement leveraging speed and long-range fires was less flawed than the timing of its implementation. Had the Pollen system been fully incorporated into the fleet, it could have provided the Royal Navy with the kind of long-range gunnery accuracy that Fisher believed he had. Moreover, only three years after Jutland, the U.S. Navy, employing wireless-equipped aircraft as spotters, produced dramatic increases in long-range naval bombardment accuracy. Aircraft would also have provided Fisher's flotilla defense forces with the scouting capability needed to concentrate against an enemy fleet approaching Britain's coast.

Conclusion

The period between the mid-nineteenth and early twentieth centuries witnessed several disruptive and overlapping shifts in the character of war at sea. These shifts challenged the Royal Navy's traditional methods of defending the British Isles, the empire, and maritime commerce.

Beginning in the late 1890s, rapid progress with submarines and torpedoes offered an entirely new way of waging war at sea. Anti-ship mines, when combined with torpedo craft, could make close—and, progressively, observational and intermediate—blockade an unacceptably risky proposition. Torpedo craft so threatened the survival of major warships that ways needed to be found to operate beyond their range, hence the all-big-gun capital ships and oceangoing destroyers operating as part of a combined-arms fleet. As Fisher foresaw, submarines proved formidable threats to battleships and commercial transports alike.

A handful of individuals identified elements of these challenges to British maritime supremacy, but only one did so comprehensively while being in a position to respond to them holistically: Admiral Jackie Fisher.

"Radical Jack's" Scheme focused on meeting these challenges by profoundly altering the Royal Navy's size, structural form, and disposition.

His vision had three basic components: battle cruisers, flotilla defense, and plunging. Fisher was willing—much more so than his colleagues at the Admiralty or Britain's political leaders—to place big bets on building a fleet that could outrange the growing torpedo threat, and exploiting submarines and torpedoes to defend Britain from direct attack when blockading the enemy's fleets was no longer a realistic option.

In a way that seems remarkable in contemporary times, Fisher succeeded in realizing a significant portion of his Scheme. The drag on Fisher's efforts, though deleterious in some ways, also had a positive side. By continuing to build dreadnought battleships, the Admiralty effectively pursued a hedging strategy against the possibility that all of Fisher's big bets might not prove out. This hedging strategy enabled the Royal Navy to adapt effectively enough to prevail when war came. Partially "wrong" about battle cruisers, Fisher proved "right" in advancing the construction of submarines and destroyers. The latter, of course, paid great dividends in the convoy operations that defeated the threat to Britain's maritime lifeline—even though they had been bought with a different mission in mind. Fisher was right to abandon the close blockade in favor of distant blockade, and his frightening predictions on the submarine threat to commerce proved prescient.

When viewed in the balance, Fisher emerges as one of the most foresighted and capable military leaders of the past two centuries. At the fleet's grand view in July 1914, on the eve of war, Rear Admiral Sir Robert Arbuthnot was moved to say, "All that is best and most modern here is the creation of Lord Fisher."[270] That fleet would pass the ultimate test: it prevented the German fleet from ever coming close to directly threatening Britain's or its allies' homelands; it maintained—albeit with difficulty—maritime commerce essential to Britain's survival; and it deterred the High Seas Fleet from challenging it in a major engagement.

As Arthur Marder concludes, "The verdict of history is that in Fisher the Navy and the nation had found their man—a strong man ready to face the tremendous responsibility and personal risk of carrying out a constructive revolution in a service rendered by the very pride of its traditions one of the most conservative in the world." "Fisher," says Marder, "whatever his defects, was a genius." Churchill concurred, writing: "His genius was deep and true."[271]

CHAPTER SEVEN

Out of the Trenches

The whole future of warfare appears to me to be in the
employment of mobile armies, relatively small but of high quality,
and rendered distinctly more effective by the addition of aircraft.

—GENERAL HANS VON SEECKT

We believe that by attacking with tanks we can achieve a higher
rate of movement than has been hitherto obtainable, and—what
is perhaps even more important—that we can keep moving once
a breakthrough has been made.

—GENERAL HEINZ GUDERIAN

ON THE MORNING OF November 8, 1918, representatives of the German
government arrived at Compiègne Forest, roughly thirty-five miles
north of Paris. There, parked along a railway siding, sat the private train
of the supreme Allied commander, Marshal Ferdinand Foch. The German delegation's mission was to obtain terms for an armistice.

There were no negotiations in the traditional sense. The Germans
were presented with a list of demands, written primarily by Foch, and

given seventy-two hours to sign. The Germans did succeed in getting the terms amended so that they were not obligated to decommission more submarines than they actually possessed and were given more time to withdraw from Allied territory. They also registered a formal protest to what they saw as a Carthaginian peace. At 5:45 a.m. on November 11, 1918, after representatives of the Allies and Germany had signed the armistice, Foch arrived and affixed his signature. After more than four years of fighting, the German Army that had dominated Europe for half a century had effectively surrendered.

The Versailles Treaty marking the war's formal end was signed on June 28, 1919. It all but disarmed Germany's military, which was forbidden from possessing aircraft, tanks, and heavy artillery. Germany's Army was reduced to 100,000 men, including 4,000 officers. Its intellectual core, the general staff, was dissolved, along with its War Academy (Kriegsakademie) and Cadet School.

It appeared to some observers that Foch's goal of rendering Germany unable to threaten France ever again had been achieved. Yet as the treaty was being signed, he remarked, "This is not a peace. It is an armistice for twenty years."[1]

Foch's words proved prophetic. In little more than two decades, the German military rose from its humiliating defeat to dominate land warfare on the Continent. In the process, the German military leadership pursued a vision of warfare that was dramatically different from the static trench warfare that dominated the Western Front in the Great War. Employing advanced military systems made possible by rapidly progressing technologies in the fields of mechanization, aviation, and radio, Germany transformed its military into an instrument capable of waging mechanized air-land warfare, popularly known as "Blitzkrieg" (or "lightning war").[2]

The Seeds of Change

Germany's military, the Reichswehr, began the postwar era in a greatly weakened state but also with a vision of waging a different kind of war, the seeds of which were sown in the latter stages of World War I.[3] The stalemate produced by static trench warfare, particularly on the Western Front, found both sides searching for ways to restore offensive maneuver at the operational (or campaign) level of war.

The German military's long-standing preference for waging a war of maneuver led it to adopt "storm" or "infiltration" tactics, the brainchild of General August von Mackensen and his chief of staff, Colonel Hans von Seeckt. Their concept centered on quickly exploiting even small breaks in the Russian lines by rushing in reserves to widen and deepen the penetration, with the goal of producing a breakout. September 1917 found General Oskar von Hutier employing these tactics successfully in operations around Riga. The Germans also discovered that using a short preparatory bombardment gave the enemy less time to concentrate forces in the sector being attacked. They began to employ specially trained troops—"storm troopers"—that were instructed to infiltrate the Russian lines, bypassing any strong points to sustain their advance into the enemy's rear area.[4]

The Allies, on the other hand, emphasized exploiting new military systems, especially the tank, a recent invention that had its proximate origins in the Royal Navy's Landship Committee, formed by the Admiralty's first lord, Winston Churchill. The French soon joined the British in this endeavor, and by 1916, both countries were producing tanks. The British Army first used tanks during the Somme offensive in September 1916. Ironically, given what transpired, the Germans only began to develop tanks after encountering them on the Somme and had only begun producing tanks in significant numbers when the armistice was signed.

The two sides' attempts at breaking the trench stalemate were on display on November 20, 1917. The British massed some 400 tanks and six infantry divisions supported by Royal Flying Corps aircraft and attacked two understrength German infantry divisions along a seven-mile front near the French town of Cambrai. Within twenty-four hours, the British drove the Germans back five miles—an unprecedented feat against well-entrenched forces on the Western Front.[5] The German counterattack at Cambrai coincidentally saw the first major use of storm tactics on the Western Front. Twenty German divisions operating without tanks erased the British breakthrough, capturing more than 150 artillery pieces and some 6,000 troops.[6]

Although the German assault did not involve tanks, German small units were now equipped with hand grenades, machine guns, grenade launchers, trench mortars, and flame-throwers, making them combined-arms units in miniature. Both massed armor and storm tactics showed promise for restoring maneuver to the battlefield, at least at the tactical level.[7] Shortly thereafter, taking a page from the British, the German high command began to use aircraft to provide mobile fire support to the storm troopers, partially offsetting their lack of tanks.[8]

No tactical system, however, could solve the German Army's fundamental operational problem in the west: the enemy's railroads and motor transport columns could move reinforcements to reestablish a new defensive line more quickly than the German storm troops—moving on foot and ever farther from their sources of supplies and artillery support—could achieve a complete breakthrough. Simply put, the Germans were losing the "concentration/counter-concentration" competition to the Allies.

When the Germans' Michel Offensive in the spring of 1918 failed to yield strategic gains, their high command, having exhausted its last major offensive reserves, found itself confronting the buildup of U.S. armies in France and the increasingly suffocating grip of the Royal Navy's economic blockade. That summer, at Soissons and Amiens, British and French forces employed tanks and aircraft together in sizeable numbers to create cracks in the German lines. Joined by the Americans, they rained a series of hammer blows on the Western Front in the summer and early autumn, increasing the stress on the German Army to the breaking point. By November, the Germans felt compelled to seek an armistice.

The Versailles Treaty left the German military with two principal operational problems. The first concerned the challenge of defending Germany's relatively long borders with a 100,000-man treaty-restricted army. In the early 1920s, Germany confronted potential threats from France and Poland, each with a military that was far superior to the Reichswehr. This problem endured until Germany's rearmament following its renunciation of the treaty in 1935. The second, more enduring problem was the one left unsolved at the end of World War I: how to restore mobility to the battlefield at the operational level of war.[9]

Hans von Seeckt

In March 1920, General Walther Reinhardt resigned as Chef der Heeresleitung of the Provisional Reichswehr and was succeeded by General Hans von Seeckt, who was appointed chief of Germany's armed forces. The change at the top of Germany's military had profound and long-lasting effects. Reinhardt believed that the recent war showed that massed firepower was king and that maneuver warfare had seen its day. Therefore,

Germany, he thought, should create a mass army based on a national militia. Reinhardt later praised the French decision to construct the Maginot Line as acknowledging the dominance of positional defense in war.[10]

Von Seeckt's views could hardly have been more different. His experience was with infiltration tactics on the Eastern Front, where better trained and led German troops had defeated numerically superior but qualitatively inferior Russian forces. This convinced him that mass armies waging positional, attrition warfare like that which dominated the Western Front would become artifacts of an era of warfare that was passing from the scene. Von Seeckt declared that "mass becomes immobile; it cannot maneuver and therefore cannot win victories, it can only crush by sheer weight." Moreover, "a conscript mass, whose training has been brief and superficial is 'cannon fodder' in the worst sense of the word, if pitted against a small number of practiced technicians on the other side." Thus, he concluded, "The whole future of warfare appears to me to be in the employment of mobile armies, relatively small but of high quality, and rendered distinctly more effective by the addition of aircraft."[11]

Whereas Reinhardt rejected the German Army's traditional emphasis on waging a war of maneuver and encircling the enemy, seeking to bring about a battle of annihilation, von Seeckt embraced it. German storm tactics were rooted in the nineteenth-century Prussian military, incorporating concepts such as *Schwerpunkt* and *Auftragstaktik*.[12] To these terms, von Seeckt added *Bewegungskrieg*—a war of movement combining high-speed operations conducted by well-integrated combined-arms formations employing both the existing and newly emerging tools of war.[13] As von Seeckt summarized his vision, "The goal of modern strategy will be to achieve a decision with highly mobile, highly capable forces, before the masses have begun to move."[14]

Von Seeckt's views were reinforced by the comprehensive study of World War I undertaken in December 1919, at his direction, by the Truppenamt (Troop Office), the shadow version of the General Staff, which was banned by the Versailles Treaty. The fifty-seven committees involving more than 400 officers produced key insights. One was that storm tactics could only enjoy success at the tactical level as long as the enemy retained advantages in operational mobility—the ability to concentrate defending forces more rapidly than the Germans could advance to prevent this from occurring. Storm tactics were further limited by the breakdown in communications that occurred as the German troops advanced, undermining the commander's ability to coordinate the attack.

Yet another problem was that the penetrating force quickly outdistanced its supporting artillery fires. Attempts to offset this problem by increasing attacking troops' weapons loads found them quickly exhausted. The study committees found that tanks, by providing mobile fire support, represented a potential solution to this problem, but only if they were not tethered to slow-moving infantry that would compromise their advantage in speed and mobility. Air forces also showed promise for providing advancing ground forces with supporting fires.[15]

These insights formed a basis for thinking about how to solve the principal task that had eluded the German Army in World War I: *restoring mobility at the operational level of warfare in such a way as to enable decisive results at the strategic level.* Von Seeckt was not alone in thinking along these lines. One of the men most responsible for developing the tank, Winston Churchill, found himself not long after the war pondering, "Suppose that the British Army sacrificed upon the Somme, the finest we ever had, had been preserved, trained and developed to its full strength until the summer of 1917, till perhaps 3,000 tanks were ready, till an overwhelming artillery barrage was prepared, till a scientific method of advance had been devised, till the apparatus was complete, might not a decisive result have been achieved at one supreme stroke?"[16]

Von Seeckt's vision did not go unchallenged within the Reichswehr. Several opposing schools of thought emerged, the most formidable being the "Defense School," led by Reinhardt, who, in 1919, ordered that preference for officer retention in the radically reduced Army go to officers who had served ably on the front lines. Von Seeckt favored General Staff officers, believing that their intellect and experience in higher command planning would help the German military identify and embrace a new way of warfare. In the end, von Seeckt prevailed, and the Reichswehr chose brains over brawn.[17]

There emerged yet a third significant faction, what might be called the "People's War School." Its advocates called for focusing the Army's efforts on the immediate danger faced by the country in its weakened state, arguing that Germany's only hope of resisting invasion by either France or Poland rested in a mass army waging guerrilla warfare. When the French occupied Germany's industrial Ruhr area in 1923 to compel it to make good on its reparations obligations, many Reichswehr officers grumbled that von Seeckt and his small "army of leaders," with its emphasis on the long term, ignored the immediate dangers to Germany's security.[18] Von Seeckt, they groused, was training a military divorced from reality, envisioning it possessing weapons that the Reichswehr neither possessed nor could hope to obtain.

In February 1924, Joachim von Stulpnagel, head of the Truppenamt's operations department, set forth his "Thoughts on the War of the Future." In it, he and a member of the People's War School noted that the Reichswehr's seven divisions had sufficient ammunition to fight for only about one hour. Rather than place faith in what they believed were von Seeckt's fantasies, they argued that Germany's best defense rested on guerrilla warfare and mass mobilization of the German population. Even then, von Stulpnagel saw such resistance as more a "heroic gesture" than a means for achieving victory.[19] One can imagine von Seeckt responding by pointing out that, if victory was out of the question in the immediate future, why not accord priority to what might be accomplished over the longer term?

In retrospect, it seems remarkable that the Reichswehr did not succumb to a defensive or People's War philosophy. The German Army had been traumatized by the carnage of World War I and all but disarmed in its wake.[20] Von Seeckt, however, did enjoy several advantages. One was his extended tenure, which ran from 1920 to 1926, allowing him time to build a foundation on which his vision could be pursued. It also helped that his vision built on the German military culture and its emphasis on wars of maneuver. By preserving the core of the German General Staff, von Seeckt also had the Army's best "brains" supporting him. His use of the shadow General Staff to analyze war operations in the Great War provided analytic rigor and support for his vision. Von Seeckt also proved adept at populating the Army with like-minded senior officers. He was succeeded by Wilhelm Heye, followed, in 1930, by Kurt von Hammerstein. Neither could match von Seeckt's intellect. But they didn't have to; they only needed to continue building on the intellectual foundation he had set in place. Future heads of the Army, including Ludwig Beck and Werner von Fritsch, embraced von Seeckt's vision, as did Oswald Lutz and Heinz Guderian, who would play key roles in developing Germany's panzer arm. They and others like them relied on von Seeckt's vision as a compass in traveling the path to Blitzkrieg.[21]

But as the general's critics pointed out, the Reichswehr needed more than a vision. It required the means to execute that vision, both human and material, and a sense of how the new military capabilities that were rapidly emerging could best be employed. Despite Germany's very modest resources, its military leadership began to establish the organizations and processes needed to do exactly that. Although banned from possessing tanks, the Reichswehr established the Inspektion der Kraftfahrtruppen (Inspectorate of Motor Transport Troops). It quickly became the center of thought on mechanized warfare in the Reichswehr outside of the Truppenamt itself. Its first inspector, General Erich von Tschischwitz, requested a General Staff–trained officer to assist him, and Captain Heinz Guderian was selected and assigned to the Seventh Motor Transport Battalion under Major Oswald Lutz. Guderian proved an ideal choice. Not only had he served in several General Staff positions after attending the Kriegsakademie, but he also had worked for nearly three years in signals units, gaining a deep understanding of and appreciation for the potential of radio to coordinate highly mobile, dispersed forces.

Von Seeckt regarded signal troops as an essential component of his war of movement. In August 1922, First Group Command in Berlin conducted the initial signal exercise of the interwar era, testing the Reichswehr's wireless capabilities and telephone network in simulated wartime conditions.[22] Three divisions contributed their signal elements to the exercise. In 1923, the Reichswehr doubled signal support to its divisions. The following year, Lieutenant Ernst Volckheim, a veteran of Germany's World War I nascent tank arm who was increasingly accepted as the Army's leading expert on armored warfare, called for mounting a radio in every tank (should the Germans ever acquire them!). By 1928, the Reichswehr was conducting major radio communications exercises involving all divisions and group headquarters.[23]

As for mechanization, the German field service regulations dedicated several sections to the tank, probably written by Volckheim.[24] Both Volckeim and the Austrian Captain Fritz Hegel, author of the influential *Pocket Book of Tanks*, envisioned fast tanks with a large radius of action as a key to reviving a war of movement. In theory, armored forces possessing these qualities could quickly mass and effect a breakthrough of the enemy front. Once the breakthrough was achieved, the armored formations could then penetrate quickly and deeply into the enemy's rear area before its defensive lines could be reestablished. If so, the operational challenge that vexed the German Army on the Western Front might be solved.

As early as October 1921, the Reichswehr conducted maneuvers of ersatz motorized units in the Harz Mountains. In the winter of 1923–24, Lieutenant Colonel Walther von Brauchitsch, who later became the Army's commander in chief, organized maneuvers employing notional motorized troops and aircraft. By 1926, the Army was conducting multi-division maneuvers, the largest since the war's end, to test aspects of these concepts.[25] These exercises were stimulated by von Seeckt's orders that focused on infantry units getting out of the trenches, waging mobile warfare, and executing flanking maneuvers, including having artillery working on ways to support mobile infantry operations. Between 1921 and 1925, the German Army issued, in three parts, a new operational doctrine, *Army Regulation 487, Leadership and Battle with Combined Arms*, conforming to von Seeckt's concept of operations.[26]

Help from Once and Future Foes

Like Blanche Dubois in *A Streetcar Named Desire*, the Reichswehr bene-fited from the "kindness" of others in effecting its transformation. Ironi-cally, the Versailles Treaty, by requiring Germany to all but demobilize its military, enabled von Seeckt to start with an elite force. In addition to retaining the Army's brightest officers, 40,000 of the 100,000-man Army were noncommissioned officers (NCOs), all regarded as "officer material."[27]

With the Reichswehr having no tanks or combat aircraft of its own, Germany's military leaders found themselves studying other armies, es-pecially the British. During the 1920s and early 1930s, the British were generally recognized as the leaders in mobile warfare concepts and prac-tice. Military theorists such as General J. F. C. Fuller and Captain Basil H. Liddell Hart were advocating military operations similar to those von Seeckt had in mind, even as British field exercises provided a vicarious "proving ground."[28]

Heinz Guderian, the self-proclaimed father of Germany's panzer forces, recalled that during this early period, "the current English hand-book on armored fighting vehicles was translated into German and for many years served as the theoretical manual for our developing ideas."[29] If the German military's path toward what became known as Blitzkrieg was dark and filled with many dead-end offshoots, it was the British who helped light the way and post the warning markers.

The 1926 British maneuvers on the Salisbury Plain proved particularly enlightening. A Reichswehr report on the exercises noted that armored ve-hicles with their increased speed now possessed the capacity to strike out independently and that motorized infantry and artillery were capable of ac-companying the tanks. The report recommended that "in exercises, armor fighting vehicles be allowed to break through repeatedly in order to portray this method of fighting and thus to collect added experience."[30] That same year, the British formed an Experimental Mechanized Force.

In no small measure because of the British exercises, a memorandum signed in January 1927 by General Werner von Fritsch, the head of the Truppenamt's operations branch, presciently concluded, "Armored, quickly moving tanks most probably will become the operationally decisive offensive weapon. From an operational perspective this weapon will be most effective if concentrated in independent units like tank brigades."[31] Shortly thereafter, in May 1927, the world's first completely mechanized combat brigade made its appearance on the Salisbury Plain. Although inferior in numbers and lacking in wireless communications, the brigade completely outmaneuvered the horse cavalry and infantry formations matched against it.[32]

Even though the British exercises impressed German military leaders, the Reichswehr had to balance its vision of future warfare with current military contingencies, primarily the threat posed to Germany's small treaty-limited army from Poland to the east, France to the west, or a coalition of the two with Czechoslovakia. War games, exercises, and studies during the winters of 1927–28 and 1928–29 focused primarily on German military operations in the event of a war with Poland. The findings clearly indicated that a war with Poland alone could be waged only for a short period and with extensive loss of territory. Major General Werner von Blomberg, head of the Truppenamt, refused to accept such an outcome and rigged the 1928 game so as to have the League of Nations intervene to force Poland to accept an armistice. This was followed by a Soviet invasion of Poland, at which time Moscow offered (and Berlin accepted) an alliance, enabling the German Army to conduct the large-scale offensive operations it longed for.[33]

For the most part, however, the Reichswehr's field exercises in the late 1920s employed cavalry, and not surrogate mechanized forces, in the leading role. As late as 1929, the Army's tank doctrine envisioned tanks primarily as an infantry support system.[34] The pattern continued with the fall 1930 maneuvers, the largest since World War I. They featured non-standard "experimental" divisional organizations and a flanking operation by a cavalry division against an infantry division.[35] Still, there was nothing particularly novel about the exercise, and for inspiration, forward-thinking German officers continued to follow the British field exercises closely. As late as 1934, Colonel Baron Geyer von Schweppenburg, Germany's military attaché in London, reported, "In the mixed tank brigade the British army created the most important mobile 'modern formation,' which it holds to be necessary for powerful, long-range, all-out strikes." That same year, British tank maneuvers in Egypt for the first time saw a tank brigade and an experimental mobile division execute large-scale penetrations.[36] When Germany began to rearm in 1935, Lutz, now a general and head of Germany's Tank Forces Command, remarked to British General Sir John Dill that "the German tank corps had been modeled on the British."[37]

A Path Not Taken: The Luftwaffe and Strategic Bombardment

In addition to proscribing a German armored force, the Versailles Treaty also banned the Germans from maintaining an air force. Nevertheless, German air-power advocates looked forward to the time when they would be free of the treaty's shackles. In thinking about what a German air force, or Luftwaffe, would look like, the Germans did not embrace the vision of air power set forth by prominent foreign military theorists—Giulio Douhet and Billy Mitchell among them—that viewed strategic aerial bombardment as a, if not *the*, decisive instrument in future wars.[38] Rather, the German military followed a different path, one that produced an air force better suited to the Blitzkrieg form of warfare than to strategic aerial bombardment.

The German Air Service's 1919–20 analysis of World War I is conspicuous for its general lack of interest in strategic bombing. This may stem from the failure of its 1917–18 strategic bombing campaign to inflict serious damage on the Allies. By 1921, it had discounted, at least for the time, bombing the enemy's homeland as a "war winning" option.[39] Although skepticism about strategic bombing's efficacy would abate over time, the Luftwaffe never fully embraced it. At best, its twin-engine bombers had sufficient range and payload capacity for major campaigns (such as attacks on an enemy's industrial base) only against Germany's proximate Continental adversaries: France, Poland, and Czechoslovakia.

Moreover, fiscal and industrial limitations also forced choices on the Luftwaffe. Germany possessed neither the production base nor the economic strength to build a bomber force on the scale of the United States and Britain's and field aircraft in the required numbers to support the Army's land campaigns.[40]

Almost from the beginning, Germany's military leaders envisioned air power enhancing the effectiveness of ground operations, and von Seeckt made funding the shadow Luftwaffe a high priority.[41] Moreover, when Germany's Air Ministry was founded in 1933, Werner von Blomberg, the minister of defense, insisted that the Army transfer high-quality officers to the new service. These included not only highly regarded pilots but first-rate General Staff officers as well.[42]

German air-power doctrine was offensive in nature, emphasizing attacking the enemy air force to achieve air superiority, conducting close air support (CAS) of ground forces, and performing interdiction operations near the front lines. These missions were well suited to supporting operations centered on rupturing the enemy's lines, followed by a fast-moving deep exploitation phase.[43]

That being said, early in the period of rearmament following Adolf Hitler's ascension to power there was considerable discussion over Germany's creating a "Risk Luftwaffe" centered on some 390 four-engine bombers supported by ten air reconnaissance squadrons. The idea was the brainchild of Dr. Robert Knauss, the head of Lufthansa, Germany's commercial airline, and a disciple of the Italian aerial-warfare theorist Giulio Douhet. Similar to Admiral Tirpitz's "Risk Fleet" concept prior to World War I, the Risk Luftwaffe's objective was to "greatly increase the risk for any conceivable enemy in a war," such that, even though it might prevail against Germany's air forces, the enemy would have suffered such loses as to become vulnerable to its other rivals.[44] Knauss argued that such a force could be fielded quickly, reducing the danger of a preemptive attack by Germany's enemies during the period of rearmament.

Only a few weeks after becoming Germany's chancellor in January 1933, Hitler voiced support for Knauss's ideas in a discussion with Reichswehr leaders. Erhard Milch, who concurred with Knauss's thinking, was appointed secretary of state of the newly formed Reich Ministry of Aviation, reporting directly to Hermann Goering, the Reich minister of aviation and a member of Hitler's inner circle. Germany's initial armament program called for a force of some 600 aircraft to be available by autumn 1935, including 250 bombers.[45] Thus, the initial air-rearmament program accorded priority to the Risk Luftwaffe concept and its emphasis on strategic bombing. The concept, however, was stillborn.

Although the German military conceded the importance of bombers, both as a deterrent and as a significant factor in air warfare, it maintained that wars would still be won primarily through cooperation among all the military services. In the winter of 1933–34, a Truppenamt war game lent support to these views, concluding that bombers alone could not eliminate the air force of a major adversary and that a balanced, combined-arms air fleet that included fighters and air defenses was needed.[46] The dominant objective in creating a powerful Luftwaffe remained fielding an "operational" force that could, both independently and in coordination with the Army and Navy, support an overall strategy designed to prevail in a conflict with Germany's immediate neighbors, France and Poland.

To sum up, from the time Hitler assumed power in 1933 through 1936, the Luftwaffe's leadership, which included men such as Milch and officers such as Walther Wever, Albert Kesselring, and Hans-Jürgen Stumpf, recognized the potential of a strategic bomber force along the lines described by Knauss. They also, however, rejected the Douhet-inspired vision of future wars being dominated by strategic bombing campaigns, supporting instead a "balanced" force with priority to supporting mechanized air-land operations.[47]

Following Wever's death in an air crash in June 1936, the Luftwaffe's leadership quality declined. Goering named Lieutenant General Kesselring to replace Wever.[48] Kesselring had a well-deserved reputation as an excellent army officer, but he lacked Wever's comprehensive vision of air power. Meanwhile, Ernst Udet was selected to serve as head of the Luftwaffe's Technical Office, even though he had little in the way of technical training or aviation experience.

As with Germany's ground forces, its air buildup borrowed from other militaries. In 1934, while in the United States, Udet became enthralled observing the U.S. Navy Curtiss Helldiver fighter conducting highly successful dive-bombing runs. Subsequently, the Germans purchased two Helldivers that were used in developing the Stuka dive-bombers that played a key role in the campaigns of 1939 and 1940.[49]

The Luftwaffe's development of dive-bombing was not without problems. When Wolfram von Richthofen took over the Development Branch of the Technical Office, he asserted that modern air defenses would make dive-bombing too risky a proposition, flatly declaring, "Diving below 6,600 feet is complete nonsense."[50] Fortunately for the Luftwaffe, several officers in von Richthofen's branch succeeded in securing support for additional field-testing, which kept the dive-bombing option alive and enabled it to prosper.

Yet if dive-bombing was a good thing, the Luftwaffe eventually pursued too much of it. Udet's enthusiasm for this form of attack saw him directing that virtually all bombers be designed for dive-bombing. The decision, James Corum notes, "bordered on aeronautical lunacy." Thus, the Ju-88 bomber could have entered production in 1938, but owing to the thousands of changes required for it to withstand the stresses entailed in dive-bombing, its production was delayed by roughly two years. Such a delay may seem like a small matter today, when aircraft development typically runs well over a decade. The rapid advance in aviation technology in the 1930s, however, resulted in a rapid turnover in aircraft as new, improved versions entered production every few years.[51]

The Luftwaffe's aerial-bombardment options were further limited when, in 1937, its four-engine bomber programs were canceled.[52] Although Germany's two-engine bombers were adequate for operations against its immediate neighbors, the decision left the Luftwaffe without a long-range bomber. A May 1939 war game showed that the Luftwaffe lacked the bombers needed to wage an "operational war" against Great Britain, a likely adversary.

In December 1938, Milch reorganized the aircraft production system. The new approach emphasized developing and producing a few bombers and fighters of superior design. The net effect was to reduce research and development on the next generation of aircraft at a time when aviation technology was advancing at a rapid rate. When the Germans realized the problem in 1942, it proved too late: the Luftwaffe confronted increasingly capable Allied aircraft with planes that were increasingly outmatched.[53] To be sure, the short-term effects of these decisions did not prove fatal to the German military's development of Blitzkrieg. In fact, if Poland and France were Germany's security problems and if the purpose of Blitzkrieg-type operations was to produce a rapid decision in the near-term future, then locking in aircraft designs to maximize the Luftwaffe's strength for a short period arguably made a great deal of sense from a strategic planning perspective. But German planners could not know that Germany would go to war in the fall of 1939, or that it could find itself waging a long war, or that it might confront new belligerents entering the conflict, thereby revealing the pitfalls of moving toward a single-point solution when developing a military capability in a time of rapid technological change.

In brief, Udet's decisions cost the Luftwaffe both time and flexibility, and Milch had locked the Luftwaffe into a force structure whose aircraft, though initially impressive, would depreciate rapidly in value as the war dragged on.[54] These shortcomings notwithstanding, the Luftwaffe achieved a great deal in a remarkably short period of time, thanks in no small measure to steps taken during the sixteen years that Germany lived under the Versailles Treaty's constraints.

When Hitler disavowed the treaty in 1935, the Luftwaffe had roughly 1,000 front-line aircraft. It was participating in full-scale maneuvers with the Army only a year later.[55] The aviation industry put the rapidly increasing military budgets to good use. The Luftwaffe expanded from three "aerial advertising squadrons" in 1933 to a force of some 4,100 front-line aircraft six years later.[56] Despite Germany's relatively late start in aviation, when war came it led the world in a number of important areas, such as high-altitude flight, aircraft cannon, and bombs.[57] When all was said and done, the Luftwaffe was well prepared to support mobile mechanized warfare against Germany's immediate neighbors. It was, however, ill prepared for longer-range bombing campaigns of the type it undertook against Great Britain in the summer of 1940 or for an extended war waged on a far greater geographic scale against the Soviet Union.[58]

Capital Stock, Manpower, and the Industrial Base

The Reichswehr's development of Blitzkrieg could not succeed without the means, both industrial and human, to field the kinds and numbers of forces needed to execute it. Germany's rearmament began following Hitler's rise to power in January 1933. By October, Germany had withdrawn from a general disarmament conference and the League of Nations. In 1935, Hitler announced full German rearmament in defiance of the Versailles Treaty, and an ambitious rearmament program followed. The pace of rearmament was limited by Germany's stunted armaments industry and the small existing military that would form the foundation for a much larger Wehrmacht. The German defense industrial base's limitations, combined with Hitler's aversion to placing Germany on a war-economy footing, meant the Wehrmacht would remain overwhelmingly reliant on horses—not machines—for its mobility.

In forcing Germany to scrap most of its World War I–era equipment, the Versailles Treaty proved a blessing in disguise, enabling the Truppenamt to design the future German military from a clean sheet of paper, as it were. Unlike the Allies, Germany was not left with large stocks of recently produced weapons that had years of service life left in them. Having spent so heavily on the war, political leaders in Britain and France were unwilling to replace weapons, even if progress in military-related technology was accelerating their depreciation. The ink was barely dry on the Versailles Treaty when the Reichswehr established the Waffenamt as its center for weapons and munitions research and development.[59]

Although the Germans were required to disestablish the General Staff, they found ways to preserve their well-educated officer corps. Reichswehr junior-officer training now featured Military District Examinations—the General Staff entrance examinations in all but name. In place of the banned Kriegsakademie, a "Leadership Assistant" course emerged. As with the Kriegsakademie, the course ran three to four years, emphasizing military history and war games. In recognition of the need to understand rapidly advancing military-related technologies, every year a dozen or so officers were sent to civilian universities to obtain engineering degrees, with many going on to achieve high rank.[60]

As early as 1924, the military districts were directed to ensure that in each unit and garrison someone would be assigned as its armor officer, with responsibility for training in mechanized warfare.[61] In 1926, the small technical course for motor officers changed its emphasis from motor technology and maintenance to armor and mechanized warfare tactics. The Inspectorate of Motor Troops School steadily evolved to become the Panzer Troops School following the onset of full-scale German rearmament.[62]

Skirting Treaty Limits

To skirt the Versailles Treaty's restrictions, additional training in armored warfare was conducted at the Reichswehr's center at Kazan in the Soviet Union. Between 1929 and 1933, it produced a cadre of qualified armor instructors.[63] Germany's "exporting" of much of its training and cadre development also extended to its pilots. Between 1925 and 1933, some 200 to 300 Germans were stationed at the Lipetsk air installation in the Soviet Union, as students, instructors, ground staff, or test pilots. Between 1929 and 1932, at least a dozen different aircraft models were put through trials there.[64] In Germany itself, pilot training was conducted through civilian "front" organizations such as Sportflug. The nation's commercial airline, Lufthansa, was, in effect, a reserve air force.[65] Thus, in 1935, when Hitler announced that Germany was rearming, the Luftwaffe already possessed some 1,000 first-line aircraft.[66]

Such training had its limits. In December 1936, Germany initiated the last comprehensive armaments plan prior to the war's outbreak. Hitler's directive to field "a powerful army in the shortest possible time" severely strained the country's manpower and industrial base.[67] Up to that point, the high level of training and quality of personnel in the treaty-limited Reichswehr had enabled Germany's Army to expand smoothly from 100,000 to 300,000. The December 1936 plan, however, called for creating a peacetime force of 830,000 that, supported by reserves, would be capable of mobilizing a force of 4,620,000 in 102 divisions, including five panzer divisions and eight motorized divisions, by October 1939.[68] Achieving this required a significant watering down of troop quality, even with a doubling of the conscription period from one year to two.

Early in von Seeckt's tenure, he directed the Army to "engage in joint planning with industry so that mass production of approved weapons and material could be begun at the strategically proper moment."[69] German industry cooperated. Krupp established armament subsidiaries abroad, including at Bofors gun plants in Sweden, Sideius A.G. shipbuilding yards in Rotterdam, and torpedo works at Utrecht and The Hague. Krupp holding companies were set up in Barcelona, Bilbao, and Cadiz in Spain, where submarine construction and experimentation went forward. Indeed, "it would be difficult to find a more perfect collaboration than that which existed between Krupp and the military establishment in these years." German officers also had access to some equipment proving grounds, such as those at Bofors.[70]

Throughout the 1920s, other countries' military industries also influenced and aided the Germans in designing and developing equipment. When the French firm Citroën was pioneering half-track technology, German firms licensed it to support the German Army.[71] Technical work on tanks began in 1925, when design specifications for a Grosstraktor ("Large Tractor," so named to deceive the Allies) were established. Between 1925 and 1929, the German industrial firms of Krupp, Daimler, and Rheinmetall were all developing tanks, with work on prototypes of half-track vehicles beginning in 1930.[72] By 1928, each firm had built two Grosstraktors for German field-testing in Soviet Russia.

Germany's industrial activities in Soviet Russia were particularly notable. In 1923, the Reichswehr launched a private holding corporation that financed a Junkers aircraft factory at Fili near Moscow, a poison-gas factory at Samara, and shell factories (under Krupp administration) at

Tula, Leningrad, and Schlusselberg. For its investment, the German Army received a share of these plants' production.[73]

Despite the sophistication of Germany's industrial base, it suffered from shortcomings relative to its future rivals, especially the United States. For example, in 1937, the German automotive industry produced 331,000 vehicles, while the United States was turning out 4.8 million. For every 1,000 Americans, there were more than 200 motor vehicles, as compared to 16 for every 1,000 Germans.[74] It thus came as no surprise to many military observers that when the Americans transformed their commercial automotive industry to military production, its output overwhelmed Germany's. Although the Wehrmacht often proved able to best its rivals in the quality of its equipment and, especially, its troops and doctrine, at some point Hitler's willingness to challenge the world's greatest economy, largest state, and greatest empire was bound to overwhelm von Seeckt's elite force.

Mechanization

Despite efforts to mitigate the effects of the Versailles Treaty, the restrictions imposed by it clearly constrained the scale and quality of German efforts toward mechanization. Although the Germans possessed nearly 1,500 Panzer (Panzerkampfwagen) I tanks by the fall of 1938, production was terminated at that time as the tank, with thin armor and two machine guns armament, was already obsolete. Nevertheless, the Panzer I formed the core of the Wehrmacht's armored force at the war's beginning.[75] The Panzer II, designed as a gap filler until state-of-the-art tanks could be produced, was nevertheless an improvement over its predecessor. The Wehrmacht had more than 1,200 Panzer IIs for the Poland campaign.[76]

By 1935, the design for the Panzer IV, a medium (twenty-ton) tank with a 75-millimeter gun, was completed. It entered mass production in 1937 and remained in production throughout the war. Only 211 of the tanks, however, were in service in September 1939. By May 1940, when the campaign in the West began, the number had only risen to around 300. The Panzer III was the last tank developed by Germany before the war, entering mass production in early 1938. It was specially designed to combat other tanks and was armed with the moderately high-velocity 37-millimeter gun. By the time the war began, Germany had 148 Panzer IIIs, and by May 1940, 432 were in service.[77]

In 1936, General Beck advocated producing a special, heavily armored "infantry" tank to supplement the main battle tank (Panzer III) and fire-support tank (Panzer IV). Guderian strongly and successfully opposed Beck's idea, arguing that an "infantry tank" was contrary to the German armored force's emphasis on speed and mobility.

Due to production limitations, the Wehrmacht incorporated other militaries' tanks into its own formations. The Austrian Army's integration into the Wehrmacht following the Anschluss in March 1938 added two infantry, two mountain, one panzer, and one light division to the German Army.[78] Following the occupation of Czechoslovakia, the Germans seized some 150 Czech tanks and the well-developed Skoda armaments works, which possessed more experience in tank design (and in production efficiency) than its German counterparts.[79] Skoda continued to produce tanks, only now for the Wehrmacht. By May 1940, some 300 Czech-built P-38(t) tanks formed the core of the newly created Seventh and Eighth Panzer Divisions.[80]

Although this hodgepodge of equipment aided the German Army's expansion, it also greatly complicated its logistics. The Wehrmacht suffered from a staggering array of vehicle and engine types. In an effort to make up for the shortcomings of German industry and Hitler's determination to go to war before the Wehrmacht was fully expanded, the tanks and other forms of mechanical transport of defeated or occupied states were often incorporated into the German Army. By 1941, more than 2,000 vehicle types participated in the German Army's assault on the Soviet Union. Army Group Center alone had to carry more than a million spare parts. One panzer division had 96 types of personnel carrier, and 111 types of truck.[81] This situation was further exacerbated by the German population's relative unfamiliarity with motor vehicles and the breakneck pace of the Army's expansion following Hitler's renunciation of the Versailles Treaty.[82]

Aviation

Germany's loss of its air force following World War I retarded the development of its aviation industry. Nonetheless, the Reichswehr exploited the nation's commercial aviation sector, providing it with subsidies to create an industrial base that could keep pace with technological developments in the field. By the mid-1920s, Germany was recognized as a world leader in commercial aviation, as Germany's airlines flew greater distances and carried more passengers than the airlines of France, Great Britain, and Italy combined.[83] German pilots gained substantial experience in long-distance flying, navigation, and instrumentation.[84]

Still, there was only so much the military could do by way of "outsourcing" research and development of new aviation technology and subsidizing its commercial airlines. These industrial capacity limitations appeared when rearmament began in the mid-1930s. Nevertheless, once the military aviation industrial base began to mobilize, the results were impressive. From a base of roughly 4,000 workers at the time Hitler came to power, the aircraft industry boasted a force of more than 200,000 in less than six years.[85] As with the ground forces, the Luftwaffe benefited greatly from the rapid advances in aviation technology during the 1930s, which had the effect of rapidly obsolescing existing stocks of combat aircraft in the air forces of Germany's rivals.

The German Military Takes the Lead

Forced by circumstance to observe the efforts of others in developing mechanized air-land warfare, the German military also positioned itself to take the lead when the opportunity arose. Toward this end, field-training exercises proved invaluable.

From the beginning, General von Seeckt insisted that tanks be represented in war games and maneuvers "as often as possible," so mock "tanks" were fabricated. Both 1926 Reichswehr field exercises employed "dummy" tanks in emphasizing maneuver, concentration, and offensive operations by the ground forces, while stressing the use of aircraft in reconnaissance, observation, and ground-attack roles. The insights derived from the exercises were significant. Following the 1927 maneuvers, the Third Cavalry Division's report concluded, "A battle without tanks is obsolete."[86]

The fall maneuvers of 1930, the largest since the war, found the Reichswehr focusing on mobile air-land operations.[87] The U.S. military attaché observing the exercise reported, "The transportation of the 5th Division was quite modern and up to date. . . . Although there were no air corps forces connected with this maneuver, all officers and men behaved exactly as though they were operating under wartime conditions in which the enemy aerial observation was very alert. . . . In accordance with the Versailles treaty, the Germans are not allowed any tanks. Yet, they had a full quota of dummy tanks with the 5th Division. These tanks were made by constructing tin covers over light automobiles."[88]

The group maneuvers, the communications exercises, and the Truppenamt's annual war games encouraged those who believed in von Seeckt's vision, while attracting converts. An American officer observing the 1926 maneuvers witnessed the Germans ignoring the "need" to maintain a continuous front, while advancing rapidly and showing a reckless disregard for protecting their flanks. He assumed these actions were the result of inept commanders. As things progressed, he was shocked to realize it was being "done by intent."[89]

The path to Blitzkrieg became a bit smoother when, on April 1, 1931, General Oswald Lutz was appointed inspector of motorized forces, with Lieutenant Colonel Guderian as his chief of staff. The two made a formidable team, with Lutz often able to gain an audience for Guderian's ideas, which, given the latter's lack of tact, was no mean feat. A railroad engineer by trade, Lutz was bright and receptive to new ideas. Earlier in his career he had served in the technical branches, commanding the motor-transport assets of one of Germany's field armies during the Great War. In the late 1920s, as a colonel, Lutz was responsible for the Reichswehr's motor-transport troops conducting experiments involving trucks, dummy tanks, and wooden artillery and antitank guns. The results led to two experimental infantry brigades being formed in 1929. They included a light "tank" battalion and three infantry battalions transported by truck.[90]

Over the next several years, under Lutz's watchful eye, these brigades participated in a series of exercises, leading him to conclude that panzer forces should be employed independent of infantry and cavalry elements. Tying them down in support of infantry would, Lutz argued, nullify the panzers' advantage in speed and range. He also pressed for employing the panzers en masse, arguing that they must be concentrated to win the breakthrough battle and lead the pursuit (or deep penetration) into the enemy's rear area. Lutz emphasized the value of surprise in panzer operations, advocated supporting the panzers with mobile combined-arms forces, and recommended that larger, multibattalion exercises be conducted to capture the effects at the operational level of warfare. The small-scale exercises conducted to date, Lutz noted, risked giving a "false picture of both weapons and troops."[91]

The field exercises of 1931 and 1932, employing dummy tanks, represented a significant step forward for Lutz and his ideas. The "panzers" operated independently from the infantry. Emphasis was placed on massed armor, surprise, and exploiting breakthroughs with mobile reserves.

Although the Reichswehr brain trust saw potential in mechanized operations, there was considerable debate over the form such operations should take. During the 1920s and early 1930s, the German military experimented with combined mechanized and horse cavalry configurations. Some officers maintained that cavalry could maneuver in terrain that was inaccessible to armored units, while allowing that mechanized forces could move more rapidly in open terrain and along roads.[92]

The 1932 Maneuvers

These concepts were tested in the 1932 maneuvers, which pitted an attack by Red (Polish) forces against Blue (German) forces and saw a substantial increase in the size of motorized formations and the scope of their operations.[93] Every major participating unit was motorized to some degree. The Red cavalry corps included dummy tanks, trucks, motorcycles, and armored cars—capabilities far more advanced than anything Poland had at that time. Red's plan was "to attack Blue forces fighting on the Oder [River] deep in the flank and rear."[94]

The exercise found the horse cavalry unable to keep up with the motorized reconnaissance detachments.[95] The maneuvers' high point found a motorized cavalry corps attempting to cross the Oder River from the east. The corps's diverse mix of horse cavalry and motorized forces proved a nightmare. Germany's president (and former field marshal) Paul von Hindenburg, on hand to witness the exercise, declared, "In war, only what is simple can succeed. I visited the staff of the Cavalry Corps. What I saw there was not simple."[96] The maneuvers' findings were so striking that although the cavalry had been among the most conservative of the Army's branches, a significant portion of its leadership began to embrace motorization.[97] Indeed, roughly 40 percent of the early Panzer Troop officers were from the cavalry. Far stiffer opposition came from the artillery, which struggled to adapt to operating on a mobile battlefield.[98]

The exercises also saw the Germans fitting their command "tanks" with radios. First-rate radio communication was integral to fast-paced operations and deep penetrations, and communications network schemes were among the Army's most widely discussed topics relating to the proper organization and employment of mobile forces.[99] The previous year's British maneuvers provided the first demonstration of tank formations controlled by a master radio transmitter, and the Germans were anxious to keep pace.[100] By the time Germany invaded Poland, all German tanks were equipped with radio receivers. Limitations on industrial output limited the number of tanks with radio transmitters, with priority going to command vehicles.

As the historian Robert Citino has observed, "What proved to be the correct application of armor—employing tanks as part of an all-mechanized combined-arms force—was something that the Germans had figured out by 1932 ... with dummy tanks, at a time when the country was officially disarmed."[101] To be sure, the proper mix of elements for mechanized formations, and the variety of these formations, would remain a matter of great debate for some time to come. For advocates of mechanized warfare like Guderian, however, the fall 1932 exercises, with their faux mechanized and motorized formations, "cheered us no end."[102]

For Lutz and Guderian, the 1932 British maneuvers offered further encouragement. The British employed tanks capable of ranges approaching 150 miles and of advancing nearly 100 miles a day.[103] Nevertheless, Germany's military leaders proceeded at a measured pace. When the new Army field manual, *Truppenführung*, was issued, it accepted the concept of employing tanks on a large scale but primarily as an adjunct to infantry-dominated maneuvers rather than in independent operations.[104]

Following the 1932 maneuvers, Guderian challenged General Ludwig Beck, chief of the Truppenamt (and who later became chief of the re-created General Staff), to accelerate the fielding of panzer divisions. Beck had chaired the committee that updated the *Truppenführung*. Despite Guderian being far junior in rank to Beck, the general and the Army as a whole were remarkably tolerant of men like Guderian, who "at one time or another antagonized virtually every senior officer in the army." Yet not only did Guderian survive despite his abrasive personality; he flourished.[105]

Although Beck would hear Guderian out, he was more cautious than his subordinate when it came to assessing the potential of massed armor operating independently deep in the enemy's rear areas. Thus, their differences were primarily over the *pace* of change, not its direction. As Guderian recalled, when he told Beck that wireless would enable command over even fast-moving formations, the general remained skeptical, declaring, "No, no, I don't want to have anything to do with you people. You move too fast for me."[106]

Hitler Quickens the Pace

The pace toward Blitzkrieg-style operations quickened following Hitler's rise to power in January 1933. Despite the Versailles Treaty restrictions, the Panzer I began to enter production, and Lutz approved plans for the Panzer II. The maneuvers that year included a cavalry division with a motorized battalion of two panzer companies and two motorcycle companies, along with a fully motorized supply train. The infantry division participating in the exercise had a motorized/mechanized element that included panzers, antitank guns, and (as with the cavalry division) a fully motorized logistics component.[107]

The pace quickened further still following Hitler's renouncing of the Versailles Treaty and the onset of rapid German rearmament in 1935. Lutz, now a major general, was assigned as head of the newly established Panzer Troops Command but lost Guderian when he took over command of one of the newly formed panzer divisions. (Guderian's successor, Friedrich von Paulus, later commanded the ill-fated Sixth Army at Stalingrad.)[108]

Still, the German military's vision exceeded what its forces could do in practice. But the gap was closing. In June, before Germany even had a single operational panzer division, General Beck conducted a General Staff planning exercise involving a panzer corps.[109] Although the exercise involved a counterattack against Czech forces with three panzer divisions, they remained under the infantry's command, to the frustration of Guderian and his fellow armor enthusiasts.[110]

Guderian, however, found an important ally in Hitler. When the führer visited Kummersdorf in early 1934 on an inspection, Guderian seized the opportunity to demonstrate the kind of equipment that would constitute a panzer division—including tanks, motorcycles, and reconnaissance cars. Following the demonstration, Hitler declared, "That's what I need! That's what I want to have."[111] Although he did not say why he wanted this type of equipment or in what quantity, Hitler also had his own vision of the next war, one not terribly dissimilar to von Seeckt's. Shortly after coming to power, Hitler declared, "The next war will be quite different from the last world war. Infantry attacks and mass formations are obsolete. Interlocked frontal struggles lasting for years on petrified fronts will not return."[112] It's also clear he understood what Guderian was proposing. Hitler's shortcomings as a military strategist were exposed over time, but his knowledge of military weapons and systems, especially their characteristics and capabilities, was widely acknowledged as remarkable.[113]

The Panzer Force

In August 1935, the first exercise of a prototype panzer division was conducted on Lüneburg Heath, near Munster. The results were impressive. At one point, Army commander in chief General von Fritsch directed the panzer division to shift ninety degrees to face an enemy that had suddenly appeared on its flank. Although specialized training had been sparse and radio equipment had not been fully issued, the division executed the maneuver in less than ninety minutes.[114] The four-week exercise convinced von Fritsch of mechanized forces' great potential and that the best defense against massed armor attack was the tank itself.[115]

The first panzer maneuvers continued to draw on contemporary British exercises. The 1934 British maneuvers saw its Army's experimental mobile division combining a four-battalion tank brigade with a motorized infantry brigade and motorized engineers, reconnaissance, and communications elements—almost exactly the same structure employed by the Wehrmacht in creating the first panzer divisions a year later.[116] It was quickly becoming clear, however, that the Germans no longer needed tutoring from the British, or any other military, in the art of mechanized warfare.

In October 1935, two months after maneuvers involving a prototype, the Wehrmacht established three panzer divisions. Reflecting General Beck's "go-slow" approach, he specified three roles for the new divisions: supporting infantry attacks, antitank defense, and "independent operational use together with other motorized forces (at present panzer division)."[117] Beck's inclusion of the third task was very much in tune with what the panzer enthusiasts had been advocating.

The first panzer divisions were composed of a tank brigade and a motorized infantry brigade, which were also similar in organization to France's light mechanized division. There were also, however, important differences. Unlike the French, the Germans emphasized combined arms: there was a complete range of supporting arms for the panzers: a motorized artillery regiment, antitank battalion, and pioneer company (later expanded to a battalion). Contrary to French doctrine, the Wehrmacht called for concentrating mechanized forces for mobile operations.[118]

Following the panzers' encouraging performance at Lüneburg, mechanized-force enthusiasts within the Wehrmacht began to campaign for establishing a panzer corps, made up of several panzer divisions.[119] Yet the proper mix of combined arms for the panzer division, let alone a panzer corps, had yet to be established. German armored-warfare advocates, like their British counterparts, initially held that panzer divisions should place overwhelming emphasis on armor. In fact, the first panzer division boasted 561 tanks.[120]

This suited panzer advocates like Guderian.[121] Field exercises, however, revealed the division to be overly "tank heavy," and steps were taken to increase the division's infantry and support elements, including logistics and engineer units, to better balance its structure.[122] By the time of Germany's invasion of Poland, the panzer division's tank strength had been reduced to between 220 and 320, and the ratio of panzer companies to infantry companies was changed from 16 to 9 to 12 to 12.[123]

In summary, the devastating combined-arms formation at the core of Blitzkrieg owed much to the insights derived from the German military's field exercises and to the Army's traditional emphasis on combined-arms cooperation. As the Wehrmacht migrated toward its panzer force, it deviated from the British path, which yielded tank-heavy, infantry-poor "unbalanced" divisions, lacking in supporting arms.[124]

The Wehrmacht also proved remarkably willing to experiment with other force structures in developing its mechanized forces. Although Guderian thought almost exclusively of panzer divisions, Beck placed greater priority on experimenting with a range of formations, including motorized infantry regiments that, he believed, could be combined rapidly into task forces tailored to the mission at hand. Beck also planned to create four fully motorized infantry divisions to work with the panzers. Here he encountered opposition from the chief of the General Army Office (Allgemeines Heeresamt), Colonel Fritz Fromm, who was responsible for carrying out the general's decision. Fromm argued that Beck's idea of *partially* motorizing infantry divisions (the motorized regiments) made no sense. Fromm was supported by Guderian and Lutz, who were concerned that mixed formations would slow the mechanized units, robbing them of a key source of advantage.

Fromm's criticism took hold. Unfortunately for panzer advocates, however, it led to the fielding of light divisions composed of two motorized rifle regiments, a reconnaissance regiment, an artillery regiment, and a panzer battalion.[125] General Guderian strongly objected to the latter's formation, arguing that their reconnaissance function could be better carried out by the Luftwaffe. But by September 1939, four light divisions were in the force. (The Polish campaign, however, later proved Guderian right, and the light divisions were converted to panzer divisions.)

The panzer divisions came into their own in the week-long 1937 fall maneuvers, which took place on the North German Plain. They were by far the largest held in Germany since the Great War. Eight infantry divisions took part, along with the Third Panzer Division and the First Panzer Division's First Panzer Brigade, some 800 tanks in all.[126]

The Third Panzer's attack plan involved employing its infantry brigade to engage enemy troops defending a bridgehead, while the division's panzer brigade struck the left flank of the defending force. The panzers, it was hoped, would make a breakthrough and advance into the enemy's rear. The division's action was part of a larger, corps-size assault planned along a twenty-five-mile front. The attack demonstrated everything the Wehrmacht's most ardent panzer advocates could have hoped for. After a sixty-mile approach march, the division went into the attack, forcing the enemy to commit its reserves. The following day, the Third Panzer broke through the enemy front and penetrated deep into its rear. The enemy position quickly became untenable, and the issue was essentially decided only four days into the planned seven-day exercise.[127]

Overseeing the maneuvers was General Franz Halder, who succeeded Beck as chief of the General Staff a year later. He came away stunned by the "fluid mobility" in the Third Panzer's operations, which were successfully coordinated with the Luftwaffe. General Beck, hardly an opponent of the panzer arm, was so taken aback by what he was seeing that he lodged a protest with the umpires, something unheard of since before the Great War. Although the division was ordered removed from further play, Beck acknowledged that it had "solved the problem allotted to it, through a well-planned, swift, and energetic use of its means."[128] Most importantly, Hitler, who observed the maneuvers, was impressed.[129]

Guderian, for his part, continued to promote his vision by placing articles in military journals, where he argued that the means for reversing the Great War's Western Front stalemate were at hand:

> The chances of an offensive based on the timetable of artillery and infantry co-operation are ... even slighter today than they were in the last war. Everything is therefore dependent on this:

to be able to move faster than has hitherto been done: to keep moving despite the enemy's defensive fire and thus to make it harder for him to build up fresh defensive positions: and finally to carry the attack deep into the enemy's defenses. . . .

As a result of surprise achieved, the March Offensive of 1918 was outstandingly successful, despite the fact that no new types of weapons were employed. If, in addition to the normal methods of achieving surprise, new weapons are also employed, then the effects of surprise will be greatly increased; but the new weapons are not a prerequisite to those effects. *We believe that by attacking with tanks we can achieve a higher rate of movement than has been hitherto obtainable, and—what is perhaps even more important—that we can keep moving once a breakthrough has been made.*[130]

Three additional "exercises" in the late 1930s also proved important in refining panzer operations. Germany's annexation of Austria in 1938 provided an opportunity to deploy some of the new panzer formations, including the entire Second Panzer Division and several panzer regiments, as part of the occupation force. During the movement, the division covered more than 400 miles in less than two days, while the SS Liebstandarte Regiment covered over 600 miles in the same period, even though the operation had been hastily improvised.[131] However, the Second Panzer Division had to abandon 30 percent of its tanks along the way, owing to problems ranging from engine difficulties and gearbox or tread damage to navigation problems (such as sliding off slick roads). Guderian recalled, "The most important weakness to make itself felt was the insufficiency of maintenance facilities, particularly for the tanks. This weakness had already been apparent during the autumn maneuvers of 1937. Proposals to remedy this state of affairs had, however, not yet been fulfilled by March of 1938. This mistake was never made again."[132] Many other tanks had to halt their advance due to a lack of fuel.[133] The experience gained employing mechanized forces in the occupation of Austria, combined with Wehrmacht operations associated with occupying the Sudetenland and Czechoslovakia in September 1938 and March 1939, respectively, resulted in greater emphasis on fuel supplies and field maintenance, which paid dividends when war began the following year.[134]

Wehrmacht field exercises continued right up to Germany's invasion of Poland in September 1939, which interrupted planning for major exercises that would have, for the first time, employed a panzer corps of five divisions. The lessons learned in these exercises were quickly incorporated into military training programs. By 1938, courses at the Kreigsakademie were being given on the principles of panzer-force operations. Panzers, students were instructed, should be employed "in mass and in great depth." Their mission was "penetration or breakthrough, enveloping the flank or encircling deep to attack from the rear." Officers were cautioned, "it is false to restrict the mobility of the [panzer] unit to that of the infantry."[135]

That same year, the position of Chef der Schnellen Truppen (chief of fast troops) was established and charged with overseeing the doctrinal development and training of all mechanized troops. Guderian was assigned the job and gave priority to developing radio networks, which he saw as central to coordinating fast-moving panzer formations.[136]

Joint Air-Land Operations

Breaking the stalemate at the operational level that had dominated the Western Front during the Great War required more than combined-arms mechanized and motorized ground formations. A high level of co-operation and integration between these ground formations was needed. Toward this end, the Luftwaffe and Army developed a partnership, with mechanized air-land operations given priority.[137] Luftwaffe commanders instructed their officers "to participate as much as possible in the command post exercises and wargames of the other services."[138] In 1935, General Wever directed, "Army training exercises should be used as much as possible as Luftwaffe exercises in order to deepen our understanding of inter-service cooperation."[139]

In fact, the German military's air arm proved crucial in resolving several challenges associated with the Wehrmacht's concept of mobile warfare. One involved developing and maintaining an accurate picture of the situation in a dynamic war of movement. Rapidly advancing panzer forces would need situation awareness, and the Luftwaffe created a force of specialized reconnaissance aircraft to function as "aerial scouts."[140] Then there was the fire-support problem. With most of the Wehrmacht's artillery being horse-drawn, the Luftwaffe's ability to provide close air support for the advancing panzers could prove critical to sustaining their momentum. These "reconnaissance-strike" operations could also warn the panzer spearheads of possible attacks on their flanks, while defending against them as well.

In 1936, the Luftwaffe and the Army participated in a five-day set of maneuvers. One entailed coordinating Luftwaffe operations with the newly formed panzer units. It found aircraft "bombing" bridges along the Main River near Frankfurt, crippling the movement of "enemy" mechanized forces. The Luftwaffe, under Generals Albert Kesselring and Hans-Jürgen Stumpf, participated in the fall 1937 maneuvers, which encompassed most of the Luftwaffe's operational force, including seventeen bomber groups, six flak regiments, seven fighter groups, and a Stuka dive-bomber group. During the exercise, a fighter group was placed in direct support of a panzer division, and for the first time in an exercise, the Luftwaffe conducted an airborne drop of paratroopers to seize a key bridge.[141]

By the summer of 1939, additional large-scale field exercises had clearly demonstrated the potential of airborne forces to contribute significantly to the Wehrmacht's vision of mobile warfare.[142] Consequently, the Twenty-Second Infantry Division was designated an air-landing division focusing on glider operations. The paratroop forces formed the Seventh Airborne Division. German glider troops went on to win fame for their capture of the Belgian fortress of Eban Emael during the campaign against France and the Low Countries in the spring of 1940, and German airborne troops proved crucial the following year in seizing the Mediterranean island of Crete.

The Spanish Civil War, which lasted from 1936 to 1939, was fought between the Nationalists, under the leadership of the fascist General Francisco Franco, and the Republicans, who supported the left-leaning Second Spanish Republic. Both sides received support from external powers, with Germany and Italy providing most of Franco's support, while the Republicans were aided primarily by Soviet Russia.

The war, won by the Nationalists, offered the Wehrmacht an opportunity to field-test, albeit in a limited way, the doctrine and equipment associated with its vision of mechanized air-land operations. As it turned out, the Germans learned little of value in the war with respect to armored warfare. The Luftwaffe fared better, deploying some 5,000 men and roughly 100 aircraft in Spain from late 1936 until the war's end in 1939. This force, known as the Condor Legion, included bombers, fighters, ground-support planes, and naval aircraft. Condor Legion aircraft conducted strategic bombing, interdiction, attacks on naval vessels, close air support, and air-superiority missions, learning to shift between them literally on the fly. Toward the war's end, German pilots developed a strong competence in supporting highly mobile ground forces on the move. By the time Germany invaded Poland, more than 19,000 Luftwaffe airmen had rotated through Europe's best "training center," gaining invaluable experience in modern air warfare.[143]

The success of close-air-support operations in Spain saw Luftwaffe leaders incorporating these lessons in numerous maneuvers with the Army. Particular emphasis was given to supporting ground units conducting river crossings and in meeting engagements, a skill that produced enormous dividends in May 1940.[144]

When Germany went to war in the late summer of 1939, the Luftwaffe was "the best-prepared air force in the world."[145] It had more veterans of modern air warfare than any other European air force. Luftwaffe pilots were more experienced in fundamental navigation and flying skills, as well as in night flying and bad-weather navigation, than their rivals. Most important for the Wehrmacht, the Luftwaffe had become the world's best-trained force for close-air-support operations.[146] When the Condor Legion returned in 1939, it was reformed as the VIII Air Corps under General von Richthofen. It soon distinguished itself both in the Polish campaign of 1939 and during the campaign against the Low Countries and France the following year.[147]

Blitzkrieg

Poland 1939

Germany's attack on Poland on September 1, 1939, which triggered war with France and Great Britain, offered the first test of the Wehrmacht's mechanized air-land operational concept. The German Army began the campaign with roughly 3,000 tanks, nearly all of which were obsolete Panzer I types, with only about 100 Panzer IIIs and 200 Panzer IVs. But the panzers incorporated the latest communications system, and many of the logistical problems that plagued them during the occupation of Austria had been fixed. The campaign produced a rapid German victory, with most Polish resistance collapsing by midmonth.

During the campaign, Guderian, now commanding the XIX Panzer Corps consisting of the Third Panzer Division and the Second and Twentieth Motorized Divisions, gave Hitler a tour of his sector. Observing some shattered Polish artillery, Hitler asked Guderian, "Our dive-bombers did that?" To which Guderian replied, "No! Our panzers!"—and, he might have mentioned, at the cost of only 150 killed in action.[148]

The close-air-support tactics that had been developed in the Spanish Civil War, such as attacking in waves and maintaining constant pressure on the enemy at the key point of decision, had a devastating effect on Polish morale. Richthofen's VIII Air Corps, with roughly half the Luft-waffe's Stuka dive-bombers and a ground-attack group, formed a "Close Battle Division" supporting the German Tenth Army, which possessed the greatest concentration of mechanized forces and had been designated the offensive's *schwerpunkt* (principal focus). The Tenth Army's commander, General Walther von Reichenau, observed that the Close Battle Division had "led to the decision [victory] on the battlefield."[149]

The campaign in Poland won over some senior-officer skeptics, such as General Gerd von Rundstedt, to the mechanized air-land war of movement that soon became known as "Blitzkrieg."[150] Many observers, however, both in the Wehrmacht and in foreign militaries, argued that Germany and Soviet Russia—which invaded Poland from the east on September 17—had the odds stacked overwhelmingly in their favor. The Poles were seen less as worthy adversaries than as victims.

France 1940

The German campaign in Poland was a striking success, but it was widely believed that the Wehrmacht's true test would come against the French Army, still counted by many observers as the world's finest. After a winter of inaction on the Western Front, the Germans opened the campaign season in April with rapid victories over Denmark and Norway, setting the stage for a showdown with the Allies: France and Great Britain.

The Wehrmacht's evolving plan for the campaign in the west—Plan Yellow—reveal an increased willingness to rely on its new methods of warfare. Two days after Poland surrendered on September 27, Halder noted in his diary, "Techniques of Polish campaign no recipe for the West. No good against a well-knit Army."[151] Early German plans called for Army Group B under General Fedor von Bock to conduct the main attack, sweeping through the Low Countries into France—a pale, unambitious revival of the 1914 Schlieffen Plan that failed in its objective of effecting a quick knockout blow to the Allies. Supporting von Bock's attack would be Army Group A, under von Rundstedt, located to the south from Aachen to the northern terminus of France's Maginot Line fortifications along its border with Luxembourg. Anticipating the German axis of attack through

Belgium and the Netherlands, the Allies' Plan D called for rushing three French armies and most of the British Expeditionary Force forward to a line between Breda and the Dyle river to prevent the loss of Antwerp and Rotterdam, while keeping the fighting away from French soil.[152]

Over the next six months, the plan changed radically, thanks to a combination of war games, debate among senior Army officers, and Hitler's personal involvement. When presented with Plan Yellow on October 22, 1939, Hitler, unimpressed, asked Generals Halder and Walther von Brauchitsch if an attack on the southern Meuse in Army Group A's sector could cut off and annihilate the main enemy forces to the north. The area was dominated by the Ardennes Forest, which appeared to pose an imposing barrier to the rapid movement of large forces, especially mechanized and motorized units. Confronted by Hitler's idea, the generals went back to reconsider their plans.[153]

Coincidentally, only a few weeks later, von Rundstedt's chief of staff, Lieutenant General Erich von Manstein, and Guderian discussed massing a panzer attack against the Allies through the Ardennes Forest to effect a breakthrough and trap the main Allied armies in Belgium. The next two months found Halder and von Rundstedt warming to the idea.[154] During a meeting at General Staff headquarters in mid-December, Halder pointed to the Ardennes Forest on a map, declaring, "Here is the weak point. Here we have to go through!" In January 1940, von Rundstedt conducted a war game to test the idea, but with infantry, not tanks, leading the way.[155]

On February 7, von Rundstedt conducted another war game to explore von Manstein's plan, this time employing a panzer and a motorized corps to attack and cross the Meuse River at Sedan. When Guderian insisted on attempting a crossing without the infantry divisions, von Rundstedt opposed the idea as too risky. Still, the game was sufficiently encouraging to keep von Manstein's concept on the table.[156]

Ten days later, Hitler met with von Manstein for a "routine" breakfast with new corps commanders. In fact, Hitler had heard of von Manstein's plan, and it piqued his interest. After the breakfast, Hitler invited the general to stay behind and describe his plan. Hitler was impressed, and their discussion extended into midafternoon. The next day, Hitler presented the plan—now "his" plan—to Halder and von Brauchitsch, with instructions to act on it. The generals, already moving toward von Manstein's approach, began to work out the details.

The revised plan called for shifting all the panzers, save one division assigned to von Bock's Army Group B for invading the Netherlands and two others ticketed for the assault on Belgium, to Army Group A and the Ardennes operation. Along with them went most of the Army's best tanks.[157] In the process, Halder created the equivalent of what would become a panzer army. It had two panzer corps but, out of deference to the infantry, was designated "Group Kleist," after its commander, General Ewald von Kleist, a cavalry veteran. Since the final version of Plan Yellow was designed to cut off the main French and British armies from their logistics support as a scythe cuts stalks of grain, it was popularly known as the "sickle-cut" plan.[158]

When the German offensive in the west opened on May 10, 1940, it was far from clear that the plan, relying heavily as it did on deception and surprise, would succeed. If the French discovered the panzer forces snaking through the Ardennes, they would be highly vulnerable to attack from the air while the French thickened their defenses along the planned breakthrough point along the Meuse.

Indeed, a general examination of the German and Allied forces opposing each other seemed, if anything, to favor the latter. Although estimates vary, the Germans possessed some 2,700 tanks in their ten panzer divisions, most of which were the obsolete Panzer I. The Allies counted some 3,500 tanks in their inventories (roughly 3,000 French and 200 British, along with some Belgian, Dutch, and Polish systems).[159] The Allies' tank forces, however, without exception included a larger proportion of models designed for infantry support, not independent mobile offensive warfare.[160]

The French tanks were heavier than those of the Germans. The latest French tanks, the Somua S35 and the heavy Char B, had twice the armor of the Panzer IVs and a superior anti-armor gun.[161] Reflecting the French military's vision of a conflict characterized by positional warfare and attrition, their tank designs emphasized firepower and armor protection more so than their German counterparts did. Heavy armor and large guns meant adding more weight. The German approach, emphasizing rapid concentration of combat power and deeply penetrating breakthrough forces, accorded priority to speed and range.[162] The German panzers' range advantage was even more pronounced considering how the Wehrmacht had extended their *effective* range though improvements in logistics, such as mobile maintenance and fuel support units.

The Germans also enjoyed an advantage in the air. Although estimates vary considerably, it appears that the Luftwaffe and the Allies each had roughly 1,000 fighters, but the Allies' 400 bombers were numerically inferior to the Germans' 1,100. The Luftwaffe also had the VIII Air Corps and 325 dive-bombers, for which the Allies had no equivalent.[163]

Germany's offensive began in the Low Countries, with the Luftwaffe dropping the Seventh Airborne Division into western Holland to seize a key airfield and bridges between Rotterdam and The Hague. The paratroopers, reinforced by glider troops of the Twenty-Second Air Landing Division, cut off Dutch forces planning to retreat within their "Fortress Holland" defense line. That same day, German glider troops landed atop the key Belgian fortress of Éban Emael, quickly capturing it and opening the way for the rapidly advancing panzers. The French and their British allies assumed that the German attack into the Low Countries represented the enemy's main line of advance. Thus, in less than forty-eight hours, the French committed their three light mechanized divisions—those with the fastest tanks—against the advancing German forces.

The real action, however, came on the Meuse. As planned, the Germans were concentrating for their main attack along a narrow front to the south, between Liege and Sedan. Four critical days passed before the French began to comprehend the true situation. Von Rundstedt's Army Group A used its clear advantage in close air support to conduct persistent Ju-87 (Stuka) dive-bombing attacks on French forces attempting to block the German Army's crossing of the Meuse River at Sedan. During the critical phase of the operation, on May 13, more than a thousand Luftwaffe aircraft kept French forces under constant attack throughout the day. The French actually took few losses, but their morale was shattered, and they proved unable to provide accurate artillery fire against the German forces crossing the river.[164]

The panzer spearhead was under the command of General Guderian, who recounted, "Instead of coolly determining just how serious the danger was around Sedan and coordinating attacks from both north and south of the area against the German bridgeheads, the French High Command dissipated its armored divisions in several hasty and ill-coordinated attacks."[165] He later recalled, "I was surprised that the French long-range artillery in the Maginot Line and its westerly extension had not laid down heavier fire and caused us more trouble during our advance. At this moment, as I looked at the ground we had come over, the success of our attack struck me as almost a miracle."[166]

Guderian's description of the breakthrough at Sedan as bordering on miraculous is understandable. Given the French Army's reputation as one of the world's best—if not *the* best—and the terrain in and around the Ardennes, which was hardly conducive to demonstrating Blitzkrieg-style operations, the relative ease of the breakthrough must have seemed extremely unlikely, especially against the backdrop of Western Front operations in the Great War.

But Guderian also recounted that, once he crossed the Meuse, he encountered one of his best commanders, Lieutenant Colonel Hermann Balck, along with his staff. Balck cheerfully greeted his commander, saying, "Joy riding in canoes on the Meuse is forbidden!" Guderian recalled that he had used those words during one of the training exercises in preparation for the operation, since at the time, his young officers' attitudes had struck him as being overly confident. "I now realized," Guderian recalled, "that they judged the situation correctly."[167]

Indeed, the speed at which the German military could adjust on the fly far surpassed that of the French. When the Germans were preparing to attempt the Meuse crossing, there was insufficient time to write and disseminate the complex orders for the Army and the Luftwaffe to integrate their actions. Guderian's chief of staff, realizing that the situation closely resembled that of a recent war game, took the game orders and crossed out "1000" (10:00 a.m.) and wrote "1600" (4:00 p.m.) in its place.[168] It worked.

In Paris, panic began to set in. On May 13, President Paul Reynaud told Churchill, appointed Britain's prime minister only three days earlier, "We have been defeated. We are beaten; we have lost the battle.... The front is broken near Sedan; they are pouring through in great numbers with tanks and armored cars." Recalling the storm-troop Michel Offensive of 1918 that soon lost momentum, Churchill told the French president not to worry: "After five or six days they will have to halt for supplies, and the opportunity for counter-attack is presented. I learned all this from the lips of Marshal Foch himself."[169]

But this was not 1918. The German military had spent a generation working to avoid a repetition of that failed offensive. And they had succeeded.

Having moved beyond the Ardennes and breached the Meuse, the German panzers could operate in the open, using their speed and range to create an irreparable rupture in the Allies' defenses. The panzer forces, in fact, advanced so rapidly that they soon became separated from the nonmotorized forces. Concerned over the prospect that the panzers might be attacked on their vulnerable flanks, von Rundstedt ordered von Kleist to slow his advance to allow the infantry forces to catch up. Upon hearing the orders, Guderian, furious, threatened to resign. General von Richthofen weighed in, pledging that his VIII Air Corps could secure the panzer spearhead's flanks, in effect substituting air power for infantry and artillery support. Von Rundstedt reluctantly agreed. The VIII Air Corps was directed to "follow Panzer Group von Kleist to the sea." Making good on von Richthofen's promise, Luftwaffe fighter and dive-bomber aircraft units were deployed with remarkable speed to support the rapidly advancing panzers, blunting several French Army attempts to mount a counterattack.[170]

To ensure continuous close air support, when necessary, maintenance personnel, aviation fuel, spare parts, and ammunition were airlifted into newly established forward operating air bases by Ju-52 transport aircraft. Thanks to insights derived from frequent prewar maneuvers and operations in Spain, the Luftwaffe had fielded some 117 motorized columns capable of moving with the Army's mechanized units. These mobile airfield-construction companies and engineer units established austere forward air bases or converted captured airfields into operational bases in a matter of hours, enabling the Luftwaffe to maintain the high sortie rates needed to support the fast-moving armored columns.[171] Robert Citino has noted, "This campaign marked the true birth of 'Air-Land battle.'"[172]

Only three days after Churchill's talk with Reynaud, the Allies' rapidly deteriorating position was becoming clear. So, too, was a growing recognition that the Wehrmacht was breaking new ground in military operations. Speaking to a joint session of Congress, President Franklin Roosevelt referred to the German methods, noting, "The element of surprise which has ever been an important tactic in warfare has become the more dangerous because of the amazing speed with which modern equipment can reach and attack the enemy's country."[173] As the panzers continued their race to the Channel, Churchill's eyes were opened. On May 24, the frustrated prime minister messaged General Hastings Ismay, his chief staff officer and adviser, remarking, "Apparently the Germans can go anywhere and do anything, and their tanks can act in twos and threes all over our rear, and even when they are located, they are not attacked. Also our tanks recoil before their field guns, but our field guns do not like to take on their tanks."[174] Years later, Churchill recalled, "I was shocked by the utter failure to grapple with the German armour which, with a few thousand vehicles, was encompassing the entire destruction of mighty armies."[175]

The panzers reached Abbeville on May 20, cutting off the main British and French armies, pinning them against the English Channel at Dunkirk. On May 28, Belgium surrendered. That day, Guderian was given command of a two-corps panzer group—Panzer Group Guderian —a panzer army in all but name. Although much of the British Expeditionary Force and some French troops were successfully evacuated to Great Britain, the Allies had suffered a devastating defeat. Having dispatched the cream of the Allies' armies in less than a month, the Wehrmacht turned south and breached the French defenses in short order. Paris was taken on June 14, and an armistice confirming France's defeat was signed on June 22. What had proved impossible to accomplish in four long years of static warfare a generation earlier had been accomplished in six short weeks in the spring of 1940.

The casualties suffered during the campaign reflected the magnitude of Germany's victory. The French suffered roughly 90,000 killed and 200,000 wounded, with 1.9 million prisoners taken. Total British, Belgian, and Dutch casualties were 68,111, 23,350, and 9,779, respectively. German losses were 27,074 killed, 111,034 wounded, and 18,384 missing.[176]

In evaluating the success of the campaign in France, General Wilhelm Ritter von Thoma of Germany cited the close cooperation of the panzer forces with the Luftwaffe, the massed use of armor, and the ability of mechanized forces to penetrate quickly and deeply into the enemy's rear areas. He found it noteworthy that although the panzer divisions had enough fuel to advance 90–120 miles, their range could be supplemented by various means, including resupply by air.[177] As for the enemy's armored forces, von Thoma concluded, "The French tanks were better than ours, and as numerous—but they were too slow. It was by speed, in exploiting surprise, that we beat the French."[178] Forced to choose between a "thick skin" (heavy armor protection) and "a fast runner" (speed), he said that Germany's panzer leaders would "always" choose the latter. Von Thoma's critique was echoed by General Günther Blumentritt, who believed that the German victory owed less to armor plate and firepower than to speed, range, and superior coordination, concluding, "Above all, German tank troops were more mobile, quicker and better at in-fighting, and able while in movement to turn wherever required by their leader. This, the French at that time were unable to do. They still fought more in the tradition of the First World War. They were not up to date either in leadership [in their concepts of modern warfare] or wireless control."[179] Indeed, during the campaign, Guderian carried out impromptu experiments with a captured

French Char B tank and found its front armor invulnerable to German tank guns. By comparison, German tank armor was perilously thin.[180]

It took several years before other militaries could match what the Germans had wrought. Not until 1942 was the Royal Air Force (RAF) able to provide the kind of close air support that the Luftwaffe had been flying since 1939. The U.S. Army Air Forces did not catch up until the latter half of 1943.[181] It took U.S., British, and Soviet mechanized forces even longer to close the gap. The Allies ultimately prevailed not by mastering this new form of warfare better than the Germans but by sheer weight of numbers and the progressively inept generalship of Corporal Hitler.

Conclusion

When did the German military truly acquire the ability to wage combined-arms mechanized air-land warfare that became Blitzkrieg? The question remains a matter of debate. For most of the period between the world wars, there was an awareness on the part of a significant element in the German officer corps that the new tools of war, especially those enabled by advances in mechanization, aviation, and radio, could transform war's character, land warfare in particular. Most of the senior officer corps, men like General Beck, accepted that mechanized forces would exert a significant influence on future wars. In the absence of a clear confirmation on the battlefield, however, relatively few officers were willing to assert that these forces would trigger a military revolution. As an impatient General Guderian wrote in 1937,

> Military literature is replete with statements that indicate that many people believe we may embark on a new war with the weapons of 1914, or at best with those available in 1918. Many authorities consider themselves forward-looking when they bring themselves to admit the value of the new weapons which appeared towards the end of the war—as auxiliaries of the old ones. This is a narrow and negative concept. Fundamentally, these men are unable to break free of the memories of positional warfare, which they persist in viewing as the combat of the future, and they are incapable of summoning up the necessary act of will to stake everything on rapid decision. In particular, they are blind to the prospects that are opened by a full exploitation of the internal combustion engine. "It is a love of comfort, not to

say sluggishness, that characterizes those who protest against revolutionary innovations that happen to demand fresh efforts in the way of intellect, physical striving and resolution." Hence, we encounter the outright assertion that motorized and mechanized weapons represent nothing revolutionary or new, and dismissive comments on the lines that their "single" chance of success came and went in 1918, that they have had their day, and that one may content oneself with standing on the defensive.[182]

Nevertheless a critical mass of the German officer corps existed, sufficient in size and stature to pursue and sustain disruptive innovation.

The German military's path to Blitzkrieg was messy. Given the difficulties involved in handicapping the prospective value of rapidly emerging military technologies, the uncertainties associated with predicting the future geopolitical environment, and the paths that potential military competitors would take in attempting to develop and exploit new sources of advantage, it is hardly surprising that the German military's path proved bumpy.

Yet thanks to von Seeckt and his acolytes, the Reichswehr established a vision of future warfare and identified the operational challenges it had to solve. Of critical importance, von Seeckt's vision fit within the German Army's tradition of waging wars of maneuver and annihilation, rather than the wars of position associated with a strategy of attrition. From an institutional perspective, the idea of mobile, mechanized airland operations was a very easy fit for the German military, especially as the Luftwaffe's leadership was populated with former Army officers.

The German military also benefited from some good fortune. Although the Versailles Treaty made developing equipment and testing operational concepts difficult, through disarmament the German military avoided being saddled with rapidly obsolescing tanks and aircraft, as were the Allied militaries following World War I. It had neither to spend scarce resources maintaining such equipment nor to feel compelled to incorporate it into its doctrine. Being disarmed also meant that the Reichswehr could avoid large production runs of equipment that would soon become outdated. Simply put, the Versailles Treaty minimized the amount of baggage the German military had to carry along its journey, lessening the drag effect on the path toward Blitzkrieg.

Ironically, Germany's wartime enemies provided insight and encouragement to pursue von Seeckt's vision. British military writings nurtured

German thinking, and British field exercises gave men like Lutz and Guderian growing confidence in their ideas. Soviet Russia aided the Reichswehr in producing, testing, and evaluating the new equipment needed to realize its vision, as well as the opportunity to train with it.

Interestingly, while the German military benefited from the actions of other great-power militaries, the Luftwaffe avoided the infatuation with strategic aerial bombardment that captured the minds of their counterparts in the United States and Great Britain. Although this yielded the "wrong" German air force for the Battle of Britain, it produced the "right" Luftwaffe for Blitzkrieg operations.[183] This again points out the situational character of disruptive military innovation: the importance of developing a vision that focuses on the *right operational problem* (or problems) at the *proper scale*.

When did the German Army become convinced that it had wrought a revolutionary new form of warfare? It was not until after the spring 1940 campaign that the officer corps as a whole accepted highly mobile, mechanized ground forces as the centerpiece of land warfare.[184] Even following the Wehrmacht's rapid victory over Poland, initial efforts at Plan Yellow assumed that the Polish campaign's success was a one-off against a weak adversary that could not be replicated against a major-power army. But given time, the General Staff came around to the ideas of von Manstein, Guderian, and Hitler. In the Polish campaign, the panzer corps operated under the control of the infantry armies. The panzer divisions were not concentrated for an operationally decisive campaign along a single axis of attack. Still, their performance greatly impressed the Wehrmacht's senior leadership.[185] Given the torpid response by the other major military organizations to German operations in Poland, it seems that widespread acceptance in military circles that a fundamental shift in the character of land warfare had occurred had to await the precipitous collapse of the celebrated French Army.

The German military's development of Blitzkrieg represented a major, or disruptive, innovation in warfare. The Reichswehr (and, later, the Wehrmacht) focused primarily on the challenge of fighting a war with Poland, France, or Czechoslovakia, alone or in combination. Blitzkrieg, as practiced by the German military, was well suited for these contingencies. But Blitzkrieg had limits, in both form and scale.

Following the fall of France, Germany's mechanized air-land force was ill-suited to address the operational challenge posed by a defiant Great Britain, an island nation. Indeed, Germany's attempt to pave the way for an amphibious assault on the island through a strategic bombing campaign revealed serious shortcomings in the Luftwaffe's capabilities in that emerging form of warfare.

There is also the matter of scale. In the fall of 1939, Germany almost certainly lacked sufficient capability to wage the kind of war against France that proved so effective against its smaller rival, Poland.[186] By 1940, however, Germany had progressed sufficiently to conduct an enhanced form of Blitzkrieg operations and on a scale sufficient to defeat the Allied forces on the Western Front. The Wehrmacht, however, never achieved the necessary scale in its mechanized air-land forces to defeat Soviet Russia in a short campaign, as it had against Poland and France. The German economy was incapable of providing the aircraft, vehicles, and fuel in the quantities necessary to wage war against Russia and the United States.[187]

That being said, the Germany military's introduction of mechanized air-land warfare enabled it to win a series of stunning victories in the war's initial campaigns. In fairness to the German military, however, it must also be pointed out that for most of the interwar period, the security problem set before it was the threat posed by France and Poland. It was only late in the day, after Hitler's rise, that Britain came to be seen as an enemy. And it was Hitler who expanded Germany's military ambitions to include warring with the globe's two emerging superpowers: Soviet Russia and the United States.

As Sir Michael Howard concludes, "The Germans were almost unique in 1939–40 in that they appreciated with the minimum of practical experience ... the full implications which the new technological developments held for military science and embodied them in their equipment and their doctrine. ... Usually everybody starts even and everybody starts wrong."[188] Simply put, Blitzkrieg represents a remarkable feat of disruptive military innovation. Perhaps Citino puts it best, observing that the Germans "are still responsible for the greatest battlefield revolution in the history of modern warfare. ... This was a new style of warfare, ... fast-paced and furious, and it left Germany's slower-moving adversaries stunned. It changed the face of warfare forever, and its principles are used today by all modern armies."[189]

CHAPTER EIGHT

Twilight of the Battle Line

To affirm that the aeroplane is going to "revolutionize" naval warfare of the future is to be guilty of the wildest exaggeration.

—SCIENTIFIC AMERICAN, 1910

A fleet whose carriers give it command of the air over the enemy fleet can defeat the latter. . . . The fast carrier is the capital ship of the future.

—ADMIRAL WILLIAM SIMS, 1925

IN THE CLOSING DAYS of World War I, the U.S. Navy had plans for a major expansion of the fleet. Top priority was given to increasing the number of battleships, widely viewed as the principal measure of naval power. Nearly a quarter of a century later, in December 1941, the Navy entered World War II against the Axis powers still viewing itself as a "battleship navy." The U.S. fleet at that time also included seven aircraft carriers, a relatively new type of warship. In fact, the first U.S. purpose-built carrier—*Ranger*—had only joined the fleet seven years earlier.

Yet during the course of the war, the United States Navy employed a new type of sea power so revolutionary, and so devastatingly effective, that the powerful Imperial Japanese Navy was, in the span of less than three years, swept from the Pacific. The core element of this new form of sea power was the U.S. carrier task force. Surface warships protected the carriers, while a revolutionary system of mobile supply bases enabled them to stay at sea for extended periods of time.[1]

When the war ended in September 1945, the Navy counted twenty-eight large "fast" carriers and seventy-one smaller carrier types in the fleet; the Navy's aviation arm had more than 41,000 planes. The fleet included fewer than a dozen battleships, and none were being built. So swift was the change from the battleship to the carrier that when the battleships damaged in Japan's attack on Pearl Harbor were repaired, they were sent back to sea as part of carrier task forces.[2] The United States Navy, which came out of World War I viewing itself, along with the Royal Navy and Imperial Japanese Navy, as one of the world's major naval forces, now stood alone with far and away the world's most powerful fleet.

A Revolutionary Vision

Barely a decade after the Wright brothers conducted the first heavier-than-air flight, in August 1913, the U.S. Navy's General Board recommended to the secretary of the Navy that "the organization of an efficient naval air service should be immediately taken in hand and pushed to fulfillment."[3] Established in 1900, the General Board served as the Navy secretary's advisory group. The original members included the Navy's senior admiral, the chief of the bureau of navigation, the chief intelligence officer, the president of the Naval War College, and three relatively junior officers. Over time, the board's composition changed, most notably to include the Marine Corps' commandant. Given its members' expertise, most issues regarding Navy policy and strategy, along with ship design and emerging technologies, were referred to the General Board for study and comment, and its recommendations carried great weight.[4]

By 1916, Navy Secretary Josephus Daniels envisioned naval aircraft enhancing the fleet's scouting ability as well as the battle line's gunnery. More expansively, he envisioned the Navy's nascent air arm engaging in "offensive operations against enemy aircraft and possibly against ships or stations." Two years later, the board recommended that airplanes be carried on scout ships, cruisers, and battle cruisers.[5] Here, as was often the case, the Navy was following in the wake of Britain's Royal Navy, which had long stood as the world's preeminent naval power. In 1918, the British launched the *Argus*, the prototype of future carriers. Operations aboard the *Argus* revealed that the British had largely solved two of the three basic challenges for employing carriers in the fleet: launching and recovering aircraft at sea. The third challenge, conducting large-scale sustained combat air operations at sea, was more formidable.[6] Although the U.S. Navy initially followed in the British footsteps, it soon diverted down its own path.

At the end of World War I, many U.S. naval officers were willing to concede that naval aviation could be useful for scouting the enemy to ensure the battleship "line of battle" was positioned to bring maximum fire against an enemy battle fleet. Moreover, by spotting the fall of the battle line's shots, aircraft could enhance naval gunfire accuracy by radioing adjustments to the battleships. To prevent enemy aircraft from performing similar functions, naval officers accepted that friendly aircraft would also be useful in screening enemy scout aircraft away from the fleet and in neutralizing enemy spotter aircraft. All this would enhance the battleship's effectiveness. In this vision of future fleet operations, the battleship remained the principal arbiter—the "capital ship"—of war at sea.

There was also a small minority of officers who believed that aircraft employed in fleet operations could revolutionize war at sea. These visionaries believed that all warships—regardless of their size, armor, and armament—would, over time, be vulnerable to attack by aircraft. When this came to pass, they asserted, it would drastically change the speed and range at which naval actions would be fought. From the beginning, these officers saw in the carrier the successor to the battleship and its ancestors, which had exercised a centuries-old domination of fleet engagements. To the carrier aircrafts' missions of reconnaissance, observation, and air defense, which in themselves would significantly alter war at sea, naval aviation enthusiasts added a game-changing operation: strikes by naval aircraft at extended ranges and of sufficient magnitude to disable an enemy fleet's capital ships.

Some of these visionaries were inspired by the Royal Navy's early carrier operations. The most prominent of these men was Rear Admiral William S. Sims, who had commanded U.S. naval forces in Europe during the war. In 1925, Sims declared, "A small, high-speed carrier alone can destroy or disable a battleship alone. . . . A fleet whose carriers give it command of the air over the enemy fleet can defeat the latter."[7] He concluded, "The fast carrier is the capital ship of the future." The admiral, a member of the General Board, went on to presciently define a fast carrier as "an airplane carrier of thirty-five knots and carrying one hundred planes."[8]

Sims's vision was shared by few of his colleagues. Naval aircraft in World War I were small and fragile, capable of flying only short distances, and could not communicate effectively with ships at extended ranges. Their bomb loads were minuscule compared with the firepower generated by a single battleship's broadside. Compounding the problem, aircraft were incapable of accurately delivering their modest payload.

Following the Armistice in 1918, the Navy was confronted with a range of options for establishing its aviation arm, which included airships, seaplanes, land-based aircraft, planes carried on existing surface combatants, and planes carried on ships specifically designed for that purpose: aircraft carriers.[9]

Two principal schools of thought emerged. Admiral William S. Benson, the chief of naval operations (CNO), belonged to the traditionalist school, believing that naval aviation could, at best, be useful in scouting and perhaps in spotting gunfire. Members of the aviation "enthusiast" school were split in their views, with the majority visualizing naval aviation principally as a key auxiliary to the battle line. Others could envision aviation becoming a central element in fleet operations but saw several major barriers that had to be overcome before naval aviation could realize its full potential. Most reflected the views of Captain Ernest J. King, who believed that unless aircraft technology continued to advance rapidly, it would not progress beyond its role as the "eyes of the fleet."[10]

Benson viewed Sims and the other air enthusiasts with deep skepticism, remarking, "The Navy doesn't need airplanes. Aviation is just a lot of noise."[11] Benson opposed Sims's recommendation that battleships be equipped with aircraft. More ominously, the CNO's postwar reorganization plan called for abolishing the naval aviation office and placing its functions under the Naval Operations Planning and Materiel divisions. A special committee convened by Benson recommended that a decision on constructing a carrier (the Navy had none) be put off.[12] Several factors, however, both internal and external to the Navy, undermined Benson's plans.

The first was the Royal Navy. Great Britain had established a commanding lead in carrier technology and planned to continue exploring the potential of naval air forces in fleet operations. For the U.S. Navy, which aspired to achieve parity with, if not superiority over, the British fleet, there was a strong institutional incentive to stay abreast with the Royal Navy in all aspects of naval warfare. This made the Royal Navy's interest in both naval aviation and carriers difficult for the Americans to ignore.

The second factor was the Navy's own embryonic testing of naval air power. Support for a carrier of some sort received a boost in March 1919, when the battleship *Texas* conducted a main-battery gunnery exercise at long range employing air spotting. Although the spotting was done by an untrained observer, the results were "many times better than was done by ship's spotters." Highly impressed with the results, the captain of the *Texas*, N. C. Twining, declared, "The Fleet that neglects aviation development will be at an enormous disadvantage in an engagement with a modern enemy fleet."[13] Suddenly, both spotter and fighter planes assumed a new importance, as did the carrier, for it alone seemed able to provide aircraft in sufficient numbers to support a major fleet engagement on the high seas.

The General Board conducted a series of confidential hearings from January to June 1919 to assess the potential role of aviation in maritime operations. At one session, Commander Kenneth Whiting, who had been in charge of the first U.S. naval air station in Britain during the war, told the board, "If the war had gone on a little longer, the bombing of Kiel, Cuxhaven and Wilhelmshaven would have been done from airplane carriers. The [British carrier] *Furious* was equipped with airplanes and made an attack on Tondern, as she steamed up and down the North Sea without hindrance."[14] Whiting declared that the increase in gunfire effectiveness with air spotting was likely to be as great as 200 percent.[15]

Testimony like Whiting's led the General Board to find that "to enable the United States to meet on at least equal terms any possible enemy . . . fleet aviation must be developed to the fullest extent. Aircraft have become an essential arm of the fleet. A Naval air service must be established, capable of accompanying and operating with the fleet in all waters of the globe. Great Britain has already accomplished this."[16]

The General Board also recommended that "airplane carriers for the fleet be provided in the proportion of one carrier to each squadron of capital ships." Despite the board's recommendation, Admiral Benson told Navy Secretary Daniels that he was "not yet prepared to admit the necessity for Spotting Planes and Short Distance Reconnaissance Planes for the fighting ships of the fleet."[17] Benson, however, was overruled.

Soon after, a third event convinced even the Navy's traditionalists to embrace aviation.

In November 1920, the Navy conducted a closely guarded aerial bombing test against the obsolete battleship *Indiana*. Owing to the classified nature of the tests (they were intended to inform future ship designs), no results were announced. The Navy was therefore stunned to see photographs of the stricken *Indiana* in the *Illustrated London News*.[18] Army Air Corps Brigadier General William "Billy" Mitchell, a strong supporter of air power's potential (and whom many suspected of leaking the photos), promptly declared to Congress, "We can tell you definitively now that we can either destroy or sink any ship in existence today."[19]

Mitchell's views had clout. He was a genuine war hero. He was the first American to fly over German lines and was the first awarded France's Croix de Guerre for bravery. Although Mitchell's claims would prove wildly exaggerated, the general had a gift for attracting attention. His exploitation of the *Indiana* test results was seen as a threat by the Navy, which began to close ranks against a common peril: the United States Army. Retired Rear Admiral Bradley A. Fiske, a strong supporter of aviation—*naval* aviation—urged the service to develop its air arm, employing the most colorful terms, declaring, "For the sake of the U.S.N. and the U.S. [of] America—let's get a Bureau of Aeronautics—as p.d.q. [pretty damned quick] as possible. ... If we don't get that Bureau next session, Gen'l Mitchell and a whole horde of politicians will get an 'Air Ministry' established, and the U.S. Navy will find itself lying in the street ... and the procession marching over it."[20]

The challenge posed to naval aviation by Mitchell in the early 1920s was real and unprecedented. Not only did Mitchell lay claim to the traditional naval function of first line of homeland defense, which he argued could be better performed by aircraft, but he also proposed that an independent air service be put in charge of aircraft carriers on the grounds that these were, properly considered, "aircraft transports."[21] As the battle lines between the Navy and Mitchell were drawn, the fight shifted to Congress. Congressman Fred C. Hicks, of the House Naval Affairs Committee, became an ardent supporter of an independent naval aviation arm, as did Senator William Borah. When General Mitchell succeeded in having an amendment inserted in a House appropriations bill for the Army in 1920 that would have put that service in control of "all aerial operations from the land bases," Secretary Daniels successfully mobilized members of Congress to oppose it.[22]

Although the Navy warded off Mitchell's initial challenge, his ideas continued to gain currency. He secured permission for a highly publicized Army bomber attack on the former German battleship *Ostfriesland* in July 1921, to which he invited senior political and military leaders. The experiment was a success, in that the ship was sunk. But the test parameters were heavily skewed in favor of the attacking aircraft. The ship's position was known in advance. It also was at anchor, which precluded it from conducting evasive maneuvers. It had no escorting air defense ships, so there was no simulated anti-aircraft fire. Naval observers discounted the significance of Mitchell's stunt, but the fact that aircraft had sent a battleship to the bottom meant that he reaped a public-relations windfall with the U.S. public and the Congress.

Despite the Navy's outrage, Mitchell's well-publicized views proved useful to the service's air enthusiasts. Like Mitchell, these men believed in the potential of air power to transform war at sea, but they sought to realize that potential *within* their service, not apart from it. In February 1921, Admiral Benson, concerned over General Mitchell's criticisms, finally agreed to establish a bureau for naval aviation. The Bureau of Aeronautics—"BuAer"—the Navy's first new bureau in sixty years, was established in August, with Rear Admiral William A. Moffett as its chief. Now the Navy had a vision for naval aviation and a home for it as well. Shortly thereafter, the General Board recommended the construction of three mammoth 39,000-ton carriers.[23]

Although a growing number of naval officers believed an air arm could be an asset, there was great uncertainty as to what form it would ultimately take, how important it would be, and whether the vision of its most ardent supporters would be realized. Moreover, while aviation technology was proceeding at a rapid rate in the early 1920s, it was impossible to know how much more progress could be made or how soon. In 1923, the General Board consulted experts in aeronautics, including Massachusetts Institute of Technology president S. W. Stratton, Johns Hopkins physicist J. S. Ames, and E. P. Warner, who chaired the Aerodynamic Department at MIT, along with leading members of the National Advisory Committee for Aeronautics (NACA), among them W. F. Durand of Stanford University; George W. Lewis, NACA's research director; and Rear Admiral David Taylor, NACA's secretary. These experts forecast that "present maximum performance of heavier-than-air craft may be increased about thirty per cent by future developments extending over an indefinite period of years. All of them consider it most unwise to base a policy of national defense on the expectation much beyond present performance."[24]

By the early 1930s, aviation had far surpassed their estimates.

The Navy's Trinity

The Navy's aviation enthusiasts needed more than a vision. They needed a sense of the operational problems or challenges that the Navy would probably face in the event of war to inform them as to *how* a naval air arm should be developed. Although the Royal Navy was considered the gold standard among the world's navies, the U.S. Navy viewed the Imperial Japanese Navy (IJN) as its principal rival. After World War I, Japan acquired several former German island chains in the Central Pacific, including the Marshalls, Carolines, and Marianas. In a war with Japan, these islands would stand as barriers to any U.S. naval advance across the Pacific. The Navy's war plan in the event of conflict with Japan, Plan Orange, called for the U.S. fleet to transit the Pacific Ocean and wage a decisive naval engagement with Japan's battle fleet in its home waters. Although the Washington Naval Treaty of 1922 would give the U.S. Navy a five-to-three advantage over the IJN in battleship tonnage, several factors worked to even the balance. First, the Navy could not entirely ignore the Atlantic Ocean, while the Japanese could focus their efforts almost exclusively on the Pacific. Moreover, raids by Japanese naval forces, such as destroyers and submarines armed with torpedoes, could be expected to whittle away at the U.S. fleet's strength during its long voyage across the Pacific. The fleet would also have to guard against strikes by Japanese land-based aircraft.

Given a disarmed Germany in Europe and good relations with Britain and France, the Navy directed the bulk of its energies to Plan Orange. As the Washington Naval Treaty precluded constructing air bases in the Western Pacific, the Navy realized it would have to bring its own air power with it to suppress the enemy's fleet air arm and shore-based air forces. This would probably require large numbers of carrier-based aircraft.[25] However, the precise role of the carriers, and of naval aviation itself, remained a source of increasingly contentious debate right up to the great Pacific naval battles in 1942.

Identifying a vision of future naval warfare, as well as a problem to measure progress against in achieving the vision, was a major step forward in naval aviation's development. But advocates of a revolution needed to determine whether advances in aviation technology would support their vision. They also needed access to the industrial and human resources necessary to sustain their vision. The answer to these challenges was found in the interrelationship between the Naval War College, the Navy's fleet exercises (called "problems"), and the Bureau of Aeronautics.

The War College

The first element of the Navy trinity was the analysis and war gaming undertaken at the Naval War College. In April 1919, Rear Admiral Sims returned from Britain to his position as president of the War College in Newport, Rhode Island. Sims informed the students that war gaming would be a major part of their education. Although Sims had gained notoriety for his work in battleship gunnery, he was forward-thinking and, having been exposed to the Royal Navy's investment in naval aviation, could envision aviation's potential threat to the battleship. He directed the college's war games to include aircraft and aircraft carriers—even though the Navy had no such ships. The games were designed to facilitate a systematic and rigorous examination of how air power might influence war at sea.[26]

Sims's ideas met with Bradley Fiske's warm approval. Fiske was the Navy's last admiral to hold the post of "Aide for Naval Operations," which he relinquished in 1915, when he was succeeded by Admiral Benson as the first chief of naval operations. Like Sims, Fiske had a well-deserved reputation as a bright, innovative thinker, credited with inventing an early version of the telescopic range finder and working out the practical aspects of aircraft torpedo bombers less than a decade after the Wright brothers' first flight. When Fiske heard of Sims's war-game initiative, he wrote the admiral, telling him, "I think your idea of having two fleets fight each other, which are exactly alike in all respects, except that whereas one fleet has sixteen battleships and the other fleet has sixteen aeroplane and torpedo-plane carriers, is bully."[27]

Sims kept the retired admiral informed of the games' progress and invited him to share his insights and suggestions, something Fiske was more than willing to do. On one occasion, Fiske told Sims, "I also believe that the aeroplane carrier is a *more powerful* ship than the present battleship—or that it will be just as soon as we have worked out a few details in the way of launching torpedoes, and landing on the decks of ships or in the water. The torpedo plane carrier *is* a capital ship." Sims asked Fiske if he would trade the "airplane carrier of the future for the battleship of the present." Fiske responded, "Yes:—I think a 35-knot torpedo plane carrier (able to shoot 20 torpedo planes 200 miles) would be a 'capital ship'—a *more* 'capital ship' than the [battleship] *New Mexico.*" Sims concurred, telling Fiske, "If I had my way, I would arrest the building of great battleships and put money into development of these new devices [aircraft carriers] and not wait to see what other countries are doing."[28]

As for the games themselves, they generated important insights for Navy theorists, planners, and practitioners, exerting strong influence on carrier design and aircraft type and mix. They showed that it was critical to maximize the number of aircraft the fleet could operate. This led to efforts to increase the number of aircraft on carriers and to compress the operating cycle for launching and recovering aircraft.[29]

"BuAer"

The Navy trinity's second element was the Bureau of Aeronautics. Its head, Rear Admiral Moffett, like Sims, was a product of the surface fleet, commanding the battleship *Mississippi* before returning to Washington to take charge of the Navy's newest bureau. Earlier in his career, Moffett had established an aviator training program during World War I while commanding the Great Lakes Naval Training Center. Sims provided the intellectual fuel that sustained the Navy along its path toward the fast carrier task force, and Moffett added BuAer's own, while providing bureaucratic and political support, especially through his forceful advocacy in the highest circles of the executive and legislative branches of the government.

Moffett saw BuAer as a think tank of sorts for naval aviation, as well as a school for the service's future aviation leaders. Moffett was a superb bureaucrat and consummate public-relations chief. His ability to cultivate the nation's political leaders' support of naval aviation was remarkable. As one observer noted, "Moffett has tackled the subject with almost fanatical zeal, supported by the whole nation from the president downwards."[30] The admiral's ceaseless efforts to win key congressional leaders' support are reflected in a note he penned at Christmastime 1931 to Congressman Carl Vinson, the new chairman of the House Naval Affairs Committee. Moffett wrote, "Upon my return from the flight of the [Airship] Akron over your district . . . the thought occurred to me . . . that the people were all your friends and how fortunate they are to have you represent them in Congress. . . . I have had the honor and pleasure of knowing you a great many years, and feel they are to be congratulated."[31] Vinson would prove an indispensable ally to the Navy in general—and naval aviation in particular—during the crucial decade of the 1930s.

By the late 1920s, Moffett had been head of BuAer for two consecutive terms spanning seven years. He knew that third terms for bureau chiefs were almost unheard of. Still, he set out to be reappointed, in part because he feared that the progress being made in naval aviation, although hard-won, remained tenuous. As BuAer's chief, Moffett become so expert at working the levers of power in Washington that there was strong bureaucratic opposition within the Navy to retaining him as BuAer's director. Undaunted, Moffett initiated a letter-writing campaign, whose message was that the Navy planned to reassign him, as the "Navy does not appreciate Aviation and its importance, and the majority still consider battleships and surface vessels of infinitely greater importance."[32] Soon President Herbert Hoover was receiving letters from key congressional and business leaders supporting Moffett's reappointment.

Hoover asked the Navy for nominations for director of BuAer. The task for responding went to Rear Admiral Richard H. "Reddy" Leigh, the head of the Navy's Bureau of Navigation (BuNav) and a Moffett rival. Leigh submitted three names to the White House, omitting Moffett's. The list was returned, with a letter asking for additional nominees. Leigh resubmitted a longer list, with Moffett's name still absent. Once again, the list was shipped back to Leigh, requesting still more nominees. At this point, articles were appearing in the press supporting Moffett's reappointment. Finally, Leigh submitted a list of all officers eligible to fill the billet, with Moffett's name at the very bottom. At last, Leigh received the president's reply: "Approved for Admiral Moffett."[33]

Moffett's early years at BuAer found him beating back Billy Mitchell's attempts to place naval aviation under a single Air Corps. Mitchell's star, however, was dimming. By early 1925, his insubordination led the Army to reject his request to be reappointed as assistant chief of staff of the Air Service and to assign him to San Antonio, Texas, as air officer to an Army corps, where he reverted to his permanent rank of colonel.

Following the crash of a Navy dirigible in September 1925, however, Mitchell publicly accused both the Army and the Navy leadership of neglecting aviation and thereby encouraging such disasters. He was brought before a court-martial for his remarks, but President Calvin Coolidge appointed an air policy board, chaired by Dwight Morrow, to study Mitchell's accusations. The board rejected Mitchell's proposal for a separate air force, recommending instead that the Army's Air Service be rechristened the Air Corps and that the War Department appoint an assistant secretary of war for air affairs. The congressional legislation that followed—the Air Corps Act of 1926—accepted the board's recommendations, including establishing the office of assistant secretary of the Navy (aeronautics), thereby giving naval aviators a voice in senior civilian circles.[34] More important, it required that all commanding officers of aircraft carriers, seaplane tenders, and naval air stations be qualified aviators.[35] This opened a path to senior positions for the young pioneers of naval aviation—men such as future admirals John H. Towers and Marc A. Mitscher. As for Mitchell, his court-martial found him guilty and, on December 17, 1925, suspended him from active duty for five years. Mitchell resigned instead.

Fleet Problems

In 1921, as Admiral Sims was beginning the war-gaming exercises at the Naval War College and BuAer was being established, the Navy's War Plans Division began to assume the presence of aircraft carriers in the fleet. It was the Navy's series of fleet problems, however, that offered the most visible, and thus perhaps the most compelling, argument for naval aviation.

The War College, BuAer, and the fleet formed a mutually supporting trinity. BuAer, through its association with industry and organizations like NACA, kept apprised of developments in aviation technology. The Naval War College tapped into BuAer for projections of future aviation capabilities and employed these projections in its war games. Insights from the college's war games were funneled into the fleet problems, whose results were studied by BuAer and the War College, creating a virtuous cycle.

The fleet problems brought together the Navy's chain of command under conditions that came as close as practicable to war itself. During the course of twenty-one fleet problems, conducted from the early 1920s until Pearl Harbor, the fleet explored a range of challenges at the strategic and operational levels of war. The exercises also offered an opportunity to identify and resolve tactical-level matters.

The initial steps were modest. Following the *Ostfriesland* experiment, Admiral Moffett saw the need to get significant numbers of aircraft operating with the fleet as soon as possible. With respect to carriers, he asserted, "We need no less than eight big ones, because a Navy today without aircraft protection and the search-patrol, scouting-patrol, and shot spotting facilities which aviation provides, is fatally weak when it puts to sea. . . . There is no argument against this statement. It is axiomatic."[36]

In March 1922, Captain Henry Mustin, BuAer's assistant chief, appeared before the General Board and, reflecting current realities, testified, "Our whole aviation program is laid out on the basis that the battleship is the dominant factor in naval warfare, provided it is properly supported by aircraft." Mustin's concept of contemporary battle fleet operations saw aircraft acting as spotters. But to do that, the Navy had to have control of the air. And control of the air meant destroying the enemy's naval air arm—and perhaps its aircraft-carrying ships as well. This required maximizing the fleet's aircraft complement. "Consequently," Mustin noted, "we put on all the combat planes we can get aboard, after leaving enough space for carrying the necessary spotting planes and a number of torpedo planes for bombing and scout work."[37]

The first fleet problem, held in the Pacific in 1923, employed two battleships in the role of carriers. It wasn't until Fleet Problem V in 1925 that the Navy's first carrier, a converted collier, the Langley, appeared, launching ten aircraft.[38] As Navy planners examined the problems associated with a potential war against Japan, they were not happy at the prospect of risking their battleships against what were anticipated to be strong defense batteries arrayed along the coast of Japan's new island possessions. Moffett, sensing an opportunity, volunteered naval aviation for the job of dealing with the island bases, declaring that "bombing aircraft, protected by fighting aircraft, both necessarily operating from carriers, could do the job of reducing the defenses."[39] The fleet exercises would be used to test the admiral's assertions.

In 1925, a critical boost to the fortunes of naval aviation occurred when Captain Joseph Reeves left the Naval War College, where he had spent time as both a student and instructor, to become commander, aircraft squadrons, battle fleet. Reeves, who possessed an insightful mind, combined with strong leadership qualities, had commanded the battleship North Dakota and, earlier in his career, coached the Naval Academy's football team to a 9-2-1 record in 1907, including a 6–0 win over Army. His experience under Admiral Sims at Newport, however, persuaded him to pursue naval aviation. Now commanding Langley, Reeves began to put into practice insights he had harvested from the War College's war games. They included the advantage accrued by conducting carrier air strikes in "pulses" rather than "streams"—a "downpour" rather than a "drizzle"—and the need to get as many aircraft aloft as possible and as rapidly as possible.[40]

Toward that end, Reeves rejected existing carrier operational procedures, which were based on Royal Navy carrier operations. The British had only one aircraft on deck at a time, whether for takeoffs or landings. When a plane landed, it was lowered to the hangar deck before the next one was allowed to land. Reeves would not abide this torpid pace of carrier operations. He fitted the *Langley* with arresting gear to halt landing aircraft on the deck and a crash barrier that would enable aircraft to remain parked on the flight deck, rather than being lowered below deck. Thus, when a plane landed on the *Langley*, the crash barrier, which had protected the planes in the "deck park" located forward, was lowered. The plane was moved forward behind the crash barrier, which was then raised as the next incoming aircraft landed. This dramatically increased aircraft operational cycle rates. From the beginning, U.S. carriers typically parked the majority of their aircraft on the flight deck, using the hangars below primarily for maintenance and repair activities.[41]

Repelling an enemy air attack was included as part of Fleet Problem VI, set for February 1926. When Reeves took command, it took fifty-two minutes to land *Langley*'s ten aircraft. By August, aircraft were being recovered at a rate of roughly ninety seconds each. Reeves soon had the ship launching ten of its fourteen aircraft in less than two minutes. Three days later, seven planes were launched in forty-one seconds.[42] During the fleet problem, the *Langley* provided the "Blue Fleet" to which it was assigned a scouting advantage over the "enemy" "Black Fleet," which relied on floatplanes stationed on battleships and cruisers. The *Langley* also demonstrated its worth operating as part of a new circular tactical formation, which would prove immensely valuable for the fast carrier task force in the Pacific War.[43] On August 9, *Langley*'s aircraft made 127 landings in a single day, demonstrating its ability to conduct sustained air operations. Thanks to the crash barrier and deck park, Reeves was able to double the ship's air complement to twenty-eight planes.[44]

Reeves's experiments aboard the *Langley* convinced the Navy that carriers would have to be constructed with an offset island superstructure, through which boiler-stack gases could pass. Other innovations saw the use of a landing signal officer to guide arriving aircraft and indirect deck lighting to facilitate night operations.[45] A carrier's elevator would be positioned on the port side, enabling aircraft to be raised and lowered so as to minimize interference with flight-deck operations. When Fleet Problem VII was conducted in the Caribbean in 1927, the *Langley* was classified as a combatant ship. Yet, despite these encouraging developments, it was not yet clear that carriers would form the backbone of naval aviation. Indeed, until the carriers *Saratoga* and *Lexington* were commissioned late that year, barely one-third of the Navy's air squadrons were associated with carriers.[46]

While offering encouragement to naval aviation enthusiasts, the Navy's early fleet problems also put paid to Billy Mitchell's extravagant claims regarding air power's current capabilities. Despite the publicity given to the sinking of the *Ostfriesland*, accurate horizontal bombing against a maneuvering ship protected by anti-aircraft fires proved highly challenging. Reeves considered the Navy's bombsight for horizontal bombing "a marvel of uncertainty and inaccuracy."[47] In July 1924, the Royal Navy undertook a similar test with the radio-controlled battleship *Agamemnon*. More than 100 bombs were dropped on the ship without the air attackers scoring a single hit. More discouragement for aviation enthusiasts came from trials of anti-aircraft guns, which scored 75 percent hits on aerial targets above 4,000 feet, suggesting that an aircraft attacking a battleship would probably not survive to drop its bomb, and if it did, the bomb would miss anyway.[48] The General Board discussed these trials at length, concluding that battleships armed with anti-aircraft guns would make the already inaccurate aerial bombing even more so.

It appeared that the only way for carrier-based aircraft to attack surface combatants effectively was with torpedoes—but the torpedoes of the time were barely faster than the ships at which they were fired. Owing to the short range of aircraft-borne torpedoes, they had to be released close to their target, making aircraft highly vulnerable to a ship's anti-aircraft defenses. Torpedoes also had a tendency to fail. Finally, early carrier aircraft could not lift torpedoes powerful enough to sink large warships.[49]

Undaunted, the Navy continued to experiment with aircraft bombing tactics. This paid dividends when, on October 22, 1926, Lieutenant Commander Frank D. Wagner led a flight of Curtiss F6C Hawks in a simulated attack on ships steaming toward San Diego. With Wagner's aircraft commencing their nearly vertical dives at an altitude of 12,000 feet, they achieved total surprise over the defenders, even though the fleet had been forewarned that it would be subjected to an air attack. The surprise was so complete and the effectiveness of the dive-bombing technique so impressive that Admiral Charles F. Hughes, commander-in-chief of the U.S. Fleet, declared that such an attack would succeed over any defense.[50]

Wagner's combination of a steep dive attack employing machine-gun fire and relatively light bombs proved far more effective than torpedo-plane attacks.[51] In exercises conducted in the fall of 1926, aircraft conducting dive-bombing attacks achieved "staggering" results. Of the 311 bombs dropped, 44.5 percent were scored as direct hits. Even more impressive, experienced pilots flying newer aircraft—the Curtiss F6C Hawks and Boeing FB-5s—achieved direct hits at a 67 percent rate. The aircraft, however, were only capable of carrying twenty-five-pound bombs, so they presented no threat to the battleship.[52]

Naval aviation enthusiasts took comfort from continuing rapid advances in aviation engine technology, which meant that aircraft would fly ever farther and carry ever heavier bombs. Two years after Wagner's demonstration, the fleet had aircraft capable of carrying 300-pound bombs, and 500-pound bomb payloads were considered well within the realm of possibility. That year found BuAer drawing up plans for an experimental plane dubbed a "diving bomber." Although the heaviest bombs employed in dive-bombing to that time topped out at 100 pounds, carrier designs called for the aircraft to deliver ordnance in the 1,000-pound range.[53] Fleet exercises in May and June 1931 off the coast of San Diego indicated that although carrier torpedo bombers would encounter heavy losses from battleship anti-aircraft batteries, dive-bombers could attack at far less risk.[54] This further tilted the scales in favor of dive-bombing for carrier strike operations. Nevertheless, the Navy, reluctant to put all its eggs in one basket, continued to pursue its horizontal- and torpedo-bombing options.

The Washington Naval Treaty

The Washington Naval Treaty of 1922 exerted significant influence on naval aviation. The treaty limited, by a fixed ratio, the amount of tonnage that each of the major naval powers—Great Britain, the United States, Japan, France, and Italy—could have in certain warship categories, including battleships and aircraft carriers, at roughly 5 to 5 to 3 to 1.75 to 1.75, respectively. Aggregate carrier tonnage was set at 135,000 tons for the U.S. and Royal Navies and 81,000 tons for the Imperial Japanese Navy. The treaty banned Britain, Japan, and the United States from constructing new fortifications or naval bases in the Pacific Ocean. This provision was widely viewed as benefiting Japan, given its location in the Western Pacific and the relative paucity of U.S. and British bases in the region.

The British proposed, and the United States and Japan accepted, allowing each country to convert two battle cruisers to aircraft carriers. Two U.S. ships under construction were designated for conversion. *Saratoga* joined the fleet in November 1927, followed by *Lexington* a month later. Each displaced 33,000 tons and had speeds in excess of thirty-three knots.[55] To reach the treaty carrier tonnage limits, the Navy's plans called for launching three 23,000-ton carriers over the following three years. Congress, however, provided no funds for new carriers between 1924 and 1928.

Moffett was skeptical of building such large carriers. BuAer's principal measure of merit for carrier design was the size of its flight deck. Moffett used it in arguing for small carriers in a report to the General Board on June 20, 1927, noting, "there is a far greater flight deck area available on a large number of small ships than a small number of large ships."[56] He concluded, "It appears that 14,000 tons approaches the upper limit of displacement which should be considered for carriers of the future."[57] In recommending carriers less than half the size of *Saratoga* and *Lexington*, the admiral argued, "Your whole air force would be more mobile. You could have the air force in a greater number of places."[58] This, Moffett believed, would provide the fleet with operational flexibility. Small carriers' aircraft could patrol a larger area, a major asset in the broad expanses of the Pacific. Relying on a few large carriers like *Saratoga* and *Lexington* risked putting too many of the fleet's aircraft eggs in a small number of baskets. Simply put, the two large converted cruisers were almost exactly the type of carrier that the Navy studies and experiments at that time were telling Moffett he should *not* want. Ironically, they were the kind of carrier the Navy would need fifteen years later in the Pacific War.

Although the Navy fretted that the *Saratoga* and *Lexington* consumed an excessive amount of the 135,000-ton treaty limit on carriers, had the Washington Treaty not been in place the steeply rising unit cost of battleships and battle cruisers would probably have produced a crowding-out effect on funding for carrier construction.[59] Indeed, when limits on total tonnage were abandoned in 1936, the Navy concentrated primarily on battleships.[60]

Looking for ways to boost the fleet's air arm within the treaty's constraints, Moffett began to explore a hybrid ship: the flying-deck cruiser. It was a bad idea whose time had come. As early as 1925, war games conducted at the Naval War College were evaluating the General Board's desire "to consider whether or not it is feasible to combine the qualities of a scout cruiser and an aircraft carrier in a new type of ship." Following the games, the president of the Naval War College reported, diplomatically, that "it would appear unwise to attempt to develop a vessel which will combine the two qualities of a cruiser and an airplane carrier."[61] The General Board shelved the concept.

Nevertheless, the flying-deck cruiser concept refused to go away. Confronted with new arms-limitations talks scheduled for 1930 in London and the Navy's strong desire to achieve carrier parity with the Royal Navy, Moffett had BuAer develop a design for a ship carrying eight catapult-launched floatplanes.[62] The idea gained traction when it became clear that the London negotiations would not increase carrier tonnage allocations. Thanks in large part to Moffett's persistence, the London agreement permitted 25 percent of each navy's cruisers to be fitted with flight decks.[63]

Armed with this agreement, in May 1930, Moffett recommended constructing five small 13,800-ton carriers and eight 10,000-ton flying-deck cruisers armed with 6-inch guns. The General Board, however, remained cool to the idea. To advance the flying-deck cruiser, Moffett ran experiments on the *Saratoga* in which aircraft used only that portion of the deck that would exist on a flying-deck cruiser. The tests were successful. The CNO, Admiral Pratt, warmed to the idea, and the General Board finally concurred with including the ship in the construction plan for fiscal year 1932.[64]

The preliminary design was completed in July 1931. Per Moffett's recommendation, it called for a 10,000-ton ship with a complement of twenty-four aircraft and nine 6-inch guns mounted in three forward turrets. The design was accepted. But Congress, faced with an economic crisis brought on by the Great Depression, refused to appropriate funds for construction, despite the vigorous efforts of Representative Carl Vinson, who chaired the House Naval Affairs Committee. Indeed, the Depression found the Navy struggling to win funds for the carrier tonnage permitted under the treaty. The fleet would have to make do with its three converted ships before its first purpose-built carrier, *Ranger*, arrived in 1934.

Moffett and Vinson's loss proved the Navy's gain. The Naval War College's assessments and General Board's misgivings proved correct. The flying-deck cruiser was neither a good cruiser nor a good carrier. It would have led the Navy down a dead end as aviation technology continued to mature. Aircraft were rapidly becoming too large and heavy to operate off the short deck of a 10,000-ton cruiser-carrier hybrid. In fact, advances were coming so quickly that even BuAer soon soured on the concept and allowed it to slip silently beneath the Navy's programmatic waves.

The "unwanted" *Saratoga* and *Lexington* proved well suited for accommodating the rapid advances in aviation, while offering higher sustained speed and better survivability than the flying-deck cruiser. And their large aircraft capacity gave the Navy freedom to mix several types of aircraft in substantial numbers. This would pay big dividends during two significant shifts in maritime warfare that occurred in rapid succession beginning in the late 1930s.[65]

As noted, the Washington Naval Treaty also created a major problem for the Navy, which had counted on establishing major forward bases on Guam, the Marianas, and the Philippines to prosecute a successful war against Japan. Without these bases, the Navy would have to bring its own air power across the Pacific, while also developing the capability to seize advanced bases to support its extended operations. Captain Frank Schofield, a member of the General Board, explained the enormous significance of this provision in an address at the Army War College in September 1923:

> *Sea Power* is not made of ships, or of ships and men, but of ships and men and *bases far and wide*. Ships without outlying bases are almost helpless—will be helpless unless they conquer bases and yet the Treaty took from us every possibility of an outlying base in the Pacific except one [Hawaii]; we gave our new capital ships and our right to build bases for a better international feeling— but no one gave us anything. Manifestly the provisions of *the Treaty presented a naval problem of the first magnitude that demanded immediate solution.* A new policy had to be formulated which would make the best possible use of the new conditions.[66] [emphasis added]

Simply put, the Navy needed a fleet capable of operating at long range and, at least initially, independent of support from forward bases.

Of course, the Washington Treaty constrained all great-power navies, only some more than others. On balance, the treaty exerted a positive—albeit serendipitous—effect on the Navy's development of the fast carrier task force. By banning battleship construction and allocating 135,000 tons for carriers, it not only permitted carrier construction but incentivized it. When the treaty collapsed in the late 1930s, the Navy had the 20,000-ton *Yorktown*-class carriers entering service and a design for the 31,000-ton *Essex* class nearly ready.[67] By allowing for the conversion of cruisers to carriers, the treaty encouraged the Navy to build large carriers, the kind that would be needed for the coming war. By also providing a ceiling on carrier tonnage, the treaty also ensured that there would be little excess baggage in the fleet in the form of small, obsolete carriers, such as the *Langley* and, later, the *Ranger*, or new battleships whose value was depreciating rapidly, to slow the final sprint to a radically different means of conducting war at sea.

Two Steps Forward . . . One Step Back

In April 1927, the Navy convened a board under Rear Admiral Montgomery Meigs Taylor to examine carrier policy for the fleet. The board included many naval aviation proponents, including Moffett, Captains Reeves and Harry Yarnell, and Lieutenant Commander Marc Mitscher. Given its composition, it's hardly surprising that the Taylor Board recommended giving priority to developing the Navy's air arm, including experimentation, noting that "the only way in which more satisfactory answers can be had is by trial along definite lines with the Fleet." The board, recognizing the growing potential of carriers, found them necessary for "service of the battle line to furnish fighting airplanes for its protection and a landing place for reservicing its airplanes; thus leaving other carriers free for scouting and offensive operations at a distance from the battle line too great to adequately serve it."[68]

Recognizing the impressive potential of dive-bombing as a means of attack, the Taylor Board recommended that dive-bombers be given priority in aircraft production. The General Board endorsed these views in November 1927, while presciently declaring that new carriers should be designed to maximize their aircraft capacity, drawing on insights from the war gaming at Newport and the fleet problems involving the *Langley*.[69] By the late 1920s, Navy planners were assigning new missions, including long-range patrolling and raids on enemy bases, to the recently commissioned *Saratoga* and *Lexington*.[70]

The Navy's vigorous exercise program continued, with *Langley* participating in several small exercises off the coast of the Hawaiian Islands during the spring of 1928 to test the carrier's proficiency in these new missions. On the evening of May 16, *Langley*, along with several other ships, steamed out of Pearl Harbor. Just before dawn the following morning, *Langley* launched its entire complement of thirty-five planes within seven minutes. Arriving over Honolulu at daybreak, the aircraft caught the Army's air component at Wheeler field by surprise, even though the Army had been forewarned. Having had to maneuver so close to the island to conduct its attack, however, the *Langley* itself was spotted by land-based torpedo planes, which attacked the vulnerable ship.[71]

Looking back over the decade since the end of World War I, it was clear that much progress had been made in the Navy's understanding and development of aviation. The carrier was now widely accepted as an important part of the fleet. But the battleship and the line of battle reigned supreme, and for good reason. Entering the 1930s, aircraft were still severely limited in their range and bomb payloads. Thus, carriers had to steam dangerously close to an enemy fleet before launching their aircraft and then loiter forward to recover those returning from their strike missions. To many observers, this level of carrier vulnerability was too great to sustain an argument for independent carrier strike operations.

The commissioning of the *Saratoga* and *Lexington* with their huge air wings moved Admiral Charles F. Hughes, the U.S. fleet commander, to assert that the fleet needed to rethink how it operated its air force, since "the advantages of suppressing an enemy air offensive before it has launched may have a far reaching effect upon the engagement of main forces."[72] The admiral's views ended up being put to the test in January 1929 during Fleet Problem IX, the first in which both sides had carriers.

The problem was conducted off Central America. During the exercise, Vice Admiral William V. Pratt (who had recently served as president of the Naval War College) authorized Rear Admiral Reeves, commanding *Saratoga*, to execute a high-speed run toward the Panama Canal. Reeves "attacked" the canal with a seventy-plane strike force launched 140 miles from the target. The attackers, arriving at 7:00 a.m., achieved complete surprise, "striking" the Miraflores and Pedro Miguel Locks before moving on to hit the Army's air base.[73] Charles A. Lindbergh, a colonel in the Army Air Corps Reserve, was aboard the *Saratoga* and took part in the flight operations.[74]

The attack succeeded despite the presence of an "enemy" fleet, which included the *Lexington*. During the *Saratoga's* approach to the Panama Canal, however, it was spotted by an "enemy" cruiser, the *Detroit*. Soon after *Saratoga* had launched its aircraft, it was engaged by battleships from the "enemy" fleet and by planes from the *Lexington* and ruled sunk. Admiral Henry V. Wiley, the fleet's commander in chief, noting the *Saratoga's* fate, concluded that there was "no analysis of Fleet Problem IX fairly made which fails to point to the battleship as the final arbiter of Naval destiny."[75] Wiley had a point. So long as carriers lacked aircraft with extended range, such an attack would expose them to great risk of destruction by the enemy fleet.

Yet others, like Admiral Pratt, took a different lesson, viewing the *Saratoga* strike not as snapshot in time but rather as a reflection of naval aviation's potential. Pratt called Reeves's raid "the most brilliantly conceived and most effectively executed naval operation" in U.S. history. Pratt declared, "I believe that when we learn more of the possibilities of the carrier we will come to an acceptance of Admiral Reeves' plan which provides for a very powerful and mobile force, . . . the nucleus of which is the carrier." Pratt flew his flag from the *Saratoga* on the return cruise, he said, "partly as a badge of distinction, but most because I want to know what makes the aircraft squadrons tick."[76] The CNO, Admiral Hughes, was also impressed. When questioned by a congressional committee on the high expense of carrier operations, the admiral declared that the two new carriers would be "the last ships he would remove from the active list."[77] Upon becoming CNO in 1930, Pratt stressed that carriers be placed on the offensive in war games and fleet exercises.

Fleet Problem IX also marked another step in the ascendency of dive-bombing at the expense of torpedo bombers. Torpedo planes were already handicapped by their relatively large size, reducing the number of aircraft a carrier could hold. More importantly, when torpedo bombers pressed their attacks, they had to maintain a straight and level attitude as they approached their target. Their fixed course exposed them to fighter-interceptors and shipborne anti-aircraft defenses. Dive-bombers operating at high altitudes were more difficult to spot, and their steep dive to their target made them a tougher target for a ship's anti-aircraft gunners. Thus, Fleet Problem X found only a single torpedo squadron out of nineteen participating in the exercise. By 1936, Fleet Problem XVII included only 12 torpedo planes out of 253 carrier-based aircraft.[78]

Fleet Problems X and XI, conducted in March and April 1930, respectively, provided the Navy with two crucial insights. First, carrier air operations were offense-dominant; and second, the battle line that lost air superiority operated at a severe and perhaps fatal disadvantage. They also confirmed Fleet Problem IX's findings regarding the carrier's vulnerabilities.

Fleet Problem X, conducted in the Caribbean, found Admiral Louis McCoy Nulton, commanding the Blue Fleet, tethering his carriers, *Saratoga* and *Langley*, to the main body. Vice Admiral William C. Cole, commanding the Black Fleet, pursued a different strategy, directing the *Lexington* to operate independently of the battle line and, in combination with his land-based aircraft, to attack the Blue Fleet. Cole's strike force dive-bombed Nulton's carriers, putting both flight decks out of action. They then proceeded to attack the Blue Fleet's battleships, dropping thirty-pound "bombs" on the *West Virginia*, *California*, and *New Mexico*.[79]

Admiral Nulton cried foul, claiming that had his air scouts located the Black Fleet first, the situation would have been reversed. Admiral Pratt rejected Nulton's claim, pointing out that Nulton's employment of his air arm as cover for his battleships precluded their use in scouting and offensive operations.[80] In Fleet Problem XI, conducted a month later, the *Saratoga* located and delivered a quick knockout blow to the *Lexington*. The exercises convinced many naval aviators that in carrier operations, it was better to "give" than "receive"—to locate and attack the enemy carriers before they could return the favor. Based on the experience in the fleet problems, Vice Admiral Cole, a member of the battleship admirals' "Gun Club," called for establishing permanent carrier "task forces" consisting of a carrier, a division of four heavy cruisers, and a squadron of eight destroyers—the forerunner of the fast carrier task forces that would dominate the coming Pacific War.[81]

The two fleet problems showed senior Navy leaders that the carriers' unarmored flight decks could be quickly put out of action, even by light bombers. Technology had yet to yield solutions for mounting an effective defense in the form of radar, long-range radio, and proximity fusing for anti-aircraft shells. Hence, it appeared that carrier operations would be relentlessly offensive-dominant: the first carrier whose aircraft spotted their adversaries' carriers and executed an attack seemed certain to reap an enormous advantage. In the critique following the conclusion of the two problems, Rear Admiral Henry V. Butler, commander of the Aircraft Squadrons, Scouting Force, noted that the opposing fleets were "like blindfolded men armed with daggers in a ring, if the bandage over the eyes of one is removed, the other [is] doomed."[82] Foreshadowing what occurred at Midway more than a decade later, Butler declared that the key to success was to be the first to locate and attack the enemy's carrier force while its planes were still on the deck.

Fleet Problem XII took place in January 1931, with the General Board on hand to observe. Blue Force, organized along the lines of Admiral Cole's "task force," included *Saratoga* and *Lexington*, along with destroyers and cruisers. It was given the mission of stopping an invading Black Force of battleships, cruisers, and destroyers, accompanied by *Langley*. Blue split its force into two carrier groups, attempting to locate and sink the transport ships carrying the landing force. Blue failed in its efforts, and Black successfully executed the landing. Once again, due to limitations on aircraft range, the carriers had to steam to within forty to seventy-five miles of their target before launching an air strike, making them highly vulnerable to ships screening the enemy's main battle force. Navy leaders felt that, given these circumstances, the carriers must continue to operate with the support of the battle line.[83] Admiral Reeves, arguably the Navy's leading practitioner of carrier operations, demurred, noting, "There is a grave possibility that these lessons may be incorrectly interpreted and that the strength and power of certain weapons may be incorrectly estimated." But the damage had been done. Admiral Pratt declared, "The battleship is the backbone of the Fleet. No clearer demonstration of the value of the battleship to the Fleet could be shown that was done in this problem."[84]

Armed with the insights from Fleet Problems X and XI, Admiral Moffett reevaluated the issue of carrier size. Three variants were examined: 13,800 tons, 18,400 tons, and 20,700 tons. The assessments concluded that carriers in the 13,800-ton *Ranger* class, then building, lacked protection against the growing threat of dive-bombing attacks. In May, Moffett reported that an 18,400-ton carrier's greater displacement would permit greater armor protection and compartmentalization, along with increased speed and a larger air wing. Admiral Pratt, however, favored the symmetry of two carriers in each class provided by *Saratoga* and *Lexington* and preferred constructing two 20,000-ton carriers and a 15,000-ton carrier (as a sister to *Ranger*).[85] Moffett, eager to secure support for more carriers, went along, as did the General Board.

Secretary of the Navy Charles Adams, however, intervened. Noting the fine performance of *Saratoga* and *Lexington* in the fleet problems, Adams directed the General Board to review the carrier-size issue once again and consider ships in the 25,000-ton range that could accommodate 8-inch guns. Moffett strenuously opposed this, particularly given the treaty tonnage limits and the fact that such heavy guns would seriously reduce the ship's complement of aircraft. Noting that the fleet problems showed that carrier warfare depended first and foremost on locating and attacking the enemy's carriers, he argued that this required planes, not guns. In presenting his views, the admiral looked beyond current carrier operations, declaring, "We can hardly visualize today the potential power of aircraft, not so much for scouting and spotting, but for bombing and torpedoing. It may readily be the deciding factor in a war."[86]

Moffett and the General Board prevailed. Congress authorized the two 20,000-ton carriers; but the Depression meant budget cuts, and no funds were appropriated for that purpose. The two carriers were commissioned in 1937 and 1938, as *Yorktown* and *Enterprise*. The smaller carrier, *Hornet*, joined the fleet in 1941.

The Emergence of Naval Aviation

On Sunday morning, February 7, 1932, 152 aircraft under the command of Rear Admiral Harry Yarnell, operating from *Saratoga* and *Lexington*, successfully executed a surprise attack on Army air bases and facilities at Pearl Harbor as part of Grand Joint Army-Navy Exercise Number 4.[87] This time, the Navy's aviation advocates found themselves challenged by the U.S. Army, whose base commanders, embarrassed over being taken by surprise, contested the carrier raid's effectiveness. They claimed that their planes had critically damaged the carriers, even though Yarnell's aircraft had conducted two bombing runs on the Army's aircraft sitting on the runways. The Army also protested the "legality" of Yarnell attacking on a Sunday.[88]

Fleet Problem XIII, following on the heels of Yarnell's Pearl Harbor attack, involved two fleets. The Blue Fleet deployed from Hawaii with the mission of supporting an expeditionary force moving against three unfortified atolls along the U.S. Pacific Coast. The Black Fleet was given the mission of defending the atolls. Yarnell commanded the Blue Fleet's air component, including the *Saratoga* and land-based aircraft in Hawaii. The carriers *Lexington* and *Langley* were assigned to the Black Fleet.

Both Yarnell and his Black Fleet counterpart, Captain Ernest King, focused on neutralizing the other's air power. The *Saratoga* and *Lexington* launched strikes on each other, with each inflicting some damage. King then received permission from his senior, Admiral William H. Standley, to operate the *Lexington* independently of his battle force. King kept the *Lexington* out of *Saratoga*'s engagement range until just the right moment. Then he launched a forty-nine-plane raid on the *Saratoga*, crippling it.

King's attack was praised by the U.S. fleet commander, Admiral Frank H. Schofield. In Captains King's and Towers's presentation of their insights from the fleet problem, both asserted that the Navy would require six to eight carriers for an offensive across the Pacific. Towers wrote Moffett that Fleet Problem XIII was "the most valuable fleet exercise carried out in recent years."[89] The offensive-dominant character of carrier air operations was now widely accepted. In a speech on October 27 at the Curtiss aircraft plant in Buffalo, Captain Arthur B. Cook, assistant chief of BuAer, declared, "the only effective way to stop the attack of bombing planes is to seek out and destroy the ships on which they are based." Only aircraft operating from carriers could accomplish this, Cook argued. "The airplane is today one of the most formidable weapons in sea warfare, the aircraft of no less importance than the battleship, cruiser, submarine, and destroyer."[90]

Only three days before Cook's presentation, Commander Hugh Douglas, the Naval War College faculty's only aviator, gave a lecture on air tactics in which he accurately foresaw the decisive engagement of the Battle of Midway, some nine years hence. Douglas had recently finished completing a two-year tour of duty as the *Saratoga*'s executive officer. During Fleet Problem XIII, his ship had been put out of action by King's aircraft. Douglas told the students, "In case an enemy carrier is encountered with planes on deck, a successful dive-bombing attack by even a small number of planes may greatly influence future operations."[91]

Fleet Problem XIV, conducted in February 1933, found the Black ("enemy") Fleet, with the *Saratoga* and *Lexington* and an escorting force, directed "to inflict maximum damage on the PEARL HARBOR NAVAL BASE in order to destroy or reduce its effectiveness."[92] The fleet, however, bypassed Hawaii in favor of strikes on the U.S. West Coast. The Black Fleet commander, Admiral Frank H. Clark (a nonaviator), split his force into three groups, with the northern group organized around the *Lexington* and the southern group around the *Saratoga*. When aircraft from the

Lexington sighted a Blue ("U.S.") submarine, Clark believed it was a scout for Blue's surface fleet and directed his cruisers to form a battle line, anticipating an engagement. In so doing, he stripped the *Lexington* of its surface-screening force. As it was preparing for a dawn aircraft launch, two Blue battleships emerged from the darkness, one on each side. The *Lexington* was quickly ruled out of action (ironically by none other than Admiral Reeves), without having launched a single aircraft. The *Saratoga* began launching its strikes against shore-based targets but was attacked and put out of commission by attacks from the *Langley* and other Blue Fleet aircraft. Once again, the fleet problems found the carriers steaming forward to launch and recover their short-legged strike aircraft. And once again, they were caught, "shelled," and sunk by enemy surface ships.[93]

In the critique that followed Fleet Problem XIV, Admiral Clark was "most severely criticized" for his handling of the carriers. Instead of employing the carriers on raids against installations ashore in violation of the time-honored dictum "a ship's a fool to fight a fort," many senior naval officers felt that the admiral should have focused on neutralizing the enemy fleet's air arm.[94]

As aircraft range and payloads continued to increase in the 1930s, concerns began to mount that the "picket line" of destroyers that had been counted on to provide warning of air attack had become inadequate to the task, given that aircraft could fly above the clouds and at high speed. Absent effective early warning, it became clear that only a successful aerial first strike against the enemy's carrier force could ensure the survival of friendly carriers. The fleet with the carrier force that struck first was almost always the winner in the fleet problems of the 1930s.[95] By 1935, a member of the General Board asserted that in any war with Japan, the struggle between carrier air forces—not the engagement between the battle lines—would decide command of the sea.[96]

Because the battle fleet was far easier to spot than a carrier at a distance from the air and because a fast carrier's speed exceeded that of the fleet, carrier commanders began to press more forcefully to operate independent of the fleet. This found the naval aviation community's relations with the Gun Club growing increasingly testy. It was suggested that with the new carriers *Yorktown* and *Enterprise* about to join the fleet, the smaller *Ranger* could support the battle force, freeing the larger carriers to operate independently.[97] Some senior Navy aviators tossed fuel on the fire, arguing that the battle fleet should be employed principally to protect the carriers. The implication, well understood by the Gun Club, was that the carrier had eclipsed the battleship as the principal arbiter of sea control.

The growing tension between the aviators and the Gun Club flared into the open during Fleet Problem XVIII. Conducted in April and May 1937, it involved 152 ships and 496 aircraft in simulating a war with Japan.[98] The White Fleet was tasked with defending the Hawaiian Islands against an attacking Black Fleet. The latter fleet included *Saratoga*, *Lexington*, and *Langley*. The White Fleet was given *Ranger*. Among those who were commanding the carrier air forces were Vice Admiral Ernest King, Vice Admiral Frederick Horne, Captain Aubrey Fitch, and Captain William Halsey. The exercise saw White Fleet flying boats conducting long-range patrol missions from the atolls between Pearl Harbor and Midway and attacks made on Black Fleet troop convoys heading to seize Midway. Aircraft from the *Ranger* attacked *Saratoga* and *Lexington*, whose air wings responded in kind. Aircraft from all three carriers conducted dive-bombing attacks using 500-pound and 1,000-pound "bombs" on warships of all types.

The fleet problem brought to a boil the debate over the proper employment of carriers. Admiral Claude C. Bloch, the Black Fleet commander, felt that the carriers were best employed in formation with the battle line, receiving protection from the surface combatants' anti-aircraft guns. The aviators hotly disputed Bloch's contention, pointing out that command of the air must be achieved *before* the opposing battle lines engaged. Vice Admiral Horne, the most senior naval aviator, argued that carriers must have freedom of movement, independent of the battle line, using evasive maneuvers at high speed to survive. Horne warned, "Once an enemy carrier is within striking distance of our fleet, no security remains until it—its squadrons—or both, are destroyed, and our carriers, if with the Main Body are at a tremendous disadvantage [in this effort to avoid detection]."[99]

Bloch rejected Horne's argument and restricted the carriers to flying patrols over the main body and covering the fleet's landing force. Horne proved correct; enemy aircraft were able to locate Bloch's carriers without much difficulty. The *Langley* was sunk, while *Saratoga* and *Lexington* were heavily damaged.[100] After the exercise, Horne circulated a paper calling for independent carrier operations. Bloch had him recall all copies.

The tension did not abate. Not long after, an argument ensued when a battleship commander accused Admiral King of essentially fighting a private war apart from the fleet, rather than providing him with air support. King, who became the chief of naval operations shortly after Pearl Harbor, was somewhat of a reformist. As a young lieutenant in 1909, he published a prize-winning article in the *Naval Institute Proceedings* criticizing the Navy's culture of "clinging on to things that are old because they are old," calling it "a drag to progress." King also highly valued military education, serving a tour as head of the Naval Postgraduate School, and advocated expanding the Naval War College and requiring all officers eligible for senior rank to attend it. In 1928, King switched to aviation, earned his pilot's wings, and became one of the first aviators to make admiral. He was tough and blunt. One of his daughters described him as "the most even-tempered man in the Navy. He was always in a rage."[101] Simply put, King never suffered those whom he considered fools (and they were many) gladly. Thus, King shot back at his Gun Club counterpart, informing him that until he, King, won the war for air superiority, he could not ensure the survival of his carriers and that without the carriers, the battle line would be bereft of air cover, scouts, and gunnery support.[102]

At the General Board hearings in October 1937 called to discuss the fiscal year 1939 aircraft procurement program, Admiral Arthur B. Cook, now BuAer's chief, testified that carriers were clearly offensive systems. While conceding the point, most Gun Club members pointed out that even though carrier aircraft could seriously damage a battleship, they could not sink a battleship; thus, battleships remained the fleet's capital ship. Nevertheless, Captain Royal Ingersoll, the director of the Navy's War Plans division, testified that strikes by carrier aircraft would be important in slowing the speed of the faster Japanese battle line. This was essential if the slower U.S. battleships were to win a fleet engagement.[103]

Fleet Problem XIX, conducted in March 1938, was designed to help resolve the growing dispute over the carrier's role. King, now the Navy's carrier commander, saw the exercise as an opportunity to correct what he felt was a serious misuse of the carrier force in Fleet Problem XVIII. The scenario divided the fleet into two opposing forces, White and Black, with the latter seeking to establish a base on White's coast following the destruction of the White Fleet. Black split its forces into two battleship groups, each accompanied by one of the two carriers in the force, *Saratoga* and *Lexington*. King objected to separating the carriers but failed to alter the scenario. *Ranger*, along with some land-based aircraft, was assigned to the White Fleet.

Aircraft from *Ranger* located and attacked *Lexington*, which was put out of commission that evening by nearly forty White land-based patrol bombers, which also dropped flares to expose Black's battle line to gunfire from the White Fleet. *Saratoga*, as King had feared, was too distant to support the *Lexington*. The exercise reaffirmed several earlier insights, including the danger posed by land-based air forces and the offensive-dominant character of carrier warfare. It did not, however, do much to resolve the dispute over carrier doctrine.

The second phase of Fleet Problem XIX tested Hawaii's defenses. Here things went better for King. The forces were again configured in two fleets. The Blue Fleet was directed to execute an amphibious landing against a Red Force on Hawaii. Red defenses included Army Air Corps planes and Navy patrol bombers. King, allowed to devise his own tactics, had both *Saratoga* and *Ranger* at his disposal with the Blue Fleet. He directed *Saratoga* to maneuver northwest of Oahu to launch a predawn attack on the island. Just before dawn on March 29, *Saratoga* launched a surprise attack on the Army's Hickam and Wheeler air fields and the Pearl Harbor Naval Air Station. As was the case with Admiral Yarnell's carrier force six years earlier, King demonstrated Pearl Harbor's vulnerability to carrier air attack.

The third and final phase of Fleet Problem XIX found the force again divided into two fleets. The Purple Fleet prepared to launch attacks on the Green Fleet's base, located at San Francisco. Assigned to the Purple Fleet, King formed *Saratoga* and *Lexington* into an independent strike force. Breaking off from the battle force, King maneuvered the carriers into position where he could begin launching air strikes on Green's base. Following the strikes, the carriers rejoined the Purple Fleet's main body, where their scouting aircraft located the Green Fleet. King's carriers then launched strikes against the Green Fleet's cruisers, destroyers, and submarines. As the exercise terminated, there was general agreement that the carriers had performed well. Still, the debate over proper carrier doctrine persisted.[104]

Radio and Radar: The Great Enablers

The introduction of radar was a key factor in the emergence of the fast carrier task force and was probably the Navy's most important technological advantage in the Pacific War. Radar was arguably the best means of providing early warning of an enemy air attack.[105] "In combination with the installation of the combat information center aboard U.S. warships, radar improved fleet air defense enormously, particularly in vectoring combat air patrols toward inbound Japanese air strikes."[106]

The Navy began to research radar during the 1930s. By the fall of 1933, the Navy understood radar's potential to enhance search operations and fire control; however, it lacked high-power vacuum tubes for the kinds of radar needed. Firms like RCA and General Electric had no need for them and were not interested in funding work in this area. Rear Admiral King, who had succeeded Moffett as head of BuAer following the latter's death in the crash of the airship *Akron*, came up with the money to fund the radar work at the Navy Research Laboratory.[107] By 1936, the Navy Research Laboratory was conducting successful demonstrations of radar equipment aboard ships. Early in 1938, a search radar was installed on a battleship and subjected to exhaustive testing during fleet maneuvers in the Caribbean the following year. The tests were a success, with approaching aircraft being detected at ranges out to fifty miles.[108] The Navy began to mount search radars on all carriers and on many surface combatants. Progress was also being made on fire-control radar.

Breakthroughs in radar technology continued apace. By July 1941, fleet exercises revealed that carrier formations equipped with radar—able to detect approaching enemy aircraft at a considerable distance—were potentially capable of tipping the balance in carrier air warfare in favor of the defense. Radar was also emerging as an indispensable navigation tool.[109] No less an authority than Fleet Admiral Chester W. Nimitz, commander of U.S. naval forces in the Pacific during the war, considered radar as revolutionary for naval warfare as the steam engine had been a century before.[110]

On the Cusp of a Revolution

In 1939, the Navy reorganized its carrier force into Carrier Division 1 (*Saratoga* and *Lexington*) and Carrier Division 2 (the newly commissioned *Yorktown* and *Enterprise*).[111] When Admiral John Towers, now BuAer's director, appeared before the General Board in July of that year, he declared that the carriers must be allowed to operate independent of the battle line, noting, "I am convinced that carriers must be considered, not as individual vessels, but as part of a striking force" consisting of two carriers, four heavy cruisers, and four destroyers.[112]

Towers abandoned small carriers. The collapse of the Washington Naval Treaty regime had removed the ceiling on carrier tonnage. In any event, modern aircraft required bigger carriers from which to operate. In his appearances before the General Board in 1939 and 1940, Towers recommended future carriers to be constructed at least as big as the recently commissioned *Yorktown* and *Enterprise*, with comparable speed (thirty-three knots) and aircraft capacity (a seventy-two-plane minimum). He also advocated increasing the carriers' fuel capacity to extend their cruising range.[113]

The General Board concurred. By January 1940, plans for the *Essex* class of carriers had been formed. The carrier would displace 27,000 tons and emphasize speed (thirty-three knots) and aircraft numbers (up to ninety) over armament (an armored flight deck was rejected) and gunfire support, which was to be provided by its escort ships.[114]

Budgets and Industry

Despite the enthusiasm of naval aviation's advocates, there were good reasons for the Navy leadership to doubt aviation's military potential, especially given the technological uncertainties involved. Extensive experimentation was one way to reduce these uncertainties. Another way was to learn from the British, who had led the way into the era of naval aviation. Designers in the Navy's Bureau of Construction and Repair benefited from access to the Royal Navy's carrier plans, enabling them to begin with a state-of-the-art design.[115]

Like other major warships, carriers had fairly long construction lead times. Even though the United States could construct warships relatively quickly, it could not match the rate at which advances in aviation technology were progressing. So the Navy was forced to make some educated guesses. *Ranger* was designed *before* Fleet Problem IX was held, and *Yorktown* and *Enterprise* were designed before the *Ranger* was commissioned. The first carrier class with a design based on extensive fleet-exercise experience was the *Essex* class.[116]

During the decade following the Washington Naval Treaty, the United States built roughly half the warship tonnage that Japan did and generally less than most other major naval powers.[117] Still, the Navy was relatively generous toward its infant aviation branch. Between 1922 and 1925, naval aviation's budget remained fixed at $14.5 million, even while the overall Navy budget was declining by some 25 percent. From 1923 to 1929, the naval air arm grew by more than 6,500 personnel, excluding the crews of the manpower-intensive *Saratoga* and *Lexington*, while overall Navy personnel strength declined by more than 1,000.[118]

Budgets became tighter during the Great Depression. Admiral Moffett, who in 1930 was pressing for more carriers, was able to get but one (the *Ranger*) authorized by Congress. Even then, the nation's deepening financial crisis delayed its being laid down.[119] In 1931, the General Board wanted to build the fleet up to the full limit permitted by the Washington Naval Treaty; at the same time, many members of Congress favored decommissioning some battleships and carriers as an economy measure. (A number of naval aviators brassily argued that, if reductions should occur, the battleships should be the first to go!)[120] Fortunately, enough carriers were in the fleet to enable their effective use in the fleet problems, while the industrial base remained strong enough to begin producing carriers in ever greater numbers as the war clouds grew close in the late 1930s.

Congress authorized constructing only three "from the keel up" carriers in the twenty years following World War I, which coincided with the Navy's period of greatest experimentation with naval aviation.[121] This had some deleterious effects. Yet it also helped the Navy to avoid locking in to a class of carriers before the rapid advances in aviation technology had begun to level off and before the character of the threat to the United States had clearly manifested itself. By enabling the Navy to build and experiment with carriers, Congress serendipitously helped to ensure that, in the late 1930s, when the danger of war was growing rapidly, the United States could quickly expand carrier production.

The Navy proved very effective at "time-based competition." The service, through a combination of design and luck, positioned itself to transform very quickly into a radically different kind of fighting force. Importantly, the Navy did not have to build carriers in large numbers to bring about a revolution in warfare at sea. Before Pearl Harbor, the Navy had constructed only eight carriers. Of those eight, only five—*Saratoga, Lexington, Yorktown, Enterprise,* and *Hornet*—approximated in size the workhorse *Essex*-class carriers that started joining the fleet in 1943. Put another way, a relatively small perturbation in the Navy's capital ship program yielded "revolutionary" results.

Following the carrier-dominated fleet engagements at Coral Sea and Midway in early 1942, the Navy moved aggressively to alter its shipbuilding priorities. Battleships were the principal casualty. The *Iowa* class was terminated at four of the six planned ships, and the *Montana* class was canceled. Sixteen fleet or fast carriers (CVs) were commissioned during the war, along with seventy-nine light (CVL) and escort (CVE) carriers. Not every ship type suffered the battleship's fate. Between 1941 and 1945, the number of submarines and destroyers in the fleet more than doubled, a feat nearly matched by the cruiser force.[122]

Of course, the carriers needed modern aircraft in large numbers. This required a capable aviation industrial base. During the 1920s and 1930s, aviation was—if not in its infancy—still very much in its adolescent stage. It was a technology marked by rapid change and not a few surprises. The Navy had experience designing ships, but it needed an industrial base that could provide it with aircraft and that could surge production when needed to meet the needs of a rapidly expanding carrier force.

The aviation industry that formed a key element in the United States' "arsenal of democracy" took decades to develop. In 1916, Secretary of the Navy Daniels suggested the Navy build its own aircraft factory to provide the fleet with prototype aircraft in small numbers for experimenting that private industry could not provide profitably. A plant for this purpose was built at the Philadelphia Naval Yard in 1917. The plant also helped the Navy validate the commercial aviation industry's claims with respect to its costs, production schedules, and technical competence.[123]

Although naval aviation benefited little in its early years from the emergence of civil aviation, NACA did, over time, promote what today is referred to as dual-use technology. Innovations such as aerodynamic streamlining, supercharged piston engines for operating at higher altitudes, and internally pressured cabins were developed under NACA auspices with financial and engineering support from the Army and Navy.[124]

The budget reductions following World War I were ameliorated to some extent by the Navy's recognition that accelerating aviation technology meant that existing aircraft represented a rapidly depreciating asset. The General Board acknowledged this in a June 1919 memo, declaring that "construction [of aircraft] should be kept as low as possible, ... but for experimental and developmental work, a liberal appropriation should be included in each yearly program." With the postwar drawdown, the Navy's requirement for aircraft dropped to just 156 planes in 1921, stressing the infant commercial aircraft industry, which depended heavily on the government for business.[125] Adding insult to injury, commercial firms had to face competition from the Navy's own Naval Aircraft Factory, which had emerged as one of the country's largest aircraft manufacturers.

In January 1922, Admiral Moffett resolved the problem, instructing the Naval Aircraft Factory to concentrate primarily on research, development, testing, and evaluation of experimental aircraft models. The factory would continue to produce aircraft, but only in limited numbers to provide a cost baseline for comparison with commercial manufacturers.[126]

Some aviation firms argued that their competitive advantage in design and innovation would be diluted by the Navy's retaining a competence in this area.[127] Indeed, BuAer's large design and engineering staff would remain a bone of contention with private industry throughout the interwar period. In any event, for the new arrangement to succeed, Congress needed to provide the funding necessary to make it work. Moffett argued that keeping the fledgling commercial industry alive and innovative was essential since, should war occur, "there would be a tremendous urge to get what we need in the shortest possible time."[128] Nevertheless, the Navy's inventory of combat aircraft fell by more than 50 percent in the seven years following World War I.

Moffett testified before the Morrow Board, "the best thing that could be done for the aircraft industry would be for the Government to have a building program in aviation ... so that the industry would know just what we would get not only this year and next year but for several years." He noted, "It is extremely difficult for aircraft manufacturers to carry out an orderly and economic procedure" without "a continuing construction policy."[129]

Moffett lobbied for his aircraft program with key members of Congress and with Morrow himself.[130] His efforts paid off. The Morrow Board report, released in December 1925, recommended that Congress authorize 1,000 modern aircraft to support naval aviation. The administration announced its support, and Moffett and his staff actually drafted the aircraft authorization bill.[131] With all the pieces in place, in 1926 Congress authorized a five-year, 1,000-aircraft naval aviation procurement program.

The Navy reached its goal of 1,000 modern (albeit rapidly obsolescing) aircraft during the summer of 1930, a year ahead of schedule. Given the relatively high number of aircraft authorized, the Navy explored a range of aircraft types that Moffett wanted for experimenting. The instructions to the Taylor Board, which was charged with reviewing aircraft types, stated, "It is necessary to assume certain risks in the purchase of new equipment, and be willing to assume these risks if we expect to advance."[132]

Naval aviation funding suffered as the Great Depression, triggered by the stock-market crash of October 1929, stretched through the 1930s. The Navy's aviation budget for fiscal year 1934, submitted in April 1932, called for $29.8 million, a reduction of $3 million from the previous year. By the time the Bureau of the Budget signed off, however, it was cut to less than $22 million.[133]

The tight Depression-era budgets had an unintended salutary effect. If the Navy's aircraft procurement budget was quite limited, so too was its ability to accumulate a large inventory of aircraft depreciating precipitously in value given the rapid progress in aviation technology. The Navy's leaders appeared to realize this and avoided locking in to large buys of a single type of aircraft. As late as October 1937, the General Board heard the director of the Navy's War Plans Division arguing against large production runs of carrier aircraft on the grounds that these became "obsolete quickly."[134] Thus, from 1932 to 1938, the Navy's inventory of combat aircraft remained essentially stagnant in number. Yet it was anything but stagnant in aircraft types. During this six-year period alone, the Navy introduced eleven new kinds of combat aircraft: two bombers, one fighter-bomber, five fighters, two scout bombers, and one torpedo bomber. Rather than invest scarce resources in maintaining a large inventory of rapidly obsolescing aircraft, the Navy emphasized keeping pace with technology.

Fortunately for the Navy, Congress passed the Vinson-Trammell Act of 1934, also known as the Naval Parity Act, authorizing the Navy to build the fleet to Washington Naval "treaty strength." Motivated primarily as a means for pulling the United States out of the Great Depression, it also helped restore the aviation industry's health by funding the construction of more than 1,000 naval aircraft over five years.[135]

The pace of events accelerated with Japan's invasion of China in 1937. Following the Washington Naval Treaty's collapse, in 1938 Congress passed the Naval Expansion Act, providing for a 20 percent increase in battle fleet ship tonnage.[136] Germany invaded Poland in September 1939, precipitating war with Great Britain and France. Following the stunning collapse of France in June 1940, Congress moved to enhance U.S. defenses, increasing the ceiling on naval aircraft to 4,500, a 50 percent boost above the level set just a few years earlier. Soon after, a third Vinson Act passed, increasing the ceiling to 10,000. In July, Congress passed the Two Ocean Bill, raising the limit to 15,000 aircraft.[137]

As the war in Europe took a turn for the worse and U.S.-Japan relations became increasingly strained, the United States' industrial base responded to the Navy's needs. From 1940 to 1944, the numbers of naval aircraft, on average, doubled each year, for an overall increase of nearly 2,000 percent.[138]

In summary, given the uncertainties and limitations the Navy faced, it adopted a hedging investment strategy. It created a "balanced" fleet in which the option remained open to expand the battle line by ramping up construction of substantially better battleships of the *Iowa* and *Montana* class or to move relatively quickly to increase the number of fast carriers with the *Essex* class. By not accumulating a large inventory of rapidly obsolescing aircraft in the 1930s, the Navy could shift more quickly to produce the modern war-winning air arm of the early 1940s.

Pilots

For the Navy to sustain the development of its aviation arm, it needed to attract and maintain sufficient numbers of capable officers as pilots. During naval aviation's infancy in the 1920s, the Navy's officer corps was dominated by graduates of the United States Naval Academy. More than 80 percent of Annapolis graduates first went to sea in battleships, the command of which was almost a prerequisite for making admiral.[139] The naval-aviation visionaries were able to expand their numbers in large part by demonstrating to the Gun Club admirals that aircraft were necessary for the battle fleet's tactical and operational effectiveness.[140] This they did, thanks to experiments like that with the battleship *Texas* and spotting. Naval-aviation enthusiasts also benefited from the claims made by General Mitchell and his supporters, and from the Navy's desire to keep pace with the Royal Navy, which had pioneered carrier aviation.

Thanks in part to BuAer's advocacy and findings like that of the Morrow Board, talented officers, among them Moffett, King, and Reeves, saw naval aviation as important and as a means of advancing their careers. Still others, like Sims and Fiske, were simply enamored of air power's potential. Then there was flying itself, which had captured the imagination of many Americans in the 1920s and '30s. Many young men jumped at the chance to fly, despite the significant risks involved. As Lindbergh and other aviation pioneers showed, flying was the exciting thing to do.

Still, developing and sustaining the manpower needed for developing naval aviation remained a struggle from the founding of the Bureau of Aeronautics right up until the eve of World War II. On November 19, 1921, only four months after becoming BuAer's head, Moffett declared, "The lack of trained naval aviators is now a serious consideration and one which requires immediate action if the efficiency of Naval Aviation is not to be impaired."[141] Three years later, with the Navy having failed to address the shortfall, a board was established to address the problem. Headed by Captain Alfred W. Johnson, the Johnson Board issued its findings in April 1925, calling for increasing the Navy's aviation training program, centered at Pensacola, Florida, and detailing additional officers into the program.[142]

Although the secretary of the Navy approved these recommendations, Moffett found himself in a fight with admirals who feared that officers who pursued aviation might become (if they were not already becoming) too detached from their primary professional development as "seafaring" officers. The ink was barely dry on the Johnson Board's recommendations when Rear Admiral William R. Shoemaker, the chief of the Bureau of Navigation with responsibility for personnel matters, including training and promotion, put forth a counterplan. Its premise was that naval aviators were no more specialized than other officers and should therefore do their share of sea duty before taking on aviation assignments. Aviator shortages, Shoemaker argued, could be eliminated by using enlisted pilots.[143] He also proposed that flight pay be drastically reduced or eliminated, as an economy measure. Moffett felt that Shoemaker's proposal, if implemented, would see aviator numbers "dwindle to a handful" and that "morale and efficiency would materially suffer." Simply put, "it would wreck Naval Aviation."[144]

The dispute went to the heart of an ongoing dispute over the BuAer's autonomy. Moffett felt that if naval aviation was to rest on a secure foundation, he had to wrest at least de facto authority over the training and assignment of officers and men from the Bureau of Navigation.[145]

With relations between the Aeronautics and Navigation bureaus growing increasingly strained, a board was convened to consider the personnel question. Its chair was Rear Admiral Montgomery Meigs Taylor.[146] The board's report, released on January 20, 1926, sought a middle ground between the two contending bureaus. It recommended that Annapolis graduates serve two years of sea duty before aviation training but that they have only one additional year of sea duty before being eligible for promotion to the rank of commander. It also recommended that, owing to the shortage of aviators in senior grades, line captains who were not aviators could be detailed to the command of aircraft carriers. If need be, such officers could be put through an abbreviated flight-training program.[147]

The report's efforts at compromise satisfied neither Moffett nor Shoemaker.[148] The matter came to a head when Shoemaker attempted to get Congress to pass legislation calling for the transfer of all naval constructors (designers) to line duties, effectively removing them from their area of specialization and depriving BuAer of their expertise. Moffett appealed directly to Navy secretary Curtis D. Wilbur, arguing that the bill went against the Morrow Board's recommendations and that "important questions of design must be handled by whole-time or permanent specialists."[149] Nowhere was the tension between the two bureaus more acute than with respect to aeronautical engineer officers. Moffett felt that they were indispensable to naval aviation's success. Without them, the service could not guarantee that advances in aviation technology would be properly exploited. He argued that "to build up a group of suitably qualified technical officers, they must be trained, must be encouraged through the recognition of their work, must be clothed with the requisite authority, and must be protected against discrimination on account of their specialization."[150]

Wilbur opposed Shoemaker's proposed legislation. A compromise was reached with Shoemaker's successor, Rear Admiral Leigh. Thirty-three naval constructors and one line officer restricted to engineering duty were assigned to BuAer on a permanent basis, with additional specialists to be assigned as necessary. In 1930, the position of aeronautical engineering duty officer was created, allowing technical specialists to pursue career paths in aviation while bypassing the time-consuming sea duty required of line officers. Moffett had won a major victory. BuAer. also scored another success as pilot classes at Pensacola were increased by 20 percent, and Annapolis graduates had their sea duty deferred until after they completed flight training.[151]

Cooperation between the two bureaus continued to improve. By 1931, BuNav was requiring all unrestricted line officers to pass a rigorous examination on the uses of naval aviation and on aircraft characteristics as a prerequisite to promotion to captain.[152] Still, if naval officers were required to understand aviation, naval aviators were required to be naval officers. This meant being experienced in fleet operations.

Although BuAer succeeded in developing a new career path for naval aviators and associated specialists, the pilot shortage continued through the 1930s. Finally, in June 1939, Congress passed legislation authorizing a civilian pilot-training program under the new Civil Aeronautics Authority (CAA). The goal, conceived by the head of the CAA, Robert H. Hinckley, was to produce 20,000 college-age pilots. The Navy strongly supported the program.[153] To facilitate the expansion, the Navy also made a conscious decision to increase the production of training aircraft at the expense of combat aircraft.[154]

These efforts paid dividends. Following the Battles of the Coral Sea and Midway, both the Americans and the Japanese faced the problem of replacing pilot losses and dealing with pilots suffering from severe fatigue. While the Japanese had no reserve of highly qualified aviators, the Americans not only were able to maintain a supply of qualified pilots but also sent their most experienced pilots back to the United States to train new pilots. As the war progressed, a large share of the U.S. carriers' success came from their pilots' skill and experience advantages over their Japanese adversaries. In brief, the Navy established a major source of competitive advantage relative to the Japanese through its pilot-training program. The defeat of Japan's carrier forces in the Pacific was won "through superiority in numbers—not in planes but in experienced pilots."[155]

Technological Change and Uncertainty

From the mid-1920s to the late 1930s, the range of naval attack aircraft increased from around 400–500 miles to between 800 and 1,200 miles, roughly a 100 percent increase in little over a decade.[156] More horsepower and improved aircraft designs meant that larger bomb loads could be carried, over greater distances. Around 1930, maximum bomb loads had leaped from a few hundred pounds a decade earlier to 1,000-pounds.[157] By the mid-1930s, aircraft capable of delivering 1,500-pound payloads were entering the fleet. When the *Yorktown* and *Enterprise* were being commissioned in the late 1930s, the Navy was introducing aircraft with 2,000-pound payloads.[158]

The combination of rapidly increasing aircraft range and payloads meant a carrier no longer had to steam close to an enemy fleet to launch an attack, while its aircraft had the potential to sink any ship afloat. When the technique of dive-bombing was combined with large payloads, dive-bombers became true ship killers. These aircraft were compact enough to be carried in substantial numbers on carriers. Exercises showed that once a dive-bomber had reached its seventy-degree dive, it was extremely difficult for a defending fighter to shoot it down.[159] The rapid progression of naval aviation found Admiral Yarnell writing to Rear Admiral Charles P. Snyder, president of the Naval War College, declaring, "New weapons are going to have a great influence on the character and outcome of the next war, and the nation which recognizes their possibilities and is prepared to use them in the most efficient manner will have a great advantage."[160]

Yet, despite the rapid progress in aviation, in 1939, a pamphlet issued by the Naval War College rejected "the idea that aviation alone can achieve decisive results against well-organized military or naval forces."[161] This was understandable. Aircraft had never sunk a battleship in combat. Tests had been conducted on the uncompleted battleship *Washington*, scheduled to be scrapped in accordance with the Washington Naval Treaty. Aircraft flying at 4,000 feet employing a 1,440-pound shell and a 2,000-pound bomb failed to penetrate its deck armor. Three additional bomb runs failed to sink the ship, which had to be sent to the bottom by the *Texas*—a battleship. There was also the matter of a battle line's anti-aircraft defenses, which played no role in the *Indiana* and *Ostfriesland* tests and which had improved markedly since the early 1920s. In 1939, the British Admiralty expressed high confidence in its ships' ability to withstand aerial attack, declaring, "Our modern ships can produce a volume of defensive fire, both long range and short range, of . . . a nature that will drive aircraft to such a height that the efficiency and accuracy of their attacking weapons will be seriously impaired. . . . Tests in peacetime as to the probable number of hits by attacking aircraft in war time are, therefore, apt to be illusory."[162]

Advances in radar-directed anti-aircraft guns also looked promising, and early warning radar, it was believed, would also aid the defense.[163] Moreover, carriers had shown very limited ability to conduct operations at night and in bad weather. Gun Club members argued that they could defend against torpedo attacks, whether delivered by aircraft or surface combatants, by armoring or adding impact-absorbing blisters to their ship hulls. It also was not clear how the carriers would replace their aircraft losses as they progressed farther across the Pacific toward Japan. Finally, critics noted that carrier aircraft were markedly inferior in speed and rate of climb to their land-based counterparts. Wouldn't it be preferable, they argued, to emphasize shore-based air forces?

Then there was firepower, not firepower as a function of range but in volume—the battle line's salvo. As late as 1940, the Naval War College was informing its students that "it takes 108 planes to carry as many large torpedoes as one squadron of destroyers and 1,200 to carry as many large bombs or large projectiles as one battleship."[164]

Given the Navy leaders' responsibilities for the nation's security and the welfare of their sailors, they could not be faulted, in the absence of a confirming event, for refusing to accept that carriers had displaced the battleship.

Baptism by Fire: The Carrier as Capital Ship

World War II presented the ultimate test of carrier aviation. It came just as technology, in the form of rapid advances in aviation, radar, and radio communications, had matured to the point where the operations anticipated by the Navy's aviation visionaries were not only possible but critical to winning the war against Japan.

Still, in the war's early days, the carrier's emerging dominance was far from clear. In 1940, two German warships caught the British carrier *Glorious* in the North Sea off Norway and sank it. Carrier-based aircraft did not figure prominently, let alone decisively, in British naval operations opposing the German invasion of Norway that same year. Naval aviation issued a wake-up call, however, in November 1940, when the Royal Navy carrier *Illustrious* launched an air strike against the Italian fleet at its harbor in Taranto. Twenty-one attacking aircraft severely damaged three battleships, putting a cruiser out of commission, damaging two destroyers, and sinking two supply ships. Remarkable as the attack was, the battleships were not sunk, even though they were immobile and weakly defended.

Other naval engagements in the European theater of war gave further hints of what was to come. In March 1941, aircraft from the British carrier *Formidable* drove off the Italian naval forces at the Battle of Cape Matapan, and in May 1941, the Royal Navy carrier *Ark Royal* played a significant role in the sinking of the German battleship *Bismarck* in the Atlantic.

Still, at the time of the Imperial Japanese Navy's surprise attack on Pearl Harbor in December 1941, the definitive case for carriers as the new capital ship had yet to be made. Admiral Husband E. Kimmel, the commander in chief at Pearl Harbor, viewed carriers as auxiliaries to the battle line. In fact, the senior air expert on Kimmel's forty-man staff held the modest rank of commander.[165] Yet in the months following the attack, the aircraft carrier established itself as the Navy's dominant weapon, not so much because Gun Club diehards experienced an epiphany but rather because the Navy, now greatly inferior in battleships to the Japanese battle fleet, was limited to hit-and-run raids best conducted by carriers, which were faster and consumed less fuel.[166]

The Battles of the Coral Sea and Midway in May and June 1942, respectively, confirmed that a transformation in naval warfare had occurred and that the United States Navy was well positioned to exploit it. The Coral Sea engagement was the first in history where the two fleets never achieved visual sight of each other. One month later, the Battle of Midway was dominated by carrier aircraft. Again, the opposing fleets did not come within sight of each other. Much as in the fleet problems of the 1930s, both sides' attacking aircraft sought out the other's carriers as their principal target, with U.S. aviators finding their targets first. In six minutes, dive-bombers from *Yorktown* and *Enterprise* destroyed three Japanese carrier flight decks with their entire aircraft complement. The Navy's decisive victory was confirmed by Japan's overall loss of four carriers. As Bernard Brodie observed at the time, "A great change had indeed fallen over the aspect of war at sea. The advent of the attack airplane was at least as revolutionary as anything which had occurred since the introduction of steam on the warship. It was clear that not only the tactics but also the whole strategy of naval warfare had been thrown off their foundations, and that, whatever new readjustments were made, the situation would never again be as it was. The airplane was bound to remain an instrument which would command first attention in any naval battle or campaign of the future."[167]

The Navy changed its shipbuilding priorities accordingly. After Pearl Harbor, the General Board wanted to increase the number of carriers but opposed converting light cruiser hulls into light or escort carriers and proposed a building program that would lay down only nine additional carriers through 1944.[168] In May, however, Admiral King, now chief of naval operations, unilaterally modified the General Board's recommendations, indefinitely deferring five battleships and replacing them with five carriers and ten cruisers.[169] Shortly after the Battle of Midway, Congressman Carl Vinson submitted a bill authorizing construction of 1.9 million tons of carriers, cruisers, and destroyers—but no additional battleships. When the chief of the Bureau of Ships testified in hearings on the bill, he concurred with Vinson's priorities. To some degree the bill reflected the shortage of battleship armor, but it also acknowledged the battleship's eclipse by the carrier as the centerpiece of the fleet.[170] In late July, King informed the chairman of the General Board that submarines would be granted first priority for construction, with battleships slipping to sixth. Only four of the planned six *Iowa*-class battleships ended up being built, and the *Montana*-class battleships were canceled in July 1943.[171]

The Navy's transformation of fleet operations in response to the emergence of the carrier as the new capital ship was so profound that by war's end, no major category of warship except mine craft was employed tactically for the purpose for which it had been built.[172] Just as dramatic were King's personnel decisions. He ruled that the aviation admiral commanding a task force would be the officer in tactical command, even if he were junior to the surface-force commander. He followed, on September 1, by creating the position of commander, aircraft, Pacific Fleet.[173] Aviators constituted nearly two-thirds of the forty officers promoted to rear admiral between November 1942 and August 1943. Admiral Towers was made Nimitz's deputy, making Towers, an aviator, his logical successor. As Clark Reynolds observed, Towers's appointment meant that "naval aviation would at last gain control of the navy."[174]

From Offense to Defense

Since neither the IJN nor the U.S. Navy had succeeded in establishing a clear lead in aircraft range, the crucial determinants of success in early carrier battles centered on the carrier task forces' scouting effectiveness and effective striking power. Early carrier operations favored the offense. To be detected and attacked was to run a high risk of being destroyed.[175] Thus, a premium was placed on stealth, deception, and dispersed forces (so as not to lose more than one carrier from one sighting). The dominance of the offense was also reflected in carrier air-wing composition. In 1942, roughly 75 percent of a U.S. carrier's air wing were attack aircraft. The U.S. fleets engaged at Coral Sea and Midway did have radar, but it was not used efficiently enough to facilitate interceptions far enough from the fleet to avert serious damage to U.S. carriers. Therefore the advantage remained with the offense, and the battles played out similar to the fleet problems in the years immediately preceding the attack on Pearl Harbor.[176]

By late 1942, however, carrier defenses were rapidly improving, thanks to extended-range communications, radar, and anti-aircraft guns. Radar and long-range radio enabled the carrier task force to receive early warning of an attack and to mass and coordinate task-force (now made up of three or four carriers) defenses. It was no longer critical to attack first, and the Navy restructured its carrier air-wing mix to approximately 65 percent fighter-interceptor aircraft. Whereas the measure of effectiveness in carrier engagements in 1942 had been the number of carriers sunk, it now became the number of naval aircraft destroyed.[177]

Carrier Limitations

In the carrier's role as the new capital ship, it also showed its limitations, as had the battleship before it. Carrier aircraft had become the chief naval weapon during the daylight hours. But when the sun set, they lost most of their effectiveness, and surface-combatant engagements remained the norm.[178] Indeed, carrier forces were quite vulnerable to surface ships at night. Following the U.S. carriers' devastating success against the Japanese carriers at Midway, they withdrew during the night, while Japanese surface ships pressed forward in an attempt to catch the carriers before they departed the area.[179] Although the carrier had clearly displaced the battleship, the latter did not suffer the horse cavalry's fate, at least not right away. The battleship dominated a number of maritime engagements. Apart from the Japanese raid on Pearl Harbor, the annihilation of a Japanese convoy and escort force by U.S. Army Air Force bombers in the Bismarck Sea, and the cruiser and battleship actions off Guadalcanal between November 12 and 15, 1942, there were seventeen named battles between Japanese and U.S. naval forces during the first two years of the war. Only four were carrier battles.[180]

Battleships were hardly sitting ducks against carrier-based aircraft, particularly once they were fitted with anti-aircraft batteries and operated as part of a carrier task force. Battleships in the latter part of the war typically had a defensive effectiveness against aircraft perhaps several orders of magnitude as great as those in the former period.[181] In the Battle of Santa Cruz in November 1942, one of the newly commissioned U.S. battleships shot down thirty-two Japanese planes in less than thirty-two minutes, while taking only one bomb hit that did little damage.[182] The fact that it proved difficult to sink a battleship in the open sea purely by employing carrier aircraft must have provided some solace to members of the Gun Club who recalled General Mitchell's boasts two decades earlier.[183]

Still, there could be no doubt as to the carrier's status as the fleet's new capital ship, reflected not only in the Navy's budgets and organization but also in its operations. They reached their pinnacle in the war with the U.S. Navy's fast carrier task force, which became capable of launching round-the-clock offensive air operations and sustaining itself for long periods in combat zones thanks to its mobile fleet train. By 1944, the U.S. Pacific Fleet had established a mobile service squadron of five major units comprising hundreds of ships positioned at strategic points in the Pacific. Logistics Support Group ships would rendezvous with carrier task-force combatants, providing them with fuel, munitions, and provisions. In so doing, the Logistics Support Groups emerged as a critical factor in the carrier task force's effectiveness.[184]

Although battleships still played a significant role in the war, they now operated without air forces at their peril. By the time the Japanese super-battleships *Musashi* and *Yamato* were sunk by U.S. air strikes in 1944 and 1945, respectively, "the destructive power of numerous U.S. Navy carrier aircraft and the combined weight of bombs and torpedoes they could hurl against any surface target would have obliterated the ships planned by any naval architects of the 1930s."[185] The long era of the battle line was over. The age of the carrier had arrived.

CHAPTER NINE

From Mass to Precision

The objective of our precision-guided weapon systems is to give us the following capabilities: to be able to see all high-value targets on the battlefield at any time, to be able to make a direct hit on any target we can see, and to be able to destroy any target we can hit.

—WILLIAM J. PERRY

We're going to dramatically change our approach, simply because it's wrong. We're now going to make defense roll-back and taking the SAMs out our first order of business. No more trying to fly past SAM sites to get to other targets. That can't be done.

—GENERAL WILBUR ("BILL") CREECH

IN 1944, THE UNITED STATES was waging a global war against the Axis powers, Germany and Japan. During that summer, forty-seven U.S. Army Air Corps B-29 bombers operating from bases in China launched a raid against the Yawata steel works in Japan. Only one plane hit the target area. And only one of the 376 bombs dropped by that B-29 hit anything of value, a powerhouse nearly three-quarters of a mile from the raid's target, a success rate of roughly 0.25 percent.[1]

The U.S. bombing effort was not faring much better in Europe. That fall, only 7 percent of the bombs dropped by the Eighth Air Force landed within 1,000 feet of their target or "aim point." Thus, a raiding force of 108 B-17 bombers armed with 648 bombs had a 96 percent chance of two bombs hitting their aim point.[2]

Until the war's final months, and particularly in Europe, the bombers found themselves confronting formidable integrated air defense systems (IADS) consisting of enemy radars, fighter-interceptors, anti-aircraft guns, and electronic jamming and counter-jamming. To counter these defenses, the Army Air Corps typically employed large numbers of fighter escorts to suppress ground-based air defenses and ward off enemy interceptors, while employing various kinds of electronic warfare. Even then, losses were often high, at times approaching prohibitive levels.[3] For nearly half a century following the bomber offensives in World War II, the U.S. Air Force (hereafter the "Air Force") and the air forces of other significant military powers confronted the formidable problem of defeating ever improving enemy air defenses.

In early 1991, however, over the skies of Iraq, in the course of several days, a handful of U.S. fighter-bomber aircraft armed with two bombs each succeeded in dismantling one of the world's most formidable integrated air defense systems. At the same time, U.S. and allied aircraft swept the skies of an enemy air force flying modern interceptor aircraft. Having achieved the air superiority that eluded it for most of the war in Europe and during wars in Korea and Southeast Asia, the Air Force went on to wreck the better part of Iraq's army in one of history's most lopsided campaigns.

How did this remarkable change in air warfare come about? Waging a successful air campaign in the face of a well-armed and determined foe is a demanding proposition, requiring the offensive force to overcome a series of challenges. To begin, the attacking force must successfully navigate its way to the target and return to a friendly base. Second, it must overcome enemy defenses without incurring unacceptable losses. Finally, having reached the target area, the attacking aircraft must employ its weapons with sufficient accuracy to destroy its assigned targets. If the air offensive force fails in any of these tasks, the campaign is likely to fail as well. Major air campaigns following World War II through the Yom

Kippur War found that the offense could be successful, but only by sustaining ever higher costs.

From World War II to Vietnam: 1945–1965

The two decades between the Allied victory in World War II and the direct U.S. intervention in the Second Indochina War found the Air Force focused on the threat posed by Soviet air power during a period of significant growth in aviation technology.

Germany fielded by far the most formidable integrated air defenses encountered by U.S. air forces in World War II. Employing a combination of fighter-interceptors, electronic warfare, and anti-aircraft artillery, the Germans at times pushed U.S. air losses close to prohibitive levels.

The IADS problem was far more manageable during the Korean War, where Chinese and North Korean air defense coverage was localized rather than integrated. Chinese defenses were concentrated primarily along the Yalu River, while Russians piloted some interceptor aircraft. Faced with a watered-down version of the German threat, the Air Force stuck to what had worked before: individual bomber raids against discrete targets involving the temporary suppression of local enemy air defenses.[4]

Air-to-Air Combat

From the onset of combat between aircraft in World War I up until the late twentieth century, success in air warfare was closely linked to leveraging a pilot's experience into an advantage in situation awareness (SA), defined as "accurate representations of where all the friendly and enemy aircraft in or near the combat arena are, what they are doing, and where they are likely to be in the immediate future."[5] Superior SA gave pilots an edge in maneuvering into a favorable attack position and surprising their enemy. Once that was achieved, a pilot only had to have that aircraft in his engagement envelope in order to get a kill. If the pilot failed to achieve surprise, he needed to engage in a far more difficult competition in outmaneuvering the enemy to achieve and maintain a firing position.

From World War I through much of the Vietnam War, pilots relied on their vision to identify the enemy, using machine guns and automatic cannon as their principal weapons. As an air-to-air "sensor," the human eye has an effective range of about two nautical miles at roughly two degrees wide. This was sufficient, as an aircraft's gun range only expanded from about 50 meters to roughly 500 meters by the mid-1960s.[6]

Surprise, enabled primarily through superior situation awareness, remained central to successful air combat through the Vietnam War. Ace pilots who fought in the two world wars strongly agreed that keeping a sharp lookout, frequently altering course to eliminate their own blind spots, and turning to meet an enemy attack rather than attempting to dive away were keys to their success. Their fundamental rule was to avoid combat in situations where surprise had not been achieved, as this was seen as a high-risk proposition. Ace pilots sought to achieve surprise.

World War II German aces Erich Hartmann (352 kills) and Gerd Barkhorn (302 kills) pursued what they called "ambush tactics" similar to those that American aces Richard Bong (40 kills) and Tommy McGuire (38 kills) were employing in the Pacific.[7] These tactics mimicked those of World War I ace pilots like the Royal Air Force's Mick Mannock and Germany's Oswald Boelcke.[8] Ambush tactics emphasized gaining greater altitude, which could be converted into speed, either to attack or to avoid combat. Pilots would approach the enemy from "up sun" (in front of the sun) to preclude being detected by the enemy pilot or approach from an enemy's "blind spot," such as from behind. Finally, they would open fire at short range to maximize hits.[9]

In the spring of 1944, the U.S. Eighth Fighter Command in England published a study that found that its most successful pilots emphasized ambush tactics. One pilot declared, "few pilots are shot down by enemies they see." Another noted, "90 percent of all fighters shot down never saw the guy who hit them." Similarly, the German fighter pilot Hartmann was "sure that eighty percent" of his kills never knew he was there until he opened fire.[10]

Pilot experience also had a significant effect on bombing accuracy. One U.S. study found that a large portion of the hits obtained were achieved by relatively few pilots, while the rest were, in the words of one pilot, "lucky to hit Germany."[11] With bombing accuracy so poor, air forces began to search for a way to enhance weapon accuracy.

Guided Weapons

Work on guided weapons, or precision-guided munitions (PGMs), began in earnest during World War II. An early U.S. effort, code-named Aphrodite, involved transforming aging bombers into robot attack aircraft using a range of technologies, including radio control and television imaging, to guide them and their 20,000-pound bomb payloads to the target. A few weeks after the D-Day invasion, General James Doolittle, commanding the U.S. Eighth Air Force in Great Britain, ordered the Third Bombardment Division to employ its "robot bombers" against German V-1 rocket sites in the Pas de Calais region of France.[12] Although the attacks showed the feasibility of using remotely guided aircraft, they failed to inflict significant damage on their assigned targets, owing primarily to German air defenses, problems associated with weather, and equipment malfunctions.[13]

Subsequent raids were similarly unsuccessful, and General Tooey Spaatz ordered the project terminated, directing that the remaining bombers be used to attack large-area industrial targets to offset the aircraft's accuracy limitations. Aphrodite, which began with the objective of achieving a precision-targeting capability, ended up with its bombers being employed as a terror weapon.[14]

The Army Air Corps was also working on Azon, a radio-guided, azimuth-only (Azon) glide bomb. Encouraging tests in early 1943 led to a request for 1,000 Azons. Beginning in 1944, Azons were employed in Western Europe, the Mediterranean, and Burma. Despite a few notable successes, including against the Avisio Viaduct near the Brenner Pass in Northern Italy in May 1944 and against rail bridges in Southeast Asia, Azon suffered from serious weather restrictions and reliability problems.[15]

German efforts to field guided weapons were more successful. On September 9, 1943, a year before the U.S. Army Air Corps began to employ guided weapons, a Luftwaffe bomber dropped a Fritz-X radio-guided bomb on the Italian battleship *Roma* as it steamed in the Mediterranean Sea, sinking it. The Germans followed up two months later, with a bomber launching an anti-ship missile, sinking a troop transport with the loss of nearly 1,200 American soldiers. That same month, the Germans scored another success when a Fritz-X guided bomb severely damaged the light cruiser *Savannah* and the British battleship *Warspite* in the Mediterranean.[16] Germany's ally, Japan, had its own "guided" bomb in the kamikazes, with pilots sacrificing themselves to maneuver their payload to its target. After making their first appearance in the fall of 1944, roughly 2,800 kamikazes sank 34 U.S. Navy ships while damaging 368 others and killing nearly 5,000 U.S. sailors. Despite being detected by U.S. radar and confronting swarms of fighter-interceptors and a wall of anti-aircraft fire, one in seven kamikazes hit a ship, and over 8 percent of these hits resulted in the ship's sinking.[17]

World War II showed glimmers of guided weapons' potential. Toward this end, in 1948, the newly established United States Air Force established the First Experimental Guided Missiles Group at Eglin Air Force Base in Florida. By year's end, the group was experimenting with four radio-controlled guided weapons.[18]

Work on perfecting the Azon continued with Razon (range and azimuth only). As its name suggests, Razon could be guided in both range and azimuth. Development began in 1942, and extensive testing in 1946. In early 1950, the Air Force began to deliver specially equipped aircraft and a supply of Razon tail assemblies to the Nineteenth Air Bombardment Group on Okinawa.[19]

When the United States went to war in Korea following North Korea's attack on South Korea on June 25, 1950, the need for weapons that could reliably destroy key fixed targets, such as bridges, remained as acute as it had been in World War II. Despite the use of increasingly sophisticated computer-assisted systems, CEPs for unguided bombs were around 500 feet.[20] Once again, the Air Force turned to guided weapons—in this case, Razon—to boost accuracy.

The first Razon missions over Korea were unsuccessful, primarily owing to bomb malfunctions and the inexperience of crew and bomb-maintenance teams. Despite its name, Razon was far more accurate in azimuth than in range. This made it attractive for use against long, narrow targets, like bridges, and Razon was employed almost exclusively against these types of targets. The results were modest. From September through the end of 1950, 489 Razons were dropped on Korean bridges, destroying fifteen, a success rate of 3 percent.[21]

The Air Force introduced another guided weapon, Tarzon, more than twelve times the size of the 1,000-pound Razon, over North Korea on December 14, 1950, and employed it through April 1951. Tarzon produced some impressive results, knocking out bridges and scoring a direct hit on a hydroelectric station. Of the twenty-eight bombs employed, six hit their targets, a success rate slightly above 20 percent. The weapon required daylight and clear weather, which rendered the bombers carrying them more vulnerable to fighter-interceptors. It also suffered from reliability problems and high maintenance costs. Most worrisome, however, was Tarzon's propensity to detonate inadvertently upon release from its aircraft, a feature that hardly endeared it to aircrews. The weapon was withdrawn from service in April, and the program was terminated in August 1951.[22]

With the signing of an armistice in July 1953, combat operations on the Korean Peninsula ended. Although guided weapons showed some promise, one expert spoke for many in declaring, "guided missiles, even in three-to-five years, . . . still will be very complicated, partly vulnerable and not as accurate as they should be." Nevertheless, weapons like Razon and Tarzon had shown enough promise to encourage their supporters. The commandant of the Air War College declared that fielding reliable and effective guided weapons "is one of the most dynamic problems facing the military forces today" and that once this was accomplished, "they will fundamentally change the whole war concept, tactically as well as strategically."[23] By the late 1950s, two critical technologies—the laser and integrated semiconductor circuits—were emerging. In time, they would make the commandant's vision a reality.

SAC Über TAC

Following World War II, the newly established Air Force consisted of three commands. Bombers were assigned to the Strategic Air Command (SAC), which was responsible for strategic bombing and aerial reconnaissance. Tactical Air Command (TAC) consisted mainly of fighters for nonnuclear operations and bomber escort missions. The Air Defense Command (ADC) was tasked with providing early warning of a Soviet nuclear-armed bomber attack and provided with interceptor aircraft to defeat it.

From the start, TAC lived in SAC's shadow, struggling for money and manpower. General Elwood Quesada, TAC's first commander, became so disillusioned with his command's red-headed-stepchild status that he requested to be reassigned, telling his pilots to abandon the command and fly bombers.[24] The Eisenhower administration's "New Look" defense strategy, with its heavy emphasis on deterring Soviet aggression with SAC's rapidly expanding nuclear strike capability, put TAC even further in the background.

General Curtis LeMay, who had commanded U.S. bomber forces in the Pacific during World War II, led SAC from 1948 to 1957. LeMay made it a priority to populate the Air Staff with "bomber guys" who had little experience with "air superiority" or air-to-air combat. Their focus was on delivering a nuclear payload on what would probably be a one-time (and perhaps even one-way) mission. When he departed SAC, LeMay became the Air Force's vice chief of staff. There he was put off disbanding TAC only by the Army's threat to develop its own tactical air force.[25] By the late 1950s, Air Force doctrine focused its fighter force on defending against enemy bombers or flying offensive tactical nuclear strike missions at low level to avoid enemy radars. With aircraft armed with nuclear weapons, bombing accuracy became far less important, as did air-to-air combat training.

In 1961, the Air Force had become so dominated by bomber generals that one of its own, General Walter C. Sweeney, Jr., was assigned as TAC's commander. Sweeney had flown B-29s under LeMay and served as SAC's first head of planning. The general chose a young fighter pilot, Major Wilbur Creech, as his aide-de-camp.

Sweeney increased TAC's training focus on air-to-air combat and close air support, while emphasizing reducing the command's accident rate.[26] Air Force leaders were so concerned about training safety that commanders could be relieved if an aircraft was lost due to accident. Since the easiest way to lose an aircraft was during realistic air-to-air combat training, TAC commanders prioritized safety over training. Sweeney proved no exception. Yet General of the Air Force Henry "Hap" Arnold, who headed the Army Air Forces during World War II, warned that an obsession with safety exacted its own price:

> If our only interest was flying safety in the United States, we would have every man fly a primary trainer on sunny days, and we could cut the accident record to almost zero. If we stopped flying and put the airplanes in hangars, we would have no accidents at all. But war is not fought that way. From the outset, the Army Air Forces have taught the men at home the maneuvers that they would execute in combat abroad. In these maneuvers a few are bound to be injured or killed, but the overwhelming proportion of the men are better prepared to defeat the enemy.[27]

Vietnam

The absence of quality training was exposed in the growing U.S. involvement in the Second Indochina War. In early 1965, Major General Gordon M. Graham, an ace pilot in World War II, now the Tactical Air

Command's director of operations, led a team to South Vietnam to "determine why jet losses occurred in a relatively unsophisticated environment." The "Graham Report" recommended that TAC's training methods should not be changed but that the commanders in the theater of war should deal with the problem. General Sweeney, now suffering from pancreatic cancer, disagreed, as did many pilots serving in Vietnam, who argued that training back in the United States should resemble the combat environment where they were being sent.[28]

Square Pegs in Round Holes

As operations in Southeast Asia heated up in the spring of 1965, the Air Force's SAC-dominated leadership realized that the air war was being dominated by TAC pilots, who were running the risks—and gaining the recognition—associated with combat. If this continued, more TAC officers would be getting combat commands, where success virtually guaranteed promotions at the SAC officers' expense. It was decided that, to spread the "burden" of the war, no aircrew member would be forced to fly a second, nonvoluntary combat tour until everyone—including the bomber pilots—had flown their first.

Unlike other major-power air forces (and the U.S. Navy), the Air Force did not separate pilots in flying school. Whereas other air forces sent the best pilots in flying school to fighter and attack aircraft, the bomber-dominated Air Force rejected the idea that fighter pilots were more skillful than bomber pilots. The Air Force believed that any pilot was a "universal pilot" capable of flying any type of aircraft. Despite the "universal" tag, once assigned to SAC's bombers, few pilots moved to fighters. The "universally assignable" SAC pilots were put in a Replacement Training Unit to learn how to fly combat fighters. Making matters worse, the training time for qualifying new fighter pilots was cut from twenty-six weeks to six. The consequences were disastrous; SAC pilots who had flown nothing but bombers their entire careers found themselves suddenly flying small fighters, with predictably poor results.[29]

The Wrong Kit: Aircraft and Missile Design

In the decade following the Korean War, TAC's focus on intercepting Soviet nuclear-armed bombers and executing high-speed penetration missions to deliver weapons saw its aircraft typically feature high wing loadings ill-suited for the maneuvering needed to prevail in air-to-air combat or survive against modern ground-based air defenses.[30] Fighter-aircraft training manuals, like that for the F-100 Super Sabre, declared that "nuclear training will in every instance take precedence over non-nuclear familiarization and qualification."[31]

As the administration of President Lyndon Johnson began to deploy ground-combat troops to Vietnam in the spring of 1965, the air threat in Southeast Asia intensified. In April, Hanoi's Vietnamese People's Air Force (VPAF) committed its MiG-15 and MiG-17 fighters to contest U.S. air operations over North Vietnam. On April 4, 1965, MiG-17s engaged Air Force fighters, downing two F-105s.[32] The fight for command of the air was under way.

The Air Force anticipated that its guided air-to-air missiles (AAMs) would give it an advantage over the VPAF. Similar missiles were first used in combat in September 1958 by Taiwanese aircraft armed with the U.S. Navy's AIM-9B Sidewinder missiles against People's Liberation Army Air Force (PLAAF) MiG-17s. In addition to the Sidewinders, work was proceeding on the AIM-7 Sparrow missile. Tests on these missiles suggested that the Air Force and Navy could expect success rates of 65 and 71 percent, respectively.[33] Both missiles, however, were designed with defeating lumbering Soviet nuclear-armed bombers in mind, not the relatively small, highly maneuverable fighter aircraft being flown by the North Vietnamese.

The first sustained use of AAMs occurred in 1965 with Rolling Thunder, the air campaign against North Vietnam. Air Force and Navy pilots employing Sidewinders found themselves pursuing tactics similar to those used in the Korean War and World War II, seeking to maneuver their aircraft into a rearward-projecting cone behind the enemy, in this case so that the missile's passive infrared (IR) seeker could detect the heat emanating from the enemy aircraft's jet engine.[34] Although the Sidewinder was an improvement over machine guns and cannons for aerial combat, it still limited the pilot to within-visual-range engagements and even then almost exclusively in daylight and in clear weather. The Sparrow III was the first air-to-air guided missile capable of engaging enemy aircraft beyond short range and from "all aspects" (from any direction: head-on, from the side, or from the rear). The Sparrow missiles achieved a kill rate of 8 percent, while the Sidewinders fared little better, at 15 percent—both far below their "advertised" performance.[35] Both missiles suffered from the challenges of maintaining them in the tropical

Southeast Asian climate. And there were technical shortcomings. For example, the missiles' electronics contained fragile vacuum tubes.[36]

As U.S. forces surged into Southeast Asia in the spring of 1965, enemy ground air defense capabilities improved dramatically. Responding to the U.S. effort, the Soviets started to deploy SA-2 surface-to-air missile (SAM) battalions to North Vietnam in April, primarily around Hanoi. On July 24, two SA-2 missiles engaged a flight of four F-4s, taking down one of them. Three days later, the Air Force conducted a large-scale raid on two SA-2 battalions located outside the Hanoi perimeter. The 100-plane strike package included forty-six F-105s supported by fifty-six other aircraft. With the SAMs threatening medium-altitude operations, the F-105s countered by employing very low-level fight profiles on their way to the target and during ordnance delivery and egress from the target area. The result was a disaster. Six F-105s were shot down by anti-aircraft artillery (AAA) batteries providing low-level coverage around the SA-2 sites.[37]

With both medium- and low-altitude operations producing unacceptable results, the Air Force and VPAF engaged in a series of moves and counter-moves, each seeking to gain an edge in the competition.[38] Of particular note, the Air Force introduced specialized F-105G "Wild Weasel" electronic warfare (EW) aircraft to warn aircraft of SAM launches. The Wild Weasels also conducted suppression attacks against active SA-2 sites, employing bombs and anti-radiation missiles. Later the Wild Weasels were equipped with jamming pods to interfere with the SA-2's target tracking and missile guidance.[39]

Generally speaking, Wild Weasels sought to induce North Vietnamese SA-2 units to turn on their radars to target U.S. aircraft. Once this occurred, the F-105Gs could trace the SA-2 radar waves back to their source, revealing the SAM site's position and facilitating an attack by U.S. aircraft, which were equipped with Shrike anti-radiation missiles (ARMs) designed to home in on the SA-2's radar emissions.

Despite the F-105Gs' impressive capabilities, they suffered heavy losses. The first Wild Weasels were deployed to Korat, Thailand, in May 1966. By mid-August, all but one of the eleven aircraft had been lost. The Air Force was also suffering from "virtual attrition," as the Wild Weasels further increased the ratio of support to attack aircraft. Efforts to maintain U.S. offensive air operations over North Vietnam at acceptable aircraft loss rates led to strike packages involving eighty aircraft or more, with only 15 to 20 percent of the planes actually dropping bombs.

Still, the Wild Weasels performed sufficiently well that the Air Force converted eighty more F-105Fs to F-105Gs in 1966 and 1967.[40]

The game of cat-and-mouse continued between the Air Force and People's Army of Vietnam (PAVN) air defense crews. The Shrike ARM proved difficult to employ effectively, as it required a distinctive maneuver in order to lock or "cage" its sensor on the SA-2's radar, and it only maintained its lock on the target radar if that radar was emitting; otherwise it would fly off course. The SA-2 crews quickly caught on and began to employ their radars intermittently. When their radar screens showed the Shrike's distinct caging maneuver, the SA-2 crews turned off their radars. To counter this move, the Wild Weasels began to carry unguided Zuni rockets. The F-105Gs would simulate the Shrike caging maneuver before launching a Zuni to deceive the SA-2 crews into shutting off their radars, taking them effectively out of action, at least for a time. The PAVN crews eventually caught on and developed a method to share data among their radars. This enabled the SA-2s to engage the Wild Weasels while minimizing the risk of being attacked. By 1968, the Air Force had developed yet another counter, deploying the Navy's AGM-78 Standard ARM, which was capable of continuing to the target's radar even *after* it ceased emitting.[41]

Guided Weapons

The Air Force made significant advances during the Vietnam War in developing and fielding guided weapons, thanks in part to progress in solid-state electronics and laser technology. Success also stemmed from actions taken by officers outside normal Air Force channels.

The Navy was the first to introduce a guided weapon, the AGM-12 "Bullpup" air-to-surface missile, which was also adopted by the Air Force. As with earlier attempts at fielding guided weapons during World War II and Korea, the Bullpup was disappointing. Its radio guidance system proved unreliable and vulnerable to jamming. The weapon also suffered from the restrictive flight parameters required to ensure its accurate delivery.[42]

Even when successfully employed, the Bullpup's warhead was typically too small to be effective against hardened targets. Their most discouraging use occurred on April 3, 1965, when seventy-nine F-105s attacked the Thanh Hoa Bridge in North Vietnam with Bullpups and more than six hundred 750-pound bombs, along with some 300 rockets and missiles. The Bullpups that were successfully guided "bounced" off the bridge. Those that detonated produced little damage. The unguided bombs failed as well. Five U.S. aircraft were lost in the attack. Over the next three years, another 869 missions were flown against the bridge, with similar results, at the cost of eleven aircraft.[43]

Another Navy guided bomb, the AGM-62 Walleye, was employed by the Air Force beginning in August 1967. Walleye represented a leap forward from earlier radio-controlled munitions, such as Razon, Tarzon, and Bullpup, and as such was classified by the Air Force as a "second generation" weapon. Its most distinguishing characteristic was its electro-optical television guidance system, enabling the Walleye to acquire and autonomously home in on a target. The Walleye produced impressive initial results, as twenty-two bombs destroyed fourteen targets without a single aircraft being lost.[44]

When the Walleye was assigned more challenging missions in October 1967, however, its shortcomings were revealed. The Walleye's TV guidance system was susceptible to failing when dealing with camouflage, smokescreens, dust, or high-contrast decoy targets, resulting in a "rash of unsatisfactory launches and attempts to launch."[45] The Walleye, however, was highly effective against high-contrast targets, such as bridges, and the Air Force continued to employ Walleyes against such targets, especially where conventional modes of attack had failed.[46]

In 1958, two years before the first working laser was successfully demonstrated, the Limited War Panel of the Air Force's Woods Hole Summer Study Group discussed using laser beams to guide air-to-ground munitions. The Air Force's growing interest in laser guidance stemmed from increasing concerns that advances in ground-based air defenses—especially radar-guided SAMs—were occurring at a rate that would lead to high and perhaps unacceptable losses of aircrews and aircraft employing unguided weapons in a war with the Soviet Union.[47]

The Air Force's efforts received important, if unsolicited, support from the Army's Missile Command (MICOM) at Redstone Arsenal in Huntsville, Alabama, and from one of its own, Colonel Joe Davis at Eglin Air Force Base (AFB) in Florida. Between 1962 and 1965, work at Redstone produced a pulsed laser generator and a detector that could identify a spot of laser light projected from the generator at considerable distance. Two MICOM engineers involved in the work began to share their findings with Davis, who became an advocate for laser guidance. Thanks in part to his efforts, in the spring of 1965 the Air Force began to explore how laser illumination could lead to a workable guided bomb. The effort was headed by the Air Force's Limited War Office, at Wright-Patterson AFB, Ohio, with a supporting detachment at Eglin. The office's objective was to identify and acquire technology that promised immediate improvements in Air Force combat operations in Southeast Asia.[48]

Texas Instruments, given the task of developing a prototype, relied heavily on existing technologies. Apart from the seeker head and the laser designator, almost every component in the laser-guided bomb used "proven technology," including the 750-pound M-117 bomb. Four guidance elements were attached to the bomb: the seeker head, guidance electronics, control assembly, and fins. Testing began at Eglin in May 1966.[49]

Over the next nine months, ten tests were conducted. The laser-guided bomb (LGB) had the potential, in Pentagon parlance, to be a "game-changing" weapon. In late 1966, Davis began to lobby key Air Force leaders for support. One particular target was Major General Andy Evans, the officer at the Pentagon responsible for research and development. As the tests continued showing promising results, Davis brought Texas Instruments representatives to Washington to brief Evans on the results. The general was won over, surmounting a key hurdle for getting the program both adopted and accelerated.

Yet the Limited War Office wanted Texas Instruments, which had produced by far the best weapon design, to stand down for a year to give another design team, headed by North American Aeronautics, an opportunity to catch up, in order to conduct another head-to-head competition. Realizing the absurdity of this approach, Davis also took the unorthodox step of arranging a "generals board" of eight high-ranking general officers from around the world, along with the recently retired Air Force chief of staff, Curtis LeMay.[50] Upon reviewing the test results, the board sent a memo to the chief of staff voicing strong support for moving forward aggressively with the program using the Texas Instruments design. Responsibility for the program was transferred from the Limited War Office to a newly created organization called the Pave Way Task Force.[51] Thanks to Davis's end run around the Air Force bureaucracy, the program moved forward quickly, and the LGB was ready for flight testing seven months later and for combat operations in Vietnam in early 1968.

The first LGB was used in combat on May 23, 1968. Half of the bombs scored direct hits. Aircrews flying the LGB missions were enthusiastic.

Paveway was appreciated by airmen, not only for its accuracy but for its simplicity. Any aircraft capable of dropping a general-purpose bomb could drop the laser-guided version of the same bomb. The use of laser guidance removed most requirements for accuracy from the delivery pilot, which was not the case with respect to dive-bombing. The Paveway I also had a very generous release point. Aircraft dropping a laser-guided bomb could deploy it from beyond an enemy's primary air defenses, thus further reducing the likelihood of incurring losses from enemy defenses. Moreover, at the bomb's recommended release altitude of 12,000 feet, the "basket" into which the bomb had to be dropped had a diameter of roughly one mile, making it "all but impossible to miss."[52]

Air Force acquisition managers declared that "the capability ... to vastly improve bombing impact accuracy was emphatically demonstrated," thereby dramatically reducing sortie requirements, aircraft attrition, aircrew losses, and operational and maintenance costs. As with most new weapons, however, problems emerged. With continued employment, the weapon's performance became less impressive. The LGB's success rate declined, and its CEP expanded to seventy-five feet.[53] It appeared that Paveway would, like its predecessors, fail to match the hype around its development.

Fortunately, a second Paveway weapon, the laser-guided Mark 84, was ready for deployment. The Mark 84 was employed with the M-117 bomb in August and September, recording an unprecedented CEP of just twenty feet, with 25 percent of the weapons scoring direct hits. By comparison, manual dive-bombing by F-105s employing unguided M117 bombs between 1965 and 1968 produced CEPs of roughly 500 feet. In 1969, the Paveway results were even better. The Air Force employed 1,601 LGBs, with 61 percent scoring direct hits, and with 85 percent of the bombs landing within ten feet, which was within the weapon's lethal radius.[54]

Concurrently, the Air Force began to field an electro-optically guided (or "TV-guided") bomb called Pave Way II, which provided a "fire-and-forget" capability to succeed the Walleye. Nicknamed "Hobo," for "homing bomb," it was more capable and accurate than Walleye and cost less.[55]

Toward the end of the Vietnam War, the Air Force started to produce an anti-armor guided weapon, the AGM-65A Maverick, a TV-guided, rocket-powered missile. Early versions achieved excellent results in conditions of good visibility. Half of the first twenty-two weapons tested achieved direct hits, with only six missing their target by more than ten feet. With an eye toward the Soviet threat, the Air Force began to develop an infrared version to improve the Maverick's ability to operate effectively in the poor visibility conditions that often prevailed in in Central Europe.[56]

Relearning Old Lessons

On November 1, 1968, a few days before the U.S. presidential election, President Johnson announced that the Rolling Thunder air campaign would be suspended, a condition imposed by North Vietnam for entering peace negotiations. Intense air operations over North Vietnam were resumed, albeit briefly, in 1972. After the war, the Air Force did a detailed assessment of 112 air-combat engagements between December 1971 and January 1973 in which an aircraft was shot down. It revealed that in more than 80 percent of the engagements, the downed aircraft's crew was unaware of the impending attack.[57] Simply put, aerial combat found the Air Force and Navy relearning what had been established in the two world wars and Korea: pilot experience, translated into situation awareness, remained the dominant factor in determining success.

Pilot Training

The overall kill ratio for Air Force and Navy pilots against enemy aircraft was 2.4 to 1, which was far worse than the Air Force's kill ratio during the Korean War (4.7 to 1 in 1950–52 and 13.9 to 1 in 1952–53). Between August 1967 and February 1968, U.S. fighters suffered an *adverse* kill ratio against the MiG-21, with eighteen U.S. aircraft lost for only five MiG-21s downed. Combat reports suggested that the Air Force's poor performance was even worse than the data suggested, as they found "little evidence that the MiG pilots ever developed real air combat maneuvering skills beyond attacking from behind and executing hard turns for both offensive and defensive maneuvers."[58]

As the surprisingly poor air-to-air-combat results piled up, in late 1967, the Navy undertook a rigorous assessment of the problem.[59] The effort, led by Captain Frank W. Ault, focused primarily on technical problems with the AIM-7 air-to-air missile. Yet it was the section on pilot tactics and training that triggered a training revolution in the Navy. It found that the service had not developed appropriate tactics to maximize the missile's effectiveness, which meant that pilots were not being trained to employ proper tactics. Solving this problem, the report found, required establishing a Navy Fighter Weapons School with an "Adversary Squadron" to fly against Navy pilots, with an eye toward providing them with realistic training.

In October 1969, the Navy established the school at Miramar Naval Air Station in California. It soon became known as "Top Gun," emphasizing dissimilar air combat training (DACT), with Navy pilots going up against aircraft similar to those being used by the enemy. In this case, Top Gun instructors flew the A-4 "Skyhawk," a small, highly maneuverable attack aircraft similar to the VPAF's MiG-17, the Navy's main rival in the skies over North Vietnam.[60]

Unlike the Navy, following Rolling Thunder, the Air Force training reverted to emphasizing avoiding accidents. The air-to-air combat training conducted typically found F-4s operating against F-4s, denying Air Force pilots experience in identifying and engaging the smaller Soviet-made aircraft employed by the VPAF.[61] More than any other man, General William W. "Spike" Momyer was responsible for this lamentable state of affairs. He had a fighter-bomber pedigree, including a stint as TAC's head of plans from 1958 to 1961. In July 1966, Momyer took command of the Seventh Air Force, which ran Air Force operations from bases in South Vietnam during Rolling Thunder. Momyer departed in August 1968 to head TAC, having witnessed firsthand the Air Force's disappointing combat performance. Hopes were high that the new commander would take the kind of action under way in the Navy.

He did not.

Momyer could not bring himself to admit that things had not gone well under his command, so he never pressed TAC to conduct DACT. He thought that the Air Force kill ratio in Vietnam from 1963 to 1968 was a "very acceptable" 2 to 1 and that the reason for the lower kill ratio was due to "political and technological factors ... with political constraints perhaps being the most significant factor."[62] Yet Air Force pilots in the Korean War had also operated under some similar political constraints and flew aircraft that were, in many ways, no more advanced than the MiGs they fought. Yet the Air Force pilots shot down roughly six Russian-piloted aircraft for every U.S. pilot lost, and their kill ratio against Chinese and Korean pilots was 25–30 to 1. Aware that DACT training would probably increase accidents, Momyer actually cut back on air-to-air training.[63]

Many Air Force leaders also remained prisoners of SAC's longstanding dominance, which focused efforts at the level of the individual raid, rather than conducting a broader campaign to suppress the North Vietnamese air defense system.[64] Simply put, the Air Force was focusing on the tactical level rather than the operational level of war.

Linebacker

Following the North Vietnamese Army's overt invasion of South Vietnam on March 30, 1972, known as the Easter Offensive, the air war over North Vietnam resumed. North Vietnam's air defenses by this time encompassed more than 200 radar installations, along with 300 SAM and several thousand AAA sites. The North Vietnamese supplemented these defenses with MiG-21 interceptors and large numbers of SAM decoys. The Soviets were also providing the North Vietnamese with enhanced SA-2 missiles.[65]

Linebacker revealed the value of Navy's new approach to pilot training. The first air strikes on Hanoi saw Navy F-4s down eight MiGs without a loss, while Air Force pilots shot down three MiGs at the cost of two F-4s. Following the three-year gap in operations since Rolling Thunder, the Air Force had difficulty coordinating complex strike packages against North Vietnam's IADS, as they had not been trained to do so. By the end of July, the MiGs enjoyed a 2-to-1 kill ratio in their favor. Air Force leaders in Washington came under pressure from President Richard Nixon, who as commander in chief had released them from many of the restrictions under which they operated in Rolling Thunder. A frustrated Nixon told his national security adviser, Henry Kissinger, that he was "disgusted" with the Air Force's performance. Meanwhile the Air Force's top brass found itself sitting in weekly Pentagon briefings with senior civilian officials where their service's performance paled in comparison to the Navy's, with the admirals praising Top Gun.[66]

Things came to a head when one of the Air Force's best pilots, Lieutenant Colonel William Kirk, told the chief of staff, General John D. Ryan, that the service's pilots were so poorly trained that he believed only 10 percent could pass a written test on the basics of air combat. Ryan told Kirk to devise a test and administer it to pilots in the field—and not to tell Momyer. More than 200 pilots took the test. The average score was ten correct answers out of twenty-five questions. Only around 10 percent of the pilots passed the test. Momyer, having learned of the test, tried to recover by recommending that TAC form an Aggressor Squadron. Ryan gave the OK. But both Ryan and Momyer were set to retire soon, and except for the promise of an Aggressor Squadron, there was little change to training.[67]

On the bright side, the Air Force's Linebacker I campaign saw guided weapons employed to devastating effect. Aircraft armed with LGBs destroyed six major bridges in North Vietnam in a single day, including the key Paul Doumer Bridge. Laser-guided bombs also proved highly effective in blunting the North Vietnamese Army's invasion, being credited with more than 20 percent of all enemy tank kills. A month later, Air Force Secretary Robert C. Seamans, Jr., declared in his "Policy Letter for Commanders," "The unprecedented accuracy of laser-guided or TV-guided 'smart' bombs and airborne sensors now being used by U.S. aircraft is making interdiction far more effective than before."[68]

Seeking to conclude a peace agreement with Hanoi, on October 23, President Nixon ordered a bombing pause above the twentieth parallel, ending Linebacker I. This exempted most of North Vietnam from attack, save for a portion of its southern "panhandle." When negotiations stalled, the United States resumed the air campaign, called Linebacker II, in late December 1972. It produced the most intense air combat of the war, involving strikes by the U.S. Strategic Air Command's B-52 bombers. Air Force losses to North Vietnamese air interceptors and ground-based air defenses were considerable. On the first night of the Linebacker II raids, on December 18, 1972, the Air Force lost three B-52s, while two others were damaged. On the campaign's second night, no B-52s were lost. On the third night, however, of the ninety-nine B-52s employed, eight were shot down. Fortunately for the Air Force, the attacks' intensity had led to the depletion of North Vietnamese SA-2 missile stocks, and losses declined dramatically thereafter.[69]

The Navy's commitment to realistic combat training paid huge dividends. Prior to Top Gun, the Navy's kill ratio was 2.42 to 1. Afterward, from 1970 to 1973, it went to 13 to 1. Navy aviators began to speak of the Vietnam air war as having two phases: "before Top Gun and after Top Gun." In contrast to the Navy's dramatic improvement in air-to-air combat, the Air Force's kill ratio, which had been 2.25 to 1 during Rolling Thunder, declined to 1.92 to 1.[70] And unlike what occurred with the North Vietnamese SAMs in Linebacker II, the Air Force could not count on Soviet forces in Europe running out of interceptor missiles.

The Yom Kippur War

The 1970s found the Soviet Union upgrading its air defense forces, including improvements to its SA-2 SAMs. It also enhanced its low-altitude defenses, introducing the SA-3 SAM, the SA-4 and SA-6 mobile SAMs, the SA-7 man-portable SAM, and the ZSU-23-4 mobile AAA system. New fighter-interceptors, including the MiG-23, MiG-25, and Su-15, appeared.

The enhanced Soviet capabilities were on display when, on October 6, 1973, Egypt and Syria launched attacks on Israel along the Suez Canal and Golan Heights, respectively. Despite suffering initial setbacks, the Israeli Defense Force (IDF) recovered quickly and launched successful counteroffensives, reclaiming all lost territory and advancing into Syria and across the Suez Canal into Egypt. Both sides suffered heavy losses in the fighting, which ended with a cease-fire on October 25.

The Israeli Air Force (IAF) performed well in air-to-air combat. The IAF also effectively employed the Maverick missile, destroying forty tanks with forty-nine Mavericks in the Sinai Desert. Of note, the IAF scored seventy-nine of its declared air-combat victories with missiles, nearly matching the eighty-three achieved with guns. The IAF, however, had problems with the Arab IADS. The low-altitude Soviet-built Egyptian SAM system's aircraft were particularly effective, with the SA-6s taking down the majority of the ninety-seven IAF aircraft lost during the war—over a third of the entire IAF.[71]

Shortly after the cease-fire went into effect, the Air Force chief of staff, General George S. Brown, directed that a study be undertaken to address the Soviet IADS threat in Europe. The result was Pave Strike, the umbrella term for eleven promising projects given special research-and-development management support.[72]

The war confirmed many of the Air Force's "lessons" from its recent experience in Southeast Asia. Foremost, perhaps, was that although a successful offensive air campaign could be waged against a modern IADS, doing so was difficult and costly. Neither the SA-2s in Southeast Asia nor the SA-2, SA-3, and SA-6 systems in the Middle East, even in combination with increasingly sophisticated AAA systems, succeeded in pushing U.S. or Israeli air forces into a defense-dominant posture. For the most part, U.S. and allied air forces were able to devise tactics and technologies to suppress, roll back, destroy, or otherwise defeat Russian-built SAMs and anti-aircraft guns while preserving the ability to deliver unguided or guided munitions using composite strike packages.

But even though the SA-2s in North Vietnam had rendered mid-altitude air operations a risky proposition in Vietnam, the low-altitude SAMs and advanced AAA systems employed by the Arab states in the Yom Kippur War were making low-attack profiles an increasingly hazardous undertaking. For attacking air forces, it was becoming a case of choose your poison. Moreover, the direct costs of these operations in the form of friendly aircraft and crews shot down, as well as the indirect costs—the growing percentage of support aircraft required for strike packages—were mounting. In a war with the Soviet-led Warsaw Pact in Central Europe, if U.S. aircraft loss rates mirrored those incurred by the IAF, NATO's air forces would be eviscerated in a matter of weeks. Based on the IAF's experience, it seemed that ground-based air defenses, not enemy interceptor aircraft, were the primary threat.[73]

On NATO's Central Front, the Soviet IADS combined MiGs, which by most counts outnumbered NATO fighters by 2 to 1, and overlapping SAM systems whose coverage extended from very low altitudes to high altitudes. Advanced AAA systems complemented the SAMs and MiGs. One major weakness of the Russian IADS, however, was its centralized command and control, which depended heavily on ground-based radars to provide its MiGs and SAMs with the location of NATO aircraft. The Air Force hoped to avoid detection by operating at very low altitudes, flying under Russian radar coverage, thereby denying the tracking information needed by the SAMs and MiGs. There was also the European weather to consider. For more than 50 percent of the year, the ceiling in Central Europe was below 3,000 feet and the visibility less than three miles. Fighter pilots had to see the targets in order to hit them. In Europe, that meant going in under the weather. And since LGBs did not perform well at low altitudes, it would be up to the pilot to put the bombs on target.[74]

Not everyone, though, was in favor of training fighter forces for low-altitude combat. The skeptics pointed out that this had been tried by the F-105s in Vietnam, and AAA had forced aircraft back to higher altitudes. Low-altitude advocates retorted that the Soviet SAM threat at medium altitude was far worse than the AAA and low-altitude SAMs. The skeptics countered by arguing that low-altitude flight profiles were dangerous and that identifying targets at low altitude was too difficult. The "go-low" advocates responded that training to improve pilot proficiency while perfecting tactics would produce success.[75] And so the debate continued.

To sum up, beginning in the late 1960s, guided weapons were emerging as a major asset in offensive air operations. Historically, the vast majority of unguided bombs had missed their aim points by hundreds of feet. Employing massed fires was the only way to compensate for such inaccuracy. This meant sending large numbers of sorties to deliver ever larger numbers of unguided munitions against a target. This began to change with LGBs, which typically landed within twenty-five feet of their aim points. Although initial estimates predicted that 30 percent of the weapons would malfunction, in 1969 only about 15 percent failed.[76]

Still, first-generation LGBs had significant limitations. Clouds, smoke, atmospheric haze, and darkness made successful employment difficult, even impossible. Initially two aircraft were required to employ LGBs. Both planes had to remain within line of sight of the target, with the aircraft doing the laser designation loitering over the target, flying a predictable flight path, making it an easier target for air defenses.

Despite the post-Vietnam congressional cuts to the U.S. defense budget that created a "hollow" military and a readiness crisis in the late 1970s, the Air Force kept Paveway alive, while continuing to develop a TV-contrast tracking system like the type used in the Hobos. By October 1978, the Air Force had stockpiled more than 30,000 guidance kits.[77]

Red Flag

The origins of the Air Force's Dissimilar Air Combat Training and Red Flag were at Nellis Air Force Base, Nevada, the largest military-controlled range in the United States. In 1949, the Air Force established its Aircraft Gunnery School at Nellis to capture and exploit the lessons and experiences that fighter pilots had learned in World War II. After the Korean War, the school was renamed the Fighter Weapons School, with the mission of providing a "doctorate in flying fighters."[78] Following the Air Force's embarrassing performance in the Linebacker campaigns, a growing number of Air Force pilots believed that the service had to make major improvements in pilot training. In 1970, Major Roger Wells, a Fighter Weapons School instructor, began to develop a threat briefing on Soviet fighter tactics, which was well received at the school and later at TAC bases around the world.[79]

Israeli Air Force pilots proved willing to share their combat experience with their American counterparts. In early 1972, two experienced

Israeli F-4 pilots, Asher Snir, one of the IAF's best, and Eytan Ben-Eliyahu (a future IAF commander), arrived at Nellis to take the Fighter Weapons School Instructor's Course. It quickly became obvious that only the best Fighter Weapons School instructors were good enough to fly with them. Snir found the course "not demanding." He and Ben-Eliyahu warned the Americans, "know your enemy" and "fly in training the way you will fly in combat."[80] One of Snir's instructors at Nellis, Richard M. "Moody" Suter, was a warm, gregarious individual and an outstanding pilot, with 232 combat missions under his belt. Suter took Snir's comments to heart.[81]

General Momyer established the Sixty-Fourth Fighter Weapons (Aggressor) Squadron at Nellis in October 1972. The Aggressors, employing Soviet fighter tactics, initially flew the T-38 Talon trainer and then the F-5E Tiger II, a better match for the MiG-21. Later, captured MiG aircraft would be flown by Aggressor pilots.[82] The change in the training environment was striking. One Air Force pilot, future chief of staff John Jumper, on confronting the MiG-21's speed and maneuverability, asked himself, "Why can't I think?"

Suter's Vision

Suter, however, saw this as a modest first step toward his emerging vision of large-scale exercises with aircrews employing live bombs and missiles while being confronted by realistic enemy air and surface-to-air missile threats. When Suter was assigned to Air Staff's Tactics Division at the Pentagon, he began working with a fellow officer, Chuck Horner (who later commanded the air campaign in the First Gulf War), in refining the concept that over time became Exercise Red Flag. His analysis also benefited from Project Red Baron, a detailed set of Air Force assessments examining air-to-air combat in Southeast Asia during the Vietnam War.[83] Red Baron confirmed, once again, that situation awareness is a critical factor in air-to-air combat success and that a fighter pilot's chance of survival in a combat environment increased dramatically after his tenth mission, validating Suter's belief in DACT.

Suter slowly built support, beginning with a briefing that he tried out on fellow staff officers, refining it until it was ready to be presented to one- and two-star generals. Their feedback enabled Suter to further polish his pitch. He put the Soviet Union's red flag on the briefing cover, and soon it was being referred to as the "Red Flag" briefing. Suter took his briefing to Nellis, where the Aggressor Squadron and the Fighter Weapons School commanders confirmed that they could execute the Red Flag concept. Word of Suter's training concept was spreading, and the Air Force chief of staff, David C. Jones, requested that Suter brief him.

Suter's presentation was designed to deflect any reason for scuppering Red Flag. He told Jones that Red Flag's cost would be minimal, since the electronic threat simulators and target hulks on various Air Force gunnery ranges could be consolidated at Nellis. The Aggressors were already based at Nellis. They would cost nothing extra. The Nellis range was already in use. Funding could be shifted to Red Flag from less effective exercises. Suter pointed out that the Air Force could claim it was promoting "jointness"—interservice cooperation—since other services could participate with their personnel and equipment. The Army had already expressed interest. Jones liked the concept and ordered Suter to brief General Robert A. Dixon, Momyer's successor at TAC.[84]

The Tidewater Alligator

Known as the "Tidewater Alligator," Dixon was "tough, demanding, and suffering no fools." Dixon was also respected for his sharp mind. He had flown fighters in World War II and again in Korea. After an assignment with SAC, in 1969 Dixon was sent to South Vietnam as the Seventh Air Force's deputy commander, flying thirty-six combat missions. Dixon was keenly interested in pilot training. When he found that many of the instructors at Nellis were more interested in "harassing and hazing" the students than in teaching them, a new group was brought in to replace them.[85]

In May 1975, a team of five Israeli pilots toured several Air Force bases and flew with U.S. pilots. Once again, they were not impressed, finding TAC's emphasis on flying safety a major barrier to improving training. Dixon agreed, comparing TAC training to doing "calisthenics—the same thing every day in a very unreal atmosphere—and betraying the purpose of training and betraying the crews."[86]

Two months later, Suter briefed Dixon, telling him that Red Flag would provide aircrews with a realistic "first ten missions" in preparing for a war against the Soviets in Europe. Red Flag, said Suter, would employ full "strike packages"—a mix of fighters, bombers, tankers, electronic warfare and reconnaissance aircraft, even search-and-rescue helicopters—against an enemy Aggressor force employing advanced radar systems,

integrated missile and AAA, along with dissimilar interceptors using Soviet tactics. Dixon liked Suter's pitch and approved Red Flag on the spot,
while informing General Jones that this would require waiving the low-
level flight and speed restrictions.[87]

The first Red Flag exercise was conducted in November 1975. Priority was given to making the training as realistic as possible. Soon Blue
Flag exercises were being conducted so that air commanders and their
staffs could master the "combined arms" planning required to conduct
successful air operations.[88]

Red Flag was an immediate success. Other Air Force commands
were soon requesting to participate. Strategic Air Command B-52s
began to fly from their bases, "launching" cruise missiles to take out
enemy defenses, then returning home. The Military Airlift Command
(MAC) cargo aircraft joined, conducting cargo drops while attempting to
evade the Aggressor forces. Tankers engaged in refueling both friendly
and Aggressor aircraft, while search-and-rescue aircraft were found pick-
ing up crewmen who were "shot down" behind enemy lines. Forward air
controllers (FACs) started directing close-air-support strikes in support
of ground forces. The Navy and Marine Corps began to participate in
the exercises, along with U.S. allies. A typical Red Flag exercise conducted in May 1977 included nineteen different types of aircraft, and 141
aircraft in all, flying more than 2,000 sorties.[89]

Given the scale and fidelity of Red Flag training, accidents were inevitable. Dixon took the heat, arguing that the realistic training at Nellis
would save many more lives in combat. The general found that he could
win over skeptics from Congress and the media by taking them out to
observe Red Flag firsthand. It also helped that the accident rate began to
drop. Still, 1979 found the Air Force suffering 2.8 accidents per 100,000
flying hours. For TAC, it was 6.3. In the cauldron of Red Flag, the figure
was 21.8.[90] By the time Dixon left command in 1978, the Air Force leadership, to its credit, had established high-fidelity pilot training, not minimizing accidents, as its top priority.

Dixon was determined not to have his work undone after departing
TAC. During his time in command, the general worked the Air Force personnel system to increase the number of general-officer slots at TAC, including two three-star-general billets for his subordinate commands, Ninth
Air Force and Twelfth Air Force. Dixon admitted that he could run TAC
without either of these numbered Air Forces but wanted to create more
senior Air Force leaders with TAC backgrounds. He actively looked for

opportunities to advance the careers of promising young officers, and the Air Staff at the Pentagon was populated by increasing numbers of fighter pilots. Dixon's own TAC staff produced a future chief of staff and a vice chief of staff, as well as several other high-ranking Air Force generals.[91]

The Vision

The three decades following World War II witnessed major changes in air warfare. The offense-defense competition continued, with both sides employing increasingly effective means to gain the upper hand, including jet aircraft, advanced forms of electronic warfare, and missiles. Neither side, however, was able to gain a clear advantage. To paraphrase the British prime minister Stanley Baldwin, the strike aircraft could always get through, but often only at high cost. Perhaps the most notable advance was the United States' introduction of reliable and effective laser- and electro-optical guided weapons.

More broadly speaking, impressive advances were being made in solid-state electronics, which, along with fantastic gains in computational capabilities, triggered the information technology (IT) revolution. These technological advances, combined with the lessons emerging from the Vietnam and Middle East wars, led some military and civilian defense leaders to envision how they might be combined to bring about a disruptive shift in the character of air warfare.

By the mid-1970s, Soviet Russia's rapidly expanding nuclear forces had achieved a rough parity with those of the United States. The loss of the United States' nuclear trump card found the U.S. defense establishment searching for ways to enhance its conventional defenses in Europe. One effort saw the Defense Advanced Research Projects Agency (DARPA) and the Defense Nuclear Agency bringing together a panel of experts to examine the problem. Its report, the Long-Range Research and Development Planning Program (LRRDPP, pronounced "lar-DEPP"), was issued in February 1975. It recommended that the country's senior leaders consider exploiting the potential of nonnuclear weapons with "near zero miss" accuracy, which were believed to be "technically feasible and militarily effective." The report noted that "the effect of this capability would be to deter limited aggression in the first place, since the credibility of a United States response with this type of [precision-guided weapon] attack would be much higher than that of a United States [nuclear] response in which millions of civilians would be killed."[92]

Interest in the potential of guided weapons was not limited to the LRRDPP study. A year after its publication, a Defense Science Board Summer Study was tasked with examining a range of emerging technologies, including those that might enhance guided weapons, along with radars, missiles, sensors, and data fusion. The task force believed that these systems could be combined into an integrated target acquisition and strike system—a kind of "reconnaissance-strike complex"—and recommended this be done.

When the administration of President Jimmy Carter assumed office in January 1977, the Pentagon's under secretary of defense for research and engineering, William J. Perry, in testifying before Congress, offered a vision of how these technologies could transform warfare:

> Precision-guided weapons, I believe, have the potential of revolutionizing warfare. More importantly, if we effectively exploit the lead we have in this field, we can greatly enhance our ability to deter war without having to compete tank for tank, missile for missile with the Soviet Union. We will effectively shift the competition to a technological area where we have a fundamental long-term advantage. ... The objective of our precision guided weapon systems is to give us the following capabilities: to be able to see all high-value targets on the battlefield at any time; to be able to make a direct hit on any target we can see, and to be able to destroy any target we can hit.[93]

Perry was convinced that, given the magnitude and scope of the enterprise he had in mind, it would take time and persistent, focused management by senior Defense Department leaders to succeed. He was supported by Defense Secretary Harold Brown, who named Perry's approach the "Offset Strategy," as its objective was to offset the United States' loss of its nuclear advantage.

Stealth

Perry also became interested in another promising IT-driven development: "stealth," which involves reducing the infrared, visual, acoustic, and radar signatures emitted by aircraft. At the time, the only successful effort at fielding an aircraft with a significantly reduced radar cross-section was the U.S. SR-71 "Blackbird" spy plane, which entered service in 1966. The Blackbird was produced by Lockheed's "Skunk Works," which specialized in advanced aircraft design and production.

In 1974, Chuck Myers, the director of Air Warfare Programs in the Pentagon's Research and Engineering Office, shared an idea that he called the "Harvey Concept" with Robert Moore, the deputy director of DARPA's Tactical Technology Office.[94] Myers advocated fielding a low-observable (stealth) combat aircraft, noting that it could greatly reduce the need for supporting jamming aircraft, which had led to the virtual attrition of strike packages.[95] Serendipitously, Malcolm Currie, the Defense Department's director of research and engineering, circulated a memo declaring his dissatisfaction with the Pentagon's lack of innovation and inviting suggestions to remedy the shortfall. Moore nominated Myers's "Harvey" idea, calling it "High Stealth Aircraft," and it was adopted.[96]

Given the radical aircraft design implied in Moore's proposal, a full-scale flight demonstration of a stealth plane would be needed to convince likely skeptics, particularly the Air Force leadership, whose support would be needed for full-scale production. If the demonstration were a success, the Air Force would need to rethink what mattered most in aircraft performance. Designing an aircraft involves making trade-offs between different desirable attributes. In the case of the High Stealth Aircraft, achieving a radically reduced radar cross-section meant sacrificing speed and maneuverability, thereby greatly reducing its air-to-air combat potential. To avoid visual detection, the aircraft would have to fly at night, counter to typical Air Force practice. Finally, in an environment of defense cutbacks, any stealth aircraft would find itself competing for scarce funding against the Air Force's preferred Advanced Combat (F-16) Fighter program.[97]

Currie had good working relationships with the Air Force leadership, including General Jones and General Alton Slay, the Air Force's R&D director. Although the generals were skeptical regarding the prospects for a stealth strike fighter, Currie won their support—with the proviso that funding for stealth not come from the Air Force's existing programs, especially the F-16.[98]

The program called for producing two one-quarter-scale stealthy manned aircraft demonstrators. In January 1975, McDonnell Douglas and Northrop were awarded contracts to design a stealthy manned aircraft. Lockheed would eventually join them.[99] Lockheed won the competition and was awarded a contract for two demonstrator aircraft. In 1976,

lead responsibility for the program, code-named Have Blue, was transferred to the Air Force Special Projects Office.

The two demonstrators were built in roughly one year, with the first
flight test occurring in April 1977. There followed a period of extensive—
and successful—testing. The moment of truth came in August 1979, when
the Have Blue aircraft participated in a classified exercise at Nellis. A Marine Corps Hawk SAM unit's radars were placed on the range and instructed to track an incoming aircraft. Although the Hawk unit was told
the target aircraft's flight path in advance, and thus where to focus its radars, the Have Blue aircraft passed undetected.[100]

Encouraged by these results, Perry wanted to incorporate stealth
combat aircraft into the Offset Strategy. Secretary Brown agreed. Perry
went to Jones and Slay, and they OK'd fielding a wing (seventy-five
planes) of stealth tactical fighter-bombers—again, as long as the funding
did not come out of the Air Force's budget. Perry set an aggressive initial
operating capability date of only four years, skipping the normal development and prototyping phases. Finally, seeking to steal the greatest possible march on the Soviets, the acquisition program, code-named Senior
Trend, was designated a highly classified "black" program. In November
1978, Lockheed received a contract to begin full-scale engineering development of a stealth aircraft, which would become the F-117. The first
F-117 was delivered, on schedule, in 1981.[101]

Barriers to Change (I)

Following Vietnam, Air Force leaders expanded their service's inventory
of guided weapons, but their efforts were rarely enthusiastic. Although
LGB performance in Vietnam demonstrated dramatic enhancements in
weapon accuracy, it was nearly two more decades before the Air Force
fully exploited guided weapons' potential. The primary reason for the
long delay was the Air Force's increasingly influential tactical-fighter
mafia.[102]

General John W. Vogt had commanded the Seventh Air Force during
Linebacker I and II. In June 1974, Vogt assumed command of U.S. Air
Forces in Europe. Given the impressive role LGBs played in Linebacker I,
Vogt seemed a likely candidate to endorse the vision of precision-strike
warfare that emerged from the LRRDPP and Defense Science Board
studies and that was adopted by Harold Brown and Bill Perry. Instead,
Vogt emphasized guided weapons' limitations:

They [LGBs] aren't very good when the weather is bad. The weather is bad most of the time in Europe so immediately you've got a severe limitation on their use over here. During Linebacker II, for example, there was only one eight-hour period during that entire eleven-day period that we were able to use those laser guided weapons. The weather wasn't adequate during all the periods of that particular operation. And I would think that the percentages would even be worse ... [in Europe] because, as you know, for nine months of the year we either have darkness or extremely bad weather. Lasers simply aren't the answer in that kind of environment nor are the electro-optical precision-guided weapons which the Air Force is buying in great quantities.[103]

Vogt's concerns regarding operational conditions in Central Europe had merit, but they were not balanced by any energetic efforts to overcome them. He also did not emphasize planning to make maximum use of LGBs in the event of war.[104]

Air Force pilots believed that they could solve the bombing-accuracy challenge through a combination of the "smart-jet, dumb-bomb" philosophy and the F-16, the first tactical fighter with an automated bombing system. The system purportedly enabled unguided bombs to be delivered with accuracy comparable to that achieved by highly skilled pilots. This led many Air Force leaders like Vogt to conclude that "dumb bombs" could be employed with sufficient accuracy and at far lower cost than LGBs. This thinking also supported the Air Force's preference to buy aircraft rather than guided weapons. After all, pilots wanted to command fighter squadrons and wings, not PGM depots. Employing LGBs and electro-optical bombs required far less pilot skill, thereby threatening to "devalue the manual dive-bombing skills that had long been at the heart of social status in Air Force [fighter] units." The Air Force, however, appeared to discount the fact that the F-16's bombing system depended on executing its bomb-release maneuver at relatively low altitudes, where it would encounter the same kind of AAA and SAM batteries that had inflicted such high losses on U.S. and Israeli aircraft in Southeast Asia and the Middle East, respectively.[105]

Despite Have Blue's impressive performance in the skies over Nellis and its rapid progression from design to production, stealth aircraft received only grudging support from the Air Force leadership. Chuck Myers, the director of Air Warfare Programs, won support for his

"Harvey" concept, not from the Air Force but from DARPA. When the Defense Department's director of research and engineering, Malcolm Currie, was searching for innovative ideas, it was DARPA that came forward with the idea for stealth, not the Air Force. And when Bill Perry approached the Air Force leadership to win support for stealth aircraft, he got it—but conditionally.

Creech

General Dixon was succeeded at TAC by General Wilbur ("Bill") Creech, a strong supporter of the realistic training embodied in the Red Flag exercises. But Creech also had a different vision of air operations and how new ways of fighting, enabled by new capabilities, could produce a disruptive boost in the Air Force's effectiveness. As TAC's commander, he intended to put his ideas to the test.

Starting his career in World War II as an enlisted man in the Army, Creech transferred to the newly formed Air Force in 1948, entering pilot school. By the late 1960s, Creech was serving in Southeast Asia as a deputy wing commander, flying 177 combat missions. By all accounts, he was an excellent pilot. There he became convinced that the Air Force idea of flying low to avoid IADS was a mistake and began to look for ways of suppressing enemy air defenses (SEAD) as part of an overall campaign. After a tour in Europe, he served as vice commander of the Air Force's Systems Command's Aeronautics Systems Division, and then as commander of its Electronic Systems Division. The latter assignment gave Creech an appreciation for electronic warfare's potential. Promoted to full general, Creech assumed command of TAC in April 1978, a position he held for an unprecedented six years.[106]

The Vision

When Creech arrived at TAC, he found that the Air Force's doctrine had stagnated. Although during the Vietnam War tactical fighters had been employed in strategic bombing operations and strategic bombers like the B-52 conducted close-air-support "tactical" missions, Air Force doctrine still viewed aircraft as linked to distinct missions, as they were in World War II. Creech's envisioned an "all day, all night, all weather, precision, standoff, interoperable force." Creech was close to General Jones, having served as his director of operations when Jones commanded the United

States Air Forces in Europe. When Jones left as Air Force chief of staff to chair the Joint Chiefs of Staff, he was succeeded by General Lew Allen, Jr. Creech and Allen soon established an "unwritten understanding" giving Creech a strong voice in procurement matters pertaining to TAC.[107]

Shortly after taking command, Creech called a Warfighter Conference of his senior commanders. The conference, viewed in retrospect as a seminal event in the Air Force's history, saw Creech outlining his vision of air power and calling on his commanders to work with him in adopting a new and very different way of meeting the challenge of increasingly sophisticated enemy air defenses.

Creech began by noting the operational problems posed by Soviet IADS and those of their proxies. Live exercises and operational analyses showed that the Air Force's strike operations could not be sustained against Soviet IADS without incurring unacceptable losses. These findings supported what the general was hearing from Israeli pilots, who described how attempting to fly below the Soviet-made IADS coverage was an exercise in futility. Creech told his commanders that the Air Force was suffering from "go-low disease." His experiences in Vietnam convinced him of two things: first, that a different way had to be found to address the IADS threat; and second, that the Air Force needed to think more expansively beyond tactics and simply "blowing by" the SAM threat on their way to and from a target. It needed to focus instead on the operational or campaign level of war.[108]

On this second point, Creech declared that air defenses had to be rolled back and suppressed on a broad level, rather than avoided or dealt with tactically within the context of a single-strike mission. Once the enemy's air defense system was suppressed, he said, air operations could be conducted at higher, more survivable altitudes, where guided munitions could be employed most effectively. For the first time in the Air Force's history, Creech said, destroying the enemy's air defense network was a prerequisite to waging an air campaign: "Our basic concept of operations rests on the fact that we must penetrate enemy defenses. To do that, we will roll back those defenses using a combination of disruptive defense suppression and selective destruction with both standoff and overflight weapons."[109]

A summary of Creech's closing remarks at the conference's conclusion is worth citing at length:

We're going to dramatically change our approach, simply because it's wrong. We're now going to make defense roll-back and taking the SAMs out our first order of business. No more trying to fly past SAM sites to get to other targets. That can't be done. Taking them out can be done, and it will be easy if we go about it right. We need to get up out of the weeds as soon as possible to avoid the AAA, a far more formidable threat. . . . Our fixation on low-altitude ingress, egress, and delivery and the systems and munitions that fit solely that approach is over.[110]

Looking back at the session, one participant, Larry D. Welch, a future Air Force chief of staff then serving on Creech's staff at TAC, recalled, "By the end of the conference, there was full agreement that low-level tactics might be necessary for a time but that we needed to get out of that mode as early as possible. Perhaps even more important for the subsequent evolution of both systems and tactics, there was a much greater appreciation for the potential of new tactical thinking . . . and the right munitions with precision guidance—all clearly within our technology capabilities."[111]

Over the next six years, Creech went about putting his vision into practice. There was resistance from the "go-low" crowd. Some argued that the war could be lost during the time it would take to dismantle the enemy's IADS. Others feared that Creech was looking for a way to avoid flying low in order to reduce Red Flag's accident rate. The general gradually identified the principal sources of resistance and either fired them or reassigned them where they would not threaten his initiatives.[112]

The results of his efforts are perhaps best judged by two senior Air Force leaders. General Jones ranked Creech "with Curtis E. LeMay as one of the two most influential men in [his] long Air Force experience."[113] More than twenty years after Jones stepped down as Air Force chief of staff, his successor, General John Jumper, declared, "No single officer has had greater influence on the Air Force in recent times than General Bill Creech. He transformed the way the Air Force conducts warfare."[114]

Many Flags

Creech's efforts centered around Red Flag. The general believed that Tactical Air Command exhibited a "propensity to put a 'realistic training' tag on *unrealistic* wartime strategy and tactics." He directed that Red Flag stop flying every mission as if it were "the first mission on the first second on the first day of a war." For example, the exercises failed to incorporate "kill removal," in which each side's losses were removed from play, after being either shot down or destroyed on the ground. Thus, every day was "Groundhog Day."[115] The threat was always at its highest, and the air wing was always fully ready. Under these conditions, pilots were compelled to fly every mission at low altitudes. Structured this way, the exercises made it impossible to explore Creech's concept for a campaign whose objective was to take down the enemy's IADS. So Creech directed that Red Flag exercises be run to reflect the first two weeks of a war rather than repeating the first day of a war every day for two weeks. This enabled Red Flag exercises to focus on rolling back enemy air defenses, followed by shifting to higher, more survivable altitudes once this was accomplished.[116]

Problems identified at the Warfighter Conference were addressed. For example, before Creech arrived, each wing commander whose unit arrived for a Red Flag exercise designed his training regimen. General Welch recalled that the wing commanders did this "with no formal benefit of others' experiences at Red Flag": "We saw the same mistakes over and over with each set of participants starting without much benefit of the lessons from prior experiences."[117] This was corrected through "Blue Flag."

Indeed, Creech continued Dixon's practice of expanding the "flags" at Nellis. He institutionalized "Blue Flag" exercises, where commanders and their staff crafted air-attack plans and simulated target lists, which were provided to the incoming wing for the next Red Flag. Black Flag trained aircraft maintenance crews, while Checkered Flag familiarized nonoperational units with the overall plan and their role in supporting it. Ultimately eighteen exercises emerged from Red Flag, as the focus shifted from the tactical to the operational level of war.

Creech added the "blue forces command element" to Red Flag, where the commander and his staff oversaw all aspects of the air effort, directing each friendly-force fighter. It made no difference if a Navy or an Air Force aircraft accomplished a mission. Air power in any form was air power. As a brigadier general, Chuck Horner had his own turn as a "blue force commander," an experience that would pay off during his command of air operations during the First Gulf War.[118]

Creech saw electronic warfare playing a prominent role in future air operations, so he instituted Green Flag, combining Air Force intelligence, jamming, and electronic warfare platforms to support the air campaign against the Aggressor force IADS. Similar to Red Flag, Green Flag exercises ran six weeks, compelling participants to focus on an extended campaign to defeat or degrade advanced Soviet IADS.[119] By the time

Creech departed TAC in 1984, Red Flag exercises typically included more than 250 aircraft and in some cases exceeded 400. By 1983, annual Aggressor training sorties at Red Flag had increased from roughly 4,300 in 1977 to 13,733, while unit-to-unit DACT training increased over the same time period to 20,612 sorties.[120]

An Enduring Legacy

Through these "Color Flag Exercises," Creech forced the Air Force to raise its eyes from the tactical level of war to the operational level as the best way to wage offensive air campaigns successfully and at an accept-able cost. When he stepped down as TAC's commander, the key elements of the SEAD campaign that dominated the start of major future U.S. air campaigns were in place.[121]

Like Dixon, Creech worked at developing a cadre of future Air Force leaders, men who he felt shared his vision and methods. His im-mediate successors at TAC, Generals Jerome F. O'Malley (1984–85) and Robert D. Russ (1985–91), continued to emphasize the realistic training exercises that Creech had either instituted or enhanced. All of the six Air Force chiefs of staff who served from 1986 through 2002 were either a TAC wing commander or on Creech's staff during the time he headed the Tactical Air Command.[122] The Air Force shift from a bomber-centric service to a fighter-dominated service was complete.

Lifting All Boats: The Air Force and the Reagan Buildup

The inauguration of President Ronald Reagan in January 1981 was fol-lowed by a major U.S. defense buildup lasting into the middle of the de-cade. The influx of resources enabled the Pentagon to avoid some difficult choices on defense priorities, providing funding for programs that, for a variety of reasons, might have been crowded out in an austere fiscal environment. This enabled the Air Force to pursue the B-1 and B-2 bomber and F-15 and F-16 fighter programs. There was room in the budget for capabilities reflecting the visions of men like Bill Perry and Bill Creech, including investments in guided weapons, precision naviga-tion, night operations, and electronic warfare. All would play key roles when the Air Force went to war early in the next decade.

The Reagan buildup saw the Air Force improving its arsenal of precision-guided weapons under the Paveway III series.[123] One, the

GBU-15 (GBU stands for "guided bomb unit"), combined television guidance and an imaging infrared system to produce a glide bomb with significantly greater standoff range than previous LGBs. It entered service in 1983.[124] The weapon could be dropped or lofted from outside the target basket, maneuvering to the target by means of an autopilot, then locating the laser designator spot using its scanning seeker. The GBU-24 and GBU-27 were developed for use with the BLU-109, a 2,000-pound weapon designed to destroy "hard" targets, like underground bunkers.[125]

The Air Force wanted Paveway III weapons released from very low altitudes to conform to the service's "go-low" survivability tactics. This required incorporating an autopilot so the weapon could maneuver itself to a position from where its laser sensor could see laser energy reflected from the target. This accommodation proved difficult and costly, and in 1985, Air Force secretary Vern Orr terminated the program after procuring only a small fraction of the originally planned kits.[126]

When Red Flag began, the Air Force lacked aircraft capable of penetrating enemy defenses and jamming enemy radar systems, a key feature of Creech's rollback concept. During the first Green Flag exercise, 72 percent of the sorties became ineffective when confronting a sophisticated jamming threat. To continue training, the Aggressor force would stop jamming. Creech told the Aggressors to keep jamming: "We always jam in Red Flag, but we stop when it starts to hurt because our purpose is to train. We jam just a few seconds to make sure people know about the jamming. [At Green Flag,] I said, 'You jam, jam, jam, jam, jam unrelentingly. People abort, it does not matter. Jam, jam, jam.' And it has had a profound effect."[127]

When the Navy demonstrated the effectiveness of its EA-6 jammers during Red Flag exercises, the Air Force began to adapt its F-111 medium bomber to a jammer version, the EF-111. The program was made part of the Air Force's Pave Strike initiative, and Creech made the EF-111 the Tactical Air Force's top equipment priority.[128]

The Air Force also began to field an improved version of the Wild Weasel. As part of the Pave Strike program, the F-4Gs were equipped with the APR-38A ECM suite, enabling them to employ multiple jamming techniques against several radars simultaneously, and armed with the AGM-88 High-Speed Anti-Radiation Missile (HARM). The supersonic HARM could be reprogrammed in flight, enabling it to strike unforeseen (or "pop-up") targets. The HARM was also capable of staying on target even after the target's radar stopped emitting.[129]

Creech backed employing C-130 cargo planes as EC-130H "Compass Call" communications-jamming aircraft, declaring, "When it [Compass Call] ... [turns] on all those jammers, he [the enemy] won't be able to talk MiG-to-MiG, MiG-to-ground, ground-to-MiG, and we can even jam some of his [surface-to-air missile] links. ... We sometimes call [the Airborne Warning and Control System] the force multiplier; Compass Call is the world's greatest force subtractor."[130]

Air-to-Air Combat

The Air Force was also looking to exploit advances in sensors to enhance its air-to-air missiles. Success here boosted efforts to shift to beyond-visual-range (BVR) engagements.

The AIM-7F Sparrow air-to-air missile, first deployed in 1976, had more than double the range of the Vietnam-era AIM-7Es. Its solid-state electronics offered greatly enhanced reliability over the vacuum tubes used in earlier versions. The follow-on AIM-7M, which came into service in 1982, improved the missile's range and effectiveness.[131] The 1980s also found the Air Force and Navy upgrading the AIM-9L Sidewinder missile, which was now capable of attacking a target aircraft from any direction, known as an "all-aspect" capability.[132]

When the Cold War ended, both U.S. and Soviet air forces had fighters capable of detecting and targeting enemy aircraft at ranges out to forty nautical miles or greater. Enemy aircraft could be targeted effectively even when flying at low altitudes in ground clutter, a capability known as "look down/shoot down." This greatly expanded the potential for BVR engagements by eliminating the "low-altitude sanctuary" due to the limitations of earlier fighter radars. It also confirmed Creech's view that the Air Force's "go-low" tactics were a losing proposition.[133]

In 1981, Creech pointed out, "This country has a decided technological edge and the technology is mature and workable and reliable enough to give us the capability to fight at night, and it provides certain advantages if we can deliver lethal firepower at night." Shortly after Creech took command at TAC, Red Flag exercises began to incorporate night operations at least twice every year. Chuck Horner recalled Creech's determination to have the Tactical Air Forces become proficient in night operations, noting that aircrews "didn't like night flying (at best an emergency procedure) and were not very good at it. ... He acknowledged we had a long way to go, but he made us start anyway with what little capability we had."[134]

Creech became a big supporter of the LANTIRN (Low-Altitude Navigation and Targeting Infrared for Night), being described by some people as "the lone champion for LANTIRN." As its name suggests, LANTIRN provided an alternative to targeting visually or by radar.[135] The Air Force also fielded Pave Tack, a laser-targeting system for F-4s and F-111s and a modified version for the F-117. Similar to LANTIRN, Pave Tack enabled nighttime target acquisition using IR imaging and automatic target tracking through its laser illuminator. Simply put, Pave Tack and LANTIRN gave Creech what he was seeking: an enhanced ability to fight at night.[136]

A Nascent Battle Network

By the mid-1980s, the Air Force was making significant strides in developing the foundation for a disruptive shift in the character of air warfare. Stealth aircraft offered the promise of penetrating enemy IADS with high confidence (if only at night). Improved radars, sensors, and air-to-air missiles were combining to shift the character of air combat to beyond-visual-range air-to-air engagements, leveraging the U.S. IT advantage over the Soviets. Advances in electronic warfare were increasing the odds of strike aircraft reaching their targets, and once there, advanced guided munitions were boosting the changes of engaging the target successfully.

Creech's vision also called for conducting operations over a wide area, both day and night, involving the integration and coordination of these systems and capabilities. This required enhancements in navigation and force integration through what became known as a "battle network."

Arguably the first integrated battle network was fielded by Great Britain in the late 1930s. It featured a system of early warning Chain Home radar transmitters and receivers linked to a central command center— Fighter Command—in London. The Royal Air Force utilized the network in defending Britain against Germany's Luftwaffe during the Battle of Britain in the summer and autumn of 1940. Thanks to its battle network, Fighter Command was able to launch its interceptor aircraft only when a Luftwaffe raid was approaching Britain, while also dispatching them to the proper intercept point.

The emergence of a battle network was also enabled by enhanced navigation. The 1950s and 1960s saw improvements in inertial guidance, improving ballistic missiles' accuracy; still, their CEPs were measured in kilometers. By the 1970s, IT-enabled advances in autonomous terrain contour matching significantly boosted cruise missiles' accuracy.[137] The greatest advance, however, came with the fielding of Navstar—more popularly known as the Global Positioning System, or simply GPS.[138]

GPS was decades in the making. In the early 1970s, the Air Force and Navy were pursuing their own navigation programs. The Navy, seeking improved submarine-launched ballistic missile accuracy, was working on its Timation satellite research program. In April 1973, it was combined with a similar Air Force project, 621B, into the Navstar Global Positioning System. Its objective was to develop a comprehensive, all-weather system capable of providing three-dimensional position, velocity, and timing accuracy.[139] The United States completed deploying the twenty-four-satellite GPS in 1993—the first navigational system offering worldwide precision. Although unforeseen at the time, GPS emerged as a key factor in enabling the disruptive shift in air warfare revealed in the First Gulf War.[140]

The same year the Navstar program was formed, the Air Force began full-scale development of the E-3 Airborne Warning and Control System (AWACS), with the first aircraft entering the Air Force four years later. The AWACS's look-down radar provided a 360-degree view of its operating area, making it capable of detecting and tracking aircraft, both friendly and hostile, operating at low altitudes—including those flying in ground clutter. Operating as part of a battle network, the AWACS shares its information with others in the network, while directing fighter-interceptors to engage enemy aircraft, thereby becoming a "third wingman" for fighter pilots.[141]

Having fielded AWACS, the Air Force began to work on the E-8 Joint Surveillance Target Attack Radar System (JSTARS). The JSTARS offered members of the emerging battle network accurate real-time location and targeting information on moving enemy ground-combat vehicular traffic. To "thicken" the network, the TR-1 reconnaissance aircraft (an upgraded U-2) was introduced to provide a deep battlefield surveillance and data-link capability.[142]

Friend or Foe?

The Air Force's efforts to use early IR and radar-homing missiles to fight beyond visual range were hampered by the challenge of distinguishing between friendly and enemy aircraft. Aircraft electronic identification, friend or foe (IFF) equipment was first employed on aircraft in World War II and was standard on nearly every combat aircraft during the Vietnam War. The IFF equipment, however, suffered from a high failure rate.[143] This understandably made Air Force and Navy aircrews reluctant to engage beyond visual range. Concerns ran so high that some commanders required pilots to have visual identification of the target aircraft before it could be engaged. Consequently, there were only two confirmed BVR kills by U.S. aircrews during Vietnam War. Solving the IFF problem became essential to exploiting the ability to engage the enemy at extended ranges.

Once again, the Israelis provided help. In the 1967 Middle East war, the Israelis recovered Soviet SRO-2 IFF transponders from downed MiGs. They shared the equipment with the Air Force, which began a covert program code-named Combat Tree, which involved building a U.S. SRO-2 interrogator system (the AN/APX-81). By 1971, the system was being mounted on Air Force fighters, enabling them to trigger a MiG's IFF response or to receive a MiG's replies to interrogations by its own ground-controlled intercept radars. Aircraft equipped with the Combat Tree system could identify enemy aircraft at ranges up to sixty nautical miles, or three times the distance that an F-4 could detect (but not positively identify) planes with its radar.[144]

The Air Force also developed the AN/ASX-1 Target Identification System Electro-Optical (TISEO), which combined a stabilized telescope with an attached TV camera that displayed images on the U.S. fighter's radarscope. Deployed on the F-4E, the TISEO enabled aircrews to identify large aircraft fifty to eighty nautical miles distant and fighter-size aircraft at distances of ten nautical miles or more. Still, long-standing pilot fears associated with "friendly fire" remained.[145] But as advances in IFF systems continued and as more effective command-and-control systems entered the force, pilots gradually gained the confidence necessary to exploit the Air Force's enhanced scouting capabilities. It soon produced a dramatic shift in the character of air-to-air combat.

Air War in the Middle East

Mole Cricket 19

On June 9, 1982, the largest single air battle since World War II occurred over the Bekaa Valley along Lebanon's central plain. The combatants were the IAF and Syria's air force and ground-based IADS. Code-named Mole Cricket 19 by the Israelis, the operation saw the IAF employing a mix of aircraft to suppress the Syrian defenses—in effect, a mini-SEAD campaign along the lines of what Creech had been advocating.

The Syrian force included nineteen SA-6 sites (the "19" in "Mole Cricket 19"), along with some SA-2 and SA-3 sites, supported by MiG-21 and MiG-23 interceptors. Against this threat, the IAF employed a squadron of Mastiff and Scout remotely piloted vehicles (RPVs, or drones). The Mastiffs acted as bait, simulating an attack by IAF fighters to get the Syrian SAMs to turn on their radars. As the SAMs fired at the RPVs, IAF fighters launched anti-radiation missiles at the sites, decimating the Syrian air defenses. In roughly ten minutes, seventeen of the nineteen SA-6 SAM sites and several SA-2 and SA-3 sites were destroyed. The remaining sites were taken out the following day. Some fifty-seven SA-6s were fired. All missed.

Scout and Mastiff RPVs also provided real-time video surveillance of Syrian fighters taxiing on their runways prior to takeoff. The information was relayed to several Israeli E-2C surveillance aircraft, as well as a Boeing 707 electronic intelligence aircraft and numerous ground and airborne jammers. The E-2Cs picked up the Syrian fighters on radar as they became airborne and relayed intercept information to IAF fighters. The Israelis began jamming the Syrian MiGs, disrupting communications with their ground-controlled intercept stations. The IAF's integrated operation, combined with the superior situation awareness of its experienced pilots, resulted in eighty-five Syrian aircraft being destroyed in the air without a single Israeli loss.[146]

Despite the IAF's impressive performance, both the IDF and many defense analysts argued that the Bekaa Valley engagements were in many ways unique. For example, the Syrian SA-6s were located in fixed positions that were well known in advance by Israeli intelligence. The operation was also extremely limited in duration, offering little opportunity for the two sides to undertake efforts aimed at offsetting the other's tactics. Nevertheless, one of the United States' foremost experts on modern air warfare concluded, "Dramatic proof of what the new technology could accomplish if skillfully wielded was offered by the crisply executed Israeli air operation."[147]

Lebanon

On December 4, 1983, eighteen months after the Israeli strikes in the Bekaa Valley, U.S. warplanes attacked Syrian anti-aircraft sites in Lebanon.

The strikes, launched from Navy carriers in the Eastern Mediterranean, were in retaliation for Syrian anti-aircraft fire against a U.S. reconnaissance aircraft supporting the U.S. Marine Corps peacekeeping force in Lebanon.

The attack, marked by confused planning and poor execution, was a debacle. One of the carriers involved, *Kennedy*, was about to depart for the Suez Canal and had already stowed its bombs when the strike order was received. Despite *Kennedy's* low operational state, and over the task force commander's objections, the time set for the attack was moved up from 11:00 a.m. to 6:30 a.m. This meant that the pilots would be attacking into the sun. Moreover, the other carrier involved, *Independence*, had loaded its strike aircraft with the wrong bombs, which had to be swapped out.

Consequently, not all aircraft could be rearmed in time for the strike. The Navy succeeded in launching twenty-eight aircraft, with stragglers attempting to catch up with those already flying to the target. Following tactics that were abandoned as ineffective during the Vietnam War, the Navy saw two of its planes shot down, while only a few Syrian sites were hit.[148] Although the strikes were a Navy operation, the poor showing could not help but raise concerns over U.S. air power in general. Fortunately, both the Air Force and the Navy took the lessons from the failed raid to heart, along with those from Mole Cricket 19.

El Dorado Canyon

In April 1986, Air Force and Navy aircraft conducted strikes against Libya in an operation code-named El Dorado Canyon. The operation followed an attack by Libyan agents against a nightclub in West Berlin that resulted in a U.S. serviceman's death.

Drawing on lessons learned from the Israeli operations in the Bekaa Valley four years before and from training at Red Flag, plans called for conducting the operation at night and employing guided weapons. The joint strike package was divided into two groups; one would hit targets around Tripoli, the other those around Benghazi. The Air Force employed eighteen F-111Fs based at Lakenheath, England, while the Navy provided aircraft specialized for SEAD to strike the Tripoli defenses. (The Navy had full responsibility for the Benghazi part of the operation.) Both packages included jamming electronic intelligence and surveillance aircraft, along with fighter escorts.[149]

Although the ground-based air defenses around Tripoli and Benghazi "were as dense and overlaid as anything that the Soviet forces maintained in Eastern Europe," only one U.S. aircraft, an F-111, was lost. Libyan air defense operators turning on their radars found themselves targeted by HARMs fired from Navy F-18s and A-7s. The strikes themselves, employing LGBs and radar-guided bombs, were highly effective.[150] Although small in scale and limited to a single day, El Dorado Canyon, like Mole Cricket 19, revealed important concepts and capabilities that would, five years hence, introduce the age of precision warfare.

Barriers to Change (II)

Attempts at disruptive innovation typically trigger significant opposition, often from the organization that is its prospective beneficiary. This was true of the Air Force. As with the service leadership's lukewarm reception to stealth, the efforts of men like Moody Suter, Bob Dixon, and Bill Creech were received skeptically by some people in the Air Force and opposed entirely by others. There was also resistance from without, however, most formidably by the Defense Reform Movement (DRM).

The movement began in the 1970s. James Fallows, Washington editor of the *Atlantic Monthly*, met John Boyd, a former Air Force pilot and defense consultant advocating, among other things, buying large numbers of low-tech systems as opposed to the high-tech aircraft and systems being pursued by the Air Force. Boyd introduced Fallows to fellow critic Pierre Sprey, along with Chuck Spinney, a former Air Force officer working as a civilian analyst in the Office of the Secretary of Defense. William Lind, who served as a staffer for Senator Robert Taft (R-Ohio) and, later, Senator Gary Hart (D-Colorado), was also a core member of the movement.

In articles and presentations, the group depicted the Air Force leadership as fools, knaves, or both. The image that Fallows painted of DRM members was one of courageous patriots exposing the unholy cabal of military brass and defense contractors who persisted in buying expensive, high-tech weapons rather than large numbers of inexpensive, easy to maintain, reliable weapons that would eliminate the Soviet quantitative advantage. This, they argued, would yield a more effective military while also saving money at the same time.

The group's influence grew along with the Reagan defense buildup. In 1981, Congress established the Military Reform Caucus, made up of more than ninety senators and representatives, split roughly equally along party lines.[151] The caucus attracted men like Senators William Cohen (R-Maine) and Sam Nunn (D-Georgia), along with Congressmen Newt Gingrich (R-Georgia), Dick Cheney (R-Wyoming), and Thomas Downey (D-New York).

The DRM's views placed the group at odds with the vision espoused by General Creech and like-minded Air Force officers. In reviewing the fiscal year 1984 defense budget, Senator Gary Hart advocated canceling production of the F-15 fighter and using the funds to procure greater numbers of less-sophisticated F-16s. Hart also called for dropping a Creech priority, the Advanced Medium-Range Air-to-Air Missile (AM-RAAM). Arguing that deep interdiction operations were ineffective, the senator recommended eliminating all weapons with a "deep combat" orientation. Finally, asserting that night-combat operations, as well as those in poor weather, were conceptually flawed, Hart advocated canceling two other Creech favorites, LANTIRN and the Maverick missile. Hart and Lind summarized these ideas in *America Can Win: The Case for Military Reform*.[152] They were joined by another reform group member, Steven Canby, who claimed that the Air Force was relying excessively on SEAD operations and precision munitions. He argued that the medium-altitude "window" for air strikes that Creech was seeking to open would remain closed. In *Atlantic Monthly* articles and the book *National Defense*, Fallows continued to push the group's agenda.[153]

In this war of ideas, the Air Force found a strong ally in the IAF and its commander, General David Ivry. With Creech's encouragement, Ivry went out of his way to tell visiting congressmen and other influential Americans how critical U.S. high-technology capabilities were to the IAF's success. He was particularly critical of the reformers' criticism of long-range aircraft. Sprey, for example, had asserted, "There's no faster way to kill the performance of a fighter than to ask for too much range." But the IAF needed range for deep-strike operations and "persistence"— the ability to extend operations at shorter ranges. During IDF exercises, F-15s would engage Mirage and F-4 fighters. When the F-15's "rivals" ran out of fuel, another group replaced them, while, thanks to their extra fuel capacity, the F-15s stayed aloft to engage the second group. On June 7, 1981, eight IAF F-16s and six F-15 escorts flew a 1,300-mile round-trip mission—a mission that would not have been possible with the DRM's short-range air force—and destroyed Iraq's nuclear reactor at Osirak near Baghdad. The IAF's operations in the Bekaa Valley a year later relied even more for their success on the kinds of high-tech capabilities that many DRM members discounted.[154]

To the reformers' great frustration, the Air Force was able to deflect most of their ideas. Yet the service's leaders often demonstrated a reluctance to consider how they might introduce new concepts and novel capabilities to boost air power's effectiveness. Creech recalled, "In attending quarterly four-star executive sessions at 'Corona Conferences' over a span of six-and-a-half years, I cannot recall a single instance where the chief of staff and the assembled four-stars, addressing a huge range of issues, ever once talked about doctrine."[155]

The same might be said of the Air Force's thinking on guided weapons. Despite the verdict of RAND analysts that LGB performance was "spectacularly good" in the 1972 Linebacker campaigns, and although major improvements in guided weapons had been achieved since the war, the Air Force went to war in January 1991 with only a small fraction of its force capable of employing them. When war did come, the Air Force was the fortunate beneficiary of efforts by officers like Dixon, Creech, and Suter. It also owed much to forward-thinking civilians like Harold Brown and William Perry, who saw the enormous potential that emerging technologies—and the IT revolution in particular—had to transform air warfare. Still others believed that new capabilities, when employed with existing capabilities in new ways, could enable dramatically different kinds of operations that would revolutionize air warfare. Among those in this latter group were Lieutenant General Chuck Horner, Colonel John Warden III, and Lieutenant Colonel David Deptula.

The First Gulf War

At midnight on August 2, 1990, Iraqi forces invaded Kuwait, quickly overwhelming its defenders. By midday, nearly all resistance had ended. President George H. W. Bush called on Iraq's leader, Saddam Hussein, to withdraw his forces. When Hussein refused, the United States began to assemble a military coalition and deploy forces to the Middle East to evict the Iraqis.

General Norman Schwarzkopf, commanding the U.S. Central Command, was in charge of overall U.S. operations for what became Operation Desert Storm (the First Gulf War). Schwarzkopf's senior airman, "Chuck" Horner, had responsibility for the air campaign but initially had little in the way of forces. Schwarzkopf and the Joint Chiefs of Staff chairman, General Colin Powell, agreed that air-campaign plans should be developed in case the Iraqis mounted an offensive into Saudi Arabia before U.S. ground forces could arrive in strength. On August 8, Schwarzkopf reached out to the Air Force for support in developing the campaign. The task ultimately went to Colonel John A. Warden III, who headed an Air Staff directorate, "Warfighting Concepts," more popularly known as "Checkmate."

Instant Thunder

Warden was one of the Air Force's leading thinkers. In his book *The Air Campaign: Planning for Combat,* Warden presented a model for air operations consisting of five concentric rings describing the enemy state as a system, with its leadership at the core.[156] He argued that by conducting air strikes against properly selected targets, air power could cripple, relatively quickly, an enemy's capacity to make war, by decapitating its leadership, fracturing its ability to control its population, reducing its ability to wage war, or some combination thereof. Drawing on his five-ring model, Warden and his team developed a plan they named Instant Thunder. It called for prosecuting an aggressive air campaign primarily against the Iraqi leadership. Warden believed that his plan, properly executed, could produce a victory in a week or so.[157]

To some people, however, Warden's concept appeared little more than a sophisticated version of arguments dating back to Giulio Douhet and Billy Mitchell on air power's ability to defeat an enemy quickly by destroying or neutralizing its center(s) of gravity. When the concept was briefed to General Powell, he declared, "I can't recommend only the strategic air campaign to the president." Nevertheless, Warden and one of the Air Force's brightest young thinkers, Lieutenant Colonel David A. Deptula, found themselves on a plane to Saudi Arabia to brief Horner.[158]

Horner, for his part, believed that "the best thing to do was to fight a ground war of maneuver and use airpower to cut the [Iraqi Army's] sustainment since [the Iraqis] were vulnerable there." As the general put it, he intended to "build a hose and point it where the ground commander sees that it's needed."[159]

Warden briefed Instant Thunder to Horner on August 20. Again, Warden asserted that the war could be won with air power in six to nine days. As with Powell, Warden immediately ran into resistance from

Horner.[160] The next day, Warden found himself on a plane back to Washington, excluded from further work on the air campaign.

Horner, however, found some of Warden's ideas attractive. During the briefing, Horner suggested that he was thinking holistically about the coming air campaign, telling Warden, "Let's not use the terms *strategic* and *tactical*. Targets are targets." And even though he rejected Instant Thunder, Horner found value in the targeting information embedded in it. Most importantly, Horner asked several of Warden's assistants to remain and assist in the planning effort. All but one—Deptula—would soon depart. The young lieutenant colonel (and later lieutenant general) emerged as one of Horner's key planners in Central Command Air Forces' Special Planning Group, whose location became popularly known as the "Black Hole."[161] The next few months saw the Black Hole planners developing an air-campaign plan unlike any before it, drawing primarily on the technological, training, and organizational innovations that had emerged over the previous two decades, as well as the operational concepts that appeared in nascent form during General Creech's tenure at TAC.

Iraq's IADS

Iraq's air defenses were formidable, even when compared to those the Air Force had encountered over Vietnam. The Iraqi IADS included four air defense sectors providing the country with overlapping SAM and anti-aircraft artillery coverage. The Iraqi Air Force, among the world's largest, boasted late-generation French and Soviet fighters, including three squadrons of advanced MiG-29 fighters. Each air defense sector had an operations center linked to subordinate operations centers, along with a network of more than 100 acquisition and tracking radars. The IADS hub was in Baghdad, which, after Moscow, had the world's highest concentration of air defenses.[162]

On paper, the balance of forces between the U.S.-led coalition and Iraq was heavily in favor of the former. Still, the balance had also been in the United States' favor in the Vietnam War and in brief operations like the 1983 strike in Lebanon. And even though Israel prevailed in the Yom Kippur War, it paid a fearful price. Saddam Hussein appeared to be betting that, like the North Vietnamese, if he could inflict heavy casualties on the coalition and drag the war on for months, he could ultimately prevail.

A Black Hole Breakthrough

There were some people at TAC who thought that they should plan the air campaign, and so they developed one. Their plan recalled Rolling Thunder, emphasizing various levels of escalation—the opposite of Instant Thunder. Perhaps with an eye toward Horner's concern over the lack of U.S. ground forces in the Middle East, the plan prioritized destroying Saddam's forces in Kuwait. This was consistent with the Air-Land Battle concept that the Air Force and Army had developed for a war in Europe, calling for air operations to focus primarily on defeating Warsaw Pact ground forces. TAC's plan also seemed to discount the potential of stealth aircraft and PGMs, defaulting to the Vietnam-era approach of massing numerous supporting aircraft to support strike aircraft attempting to penetrate enemy IADS to attack discrete targets.[163]

Fortunately, forward-thinking airmen gave Air Force leaders an alternative: waging a new kind of broad-based campaign with SEAD as its initial objective. In fact, the air campaign plan crafted in the Black Hole was not the product of Air Force doctrine. Rather, it was designed to combine stealth, guided weapons, and other advanced capabilities within the context of the Red Flag high-fidelity training to create a new and devastatingly effective form of air operations.[164]

Prior to the First Gulf War, few Air Force planners envisioned a single aircraft taking out multiple targets in a single sortie or a strike aircraft operating alone, without clusters of escort aircraft, against advanced air defenses. Sitting in the Black Hole, however, Deptula focused his planning around the handful of stealth F-117s at his disposal, each armed with two guided weapons, designating them as the air campaign's spearhead. Combining stealth and precision would enable the Air Force to accelerate the SEAD campaign, compressing Creech's "roll-back" concept to something approaching Warden's "instant" success timeline. Once the SEAD phase of the air campaign was accomplished, the skies over Iraq would be clear for all coalition air forces to conduct the full range of air-warfare missions nearly simultaneously. The plan also incorporated advances in command and control, navigation, and unmanned systems. Horner thus received an alternative to the Air Force's "go-low, smart-jet, dumb-bomb" single-strike package mind-set for employing air power.[165]

To Horner's credit, he adopted it.

In its final form, the air campaign was made up of four distinct phases. Phase I, lasting roughly seven days, emphasized Creech's SEAD campaign concept, focusing on Iraq's IADS. Phase II, planned to last three days, had air forces concentrating on suppressing Iraqi air defenses in the Kuwait Theater of Operations. Phase III, anticipated to last roughly a month, gave priority to inflicting attrition on the Iraqi army and isolating it from its sources of support. This would pave the way for the coalition ground offensive. Phase IV envisioned coalition air forces performing a range of missions during the coalition's ground-force offensive.

Desert Storm

The air campaign began the night of January 17, 1991, with the daunting objective of neutralizing Iraq's IADS within twenty-four hours. Led by a combination of Air Force reconnaissance systems, precision munitions, and stealthy F-117s, the mission was accomplished in the war's first eight hours.

The stealth F-117s, each armed with two PGMs, were assigned to strike high-value targets in and around Baghdad, including critical Iraqi communications and air defense nodes. The air campaign's initial hours also included a key deception operation code-named Scathe Mean. Shortly after the F-117A's guided-weapon attacks on Baghdad, a wave of long-range, radio-controlled, aerial drones and air-launched decoys arrived over the city. The drones simulated the electronic radar signatures of various coalition aircraft, inducing Iraqi air defense units to activate their radars, thereby revealing their position, whereupon they were promptly attacked with HARMS launched from F-4G Wild Weasels.[166] Operations were coordinated by the U.S. military's nascent battle network, including GPS, as well as AWACS and JSTARS aircraft. After the first night, Iraqi air defense sectors were forced into autonomous operations. Hardened SAM and interceptor operations centers were neutralized within four days.[167]

With the SEAD mission accomplished, coalition aircraft were able to operate effectively at acceptable risk at medium and high altitudes. The Air Force then began to employ a wide range of aircraft to suppress any remaining Iraqi early warning and ground-controlled intercept radar sites, command-and-control nodes, SAM sites, and air bases. Thanks to superior training, tactics, and equipment, Air Force losses were substantially lower than those suffered by allied air forces that persisted in "go-low" tactics. The Royal Air Force quickly lost 10 percent of its seventy Tornadoes supporting the coalition. The French Air Force, also "going low," saw two separate flights suffer serious damage early on. In forty-three days of intense day and night combat, the Air Force lost thirteen fighters, by far the lowest loss rate of any coalition air force. The Royal Air Force's Tornado had a loss rate of roughly ten per 1,000 sorties, eleven times that of the F-15E, which flew similar missions.[168]

General Horner's air operations center created a daily air tasking order, including every coalition aircraft flying over the area of operations. This enabled Horner to exercise overall control—unity of command—over the air campaign, a critical factor given its scale and scope.[169] Horner also benefited from the technological advances made in the two decades since Vietnam. Space-based systems provided accurate and timely weather forecasts. GPS satellites proved indispensable as navigational aids in guiding many coalition aircraft to their targets. This support was especially key at night and during the first week of the campaign, when air operations were hampered by poor weather over much of Iraq and Kuwait.[170]

Elsewhere on the air campaign's first night, thirteen B-52s, navigating with their forward-looking infrared sensors and GPS, flew at altitudes less than 400 feet to attack five Iraqi forward-operating airfields. According to a B-52G radar navigator, "[The GPS's] super-accurate navigation data kept our systems reliable as we crossed Iraq with our radars off, and the final radar aiming on our bomb runs needed little or no adjustment by the bombardier."[171]

The Air Force's U-2R/TR-1 reconnaissance aircraft relied on its GPS-assisted radar to locate targets and transmit their precise coordinates to an AWACS orbiting over Saudi airspace. The AWACS forwarded this near-real-time intelligence information to B-52s via coded messages, enabling the bombers to fly directly to their targets. More broadly speaking, GPS also allowed coalition air forces to update their inertial navigation systems, thereby improving the accuracy of their attacks with unguided weapons by an order of magnitude against fixed targets.[172] The AWACS proved capable of detecting enemy aircraft flying at low altitudes at distances more than 200 nautical miles and identifying Iraqi aircraft during their takeoff runs, enabling them to be tagged as hostile and the information provided to coalition pilots. The U.S. network of airborne sensors, weapons, and command, control, and communications links gave coalition aircrews an enormous advantage in situation awareness, alleviating much of the resistance pilots had exhibited in earlier conflicts with respect to BVR engagements.[173] The improvements in navigation, including the use of LANTIRN, combined with enhanced command and control, enabled the Air Force to operate effectively at night. Indeed, the F-117 operated *solely* at night.[174]

This nascent U.S. battle network provided coalition commanders with inter- and intratheater communications links, secure data transmission, weather information, ballistic missile early warning, surveillance and reconnaissance imagery, and signals intelligence. Looking back on the role that GPS and satellite-based communications played in coalition operations, Air Force chief of staff General Merrill A. McPeak declared it "the first space war."[175]

The Payoff

Coalition air forces rapidly eliminated Iraq's air force as a significant threat. Thirty-three Iraqi fixed-wing aircraft were downed during the war, at a loss of a single Navy F/A-18. This 16.5-to-1 exchange represented an enormous improvement over the roughly 2-to-1 rate achieved in the Vietnam War. Although many combat-experienced Iraqi pilots were flying modern Soviet fighters, they proved no match for Air Force aircrews drawing on their training at Red Flag. Every coalition air-combat victory was achieved with advanced IR-guided Sidewinder and radar-guided Sparrow missiles. The Sparrows employed by Air Force aircrews were more than six times more reliable in 1991 than they had been during the Rolling Thunder campaign and roughly five times more reliable than those used during Linebacker I and II. Overall, air-to-air missiles in the First Gulf War were approximately three times more likely to achieve a kill than those employed during the Vietnam War.[176]

During the war's first three days, Iraqi pilots employed tactics that would have been recognized by North Vietnamese pilots two decades before. In 82 percent of coalition air engagements against Iraqi fixed-wing aircraft, AWACS provided target information and identification well before U.S. fighters had even detected enemy aircraft.[177] The Air Force's superior target identification and enhanced air-to-air missiles enabled U.S. aircrews to attack Iraqi aircraft beyond visual range and gave them the confidence to do so. During the war, sixteen of thirty-three engagements, or 48 percent, between fixed-wing aircraft occurred BVR. The war revealed that an aircrew's SA was no longer primarily limited to what they could physically see but rather what they received from information provided by other sources, such as the AWACS.[178]

The Air Force's performance in BVR air-to-air combat discredited yet another Defense Reform Movement pillar: its emphasis on close-in, high-maneuver engagements. In the First Gulf War, no Air Force aircraft were downed in air-to-air engagements. Air Force crews shot down 37 Iraqi aircraft. Only three engagements involved any maneuvering. More than 250 enemy aircraft were destroyed on the ground, including those in shelters, by the hard-target penetrating guided weapons developed during the 1980s, which DRM members generally opposed. With their hardened shelters no longer affording protection, 148 Iraqi pilots took their aircraft to Iran. Thus, ground attack—not air combat and especially not maneuvering air combat—posed the greatest danger to Iraq's air force. The trend away from the maneuvering dogfight has continued since the First Gulf War.[179]

Stealth and Precision

As then–major general David Deptula, one of the key figures in planning the Desert Storm air campaign, concluded, "Prior to 1991, two separate, leap-ahead military technologies had matured enough to offer an order-of-magnitude breakthrough. The first was low-observable (i.e., stealth) technology, and the second was the development of precision-guided munitions."[180]

The F-117 stealth aircraft carrying two LGBs was a—and arguably *the*—crucial factor in the astounding success achieved in the SEAD campaign. The F-117s attacked the most heavily defended targets in Iraq, against more advanced versions of the Soviet-built IADS that were so effective in the Vietnam and Yom Kippur Wars. Although F-117s flew only 2 percent of the sorties during the air campaign, they struck approximately 40 percent of the strategic targets, achieving a success rate of roughly 80 percent.[181] According to Lieutenant General Horner's director of campaign plans, Brigadier General Buster C. Glosson, "One need only look back to our raids on Schweinfurt, Germany, in World War II to see how dramatically precision weapons have enhanced our capabilities over the last 50 years. Two raids of 300 B-17 bombers could not achieve with 3,000 bombs what two F-117s can do with only four."[182]

As Glosson noted, the F-117s were clearly a terrific "force multiplier." Their stealth and ability to employ guided weapons eliminated the need to generate the large strike-force packages that characterized earlier wars. During Operation Desert Storm, a typical nonstealth strike package employed thirty-eight Air Force, Navy, Marine, and Saudi air-craft, with only eight (21 percent) being strike aircraft: roughly the same ratio of strike to support aircraft employed during the final stages of the Vietnam War.[183] During the First Gulf War, the U.S. military—primarily the Air Force—dropped more than 9,500 LGBs—more than double the number released over North Vietnam from 1968 to 1972.[184] Some 17,000 guided weapons of all types were employed in the First Gulf War, but they constituted only 8 percent of the total bombs expended. Yet they produced more than 75 percent of the serious damage inflicted on Iraqi targets.[185] A 1993 Defense Science Board study concluded that air operation's effectiveness had increased by an order of magnitude in the First Gulf War, noting that "for many target types, a ton of PGMs typi-cally replaced 12–20 tons of unguided munitions on a tonnage per target kill basis as well as saving as much as 35–40 tons of fuel per ton of PGMs delivered."[186]

As for the weapons themselves, some—the Paveway LGBs, Walleye, Maverick, Hellfire, and Shrike—had their roots in the Vietnam War and its immediate aftermath. By far the majority of guided weapons em-ployed in Operation Desert Storm were LGBs and Mavericks. Never-theless, the improvements in guided weapons were significant. For exam-ple, during the Vietnam War, Paveway I LGBs enabled the Air Force to take down bridges that had withstood repeated attacks. In Operation Desert Storm, Paveway II and III munitions with BLU-109/B "penetra-tor" warheads breached hardened aircraft shelters that were purportedly invulnerable to conventional bombing. And the 500-pound GBU-12 guided weapon with the Mark-82 warhead took out individual Iraqi tanks, even when they were sheltered in sand revetments.[187]

Although consigned to the outer ring in Warden's Instant Thunder concept, air attacks devastated Iraq's army. For example, prior to the be-ginning of the ground offensive, on the night of February 9, 40 F-111Fs armed with guided weapons destroyed more than 100 Iraqi armored ve-hicles. Four days later, during the night of February 13–14, 46 F-111Fs dropped 184 GBU-12 LGBs, destroying another 132 armored fighting vehicles, a 72 percent kill rate. Overall, during the war, Air Force F-111Fs destroyed 920 Iraqi armored fighting vehicles, out of an estimated total of 6,100, making them a leader in the "tank plinking" air campaign preceding the coalition's ground offensive.[188]

The success of the F-111s and F-15s put to rest still another Defense Reform Movement assertion: that the advanced aircraft favored by the

Air Force were too sophisticated and expensive to perform reliably in combat. At the onset of the air campaign, the F-15s and F-111Fs had 95.8 percent and 98.4 percent fully mission-capable rates, respectively. After some six weeks of combat, the rates had fallen to 93.8 percent and 93.9 percent, respectively, hardly a precipitous decline.[189]

The air campaign also witnessed a dramatic improvement in interdiction operations. In the Vietnam War, prior to the introduction of LGBs, it often took hundreds of sorties to destroy a bridge. In Operation Desert Storm, guided weapons destroyed forty-one of fifty-four key Iraqi bridges and thirty-one pontoon bridges in approximately four weeks. Postwar analysis revealed that Iraq's ability to move supplies from Baghdad to the Kuwaiti theater of operations dropped by more than 90 percent, from a potential capacity of 216,000 metric tons per day prior to the war to roughly 20,000 tons. The Air Force's successful interdiction campaign discredited Defense Reform Movement arguments, like those of Senator Hart, that all weapons with a "deep combat" focus, such as those employed in deep interdiction operations, should be canceled.[190]

The Big Picture

The air campaign in Operation Desert Storm reflected a disruptive shift in air warfare's character. Admittedly, Colonel Warden's vision of a short, decisive campaign lasting less than ten days proved an illusion. There was little evidence to support Warden's contention that the air campaign's infrastructure attacks against Baghdad and other targets north of the Euphrates River by themselves would produce a coalition victory.[191]

The de facto Air Force doctrine that emerged in the First Gulf War had several fathers, none more important than General Creech. The air war was waged as a campaign. Creech's vision of a SEAD campaign combined with medium- and high-altitude operations was realized, the product of forward-thinking airmen like Horner, Warden, and Deptula. Thanks to the SEAD campaign, which fractured Iraq's IADS, coalition aircraft could minimize operating at low altitudes, rendering Iraqi AAA relatively ineffective.[192]

Creech's emphasis on night operations also paid enormous dividends, as the air campaign's key initial strikes and many thereafter were conducted under cover of darkness. Indeed, after the First Gulf War, airmen began to refer to "the first night" rather than "the first day" of an air operation.[193] Looking back, General Horner declared,

It's hard to sum up . . . our success in a single sentence, but one of our commanders came as close as anyone could. A few days after the war was over, I was visiting one of our bases. The wing commander and I were visiting with the people who had performed so brilliantly, basking in the glow of our success, and reminiscing about the events that had contributed to it. As we talked more and more about how it had all been put together the wing commander turned to me and put it in these words: *"You know, General Horner, after all that General Creech did for us, we couldn't miss."*[194]

Major General John Corder, who had served as Central Command's deputy director of air operations during the war and who had administered the infamous written test to TAC crews in 1972 that led to the Air Force creating its Aggressor squadron at Nellis, called General Dixon when he returned home. Corder told Dixon that the Air Force's success in the war was the result of what Dixon had done in instituting Red Flag during his time as commander of TAC. Corder recalled that at the call's conclusion, the crusty Dixon was on the verge of tears.[195]

Air operations in the First Gulf War were closely studied by the U.S. military's Cold War rivals in Soviet Russia. The U.S. air campaign confirmed the vision of Soviet military theorists, including Marshal Ogarkov, that a "revolution in military affairs" was under way, with the reconnaissance-strike complex at its core. They concluded that "a new line in non-nuclear means of armed struggle had been developed," one based on the "intellectualization" of weapons.[196] In an assessment of U.S. air operations, the Soviet Air Force chief declared, "It should be noted that the conception of unification of automated control systems, communications, monitoring, reconnaissance, and electronic combat assets of varied nationality into a single whole and access to a global operational control system was fully realized in practice." Another Russian military theorist concluded that, regarding air operations, "the scale of its employment rose to the operational-strategic level. This indubitably is an important innovation."[197]

The Russian military theorists might also have noted that the air campaign in Operation Desert Storm reflected, in some sense, an incomplete air-power revolution. Although most of the elements of "reconnaissance-strike complexes"—guided-weapons battle networks—were on display, they were not sufficiently integrated to enable the Air Force to identify fleeting, or "time-sensitive," targets and strike them effectively. Over the next two decades, the U.S. military, and the U.S. Air Force in particular, would make significant progress in meeting this challenge, albeit in "benign" or relatively "uncontested" air environments.

The LGBs employed in the First Gulf War were limited to employment in clear weather, while other guided weapons relied on IR signatures or radar emissions to identify a target. By the end of the 1990s, new guided weapons were fielded, notably the Joint Direct Attack Munition (JDAM) and the Joint Standoff Weapon (JSOW). As "seekerless" guided weapons, the JDAM ("Jay-dam") and JSOW ("Jay-sow") use GPS for inertial guidance and to provide the target's coordinates. These guided weapons cost less than similar guided weapons and, unlike LGBs, can be employed through clouds, smoke, or other forms of obscuration and at night. They do not require target designation (as with a laser), so, once they are dropped, aircrews can move on to other missions or employ additional weapons. Both JDAMs and JSOWs are also capable of receiving GPS updates after launch. In brief, they give aircrews an all-weather "launch-and-leave" capability.[198]

New air-to-air guided weapons were fielded, enhancing the Air Force's effectiveness in air-to-air combat. The AMRAAM gave aircrews a major boost in performance over the Sparrow. Both had roughly the same range, but unlike the Sparrow, the AMRAAM is a "fire-and-forget" weapon, enabling its aircrew to engage in evasive maneuvers or to move on to perform additional tasks. The AMRAAM also weighs far less than the Sparrow while having a higher speed, giving the enemy less time to react and engage in defensive maneuvers.[199]

Significant advances in what have come to be known as "battle networks" occurred following the First Gulf War. Experience in the war suggested that compressing the engagement cycle or "kill chain" would become increasingly important, especially against time-sensitive targets, such as a mobile missile launcher fleeing the site of a launch.[200] During Operation Desert Storm, it typically took about seventy-two hours to compile the air tasking order that determined the targets that would be attacked. The process of identifying targets, executing attacks against them, and assessing the attacks' success typically spanned several days.

Eight years later, during the Air Force's participation in Operation Allied Force against Serbian forces in Yugoslavia, progress had clearly been made. The average "sensor-to-shooter" cycle was reduced from the three days it took to create the air tasking order to about three to four hours. Tomahawk targeting time was reduced to less than two hours. By the time of the Second Gulf War (Operation Iraqi Freedom) in 2003, further refinements to the U.S. battle networks had been made. Ten types of scout drones were employed, and in unprecedented numbers. They joined U.S. manned intelligence, surveillance, and reconnaissance (ISR) assets, including U-2, JSTARS, and AWACS aircraft. Many coalition strike aircraft were able to monitor the movement of Iraqi forces by using radar images transmitted directly to them from these ISR aircraft, even in sandstorms. The drones occasionally executed strike missions, continuing a role they first played in Afghanistan, with Predator UAVs firing Hellfire antitank missiles against Iraqi targets.[201]

To move scouting data quickly to strike elements, the Air Force established a Time-Sensitive Targeting Cell (TSTC) at Prince Sultan Air Base in Saudi Arabia. The air attack on the Ba'ath Party headquarters, where General Ali Hassan al-Majid, the dreaded cousin of Saddam Hussein known as "Chemical Ali," was reported to be located, was executed in less than half an hour from the time the general was spotted heading into his villa by a British special operations soldier. The information was relayed to the TSTC, which cued an F-16 strike aircraft that destroyed the villa using PGMs. In some instances, the TSTC put bombs on target within twenty minutes of being alerted by intelligence. In all, coalition air forces struck nearly 700 targets based on "dynamic retargeting" and executed more than 150 missions against time-sensitive targets, such as Iraqi leaders and suspected weapons of mass destruction.[202]

For nearly half a century following the bomber offensives in World War II, the U.S. Air Force and the air forces of other significant military powers confronted the problem of overcoming ever improving enemy air defenses. Losses were often high and at times bordered on unsustainable.

In early 1991, however, over the skies of Iraq, in the course of several days, an air campaign, led by a handful of U.S. fighter-bomber aircraft armed with two bombs each, succeeded in dismantling one of the world's most formidable integrated air defense systems. At the same time, U.S. and allied aircraft swept the skies of an enemy air force flying modern interceptor aircraft. With the Air Force having achieved the air superiority that eluded it over North Vietnam twenty years earlier, it went on to wreck the better part of the Iraqi Army in one of the most lopsided campaigns in the history of war.

The First Gulf War revealed a disruptive shift in the character of air warfare. New capabilities, including guided weapons, stealth aircraft, and advanced means of navigation and communication, were combined into a nascent guided-weapons battle network. These capabilities were employed in a campaign based on an innovative operational concept, the brainchild of Air Force leaders—and thinkers—that spanned from senior generals to midlevel officers. The campaign's execution benefited enormously from a revolution in training that enabled aircrews to gain the kind of competence that previously could only be acquired through extended combat. By several measures of merit, the air campaign conducted in Operation Desert Storm yielded orders of magnitude or greater improvements in operational effectiveness. As Russian military theorists concluded, the "revolution in military affairs" they had foreseen was now a reality.

CHAPTER TEN

Echoes of History

Victory will smile upon those who anticipate changes in the character of war, not upon those who wait to adapt themselves after changes occur.

—GENERAL GIULIO DOUHET

He who will not apply new remedies must expect new evils.

—SIR FRANCIS BACON

SENIOR DEFENSE POLICY MAKERS want to know how their country stands in key areas of the military competition. They are particularly interested in knowing when they face disruptive shifts in the competition and how to exploit them to their advantage. Part 1 of this study argues that we are in such a period of disruptive change. Not only is the precision-warfare regime reaching its mature phase, but it appears to be overlapping with the onset of a new military revolution. It seems that we can discern, if only dimly, the new regime's characteristics.

The preceding four chapters describe how military organizations engaged in disruptive innovation to trigger a military revolution and, along with it, a large and rapid shift in the military balance in their favor. If policy makers accept that they are in a period of disruptive change in warfare, they need to know how well their military and the militaries of their rivals are positioned to exploit the next big thing (or things) in warfare. Although a detailed assessment of this question is beyond the scope of this inquiry, it's possible to provide some preliminary thoughts on the matter.

By examining the histories presented in the previous chapters, it's possible to identify characteristics common to the four military organizations that succeeded in pursuing disruptive innovation and that led the way in navigating the shift in warfare from one regime to another. Two general observations emerge. First, despite the term "military revolution," disruptive innovation did not yield results overnight. The path that each military organization took was long, typically taking a decade or two to traverse. That being said, when the new warfare regime emerged, it typically caught other militaries—and even the military organization that introduced it—somewhat by surprise.

Second, the process that each of the four militaries followed was invariably messy and bumpy, neither straight nor smooth. Detours and setbacks were common. It was often a case of two steps forward, one step back. The role that chance, or luck, played in each history was often significant.

A closer inspection of the four histories finds that those military organizations that led the way toward realizing a quantum leap in military effectiveness share certain characteristics. The balance of this chapter is devoted to describing these characteristics and their possible implications for the current military competition.

A Guiding Vision

Each of the four military organizations profiled in the histories had a guiding vision of the new warfare regime. This vision addressed two questions of fundamental importance: What are we trying to do? and How can we accomplish this in a far more effective way than we can at present? The vision is relatively brief and unambiguous, serving to focus and inform the organization's efforts.

In the Royal Navy's case, Admiral Fisher argued that the existing naval-warfare regime, centered on battleships and the simple line of battle, was doomed unless (and perhaps even if) major changes were made. Fisher declared, "The battleship of the olden days was necessary because it was the one and only vessel that nothing could sink except another battleship. Now every battleship is open to attack by fast torpedo-craft and submarines."[1] Consequently, Fisher argued, "There is good ground for enquiry whether naval supremacy of a country can any longer be assessed by its battleships."[2]

The admiral's vision of future war at sea was clear and unambiguous: for the surface fleet, he wanted ships with superior speed and long-range strike capabilities to operate effectively beyond the enemy's rapidly growing torpedo range. Fisher also envisioned submarines armed with torpedoes performing a new mission: flotilla defense. The fleet's actions would be coordinated by a global command-and-control network.

In the case of the German military and Blitzkrieg, General von Seeckt's vision was succinct: "The goal of modern strategy will be to achieve a decision with highly mobile, highly capable forces, before the masses have begun to move."[3] Simply put, von Seeckt envisioned overturning the positional, attrition warfare that prevailed on the Western Front in World War I with "highly mobile" and "highly capable" forces (which eventually became the elite panzer units combined with air support) capable of not only penetrating the enemy front but also rupturing it "before the masses have begun to move," or counter-concentrate to stop them. Over time, leaders like General Guderian added clarity to the vision, stating, *"We believe that by attacking with tanks we can achieve a higher rate of movement than has been hitherto obtainable, and—what is perhaps even more important—that we can keep moving once a breakthrough has been made."*[4]

The U.S. Navy was blessed with its own visionaries in the years between the world wars. One was Admiral Sims, who, nearly a decade before the United States launched its first purpose-built carrier, asserted, "A small, high-speed carrier alone can destroy or disable a battleship alone. . . . A fleet whose carriers give it command of the air over the enemy fleet can defeat the latter. [Consequently], the fast carrier is the capital ship of the future."[5] Sims's vision was shared by Admiral Moffett, who proclaimed, "We can hardly visualize today the potential power of aircraft, not so much for scouting and spotting, but for bombing and torpedoing. It may readily be the deciding factor in a war."[6]

The U.S. Air Force's leading visionary was General Creech. The general was convinced that a different way had to be found to address the integrated air defense system (IADS) threat that had inflicted such high casualties on the U.S. Air Force and Navy during the Vietnam War and on the Israeli Air Force in the Yom Kippur War that followed. Creech's vision was of an all-day, all-night, all-weather, precision, stand-off, integrated force that would wage a campaign whose goal was to suppress enemy air defenses, not "fly past" them.[7]

In summary, in each case where a military organization led the way to a disruptive shift in the competition, it enjoyed the benefit of a clear vision of the envisioned end state—what it was trying to do and how it would go about accomplishing it.

Extended Tenure and Institutionalization

In each of the four cases examined, the senior leaders most associated with disruptive innovation enjoyed what in today's U.S. military would be considered an unusually long tenure. This makes intuitive sense, as large-scale innovation takes an extended period to bring about.

Admiral Fisher served as first sea lord from 1904 to 1910 and then again from 1914 to 1915, roughly eight years over a twelve-year span. Rear Admiral Moffett, arguably the key figure in the development of U.S. naval aviation, served as head of the Navy's Bureau of Aeronautics for an astounding twelve years, from its inception in 1921 until 1933.[8] (His tenure would have been even longer had he not perished in an airship crash.) Similarly, General von Seeckt, head of the German Army from 1920 to 1926, would have served longer save for a political scandal that erupted when he invited the grandson of Germany's former emperor to observe maneuvers. Perhaps most remarkable is General Creech, who headed the Air Force's Tactical Air Command for six years, from 1978 to 1984.

Each of these leaders cultivated acolytes and advanced their careers. Fisher established what became known as the "Fishpond." He declared, "Favouritism was the secret of our efficiency in the old days and got us young Admirals. . . . *'Buggins's turn' has been our ruin and will be disastrous hereafter!*"[9] Among the Fishpond members was John Jellicoe, who commanded Britain's Grand Fleet at Jutland, and officers like Rear Admiral Reginald Bacon, whom Fisher described as the "cleverest man in the Navy."[10] Fisher's efforts are well expressed by his declaration, "I have in my drawer letters from 24 Captains and Commanders, the very pick of the service, in favor of the scheme. I prefer these 24 opinions of the coming admirals, who are going to command our fleets and administer the Admiralty, to any 24 admirals now existing but who are passing away."[11]

Admiral Moffett succeeded in ensuring that all aviators were officers and that certain commands, such as those of naval air stations and aircraft carriers, were reserved for pilots. The BuAer staff provided slots for aviators and a place for them to gain experience. During the 1920s, future Navy admirals such as Mitscher and Towers found a home in BuAer. The chief of naval operations during World War II, Fleet Admiral Ernest King, whom Moffett convinced to transfer to naval aviation, succeeded Moffett as head of BuAer in 1933.

General von Seeckt's crucial contribution came early in his tenure. It was then that the decision was made to prioritize keeping General Staff officers—the "brains" of Germany's Army—on active duty rather than those officers who had gained extensive operational experience during the Great War. This aided von Seeckt's efforts to keep the Army focused on future possibilities, rather than past experiences.

Whether by luck or design, a remarkable number of Air Force future leaders worked for General Creech during his tenure as head of the Tactical Air Command. All six of the Air Force chiefs of staff who served from 1986 through 2001 were either a wing commander or on Creech's staff during the time he headed the Tactical Air Command. Over time, twenty-one of the officers Creech had a hand in developing rose to the rank of full general.[12]

Technologies Are a Key Enabler

In each of the four cases, disruptive innovation was either driven or enabled by significant advances in military-related technologies. In some instances, it was a case of "technological push"—new technologies emerged, leaving militaries to figure out how to best exploit them. There were examples of "technological pull," where militaries were actively—at times desperately—seeking out technologies that would enable them to exploit big opportunities that they had identified but lacked the means to exploit.

During Fisher's tenure as first sea lord, maturing torpedo technology and the ability of submarines to operate at progressively greater ranges made the Royal Navy's close blockade operations an increasingly risky, if not suicidal, proposition. Fisher sought to leverage this technological "push" to his benefit through flotilla defense of the British Isles. Other advances, such as those in metallurgy, wireless, turbine engines, and propulsion—shifting from coal to oil as the fleet's fuel—were crucial to Fisher's Scheme in three ways: first, in making possible his fast, all-big-gun line of battle to move engagement beyond torpedo range; second, in creating a different way of employing capital ships in the form of the flying wing of fast battle cruisers; and third, by enabling a radical shift in the Royal Navy's basing posture to enhance imperial defense and protection against commerce raiders. Absent the advances being made with these technologies, Fisher's Scheme would have been far more difficult to realize, if it were possible at all.

During the period between the world wars, both the German Army and Luftwaffe and the U.S. Navy benefited greatly from the introduction of mechanization, aviation, radio, and, especially in the Navy's case, radar. Regarding the Wehrmacht, the automotive industry's maturation made it possible to field armored vehicles with the necessary speed and range to restore mobility at the operational level of war. Modern aircraft proved essential in providing rapidly advancing ground forces with scouting information on threats to their flanks, as well as a highly mobile form of artillery "close air support." Radio proved indispensable for maintaining command and control over highly dispersed forces on the move.

The U.S. Navy found itself leveraging these same technologies, although in a very different way. Advances in aviation technology were fundamental to the shift from a battleship-centered fleet to one organized around the carrier as its capital ship and the fast carrier task force as the successor to the line of battle. Long-range radio and radar further transformed war at sea by providing the carrier task force with early warning of approaching enemy aircraft and a means to coordinate friendly aircraft operations over extended ranges. This enabled the Navy to shift from an offense-dominant regime, in which it was crucial to locate and sink the enemy's carriers, to a defense-dominant regime centered on early warning of enemy air attacks and employing fighter-interceptors and anti-aircraft-artillery escort ships to defeat them.

In the quarter century prior to the First Gulf War, the U.S. Air Force's dramatic change in the character of air operations found it relying heavily on advances in technology, especially those emerging from the IT revolution, which was just then gathering momentum. The introduction of solid-state electronics, enhanced sensors, and laser technology in the late 1960s made effective guided weapons possible. The IT revolution also proved crucial in fielding stealth aircraft, as well as the GPS satellite constellation and advanced scouting and command-and-control systems, such as AWACS and JSTARS, that provided aircrews with an enormous boost in situation awareness.

New and Novel Operational Concepts

Operational concepts provide the basis for planning at the theater or campaign level of war, including describing how forces will operate to achieve strategic goals. As such, they offer possible solutions to existing and emerging military challenges. Dramatic shifts in the character of military competitions, such as those described in the four histories, find the most successful military organizations developing and refining operational concepts that are very different from those that dominate the existing warfare regime. These concepts informed and guided analysis, war gaming, field and fleet exercises, and experiments and were in turn informed by them. In this way, they shaped a military's doctrine, as well as its size, force mix, organization, structure, and investment priorities.

In each instance, innovative operational concepts enabled the militaries to realize far more effective ways of competing at the campaign level of war. They also directly or indirectly created "winners" and "losers" with respect to particular capabilities, systems, force types, and structures, as well as among the organization's subcultures. Indeed, the "losing" subcultures often presented a major barrier to efforts at disruptive innovation, as was the case with Admiral Beresford and the Syndicate of Discontent, General Reinhardt, the U.S. Navy's "Gun Club," and the U.S. Air Force's bomber-pilot-dominated leadership.

For Admiral Fisher, flotilla defense offered a new way of defending the British Isles. His concept of employing a global surveillance and intelligence network with a mobile "flying wing" of fast, heavily armed battle cruisers enabled the Royal Navy to transform the fleet's global posture. Fisher's best-known operational concept saw the fleet operating as a "combined arms" battle force with "flotilla craft" as its screening force, and all-big-gun battleships and battle cruisers firing at long range to gain an advantage over the enemy battle line and offset the threat posed by the enemy's torpedo-armed destroyers and submarines.

The German Army confronted the unsolved problem that emerged on the Western Front during World War I: restoring mobility at the operational level of war to avoid losing a war of attrition. To this end, forward-thinking German Army leaders, in conjunction with the Luftwaffe, developed an operational concept in line with the military's tradition of emphasizing maneuver over positional warfare. Leveraging advances in aviation, mechanization, and radios, the Germans developed a form of mechanized air-land warfare operations known as Blitzkrieg, enabling the Germans to accomplish in six weeks in the spring of 1940 what they could not achieve in four years during the First World War and to dominate land warfare in Europe for nearly three years.

Meanwhile, the U.S. Navy was engaged in efforts to address the problem of conducting a campaign extending across the Pacific Ocean to Japan's home waters, where it envisioned fighting a decisive battle against the Imperial Japanese Navy. Lacking advanced bases, Navy leaders knew that the fleet would need to bring its own air power and logistics with it, while maintaining extended sea lines of communication. The Americans exploited advances in aviation and radio, as well as radar, in developing the fast carrier task force that, in the months following the attack on Pearl Harbor, rendered the line of battle obsolete, with the carrier emerging as the fleet's new capital ship.

In the 1960s and '70s, modern air forces like those of the Americans and Israelis confronted the growing challenge of rapidly improving IADS. Both the U.S. and Israeli air forces persisted in conducting offensive air operations, but at a high cost in actual and virtual attrition, even against minor powers like North Vietnam and Egypt.

General Creech and like-minded officers envisioned a campaign to suppress the enemy's IADS, rather than trying to bypass it. In addition to introducing high-fidelity training, the Air Force drew on the IT revolution that proved essential to advances in guided weapons, fielding stealth aircraft, conducting effective night operations, and achieving advanced situation awareness. The combination of capabilities that emerged from this effort enabled Creech's vision to become a reality in the First Gulf War.

Different Measures of Effectiveness

New problems at the operational level of war and the novel operational concepts and capabilities developed to overcome them found militaries adopting new measures of effectiveness (MOEs). Admiral Fisher's Scheme introduced a new concept for the fleet's global posture. Prior to Fisher, a key metric in assessing imperial defense was the number of ships in squadrons on distant stations, in places like Asia and North America. Fisher's transformation of the Royal Navy's posture discounted ship numbers. Indeed, more than 150 obsolete ships were *withdrawn* from service. Instead, he emphasized near-real-time information provided by the Admiralty's global communications network, enabled by undersea cables and wireless, and the number of modern, fast battle cruisers capable of rapidly deploying to threatened spots around the globe.

For Fisher to realize his concept of battle fleet engagement, he markedly increased the emphasis on ship speed and engagement range, sacrificing armor to get it. The admiral was especially keen on his battle line enjoying an advantage of speed over its rivals, declaring, "There is no question whatever that the first desideratum in every type of fighting vessel is speed. . . . It is absolutely impossible to exaggerate the supreme importance of speed."[13]

Fisher's concept of flotilla defense measured its effectiveness in terms of submarines and destroyers armed with torpedoes rather than a surface fleet defending Britain's shores. Here we find Fisher again sacrificing armor (as well as speed and firepower) to exploit the submarine's greatest advantage: stealth.

Similarly, the German Army emphasized new MOEs in abandoning the positional, firepower-heavy attrition warfare that dominated the Western Front during the Great War and moving toward mechanized air-land operations. In designing mechanized forces, the Germans emphasized tank speed and operational range over firepower and armor protection. As Guderian described it, "*The chances of an offensive based on the timetable of artillery and infantry co-operation are . . . even slighter today than they were in the last war. Everything is therefore dependent on this: to be able to move faster than has hitherto been done: to keep moving despite the enemy's defensive fire and thus to make it harder for him to build up fresh defensive positions: and finally to carry the attack deep into the enemy's defenses.*"[14] This contrasted starkly with French tank design, which was wedded to a war-fighting concept closely aligned to positional warfare and thus gave priority to armor and armament. Not surprisingly, the German concept of a highly mobile war of maneuver required greater emphasis on command and control, so MOEs like the percentage of tanks equipped with radio transmitters and receivers became increasingly important. This is not to say that the German Army was happy with its weakly armed Panzer Is and IIs, only to note that when it came to setting priorities, speed and range generally trumped firepower and armor plate.

Dramatically altered MOEs also characterized the U.S. Navy's shift from a battleship-centric to a carrier-centric fleet. The Gun Club emphasized the weight of a broadside that could be fired at the maximum range of the largest guns. As long as this measure of merit prevailed, the battleships would always compare favorably with carriers.

Those naval officers who envisioned the carrier as the capital ship advocated different metrics. Like Fisher and the Germans, American naval visionaries were willing to trade armor and firepower for speed and range. Toward this end, U.S. carriers dispensed with armor-plated decks. American naval air enthusiasts valued the carrier air wing's extended-range fires over the battle line's volume fires. A carrier could only deliver a fraction of the firepower inherent in the line of battle, they admitted, but it could do so at a range ten times greater. During the 1930s, when it was clear that carrier warfare was "offense dominant" and that the key to success was to find and sink the enemy's carrier before it found yours, the Navy emphasized scouting to find the enemy carriers and sinking them, over armor-plated decks and onboard anti-aircraft defenses. Consequently, the Navy sought to maximize the number of aircraft and their launch and recovery speed on its carriers.

The First Gulf War yielded a major shift in several key MOEs used by the Air Force to determine military effectiveness. For example, the growing dominance of beyond-visual-range engagements required less in the way of aircraft maneuverability and speed in a dogfight and more ability in scouting—detecting an enemy aircraft at the moment it enters a friendly aircraft's missile range. As scouting (and defeating the enemy's scouting) became more important, so did stealth.

The combination of stealth and guided weapons produced a shift away from large-strike packages, where a large majority of aircraft were in support roles, and toward small numbers of stealthy aircraft armed with guided weapons. The MOE for these operations shifted from the number of aircraft that could be assigned to strike a target to the number of guided weapons employed on stealth aircraft. Similarly, the measure of bomb tonnage dropped gave way to bomb accuracy. This can be seen by the rapidly growing percentage of guided weapons relative to unguided bombs employed in Air Force operations following the First Gulf War. Precision-guided munitions constituted less than 10 percent of the munitions employed by the U.S. aircraft in the First Gulf War. This figure grew to roughly 30 percent in the 1999 Balkan War, exceeded 50 percent in air operations in Afghanistan in 2001–2 (Operation Enduring Freedom), and surpassed 60 percent in the Second Gulf War.[15]

Scouting in the form of situation awareness remained crucial to effective air operations, but in a different way. The shift away from visual engagements to BVR engagements was made possible by linking an aircraft (including its radar and sensors) into a battle network and arming it with increasingly reliable extended-range air-to-air missiles.

Exercises and Experimentation

Professional analysis, simulations, and war games, although important in their own right, can only go so far in identifying, developing, and validating new concepts of operation and new military system requirements. They lack the detailed level of resolution (and "friction") realized from well designed and executed field exercises and fleet maneuvers. This is critical because, in war, the devil is often in the details, and Murphy's Law is often the order of the day.

For example, war games conducted at the Naval War College in the early 1920s identified the importance of maximizing the number of aircraft on a carrier, as well as aircraft sortie rates. It was not, however, until the *Langley* was launched and participated in exercises that the Navy could determine precisely *how* this goal was to be achieved (or, indeed, *whether* it could be achieved at all). Under Captain Joseph Reeves, the *Langley* conducted a series of exercises and experiments that led to such innovations as crash barriers and the deck park, enabling the ship to more than double its aircraft complement while dramatically increasing its sortie rate.[16] Similarly, the German military's exercises and operations, including those during the Spanish Civil War and as part of the occupation of Austria and Czechoslovakia, enabled it to identify panzer divisions' fuel and spare-parts requirements more accurately and how the Luftwaffe could best function as a highly mobile source of reconnaissance and strike support for Germany's ground forces. The Royal Navy's fleet exercises in the years prior to World War I revealed the limitations of its torpedo-boat destroyers in defeating enemy torpedo boats in close blockade operations. They also identified significant problems associated with the long-range gunnery accuracy that was crucial to Fisher's vision of battle fleet engagements. General Creech's Red Flag exercises showed just how much the Air Force had to learn with respect to conducting a suppression of enemy air defenses (SEAD) campaign in general and under conditions of aggressive enemy jamming in particular.

Field and fleet exercises also helped to vet and refine operational concepts. The U.S. Navy's series of fleet problems enabled it to develop the principles of the fast carrier task force, making possible its prompt introduction following the attack on Pearl Harbor. This also proved the case with the Air Force's Red Flag exercises and those conducted by the German Army and Luftwaffe. Red Flag aided the Air Force in developing, almost on the fly, the innovative air campaign for Operation Desert Storm. In the German military's case, field exercises facilitated the blending of combined arms in panzer divisions and their integration with the Luftwaffe. The Royal Navy's exercises were crucial to its shift from close blockade to distant blockade operations that proved successful against Germany.

Field and fleet exercises were indispensable in each military's maintaining an awareness of significant shifts in the character of military competition that sometimes occur during periods of revolutionary change but that are not themselves revolutionary. This was the case with the U.S. Navy and Air Force. The U.S. Navy's fleet problems and experiments identified several such shifts. Tests on the battleship *Texas* in 1919 showed that aircraft acting as spotters greatly enhanced the battle line's gunnery at extended ranges. Ten years later, Fleet Problem IX revealed that carriers could function as an independent strike force by conducting raids, even though they still had not displaced the battle line as the arbiter of sea control. In the absence of fleet exercises and experiments, it is doubtful the Navy would have either identified these shifts in the military competition or adapted to them as quickly and as well as it did.

Similarly, the U.S. Air Force benefited considerably from its experience and that of the Israeli Air Force (IAF) in several wars—the ultimate "field exercises." The Vietnam War showed that guided weapons could enable the existing form of air operations—large-strike packages focused on individual missions at the tactical level of warfare—to be executed more effectively. The IAF's operation in the Bekaa Valley demonstrated the boost in effectiveness that a nascent battle network employing unmanned aircraft could provide.

One reason why disruptive military innovation typically requires a decade or more to bring about is that it typically must overcome individual and institutional resistance. Properly structured field exercises and fleet maneuvers, involving actual forces in an environment that is as close to combat as possible, are arguably unsurpassed in their ability to generate support, and even enthusiasm, within the officer corps for new operational concepts. The *Saratoga's* raid on the Panama Canal in Fleet Problem IX and the Third Panzer Division's performance in the German Army's 1937 North German Plain maneuvers convinced many officers who witnessed these exercises—in a way that no war game or simulation could have—that they were on to something special and that a new and far more effective way of conducting military operations was possible.[17] The same can be said regarding the effect on the officer corps that occurred following "real-world" operations like the German Condor Legion's operations during the Spanish Civil War, the IAF's brief campaign against Syrian forces in the Bekaa Valley, and the U.S. air strikes in Operation El Dorado Canyon and its Red Flag exercises.

Investment Strategies: Options and Hedges

For navies that believe they are in a period of disruptive change, Admiral Fisher offers excellent guidance: "The first essential is to divest our minds totally of the idea that a single ship type as now built is necessary."[18] To various degrees, through serendipity or design, each of the four military organizations examined pursued investment strategies emphasizing hedging against the uncertainties inherent in a highly dynamic competitive environment, in part by creating options in potentially revolutionary capabilities that could be exercised quickly if they proved out.

To the maximum extent possible, a hedging strategy avoids locking in, via large production runs, to current or emerging military systems. With respect to the latter, it is important to recognize the dangers of "false starts" and "dead ends," as well as the value of "wildcatting." False starts occur when systems or capabilities are purchased in quantity before they have reached the point where they prove themselves. Dead ends are those systems and capabilities that may appear attractive but never fulfill their promise within the planning horizon. Wildcatting prioritizes exploring a wide range of potentially attractive systems and capabilities that have the potential to advance disruptive innovation.

Thus, wildcatting expands opportunities for exploring new operational concepts in field and fleet exercises, enabling military organizations to buy options, or insurance, against an uncertain future, thereby reducing risk. This boosts a military's feedback from exercises, reducing the danger of locking in to current systems that may depreciate rapidly following a disruptive shift in the military competition. Wildcatting also helps to avoid investing in false starts or dead ends.

Two of the four military organizations examined here avoided locking in to large production runs of major military systems that would greatly depreciate in value or that visionaries believed would enable a major boost in combat effectiveness. In the case of the U.S. Navy and

German Army, this was facilitated by treaty obligations. The Washington Naval Treaty prohibited the construction of battleships and placed a relatively low ceiling on carrier tonnage. With respect to naval aviation, the U.S. Navy consciously tried to limit its purchase of large numbers of aircraft, since the rapid advances being made in aviation technology ensured that they would become quickly outdated. The Versailles Treaty produced a similar effect by banning the German military from possessing tanks and aircraft.

In the Royal Navy's case, given that it confronted a very dynamic and ongoing competition for maritime supremacy, it needed to maintain a powerful active fleet while it worked to exploit the opportunities Fisher believed would sustain Britain's maritime dominance. Still, where possible, Fisher avoided large production runs, particularly with respect to battleships. Indeed, *Dreadnought* was the only ship of its class. Although construction of battleships and battle cruisers was necessary in light of improvements in rival fleets, the numbers in each successive ship class were relatively small.

In the U.S. Navy's case, arms control and the Great Depression helped keep it from investing heavily in the *Ranger* class of carriers, which proved a false start—the right *kind* of ship but the *wrong ship design* for the kind of war that would be waged in the Pacific. Moffett's flying-deck cruisers were dead-end ships that, despite the admiral's affection for them, fortunately were never built. The same can be said of the Navy's airships. As for the German military, it enjoyed the "benefit" of more than fifteen years of disarmament that precluded significant production runs of aircraft and tanks.

The Royal Navy suffered a major false start in its torpedo-boat destroyers. These ships were specifically designed to defeat the threat posed by torpedo boats that emerged in the mid-1880s. Four classes of torpedo-boat destroyers were launched and began to enter the fleet in 1892.[19] Fleet maneuvers revealed these ships as unable to accomplish the mission for which they were designed. Over time, larger versions of the ships, now simply called "destroyers," proved their value, although in convoy missions that were very different from those originally envisioned for their ancestors.

The U.S. Air Force, like the Royal Navy, had to account for the ongoing improvements in Soviet Russia's military capabilities, and hence the large production runs necessary to maintain a great power's modern air arm were unavoidable. It did, however, make a substantial investment in wildcatting, although Air Force leaders generally had to be coaxed into investing in stealth aircraft and guided munitions, which were purchased in relatively small numbers.

In summary, all four military organizations devoted considerable resources to creating options that enabled them to move with relative speed to exploit a discontinuous shift in the character of warfare. In the Royal Navy's case, this manifested itself in several ways, including its investment in destroyers, submarines, battle cruisers, and the new-age battleships heralded by *Dreadnought*.

Despite the limits imposed by the Washington Naval Treaty and severe fiscal austerity, in the decade prior to World War II, the U.S. Navy introduced four different carrier classes into the fleet, the converted "Sara-Lex" cruisers (the *Lexington* class at 33,000 tons), the *Ranger* (13,800 tons), the *Yorktown* class (roughly 20,000 tons), and the *Wasp* (14,900 tons). The Navy also hedged against the uncertainties associated with the development of air power, investing in various types of attack aircraft, including those designed for horizontal- and dive-bombing attacks, as well as torpedo bombers.

The German Army developed four types of tanks in the short period between the onset of rearmament in 1935 and 1939, while also exploring a variety of ground formations to determine the ideal mix of combat and combat-support arms for waging mechanized warfare. They included the panzer division, motorized (panzer grenadier) division, light divisions, an airborne division, and glider-troop formations.

In the two decades preceding the First Gulf War, the U.S. Air Force fielded the basic elements of its battle network and missiles that would enable a shift to BVR air-to-air engagements, while enhancing its counterscouting efforts by fielding a wing of stealth aircraft. It also created a major alternative to its "smart pilot, dumb bomb" strike arm in the form of precision-guided munitions.

Time-Based Competition: The First- and Second-Move Advantage

Like manpower, money, and matériel, time can play an important role in determining military advantage. The ability to compete based on time involves employing time more efficiently and effectively than one's rivals. Militaries that develop a world-class competence in time-based competition are more agile than their rivals. They introduce new capabilities more rapidly and alter their force structure and doctrine more quickly than their competitors. The ability to compete based on time is especially advantageous during periods of disruptive change, which require a far greater degree of adaptation than is the case in periods of evolutionary change.

Since time is a resource, employing it effectively can reduce the risk associated with a military organization's strategy when it comes to investment priorities. The faster a military can introduce new capabilities into the force, the less need it has to field a large standing military. This is particularly important in periods of disruptive change, when existing military capital stock is prone to depreciate at an accelerated rate.

Of course, the troops that operate military systems must be familiar with them in order to maximize their effectiveness. The same can be said of the need to train them to execute a military's doctrine—especially one based on innovative operational concepts. The histories examined in this study, however, suggest that this does not require a lengthy period of time to achieve. Within the span of five years, the German Army went from its Versailles Treaty disarmed state to conducting sophisticated mechanized air-land operations in two large-scale campaigns resulting in decisive victories. Within five years, the U.S. Navy, which until the late 1930s had a carrier force made up of a converted collier, two converted cruisers, and one undersized purpose-built carrier, found itself operating more than eighty carriers of all types while waging a fundamentally new type of war at sea on the way to destroying the formidable Imperial Japanese Navy.

Military organizations enjoying a superior position in time-based competition are well placed to adopt strategies based on exploiting the first- and second-move advantage. As the term suggests, the first-move advantage involves shifting to a new, more effective way of competing before rivals can react and keep pace. The second-move advantage finds a military organization confronting a situation where a rival has begun fielding new capabilities, forces, and operational concepts with an eye toward effecting a disruptive shift in the competition in its favor. If the lagging military enjoys an advantage in time-based competition, it can use it to catch up—and surpass—the rival that is seeking to exploit the first-move advantage.

The benefits associated with the second-move advantage are several. For one, it allows the "second mover" to see with relative clarity the "first mover's" plans for gaining a competitive advantage. This reduces considerably the uncertainty confronting the second mover. Another benefit accruing to the second mover occurs in situations where it enjoys a dominant position in the existing competition and thus has no need to introduce new capabilities that would lead to the premature depreciation of a considerable portion of its existing military capital stock.

The four militaries in this study, to varying degrees, employed time-based competition to their advantage. The Royal Navy case provides perhaps the best example. Recall that for much of the nineteenth century the Admiralty leveraged its command of money and Britain's large and technically advanced industrial base to pursue a strategy of the second-move advantage. This saw Britain's principal naval rival at that time, France, seeking and failing to exploit the first-move advantage by introducing steam propulsion in its warships and then ironclad ships. The British produced a militarily significant number of the new type of warships more quickly than the French, even though La Marine Nationale had moved first.

Enjoying an advantage in time-based competition also enables a military organization to pursue a strategy of the first move, which Admiral Fisher did most famously by constructing *Dreadnought*. This all-big-gun, turbine-engine battleship effectively "wrecked" the German Navy's construction program. Fisher explained his strategy this way: "Put off to the very last hour the ship (big or little) that you mean to build (or perhaps not build her at all!). You see all your rival's plans fully developed, their vessels started beyond recall, and then in each individual answer to each such rival vessel you PLUNGE with a design 50 per cent. better! knowing that your rapid shipbuilding and command of money will enable you to have your vessel fit to fight as soon if not sooner than the rival vessel."[20] Once the Germans began to build dreadnoughts, Fisher was "plunging" yet again with fast battle cruisers.

The German Army and Luftwaffe serendipitously found themselves enjoying a second-move advantage in that, being disarmed for most of the interwar period, they were able to see the investment priorities of Germany's principal rivals. Similarly, the U.S. Navy had the good fortune of following in the Royal Navy's wake after World War I, when the British had a monopoly on aircraft carriers.[21] This represented a near-term advantage for the Royal Navy, but it proved ephemeral. Aviation technology was advancing at breakneck speed, and the Royal Navy's carriers were depreciating in value at an accelerated rate. Moreover, tight budgets, combined with a desire to get full value out of the newly constructed carriers, found British political leaders reluctant to update the class. The U.S. Navy, on the other hand, was better able to keep pace with advances in naval aviation owing to its late arrival to the competition.

The U.S. Air Force offers perhaps the best example of a military organization pursuing the first-move advantage. The U.S. military under Defense Secretary Harold Brown explicitly sought to leverage the country's competitive IT advantage over Soviet Russia in pursuing its Offset Strategy, developing stealth and battle-management aircraft, guided weapons, advanced sensors, and a space-based navigation and positioning system. In combination, they enabled the Air Force in particular, and the U.S. military more broadly, to exploit the first-move advantage and gain a dramatic boost in effectiveness.

Little Things Mean a Lot

The shift from one warfare regime to another often occurs after a relatively small shift in a military's structure and equipment. Put another way, the phenomenon is highly nonlinear: even a relatively small percentage of the total force capable of waging the new form of warfare can achieve levels of effectiveness far greater than much larger forces fighting within the construct of the passing regime.

With the possible exception of the Royal Navy, each of the militaries examined in the case studies brought about a disruptive shift in the military balance with a small shift in the composition of its capital stock. For example, only 12 percent of the German Army that defeated the combined Belgian, British, Dutch, and French forces in a campaign lasting but six weeks was mechanized or motorized.[22] In late 1941, the U.S. Navy included 352 major combatants, of which only 7 were aircraft carriers.[23] During the First Gulf War, the U.S. Air Force's fifty-nine F-117 Nighthawks represented only 2.5 percent of combat aircraft in the theater. Moreover, during the air campaign in Operation Desert Storm, less than 10 percent of the bombs dropped by the Air Force were guided weapons, yet they produced more than 75 percent of the damage inflicted on Iraqi targets.[24]

The phenomenon is less apparent with respect to the Royal Navy and the so-called *Dreadnought* revolution. That being said, the construction of a single ship, *Dreadnought,* had a profound effect on the maritime competition. Once it appeared, it became clear that pre-dreadnought battleships were greatly inferior in speed, range, and long-range fires. A line of battle made from pre-dreadnought battleships risked being hopelessly outclassed by only a handful of dreadnoughts. The submarine's emergence enabled Germany to introduce a new form of blockade. At the war's start, of the 334 combatants in the Imperial German Navy, less than 10 percent, only 31, were submarines.[25]

The Incomplete Revolution

In all of the instances when a military organization's disruptive innovation produced a dramatic boost in its effectiveness, significant parts of its authors' vision of future warfare remained unfulfilled. In the case of the Royal Navy, for instance, Fisher's vision, combining uniform big guns, and hence long-range fires, with an advantage in speed to set and maintain a favorable engagement range, assumed that the problem of range-finding would be solved. This proved wrong. At Jutland, the Grand Fleet's gunnery was generally poor. Moreover, the weather in the North Sea, where the fleet would be most likely to engage the German High Seas Fleet, was often cloudy, creating additional problems for ships counting on being able to engage the enemy accurately at very long range. In a sense, the war came a bit too early for Fisher's vision to be fully realized. In 1919, only three years after Jutland, rudimentary tests involving U.S. aircraft acting as spotters for the battleship *Texas* dramatically increased the ship's gunnery accuracy. That being said, perhaps the greatest affirmation of Fisher's vision came from Britain's rivals. After the launch of the *Dreadnought*, all the major navies shifted to producing the New Model capital ship. Indeed, from then on, "battleships" were often referred to as "dreadnoughts." Fisher's vision of the submarine's fundamental reshaping of the maritime competition also proved correct, although not exactly in the way he anticipated.

As with Fisher's transformed fleet, Germany's Blitzkrieg force proved incomplete in at least one important respect. The problem resided in the lack of motorized or mechanized infantry in the form of panzer grenadier divisions. Their absence in sufficient numbers found German armored units unable, at times, to exploit fully the breakthroughs made in the enemy lines. In France, for example, following the breakthrough of Guderian's XIX Panzer Corps at Sedan, the armored force risked being halted owing to concerns that further advances without infantry support would pose unacceptable risks to its flanks.[26] The problem was again confronted, with a far less happy outcome for the Germans, in the first month of the Barbarossa campaign in Russia. By mid-July 1941, only three weeks into the campaign, Army Group Center's two panzer groups (later "armies") had advanced to Smolensk, roughly halfway from the invasion's jump-off point and Moscow. Those Russian forces not already destroyed or captured were mostly in disarray. But as Alan Clark notes, "The extent to which the Panzer armies of [Generals] Hoth and Guderian were outrunning their supporting infantry was a constant source of worry to OKH [Oberkommando des Heeres, the German Army's high command]. The Germans were very short of motorized infantry units, and those that they had operated close up with the tanks as part of the armoured spearhead. . . . During the last week in July, both at OKH and OKW [Oberkommando der Wehrmacht, the armed forces' high command], opinions were united in the view that the advance of Army Group Center should be slowed down."[27]

The U.S. Navy's carriers also had limitations. Carrier aircraft dominated the daylight hours, but at night, surface-combatant engagements were the norm.[28] Following the devastating success of U.S. flattops against Japanese carriers in the Battle of Midway, they withdrew during the night, while Japanese surface ships pressed ahead, attempting to engage them.[29] Although the carrier had clearly displaced the battleship as the capital ship, the latter did not quickly go the way of the horse cavalry. In several maritime engagements during World War II, the battleship dominated.

The U.S. Air Force's introduction of precision warfare in the First Gulf War also had its limitations. The stealthy F-117 aircraft only operated at night. Their laser-guided bombs were generally ineffective in poor weather, including conditions involving smoke and cloud cover. Furthermore, in early 1991, GPS coverage was limited, and there were times when it was unavailable. Finally, the Air Force's ability to strike mobile or "time-sensitive" targets in near real time was exceedingly modest.

In summary, although war provides the ultimate validation of the vision of a dramatically new and more effective form of military operation, it typically also reveals gaps in the vision that remain to be addressed.

One Size Does Not Fit All

Our four militaries that were engaged in disruptive innovation were focused on addressing specific problems, or challenges, at the operational level of war. These problems were overcome thanks to these militaries' ability to identify, develop, and exploit major new sources of competitive advantage. That being said, the new forms of warfare that emerged, though remarkably effective in certain aspects of the overall competition, were considerably less effective in other situations. These limitations appear in form and scale: either the form of military challenge was materially different from the one that was the focus of disruptive innovation, or the magnitude of the challenge was so great that the new form of warfare could not be executed at the necessary scale to address it successfully.

For example, Blitzkrieg proved enormously successful in defeating Poland and France in short campaigns. Having succeeded in these, the German military was confronted with a challenge quite different in form from the one for which it was designed—conducting a seaborne invasion of the British Isles. When, in 1941, Hitler declared war on the Soviet Union, the Wehrmacht faced forces roughly similar in form to those it had encountered earlier in Poland and France. Yet despite their great success against the Soviets, the German armed forces lacked the size to defeat a modern military on the scale the Russians could field or to exercise effective control over an area an order of magnitude greater than that of Poland or France.

Similarly, owing to the enormous size and industrial might of the U.S. Navy, it hardly lacked the ability to compete at any scale the Axis powers presented. Nevertheless, although the fast carrier task forces dominated surface-fleet operations—especially during daylight—they were far from ideal for solving the problem being posed by Germany's submarine force, which was waging a commerce-raiding campaign popularly known as the Battle of the Atlantic.

The Royal Navy under Fisher succeeded in transforming the battle fleet into a far more powerful force than it had been in the pre-dreadnought era, thereby succeeding in accomplishing its principal mission: keeping the Kaiser's surface fleet at bay. That said, Fisher's New Model battleships, battle cruisers, and flotilla defense force did not solve the problem posed by the emergence of a new form of commerce raiding in the form of Germany's submarine force.

The U.S. Air Force represents an interesting case in that other militaries—the People's Liberation Army, in particular—are only now fielding many of the capabilities associated with the precision-warfare revolution. The threat emerging from the PLA, for example, is substantially different from that presented by Iraq in the First Gulf War or the Soviets during the Cold War. The Chinese fielding of anti-access/

area-denial forces is shifting the form of the air competition, from one in which the Air Force could count on assured access to the theater of operations to one in which access is now highly contested, in large part from the threat of air and missile attack on forward U.S. air bases. Moreover, the PLA Air Force can compete on a far greater scale than any rival the U.S. Air Force has encountered since the Cold War. The U.S. Air Force—along with the rest of the U.S. military—is only now beginning to confront the problems posed by the emergence of a mature precision-warfare regime.

To sum up, each of the four militaries examined here was the first to engage in disruptive innovation to realize a major boost in its competitive advantage *in a particular aspect* of the military competition. This reinforces the importance of military organizations' need to focus on addressing the questions, What is it we are trying to do? and What is the particular challenge at the operational level of war that we are trying to address?

Serendipity

In reviewing the four histories presented in this study, one is struck by the role that chance, or good fortune, plays in successful disruptive innovation. Serendipity seems to have its greatest effect with respect to the individuals who lead the effort. In the German military's case, it seems unlikely that its progression toward Blitzkrieg would have proceeded as quickly or effectively as it did if General Reinhardt rather than General von Seeckt had led the Reichswehr. The same might be said of Admirals Fisher and Moffett and of Generals Creech and Dixon and their respective military organizations.

At times, exogenous factors precluded a military organization from pursuing an ill-advised course of action. Although viewed as an unwelcome development by many U.S. naval officers, the Washington Navy Treaty prevented the United States from building battleships at the expense of carrier construction. On the other hand, the treaty limits also encouraged Moffett to argue for dead-end systems like flying-deck cruisers and constructing false-start carriers like *Ranger*. In this case, however, the Great Depression's austere budgets precluded Moffett from pursuing his plans. Similarly, the Versailles Treaty prevented the German military from aggressively pursuing von Seeckt's agenda in the 1920s. So when Germany began to rearm in the mid-1930s, the Wehrmacht was not burdened with the expense of maintaining and operating (or even disposing of) large quantities of outdated or rapidly obsolescing tanks and planes.

Outsiders nudged the U.S. Air Force toward disruptive innovation. William Perry's support for stealth aircraft and guided weapons and the OK he received from Secretary of Defense Harold Brown were crucial to creating the new form of air operations that the Air Force introduced in Operation Desert Storm. During Admiral Fisher's tenure as first sea lord, he benefited greatly from the backing provided by King Edward VII and, following his retirement, by the first lord of the Admiralty, Winston Churchill. German Army panzer enthusiasts, Guderian in particular, profited significantly from Hitler's support. Congressman Carl Vinson, chairing Congress's Naval Affairs Committee, backed a series of bills in the years leading up to Pearl Harbor that were crucial in maintaining naval aviation's momentum.

Although each military was aided significantly by good fortune, as Branch Rickey once observed, "Luck is the residue of design." The role played by luck was not insignificant, but it was one element of many that led to success. Those other elements were often the product of conscious design.

Speed, Range, and Scouting

The assessment of the four militaries reveals a *general, but not uniform,* emphasis on increased engagement range and platform speed at the expense of physical protection (armor) and, in some instances, firepower (armament). These militaries also generally favored range and accuracy in fires relative to volume fires ("firepower"). In the Royal Navy's case, the all-big-gun capital ship favored by Fisher prized speed and extended-range gunfire, sacrificing ship armor and rapid-fire guns to obtain it. The German Army's vision of mobile warfare found it emphasizing speed and range in its tanks, again sacrificing armor and armament, especially relative to the French Army's tanks. In a similar vein, the U.S. Navy discounted its carriers' active and passive ship defenses—guns and armor-plated decks—to increase their speed and expand the number of aircraft they could carry. Obviously, when compared to a battleship, the carrier itself sacrificed firepower in favor of being able to execute air strikes at high speed over extended distances. The First Gulf War found the U.S. Air Force boosting its emphasis on precision accuracy. The F-117s, however, were significantly slower than their F-15 and F-16 counterparts, a shortcoming that was offset to a considerable extent by their stealth. The Nighthawks were valued for the enormous advantage they offered in winning the scouting competition, which partially offset the need for speed.

With advances in engagement speed and modern communications, scouting grew in importance. Fisher relied on his global communications network to provide information on rival fleet movements and to enable his fast battle cruisers to arrive quickly where needed to address threats to the empire. In the German military's case, its operations—particularly in addressing concerns over flank protection following breakthrough operations—relied on the Luftwaffe for scouting support and on radios to move information among the panzer forces. For the U.S. Navy's carrier forces, especially early in the Pacific War, scouting was crucial. In the offense-dominant regime that characterized the war's first eighteen months or so, finding Japan's carriers before they discovered their U.S. counterparts was the key to success. In this context, it's easy to see why the Navy was willing to sacrifice defensive armor and armament to augment its carrier air wing: the more aircraft, the greater the number available for scouting.[30] The introduction of long-range radio and radar into the fleet provided it with significant scouting advantages. Regarding the U.S. Air Force, establishing and maintaining situation awareness through various scouting means, especially the nascent battle network that included systems like GPS, AWACS, and JSTARS, was essential. Stealth aircraft proved crucial in defeating the enemy's scouting efforts.

Organizational Innovation

As described above, there is a significant number of common features characterizing military organizations that led the way in effecting a military revolution through disruptive innovation. Still, it's important to understand that these characteristics are not definitive, only suggestive. The militaries examined in this study are small in number, in part because military revolutions are relatively rare phenomena. That said, there are others that could be examined to confirm or challenge these findings. For example, between the world wars, the Imperial Japanese Navy engaged in disruptive innovation, creating the carrier air arm that proved a formidable match for the U.S. Navy's fast carrier task forces. During the same period, the U.S. Army Air Force and British Royal Air Force created strategic aerial-bombardment forces, enabling for the first time large-scale, prompt, direct attacks on an enemy's population and industry, even before its ground and naval forces were defeated. It's possible that an examination of these militaries' success at disruptive innovation could yield significantly different findings or confirm those reached in Part 2 of this book.

On a more encouraging note, the characteristics derived from the four militaries examined here do correlate remarkably well to those identified as resident in business organizations that have successfully pursued disruptive innovation. Although military and business organizations have important differences, corporations, like their military counterparts, are constantly on the lookout for new sources of competitive advantage, even as they maintain a vigilant eye on products, services, and other sources of advantage that risk becoming wasting assets.[31]

For example, in the 1970s, the Boston Consulting Group developed a two-by-two matrix that classifies a corporation's assets. Although it is rather simplistic, the matrix offers a useful framework for thinking about a business's products and competitive advantages. The matrix is defined on its two sides by increases in levels of market share and by market growth rate. A firm's "Stars" are those that have great potential to provide a major source of advantage (and profit) but have yet to realize that potential. They are roughly analogous, for example, to the U.S. Navy's carrier force in the 1920s and '30s and the U.S. Air Force's stealth aircraft and precision munitions during the 1980s. "Cash Cows" are assets that enjoy large market share and generate substantial profits in mature, stable markets. They might be compared to the military systems or capabilities that dominate an existing form of warfare.

A business's "Question Marks" are assets that are in areas of high market growth but have a weak competitive position and are behind in the race to exploit the emerging market. The comparison here to military competitions is tenuous. A useful comparison might be to militaries pursuing the second-move advantage: they are "behind in the race," but in the case of an emerging "market" in a new form of warfare, they cannot abandon the race the way a corporation can, save in situations where a better alternative exists. Finally, there are the "Dogs," assets that enjoy low market share in stable, mature markets. In terms of disruptive military innovation, these might be classified as "wasting assets"—systems and capabilities that offer little in the way of competitive advantage and that need to be divested so that the resources sustaining them can be better employed elsewhere. Fisher's scrapping of more than 150 ships that were deemed obsolete provides an example.

In a period of disruptive innovation, some Question Marks will eventually become Stars, dominating new warfare "markets" and establishing themselves as Cash Cows. Question Marks that fail to pan out—such as the Royal Navy's torpedo-boat destroyers and the U.S. Navy's airships—will become Dogs and be divested. Cash Cows like the battleships during the dreadnought era up until World War II eventually ended up as Dogs. The churn is constant. As Michael Porter notes, "A nation's competitiveness depends on the capacity of its industry to innovate and upgrade."[32] George Stalk concurs, finding that "the best competitors, the most successful ones, know how to keep moving and always stay on the cutting edge."[33]

As with disruptive military innovation, firms in free-market economies have found advancing a vision of the new competitive environment essential to successful innovation. John Kotter found in his study of the corporate sector that, for disruptive innovation to occur, a vision is needed: "In every successful transformation that I have seen, the guiding coalition develops a picture of the future that is relatively easy to communicate and appeals to customers, stockholders, and employees. ... Without a sensible vision, a transformation effort can easily dissolve into a list of confusing and incompatible projects that can take the organization in the wrong direction or nowhere at all." Kotter discovered that "in failed transformations, you often find plenty of plans and directives and programs, but no vision."[34]

Kotter's findings are supported in the pathbreaking work on disruptive innovation of Joseph Bower and Clayton Christensen. They confirmed the importance of having a vision of how the competitive environment might change dramatically, concluding that "managers of companies that have championed disruptive technologies in emerging markets look at the world quite differently." Those leaders who prove unable to exploit the "next big thing ... fail—not because they make the wrong decisions, but because they make the right decisions for circumstances that are about to become history."[35]

As with our four militaries, disruptive change in the corporate sector does not occur overnight, and it also encounters resistance, both internal and external. Porter's research on the competitive advantage of nations finds that "with few exceptions, innovation is the result of unusual effort. The company that successfully implements a new or better way of competing pursues its approach with dogged determination, often in the face of harsh criticism and tough obstacles."[36] Kotter echoes Porter, concluding that "the most general lesson to be learned ... is that the change process goes through a series of phases that, in total, usually require a considerable length of time."[37]

Similar to military organizations that succeed in effecting disruptive change, those in the private sector that succeed look to exploit a new way of doing business. For militaries, this means *new operational concepts*, or ways of operating. As Porter puts it, "Some innovations create competitive advantage by perceiving an entirely new market opportunity or by serving a market segment that others have ignored. When competitors are slow to respond, such innovation yields competitive advantage."[38] Disruptive military innovation leads to a new "market opportunity" through new forms of warfare, such as the Royal Navy's concept of flotilla defense (and the German Navy's strategic submarine blockade), the German military's mechanized air-land operations, the U.S. Navy's fast carrier strike task force, and the U.S. Air Force's "reconnaissance-strike" operations. Not surprisingly, innovation in the modern business world typically involves using emerging technologies in novel ways. As Porter describes it, companies "approach innovation in its broadest sense, including both new technologies and new ways of doing things."[39]

The experience with field exercises of the four militaries in this study finds support from some of the nation's top business-school academics researching organizational innovation. Bower and Christensen found, "Because disruptive technologies frequently signal the emergence of new markets or market segments, managers must create information about such markets—who the customers will be, which dimensions of product performance will matter most to which customers, and what the right price points will be. Managers can create this kind of information only by experimenting rapidly, interactively, and inexpensively with both the product and the market."[40] In military terminology, "product" appears in the form of doctrine and capabilities and how they are applied. Addressing a "market" refers to either an operational challenge against which these capabilities are directed or an opportunity to introduce a new and far more effective way of operating—creating a new "market."

Experiments conducted by the four military organizations presented in this study helped refine their operational concepts, while also building support within the officer corps for the new vision of warfare. Kotter found a similar phenomenon in the corporate sector. Similar to the enthusiasm generated by the German Army's field exercise on the North German Plain in the fall of 1937, the U.S. Air Force's Red Flag exercises under General Creech, or the *Saratoga*'s strike on the Panama Canal in Fleet Problem IX, Kotter discovered that, in the corporate sector, "most people won't go on the long march unless they see compelling evidence within 12 to 24 months that the journey is producing expected results. Without short-term wins, too many people give up or actively join the ranks of those people who have been resisting change."[41]

Our four militaries that successfully pursued disruptive innovation were characterized by visionary leaders receiving extended tenure. These leaders typically cultivated acolytes to carry the vision of disruptive change beyond the leader's tenure. Research on the corporate sector comes to a similar conclusion. Kotter notes that effecting "transformational" change requires "taking sufficient time to make sure that the next generation of top management really does personify the new approach." Echoing Fisher's admonition against following "Buggins's turn," Kotter finds that "if the requirements for promotion don't change, renewal rarely lasts. One bad succession decision at the top of an organization can undermine a decade of hard work. ... [Disruptive innovation] typically goes nowhere until enough real leaders are promoted or hired into senior-level jobs."[42]

Regarding measures of effectiveness, Bower and Christensen's findings are worth summarizing at length:

> Disruptive technologies introduce a very different package of attributes from the one mainstream customers historically value, and they often perform far worse along one or two dimensions that are particularly important to customers. As a rule, mainstream customers are reluctant to use a disruptive product in applications they know and understand. At first, then, disruptive technologies tend to be used and valued only in new markets or new applications; in fact, they generally make possible the emergence of new markets. ...
>
> Many of the disruptive technologies we studied *never* surpassed the capability of the old technology. It is the trajectory of the disruptive technology compared with that of the *market* that is significant.[43]

So it is with our four militaries. In each instance, the new "tools" of war underperformed established systems that dominated the existing warfare regime. Fisher's submarine flotilla defense boats lacked just about everything that was valued in a modern battleship, including speed, firepower, and range. What they had was stealth. The German Army's panzer formations lacked the firepower of the artillery, the "king of battle" on the Great War's Western Front. What the panzers had, which seemed of minor significance in static, positional warfare, was speed and range. The air wing that flew off the decks of the *Enterprise* at Midway could not dream of matching the firepower of a battleship or its ability to take a hit. What it offered was greatly superior range and speed, which could bring about a disruptive shift in war at sea *if* carrier aircraft could sink battleships. In the First Gulf War, the U.S. Air Force's F-117 stealth aircraft lacked the speed and maneuverability associated with modern jet strike aircraft. What the Nighthawk offered was stealth and the ability to employ precision-guided munitions—two attributes that appeared marginal to many pilots trained to survive by outmaneuvering their opponents and achieving "pickle barrel" accuracy through a combination of computer support and pilot skill.[44]

This dynamic highlights the importance of placing a military capability within the context of a vision of the new competitive environment and its new operational concept to assess its true value. It's important for senior leaders to have these "disruptive MOEs" in mind as they proceed. As Bower and Christensen conclude, "Disruptive technologies tend to stall early in strategic reviews because managers either ask the wrong questions or ask the wrong people the right questions."[45] In other words, shortsighted leaders frame the discussion of MOEs in terms of the current competitive environment, rather than the environment that will exist. For leaders who fall into this trap, carriers remain locked into their role of enhancing the battle line's effectiveness, tanks are consigned to support infantry operations, and stealth aircraft are assigned to strike packages.

The histories of our four militaries that led the way in bringing about a military revolution yield valuable insights for contemporary military organizations anticipating discontinuous shifts in warfare. That being said, the findings are not definitive. At best, they are highly suggestive. We are well served by remembering Richard Feynman's injunctions that, even in the hard sciences such as physics, the "laws" stated in textbooks are really approximations and always subject to revision. So it is, too, with the study of war and organizational behavior. Still, as conditional as these findings are, they are arguably more useful than simply "awaiting events" or "muddling through."

CHAPTER ELEVEN

Where Do We Stand?

"Would you tell me, please, which way I ought to go from here?"
said Alice to the Cheshire Cat. "That depends a good deal on
where you want to get to," said the Cat.

—LEWIS CARROLL, *Alice's Adventures in Wonderland*

How many types of ships do we want? This is quite easy to answer if
we make up our minds *how we are going to fight!* Who has made
up his mind? *How many of our admirals have got minds?*

—ADMIRAL OF THE FLEET JOHN "JACKIE" FISHER

SENIOR U.S. NATIONAL SECURITY policy makers need to know how the
U.S. military stacks up against rival militaries in the balance of power.
The Pentagon's Office of Net Assessment (ONA) is charged with providing this analysis. It typically does so in one of two ways. One kind of assessment focuses on the balance in key regions where the United States
has vital interests, such as in the Western Pacific and in Europe. The second kind examines so-called functional balances, such as the state of the
competition in space, in the undersea, and in strategic forces. There
are, however, some assessments that do not fit neatly into either bin. For

example, during the Cold War, ONA produced comparative assessments of U.S. and Soviet military training and of the economic burden of generating and maintaining military forces. Thus, it would come as no surprise were it to address the U.S. military's relative competence with respect to disruptive military innovation.

As the level of effort involved in crafting a net assessment has been compared to undertaking a doctoral dissertation, a thorough treatment of this important issue lies well beyond the bounds of this book. That being said, it's possible to use the metrics identified in the preceding chapter to present some general observations regarding the U.S. military's ability to engage in innovation on a grand scale. Of course, its position must be judged not in absolute terms but in relation to the competence of its rivals.

What Are We Trying to Do?

Not long after the *Military-Technical Revolution* assessment was completed in 1992, Andrew Marshall sent me on the road to get reaction from some colleagues whose views he regarded highly. One such venture found me briefing a group that included one of the titans of political science, Sam Huntington. Following my presentation, Huntington, who had read my book on the U.S. Army's unsuccessful effort to adapt to wage counterinsurgency effectively during the Vietnam War, asked, "So, Andy, tell me: If we had developed this military-technical revolution at the time of Vietnam, would it have made a difference?" Huntington's point was well put. Indeed, Marshall would typically begin discussion on new work by asking, "What is it we are trying to do?" As Chapter 10 notes, and as Huntington was kindly pointing out, success in disruptive military innovation is highly dependent on the challenge that a military sets for itself. What is it trying to accomplish? Simply put, success in one attempt at disruptive innovation does not provide an advantage in all circumstances. Consequently identifying the right challenge against which to focus a military's efforts at disruptive innovation is critical. The more accurately and precisely you can define it, the greater the chances that you will be able to address it successfully.

Each of the four military organizations examined in this book addressed this fundamental question: What key challenges do we confront at the operational (or theater) level of war? In each case, the question was posed during a major shift in the character of warfare.

Absent a clear statement of the problem, it's difficult to establish the "virtuous cycle" of analysis, war-gaming, field exercises, and interaction with industry important to disruptive innovation. Recall that the operational challenge informs thinking about operational concepts, which identifies the kinds of war games and exercises that should be conducted to subject the concept to testing and evaluation. The results are used to adapt the concept and its associated performance metrics, while also informing defense policy, resource, and program priorities. Absent a clear statement of the operational challenge and an operational concept that describes how it will be addressed, it truly is a case of "if you don't know where you want to go, any road will get you there."

Operational Challenges

When it comes to operational challenges, the U.S. military operates at a disadvantage. Recent administrations have been silent on the operational challenges for which the U.S. military should prepare, complicating its efforts to develop operational concepts. The most recent National Defense Strategy does not even define the term.[1] As used here, "operational challenges" are *compelling real-world problems posed by adversaries at the operational (or campaign) level of war.*

During the Cold War, for example, Central Europe was the location of the key regional military competition between NATO and the Soviet-led Warsaw Pact. Consequently, the U.S. military's principal operational challenge involved *defending NATO's Central European frontiers against a numerically superior foe (Soviet Russia and its Warsaw Pact allies) in a high-intensity conflict environment while avoiding employing nuclear weapons.* This clear statement of the problem enabled the U.S. military, over the course of the forty-year standoff between the two superpowers, to develop a series of operational concepts that informed the crafting of military doctrine. These concepts were adapted and, at times, even abandoned, as circumstances required.

Given the current geopolitical environment, a contemporary set of core operational challenges for the U.S. military might include the following:

- Deterring and, if necessary, defending the U.S. homeland and its treaty allies from catastrophic strategic attack, including by weapons of mass destruction, as well as by advanced conventional and cyber weapons (i.e., against technically advanced, numerically comparable enemies).

- Deterring and, if necessary, defending U.S. allies and security partners in the Indo-Pacific region, especially those along the first island chain, from Chinese aggression and coercion (i.e., against a technically advanced, locally numerically superior enemy) without resorting to the use of nuclear weapons.
- Deterring and, if necessary, defending NATO's Eastern European frontiers from Russian aggression and coercion (i.e., against a technically advanced, locally numerically superior enemy) without resorting to the use of nuclear weapons.
- Deterring and, if necessary, defending against attempts to sever lines of communication via the global commons linking the United States to key overseas theaters of operation and key trading partners/resources (i.e., against technically advanced, numerically comparable enemies) without resorting to the use of nuclear weapons.

There should be no more than five or six core operational challenges—not every challenge can be a "core" challenge. Even these challenges should be prioritized to inform choices regarding resource allocation.

New and Innovative Operational Concepts

Operational concepts provide the conceptual basis for planning at the theater or campaign level of war, including describing how joint and combined forces will operate to achieve strategic goals. Put simply, they offer possible solutions to core operational challenges, both existing and emerging. Periods of dramatic change in the character of military competition, such as those described in the histories of disruptive military innovation in this book, find the most successful military organizations developing and refining new and innovative operational concepts. Properly applied, operational concepts inform (and are informed by) military planning, war gaming, field exercises, and experiments. In combination, these efforts inform military doctrine, the military's size and structure, and its investment priorities. In each history examined in Part 2 of this book, the pathbreaking military organization leveraged emerging technologies embedded in new military systems and capabilities to identify, develop, and refine operational concepts that provided them with far more effective ways of meeting the challenges posed by their rivals at the campaign level of war.

At present, the U.S. military, lacking a clear statement of the principal operational challenges it confronts at the theater level of war, is ill positioned to develop operational concepts capable of effecting a quantum boost in its effectiveness. The causes of this omission are difficult to discern. After all, the United States has identified its principal great-power rivals. Senior policy makers on both sides of the political divide know the key military theaters of operation. Yet the U.S. Joint Staff and military services are proceeding with concept development at a pace and level of abstraction that are both unnecessary and unhelpful.

A Lack of Practice?

Part of the problem may be that the U.S. political leadership and military are out of practice. The decade following the Cold War found the United States enjoying a dominant advantage over any existing or prospective major-power rival. There were no pressing major conventional-war operational challenges against which U.S. military planners could focus their efforts. The emphasis was on planning for "major regional contingencies," "major theater wars," and "major combat operations"— synonyms for war against minor powers like Iran, Iraq, and North Korea. Evidence of this is found in the emphasis at the time on planning based on "capabilities" (as opposed to "threats").[2]

Moreover, after the U.S. military's phenomenal success in the First Gulf War, it understandably, if not wisely, adopted an attitude of "if it isn't broke, why fix it?" General Colin Powell, chairman of the Joint Chiefs of Staff during the war, remarked that it was tailor-made for what the U.S. military had done to prepare for the kind of operational challenge posed by the Soviets in Europe. The war, he said, "was that Cold War battle that didn't come, without trees and mountains. We got a nice desert, and we got a very, very incompetent enemy to work against."[3] The Second Gulf War found the U.S. military arguably winning an even more lopsided victory, this time with an enhanced version of the war-fighting concepts that had succeeded spectacularly twelve years earlier.

Following the 9/11 attacks, U.S. military planning priorities shifted to addressing the challenges posed by radical Islamist terrorist organizations and insurgents, particularly in Afghanistan and Iraq. Here the services found themselves playing a game of catch-up following nearly three decades of benign neglect of counterinsurgency warfare.[4] Yet at the same time the U.S. military was becoming absorbed by irregular wars in Central Asia and the Middle East, both China and Russia were beginning to stir. The lack of resources to challenge U.S. military dominance that had plagued them for much of the 1990s was greatly alleviated by rapid economic growth in the case of the former and a surge in oil prices with regard to the latter. Their common objective was to end the Americans' dominance of the precision-warfare regime.

The signs were clear for those who were willing to see them, and I played a role in efforts to develop a new operational concept to meet the challenge posed by China to the military balance in the Western Pacific Theater of Operations (WPTO). The Center for Strategic and Budgetary Assessments (CSBA), a Washington public-policy institute (commonly known as a "think tank") where I was serving as president at the time, took on the task. The result was presented in two publications, *Why AirSea Battle?* and *AirSea Battle: A Point-of-Departure Operational Concept.*[5] To our surprise, and encouragement, the Pentagon soon established an Air-Sea Battle Office with a similar goal in mind.

Joint Forces Command, R.I.P.

Not long after, in 2011, Joint Forces Command (JFCOM) was disestablished.[6] The command was formed in 1999 with the mission of leading the military's innovation efforts. For all its warts, "Jiff-Com" as it was called, was the only four-star command charged with developing joint concepts of operation for the U.S. military. Now the task was assigned not to a command but to the Joint Staff's J-7 (Joint Force Development) element. Joint concepts would now be fostered through a deliberative, consensus-based process.[7] The requirement for consensus has been lethal to the enterprise, as new operational concepts directly or indirectly create classes of "winners" and "losers" with respect to particular capabilities, force types, and structures, as well as within the subcultures of the military service in question. With innovative concepts, these effects are magnified. Mandating consensus is a sure way for those who envision themselves as "losers" in the new way of war to block change. As one senior officer involved in the effort observed, the process was designed to produce "tapioca" (pudding) as each service moved to defend its programs and budgets against any concept that risked compromising them.

CSBA's AirSea Battle concept, similar to the Cold War–era operational concepts noted earlier, focused on a specific operational problem—in this case, defending the WPTO, particularly along the first island chain, against Chinese aggression and coercion. The Defense Department's Air-Sea Battle concept, however, was abstract. Rather than focusing on an operational challenge, it attempted to address the full spectrum of conflict, up to but not including nuclear warfare, but in no particular geographic theater and against no specific adversary.[8]

In 2015, the Defense Department closed the Air-Sea Battle Office, folding it into the Joint Concept for Access and Maneuver in the Global Commons (JAM-GC, pronounced "Jam, Gee-Cee") effort. The Pentagon stated that the change was needed because "the missing part of the Air-Sea Battle concept was the land portion, basically how the land forces could be used to allow U.S. forces to gain access to a contested area."[9]

Archipelagic Defense

Once again, the Joint Staff found itself playing catch-up. The previous year, the Pentagon's Office of Net Assessment, responding to concerns from the Office of the Secretary of Defense (Policy) over the lack of progress being made by the military with its Air-Sea Battle concept, approached me about leading a "Summer Study": a two-week effort bringing together a small team of experts to focus on an issue of strategic importance to the department's leadership.[10] The task: develop a preliminary operational concept for the WPTO that leveraged the military's full capabilities, including those of the Army and Marine Corps. Our work yielded a basic concept of operations, which my colleague Jim Thomas christened "Archipelagic Defense."

The journal *Foreign Affairs* published my summary of Archipelagic Defense in early 2015.[11] Shortly thereafter, at the invitation of the Japanese government, I traveled to Japan to give a series of briefings on the concept to senior government and military leaders. The Japanese encouraged me to elaborate on Archipelagic Defense, and in 2017, my detailed version of the concept, which drew on the Summer Study effort, was published.[12] Shortly thereafter, in March 2018, again at the Japanese government's request, I traveled to Tokyo and gave the keynote address at the "Group of Five Strategic Dialogue."[13] I was one of only two nonmilitary participants, the other being Japan's deputy national security adviser, Nobukatsu Kanehara. The U.S. military was not invited to brief on its JAM-GC concept.

The attention given to Archipelagic Defense led to a series of briefings with senior U.S. defense officials and military leaders, who were engaged in preparing the National Defense Strategy. Secretary of Defense James Mattis retasked the military with "developing operational concepts to sharpen our competitive advantages and enhance our lethality."[14]

More Heat than Light

Throughout the Trump administration, however, the military still experienced difficulty making progress on this front. Perhaps not surprisingly, the congressional Commission on the National Defense Strategy was highly critical of the Defense Department's inability to develop such concepts, noting, "DOD [Department of Defense] and the White House have not yet articulated clear operational concepts for achieving U.S. security objectives in the face of ongoing competition and potential military confrontation with China and Russia. . . . We found that DOD struggled to link objectives to operational concepts to capabilities to programs and resources. This deficit in analytical capability, expertise, and processes is intolerable in an organization responsible for such complex, expensive, and important tasks, and it must be remedied."[15] The frustration with the lack of progress extended to the strategic studies community. One highly regarded expert, Colonel (Retired) David Johnson, explained why the U.S. military's efforts were floundering:

> A key strength of . . . AirLand Battle was that [it was] . . . designed to solve one problem: the defense of Western Europe against the Warsaw Pact. This enabled the Army and the Air Force to focus their concept- and capability-development efforts on a known enemy, in a specific place, with understood weapons. By contrast, the various multi-domain concepts now under development are generic. They focus on domains rather than adversaries. . . . Absent JFCOM [Joint Forces Command], it is not surprising that there is no joint force [operational] concept, much less a common lexicon, for multi-domain concepts. Instead, there are multiple competing concepts: Multi-Domain Battle, Multi-Domain Operations, Multi-Domain Command and Control, and Multi-Domain Maneuver, and more are likely

in the offing as the services vie to solve challenges posed by Russia and China in ways that are in keeping with their respective service institutional ethos.[16]

Following Secretary Mattis's departure in December 2018, the U.S. military began yet another effort at developing operational concepts. The newly appointed defense secretary, Mark Esper, directed the four services and the Joint Staff to create a "Joint Warfighting Concept for All-Domain Operations." According to the vice chairman of the Joint Chiefs of Staff, General John Hyten, the effort built on former Joint Chiefs chairman General Joseph Dunford's ideas on "global force management" and "global fires" (weapons that could be launched from *outside* a theater of war to generate effects within it). The new Joint Chiefs chairman, General Mark Milley, added four new elements: global plans (planning for rapid crisis response); global operations short of fires (operations in the so-called gray zone between peace and open war); global messaging integration (the use of both words and actions to reassure allies and deter adversaries); and global integration of deterrence (the use of all means, not just nuclear, to deter adversaries from undertaking aggression).

All-Domain Operations was also viewed by some people as an evolution of "Multi-Domain Battle" and "Multi-Domain Operations." Work on another concept, Joint All-Domain Command and Control (JADC2), was undertaken for the purpose of enabling All-Domain Operations.[17]

In July 2020, General Milley requested that each of the services take on a piece of the effort to develop the Joint Warfighting Concept. The Army took contested logistics; the Air Force, JADC2; the Navy, joint fires. No service volunteered to lead the effort on information advantage, so it was assigned to the Joint Staff.[18] Each of these concepts contains different key assumptions while focusing on a different aspect of military operations, making the task of combining them into a coherent whole challenging, to say the least. As with previous failed efforts, the Joint Warfighting Concept is not focused on a real-world military challenge, and suffers from relying too heavily on the services and paying insufficient attention to how their disparate efforts will be fused into a holistic war-fighting concept.[19]

There have been a few bright spots. Admiral Philip Davidson, then head of Indo-Pacific Command, proposed developing an "Indo-Pacific Warfighting Concept" focused on the real-world operational problem that confronted his command: deterring and, if necessary, defeating Chinese aggression against U.S. allies and security partners in the WPTO. Realizing the need to create a process characterized by a virtuous cycle, Davidson envisioned testing and refining the concept through a "joint network of training ranges." In an implicit criticism of the ongoing Joint Staff efforts, the admiral declared that any "new warfighting concept must deliver a similar sense of assurance to our allies and partners today that AirLand Battle provided to NATO member states in Europe in the 70s and 80s."[20] The admiral, however, retired in May 2021 as the Pentagon's effort to develop operational concepts was undergoing yet another change.

When the Biden administration entered office in January 2021, the military once again hit the now well-worn reset button as the new secretary of defense, General (Retired) Lloyd Austin III, signed off on a new version of the JWC. In July, a new concept, "Expanded Maneuver," was introduced. As described by General Hyten, the concept is designed to expand maneuver "in space and time. In every area that an adversary can move, you have to figure out how to fill that space in time, before they can move." This requires figuring out, "how do I aggregate my capabilities to provide significant effect, and then how do I disaggregate to survive any kind of threat?"[21]

The concept is composed of four "functional battle areas": "contested logistics," "joint fires," "all-domain command and control," and "information advantage." The change was apparently motivated by the military leadership's inexplicably belated realization that access to space and cyberspace would be heavily contested in a war with another great power. As General Hyten described it, U.S. forces were being defeated in war games because "we had basically attempted [i.e., 'assumed'] an 'information dominance' structure where information was ubiquitous to our forces just like it was in the first Gulf War, and just like it has been for the last 20 years."[22]

As with previous attempts, the U.S. military's current efforts shy away from focusing on a real-world problem at the campaign level of warfare, where important factors such as geography, force mobilization, and the absence (or presence) of allies are taken into account. As General Hyten described it, the Joint Warfighting Concept should be viewed as an "aspirational" document whose planning horizon extends thirty years into the future, rather than an operational concept designed to address any of today's existing and emerging key operational challenges.[23]

In the Absence of a Compelling Concept

The lack of U.S. operational concepts focused on real-world contingencies works to undermine other key factors supporting disruptive innovation. For example, take the Western Pacific Theater of Operations. The absence of a clear operational challenge, such as defending the first island chain from Chinese aggression, makes establishing a "virtuous cycle" difficult, if not impossible.

At the risk of stating the obvious, it makes a difference whether the Pentagon's Joint Warfighting Concept is intended to deter and defeat the Russian or the Chinese military; whether it will be executed in Eastern Europe or the Western Pacific. One only has to look at U.S. operations in these two theaters during World War II to see the great variance in fighting methods. Patton's highly mechanized Third Army, which proved central to U.S. operations in Western Europe that led to Germany's defeat, had no equivalent in the Pacific—not because the Americans could not field such a force but because it would have been of marginal effectiveness. Similarly, the U.S. Navy's fast carrier task forces that dominated war in the Central Pacific were not replicated for the Battle of the Atlantic, for the simple reason that they would have been far less effective than the combination of convoy escorts, light carriers, and land-based aircraft employed to defeat the German submarine threat.

As this study's histories reveal, new operational challenges and the novel operational concepts that new technologies and capabilities enable typically lead to changes in key measures of effectiveness. This is especially true in situations where technological advances enable militaries to field new and different military capabilities. For example, today the U.S. Navy sees itself serving as a maneuver force in the WPTO. Depending on how the Navy's thinking develops, the range of its weapons—aircraft and missiles—could become an increasingly important MOE relative to, say, the number of ships in the fleet.[24]

Until the U.S. military devises a concept for how it is going to fight, it also risks making poor investment choices, a luxury it can ill afford when confronted with two great military-power rivals in a period of rapidly growing domestic public debt. Absent an operational concept that takes into account the major changes that are occurring in war's character, the Pentagon risks operating off "program momentum": simply continuing to field capabilities that are moving through the production pipeline. Yet these programs were initiated years, and in some cases well over a decade, ago, when the United States' geopolitical situation was far more favorable, and the threats it confronted far less advanced, than those of today.

Which capabilities merit continued production? Which should be canceled? Which should be retained as hedges? Absent a decision on how the U.S. military plans to address real-world operational challenges and to create a "virtuous cycle" for testing and refining new operational concepts, answering these questions becomes far more difficult than it need be.

Speed—and the Lack Thereof

There is also the matter of time. The more quickly a military can introduce new capabilities into the force, the less need it has to field these capabilities in large numbers as a hedge against uncertainty, thereby saving material resources. As our histories show, the ability to field new systems and capabilities rapidly is particularly important in periods when existing military capital stock is prone to depreciate at an accelerated rate, as is characteristic in periods of disruptive change in the military competition.

The U.S. military's ability to compete based on time, once a formidable source of competitive advantage, has eroded precipitously. As General Hyten candidly admitted, "I'm very concerned that our nation has lost the ability to go fast. And we have adversaries now, and we see proof in those adversaries that they're going faster than we are. . . . Slow, expensive, that's the way it is [for us]. . . . I'm criticizing the entire process. . . . The entire process is broken."[25] The general's concerns are well founded. Not only is the U.S. military slow to field new capabilities, but it has also compiled an unenviable record of spending tens of billions of dollars on "failure to launch" systems that have stumbled through their development process only to be canceled for being impractical, far over their initial cost projections, or both.[26]

Hello, I Must Be Going

Shortly after assuming command of Joint Forces Command in November 2007, General James Mattis asked my colleague Barry Watts and me to conduct an independent assessment of the command. Having been a member of the 1997 National Defense Panel, whose recommendation led to JFCOM's creation, and having served as a long-standing member of the command's Transformation Advisory Group, I was familiar with JFCOM's operations. As it turned out, we discovered what General Mattis had suspected: the command was suffering from numerous problems.

One particularly acute problem concerned the disconnect between the length of time it typically takes to bring about disruptive change—typically a decade or longer—and the length of the JFCOM commander's tour, which averaged less than two years. As one senior member of the command put it, "It takes a year to figure out the job. By the time you're here eighteen months, you're a lame duck." In each of the four histories examined in this study, senior leaders closely associated with disruptive innovation typically served in their billets substantially longer than two years. Earlier successful attempts at disruptive innovation by the U.S. military found senior leaders like Creech, Moffett, and Admiral Hyman Rickover enjoying extended tenure lasting at least six years and, in Moffett's and Rickover's cases, much longer. Yet Mattis was probably going to have two years to accomplish a task that history suggests requires at least three times as long just to generate and sustain momentum.

My recommendation to Mattis was that the JFCOM commander should have the opportunity to serve two consecutive three-year terms, six years in all. Assuming that the commander's tenure proved successful, he would then be assigned a four-year term as vice chairman of the Joint Chiefs of Staff to ensure that the groundwork laid in the previous six years was brought to fruition. Although it was clear to me that something along these lines was needed, I also knew that the chances of my recommendation being adopted were slim. Apparently so did Mattis. Rather than maintain the fiction that Joint Forces Command was succeeding in its mission, he recommended it be disbanded, which it was, three years later.

Today the U.S. military continues to rotate senior civilian and military leaders in and out of positions at a rapid rate, for terms lasting as long as four years but typically less. This may be appropriate in some cases. But the findings of this study indicate that there must be exceptions. Disruptive U.S. military innovation will occur, if it occurs at all, over a significantly longer period. To maintain a foolish consistency in the tour lengths of senior officers responsible for pursuing disruptive innovation is to ignore the American military's own history as well as the experience of other successful military organizations.

Exercises and Experimentation

Field exercises focused on testing and refining innovative operational concepts designed to address real-world contingencies, and the experiments they make possible, play a critical role in enabling large-scale military innovation. Each of the military organizations examined in the four histories here derived significant benefits from these activities, which proved indispensable assets in identifying key measures of effectiveness and determining investment (and divestment) priorities.

Joint Forces Command was established to promote these kinds of exercises and experiments. Following the 9/11 attacks, however, such exercises were all but forgotten as the command shifted to supporting forces preparing for operations against enemies as part of the so-called Global War on Terror. JFCOM priorities also took a backseat to "shaping" activities, in which exercises were designed primarily to promote goodwill with active and prospective security partners. As Admiral Davidson pointed out, even today, a decade after JFCOM's demise, despite the major reduction in U.S. forces dedicated to counter-terror and counterinsurgency operations over the past ten years and even given the rise of great-power rivals, a regular series of joint exercises focusing on refining innovative operational concepts addressing real-world operational challenges has yet to be established.

Closing Thoughts

This study yields four significant findings with respect to the U.S. military in particular and the current military competition generally. These findings are suggestive, not definitive, which is another way of saying that the range of significant variables influencing military affairs is so great as to preclude the authoritative conclusions reached in the hard sciences—although Richard Feynman would no doubt warn us that even findings in the hard sciences can still be rather soft in spots.

First, the world is in a period of disruptive change in the character of warfare, or what has come to be known as a military revolution. This is primarily the result of geopolitical and military-technical change. The return of China and Russia as active, revisionist great military powers finds the military competition escalating to a level not seen since the Cold War. Simultaneously, the advance of a range of new military-related technologies that can be employed by themselves, or more likely in combination, through new war-fighting concepts of operation, offer the promise of waging war far more effectively than ever before. This situation finds the U.S. military especially challenged. It has spent most of the past three decades focusing on waging war against minor powers, such as Iraq, Libya, and Serbia, and on counterinsurgency and counter-terror campaigns against nonstate groups while its great-power rivals, China and Russia, have devoted intense effort to offsetting the United States' dominant position in precision warfare. Their efforts have paid off: the Americans no longer enjoy a near monopoly in this form of warfare. Therefore, the U.S. military must address how to adjust to the maturing Precision-Warfare Revolution while figuring out how to meet the challenge of an overlapping emerging revolution.

Second, under these conditions of radical change in the competitive environment, the need to engage in disruptive innovation is both compelling and profound. This is because, as our histories show, militaries that succeed in leading the way into a new and far more effective way of waging war during periods of military revolution can gain an enormous advantage over their rivals. Correspondingly, those that fail to keep pace can find themselves operating at a severe disadvantage.

Third, analysis of military organizations that succeeded in engaging in acts of disruptive innovation during periods of revolutionary change in warfare reveals a number of common attributes. These characteristics exhibit similarities to those exhibited by highly innovative organizations in the business world. At a minimum, military organizations attempting disruptive innovation would benefit from examining how well they embody these attributes.

Finally, we have a preliminary assessment of the U.S. military's efforts at disruptive innovation. It finds that, from the "Revolution in Military Affairs" and efforts at "transformation" in the decade following the Soviet Union's collapse, to the rise and fall of Joint Forces Command, to the repeated attempts to develop operational concepts over the past decade, the United States' armed forces exhibit few, if any, of the characteristics of military organizations that succeed in this endeavor.

Notes

Introduction

1. The U.S. Defense Department defines "general war" as "armed conflict between major powers in which the total resources of the belligerents are employed, and the national survival of a major belligerent is in jeopardy." U.S. Department of Defense, "Dictionary of Military and Associated Terms," Joint Publication 1-02, April 12, 2001 (amended through June 9, 2004), 219.

2. John Newhouse, *War and Peace in the Nuclear Age* (New York: Vintage, 1988), 184.

Chapter One. Come the Revolution

1. U.S. General Accounting Office, "Operation Desert Storm: Problems with Air Force Medical Readiness," December 1993, 3; "Potential War Casualties Put at 100,000; Fewer U.S. Troops Would Be Killed or Wounded than Iraqi Soldiers, Military Experts Predict," *Los Angeles Times*, September 5, 1990, http://articles.latimes.com/1990-09-05/news/mn-776_1_military-experts.

2. As employed in this study, the term "battle network" refers to a military organization's command and control (C2) systems and capabilities (to which are often added "communications and computers," giving us "C4"). Battle networks coordinate and integrate the actions of their military's "scouting" and strike forces. Scouting forces comprise a military's intelligence, surveillance, and reconnaissance (ISR) capabilities used to ascertain knowledge of the enemy. Counter-scouting is those actions taken to defeat scouting. These three elements combine to form a "reconnaissance-strike complex." Captain (Retired) Wayne P. Hughes, *Fleet Tactics and Coastal Combat* (Annapolis, Md.: Naval Institute Press, 2000), 11–12, 175–76; Andrew F. Krepinevich, Jr., and Barry D. Watts, *The Last Warrior* (New York: Basic, 2015), 193–226; Marshal V. D. Sokolovsky, chief ed., *Soviet Military Strategy*, trans. Harriet Fast Scott,

3rd ed. (New York: Crane, 1975), 227; Marshal N. V. Ogarkov, "The Defense of Socialism: Experience of History and the Present Day," *Red Star*, May 9, 1984, trans. U.S. Foreign Broadcast Information Service (FBIS).

3. U.S. Air Force, "U.S. Manned Aircraft Combat Losses, 1990–2002," Air Force Historical Research Agency, Maxwell Air Force Base, December 9, 2002, 1. A "sortie" is a single mission flown by a single aircraft.

4. The use of the phrase "character of warfare" is instructive. Through the ages and across military revolutions, war's *nature* has remained immutable.

5. Interview with Marshal of the Soviet Union N. V. Ogarkov, chief of the General Staff, "The Defense of Socialism: Experience of History and the Present Day," *Krasnaya Zvezda*, May 9, 1984, 2–3, quoted in Barry D. Watts, *Six Decades of Guided Munitions and Battle Networks: Progress and Prospects* (Washington, D.C.: CSBA, 2007), 25.

6. Dominic A. Paolucci, *Summary Report of the Long Range Research and Development Planning Program* (Falls Church, Va.: Lulejian and Associates, February 7, 1975), 45, quoted in Barry D. Watts, *Nuclear-Conventional Firebreaks and the Nuclear Taboo* (Washington, D.C.: CSBA, 2013), 17.

7. Patrick J. Garrity, "Why the Gulf War Still Matters: Foreign Perspectives on the War and the Future of International Security," Center for National Security Studies, July 1994, xvi, 59–60; Defense Intelligence Agency, "Soviet Analysis of Operation Desert Shield and Operation Desert Storm," trans. LN 006-92, October 28, 1991, 32.

8. A. W. Marshall, Memorandum for Fred Ikle, "Future Security Environment Workshop Group: Some Themes for Special Papers and Some Concerns," September 21, 1987; Krepinevich and Watts, *Last Warrior*, 193–226.

9. "Anti-access" refers to "those actions and capabilities, usually long range, designed to prevent an opposing force from entering an operational area," while "area-denial" refers to "those actions and capabilities, usually of shorter range, designed to limit an opposing force's freedom of action within an operational area." U.S. Department of Defense, *Joint Operational Access Concept (JOAC)*, version 1.0 (Washington, D.C.: U.S. Department of Defense, 2012), 1; Andrew F. Krepinevich, *The Military-Technical Revolution: A Preliminary Assessment* (Washington, D.C.: CSBA, 2002), 30, 44; Roger Cliff, Mark Burles, Michael S. Chase, Derek Eaton, and Kevin L. Pollpeter, *Entering the Dragon's Lair* (Santa Monica, Calif.: RAND, 2007), 1. The term "system of systems" was originally used to describe the emergence of battle networks that brought together weapon systems that were the product of "systems integration," which combines large numbers of different components. Systems integration was generally limited to military powers with an advanced industrial base. Thus, a "system of systems" described the linking together of individual integrated systems into systems architectures.

10. Shortly after I departed Marshall's staff in the summer of 1993, he dropped the term "military-technical revolution" in favor of another Russian term, "revolution in military affairs." This stemmed from his concerns that U.S.

senior officials and military leaders would not give sufficient attention to the need for organizational and doctrinal innovation—which the assessment found to be critical to success—but would emphasize technology. Despite the shift from "MTR" to "RMA," Marshall's fears were realized.

11. Krepinevich, *Military-Technical Revolution*, 32, 34. This is a reprint of the original work produced by the Pentagon's Office of Net Assessment in July 1992. Two more fully developed assessments with the same title were produced, which have not been published, one in July 1993 and the other in November 1993.

12. Bernard Brodie and Fawn M. Brodie, *From Crossbow to H-Bomb* (Bloomington: Indiana University Press, 1962), 213–15; Thomas Wildenberg, *Destined for Glory* (Annapolis, Md.: Naval Institute Press, 1998), 169–70; Ronald H. Spector, *Eagle Against the Sun* (New York: Free Press, 1985), 148, 174; Andrew F. Krepinevich, *The Army and Vietnam* (Baltimore: Johns Hopkins University Press, 1986), 115–27.

13. See Geoffrey Parker, *The Military Revolution: Military Innovation and the Rise of the West, 1500–1800* (Cambridge: Cambridge University Press, 1988). See also Krepinevich, *Military-Technical Revolution*, 32, 34; and Andrew F. Krepinevich, "Cavalry to Computer: The Pattern of Military Revolutions," *National Interest*, Fall 1994, 30–42.

14. *Encyclopaedia Britannica*, s.v. "Revolution: Politics," https://www.britannica.com/topic/revolution-politics.

15. Robert Forster and Jack P. Greene, introduction to *Preconditions of Revolution in Early Modern Europe*, ed. Forster and Greene (Baltimore: Johns Hopkins University Press, 1970), 1. The contributors to this edited work could only identify two instances in early modern Europe that fit the definition of "revolution": the Netherlands in the 1570s and England in the 1640s. Quoted in Geoffrey Parker, "In Defense of *The Military Revolution*," in *The Military Revolution Debate: Readings on the Military Transformation of Early Modern Europe*, ed. Clifford J. Rogers (Boulder, Colo.: Westview, 1994), 339, 357.

16. For a discussion of the characteristics of the term "revolution" in scientific and political revolutions, see Thomas S. Kuhn, *The Structure of Scientific Revolutions*, 4th ed. (Chicago: University of Chicago Press, 2012), 92–94.

17. Richard P. Feynman, *Six Easy Pieces* (New York: Basic, 2011), 3.

18. Ibid., 2.

19. Ibid., 10.

20. Joseph L. Bower and Clayton M. Christensen, "Disruptive Technologies: Catching the Wave," *Harvard Business Review*, January–February 1995, 43.

21. Ibid., 48.

22. Clayton M. Christensen, *The Innovator's Dilemma* (New York: HarperBusiness Essentials, 2003).

23. Barry R. Posen, *The Sources of Military Doctrine: France, Britain, and Germany Between the World Wars* (Ithaca, N.Y.: Cornell University Press, 1984); Stephen Peter Rosen, *Winning the Next War* (Ithaca, N.Y.: Cornell University

Press, 1991); Williamson Murray, *America and the Future of War* (Stanford, Calif.: Hoover Institute Press, 2017).

24. Michael Roberts, "The Military Revolution, 1560–1660," in Rogers, *Military Revolution Debate*, 13, 19.

25. Parker, *Military Revolution*, 9–10; Parker, "In Defense of *The Military Revolution*," 345–46.

26. Parker, *Military Revolution*, 4.

27. Jeremy Black, *European Warfare: 1660–1815* (New Haven: Yale University Press, 1995); Black, "A Military Revolution? A 1660–1792 Perspective," in Rogers, *Military Revolution Debate*, 95–116. Other scholars have still different interpretations of what occurred during the period between 1500 and 1815. See, for example, Rogers, *Military Revolution Debate*. Of note, these scholars' "revolutions" spanned from 100 years (in Rogers's case) to three centuries (as posited by Parker).

28. Parker, *Military Revolution*, 146.

29. Krepinevich, *Military-Technical Revolution*, 45–49.

30. Andrew. F. Krepinevich, Jr., "The Pentagon's Wasting Assets," *Foreign Affairs*, July–August 2009, 18–33.

Chapter Two. The Shape of Things to Come

1. Andrew F. Krepinevich, Jr., "The Stealth Battleship," *Issues in Science & Technology* 15, no. 3 (Spring 1999), https://issues.org/p_krepinevich.

2. The U.S. Navy did convert four Trident boats into cruise-missile carriers, or "SSGNs." Of course, the carriers and submarines would be moving targets. My simple example did not address, among other factors, the cruise missile's ability (or lack thereof) to track its carrier target all the way through to striking it.

3. Dierk Walter, "A Military Revolution? Prussian Military Reforms Before the Wars of German Unification," Institutt for Frosvarsstudier, February 2001, 20.

4. Ibid., 14.

5. Michael Howard, *War in European History* (Oxford: Oxford University Press, 2009), 97.

6. Walter, "Military Revolution?," 13–14.

7. Howard, *War in European History*, 97–98; Brodie and Brodie, *Crossbow to H-Bomb*, 130–31.

8. William H. McNeill, *The Pursuit of Power* (Chicago: University of Chicago Press, 1982), 248–49.

9. Brodie and Brodie, *Crossbow to H-Bomb*, 132; McNeill, *Pursuit of Power*, 231; James M. McPherson, *Battle Cry of Freedom* (Oxford: Oxford University Press, 1988), 473.

10. Brodie and Brodie, *Crossbow to H-Bomb*, 132, 135; "Civil War Technology," *History.com*, August 21, 2018, https://www.history.com/topics/american-civil-war/civil-war-technology.

11. Shelby Foote, *The Civil War: Red River to Appomattox* (New York: Vintage, 1974), 872.

12. Herman Hattaway and Archer Jones, *How the North Won* (Urbana: University of Illinois Press, 1991), 584, 597, 674.

13. Howard, *War in European History*, 102–3.

14. Brodie and Brodie, *Crossbow to H-Bomb*, 152; Ernest R. May, *Strange Victory: Hitler's Conquest of France* (New York: Hill and Wang, 2000), 118–20, 395–96, 435–36.

15. May, *Strange Victory*, 120; Walter, "Military Revolution?," 20; Brodie and Brodie, *Crossbow to H-Bomb*, 139.

16. Howard, *War in European History*, 106.

17. Ibid., 103–4.

18. Paul Kennedy, "Britain in the First World War," in *Military Effectiveness*, vol. 1, *The First World War*, ed. Alan R. Millett and Williamson Murray (Boston: Unwin Hyman, 1988), 49, 51, 54, 56; Timothy K. Nenninger, "American Military Effectiveness in the First World War," ibid., 140.

19. Brodie and Brodie, *Crossbow to H-Bomb*, 109.

20. Ibid., 137. At Fredericksburg, Union casualties were greater than 13,000, while the Confederates suffered fewer than 5,000. Pickett's Charge resulted in more than 5,000 Confederate casualties, against roughly 1,500 for the Union. Earl J. Hess, *Pickett's Charge: The Last Attack at Gettysburg* (Chapel Hill: University of North Carolina Press, 2001), 333–35; McPherson, *Battle Cry of Freedom*, 572.

21. Consider a simple thought experiment involving two armies of 10,000 men each. Army A is armed with *repeating* muskets, giving it a high rate of fire, while Army B is equipped with *rifled* muskets, translating to an advantage in range and accuracy. The Spencer repeating rifle could be fired seven times in thirty seconds before reloading, while the Dreyse needle gun could be fired five to seven times per minute. An experienced soldier could fire a musket about three rounds a minute. A reasonable assumption finds Army A enjoying a five-to-one rate-of-fire (volume fires) advantage over Army B's rifled muskets. But Army A's smoothbore rapid-fire muskets are effective at only 100 yards, while Army B's rifled muskets can engage effectively at 500 yards. Thus Army A needs to close to within 100 yards of Army B before it reaches its effective engagement range, while Army B can begin engaging Army A at 500 yards. An average soldier took roughly twenty-five seconds to reload a muzzle loader, and troops advancing at quick-time could cover roughly 80 yards during that time interval. Thus, in the time it would take Army A's troops to cover 400 yards, Army B's troops could get off five or six shots (at 500, 420, 340, 260, 180, and perhaps 100 yards) before Army A could engage effectively. Given the rate-of-fire disparity, for Army B to have an advantage in effective fires at the point where Army A reaches its effective fire range of 100 yards, it would have to outnumber Army A by more than five to one. This means Army A would have had to suffer 80 percent

casualties, reducing its effective strength to 2,000. What would Army B need to do to accomplish this? Again, assuming Army B's 10,000 troops get off between five and six rounds (let's split the difference and say five and a half) before Army A closes to its effective engagement range, they would have fired 55,000 rounds, needing 8,000 hits, a success rate of less than 15 percent, or roughly one out of every six rifled bullets fired. Could Army B's riflemen have accomplished this? It depends on myriad factors, such as terrain, visibility, training, and leadership. An Army B composed of well-trained marksmen, ably led and confronting an enemy advancing on open ground in broad daylight, would stand a much better chance than an Army B populated by ill-trained and poorly led recruits, positioned in a forest, and confronting Army A's advance on a foggy morn. Of course, we'd have to look at Army A's training and leadership as well. There's also the issue of Army B's mobility. On the defensive, it's possible it could extend its range advantage by forming into three ranks and volley firing, with one rank firing, another moving back, and a third reloading. This might enable it to fire another volley or two before Army A could close to its effective range. (Alternatively, if Army A assumed the defense, Army B could move within its engagement range while staying beyond Army A's effective range and firing away.) What about artillery? The three-inch Parrott gun was the most widely used rifled gun during the Civil War. In addition to being rifled, it enjoyed a 250-yard range advantage over the twelve-pound Napoleon, the war's most popular smoothbore cannon. Still, artillery accuracy at very long range remained poor, and guns could not easily advance close to enemy lines, lest gunners come within range of enemy sharpshooters. As was often the case in the Great War, preliminary and assault bombardment in the Civil War could not carry the day for the offense, although artillery could greatly aid the defense. As Bernard and Fawn Brodie conclude, ultimately "the rifle and trench ruled Civil War battlefields as thoroughly as the machine-gun and trench rule those of World War I." Brodie and Brodie, *Crossbow to H-Bomb*, 105; McNeill, *Pursuit of Power*, 245; McPherson, *Battle Cry of Freedom*, 474–77; James C. Hazlett, Edwin Olmstead, and M. Hume Parks, *Field Artillery Weapons of the American Civil War* (Urbana: University of Illinois Press, 1983); Phillip M. Cole, *Civil War Artillery at Gettysburg* (Cambridge, Mass.: Da Capo, 2002), 298.

22. Howard, *War in European History*, 123.
23. Brodie and Brodie, *Crossbow to H-Bomb*, 162.
24. Arthur Herman, *To Rule the Waves* (New York: HarperCollins, 2004), 459.
25. Jon Tetsuro Sumida, *In Defence of Naval Supremacy: Finance, Technology and British Naval Policy, 1889–1914* (Boston: Unwin Hyman, 1989), 41.
26. Ibid., 50.
27. Fisher, in fact, preferred battle cruisers to battleships, as they traded armor for speed and long-range fires to an even greater degree than dreadnoughts. The *Lion*-class battlecruisers commissioned in 1912 boosted armament from

12-inch guns to 13.5-inch guns, nearly doubling the shell weight that could be fired in a single broadside, while steaming at twenty-seven knots. Its armor belt, however, was but nine inches.

28. Karl Lautenschläger, "The Dreadnought Revolution Reconsidered," in *Naval History: The Sixth Symposium of the U.S. Naval War College*, ed. Daniel M. Masterson (Wilmington, Del.: Scholarly Resources, 1987), 129; Geoffrey Penn, *Infighting Admirals* (Yorkshire, U.K.: Leo Cooper, 2000), 138; Robert K. Massie, *Dreadnought* (New York: Random House, 1991), 469.

29. Admiral Sir Reginald Bacon, *The Life of Lord Fisher of Kilverstone*, 2 vols. (London: Hodder and Stoughton, 1929), 1:255.

30. Edwin Gray, *The Devil's Device* (Annapolis, Md.: Naval Institute Press, 1975), 178, 182, 259, 264; Bernard Brodie, *Sea Power in the Machine Age* (New York: Greenwood, 1969), 298.

31. Brodie, *Sea Power*, 277; Edwyn Gray, *The Devil's Device* (Annapolis, Md.: Naval Institute Press, 1991), 178–79, 182, 259–60.

32. Nicholas A. Lambert, *Sir John Fisher's Naval Revolution* (Columbia: University of South Carolina Press, 1999), 79.

33. Roger Parkinson, *Dreadnought: The Ship That Changed the World* (London: I. B. Tauris, 2015), 84–85.

34. Sumida, *Naval Supremacy*, 153; Brodie and Brodie, *Crossbow to H-Bomb*, 188.

35. Nicholas Lambert, "Dreadnought—The Revolution That Never Was," unpublished paper, 2002, 1–2.

36. Brodie, *Sea Power*, 96.

37. Martin Gilbert, *The First World War* (New York: Henry Holt, 1994), 102, 127, 431; Anthony Wells, "Naval Intelligence and Decision Making in an Era of Technical Change," in *Technical Change and British Naval Policy, 1860–1939*, ed. Bryan Ranft (London: Hodder and Stoughton, 1977), 125.

38. General Heinz Guderian, *Panzer Leader*, trans. Constantine Fitzgibbon (Costa Mesa, Calif.: Noontide, 1990), 39, 41.

39. Robert M. Citino, *Quest for Decisive Victory* (Lawrence: University Press of Kansas, 2002), 244.

40. Ronald Spector, "The Military Effectiveness of U.S. Forces: 1919–1939," in *Military Effectiveness*, vol. 2, *The Interwar Period*, ed. Allan R. Millett and Williamson Murray (Boston: Unwin Hyman, 1988), 84.

41. Roy A. Grosnick, *Dictionary of American Naval Squadrons*, vol. 1 (Washington, D.C.: Naval Historical Center, Department of the Navy, 1995), 453–508.

42. John T. Correll, "Daylight Precision Bombing," *Air Force Magazine*, October 2008, 62.

43. Difficulty in obtaining data on the kamikazes has produced some significantly differing estimates regarding their operation and performance. For example, a postwar assessment concluded that roughly one-third of all kamikaze fighters who left their bases succeeded in hitting a ship—a success rate seven to ten times that of a conventional sortie but also more than twice the

rate cited in other assessments. Ronald H. Spector, *At War, at Sea* (New York: Viking, 2001), 312.

44. Smithsonian National Air and Space Museum, "V-2 Missile," accessed February 19, 2022, https://airandspace.si.edu/collection-objects/v-2-missile/nasm_A19600342000.

45. Howard, *War in European History*, 127.

46. Andrew Roberts, *Masters and Commanders* (New York: HarperCollins, 2009), 92–93.

47. Philip Ball, *Beyond Weird* (Chicago: University of Chicago Press, 2018), 6.

48. Bernard Brodie, "Implications for Military Policy," in *The Absolute Weapon*, ed. Brodie (New York: Harcourt, Brace, 1946), 76.

49. President John F. Kennedy, "Radio and Television Report to the American People on the Soviet Arms Buildup in Cuba," October 22, 1962, John F. Kennedy Presidential Library, https://www.jfklibrary.org/Asset-Viewer/sUVmCh-sBomoLfrBcaHaSg.aspx.

50. Frank C. Carlucci, *Annual Report to the Congress, FY 1990* (Washington, D.C.: GPO, January 17, 1989), 77; U.S. Department of Energy, "Megatonnage of U.S. Nuclear Arsenal," September 2021; Natural Resources Defense Council and Committee on International Security and Arms Control, *The Future of U.S. Nuclear Weapons Policy* (Washington, D.C.: National Academy Press, 1997), 109.

51. William Robert Johnson, "Megaton Weapons," Johnston's Archive, April 6, 2009, http://www.johnstonsarchive.net/nuclear/multimeg.html.

52. Paul G. Gillespie, "Precision Guided Munitions: Constructing a Bomb More Potent than the A-bomb" (Ph.D. diss., Lehigh University, 2002), 87.

53. Ibid., 163, 165; Barry D. Watts, *The Evolution of Precision Strike* (Washington, D.C.: CSBA, 2013), 183–84.

54. Gillespie, "Precision Guided Munitions," 203; Watts, *Precision Strike*, 183–84; Benjamin S. Lambeth, *The Transformation of American Air Power* (Ithaca, N.Y.: Cornell University Press, 2000), 160; David R. Mets, "The Long Search for Surgical Strike: Precision Munitions and the Revolution in Military Affairs," CADRE Paper Number 12, Maxwell Air Force Base, Ala., Air University Press, October 2001, 36.

55. Tom Bowman, "Strike Team Advances Precision, Pace of War," *Baltimore Sun*, April 20, 2003, 1A; Lieutenant General T. Michael Moseley, "Operation Iraqi Freedom—By the Numbers," U.S. Air Forces Central Command, Assessment and Analysis Division, April 30, 2003, 9.

56. Douglas Jehl, "Digital Links Are Giving Old Weapons New Power," *New York Times*, April 7, 2003, 2.

57. John Stillion, *Trends in Air-to-Air Combat: Implications for Future Air Superiority* (Washington, D.C.: CSBA, 2015), i, 57.

58. Ibid., 28–29; Watts, *Precision Strike*, 144.

59. Stillion, *Air-to-Air Combat*, ii.

60. Lambeth, *American Air Power*, 125.

61. Chris Rohlfs and Ryan Sullivan, "The MRAP Boondoggle," *Foreign Affairs*, July 26, 2012, https://www.foreignaffairs.com/print/node/1070487; Christopher Lamb and Sally Scudder, "Why the MRAP Is Worth the Money," *Foreign Affairs*, August 23, 2012, https://www.foreignaffairs.com/articles/afghanistan/2012-08-23/why-mrap-worth-money; "Mine Resistant Ambush Protected Program," GlobalSecurity.org, last modified August 8, 2016, https://www.globalsecurity.org/military/systems/ground/mrap.htm; Natalya Anfilofyeva, "Majority of U.S. MRAPs to Be Scrapped or Stored," CSBA, January 5, 2014, https://csbaonline.org/about/news/majority-of-us-mraps-to-be-scrapped-or-stored.

62. Sydney J. Freedberg, Jr., "Milley's Future Tank: Railguns, Robotics & Ultra-Light Armor," *Breaking Defense*, July 27, 2017, https://breakingdefense.com/2017/07/railguns-robotics-ultra-light-armor-general-milleys-future-tank.

63. Megan Eckstein, "New Marine Corps Cuts Will Slash All Tanks, Many Heavy Weapons as Focus Shifts to Lighter, Littoral Forces," U.S. Naval Institute, March 23, 2020, https://news.usni.org/2020/03/23/new-marine-corps-cuts-will-slash-all-tanks-many-heavy-weapons-as-focus-shifts-to-lighter-littoral-forces.

Chapter Three. The Mature Precision-Warfare Regime

1. Krepinevich, *Military-Technical Revolution*, 15.

2. Ibid., 12.

3. Ibid., 22. China's People's Liberation Army has adopted the term "information dominance" in its writings. The PLA believes it must be achieved to enable air and sea dominance, which are necessary to support offensive operations. *Lectures on the Command of Joint Campaigns* (Military Science Press, 2013), 165, cited in Elsa B. Kania and John K. Costello, "The Strategic Support Force and the Future of Chinese Information Operations," *Cyber Defense Review*, Spring 2018, 117.

4. Krepinevich, *Military-Technical Revolution*, 22.

5. Ibid., 32.

6. Andrew F. Krepinevich, "The Military-Technical Revolution: A Preliminary Assessment," unpublished paper, July 1993, III-24.

7. Edmund J. Burke, Kristen Gunness, Cortez A. Cooper III, and Mark Cozad, *People's Liberation Army Operational Concepts* (Santa Monica, Calif.: RAND, 2020), 11.

8. Space is overwhelmingly used as a domain in which to exploit capabilities in the electromagnetic and cyber domains.

9. Burke et al., *PLA Operational Concepts*, 11.

10. Ibid., 7, 13.

11. Ibid., 7; Roger Cliff, John Fei, Jeff Hagen, Elizabeth Hague, Eric Heginbotham, and John Stillion, *Shaking the Heavens and Splitting the Earth: Chinese*

Air Force Employment Concepts in the 21st Century (Santa Monica, Calif.: RAND, 2011), 61–64.

12. U.S.-China Economic and Security Review Commission, *2020 Report to Congress of the U.S.-China Economic and Security Review Commission* (Washington, D.C.: U.S. Government Printing Office, December 2020), 393–94. PLA strategists view the cyber domain as particularly critical to power projection, and China's dominance of global telecommunications infrastructure could bolster that capability. Defense Intelligence Agency, *China Military Power: Modernizing a Force to Fight and Win* (Defense Intelligence Agency, 2019), 43, www.dia. mil/Military-Power-Publications; Cliff et al., *Shaking the Heavens*, 60–61; Todd Harrison, Kaitlin Johnson, and Thomas G. Roberts, "Space Threat 2018: China Assessment," Aerospace Security Project, Center for Strategic and International Studies, April 12, 2018, https://aerospace .csis.org/space-threat-2018-china; Burke et al., *PLA Operational Concepts*, 8.

13. Kevin L. Pollpeter, Michael S. Chase, and Eric Heginbotham, *Strategic Support Force and Its Implications for Chinese Military Space Operations* (Santa Monica, Calif.: RAND, 2017), 2, 32, 35, https://www.rand.org/pubs/ research_reports/RR2058.html; Burke et al., *PLA Operational Concepts*, 13. See also Robert O. Work and Greg Grant, *Beating Americans at Their Own Game* (Washington, D.C.: Center for a New American Security, 2019), 8.

14. Burke et al., *PLA Operational Concepts*, 7, 10; Cliff et al., *Shaking the Heavens*, 61–62; Scott W. Harold, *Defeat, Not Merely Compete* (Santa Monica, Calif.: RAND, 2018), 35; Michael S. Chase, testimony for the U.S.-China Economic and Security Review Commission, *Hearing on China's Military Reforms and Modernization: Implications for the United States*, February 15, 2018, 6.

15. Cliff et al., *Shaking the Heavens*, 56–60.

16. U.S. Office of the Secretary of Defense, *Military and Security Developments Involving the People's Republic of China 2020* (Washington, D.C.: U.S. Department of Defense, 2020), 161; Burke et al., *PLA Operational Concepts*, 21–22.

17. U.S. Office of the Secretary of Defense, *Military and Security Developments*, 161.

18. "Finlandization" refers to a situation in which a powerful state indirectly controls the foreign policy of a smaller neighboring country or group of countries, while allowing them to maintain their nominal independence. The term was coined in reference to the Soviet Union's control over Finland's foreign policies during the Cold War.

19. Andrew F. Krepinevich, Jr., *Archipelagic Defense: The Japan-U.S. Alliance and Preserving Peace and Stability in the Western Pacific* (Tokyo: Sasakawa Peace Foundation, 2017), 62–99.

20. Andrew F. Krepinevich, Jr., and Eric Lindsey, *The Road Ahead: Future Challenges and Their Implications for Ground Vehicle Modernization* (Washington, D.C.: CSBA, 2012), 17, 33.

21. The nuclear competition, as it has since the advent of this form of warfare in 1945, seems certain to continue favoring the offense for the foreseeable future.

22. David Axe, "The U.S. Navy Wants a New Guided-Missile Submarine," *National Interest*, November 27, 2017, https://nationalinterest.org/blog/the-buzz/the-us-navy-wants-new-guided-missile-submarine-23372.

23. An aircraft's range is a function of several factors, including its payload and flight profile. Its range can also be extended through in-flight refueling from tanker aircraft. The Vietnam-era A-6's combat mission radius was roughly 890 miles carrying a 2,080-pound payload with two external fuel tanks. The F-18 Super Hornet aircraft on today's carriers has a range of roughly 500 miles, while the F-18 Advanced Super Hornet's range, with its external conformal fuel tanks, is estimated at approximately 800 miles. "A-6 Intruder," GlobalSecurity.org, last modified July 7, 2011, https://www.globalsecurity.org/military/systems/aircraft/a-6.htm. Kyle Mizokami, "The F/A-18 Super Hornet Is About to Fly Farther than Ever Before," *Popular Mechanics*, February 16, 2018, https://www.popularmechanics.com/military/aviation/a18211702/fa-18-super-hornet-longer-legs-fuel-tanks-range. The Navy's new F-35C aircraft is listed as having a combat range of 615 miles. Sydney J. Friedberg, "F-35C & Ford Carriers—A Wrong Turn for Navy: CNAS," *Breaking Defense*, October 19, 2015, https://breakingdefense.com/2015/10/f-35c-a-wrong-turn-for-navy-cnas.

24. Krepinevich, *Military-Technical Revolution*, 14.

25. Ibid., 23.

26. Ibid., 14.

27. Ibid., 23.

28. Gregory Falco, "Our Satellites Are Prime Targets for a Cyberattack. And Things Could Get Worse," *Washington Post*, May 7, 2019, https://www.washingtonpost.com/opinions/our-satellites-are-prime-targets-for-a-cyberattack-and-things-could-get-worse/2019/05/07/31c85438-7041-11e9-8be0-ca575670e91c_story.html?utm_term=.be33f7bec97f. See also Alyssa Newcomb, "Hacked in Space: Are Satellites the Next Cybersecurity Battleground?," *NBC News*, October 3, 2016, https://www.nbcnews.com/storyline/hacking-in-america/hacked-space-are-satellites-next-cybersecurity-battleground-n658231.

29. Tony Girard, "The Attack-Counterattack Game," *Aerospace and Defense Technology*, April 1, 2014, https://www.aerodefensetech.com/component/content/article/adt/features/articles/19412.

30. For a detailed discussion of this topic, see Stephen Budiansky, *Blackett's War* (New York: Vintage, 2013).

31. Even fixed assets, such as forward air bases, may benefit from significantly diminishing the enemy's scouting forces. See, for example, the discussion in Krepinevich, *Archipelagic Defense*, 80–84.

32. The U.S. Navy's Haystack and UPTIDE exercises in the 1950s and '60s were predicated on the belief that such "gaps" could be created and exploited. Robert G. Angevine, "Hiding in Plain Sight: The U.S. Navy and Dispersed Operations Under EMCON, 1956–1972," *Naval War College*

Review, Spring 2011. See also Operations Evaluation Group, "OEG Report 77: The Sixth Fleet Concept and Analysis of Haystack Operations," January 24, 1958.

33. The Doolittle Raid, conducted on April 18, 1942, was the culmination of a series of raids by U.S. carrier forces. The U.S. carrier *Hornet* steamed within Japan's inner maritime defenses to a position roughly 650 miles away from the homeland and launched sixteen Army Air Corps bombers for an attack on Tokyo. Intensive U.S. scouting preceded the U.S. strike to ensure that Japanese scouting forces had not uncovered the operation. Submarines were sent deep into Japanese waters, while the carrier *Enterprise* sent scout aircraft out to determine if the U.S. task force had been spotted. *Enterprise* and *Hornet* detected several "enemy surface craft" as they approached the attack launch point. Upon sighting one within visual range, the attack was immediately launched—roughly 250 miles away from the planned launch point. George W. Baer, *The U.S. Navy: One Hundred Years of Sea Power* (Stanford, Calif.: Stanford University Press, 1993), 216–17; Lisle A. Rose, *Power at Sea: The Breaking Storm, 1919–1945* (Columbia: University of Missouri Press, 2007), 200, 250–51; Norman Polmar, *Aircraft Carriers* (Dulles, Va.: Potomac, 2006), 205–6, 209; James G. Roche and Barry D. Watts, "Choosing Analytic Measures," *Journal of Strategic Studies* 14, no. 2 (1991): 184–89.

34. The bombers' range far exceeded that of their naval counterparts. Interestingly, the Japanese "picket line" of scout ships did succeed in warning of the approaching attack; however, the Japanese air defense command assumed that the strike would be conducted by naval aircraft and, based on the reported sightings and shorter range of naval carrier–based strike aircraft, believed the attack would occur one or two days later than it did. Polmar, *Aircraft Carriers*, 206. Only a few months earlier, at Pearl Harbor, the U.S. side suffered from a similar problem with respect to interpreting scouting information. Roberta Wohlstetter, *Pearl Harbor: Warning and Decision* (Stanford, Calif.: Stanford University Press, 1962).

35. Krepinevich, *Military-Technical Revolution*, 26.

36. "U.S. Combat Pilots on Speed," *ABC News*, December 20, 2002, https://abcnews.go.com/2020/story?id=123778&page=1.

37. There are arguably eight domains in which warfare occurs. The land, sea surface, undersea, electromagnetic, and air domains featured prominently in World War II. Since then, three additional domains—space, the seabed, and cyberspace—have become major military competition venues. The expansion from five domains to eight since 1945 represents a 60 percent increase.

38. Andrew Roberts, *The Storm of War* (New York: HarperCollins, 2011), 463.

39. The enemy might choose to employ relatively novel forms of scouting, such as spies providing information via the internet or cell phones. This assumes that friendly forces have not taken effective countermeasures and that it is still possible to communicate via cellular transmissions and the internet in the midst of an intense electronic combat to gain information superiority.

40. For a more detailed discussion of the "shell-game" concept in a conflict between the United States and its allies in the Western Pacific and China, see Krepinevich, *Archipelagic Defense*, 82–83.

41. One of the first acts of war by Great Britain against Germany in 1914 was to cut its overseas telecommunications cables. On August 5, 1914, the Royal Post Office Cable Ship *Alert* cut the five German Atlantic submarine telegraph cables. Jonathan Reed Winkler, *Nexus: Strategic Communications and American Security in World War I* (Cambridge, Mass.: Harvard University Press, 2008), 5–6, 10.

42. Joshua T. White, "China's Indian Ocean Ambitions: Investment, Influence, and Military Advantage," Brookings Institution, June 2020, 1, 4–7, 10–11.

43. This is one reason that Germany proved much less vulnerable to blockade in World War II than it did in World War I, when the Allied blockade contributed significantly to its defeat. During the first twenty-two months of World War II, the Germans could rely on the Soviet Union for raw materials, which greatly reduced the effectiveness of the British blockade. In World War I, Russia was an active ally of Britain from the beginning.

44. For a detailed treatment of the potential complexities associated with executing a blockade against a neutral major power, see Nicholas A. Lambert, *Planning Armageddon* (Cambridge, Mass.: Harvard University Press, 2012). Generally speaking, a land blockade can be pursued along the same general lines as a maritime blockade, imposing similar costs on the enemy. Friendly forces would probably impose a distant land blockade in their own rear area or where they enjoy a local advantage, enabling them to employ less expensive, shorter-range scouting and strike systems. To contest this distant blockade, the enemy would probably be compelled to deploy a relatively high percentage of its scarce long-range scouting and strike forces.

45. For a discussion of this issue, see Andrew F. Krepinevich, Jr., *Protracted Great Power War* (Washington, D.C.: Center for a New American Security, 2020).

46. Estimates place Chinese losses at roughly 19,000 combat casualties, and 29,000 noncombat casualties, with the latter being attributed primarily to weather and lack of food. The historian Yan Xue of the People's Liberation Army National Defense University states that the Chinese Ninth Army was out of action for three months following the engagement. Patrick C. Roe, *The Dragon Strikes: China and the Korean War, June–December 1950* (Novato, Calif.: Presidio, 2000), 394; Yan Xue, *First Confrontation: Reviews and Reflections on the History of War to Resist America and Aid Korea* (Beijing: Chinese Radio and Television Publishing House, 1990), 59. See also Roy Appleman, *Escaping the Trap: The US Army X Corps in Northeast Korea, 1950* (College Station: Texas A&M University Press, 1990). In taking Berlin, Soviet casualties were estimated at roughly 80,000 killed or missing and 280,000 sick or wounded. Grigori F. Krivosheev, ed., *Soviet Casualties and Combat Losses in the Twentieth Century* (London: Greenhill, 1997), 157.

47. Krepinevich, *Army and Vietnam*, 238, 248. The U.S. forces suffered roughly 1,500 killed in action. The U.S. command asserted that the Communists had lost some 32,000 to 37,000 killed and 6,000 captured.

48. Lieutenant General N. Korenevskiy, "The Role of Space Weapons in a Future War," U.S. Central Intelligence Agency, December 1961, 6, https://www.cia.gov/library/readingroom/docs/CIA-RDP33-02415A000500190011-3.pdf (originally published by the Russian military journal *Voyennaya Msyl* (Military Thought).

49. Ibid., 8.

50. Ibid., 9.

51. Ibid., 12. The general anticipated that the Americans might engage in a race to the moon to create military bases there that would "preclude the possibility to destroying the U.S. military might in case of surprise attack." Earlier that year, President Kennedy had established the goal of sending a man to the moon and returning him safely before the end of the decade.

52. Ibid., 21.

53. Paul Tullus, "The World Economy Runs on GPS. It Needs a Backup Plan," *Bloomberg Business Week*, July 25, 2018, https://www.bloomberg.com/news/features/2018-07-25/the-world-economy-runs-on-gps-it-needs-a-backup-plan.

54. William J. Broad, "How Space Became the Next 'Great Power' Contest Between the U.S. and China," *New York Times*, January 24, 2021, https://www.nytimes.com/2021/01/24/us/politics/trump-biden-pentagon-space-missiles-satellite.html; "Nanosats Are Go!," *Economist*, June 5, 2014, https://www.economist.com/technology-quarterly/2014/06/07/nanosats-are-go.

55. *Nanosats Database*, accessed February 19, 2022, https://www.nanosats.eu; Michael Sheetz, "SpaceX Is Manufacturing 120 Starlink Internet Satellites per Month," *SpaceNews*, August 10, 2020, https://spacenews.com/u-s-military-space-architecture-to-bring-in-commercial-systems-small-satellites; Jonathan O'Callaghan, "SpaceX Launches Rocket with 143 Satellites—The Most Ever Flown on a Single Mission," *Forbes*, Jan 24, 2021, https://www.forbes.com/sites/jonathanocallaghan/2021/01/24/spacex-launches-rocket-with-143-satellites--the-most-ever-flown-on-a-single-mission/?sh=387291be27fd; Amy Thompson, "SpaceX Launches 60 Starlink Satellites on Record-Setting Used Rocket, Nails Landing," *Space.com*, February 4, 2021, https://www.space.com/spacex-starlink-18-satellites-launch-rocket-landing. Iridium, which had held the record for the largest commercial satellite constellation, was manufacturing roughly six satellites per month at peak production. Even accounting for the fact that each Starlink is smaller than an Iridium satellite, SpaceX's build rate is twenty times as fast. A Starlink satellite weighs roughly 575 pounds.

56. Microsatellites are those weighing about 100 kilograms, or around 225 pounds, while nanosatellites weigh only a few kilograms, or less than 10 pounds. "Nanosats Are Go!"; Mike Wall, "Rocket Lab Launches 13 CubeSats

on 1st Mission for NASA," *Space.com*, December 16, 2018, https://www.space
.com/42714-rocket-lab-launches-cubesats-nasa.html; "Orbital Ecosystem,"
Economist, June 15, 2019, 71–72; Anna Esher, "Inside Planet Labs' New Satellite Manufacturing Site," *TechCrunch*, September 14, 2018, https://
techcrunch.com/2018/09/14/inside-planet-labs-new-satellite-manufacturing-
site; Josef S. Koller, "The Future of Ubiquitous, Realtime Intelligence: A
GEOINT Singularity," Aerospace Corporation Center for Space Policy and
Strategy, August 2019, 3.

57. Robert Cardillo, remarks at GEOINT 2017, https://www.nga.mil/Media
Room/SpeechesRemarks/Pages/GEOINT-2017-Symposium.aspx, cited in
United States Geospatial Intelligence Foundation, "2018 State and Future
of GEOINT Report," February 2018, 45, https://www.researchgate.net/
publication/322962399_Discipline-Based_Education_Research_A_new_
approach_to_teaching_and_learning_in_geospatial_intelligence_in_the_
United_States_Geospatial_Intelligence_Foundation_2018_STATE_AND_
FUTURE_OF_GEOINT_REPORT.

58. Koller, "Future of Ubiquitous, Realtime Intelligence," 4; "Orbital Ecosystem," 72.

59. Jim Vinoski, "Space Truckin': Thanks to D-Orbit, It's Not Just a Great Old
Deep Purple Song Anymore," *Forbes*, June 10, 2021, https://www.forbes.
com/sites/jimvinoski/2021/06/10/space-truckin-thanks-to-d-orbit-its-not-
just-a-great-old-deep-purple-song-anymore/?sh=1d4f9aa113c0.

60. Air University Assessment Team, "Fast Space: Leveraging Ultra Low-Cost
Space Access for 21st Century Challenges," U.S. Air University, January 13,
2017, A-2; Katie Hunt, "Mission to Clean Up Space Junk with Magnets
Set for Launch," *CNN Business*, April 1, 2021, https://www.cnn.com/
2021/03/19/business/space-junk-mission-astroscale-scn/index.html.

61. Harry W. Jones, "The Recent Large Reduction in Space Launch Cost,"
paper presented at the 48th International Conference on Environmental
Systems, July 12, 2018, Albuquerque, New Mexico.

62. Eric Berger, "Russia Appears to Have Surrendered to SpaceX in the Global
Launch Market," *Ars Technica*, April 18, 2018, https://arstechnica.com/
science/2018/04/russia-appears-to-have-surrendered-to-spacex-in-the-
global-launch-market; Charlie Campbell, "From Satellites to the Moon and
Mars, China Is Quickly Becoming a Space Superpower," *Time*, July 17,
2019, https://time.com/5623537/china-space.

63. U.S. Department of Defense, "Final Report on Organizational and Management Structure for the National Security Space Components of the Department of Defense," August 9, 2018, 4. "Dazzling" involves the use of directed
radiation to temporarily disable (or "blind") a target, which is usually some
sort of sensor, including human vision.

64. Namrata Goswami, "China's Grand Strategy in Space: To Establish Compelling Standards of Behavior," *Space Review*, August 5, 2019, http://www.
thespacereview.com/article/3773/1.

65. Michael R. Gordon, "Russia Tests an Anti-Satellite Weapon, U.S. Officials Say," *Wall Street Journal*, July 23, 2020, https://www.wsj.com/articles/russia-tests-an-anti-satellite-weapon-u-s-officials-say-11595545670; Christian Davenport, "The Battlefield 22,000 Miles Above Earth," *Wilson Quarterly*, Winter 2019, https://wilsonquarterly.com/quarterly/the-new-landscape-in-space/the-battlefield-22-000-miles-above-earth.

66. "Using the Force," *Economist*, July 20, 2019.

67. Broad, "Next 'Great Power' Contest."

68. Olivia Beavers, "Rising Concerns over Hackers Using Satellites to Target U.S.," *The Hill*, June 26, 2018, https://thehill.com/policy/cybersecurity/394037-satellites-become-latest-tool-for-hackers-targeting-businesses-consumers.

69. Tullus, "World Economy Runs on GPS."

70. "Finland's GPS Was Disrupted During NATO War Games and Russian Could Be Responsible," *Reuters.com*, November 11, 2018, https://www.reuters.com/article/us-finland-russia-defence-idUSKCN1NG0TG.

71. U.S. Department of Defense, "Final Report on Organizational and Management Structure," 4–5.

72. Patrick M. Shanahan, "Remarks by Acting Secretary Shanahan at the 35th Space Symposium, Colorado Springs, Colorado," April 9, 2019, available at https://www.defense.gov/Newsroom/Transcripts/Transcript/Article/1809882/remarks-by-acting-secretary-shanahan-at-the-35th-space-symposium-colorado-sprin/source/GovDelivery.

73. Most of this jamming involved truckers and various types of cab drivers trying to conceal their locations from their employers, presumably to take breaks.

74. "Using the Force," 19; Tullus, "World Economy Runs on GPS." Fortunately, every plane landed safely, with the pilots manually "eyeballing" their approaches. One wonders what would have happened had the weather precluded this method.

75. Tulles, "World Economy Runs on GPS."

76. For example, see "Tactical High-Energy Laser (THEL)," *Jane's Land Warfare Platforms*, August 14, 2012; "Northrop Grumman Skyguard," *Jane's Electro-Optic Systems*, September 3, 2010; "Skyguard (Laser Air Defence)," *Jane's Land Warfare Platforms*, March 10, 2015; "HEL MD Laser Continues Testing, Moves Towards 60 kW System," *Jane's Defence Weekly*, September 10, 2014; U.S. Air Force, "Starfire Optical Range at Kirtland Air Force Base," fact sheet, March 9, 2009. See U.S. Office of Naval Research, "Navy Solid State Laser Program Overview," February 22, 2013. See also "Northrop Grumman Mid-InfraRed Advanced Chemical Laser (MIRACL)," *Jane's Electro-Optic Systems*, September 21, 2010; and "Ship-Based Laser," *Jane's Strategic Weapon Systems*, July 25, 2014, cited in Eric Heginbotham et al., *The U.S.-China Military Scorecard* (Santa Monica, Calif.: RAND, 2015), 235–36.

77. Valerie Insinna, "The US Air Force's X-37B Spaceplane Lands After Spending Two Years in Space," *Defense News*, October 28, 2019, https://www.defensenews.com/space/2019/10/28/the-air-forces-x-37b-spaceplane-finally-landed-after-spending-two-years-in-space; U.S. Air Force, "X-37B Orbital Test Vehicle," fact sheet, August 7, 2020, https://www.af.mil/About-Us/Fact-Sheets/Display/Article/104539/x-37b-orbital-test-vehicle.

78. Mike Wall, "X-37B Military Space Plane's Latest Mystery Mission Hits 700 Days," *Space.com*, August 8, 2019, https://www.space.com/x-37b-military-space-plane-otv5-700-days.html; Kyle Mizokami, "Here's How the X-37B Spaceplane 'Disappears,'" *Popular Mechanics*, July 24, 2019, https://www.popularmechanics.com/military/a28496447/x-37b-disappear.

79. Mizokami, "X-37B Spaceplane."

80. Pratik Jakhar, "China Claims 'Important Breakthrough' in Space Mission Shrouded in Mystery," *BBC.com*, September 9, 2020, https://www.bbc.com/news/science-environment-54076895; Andrew Jones, "China Carries Out Secretive Launch of 'Reusable Experimental Spacecraft,'" *SpaceNews*, September 4, 2020, https://spacenews.com/china-carries-out-secretive-launch-of-reusable-experimental-spacecraft; Andrew Jones, "China Launches Secretive Suborbital Vehicle for Reusable Space Transportation System," *SpaceNews*, July 16, 2021, https://spacenews.com/china-launches-secretive-suborbital-vehicle-for-reusable-space-transportation-system.

81. Sandra Erwin, "Report: Nuclear Propulsion Would Help Military Satellites Maneuver Out of Harm's Way," *SpaceNews*, January 14, 2022, https://spacenews.com/report-nuclear-propulsion-would-help-military-satellites-maneuver-out-of-harms-way.

82. Broad, "Next 'Great Power' Contest."

83. Davenport, "Battlefield 22,000 Miles Above Earth." The general was guilty of an overstatement. Precision-guided munitions, such as laser-guided bombs, were used effectively decades before GPS and do not require the precision navigation and timing provided by that constellation, as do weapons such as the U.S. Joint Direct Attack Munition (JDAM).

84. "Air Breaking," *Economist*, March 9, 2019, 71.

85. Ibid., 72.

86. Krepinevich, *Military-Technical Revolution*, 23.

Chapter Four. Disruptive Technologies

1. During my service in the Army, I was assigned to the Office of Net Assessment from 1989 to 1993. I have served as a consultant for ONA since 1995.

2. Greg Allen and Taniel Chan, "Artificial Intelligence and National Security," Belfer Center, Harvard University, July 2017, 7.

3. Miles Brundage, Shahar Avin, et al., "The Malicious Use of Artificial Intelligence: Forecasting, Prevention, and Mitigation," University of Oxford,

University of Cambridge, the Center for a New American Security, and the Electronic Frontier Foundation, February 2018, 9.

4. Eric Schmidt, "Remarks at the Techonomy Conference in Lake Tahoe," *TechCrunch*, August 4, 2010, http://techcrunch.com/2010/08/04/schmidt-data.

5. National Security Telecommunications Advisory Committee (NSTAC), "NSTAC Report to the President on Big Data Analytics," May 11, 2016, ES-1.

6. NSTAC, "NSTAC Report to the President on the Internet of Things," November 19, 2014, 1, https://www.cisa.gov/sites/default/files/publications/ NSTAC%20Report%20to%20the%20President%20on%20the%20Internet %20of%20Things%20Nov%202014%20%28updat%20%20%20.pdf.

7. Gartner Inc., "Gartner Says 6.4 Billion Connected 'Things' Will Be in Use in 2016, Up 30 Percent from 2015," November 10, 2015, http://www.gartner .com/newsroom/id/3165317; Juniper Research, " 'Internet of Things' Connected Devices to Almost Triple to Over 38 Billion Units by 2020," July 28, 2015, http://www.juniperresearch.com/press/press-releases/iot-connected-devices-to-triple-to-38-bn-by-2020; Sagar Bhat, Omkar Bhat, and Pradyumma Gokhale, "Applications of IoT and IoT: Vision 2020," *International Advanced Research Journal in Science, Engineering and Technology*, January 2018, 36.

8. James Somers, "How the Artificial-Intelligence Program AlphaZero Mastered Its Games," *New Yorker*, December 28, 2018, https://www.newyorker .com/science/elements/how-the-artificial-intelligence-program-alphazero-mastered-its-games; Larry Greenemeier, "AI Versus AI: Self-Taught AlphaGo Zero Vanquishes Its Predecessor," *Scientific American*, October 18, 2017, https://www.scientificamerican.com/article/ai-versus-ai-self-taught-alphago-zero-vanquishes-its-predecessor.

9. Cade Metz, "Hold 'Em or Fold 'Em? This A.I. Bluffs with the Best," *New York Times*, July 11, 2019, https://www.nytimes.com/2019/07/11/science/ poker-robot-ai-artificial-intelligence.html.

10. Zachary Kallenborn, "The Race Is On: Assessing the U.S.-China Artificial Intelligence Competition," Modern War Institute, April 16, 2019, https:// mwi.usma.edu/race-assessing-us-china-artificial-intelligence-competition.

11. Peter Sondergaard, "Remarks at the Gartner Symposium/ITxpo," Gartner, October 2011, http://www.gartner.com/newsroom/id/1824919. See also NSTAC, "Big Data Analytics," 10.

12. Defense Science Board, "Summer Study on Autonomy," Office of the Under Secretary of Defense for Acquisition, Technology and Logistics, June 2016, 4–5. Definitions for *intelligent system, autonomy, automation, robots,* and *agents* can be found in L. G. Shattuck, "Transitioning to Autonomy: A Human Systems Integration Perspective," presentation at *Transitioning to Autonomy: Changes in the Role of Humans in Air Transportation*, March 11, 2015, https:// human-factors.arc.nasa.gov/workshop/autonomy/download/presentations/ Shaddock%20.pdf.

13. Jack Corrigan, "Three-Star General Wants AI in Every New Weapon System," *Nextgov*, November 2, 2017, https://www.nextgov.com/cio-briefing/2017/11/three-star-general-wants-artificial-intelligence-every-new-weapon-system/142225; Richard H. Schultz and General Richard D. Clarke, "Big Data at War: Special Operations Forces, Project Maven, and Twenty-First Century Warfare," Modern Warfare Institute, August 25, 2020, https://mwi.usma.edu/big-data-at-war-special-operations-forces-project-maven-and-twenty-first-century-warfare.

14. Defense Science Board, "Autonomy," 42; Dave Gershgorn, "The Era of Easily Faked, AI-Generated Photos Is Quickly Emerging," *Quartz*, October 30, 2017; https://qz.com/1115353/new-research-from-nvidia-shows-that-the-era-of-easily-faked-ai-generated-photos-is-quickly-emerging.

15. National Reconnaissance Office, "Sentient Program," https://www.nro.gov/Portals/65/documents/foia/declass/ForAll/051719/F-2018-00108_C05113688.pdf; Edward Giest and Andrew J. Lohn, *How Might Artificial Intelligence Affect the Risk of Nuclear War?* (Santa Monica, Calif.: RAND, 2018), 10.

16. Sarah Scoles, "Meet the U.S.'s Spy System of the Future—It's Sentient," *Fortuna's Corner*, July 31, 2019, https://fortunascorner.com/2019/08/01/meet-the-u-s-s-spy-system-of-the-future-its-sentient.

17. Ibid.

18. Defense Science Board, "Autonomy," 53.

19. Ibid.; Giest and Lohn, *Nuclear War?*, 10; Allen and Chan, "Artificial Intelligence," 24.

20. "The Fog of War May Confound Weapons That Think for Themselves," *Economist*, May 29, 2021, https://www.economist.com/science-and-technology/2021/05/26/the-fog-of-war-may-confound-weapons-that-think-for-themselves.

21. "Russia Says 13 Drones Used in Attack on Its Air Base, Naval Facility in Syria," Radio Free Europe/RadioLiberty, January 8, 2018, https://www.rferl.org/a/syria-russia-says-drones-used-attack-bases/28963399.html.

22. Spencer Jakab, "Saudi Oil Attack: This Is the Big One," *Wall Street Journal*, September 14, 2019, https://www.wsj.com/articles/saudi-oil-attack-this-is-the-big-one-11568480576; Dion Nissenbaum, Summer Said, and Jared Malsin, "U.S. Tells Saudi Arabia Oil Attacks Were Launched from Iran," *Wall Street Journal*, September 16, 2019, https://www.wsj.com/articles/u-s-tells-saudi-arabia-oil-attacks-were-launched-from-iran-11568644126.

23. Defense Science Board, "Autonomy," 83; Allen and Chan, "Artificial Intelligence," 16; Brundage et al., "Artificial Intelligence," 19.

24. Defense Science Board, "Autonomy," 83. See also John Arquilla and David Ronfeldt, *Swarming and the Future of Conflict* (Santa Monica, Calif.: RAND, 2000), https://www.rand.org/pubs/documented_briefings/DB311.html.

25. Brundage et al., "Artificial Intelligence," 20.

26. General (Retired) John Allen and Amir Husain, "AI Will Change the Balance of Power," *U.S. Naval Institute Proceedings*, August 2018, https://www

.usni.org/magazines/proceedings/2018/august/ai-will-change-balance-power.

27. Seth J. Frantzman, "50 Iranian Drones Conduct Massive 'Way to Jerusalem' Exercise," *Jerusalem Post*, March 14, 2019, https://www.jpost.com/Middle-East/50-Iranian-drones-conduct-massive-way-to-Jerusalem-exercise-report-583387.

28. Aaron Mehta, "Pentagon Launches 103 Unit Drone Swarm," *DefenseNews*, January 10, 2017, https://www.defensenews.com/air/2017/01/10/pentagon-launches-103-unit-drone-swarm; Shawn Snow, "Pentagon Successfully Tests World's Largest Micro-Drone Swarm," *Military Times*, January 9, 2017, https://www.militarytimes.com/news/pentagon-congress/2017/01/09/pentagon-successfully-tests-world-s-largest-micro-drone-swarm. "Self-healing" occurs when the swarm reconfigures itself to account for the loss of one or more members.

29. Joseph Trevithick, "USAF Wants to Network Its Precision Munitions Together into a 'Golden Horde' Swarm," *The War Zone*, June 26, 2019, https://www.thedrive.com/the-war-zone/28706/usaf-wants-to-network-its-precision-munitions-together-into-a-golden-horde-swarm; Peter Suciu, "The Air Force's New Golden Horde Swarming Munitions: A Game Changer?," *1945*, June 10, 2021, https://www.19fortyfive.com/2021/06/the-air-forces-new-golden-horde-swarming-munitions-a-game-changer.

30. Jeffrey Lin and P. W. Singer, "China Is Making 1,000-UAV Drone Swarms Now," *Popular Science*, January 8, 2018, https://www.popsci.com/china-drone-swarms.

31. Ibid.

32. Defense Science Board, "Autonomy," 85–86.

33. Joseph Hanacek, "The Perfect Can Wait: Good Solutions to the 'Drone Swarm' Problem," *War on the Rocks*, August 14, 2018, https://warontherocks.com/2018/08/the-perfect-can-wait-good-solutions-to-the-drone-swarm-problem.

34. Brundage et al., "Artificial Intelligence," 18.

35. Andrew F. Krepinevich, Jr., "Get Ready for the Democratization of Destruction," *Foreign Policy*, February 15, 2011, http://www.foreignpolicy.com/2011/08/15/get-ready-for-the-democratization-of-destruction. Recent Russian military operations in Ukraine have been characterized by the widespread use of unmanned aerial vehicles for operational intelligence and tactical targeting. Russian artillery and multiple-rocket launchers employ advanced munitions to strike targets identified by UAVs promptly. Such strikes have reportedly produced the majority of all Ukrainian casualties, while making it difficult for light infantry fighting vehicles to survive. Consequently, special forces and irregular forces were often forming the ground maneuver force, rather than "traditional" mechanized formations. See Phillip A. Karber, *"Lessons Learned" from the Russo-Ukrainian War: Personal Observations*, draft (Vienna, Va.: Potomac Foundation, July 8, 2015),

https://prodev2go.files.wordpress.com/2015/10/rus-ukr-lessons-draft.pdf; Mary Ellen Connell and Ryan Evans, *Russia's "Ambiguous Warfare" and Implications for the U.S. Marine Corps* (Arlington, Va.: CNA, May 2015), https://www.cna.org/CNA_files/PDF/DOP-2015-U-010447-Final.pdf; Can Kasapoglu, *Russia's Renewed Military Thinking: Non-Linear Warfare and Reflexive Control*, Research Paper 121 (Rome: NATO Defense College, November 2015); Peter Pomerantsev, "Brave New War," *Atlantic*, December 29, 2015, http://www.theatlantic.com/international/archive/2015/12/war-2015-china-russia-isis/422085.

In the course of the thirty-four-day Second Lebanon War, fought in the summer of 2006 between Hezbollah and the Israeli Defense Forces (IDF), Hezbollah fought Israel, a larger, better-equipped enemy, to a standstill with the aid of numerous guided defensive weapons. Hezbollah sustained the volume of its rocket fire during the course of the war, firing more than 4,000 of its estimated 12,000 nonprecision rockets into Israel, including a salvo of some 250 weapons in the war's final hours. Matt Matthews, *We Were Caught Unprepared: The 2006 Hezbollah-Israeli War* (Fort Leavenworth, Kan.: U.S. Army Combined Arms Center Combat Studies Institute Press, 2007), 1, 38–40, 43–56; Frank G. Hoffman, *Conflict in the 21st Century: The Rise of Hybrid Wars* (Arlington, Va.: Potomac Institute for Policy Analysis, December, 2007), 22; David E. Johnson, *Military Capabilities for Hybrid War: Insights from the Israel Defense Forces in Lebanon and Gaza* (Santa Monica, Calif.: RAND, 2010).

In 2021, Colonial Pipeline, an American firm, was subjected to a ransomware attack. The cyber attack disrupted supplies of gasoline, jet fuel, and diesel along the East Coast of the United States, leading to widespread shortages, which were resolved only after Colonial Pipeline paid the ransom of $4.4 million in Bitcoin. Brian Fung and Geneva Sands, "Ransomware Attackers Used Compromised Password to Access Colonial Pipeline Network," *CNN.com*, June 4, 2021, https://www.cnn.com/2021/06/04/politics/colonial-pipeline-ransomware-attack-password/index.html.

36. "Business Is Booming as Regulators Relax Drone Laws," *Economist*, June 19, 2021, https://www.economist.com/science-and-technology/2021/06/17/business-is-booming-as-regulators-relax-drone-laws.

37. Defense Science Board, "Autonomy," 43.

38. Alan Phillips, "Drone Sales Numbers: Nobody Knows, So We Venture a Guess," *Drone Life*, April 16, 2015, https://dronelife.com/2015/04/16/drone-sales-numbers-nobody-knows-so-we-venture-a-guess. See also Rob Lever, "Drones Swoop into Electronics Show as Interest Surges," *YahooTech*, January 7, 2015, https://www.yahoo.com/tech/s/drones-swoop-electronics-show-interest-surges-061549575.html.

39. James Adams, "How Drones Are Dramatically Changing Warfare," *Spectator*, September 15, 2019, https://spectator.us/drones-dramatically-changing-warfare.

40. Defense Science Board, "Autonomy," 43.
41. Brundage et al., "Artificial Intelligence," 17.
42. Carlo Pinciroli, Adam Lee-Brown, and Giovanni Beltrame, "Buzz: A Novel Programming Language for Heterogeneous Robot Swarms," *Robohub*, August 10, 2015, https://robohub.org/buzz-a-novel-programming-language-for-heterogeneous-robot-swarms; Defense Science Board, "Autonomy," 86.
43. Defense Science Board, "Autonomy," 85.
44. Ibid., 86.
45. Ibid., 13.
46. Allen and Chan, "Artificial Intelligence," 14.
47. "Trying to Restrain the Robots," *Economist*, January 19, 2019, 23–24.
48. Defense Science Board, "Autonomy," 27.
49. Brundage et al., "Artificial Intelligence," 10.
50. Defense Science Board, "Autonomy," 28; Allen and Chan, "Artificial Intelligence," 19.
51. Brundage et al., "Artificial Intelligence," 19, 21; "The Methods and Menace of the New Bank Robbers," *Economist*, June 19, 2021, https://www.economist.com/finance-and-economics/2021/06/16/the-methods-and-menace-of-the-new-bank-robbers.
52. NSTAC, "Big Data," 27–28.
53. Defense Science Board, "Autonomy," 92.
54. Allen and Chan, "Artificial Intelligence," 19.
55. NSTAC, "Big Data," 33–34.
56. Kris Osborn, "DARPA Prototypes New AI-Enabled 'Breakthrough' Cyberattack 'Hunting' Technology," *Warrior Maven*, December 18, 2018, https://defensemaven.io/warriormaven/cyber/darpa-prototypes-new-ai-enabled-breakthrough-cyberattack-hunting-technology-6yKXpdVGuUupUV-xgIJ9cA.
57. Ibid. A denial-of-service attack involves an attacker rendering a computer or network unavailable to its intended users, typically by flooding the targeted machine with erroneous traffic that overloads the system. Denial-of-service attacks have been used against online betting firms, which are particularly attractive targets as they require timely access to their customers, who often wait until just before a sporting event to place their bets. A successful attack typically has the attacker communicating to the target an offer to cease the attack in exchange for money. A distributed denial-of-service attack finds the attacker mounting an attack from many different sources, often with "botnets," a kind of "zombie army" of computers that have been compromised and used to flood the target's system with email messages.
58. NSTAC, "Big Data," 19.
59. Ibid., 11.
60. Ibid., 12.
61. Praveen Kopalle, "Why Amazon's Anticipatory Shipping Is Pure Genius," *Forbes*, January 28, 2014, https://www.forbes.com/sites/onmarketing/2014/

01/28/why-amazons-anticipatory-shipping-is-pure-genius. See also Defense Science Board, "Autonomy," 70.

62. Defense Science Board, "Autonomy," 70. Walmart has similarly employed enterprise inventory management for predictive supply-chain management. Big-data analytics at Walmart Labs gather information from sources, including online purchase transactions, the long-term online shopping records or customer life cycles of online consumers, and information on industry trends in e-commerce.

63. Ibid., 71; Justine Brown, "Forecasting the Unexpected: Home Improvement Retailers and Emergency Response," *Inbound Logistics*, July 29, 2014, https://www.inboundlogistics.com/cms/article/forecasting-the-unexpected-home-improvement-retailers-and-emergency-response. Ace Hardware employs a similar approach to that of Home Depot.

64. Adam Stone, "Army Logistics Integrating New AI, Cloud Capabilities," *C4ISRnet*, September 7, 2017, https://www.c4isrnet.com/home/2017/09/07/army-logistics-integrating-new-ai-cloud-capabilities.

65. Giest and Lohn, *Nuclear War?*, 1.

66. Andrew Ilachinski, "AI, Robots and Swarms: Issues, Questions and Recommended Studies," CNA, January 2017, vi–vii.

67. Sydney J. Friedberg, Jr., "Big Bad Data: Achilles' Heel of Artificial Intelligence," *Breaking Defense*, November 13, 2018, https://breakingdefense.com/2018/11/big-bad-data-achilles-heel-of-artificial-intelligence.

68. Henry A. Kissinger, Eric Schmidt, and Daniel Huttenlocher, "The Coming AI Metamorphosis," *Atlantic*, August 2019, https://www.theatlantic.com/magazine/archive/2019/08/henry-kissinger-the-metamorphosis-ai/592771; Sydney J. Friedberg, Jr., "War Without Fear: DepSecDef Work on How AI Changes Conflict," *Breaking Defense*, May 31, 2017, https://breakingdefense.com/2017/05/killer-robots-arent-the-problem-its-unpredictable-ai.

69. Friedberg, "Big Bad Data."

70. Brundage et al., "Artificial Intelligence," 20.

71. The phrase "ghost in the machine" was coined by the British philosopher Gilbert Ryle. His use of the phrase is in reference to the mind-body relationship, calling a person's mind the "ghost in the machine." Computer programmers use the term when referring to a program that runs contrary to their expectations. "Ghost in the Machine," *Grammarist*, accessed February 19, 2022, https://grammarist.com/idiom/ghost-in-the-machine. See also Friedberg, "Big Bad Data."

72. Defense Science Board, "Autonomy," 14–15.

73. U.S. National Intelligence Council, *Global Trends: Paradox of Progress* (Washington, D.C.: Director of National Intelligence, 2017), 218.

74. In 1925, the Russian economist Nikolai Kondratiev was the first to propose the phenomenon of major cycles, or waves, of innovation, hence a "Kondratiev Wave." The five initial major economic cycles have been defined as the Industrial Revolution; the age of steam and railways; the age of steel and electricity;

the age of oil, cars, and mass production; and the age of information and communication. Each cycle ran between forty and sixty years. The sixth cycle is postulated by some people as an increase in resource efficiency. This sixth wave is anticipated to be driven by the internet of things, combined with new industrial applications, business models, and services. Josef S. Koller, "The Future of Ubiquitous, Realtime Intelligence: A GEOINT Singularity," Aerospace Corporation Center for Space Policy and Strategy, August 2019, 5. See also James Bradford Moody and Bianca Nogrady, *The Sixth Wave: How to Succeed in a Resource-Limited World* (Sydney: Random House Australia, 2010).

75. A. T. Kearney, "3D Printing: Ensuring Manufacturing Leadership in the 21st Century," Hewlett Packard, 2017, 6, https://www8.hp.com/us/en/images/3D_Printing___Ensuring_Manufacturing_Leadership_in_the_21st_Century_tcm245_2547663_tcm245_2442804_tcm245-2547663.pdf.

76. Ibid.

77. Connor M. McNulty, Neyla Arnas, and Thomas A. Campbell, "Toward the Printed World: Additive Manufacturing and Implications for National Security," *Defense Horizons* (Institute for National Strategic Studies, National Defense University), September 2012, 4.

78. Photo-polymerization is a technique that uses light (visible or ultraviolet) to initiate and propagate a polymerization reaction to form a linear or cross-linked polymer structure.

79. McNulty, Arnas, and Campbell, "Toward the Printed World," 9.

80. Lieutenant Colonel Benjamin D. Forest, "The Future of Additive Manufacturing in Air Force Acquisition," unpublished paper, Air War College, March 22, 2017, 8.

81. U.S. Department of Energy (DoE), "Additive Manufacturing: Pursuing the Promise," August 2012, 1, https://www.energy.gov/sites/prod/files/2013/12/f5/additive_manufacturing.pdf; McNulty, Arnas, and Campbell, "Toward the Printed World," 3; Trevor Johnston, Troy D. Smith, and J. Luke Irwin, *Additive Manufacturing in 2040* (Santa Monica, Calif.: RAND, 2018), 5.

82. Maryne Dijkstra, Alexandra Krause, Layann Masri, Gordon McCambridge, Jarrell Ng, Shi Bao Pek, Eun Sung Yang, and Yiting Zheng, "U.S. National Strategy for Additive Manufacturing," Jackson Institute for Global Affairs, Yale University, 2014, 8; DoE, "Additive Manufacturing," 1.

83. Richard, D'Aveni, "The 3-D Printing Revolution," *Harvard Business Review*, May 2015, https://hbr.org/2015/05/the-3-d-printing-revolution.

84. McNulty, Arnas, and Campbell, "Toward the Printed World," 3; Johnston, Smith, and Irwin, *Additive Manufacturing*, 5.

85. D'Aveni, "3-D Printing Revolution."

86. Johnston, Smith, and Irwin, *Additive Manufacturing*, 11.

87. Institute for Defense and Government Advancement, "Top Ten Uses for Additive Manufacturing for Defense," June 29, 2015, https://www.idga.org/military-equipment-platforms/news/top-ten-uses-for-additive-manufacturing-for-defe.

88. McNulty, Arnas, and Campbell, "Toward a Printed World," 3; Johnston, Smith, and Irwin, *Additive Manufacturing*, 5.

89. Johnston, Smith, and Irwin, *Additive Manufacturing*, 4.

90. Ibid., 12; Colonel Leslie D. Begley, "Increasing Capabilities and Improving Readiness Through Additive Manufacturing Techniques," unpublished paper, U.S. Army War College, January 4, 2017, 7; Forest, "Future of Additive Manufacturing," 14.

91. Institute for Defense and Government Advancement, "Top Ten Uses."

92. Begley, "Increasing Capabilities," 7.

93. McNulty, Arnas, and Campbell, "Toward a Printed World," 5.

94. Dijkstra et al., "U.S. National Strategy," 7.

95. Kearney, "3D Printing," 9; Simon Véronneau, Geoffrey Torrington, and Jakub P. Hlávka, *3D Printing: Downstream Production Transforming the Supply Chain* (Santa Monica, Calif.: RAND, 2017), 17.

96. Begley, "Increasing Capabilities," 10.

97. Ibid., 9.

98. Kearney, "3D Printing," 24.

99. Institute for Defense and Government Advancement, "Top Ten Uses."

100. Johnston, Smith, and Irwin, *Additive Manufacturing*, 12; ME5 Calvin Seah Ser Thong and ME4 Choo Wei Wen, "3D Printing—Revolutionising Military Operations," *Pointer* (Singapore Armed Forces) 42, no. 2 (2016): 39, https://www.mindef.gov.sg/oms/safti/pointer/documents/pdf/Vol42No2_4%203D%20Printing.pdf.

101. Forest, "Future of Additive Manufacturing," 18.

102. U.S. Senate Armed Services Committee, *Inquiry into Counterfeit Electronic Parts in the Department of Defense Supply Chain, United States Senate, 112th Congress*, S. Rep. No. 112-167, May 21, 2012.

103. U.S. National Intelligence Council, *Global Trends*, 180.

104. Seth Augenstein, "Rise of Synthetic Biology Means U.S. Government Unprepared for Biowarfare," *Laboratory Equipment*, June 20, 2018, https://www.laboratoryequipment.com/news/2018/06/rise-synthetic-biology-means-us-government-unprepared-biowarfare (accessed July 19, 2019).

105. Seth Augenstein, "Scientists Synthesize Pox Virus, Unleashing Controversy," *Laboratory Equipment*, January 22, 2018, https://www.laboratoryequipment.com/news/2018/01/scientists-synthesize-pox-virus-unleashing-controversy (accessed July 19, 2019).

106. Ibid.

107. Royal Society, "Synthetic Biology," accessed February 19, 2022, https://royalsociety.org/topics-policy/projects/synthetic-biology.

108. "A Whole New World," Technology Quarterly, *Economist*, April 6, 2019, 4, 6.

109. Zyg Dembek, "The Genie Is Out of the Lamp," *CBNW*, January 2019, 53; Patrick Tucker, "U.S. Army Making Synthetic Biology a Priority," *Defense One*, July 1, 2019, https://www.defenseone.com/technology/2019/07/us-army-making-synthetic-biology-priority/158129/?oref=defenseone_today_nl.

110. Nucleases belong to a class of enzymes that cleave nucleic acids into nucleotides and other products. They are capable of effecting single- and double-stranded breaks in their target molecules. In living organisms, nucleases are needed for many aspects of DNA repair. Ribonucleases act only on ribonucleic acids (RNA), and deoxyribonucleases act only on deoxyribonucleic acids (DNA).

111. Marcy E. Gallo, John F. Sargent, Jr., Amanda K. Sarata, and Tadlock Cowan, "Advanced Gene Editing: CRISPR-Cas9," Congressional Research Service, April 28, 2017, 2–3.

112. John Travis, "Making the Cut: CRISPR Genome-Editing Technology Shows Its Power," *Science*, December 2015, 1456.

113. Gallo et al., "Advanced Gene Editing," 12.

114. Ibid., 20. For the origins of the "Green Revolution" and Charles Borlaug, the man most responsible for triggering it, see Charles C. Mann, *The Wizard and the Prophet* (New York: Knopf, 2018), 95–155.

115. A "cultivar" is a group of plants selected for their desirable characteristics that are maintained during propagation. For example, trees cultivated in the forestry industry are selected with an eye toward their yield of commercial timber.

116. Yanpeng Wang, Xi Cheng, Qiwei Shan, et al., "Simultaneous Editing of Three Homoeoalleles in Hexaploid Bread Wheat Confers Heritable Resistance to Powdery Mildew," *Nature Biotechnology*, July 20, 2014, 947–51.

117. Keith Edmisten, "CRISPR Is Coming to Agriculture—With Big Implications for Food, Farmers, Consumers, and Nature," NC State Extension, January 28, 2016.

118. More broadly speaking, transgenesis is the process by which genetic material from one species or breed is transferred to another.

119. Rob Stein, "CRISPR Bacon: Chinese Scientists Create Genetically Modified Low-Fat Pigs," *NPR.org*, October 23, 2017, https://www.npr.org/sections/thesalt/2017/10/23/559060166/crispr-bacon-chinese-scientists-create-genetically-modified-low-fat-pigs; Gallo et al., "Advanced Gene Editing," 21.

120. Stella K. Vasiliou and Eleftherios P. Diamandis, moderators, "CRISPR-Cas9 System: Opportunities and Concerns," *Clinical Chemistry*, August 22, 2016, http://hwmaint.clinchem.org/cgi/doi/10.1373/clinchem.2016.263186.

121. Gallo et al., "Advanced Gene Editing," 18–19.

122. Lon Augustenborg, "Genetics: An Emerging Global Threat," *Teneo*, January 1, 2017, https://www.teneo.com/genetics-an-emerging-global-threat.

123. Robert H. Latiff, *Future War: Preparing for the New Global Battlefield* (New York: Knopf, 2017), 33.

124. Antonio Regalado, "Chinese Scientists Are Creating CRISPR Babies," *MIT Technology Review*, November 25, 2018, https://www.technologyreview.com/s/612458/exclusive-chinese-scientists-are-creating-crispr-babies;

"Jump Start," *Economist*, June 15, 2019, 73; "A Moment for Reflection," *Economist*, December 1, 2018, 70–71.

125. Tucker, "Synthetic Biology."

126. Prashant Mali, Kevin M. Esvelt, and George M. Church, "Cas9 as a Versatile Tool for Engineering Biology," *Nature Methods*, October 2013, 962; "Jump Start," 73.

127. U.S. National Intelligence Council, *Global Trends*, 178. "Gene drives" are genetic elements for which inheritance is favorably biased. U.S. National Academies of Sciences, Engineering, and Medicine (NAS), *Biodefense in the Age of Synthetic Biology* (Washington, D.C.: National Academies Press, 2018), 18, https://doi.org/10.17226/24890.

128. Vladimír Pitschmann and Zdeněk Hon, "Military Importance of Natural Toxins and Their Analogs," *Molecules* 21 (April 28, 2016): 556.

129. Jerry Warner et al., "Analysis of the Threat of Genetically Modified Organisms for Biological Warfare," Defense Technical Information Center, 2011, http://oai.dtic.mil/oai/oai?verb=getRecord&metadataPrefix=html&identifier=ADA547199; Spiez Laboratory, *Spiez Convergence: Report on the Second Workshop* (Spiez, Switzerland: Swiss Federal Office for Civil Protection, 2016), 21–26; Erik Frinking, Tim Sweijs, Paul Sinning, Eva Bontje, Christopher Frattina della Frattina, and Mercedes Abdalla, "The Increasing Threat of Biological Weapons," Hague Centre for Strategic Studies, 2016, 10.

130. U.S. National Intelligence Council, *Global Trends*, 53.

131. Dembek, "Genie," 53.

132. Ibid.

133. "Improvised Weapons. Hell's Kitchens," *Economist*, May 21, 2016, http://www.economist.com/news/science-and-technology/21699098-makeshift-weapons-are-becoming-more-dangerous-highly-sophisticated.

134. Latiff, *Future War*, 32.

135. Upon reading this section of the manuscript while in draft form, my son and namesake decided to check this out for himself. He found that he could purchase a CRISPR kit for $159 online at http://www.the-odin.com/diy-crispr-kit. Harvard University is offering a course online titled "CRISPR: Gene-Editing Applications," https://gs.harvardx.harvard.edu/harvard-crispr-gene-editing-applications-online-short-course-sf/?ef_id=c%3A318503670128_d%3Ac_n%3Ag_ti%3Akwd-317599818853_p%3A_k%3A%2Bcrispr_m%3Ab_a%3A62703010079&gclid=CjoKCQjwiILsBRCGARIsAHKQWLNeC70KN8wmkx-owEZUV9eOxg79xkvZWYPoIgcspqFYs4f6v9yT9EaAhWpEALw_wcB.

136. Daniel M. Gerstein, "Can the Bioweapons Convention Survive Crispr?," *Bulletin of the Atomic Scientists*, July 25, 2016, https://thebulletin.org/2016/07/can-the-bioweapons-convention-survive-crispr.

137. Augustenborg, "Genetics."

138. Vasiliou and Diamandis, "CRISPR-Cas9 System."

139. Augustenborg, "Genetics"; Zeynep Tufekci, "Where Did the Coronavirus Come From? What We Already Know Is Troubling," *New York Times*, June 25, 2021, https://www.nytimes.com/2021/06/25/opinion/coronavirus-lab.html.
140. Frinking et al., "Increasing Threat of Biological Weapons," 8.
141. NAS, *Biodefense*, 86.
142. Ibid., 91.
143. Ibid., 86.
144. U.S. National Intelligence Council, *Global Trends*, 178.
145. NAS, *Biodefense*, 86, 89.
146. Flippa Lentzos, "How to Protect the World from Ultra-Targeted Biological Weapons," *Bulletin of Atomic Scientists*, December 7, 2020, https://thebulletin.org/premium/2020-12/how-to-protect-the-world-from-ultra-targeted-biological-weapons.
147. Matthew Harper, "Ilumina Promises to Sequence Human Genome for $100—But Not Quite Yet," *Forbes*, January 9, 2017, https://www.forbes.com/sites/matthewherper/2017/01/09/illumina-promises-to-sequence-human-genome-for-100-but-not-quite-yet/#6fd8c72d386d.
148. Alexandra Ossola, "Welcome to the Future, a Place Where Everyone Knows Your Genetic Code," *Futurism*, December 14, 2017, https://futurism.com/genetic-privacy-hacking.
149. A report from Reuters finds that Chinese investment currently makes up about 43 percent of the funds going into U.S. biotech start-ups, or over $5 billion a year. Tucker, "Synthetic Biology"; "Biotechnology Market Size Worth $727.1 Billion By 2025," Grand View Research, August 2017, https://www.grandviewresearch.com/press-release/global-biotechnology-market.
150. NAS, *Biodefense*, 11, 18.
151. "Gene Machines," *Economist*, March 3, 2018, 71.
152. "Whole New World," 8.
153. NAS, *Biodefense*, 91.
154. For a history of the Spanish influenza, see John M. Barry, *The Great Influenza* (New York: Penguin, 2005).
155. Brooke Borel and Quanta Magazine, "When Evolution Fights Back Against Genetic Engineering," *Atlantic*, September 12, 2016, https://www.theatlantic.com/science/archive/2016/09/gene-drives/499574.
156. William Manchester and Paul Reid, *The Last Lion: Winston Spencer Churchill*, vol. 3, *Defender of the Realm, 1940–1965* (New York: Little, Brown, 2012), 114.
157. Dave Deptula, "Hypersonic Weapons Could Transform Warfare. The U.S. Is Behind," *Forbes*, October 5, 2018, https://www.forbes.com/sites/davedeptula/2018/10/05/faster-than-a-speeding-bullet/#353d7e905ca6; "Speed Is the New Stealth," *Economist*, June 1, 2013, https://www.economist.com/technology-quarterly/2013/06/01/speed-is-the-new-stealth.

158. R. Jeffrey Smith, "Hypersonic Missiles Are Unstoppable: And They're Starting a New Global Arms Race," *New York Times Magazine*, June 19, 2019, https://www.nytimes.com/2019/06/19/magazine/hypersonic-missiles .html; Jon Isaac, "The Navy's Newest Nemesis: Hypersonic Weapons," Center for International Maritime Security, April 15, 2019, http://cimsec. org/the-navys-newest-nemesis-hypersonic-weapons/40135; Eliot Gardner, "Hypersonic Weapons: Can Anyone Stop Them?," *Air Force Technology*, October 16, 2018, https://www.airforce-technology.com/features/hypersonic-weapons-can-anyone-stop.

159. Eleanor Peake, "Hypersonic Missiles Are Coming to Change Warfare Forever," *Wired*, October 29, 2017, https://www.wired.co.uk/article/this-is-how-hypersonic-missiles-could-change-the-future-of-warfare; James Clad, "China's Hypersonic Weapons Leave U.S. Defenseless, for Now," *The Hill*, May 1, 2019, https://thehill.com/opinion/national-security/441542-china-hypersonic-weapons-leave-us-defenseless-for-now; Smith, "Hypersonic Missiles Are Unstoppable."

160. Smith, "Hypersonic Missiles Are Unstoppable." Of course, a hypersonic missile's ability to disable or destroy a target will remain a function of the weapon's weight and shape and the target's armor form and density, among other things. Gardner, "Hypersonic Weapons."

161. Isaac, "Navy's Newest Nemesis."

162. In testimony before the Senate Armed Services Committee, General John Hyten, then head of the U.S. Strategic Command, conceded, "We don't have any defense that could deny the employment of such a weapon against us, so our response would be our deterrent force, which would be the triad and the nuclear capabilities that we have to respond to such a threat." Aaron Mehta, "Hypersonics 'Highest Technical Priority' for Pentagon R&D Head," *Defense News*, March 6, 2018, https://www.defensenews.com/pentagon/2018/03/06/hypersonics-highest-technical-priority-for-pentagon-rd-head; Rebecca Kheel, "Russia, China Eclipse U.S. in Hypersonic Missiles, Prompting Fears," *The Hill*, March 27, 2018, http://thehill.com/policy/defense/380364-china-russia-eclipse-us-in-hypersonic-missiles-prompting-fears.

163. Gardner, "Hypersonic Weapons"; Isaac, "Navy's Newest Nemesis"; Joseph Trevithick and Tyler Rogoway, "Air Force to Turn Navy Air Defense Busting Missile into High-Speed Critical Strike Weapon," *The War Zone*, March 18, 2019, https://www.thedrive.com/the-war-zone/27022/air-force-to-turn-navy-air-defense-busting-missile-into-high-speed-critical-strike-weapon.

164. "Speed Is the New Stealth."

165. Gardner, "Hypersonic Weapons"; Smith, "Hypersonic Missiles Are Unstoppable," "Hypersonic Boom," *Economist*, April 6, 2019, 68.

166. Sydney J. Freedberg, Jr., "3D Printing Key to Hypersonic Weapons: Raytheon," *Breaking Defense*, March 30, 2016, https://breakingdefense.com/2016/03/3d-printing-key-to-hypersonic-weapons-raytheon.

167. "Hypersonic Boom," 68.

168. Smith, "Hypersonic Missiles Are Unstoppable."

169. Tom Simonite, "The *Wired* Guide to Quantum Computing," *Wired*, August 24, 2018, https://www.wired.com/story/wired-guide-to-quantum-computing.

170. "Here, There and Everywhere," Technology Quarterly, *Economist*, March 11, 2017, 7–8. In simple terms, Shor's algorithm solves the following problem: "For a given integer 'N,' find its prime factors." Prime factors are the prime numbers that, when multiplied together, make the original number 'N.' Cryptologists use prime factorization because it is very hard to identify the prime factors of very large numbers, a problem that frustrates even modern computers. For a detailed and highly technical treatment of this issue, see Michael A. Nielsen and Isaac L. Chuang, *Quantum Computation and Quantum Information* (Cambridge: Cambridge University Press, 2010); and Phillip Kaye, Raymond Laflamme, and Michele Mosca, *An Introduction to Quantum Computing* (Oxford: Oxford University Press, 2007).

171. David Cardinal, "How Does Quantum Computing Work?," *Extreme Tech*, January 30, 2019, https://www.extremetech.com/extreme/284306-how-quantum-computing-works. See also "Qubits—Superimposition and Entanglement," accessed February 19, 2022, https://hego.redbrick.dcu.ie/technicalmanual/node34.html.

172. Will Hurd, "Quantum Computing Is the Next Big Security Risk," *Wired*, December 7, 2017, https://www.wired.com/story/quantum-computing-is-the-next-big-security-risk; Jack Nicas, "How Google's Quantum Computer Could Change the World," *Wall Street Journal*, October 16, 2017, https://www.wsj.com/articles/how-googles-quantum-computer-could-change-the-world-1508158847.

173. Cardinal, "How Does Quantum Computing Work?"

174. Nicas, "Google's Quantum Computer."

175. Simonite, "*Wired* Guide to Quantum Computing."

176. Ibid.

177. Nicas, "Google's Quantum Computer."

178. Simonite, "*Wired* Guide to Quantum Computing."

179. George Musser, "Job One for Quantum Computers: Boost Artificial Intelligence," *Wired*, February 10, 2018, https://www.wired.com/story/job-one-for-quantum-computers-boost-artificial-intelligence.

180. Hurd, "Quantum Computing."

181. Nicas, "Google's Quantum Computer"; Mikhail Dyakonov, "The Case Against Quantum Computing," *IEEE Spectrum*, November 15, 2018, https://spectrum.ieee.org/computing/hardware/the-case-against-quantum-computing.

182. Nicas, "Google's Quantum Computer."

183. Dyakonov, "Case Against Quantum Computing."

184. Emily Grumbling and Mark Horowitz, eds., *Quantum Computing: Progress and Prospects* (Washington, D.C.: National Academies Press, 2019), 21.

185. Dyakonov, "Case Against Quantum Computing."

186. Grumbling and Horowitz, *Quantum Computing*, 2–5.

187. Nicas, "Google's Quantum Computer."

188. Dyakonov, "Case Against Quantum Computing"; Grumbling and Horowitz, *Quantum Computing*, 3, 5.

189. Grumbling and Horowitz, *Quantum Computing*, 3–4.

190. Dyakonov, "Case Against Quantum Computing."

191. Missouri's nickname is the "Show Me State." Schlesinger was reiterating his skepticism and, in effect, telling me that he would need a lot more "proof" than I was providing before he would get excited about directed-energy weapons.

192. Annah Ahronheim, "Israel Unveils Breakthrough Laser to Intercept Missiles, Aerial Threats," *Jerusalem Post*, January 9, 2020, https://www.jpost.com/Israel-News/Israels-Defense-Ministry-announces-breakthrough-in-laser-technology-613568; Tyler Rogoway, "How the Once Elusive Dream of Laser Weapons Suddenly Became a Reality," *The War Zone*, November 25, 2020, https://www.thedrive.com/the-war-zone/37775/how-the-once-elusive-dream-of-laser-weapons-suddenly-became-a-reality; Andrew Feickert, "U.S. Army Weapons-Related Directed Energy (DE) Programs: Background and Potential Issues for Congress," Congressional Research Service, February 12, 2018, 5.

193. Andy Extance, "Military Technology: Laser Weapons Get Real," *Nature*, May 27, 2015, https://www.nature.com/news/military-technology-laser-weapons-get-real-1.17613.

194. U.S. Defense Intelligence Agency, "Challenges to Security in Space," 2019, 20–21, https://www.dia.mil/Portals/27/Documents/News/Military%20Power%20Publications/Space_Threat_V14_020119_sm.pdf.

195. Bart Hendrickx, "Peresvet: A Russian Mobile Laser System to Dazzle Enemy Satellites," *Space Review*, June 15, 2020, https://www.thespacereview.com/article/3967/1; Chreis Zappone, "Space Lasers and the New Battlefield Emerging Under China's Anti-Satellite Tactics," *Sydney Morning Herald*, August 9, 2021, https://www.smh.com.au/world/asia/space-lasers-and-the-new-battlefield-emerging-under-china-s-anti-satellite-tactics-20210804-p58ft2.html.

196. Kris Osborn, "The U.S. Military Has a New Master Plan to Use Lasers in a War," *National Interest*, March 9, 2021, https://nationalinterest.org/blog/buzz/us-military-has-new-master-plan-use-lasers-war-179699.

197. Liam Stoker, "Electromagnetic Pulse Weaponry: Boeing CHAMP Video and Jammer Grenades," *Army-Technology.com*, November 27, 2012, http://www.army-technology.com/features/featureelectromagnetic-pulse-weaponry-boeing-champ-jammer-grenades; Devin Coldewey, "Boeing's New Missile Takes Down Electronics Without Touching Them," *NBCNews.com*, October 24, 2012, https://www.nbcnews.com/tech/tech-news/boeings-new-missile-takes-down-electronics-without-touching-them-flna1C6663618.

198. David Axe, "How 'Revolutionary' Is CHAMP, New Air Force Microwave Weapon?," *AOL Defense*, November 28, 2012, http://defense.aol.com/2012/11/28/how-revolutionary-is-champ-new-air-force-microwave-weapon; Sydney J. Freedberg, Jr., " 'A Golden Age for Collaboration': On Lasers & Microwaves: But Watch the Cheetos!," *Breaking Defense*, July 7, 2020, https://breakingdefense.com/2020/07/a-golden-age-for-collaboration-on-lasers-microwaves-but-watch-the-cheetos.

199. Alex Hempel, "The SM-2, SM-3, SM-6, ESSM, and RAM: A Guide to U.S. Naval Air Defense Missiles, *WhiteFleet.net*, August 5, 2016, https://whitefleet.net/2016/08/05/sm-2-sm-3-sm-6-and-essm-a-guide-to-us-naval-air-defense-missiles.

200. Ballistic missile warheads, which must be hardened to withstand the extreme heat associated with reentering the atmosphere, pose yet another problem for laser defenses.

201. Hughes, *Fleet Tactics*, 99–108.

202. Karl Kristian Steincke, *Ogsaa en Tilvaerelse*, vol. 4, *Farvel Og Tak: Minder Og Meninger* (Copenhagen: Fremad, 1948), 227, https://quoteinvestigator.com/2013/10/20/no-predict.

Chapter Five. W(h)ither Deterrence?

1. Andrew Roberts, *Churchill: Walking with History* (New York: Viking, 2018), 361.
2. Bernard Brodie, "War in the Atomic Age," in Brodie, *Absolute Weapon*, 62.
3. Andrew F. Krepinevich, Jr., *The Decline of Deterrence* (Washington, D.C.: Hudson Institute, 2019), 50–52.
4. A. Roberts, *Churchill*, 399.
5. Barack Obama, *National Security Strategy*, White House, February 2015, 7–8, 29.
6. Barack Obama, *Sustaining Global Leadership: Priorities for 21st Century Defense*, White House, January 3, 2012, 8, 10–13.
7. James Mattis, *Summary of the 2018 National Defense Strategy*, Department of Defense, 2018, 1, 5.
8. Sebastian Roblin, "China Is Building Over 100 Missile Silos in the Desert—Is It Playing a Nuclear 'Shell Game'?," *National Interest*, June 12, 2021, https://nationalinterest.org/blog/buzz/china-building-over-100-missile-silos-desert—-it-playing-nuclear-"shell-game"-189506; Bill Gertz, "China Building Third Missile Field for Hundreds of New ICBMs," *Washington Times*, August 12, 2021, https://www.washingtontimes.com/news/2021/aug/12/china-engaged-breathtaking-nuclear-breakout-us-str. "Crisis stability" refers to a situation where the potential for a decisive change in the security fortunes of two or more rivals exists and yet even risk-tolerant decision-makers view the anticipated costs of attacking as far outweighing the prospective benefits. In simple terms, crisis stability means that even under

circumstances where two rivals are playing for high stakes under intense pressure, neither has an incentive to "shoot first." Michael S. Gerson, "The Origins of Strategic Stability: The United States and the Threat of Surprise Attack," in *Strategic Stability: Contending Interpretations*, ed. Elbridge A. Colby and Michael S. Gerson (Carlisle, Pa.: U.S. Army War College Press, February 2013), 2, 26–27; Glenn A. Kent and David E. Thaler, *First-Strike Stability: A Methodology for Evaluating Strategic Forces* (Santa Monica, Calif.: RAND, 1989), v; Elbridge Colby, "Defining Strategic Stability: Reconciling Stability and Deterrence," in Colby and Gerson, *Strategic Stability*, 49.

9. W. J. Hennigan and John Walcott, "The U.S. Expects China Will Quickly Double Its Nuclear Stockpile," *Time*, May 29, 2019, https://time.com/5597955/china-nuclear-weapons-intelligence; Liu Xuanzun, "China Urged to Expand Nuclear Arsenal to Deter U.S. Warmongers," *Global Times*, May 8, 2020, https://www.globaltimes.cn/content/1187775.shtml.

10. Dean Cheng, "Chinese Views on Deterrence," *Joint Forces Quarterly*, First Quarter, 2011, 92; Thomas Schelling, *Arms and Influence* (New Haven: Yale University Press, 1967), 69.

11. Watts, *Six Decades*, 25.

12. For a discussion of a general thermonuclear war's prospective characteristics, see Herman Kahn, *Thinking About the Unthinkable in the 1980s* (New York: Simon and Schuster, 1984).

13. Krepinevich, *Decline of Deterrence*, 20–23.

14. Ibid., 37–45.

15. Richard A. Clarke and Robert K. Knake, *Cyber War* (New York: HarperCollins, 2010), 7.

16. Evgeny Myasnikov, "Counterforce Potential of High-Precision Weapons," in *Nuclear Disarmament: New Technology, Weapons and Treaties*, ed. Alexei Arbatov and Vladimir Dvorkin (Moscow: Carnegie Moscow Center, 2009), 107; Alexei Arbatov, *Gambit or Endgame? The New State of Arms Control* (Washington, D.C.: Carnegie Endowment for International Peace, 2011), 9.

17. Arbatov, *Gambit or Endgame?*, 17, 21.

18. Military Doctrine of the Russian Federation (in Russian), 2014, http://news.kremlin.ru/media/events/files/41d527556bec8deb3530.pdf, quoted in Alexey Arbatov, "Nuclear Deterrence: A Guarantee or Threat to Strategic Stability?," Carnegie Moscow Center, March 22, 2019, https://carnegie.ru/2019/03/22/nuclear-deterrence-guarantee-or-threat-to-strategic-stability-pub-78663.

19. Russian doctrine also includes the possibility of launching a retaliatory strike should it detect that a nuclear attack is under way against it, typically referred to as "launch on warning." The June 2020 policy document describes a number of circumstances under which Moscow might consider the use of nuclear weapons, including when it has received "reliable data on a launch of ballistic missiles attacking the territory of the Russian Federation

and/or its allies" and in response to the "use of nuclear weapons or other types of weapons of mass destruction by an adversary against the Russian Federation and/or its allies." Russia also reserves the right to respond with nuclear weapons following an "attack by [an] adversary against critical governmental or military sites of the Russian Federation, disruption of which would undermine nuclear forces' response actions" and "aggression against the Russian Federation with the use of conventional weapons when the very existence of the state is in jeopardy." Ministry of Foreign Affairs of the Russian Federation, *On Basic Principles of State Policy of the Russian Federation*, Moscow, June 2, 2020, paras. 4, 5, 10, and 19, https://www.mid.ru/en/web/guest/foreign_policy/international_safety/disarmament/-/asset_publisher/rpofiUBmANaH/content/id/4152094, quoted in Amy F. Woolf, "Russia's Nuclear Weapons: Doctrine, Forces and Modernization," Congressional Research Service, July 20, 2020, 4–5. See also Woolf, "Russia's Nuclear Weapons," 6–7; and Michael Kofman and Anya Loukianova Fink, "Escalation Management and Nuclear Employment in Russian Military Strategy," *War on the Rocks*, June 23, 2020, https://warontherocks.com/2020/06/escalation-management-and-nuclear-employment-in-russian-military-strategy; Admiral Charles A. Richard, Testimony, Senate Committee on Armed Services, April 20, 2021, 10.

20. James Mattis, *U.S. Nuclear Posture Review* (Washington, D.C.: Office of the Secretary of Defense, February 2018), xii, 8, https://media.defense.gov/2018/Feb/02/2001872886/-1/-1/1/2018-NUCLEAR-POSTURE-REVIEW-FINAL-REPORT.pdf.

21. Mingda Qiu, "China's Science of Military Strategy: Cross-Domain Concepts in the 2013 Edition," Cross Domain Deterrence Working Paper, University of California at San Diego, La Jolla, Calif., September 2015, 14.

22. Research Department of Military Strategy, *Science of Military Strategy*, 148, quoted in Mingda Qiu, "China's Science of Military Strategy," 13.

23. Krepinevich, *Decline of Deterrence*, 50–52.

24. Nevil Shute, *On the Beach* (New York: William Morrow, 1957).

25. Martin Shubik, "Terrorism, Technology and the Socioeconomics of Death," *Comparative Strategy* 16, no. 4 (1997): 399–414.

26. "*The Dark Knight* (2008): Michael Caine: Alfred," *IMDb*, accessed February 19, 2022, https://www.imdb.com/title/tt0468569/characters/nm0000323.

27. This is the basis for insurance. A risk-averse person accepts an expected value that is less than that of the gamble in order to obtain a sure thing; that is to say, the person pays a premium to avoid risk. Uncertainty exists when the decision-makers do not know the possible outcome of their decision in advance or the probabilities. On the other hand, risk exists when the decision-makers have some sense of the probabilities of potential outcomes in advance. For example, before rolling a pair of dice, an individual knows the odds of rolling snake eyes (two ones). (The odds are one in thirty-six.) In a game of poker, the players are less certain of the outcome of a particular

hand, but expert players have a sense of the range of the odds in choosing a particular course of action. Richard E. Nisbett, Kaiping Peng, Incheol Choi, and Ara Norenzayan, "Culture and Systems of Thought: Holistic Versus Analytic Cognition," *Psychological Review* 108, no. 2 (2001): 291.

28. Herbert A. Simon, "A Behavioral Model of Rational Choice," RAND P-365, January 20, 1953; Herbert A. Simon, "Rational Choice and the Structure of the Environment," *Psychological Review* 63 (March 1956): 129–38. See also Daniel Kahneman, "Maps of Bounded Rationality: Psychology for Behavioral Economics," *American Economic Review* 93 (December 2003): 1449–75.

29. James March and Herbert Simon, with the collaboration of Harold Guetzkow, *Organizations*, 2nd ed. (Cambridge: Blackwell, 1993), 3–4.

30. Richard M. Cyert and James March, *A Behavioral Theory of the Firm*, 2nd ed. (Cambridge: Blackwell, 1992), 120–22, 214–15.

31. Daniel Kahneman, *Thinking Fast and Slow* (New York: Farrar, Straus and Giroux, 2011), 334; Jack S. Levy, "Applications of Prospect Theory to Political Science," *Synthese*, May 2003, 217. Tversky and Kahneman also found that individuals exhibit *diminishing sensitivity* to gains and losses (or anticipated benefits and costs) and that decision-makers overweight low-probability outcomes and underweight high-probability outcomes.

32. R. H. Thaler, "Toward a Positive Theory of Consumer Choice," *Journal of Economic Behavior and Organization* 1 (1980): 39–60.

33. Kahneman, *Thinking Fast and Slow*, 250, 256–57.

34. Henry Kissinger, *Diplomacy* (New York: Simon and Schuster, 1994), 248.

35. The fact that one of those who seeks power obtains it does not necessarily tell us anything about the winner's skill. If ten contestants compete in a "winner-take-all" game, one of them will necessarily emerge as the ultimate winner, even if all ten are absolutely equal in skill.

36. Nisbett et al., "Culture," 291.

37. Ethan Watters, "We Aren't the World," *Pacific Standard Magazine*, February 25, 2013, https://psmag.com/social-justice/joe-henrich-weird-ultimatum-game-shaking-up-psychology-economics-53135.

38. Ibid.

39. Joseph Henrich, Robert Boyd, Samuel Boyles, Colin Camerer, et al., " 'Economic Man' in Cross-Cultural Perspective: Behavioral Experiments in 15 Small-Scale Societies," *Behavioral and Brain Sciences* 28 (2005): 7.

40. It may also be that in cases where Player A is risk seeking, A may make an "unfair" offer to Player B, anticipating that B's self-interest will lead B to accept the offer.

41. Donald Kagan, *On the Origins of War* (New York: Doubleday, 1995), 38–39, 204.

42. Alistair Horne, *To Lose a Battle: France 1940* (New York: Penguin, 1990), 95.

43. William Taubman, *Khrushchev* (New York: Norton, 2003), 541, 546.

44. Ibid., 574, 576.

45. Evan Thomas, *Ike's Bluff* (New York: Little, Brown, 2012), 105.

Chapter Six. Fisher's Scheme

1. Paul M. Kennedy, *The Rise and Fall of British Naval Mastery* (London: Ashfield, 1976), 205.
2. Peter Padfield, *Battleship* (Edinburgh, U.K.: Birlinn, 2000), 154. Admiral Richards served as First Sea Lord—the Royal Navy's most senior officer—from 1893 to 1899.
3. Ibid., 150–51.
4. Lambert, "Dreadnought," 7.
5. Ibid., 9; Parkinson, *Dreadnought*, 5.
6. Padfield, *Battleship*, 11.
7. Ibid.
8. Ibid., 11–12.
9. Ibid., 62; Jan Morris, *Fisher's Face* (New York: Random House, 1995), 89.
10. Padfield, *Battleship*, 61–62.
11. Spector, *At War, at Sea*, 34–35.
12. Ibid., 22–23; Morris, *Fisher's Face*, 90.
13. Alan Cowpe, "The Royal Navy and the Whitehead Torpedo," in *Technical Change and British Naval Policy, 1860–1939*, ed. Bryan Ranft (London: Hodder and Stoughton, 1977), 23–25; Padfield, *Battleship*, 58.
14. Padfield, *Battleship*, 57, 109–10.
15. Cowpe, "Whitehead Torpedo," 28–29.
16. Bryan Ranft, "The Protection of British Seaborne Trade and the Development of Systematic Planning for War, 1860–1906," in Ranft, *Technical Change*, 30.
17. Ibid., 28–29.
18. Ibid., 30–31.
19. Penn, *Infighting Admirals*, 45–46.
20. Cowpe, "Whitehead Torpedo," 31.
21. Massie, *Dreadnought*, 501–8; Richard Freeman, *The Great Edwardian Naval Feud* (Barnsley, U.K.: Pen and Sword Maritime, 2009), 12–15, 23–25, 29, 32–34.
22. Britain's sea lord is the rough equivalent of the U.S. Secretary of the Navy. A junior sea lord is a senior civilian serving under the sea lord.
23. Penn, *Infighting Admirals*, 41.
24. Freeman, *Naval Feud*, 37.
25. Penn, *Infighting Admirals*, 58.
26. Ibid., 44.
27. Reflecting the Navy's offensive traditions, the admirals declared that "with regard to furnishing convoys for protection of commerce, the days of convoy are past." Cowpe, "Whitehead Torpedo," 31; Penn, *Infighting Admirals*, 47; Parkinson, *Dreadnought*, 10.
28. C. J. Bartlett, *Great Britain and Sea Power, 1815–1853* (Oxford, U.K.: Clarendon, 1963), 23.
29. Aaron L. Friedberg, *The Weary Titan: Britain and the Experience of Decline, 1895–1905* (Princeton, N.J.: Princeton University Press, 1988), 147.

30. Sumida, *Naval Supremacy*, 14.

31. E. L. Woodward, *Great Britain and the Royal Navy* (Hamden, Conn.: Archon, 1964), 456; Friedberg, *Weary Titan*, 149–50.

32. Friedberg, *Weary Titan*, 149.

33. Ibid., 150.

34. Kennedy, *British Naval Mastery*, 222.

35. Padfield, *Battleship*, 145–46.

36. Spector, *At War, at Sea*, 25.

37. Shawn T. Grimes, *Strategy and War Planning in the British Navy, 1887–1918* (Woodbridge, U.K.: Boydell, 2012), 24.

38. Cowpe, "Whitehead Torpedo," 32–33; Lord John Fisher, *Fear God and Dread Nought: The Correspondence of Admiral of the Fleet Lord Fisher of Kilverstone*, vol. 1, *The Making of an Admiral, 1854–1904*, ed. Arthur Marder (Cambridge, Mass.: Harvard University Press, 1952), 100.

39. Grimes, *Strategy*, 24–25.

40. Ibid.

41. Ibid.

42. Arthur J. Marder, *The Anatomy of British Sea Power* (London: Frank Cass, 1964), 220. The four naval lords were renamed "sea lords" in 1904.

43. Parkinson, *Dreadnought*, 42.

44. Lambert, *Planning Armageddon*, 29; Penn, *Infighting Admirals*, 48.

45. Parkinson, *Dreadnought*, 22–23, 33.

46. Cowpe, "Whitehead Torpedo," 32; Grimes, *Strategy*, 27–28; Penn, *Infighting Admirals*, 51.

47. Grimes, *Strategy*, 28, 228–29; Cowpe, "Whitehead Torpedo," 33.

48. Padfield, *Battleship*, 116–17, 119; Parkinson, *Dreadnought*, 44; Penn, *Infighting Admirals*, 48.

49. Lambert, *Fisher's Revolution*, 27.

50. Gray, *Devil's Device*, 152–54. The United States Navy purchased the rights to use Obry's gyroscope in 1896, with the Royal Navy following two years later. By 1900, the Royal Navy's entire inventory of over 4,000 torpedoes, spread in squadrons spanning the globe, had been fitted with the gyroscope, an indication of the Admiralty's belief that Obry's technology was, in today's military parlance, a game changer.

51. Lambert, "Dreadnought," 27–28; Theodore Ropp, *Development of a Modern Navy: French Naval Policy, 1871–1904*, ed. Stephen S. Roberts (Annapolis, Md.: Naval Institute Press, 1987), 350–51.

52. Lambert, *Fisher's Revolution*, 22; Lambert, *Planning Armageddon*, 24–25; Spector, *At War, at Sea*, 56–57.

53. Nicholas Lambert, "Economy or Empire? The Fleet Unit Concept and the Quest for Collective Security in the Pacific, 1909–1914," in *Far Flung Lines*, ed. Greg Kennedy and Keith Neilson (London: Frank Cass, 1997), 56–57.

54. Lambert, "Dreadnought," 14.

55. Grimes, *Strategy*, 28–29, 41.

56. Ibid., 30–32.

57. Ibid., 32–33.

58. Freeman, *Naval Feud*, 51–52.

59. Penn, *Infighting Admirals*, 58, 67; Massie, *Dreadnought*, 513–14.

60. Cowpe, "Whitehead Torpedo," 34–35; Grimes, *Strategy*, 33–34.

61. Cowpe, "Whitehead Torpedo," 34–35; Grimes, *Strategy*, 34.

62. Padfield, *Battleship*, 154.

63. Spector, *At War, at Sea*, 104.

64. Lambert, *Fisher's Revolution*, 48–49.

65. Ibid., 123.

66. Spector, *At War, at Sea*, 104.

67. Lambert, *Fisher's Revolution*, 79.

68. Ibid., 49–50. Arnold-Forster later served as Britain's secretary of state for war from 1903 to 1905.

69. Marder, *Anatomy*, 370–71, quoted in ibid., 64. The admiral was born in Austria and was related to Britain's royal family. He joined the Royal Navy at the age of fourteen. Battenberg had a distinguished Navy career, capped by his service as first sea lord from 1912 to 1914.

70. Bacon, *Fisher*, 1:152, quoted in Penn, *Infighting Admirals*, 94–95.

71. Lambert, *Fisher's Revolution*, 67; Arthur J. Marder, *From the Dreadnought to Scapa Flow: The Road to War, 1904–1914* (Annapolis, Md.: Naval Institute Press, 2013), 334.

72. Lambert, *Fisher's Revolution*, 67.

73. Gray, *Devil's Device*, 178–79, 182. The torpedo's speed could be increased at the expense of reduced range. Thus, to boost the speed to thirty-three knots required a sacrifice in range to roughly 1,000 yards. Marder, *Dreadnought*, 329.

74. Bacon, *Fisher*, 1:247.

75. Whitehall is the road in London along which the center of the United Kingdom's government is located, so "Whitehall" is popularly used as a figure of speech in referring to the British government.

76. Friedberg, *Weary Titan*, 178–79.

77. Archive of William Waldegrave Palmer, 2nd Earl of Selborne, Oxford Bodlesian Libraries, 142. Hereafter cited as "Selborne Papers."

78. Friedberg, *Weary Titan*, 197.

79. There seemed to be an affinity among a number of officials in Admiralty for an unofficial alliance with the United States Navy, or at least some kind of intelligence sharing, so that both services could act in concert to maintain free trade and the status quo in the Pacific. Padfield, *Battleship*, 139.

80. Friedberg, *Weary Titan*, 166.

81. Padfield, *Battleship*, 138–39.

82. Friedberg, *Weary Titan*, 175.

83. Selborne Papers, 161, quoted in ibid., 176.

84. Friedberg, *Weary Titan*, 191.

85. Kennedy, *British Naval Mastery*, 206.

86. Padfield, *Battleship*, 156–57.

87. Ibid., 158–59.

88. A. J. P. Taylor, *The Struggle for Mastery in Europe, 1848–1918* (Oxford: Oxford University Press, 1971), 408–17.

89. Grimes, *Strategy*, 64.

90. Friedberg, *Weary Titan*, 97.

91. Ibid., 99, 106.

92. Parkinson, *Dreadnought*, 50; Lambert, *Planning Armageddon*, 497.

93. Lambert, *Fisher's Revolution*, 111, 113; Spector, *At War, at Sea*, 33.

94. Spector, *At War, at Sea*, 27–28.

95. Ibid., 55. Standing the notion of financial incentives on its head, at this time roughly 1,000 men a year purchased their early discharge from the Royal Navy by making a lump-sum payment to the Admiralty!

96. Lambert, "Dreadnought," 27–28.

97. Spector, *At War, at Sea*, 44–45; Lambert, *Fisher's Revolution*, 112. The introduction of larger engines increased the demand for coal stokers. Indeed, one major reason for the Royal Navy's early shift to oil-fired engines was to relieve some of the stress on manpower requirements.

98. The Royal Navy did not keep its entire fleet in full commission in peacetime. Typically around one-third of its personnel were billeted ashore. Almost half of the "War Fleet" was in reserve. To develop its full "two-power strength," the Royal Navy had to mobilize the reserve. Lambert, *Fisher's Revolution*, 111.

99. Friedberg, *Weary Titan*, 89.

100. The first lord, a civilian member of the Cabinet, had ultimate authority and responsibility for the Royal Navy. However, he did not have the authority to make independent decisions; that power rested with the Board of Admiralty itself. Thus, the first lord needed the support of his naval lords to act. Lambert, *Fisher's Revolution*, 16.

101. Lord Hankey, *The Supreme Command, 1914–1918*, vol. 1 (London: Allen and Unwin, 1961), 19, quoted in ibid., 75.

102. Freeman, *Naval Feud*, 52; Parkinson, *Dreadnought*, 46.

103. Lambert, *Planning Armageddon*, 30.

104. Morris, *Fisher's Face*, 51, 53, 79.

105. Ibid., 66, 237; Penn, *Infighting Admirals*, 10.

106. Morris, *Fisher's Face*, 66, 69.

107. Ibid., 82, 117; Herman, *To Rule the Waves*, 477.

108. Bacon, *Fisher*, 1:122.

109. John Fisher, *The Papers of Admiral Sir John Fisher*, ed. Lieutenant Commander P. K. Kemp, 2 vols. (New York: Routledge, 1960), 1:20. Hereafter cited as *Fisher Papers*.

110. Ibid, 40–41.

111. Ibid., 40.

112. Fisher, *Fear God and Dread Nought*, 1:156.

113. Ibid., 1:308.
114. Parkinson, *Dreadnought*, 50.
115. Sumida, *Naval Supremacy*, 51.
116. Ibid., 117.
117. Herman, *To Rule the Waves*, 480.
118. Lambert, *Fisher's Revolution*, 125.
119. Ibid., 122.
120. Ibid., 163.
121. Ruddock Mackay, "The Admiralty, the German Navy and the Redistribution of the British Fleet, 1904–1905," *Mariner's Mirror*, August 1970, 341.
122. *Fisher Papers*, 1:20.
123. Ibid., 1:191.
124. Ibid., 1:192.
125. Mackay, "Admiralty," 342–43.
126. In February 1905, Selborne also announced cutbacks in Britain's dockyards at Halifax and Esquimalt in Canada, Jamaica in the Caribbean, and Trincomalee in South Asia.
127. Kennedy, *British Naval Mastery*, 217; Mackay, "Admiralty," 345.
128. Lambert, *Fisher's Revolution*, 100; Lambert, *Planning Armageddon*, 35.
129. Fisher, *Fear God and Dread Nought*, 2:23.
130. *Fisher Papers*, 1:196.
131. The introduction of the Scheme in 1905 and the subsequent scrapping of 154 old ships were later calculated to have freed up no fewer than 950 officers and 11,000 men for other assignments. Lambert, *Fisher's Revolution*, 112.
132. Lambert, *Fisher's Revolution*, 115; Penn, *Infighting Admirals*, 114; Philip Towle, "The Evaluation of the Experience of the Russo-Japanese War," in Ranft, *Technical Change*, 76–77.
133. Lambert, "Dreadnought," 1–2.
134. Lambert, "Economy or Empire?," 62.
135. British cable companies carried about 80 percent of cable traffic outside of Europe. Lambert, "Dreadnought," 11.
136. Ibid., 18–19.
137. Lambert, "Economy or Empire?," 57–58.
138. *Fisher Papers*, 1:30–31.
139. Parkinson, *Dreadnought*, 84–85.
140. Charles H. Fairbanks, Jr., "Choosing Among Technologies in the Anglo-German Naval Arms Competition, 1898–1915," in *Naval History: The Seventh Symposium of the U.S. Naval Academy*, ed. William Cogar (Wilmington, Del.: Scholarly Resources, 1988), 128.
141. Jon Tetsuro Sumida, "British Capital Ship Design and Fire Control in the Dreadnought Era: Sir John Fisher, Arthur Hungerford Pollen, and the Battle Cruiser," *Journal of Modern History* 51 (June 1979): 226–27; Sumida, *Naval Supremacy*, 259.
142. Penn, *Infighting Admirals*, 138; Massie, *Dreadnought*, 469.

143. Penn, *Infighting Admirals*, 135.

144. Sumida, "British Capital Ship Design," 210; Parkinson, *Dreadnought*, 82.

145. Fairbanks, "Choosing Among Technologies," 127; Keith Neilson, " 'The British Empire Floats on the British Navy': British Naval Policy, Belligerent Rights, and Disarmament, 1902–1909," in *Arms Limitations and Disarmament: Restraints on War, 1899–1939*, ed. B. J. C. McKercher (Westport, Conn.: Praeger, 1992), 24.

146. Massie, *Dreadnought*, 495; Sumida, *Naval Supremacy*, 158.

147. Sumida, "British Capital Ship Design," 220–21. A ship's speed is reduced as its bottom becomes dirty, such as with accumulated barnacles; thus the need for a significant margin in ship speed to offset the drag effect of a dirty bottom.

148. Sumida, *Naval Supremacy*, 162.

149. Lambert, "Economy or Empire?," 61–62.

150. Britain's "Welsh Cardiff" coal was preferred by most major navies. Moreover, Britain had already incurred substantial sunk costs in developing the world's best network of coaling stations. Finally, coal had its tactical advantages, as it was inert under the action of explosives and actually acted to reduce their impact.

151. Massie, *Dreadnought*, 784; CDR Erik Dahl, "The Limits of Technological Innovation: The Change from Coal to Oil Under Churchill," unpublished paper, 2002, 1–4.

152. Dahl, "Limits of Technological Innovation," 16.

153. Ibid., 4.

154. Ibid., 8–9. Government ownership of a private company was highly unusual but was sanctioned in rare instances in order to secure a strategic advantage. For example, the government had purchased shares in the Suez Canal in the mid-nineteenth century.

155. Ibid., 13–14.

156. Sumida, *Naval Supremacy*, 261.

157. Ibid.; Herman, *To Rule the Waves*, 479; Lambert, *Fisher's Revolution*, 78.

158. Lambert, *Fisher's Revolution*, 136.

159. Sumida, *Naval Supremacy*, 153.

160. Ibid., 135, 149–50, 251; Morris, *Fisher's Face*, 202; Parkinson, *Dreadnought*, 170–73.

161. *Fisher Papers*, 2:106; Lambert, *Planning Armageddon*, 53.

162. Lambert, *Planning Armageddon*, 53, 59; Penn, *Infighting Admirals*, 201–2; Grimes, *Strategy*, 61.

163. Holger H. Herwig, "The German Reaction to the Dreadnought Revolution," *International History Review* 13 (May 1991): 282.

164. Padfield, *Battleship*, 189; Morris, *Fisher's Face*, 186.

165. Massie, *Dreadnought*, 485; Herwig, "German Reaction," 277, 279–80.

166. *Fisher Papers*, 2:279. While Fisher hoped to upset Germany's shipbuilding plans, there is no evidence that he knew of the problems it would pose

Tirpitz with respect to the Kiel Canal. The canal was widened and finally completed, at great cost, in August 1914.

167. Massie, *Dreadnought*, 486; Herwig, "German Reaction," 278.

168. Fisher, *Fear God and Dread Nought*, 2:431.

169. Massie, *Dreadnought*, 520.

170. Bacon, *Fisher*, 2:98; Morris, *Fisher's Face*, 190.

171. Lambert, *Fisher's Revolution*, 8. Indeed, Fisher was constantly being tempted by his industry friends, who offered him huge salaries if he would forsake the Navy and enter the private sector.

172. The four major firms were Vickers, Armstrong-Whitworth, the Fairfield Shipbuilding Company, and John Brown & Co. Ltd.

173. Lambert, *Fisher's Revolution*, 24, 147. Interestingly, this relationship survived Fisher's tenure on through World War I.

174. Ibid., 132.

175. Privately, senior Admiralty officials admitted (though not to politicians) that the process of calculating naval balance was "one of extreme complexity." In public, however, the Navy maintained that in future naval engagements "only dreadnoughts would matter." Ibid., 135–36.

176. Fisher, *Fear God and Dread Nought*, 2:141.

177. Lambert, *Fisher's Revolution*, 142.

178. Ibid., 148.

179. Parkinson, *Dreadnought*, 103.

180. Sumida, *Naval Supremacy*, 113.

181. Spector, *At War, at Sea*, 21.

182. Parkinson, *Dreadnought*, 76; Padfield, *Battleship*, 181–82; Towle, "Russo-Japanese War," 72.

183. Towle, "Russo-Japanese War," 71.

184. Gray, *Devil's Device*, 167–70, 172.

185. Ibid., 68; Padfield, *Battleship*, 171; Cowpe, "Whitehead Torpedo," 66; Towle, "Russo-Japanese War," 66.

186. Lambert, *Fisher's Revolution*, 83–85; Robert K. Massie, *Castles of Steel* (New York: Random House, 2003), 124.

187. Grimes, *Strategy*, 37.

188. Herman, *To Rule the Waves*, 480.

189. Lambert, *Planning Armageddon*, 46.

190. Ranft, "Protection," 20–21.

191. Lambert, *Planning Armageddon*, 71–75; Grimes, *Strategy*, 86.

192. The designations "A" and "A1" reflect France's status, either as a neutral (A) or an active ally (A1) in a war between Britain and Germany. Grimes, *Strategy*, 89–90.

193. Ibid., 99.

194. Ibid.

195. Ibid., 99, 127–28.

196. Lambert, *Planning Armageddon*, 4–5.

197. Ibid., 75–77.
198. During one inquiry session, Fisher wrote a colleague, "I am here wasting my time considering an invasion of England by Germany under the inconceivable conditions of the 'bolt from the blue' school." Lambert, *Fisher's Revolution*, 172, 180.
199. Ibid.
200. Ibid., 180.
201. Fisher, *Fear God and Dread Nought*, 1:412, 172, 181. However, Fisher's behavior at the CID meetings, which he was required to attend, was far from perfect. The admiral refused to hide his disdain for the proceedings and used the meetings as an opportunity to catch up on his correspondence.
202. Grimes, *Strategy*, 118
203. Ibid., 115, 118, 121.
204. Shawn T. Grimes, "War Planning and Strategic Development in the Royal Navy, 1887–1918" (Ph.D. diss., King's College, University of London, 2003), 151–52. Plans W4, W5, and W6 posited a war between Britain and a U.S.-German alliance.
205. Grimes, *Strategy*, 126.
206. Morris, *Fisher's Face*, 97.
207. Grimes, *Strategy*, 101–2.
208. Ibid., 134; Freeman, *Naval Feud*, 168.
209. Sumida, *Naval Supremacy*, 193, 195–96. During the same period, expenditures on social welfare increased by roughly 900 percent. This, however, did not raise total social-welfare spending to match that on the Army and Navy. Unknown to the British, the German government's budget woes were comparatively greater.
210. William Manchester, *The Last Lion: Winston Spencer Churchill*, vol. 1, *Visions of Glory, 1874–1932* (New York: Little, Brown, 1983), 407.
211. Marder, *Dreadnought*, 21–22.
212. Morris, *Fisher's Face*, 161.
213. Marder, *Anatomy*, 65, 78.
214. Grimes, *Strategy*, 143.
215. Fairbanks, "Choosing Among Technologies," 139.
216. Massie, *Dreadnought*, 520.
217. Freeman, *Naval Feud*, 114. Fisher described his meeting with Beresford as follows:

> I had three hours with Beresford yesterday and all is settled and the Admiralty don't give in one inch to his demands; but I had as a preliminary to agree to three things:
> Lord Charles Beresford is a greater man than Nelson.
> No one knows anything about naval war except Lord Charles Beresford.
> The Admiralty haven't done a single d——d thing right.

218. Lambert, *Fisher's Revolution*, 188.

219. Ibid., 193; Grimes, *Strategy*, 151.

220. Penn, *Infighting Admirals*, 218.

221. Bacon, *Fisher*, 2:53; Morris, *Fisher's Face*, 178.

222. National Archives (NA), *Beresford Enquiry*, CAB, 10, quoted in Lambert, *Fisher's Revolution*, 191; Freeman, *Naval Feud*, 190, 192.

223. Grimes, *Strategy*, 150–51.

224. NA, *Beresford Enquiry*, 51, quoted in Lambert, *Fisher's Revolution*, 191–92; Marder, *Dreadnought*, 196.

225. Freeman, *Naval Feud*, 206.

226. Penn, *Infighting Admirals*, 17.

227. Bacon, *Fisher*, 2:103; Freedman, *Naval Feud*, 215–16; Grimes, *Strategy*, 152; Lambert, *Fisher's Revolution*, 194.

228. Freeman, *Naval Feud*, 219–20; Penn, *Infighting Admirals*, 225.

229. Lambert, *Fisher's Revolution*, 194.

230. Fisher, *Fear God and Dread Nought*, 2:262. As for the four committee members, which included Asquith himself, Fisher wished them all hell "on earth . . . instead of waiting."

231. Lambert, *Fisher's Revolution*, 202.

232. Massie, *Dreadnought*, 541.

233. Ibid., 542.

234. Lambert, *Fisher's Revolution*, 195.

235. Lambert, "Economy or Empire?," 62.

236. Neilson, "British Empire Floats," 26.

237. Lambert, *Fisher's Revolution*, 78.

238. Grimes, *Strategy*, 158; Lambert, *Planning Armageddon*, 133.

239. Morris, *Fisher's Face*, 229.

240. Wilson's early retirement also resulted in his opposition to Churchill's creation of a naval staff. Fisher also continued to promote members of the Fishpond to Churchill. He successfully advised Churchill to appoint Admiral John Jellicoe—twenty-first in seniority among the Navy's vice admirals—as second in command of the Home Fleet, thereby giving him the experience and seniority necessary to assume command of the Royal Navy's primary fleet when war came. Jackie also proved a strong supporter of Admiral Battenberg, who succeeded Bridgeman as first sea lord in 1912. Both of these successors to Wilson lacked Fisher's dynamism, which may explain why Jackie, who was trying to work his will through Churchill, supported their appointment.

241. Lambert, *Fisher's Revolution*, 239, 244–45.

242. Kennedy, *British Naval Mastery*, 223–24.

243. Lambert, *Fisher's Revolution*, 248, 250–52. In referring to Churchill's retreat, Fisher sadly noted to one colleague, "[He] can't go quite as far as I urge him, as his instruments [i.e., the other members of the Board of Admiralty] are inadequate. They shiver on the brink and won't take the great plunge. He can't well plunge alone." (ibid., 248).

244. Sumida, *Naval Supremacy*, 258–60.

245. Manchester, *Last Lion*, 1:441, 443.

246. Kennedy, *British Naval Mastery*, 226; Massie, *Dreadnought*, 825.

247. Manchester, *Last Lion*, 1:451. See also Massie, *Dreadnought*, 836.

248. John H. Maurer, "Churchill's Naval Holiday: Arms Control and the Anglo-German Naval Race 1912–1914," *Journal of Strategic Studies* 15 (March 1992): 105.

249. Grimes, *Strategy*, 164.

250. Lambert, *Fisher's Revolution*, 207.

251. Ibid., 263.

252. Ibid., 263–64, 277–80; Grimes, *Strategy*, 176–77.

253. Grimes, *Strategy*, 179–80; Lambert, *Fisher's Revolution*, 286.

254. Lambert, *Fisher's Revolution*, 284–87.

255. Sumida, *Naval Supremacy*, 263–64; Massie, *Castles*, 125; Lambert, *Fisher's Revolution*, 293; Spector, *At War, at Sea*, 105.

256. Lambert, *Fisher's Revolution*, 298–303.

257. Italy, the third member of the Triple Alliance, initially remained neutral. It entered the war on the side of the Allies in 1915.

258. Spector, *At War, at Sea*, 108; John H. Maurer, "Imperial Germany's Naval Challenge and the Renewal of British Power," in *British World Policy and the Projection of Global Power, c. 1830–1960*, ed. T. G. Otte (Cambridge: Cambridge University Press, 2019), 172; Gray, *Devil's Device*, 188.

259. Grimes, *Strategy*, 196–97, 201; Herman, *To Rule the Waves*, 495.

260. Herman, *To Rule the Waves*, 498.

261. Grimes, *Strategy*, 189, 200–201, 204, 206.

262. Massie, *Castles*, 432, 441–43.

263. Sumida, "British Capital Ship Design," 228; Sumida, *Naval Supremacy*, 289; Massie, *Castles*, 417, 419.

264. The reader will recall that Churchill, Fisher, and members of the Fishpond were attempting to move toward a homogeneous battle line and retire older, slower battleships at the time that Tirpitz introduced his 1912 naval bill. The German bill led to an increase in the Royal Navy's battleship force, and the older ships were retained.

265. Lord Ernie Chatfield, *The Navy and Defence: An Autobiography* (London: William Heinemann, 1942), 143, quoted in Massie, *Castles*, 596.

266. During the same period, the *Lion, Princess Royal, Tiger, New Zealand,* and *Indefatigable* scored a total of five hits. Sumida, "British Capital Ship Design," 229.

267. German pre-dreadnoughts were, as a rule, less well protected than their Royal Navy counterparts. When the British launched *Dreadnought*, Germany responded by imitating Fisher's gambit, but only in the broadest sense. To be sure, the German Navy built dreadnoughts and modern battle cruisers. But Tirpitz set different priorities in making his design trade-offs. First off, the German fleet did not value endurance as highly as the Royal

Navy; the British needed endurance to send ships long distances to protect the outer reaches of the empire. The major shift in German design, however, was its according a far higher priority to ship protection. The share of displacement devoted to armor rose from 33 percent in the *Deutschland* class to 35 percent in the *Nassau* class, then to 37 percent in the *Ostfriesland* class and to 40 percent in the *Koenig* class. If Fisher was betting on speed and range to fight at a gentleman's distance, the Imperial German Navy cast its lot with the ability to take punishment and survive a brawl. Before World War I, only Germany conducted systematic experiments on ship protection. Not only would British warships prove more vulnerable to underwater hits, but they were also less able to deal with flooding. The *Queen Elizabeth* super-dreadnought, for example, could pump out 950 tons of water per hour, while its German contemporary, the *Bayern*, could pump at a rate *nearly six times greater.* Finally, the Germans had learned an important lesson at the Dogger Bank engagement. There a shell had penetrated *Seydlitz's* aft turret, triggering powder in the turret to catch fire, flash below, and kill everyone in two aft turret systems. The ship would have blown up if its magazines had not been flooded to extinguish the flames. The Germans installed antiflash protection on the hatches between handling room and magazines—something Beatty's ships lacked at Jutland. Fairbanks, "Choosing Among Technologies," 129–30, 132, 135; Massie, *Castles,* 667.

268. Massie, *Dreadnought,* 781.
269. Parkinson, *Dreadnought,* 235, 237; Padfield, *Battleship,* 228, 240.
270. Marder, *Dreadnought,* 206.
271. Ibid., 13, 406; Freeman, *Naval Feud,* 235.

Chapter Seven. Out of the Trenches

1. Winston S. Churchill, *The Second World War: The Gathering Storm* (New York: Houghton Mifflin, 1948), 6.
2. Although the term "Blitzkrieg" has become synonymous with the form of mechanized air-land operations conducted by the German military in World War II, the Germans themselves did not use the term, or invent it.
3. The term *Reichswehr* is translated as "Realm Defense." It was renamed the *Wehrmacht* ("Defense Force") in 1935.
4. Kenneth Macksey, *Guderian: Panzer General* (Mechanicsburg, Pa.: Stackpole, 2003), 19–20.
5. Bruce I. Gudmundson, *Stormtroop Tactics* (New York: Praeger, 1989), 139.
6. James S. Corum, *The Roots of Blitzkrieg* (Lawrence: University Press of Kansas, 1992), 9.
7. Gudmundson, *Stormtroop Tactics,* 172.
8. Corum, *Blitzkrieg,* 16.

9. Williamson Murray, "Armored Warfare: The British, French, and German Experiences," in *Military Innovation in the Interwar Period*, ed. Williamson Murray and Allan R. Millett (New York: Cambridge University Press, 1996), 36.

10. Gordon A. Craig, *The Politics of the Prussian Army, 1640–1945* (Oxford: Oxford University Press, 1955), 96–97; James S. Corum, "A Comprehensive Approach to Change," in *The Challenge of Change*, ed. Harold R. Winton and Dave R. Mets (Lincoln: University of Nebraska Press, 2000), 38.

11. Hans von Seeckt, *Gedanken eines Soldaten* (Leipzig: von Hase and Koehler, 1935), 56, quoted in Robert M. Citino, *The Evolution of Blitzkrieg Tactics: Germany Defends Itself Against Poland, 1918–1933* (New York: Greenwood, 1987), 71; B. H. Liddell Hart, *The German Generals Talk* (New York: Harper-Collins, 1948), 15; Horne, *To Lose a Battle*, 89.

12. *Auftragstaktik* (mission tactics) were developed by the Prussian army following the Napoleonic Wars. Emphasis is placed on commanders giving their subordinate a clearly defined mission and a time frame within which it must be accomplished. The subordinate commander is given wide latitude as to how he accomplishes the mission. *Schwerpunkt* refers to an operation's principal focus or weight of effort. Milan Vego, "Clausewitz's Schwerpunkt: Mistranslated from German—Misunderstood in English," *Military Review* 87 (January–February 2007): 101–9.

13. Robert M. Citino, *The Path to Blitzkrieg* (Boulder, Colo.: Lynne Rienner, 1999), 43.

14. Von Seeckt, *Gedanken eines Soldaten*, 77, quoted in Citino, *Evolution of Blitzkrieg*, 72.

15. Major Dakota L. Wood, "Breakthrough! The German Search for Mobility," unpublished paper, December 23, 1998, 9–10.

16. Winston S. Churchill, *The World Crisis, 1916–1918*, part 2 (New York: Charles Scribner's Sons, 1927), 61–62, quoted in Carlo D'Este, *Warlord* (New York: HarperCollins, 2008), 297.

17. Von Seeckt's approach "was less democratic than Reinhardt's vision, but von Seeckt was correct in recognizing the organizational and technical abilities of the General Staff as having first priority." Corum, *Blitzkrieg*, 33–34. Von Seeckt's victory was won with the support of General Wilhelm Groener, who had replaced General Erich Ludendorff, Germany's de facto wartime dictator, as the Army's quartermaster general. (Ludendorff was a Reinhardt supporter.)

18. Citino, *Path to Blitzkrieg*, 148.

19. William Deist, "The Rearmament of the Wehrmacht," in *Germany and the Second World War*, trans. P. S. Falla, Dean S. McMurry, and Ewald Osers (Oxford, U.K.: Clarendon, 1990), 377–78.

20. Larry H. Addington, *The Blitzkrieg Era and the German General Staff, 1865–1941* (New Brunswick, N.J.: Rutgers University Press, 1971), 30–31.

21. Corum, "Change," 64; Hart, *German Generals Talk*, 20.

22. Citino, *Path to Blitzkrieg*, 116.

23. Corum, *Blitzkrieg*, 45, 108, 187–88.

24. Citino, *Path to Blitzkrieg*, 154.

25. Craig, *Prussian Army*, 396; Corum, "Change," 49.

26. Corum, "Change," 40–41.

27. Horne, *To Lose a Battle*, 88.

28. Azar Gat, "British Influence and the Evolution of the Panzer Arm: Myth or Reality? Part I," *War in History* 4 (April 1997): 162–63.

29. Ibid., 160.

30. Murray, "Armored Warfare," 39–40.

31. Gat, "British Influence, Part I," 159.

32. Harold R. Winton, "Tanks, Votes, and Budgets: The Politics of Mechanization and Armored Warfare in Britain, 1919–1939," in Winton and Mets, *Challenge of Change*, 80; Corum, "Change," 56; Macksey, *Guderian*, 42.

33. Deist, "Wehrmacht," 389, 391.

34. Corum, *Blitzkrieg*, 194.

35. Citino, *Path to Blitzkrieg*, 187, 189.

36. Following the 1932 British maneuvers, an article on the subject published in the *Militar-Wochenblatt* opened with the following words: "The British army undoubtedly stands today ahead of all armies in the field of mechanization. ... The frequent maneuvers of the armored formations at Salisbury are today the object of curiosity for all men of cultivation. They are in fact the highest school of mechanization." Gat, "British Influence, Part I," 167–68.

37. Ibid., 173.

38. David MacIsaac, "Voices from the Central Blue: The Air Power Theorists," in *Makers of Modern Strategy: From Machiavelli to the Nuclear Age*, ed. Peter Paret (Princeton, N.J.: Princeton University Press, 1986), 629–35.

39. Corum, *Blitzkrieg*, 145–46; James S. Corum, "The Luftwaffe's Army Support Doctrine, 1918–1941," *Journal of Military History* 59 (January 1995): 53.

40. Williamson Murray, *Strategy for Defeat: The Luftwaffe, 1933–1945* (Maxwell AFB, Ala.: Air University Press, 1983), 10–11.

41. James S. Corum, *The Luftwaffe: Creating the Operational Air War, 1918–1940* (Lawrence: University Press of Kansas, 1997), 52.

42. Murray, *Strategy for Defeat*, 5–6. Blomberg offered Hermann Goering, the minister of aviation, a choice between Walther Wever and Erich von Manstein. Goering chose Wever, who proved a superb chief until his untimely death in 1936, while von Manstein went on to achieve the rank of field marshal and compile one of the most impressive records of any senior officer in any military during World War II.

43. Luftwaffe Regulation 16, *Command of the Air War*, declared, "The mission of the armed forces in war is to break the enemy will. The will of the nations is most strongly embodied in its armed forces. Therefore, the destruction of the enemy armed forces is the primary goal in war." Corum, "Luftwaffe's Army Support Doctrine," 57–58.

44. Deist, "Wehrmacht," 482–84.

45. Ibid.

46. Ibid., 489–90.

47. Ibid., 493.

48. Kesselring would be replaced after only a year by General Stumpf, who in turn was replaced by Colonel Hans Jeschonnek in 1939.

49. General der Flieger Paul Deichmann, *Spearhead for Blitzkrieg*, ed. Alfred Pierce (London: Greenhill, 1996), 41–42.

50. Ibid., 42.

51. Corum, *Luftwaffe*, 266–68.

52. Manfred Messerschmidt, "German Military Effectiveness Between 1919 and 1939," in Millett and Murray, *Military Effectiveness*, vol. 2, 232.

53. Murray, *Strategy for Defeat*, 20.

54. Despite the shortcomings noted here, the German Air Ministry did pursue a number of revolutionary systems. Development of the V-1 and V-2 rockets began in the mid-1930s. The Heinkel Company developed the world's first jet engine in 1937. The jet-powered He-176 first flew at Peenemunde in 1939.

55. Horne, *To Lose a Battle*, 120–21.

56. Deist, "Wehrmacht," 481.

57. Corum, *Luftwaffe*, 269–70.

58. W. Heineman, "The Development of the German Armoured Forces, 1918–1940," in *Armoured Warfare*, ed. J. Harris and F. H. Toase (New York: St. Martin's, 1990), 54.

59. The Waffenamt was established on November 8, 1919, as "Reichwaffenamt." On May 5, 1922, the name was changed to "Heereswaffenamt" (Army Ordnance Office).

60. Corum, *Blitzkrieg*, 85; Corum, "Change," 66–67.

61. Corum, *Blitzkrieg*, 132–33. Corum notes, "The job of the unit armor officer was not just another extra duty for motor officers. The high command ordered that the transfer of tank officers was to be avoided and that those who had served a term as tank officer could serve for a second tour of duty in that assignment."

62. Ibid., 136.

63. Ibid., 190–95.

64. Ibid., 162, 167.

65. Ibid., 151.

66. Horne, *To Lose a Battle*, 121.

67. Deist, "Wehrmacht," 445–47.

68. Ibid., 449.

69. Craig, *Prussian Army*, 406.

70. Ibid., 406–7.

71. Corum, "Change," 48.

72. Corum, *Blitzkrieg*, 112, 118.

73. Craig, *Prussian Army*, 410.

74. Richard Overy, *Why the Allies Won* (New York: Norton, 1995), 224. Germany also lacked a large tractor industry for producing tracked or half-tracked vehicles, a secure source of oil, a large oil-refining industry, and a robust mechanical-maintenance service industry. There apparently was no system in place for converting Germany's automobile industry to war production. Even with the limited mechanization of the German Army, it was continuously short of drivers and personnel for salvage and maintenance units. R. L. DiNardo, *Mechanized Juggernaut or Military Anachronism?* (New York: Greenwood, 1991), 7, 9–10.

75. Russell H. S. Stolfi, "Equipment for Victory in France in 1940," *History Journal of the Historical Association* 55 (February 1970): 6. The Panzer I's limitations were highlighted in the Polish campaign. Some 150 Panzer Is were knocked out by the Poles.

76. Ibid., 7. Reflecting in part the Panzer II's improved capabilities relative to the Panzer I, the Panzer II remained in production until 1944.

77. Ibid.

78. Deist, "Wehrmacht," 450.

79. Heineman, "Armoured Forces," 60.

80. Stolfi, "Equipment," 8; Werner Haupt, *A History of the Panzer Troops* (West Chester, Pa.: Schiffer Military History, 1990), 45. The Germans also outfitted fifteen infantry divisions with confiscated Czech equipment. Deist, "Wehrmacht," 451.

81. Overy, *Why the Allies Won*, 217.

82. DiNardo, *Juggernaut or Anachronism?*, 7, 9–10.

83. Corum, *Luftwaffe*, 84, 113.

84. Murray, *Strategy for Defeat*, 4.

85. Ibid., 7.

86. Corum, *Blitzkrieg*, 186.

87. Citino, *Evolution of Blitzkrieg*, 184.

88. Ibid.

89. Corum, *Blitzkrieg*, 185–89.

90. Heinz Guderian, *Achtung—Panzer!*, trans. Christopher Duffy (London: Arms and Armour, 1992), 142.

91. Citino, *Evolution of Blitzkrieg*, 203.

92. Haupt, *Panzer Troops*, 70–71.

93. Citino, *Evolution of Blitzkrieg*, 184.

94. Ibid.

95. Ibid., 214.

96. Citino, *Decisive Victory*, 203–4.

97. Haupt, *Panzer Troops*, 70–71.

98. Macksey, *Guderian*, 62–63.

99. Haupt, *Panzer Troops*, 59; Macksey, *Guderian*, 50.

100. Citino, *Decisive Victory*, 191.

101. Citino, *Path to Blitzkrieg*, 252.

102. Guderian, *Achtung—Panzer!*, 162.
103. Gat, "British Influence, Part I," 167.
104. Heineman, "Armoured Forces," 57–58.
105. David E. Johnson, *Fast Tanks and Heavy Bombers* (Ithaca, N.Y.: Cornell University Press, 1998), 10–11.
106. Guderian, *Panzer Leader*, 32.
107. Citino, *Path to Blitzkrieg*, 215, 252.
108. Haupt, *Panzer Troops*, 23, 29. The Army Motor Vehicle School in Berlin, established in 1934, was soon transferred to a new barracks. Revealingly, it was renamed "Cambrai Barracks" in 1935.
109. Murray, "Armored Warfare," 40.
110. Azar Gat, "British Influence and the Evolution of the Panzer Arm: Myth or Reality? Part II," *War in History* 4 (July 1997): 318.
111. Macksey, *Guderian*, 58,
112. Horne, *To Lose a Battle*, 94.
113. A. Roberts, *Storm*, 50.
114. Heineman, "Armoured Forces," 58.
115. Deist, "Wehrmacht," 433.
116. Gat, "British Influence, Part II," 334.
117. Deist, "Wehrmacht," 435.
118. Citino, *Path to Blitzkrieg*, 231.
119. Heineman, "Armoured Forces," 40.
120. Gat, "British Influence, Part II," 335.
121. Heineman, "Armoured Forces," 55; Guderian, *Panzer Leader*, 39–45.
122. Haupt, *Panzer Troops*, 72.
123. Corum, "Change," 51.
124. Gat, "British Influence, Part II," 334.
125. Deist, "Wehrmacht," 436; Guderian, *Panzer Leader*, 36.
126. Citino, *Path to Blitzkrieg*, 239–40. Note that the 1935 maneuvers had taken place before the panzer divisions had been created, while the 1936 maneuvers focused primarily on testing the quality of noncommissioned officers and men in a rapidly expanding Army.
127. Citino, *Decisive Victory*, 208–10; Corum, "Change," 51.
128. Citino, *Evolution of Blitzkrieg*, 241.
129. May, *Strange Victory*, 88, 235; Citino, *Decisive Victory*, 207–8.
130. Guderian, *Panzer Leader*, 39, 41.
131. Messerschmidt, "German Military Effectiveness," 245.
132. Heineman, "Armoured Forces," 40–41; Guderian, *Panzer Leader*, 54. During this period, the Army's first three panzer divisions were still being fleshed out with support troops (such as engineers) and equipment. On November 10, 1938, the Wehrmacht activated two new panzer divisions and four new panzer brigades.
133. Guderian, *Panzer Leader*, 54.
134. Ibid., 49–54.

135. Citino, *Evolution of Blitzkrieg*, 242–43.

136. Heineman, "Armoured Forces," 59.

137. Corum, *Luftwaffe*, 245.

138. Corum, "Luftwaffe's Army Support Doctrine," 61.

139. Corum, "Change," 76.

140. "Situation awareness," broadly defined, is the capability of one's forces to possess accurate knowledge of the location of friendly and enemy forces in or near the operational area, their activities, and where they are likely to be in the immediate future.

141. Corum, *Luftwaffe*, 234–35.

142. Ibid., 238.

143. James S. Corum, "The Spanish Civil War: Lessons Learned and Not Learned by the Great Powers," *Journal of Military History* 62 (April 1998): 313–34; Citino, *Decisive Victory*, 243.

144. Corum, *Luftwaffe*, 247.

145. Citino, *Decisive Victory*, 249–50.

146. Corum, *Luftwaffe*, 220, 223.

147. Corum, "Spanish Civil War," 326.

148. Macksey, *Guderian*, 80.

149. Corum, *Luftwaffe*, 223, 272, 274.

150. Williamson Murray, *The Change in the European Balance of Power, 1938–1939* (Princeton, N.J.: Princeton University Press, 1984), 36.

151. Robert A. Doughty, *The Breaking Point: Sedan and the Fall of France, 1940* (Mechanicsburg, Pa.: Stackpole, 1990), 13.

152. A. Roberts, *Storm*, 53; May, *Strange Victory*, 356.

153. Horne, *To Lose a Battle*, 187.

154. Macksey, *Guderian*, 98.

155. May, *Strange Victory*, 227.

156. Horne, *To Lose a Battle*, 204–5.

157. Ibid., 205–6.

158. May, *Strange Victory*, 233, 265.

159. The French possessed an even greater advantage in overall tank tonnage. Prior to May 1940, France had produced roughly 61,650 tons of tanks, whereas combined German and Czech production yielded only 36,650 tons. Simply put, the French Army's tanks were heavier than those of their German enemies. Stolfi, "Equipment," 2, 9–11, 16.

160. Karl Hardach, *The Political Economy of Germany in the Twentieth Century* (Berkeley: University of California Press, 1980), 76.

161. Macksey, *Guderian*, 100.

162. Stolfi, "Equipment," 13. Interestingly, the panzer divisions had no clear advantage in speed over the French light mechanized divisions, of which there were three, comprising some 240 tanks each.

163. Horne, *To Lose a Battle*, 233; A. Roberts, *Storm*, 54.

164. Corum, *Luftwaffe*, 277.
165. Stolfi, "Equipment," 20.
166. Guderian, *Panzer Leader*, 106.
167. Ibid., 102.
168. Macksey, *Guderian*, 105.
169. Horne, *To Lose a Battle*, 445–46.
170. Corum, *Luftwaffe*, 277.
171. Ibid., 249.
172. Citino, *Decisive Victory*, 257.
173. Doughty, *Breaking Point*, xvi.
174. Winston S. Churchill, *Their Finest Hour* (New York: Houghton Mifflin, 1949), 70.
175. Ibid., 53.
176. Horne, *To Lose a Battle*, 666–67.
177. Hart, *German Generals Talk*, 95–96.
178. Ibid., 94.
179. Ibid., 143–44.
180. Macksey, *Guderian*, 122.
181. Corum, *Luftwaffe*, 286.
182. Guderian, *Achtung—Panzer!*, 24.
183. Corum, "Luftwaffe's Army Support Doctrine," 71–72, 76.
184. Murray, "Armored Warfare," 43. Indeed, the famed German panzer commander Erwin Rommel was not converted to this new form of warfare until the French campaign.
185. Heineman, "Armoured Forces," 61.
186. Addington, *Blitzkrieg Era*, 123.
187. Overy, *Why the Allies Won*, 215, 218, 224, 243.
188. Macksey, *Guderian*, 80–81.
189. Citino, *Decisive Victory*, 256, 283.

Chapter Eight. Twilight of the Battle Line

1. David C. Evans and Mark R. Peattie, *Kaigun* (Annapolis, Md.: Naval Institute Press, 1997), 491.
2. Baer, *U.S. Navy*, 144.
3. Thomas C. Hone, Norman Friedman, and Mark D. Mandeles, *American and British Aircraft Carrier Development* (Annapolis, Md.: Naval Institute Press, 1999), 17.
4. John T. Kuehn, *Agents of Innovation: The General Board and the Design of the Fleet That Defeated the Japanese Navy* (Annapolis, Md.: Naval Institute Press, 2008), 11, 14, 18.
5. William M. McBride, *Technological Change and the United States Navy, 1865–1945* (Baltimore: Johns Hopkins University Press, 2000), 130–31.

6. Norman Friedman, "The Aircraft Carrier," in *The Eclipse of the Big Gun: The Warship, 1906–45*, ed. Robert Gardiner (Annapolis, Md.: Naval Institute Press, 1992), 38.

7. Quoted in Clark G. Reynolds, *The Fast Carriers* (Annapolis, Md.: Naval Institute Press, 1968), 1.

8. Ibid.; Charles M. Melhorn, *Two-Block Fox* (Annapolis, Md.: Naval Institute Press, 1974), 30–31.

9. Admiral William Moffett, who became the first head of the Navy's Bureau of Aeronautics, actually proposed experimenting with aircraft deployed on submarines. See William F. Trimble, *Admiral William A. Moffett: Architect of Naval Aviation* (Washington, D.C.: Smithsonian Institution Press, 1994), 108.

10. Melhorn, *Two-Block Fox*, 33.

11. Trimble, Moffett, 71.

12. Melhorn, *Two-Block Fox*, 28–29, 33.

13. Ibid., 37.

14. Hone, Friedman, and Mandeles, *Aircraft Carrier Development*, 22–23.

15. Thomas C. Hone and Trent Hone, *Battle Line: The United States Navy, 1919–1939* (Annapolis, Md.: Naval Institute Press, 2006), 81. By 1935, the Navy concluded that aerial spotting produced six times as many hits as spotters placed in a ship's top mast position.

16. Melhorn, *Two-Block Fox*, 26; Norman Friedman, Thomas C. Hone, and Mark D. Mandeles, "The Introduction of Carrier Aviation into the U.S. Navy and Royal Navy: Military-Technical Revolutions, Organizations, and the Problems of Decision," unpublished paper, May 12, 1994, 57.

17. Melhorn, *Two-Block Fox*, 26, 38.

18. Ibid., 60.

19. Ibid.

20. William M. McBride, "Challenging a Strategic Paradigm: Aviation and the U.S. Navy Special Policy Board of 1924," *Journal of Strategic Studies* 14 (September 1991): 75, quoted in Geoffrey Till, "Adopting the Aircraft Carrier," in Murray and Millett, *Military Innovation in the Interwar Period*, 209–10.

21. Spector, *Eagle*, 22.

22. Melhorn, *Two-Block Fox*, 56.

23. Hone, Friedman, and Mandeles, *Aircraft Carrier Development*, 29.

24. McBride, *Technological Change*, 144, 182.

25. Melhorn, *Two-Block Fox*, 88; Thomas C. Hone and Mark D. Mandeles, "Interwar Innovation in Three Navies: U.S. Navy, Royal Navy, Imperial Japanese Navy," *Naval War College Review* 40 (Spring 1987): 63–83.

26. Friedman, Hone, and Mandeles, "Carrier Aviation," 22.

27. McBride, *Technological Change*, 135.

28. Ibid., 135–36.

29. Friedman, "Aircraft Carrier," 39.

30. Till, "Aircraft Carrier," 210–11.

31. Hone, Friedman, and Mandeles, *Aircraft Carrier Development*, 166.
32. Trimble, *Moffett*, 193–95.
33. Ibid.
34. The office was abolished in 1932, a victim of the Depression.
35. Reynolds, *Fast Carriers*, 15.
36. Trimble, *Moffett*, 89.
37. Ibid., 101.
38. Reynolds, *Fast Carriers*, 17.
39. Ronald H. Spector, "Winning with Second Best Technology: Naval Aviation in the Pacific, 1941–1944," unpublished paper, n.d., 7.
40. Thomas Wildenberg, *All the Factors of Victory* (Dulles, Va.: Brassy's, 2003), 128–29. Ironically, the collier *Jupiter*, which had been converted to the *Langley*, had been Reeves's first command.
41. Evans and Peattie, *Kaigun*, 323–24.
42. Wildenberg, *Factors*, 129.
43. Albert A. Nofi, *To Train the Fleet for War* (Newport, R.I.: U.S. Naval War College Press, 2010), 86–87.
44. Friedman, "Aircraft Carrier," 39; Wildenberg, *Factors*, 139; Clark G. Reynolds, *Admiral John H. Towers* (Annapolis, Md.: Naval Institute Press, 1991), 205.
45. Trimble, *Moffett*, 107.
46. Baer, *U.S. Navy*, 140.
47. Wildenberg, *Destined for Glory*, 9.
48. McBride, *Technological Change*, 145.
49. Polmar, *Aircraft Carriers*, 67.
50. Wildenberg, *Destined for Glory*, 10; Reynolds, *Fast Carriers*, 17; Friedman, Hone, and Mandeles, "Carrier Aviation," 90, 188. While Wagner's demonstration helped pave the way for carrier strike operations, Marine Corps aviators pioneered dive-bombing in Haiti in 1919. See Trimble, *Moffett*, 209.
51. Friedman, Hone, and Mandeles, "Carrier Aviation," 90; Wildenberg, *Destined for Glory*, 100–102.
52. Wildenberg, *Destined for Glory*, 16.
53. Ibid., 70.
54. Trimble, *Moffett*, 210.
55. Ibid., 203.
56. Ibid., 212.
57. Ibid., 205.
58. Ibid., 206.
59. Friedman, "Aircraft Carrier," 50.
60. Ibid., 50–52.
61. Hone, Friedman, and Mandeles, *Aircraft Carrier Development*, 37.
62. Trimble, *Moffett*, 210.
63. The treaty actually permitted flight decks to be incorporated on existing capital ships and on destroyers and cruisers. But since the treaty also banned

the construction of new capital ships, and destroyers were too small to undergo conversion, the net effect was solely on cruisers. Ibid., 220–21.

64. Ibid., 223.

65. Friedman, "Aircraft Carrier," 50. This latter characteristic would be particularly important as the Navy shifted its aircraft mix during the transition period from an offensive-dominant mini-regime to a more defense-dominant regime between 1942 and 1944.

66. Kuehn, *Agents of Innovation*, 38.

67. Friedman, Hone, and Mandeles, "Carrier Aviation," 181; Polmar, *Aircraft Carrier*, 74–75; Sebastian Roblin, "Why the Navy's Essex-Class Carriers Were So Good," *National Interest*, April 9, 2020, https://nationalinterest.org/blog/buzz/why-navys-essex-class-aircraft-carriers-were-so-good-142767.

68. Trimble, *Moffett*, 204; Reynolds, *Fast Carriers*, 16.

69. Trimble, *Moffett*, 204.

70. Edward S. Miller, *War Plan Orange* (Annapolis, Md.: Naval Institute Press, 1991), 348.

71. Wildenberg, *Destined for Glory*, 52.

72. Craig C. Felker, *Testing American Sea Power: U.S. Navy Strategic Exercises, 1923–1940* (College Station: Texas A&M University Press, 2007), 49.

73. *Saratoga* carried 110 planes and 100 pilots, an enormous leap in capability from the *Langley*'s few dozen aircraft. *Fleet Problem IX*, National Archives Publication M964, "Report of the CINC, U.S. Fleet," 23, 26, 71, cited in Friedman, Hone, and Mandeles, "Carrier Aviation," 94; Nofi, *To Train the Fleet*, 113. The *Saratoga*'s exploit was partly the product of chance: it was detached from the battleship force because the battleships' destroyer screen did not have sufficient fuel to keep up with it.

74. Nofi, *To Train the Fleet*, 110.

75. Reynolds, *Fast Carriers*, 17.

76. Ibid.; Robert L. O'Connell, *Sacred Vessels: The Cult of the Battleship and the Rise of the U.S. Navy* (Boulder, Colo.: Westview, 1991), 285.

77. Nofi, *To Train the Fleet*, 117.

78. Felker, *Testing*, 51.

79. Ibid., 54.

80. Ibid., 56.

81. Hone and Hone, *Battle Line*, 74, 76; Nofi, *To Train the Fleet*, 134–35.

82. Wildenberg, *Destined for Glory*, 83–85.

83. Ibid., 92.

84. O'Connell, *Sacred Vessels*, 286.

85. Trimble, *Moffett*, 226–27.

86. Ibid., 228.

87. Pearl Harbor was also subjected to another "attack" by the *Saratoga* in 1938. The Japanese war-gamed carrier-led attacks against Pearl Harbor as early as autumn 1927. Evans and Peattie, *Kaigun*, 473.

88. Reynolds, *Towers*, 237–38.

89. Ibid., 238–39.
90. Wildenberg, *Destined for Glory*, 128.
91. Ibid., 127–28.
92. Reynolds, *Towers*, 238–39.
93. Hone, Friedman, and Mandeles, *Aircraft Carrier Development*, 135.
94. Reynolds, *Towers*, 245–47.
95. Hone, Friedman, and Mandeles, *Aircraft Carrier Development*, 50.
96. Ibid., 66.
97. Reynolds, *Towers*, 272.
98. Felker, *Testing*, 58.
99. Wildenberg, *Destined for Glory*, 163.
100. Reynolds, *Fast Carriers*, 18.
101. Ian W. Toll, *Pacific Crucible* (New York: Norton, 2012), 164, 167.
102. Friedman, "Aircraft Carrier," 44.
103. Wildenberg, *Destined for Glory*, 158.
104. Reynolds, *Towers*, 276–79.
105. Hughes, *Fleet Tactics*, 87.
106. Evans and Peattie, *Kaigun*, 508.
107. Hone and Hone, *Battle Line*, 135–36.
108. Ironically, the Japanese had initiated research on radar around the same time as the Americans. However, "official indifference, haphazard mobilization of scientific talent, and—as always—the absence of interservice cooperation fatally delayed the practical military application of Japanese radar research." Evans and Peattie, *Kaigun*, 394, 411.
109. Hone, Friedman, and Mandeles, *Aircraft Carrier Development*, 67; Hughes, *Fleet Tactics*, 116–17. For example, in the Battle of the Eastern Solomons, U.S. air-search radar detected the Japanese approaching at eighty-eight miles, allowing the Americans to put fighters in the air and to direct them to intercept the enemy without fear of being surprised by enemy aircraft arriving from another direction.
110. Miller, *War Plan Orange*, 350.
111. Ibid., 291.
112. Ibid., 292.
113. Ibid. The Navy was aware of the implications of fighting the Imperial Japanese Navy in its home waters and at a great distance from its own bases and began to experiment with underway refueling as early as 1936 and was perfecting refueling techniques for large warships by the time of Pearl Harbor. Evans and Peattie, *Kaigun*, 393.
114. Reynolds, *Towers*, 292–93.
115. Norman Friedman, *U.S. Aircraft Carriers: An Illustrated Design History* (Annapolis, Md.: Naval Institute Press, 1983), 33.
116. Spector, *Eagle*, 23.
117. Evans and Peattie, *Kaigun*, 353.
118. Hughes, *Fleet Tactics*, 86.

119. Reynolds, *Towers*, 227.

120. The argument put forth is reflected in the exchange at a General Board session between Captain Towers and Admiral Meigs Taylor of the Navy's War Plans Division:

> TOWERS: Don't you think though that in view of the fact that air-craft carriers are the newest type of vessels in the Fleet that they should be *continued?*
> TAYLOR: At the expense of other ships?
> TOWERS: Yes, sir.
> TAYLOR: I wouldn't say so. . . . That is a statement that the most important development in the fleet is aviation.
> TOWERS: I don't think it is quite that.
> TAYLOR: Pretty nearly.
> TOWERS: It is an important element to have experience with at the present time because there is less history behind it.

General Board hearings, May 1, 1931, 152, quoted in ibid., 228.

121. Bureau of Ships, Navy Department, *Ships Data U.S. Naval Vessels* (Washington, D.C.: GPO, 1945), vol. 1, 75–113. The carrier *Langley*, a converted collier, was commissioned in 1922.

122. Naval History and Heritage Command, "U.S. Ship Force Levels: 1886–Present," accessed February 19, 2022, https://www.history.navy.mil/research/histories/ship-histories/us-ship-force-levels.html.

123. W. F. Trimble, *Wings for the Navy: A History of the Naval Aircraft Factory, 1917–1956* (Annapolis, Md.: Naval Institute Press, 1990), 7–8, cited in Friedman, Hone, and Mandeles, "Carrier Aviation," 54–55.

124. One area where promising developments were not being exploited was the turbojet, whose potential was understood as early as 1935. But Congress would not provide funding for industry to do the necessary research and development. I. B. Holley, Jr., "Jet Lag in the Army Air Corps," in *Military Planning in the Twentieth Century*, ed. H. R. Borowski (Washington, D.C.: Office of Air Force History, 1986), 123–53, cited in Friedman, Hone, and Mandeles, "Carrier Aviation," 196–97. Torpedo production also suffered from financial shortfalls and lack of attention. Between 1923 and 1940, the Navy had but one source for its torpedoes. The contractor had no competition and little incentive to improve production standards. Torpedo testing was not carried out under operational conditions. Production levels were small, even in the late 1930s. The Navy would pay a terrible price during the war for the failure to develop effective torpedoes. Baer, *U.S. Navy*, 138–39.

125. Trimble, *Moffett*, 112.

126. Ibid.

127. Ibid., 113.

128. Ibid., 116.

129. Ibid., 170.

130. Ibid., 175–76.
131. Ibid., 178.
132. Reynolds, *Towers*, 226.
133. Trimble, *Moffett*, 249.
134. Friedman, Hone, and Mandeles, "Carrier Aviation," 106.
135. Hone, Friedman, and Mandeles, *Aircraft Carrier Development*, 58.
136. Wildenberg, *Destined for Glory*, 162.
137. Ibid., 162–63.
138. Deputy Chief of Naval Operations and The Commander, Naval Air Systems Command, *United States Naval Aviation, 1910–1980* (Washington, D.C.: GPO, 1981), 381–82.
139. Friedman, Hone, and Mandeles, "Carrier Aviation," 19.
140. Stephen Peter Rosen, *Winning the Next War: Innovation and the Modern Military* (Ithaca, N.Y.: Cornell University Press, 1991), 76–80.
141. Trimble, *Moffett*, 135.
142. Ibid., 139–40.
143. Ibid., 140.
144. Ibid., 184, 186.
145. Ibid., 183.
146. There were two Taylor Boards on naval aviation. The first was established in 1925 and reported out in January 1926. The second board was established in April 1927, and its report was endorsed by the General Board in November of that year. Wildenberg, *Destined for Glory*, 28–31.
147. Trimble, *Moffett*, 187.
148. Ibid., 188.
149. Ibid., 191.
150. Ibid., 190.
151. Ibid., 192, 199.
152. Friedman, Hone, and Mandeles, "Carrier Aviation," 107.
153. Reynolds, *Towers*, 295.
154. Evans and Peattie, *Kaigun*, 326. The Japanese did not institute a comparable training program until 1941.
155. Spector, "Second Best Technology," 30–31.
156. Roy A. Grosnick, *Dictionary of American Naval Aviation Squadrons* (Washington, D.C.: Naval Historical Center, Department of the Navy, 1955), vol. 1, 453–508; Gordon Swanborough and Peter M. Bowens, *United States Navy Aircraft Since 1911* (Annapolis, Md.: Naval Institute Press, 1990).
157. Grosnick, *Naval Aviation Squadrons*, 453–508.
158. Ibid.; Swanborough and Bowens, *Navy Aircraft*, 103.
159. Interestingly, since the U.S. carriers *Wasp* and *Ranger* were both too small to carry torpedo bombers, the development of dive-bombing was essential if these ships were to emerge as major offensive strike platforms. Swanborough and Bowens, *Navy Aircraft*, 103–4; Wildenberg, *Destined for Glory*, 194. The Navy did not develop a radio-controlled drone aircraft that could

simulate a dive-bombing attack until October 1939. Tests with the drone revealed that fleet defenses against this form of attack were "quite inadequate." Hone, Friedman, and Mandeles, *Aircraft Carrier Development*, 164.

160. O'Connell, *Sacred Vessels*, 310.

161. Spector, *Eagle*, 22–23.

162. Brodie, *Sea Power*, 402, 405.

163. Thomas C. Hone and Mark Mandeles, "Managerial Style in the Interwar Navy: A Reappraisal," *Naval War College Review* 32 (September–October 1980): 95–96.

164. Ronald Spector, "The Military Effectiveness of the U.S. Armed Forces, 1919–1939," in Millet and Murray, *Military Effectiveness*, vol. 2, 84.

165. Evans and Peattie, *Kaigun*, 307.

166. Spector, "Second Best Technology," 15.

167. Brodie, *Sea Power*, 410–11.

168. Joel R. Davidson, *The Unsinkable Fleet* (Annapolis, Md.: Naval Institute Press, 1996), 34.

169. Ibid., 34, 60. When shipbuilding accelerated in 1940, the Navy's planners realized that armor-plate production capacity represented the critical bottleneck in expanding the fleet. This led to lighter ships (which could be built more quickly) being given greater priority at the expense of battleship construction. In the end, the shortage may have proved serendipitous, arresting as it did the production of the soon-to-be-displaced battleships and providing modest boost to carrier construction.

170. Ibid., 36.

171. Ibid., 35; O'Connell, *Sacred Vessels*, 316; McBride, *Technological Change*, 185. Interestingly, in the summer of 1942, President Roosevelt opposed building the large *Midway*-class (45,000-ton) carriers, arguing that the ships would use too much steel and take too long to build. In December, the president approved their construction after much Navy lobbying. Roosevelt, however, proved correct: none of the *Midway*-class carriers were completed in time to see action in the war.

172. Hughes, *Fleet Tactics*, 94.

173. Friedman, Hone, and Mandeles, "Carrier Aviation," 108–9. Before 1942, the only other such command in the Navy had been that for battleships.

174. McBride, *Technological Change*, 206, 208.

175. In December 1941, the United States possessed seven fleet carriers: *Saratoga, Lexington, Ranger, Yorktown, Enterprise, Wasp,* and *Hornet.* A year later, only one—*Ranger*—had not been sunk or seriously damaged.

176. Friedman, "Aircraft Carrier," 47.

177. Hughes, *Fleet Tactics*, 102, 105.

178. Ibid., 118.

179. Hone, Friedman, and Mandeles, *Aircraft Carrier Development*, 162.

180. Evans and Peattie, *Kaigun*, 503.

181. Brodie, *Sea Power*, 407, 417.

182. Ibid., 418–19.

183. The British battleships *Prince of Wales* and *Repulse* were sunk in December 1941 by Japanese *land*-based aircraft.

184. Hone, Friedman, and Mandeles, *Aircraft Carrier Development*, 69. The IJN's formation of the First Mobile Fleet in 1944 was a belated attempt to imitate the Americans' fast carrier task forces. Evans and Peattie, *Kaigun*, 501.

185. Evans and Peattie, *Kaigun*, 380.

Chapter Nine. From Mass to Precision

1. Richard P. Hallion, "Precision Guided Munitions and the New Era of Warfare," APSC Paper Number 53, Air Power Studies Centre, Fairbairn, Australia, https://fas.org/man/dod-101/sys/smart/docs/paper53.htm.

2. Ibid.

3. Adam R. Grissom, Caitlin Lee, and Karl P. Mueller, *Innovation in the United States Air Force: Evidence from Six Cases* (Santa Monica, Calif.: RAND, 2016), 43.

4. Ibid., 44.

5. Watts, *Precision Strike*, 45–46; Stillion, *Air-to-Air Combat*, i.

6. Stillion, *Air-to-Air Combat*, i.

7. Barkhorn characterized maneuvering combat as a high-risk, low-payoff activity and estimated that between 80 and 90 percent of his victories were against unsuspecting targets.

8. Stillion, *Air-to-Air Combat*, 6.

9. Ibid.

10. Watts, *Precision Strike*, 48.

11. Lieutenant Colonel James C. Slife, "Creech Blue: Gen. Bill Creech and the Reformation of the Tactical Air Forces, 1978–1984," *Air University Press*, October 2004, 77.

12. Gillespie, "Precision Guided Munitions," 47–48.

13. Ibid.

14. Spaatz wanted "to leave in the minds of the Germans the threat of robot attacks against cities [by attacking] an industrial objective in a large German city as far inland as practicable." General "Hap" Arnold, commander of the U.S. Army Air Forces, wanted to go even further. In a November 23, 1944, letter to General Spaatz, Arnold proposed, "turn them [the Aphrodite bombers] loose to land all over Germany so that the Germans would be just as much afraid of our war weary planes on account of not knowing just where they were going to hit, as are the people in England from the [V-1] buzz bombs and [V-2] rockets." Ibid., 48–49, 57.

15. Ibid., 54–56.

16. Ibid., 58; Richard P. Hallion, "Precision Weapons, Power Projection and the Revolution in Military Affairs," unpublished paper, USAF Air Armament Summit, Eglin Air Force Base, Florida, May 26, 1999, http://www.airforcehistory.hq.af.mil/oldsite/Hallionpapers/precisionweaponspower.htm. Nevertheless, between December 1944 and March 1945, the Air Force's Seventh Bombardment

Group employed 459 Azons, with roughly 15 percent achieving direct hits. The Fritz-X had an estimated circular error probable (CEP) of fifteen feet and a 30 percent hit rate. CEP is defined as the radius of a circle within which 50 percent of the weapons employed are expected to fall. Thus, an aircraft carrying a bomb load of sixteen weapons with a CEP of 500 feet can—on average—expect half of those weapons (eight) to fall within 500 feet of the target. Yet despite the weapon's impressive performance, the Luftwaffe discontinued using it after 1943. This may have stemmed from parochial concerns within the Luftwaffe that the weapon could lead to a shift from fighter to bomber production or from an Allied bombing raid that destroyed on the ground the only Luftwaffe squadron capable of employing the Fritz-X.

17. Difficulty in obtaining data on the kamikazes has produced some significantly differing estimates regarding their operation and performance. For example, a postwar assessment concluded that roughly one-third of all kamikaze fighters who left their bases succeeded in hitting a ship—a success rate seven to ten times that of a conventional sortie but also more than twice the rate cited in other assessments. Spector, *At War, at Sea,* 312.

18. Gillespie, "Precision Guided Munitions," 79–80. One of the four experiments involving a "missile-like" weapon was a variant of the German V-1 "buzz bomb."

19. Mary R. Self, "History of the Development of Guided Missiles, 1946–1950," Wright-Patterson AFB, Ohio, December 1951, 32–34; Jacob Neufeld, "The Development of Ballistic Missiles in the United States Air Force 1945–1960," Office of Air Force History, United States Air Force, Washington, D.C., 1990, 11.

20. Gillespie, "Precision Guided Munitions," 87.

21. Ibid., 88.

22. Ibid., 91, 93. The name "Tarzon" is a combination of "Tallboy" (a 12,500-pound British-developed bomb) and "azimuth and range only." Troops pronounced it "Tarzan."

23. Ibid., 97.

24. Brian Daniel Laslie, "Red Flag: How the Rise of 'Realistic Training' After Vietnam Changed the Air Force's Way of War, 1975–1999" (Ph.D. diss., Kansas State University, 2013), 48; Paul R. Schratz, *Evolution of the American Military Establishment Since World War II* (Lexington, Va.: George C. Marshall Research Foundation, 1978), 63; Marshall L. Michel III, "Revolt of the Majors: How the Air Force Changed After Vietnam" (Ph.D. diss., Auburn University, 2006), 24.

25. Michel, "Revolt," 24–25.

26. Laslie, "Red Flag," 77–78.

27. Laslie, "Red Flag," 49–50, 77–78; Michel, "Revolt," 45, 194. See also Richard P. Hallion, "A Troubling Past: Air Force Fighter Acquisition Since 1945," *Air Power Journal* 4 (Winter 1990): 54–64.

28. Laslie, "Red Flag," 24–27.

29. Ibid., 14; Michel, "Revolt," 58–59, 62–64.

30. Grissom, Lee, and Mueller, *Innovation*, 45–46.
31. Gillespie, "Precision Guided Munitions," 104.
32. Grissom, Lee, and Mueller, *Innovation*, 46–47.
33. Stillion, *Air-to-Air Combat*, 10.
34. Watts, *Precision Strike*, 128.
35. Watts, *Precision Strike*, 112; Stillion, *Air-to-Air Combat*, 10. The Sparrow and Sidewinder may also have underperformed due to a lack of aircrew training with the missile. Lambeth, *American Air Power*, 43. The Air Force inventory also included the AIM-4 Falcon family of missiles. Like the Sparrow and Sidewinder, these missiles were designed with defeating Soviet bombers in mind. They were employed briefly to Southeast Asia but performed so poorly that they were soon abandoned in favor on the Sidewinder.
36. Watts, *Precision Strike*, 12–13.
37. Grissom, Lee, and Mueller, *Innovation*, 46–47. The SA-2 sites turned out to be decoys.
38. In August, Air Force chief of staff General John McConnell formed the Dempster Commission, named after its chairman, Brigadier General Kenneth Dempster, with the mission of "solving" the SA-2 problem. A Quick Reaction Capability program was used to procure new equipment on accelerated timelines. The Electronic Countermeasure Commission recommended that the Air Force procure Radar Homing and Warning Systems, ECM pods, and Navy Shrike anti-radiation missiles, systems already developed by the Strategic Air Command and the Navy that could be provided immediately to units in the field. The commission also recommended fielding what became known as the Wild Weasels. Ibid., 48–49.
39. Watts, *Precision Strike*, 6.
40. Grissom, Lee, and Mueller, *Innovation*, 50; Gillespie, "Precision Guided Munitions," 146.
41. Grissom, Lee, and Mueller, *Innovation*, 50.
42. Gillespie, "Precision Guided Munitions," 151.
43. Ibid., 29, 122, 152.
44. Ibid., 154, 156.
45. Ibid., 155–56.
46. Ibid., 157.
47. Watts, *Precision Strike*, 180.
48. Ibid., 181–82; Gillespie, "Precision Guided Munitions," 117.
49. Gillespie, "Precision Guided Munitions," 132.
50. Ibid., 133.
51. "Pave" is an acronym for "precision avionics vectoring equipment," which became nicknamed "Pave Way" and eventually "Paveway" for describing the entire family of laser-guided bombs. Ibid., 159–61; C. R. Anderegg, *Sierra Hotel: Flying Air Force Fighters in the Decade After Vietnam* (Washington, D.C.: United States Air Force History and Museums Program, 2001), 123.
52. Gillespie, "Precision Guided Munitions," 169.

53. Ibid., 163; Anderegg, *Sierra Hotel,* 124.

54. Gillespie, "Precision Guided Munitions," 163, 165; Watts, *Precision Strike,* 183–84.

55. The Air Force continued to make improvements as part of the "Pave" effort through the end of its combat operations in Southeast Asia in 1973. Some improvements focused on making aircraft employing LGBs more survivable. Pave Knife and its improved follow-on version, Pave Spike, led to the fielding of a laser designating pod carried beneath the aircraft that enabled self-designation, thereby reducing the number of aircraft required for a given mission. Pave Sword, which linked the designator to an IR targeting television aboard an AC-130 gunship, made night operations possible. This innovation robbed the enemy of its nighttime sanctuary while simultaneously exploiting the cover of darkness. Gillespie, "Precision Guided Munitions," 166, 173.

56. Ibid., 166; Slife, "Creech Blue," 18.

57. *Project Red Baron III: Air-to-Air Encounters in Southeast Asia (U),* vol. 3, part 1, *Tactics, Command and Control, and Training* (Nellis Air Force Base, Nev.: U.S. Air Force Tactical Fighter Weapons Center, June 1974), 61, cited in Watts, *Six Decades,* 45–46. The engagements analyzed all those occurring between U.S. and enemy fighters in Southeast Asia from December 1971 through January 1973. In these 112 encounters, 75 MiGs and 37 U.S. aircraft were lost.

58. Lambeth, *Air Power,* 45–46.

59. During the final thirteen months of Rolling Thunder, from October 1967 to October 1968, Navy pilots shot down nine MiGs against six losses, for a loss ratio of 1.5 to 1. Watts, *Precision Strike,* 136, 155.

60. Michel, "Revolt," 98–100.

61. Ibid., 103–4.

62. General William Momyer, USAF, *Air Power in Three Wars: WWII, Korea, Vietnam* (Washington, D.C.: Air Force History and Museums Program, 1978), 176–78.

63. Michel, "Revolt," 106–7.

64. Ibid., 51.

65. Grissom, Lee, and Mueller, *Innovation,* 51–52.

66. Michel, "Revolt," 144–46.

67. Ibid., 147, 149, 154.

68. Gillespie, "Precision Guided Munitions," 176.

69. Grissom, Lee, and Mueller, *Innovation,* 52.

70. Lambeth, *Air Power,* 48.

71. Ibid., 53; Slife, "Creech Blue," 18; Mets, "Search for Surgical Strike"; Lambeth, *Air Power,* 55–56; Stillion, *Air-to-Air Combat,* 16.

72. Grissom, Lee, and Mueller, *Innovation,* 53; Slife, "Creech Blue," 18.

73. Lambeth, *Air Power,* 69, 74.

74. Anderegg, *Sierra Hotel,* 127–28; Watts, *Precision Strike,* 7; Richard H. Van Atta, Michael J. Lippitz, Jasper C. Lupo, Rob Mahoney, and Jack H. Nunn, "Transformation and Transition: DARPA's Role in Fostering an Emerging

Revolution in Military Affairs: Volume 1—Overall Assessment," IDA Paper P-3698, Institute for Defense Analysis, April 2003, S-2.

75. Anderegg, *Sierra Hotel*, 61.

76. Watts, *Precision Strike*, 10, 184–85.

77. Gillespie, "Precision Guided Munitions," 191; Anderegg, *Sierra Hotel*, 135; Slife, "Creech Blue," 18.

78. Today it is known as the United States Air Force Warfare Center.

79. Anderegg, *Sierra Hotel*, 73–74.

80. Michel, "Revolt," 111–12.

81. Ibid., 112.

82. The MiGs were referred to as the "Red Eagles" and were assigned to the Air Force's 4477th Test and Evaluation Squadron, which began flying at Nellis in 1977. The first MiG-21 was given to the United States by Israel in 1966 and flown against Air Force and Navy aircraft in a program called HAVE DONUT. In 1968, the Israelis provided two MiG-17s, which underwent similar exercises, known as HAVE DRILL, which informed the Navy's Top Gun school. Maj. Ronald L. Rusing, USAF, "Prepare the Fighter-Red Flag/Composite Force" (master's thesis, U.S. Army Command and General Staff College, Fort Leavenworth, Kan., 1980), 12; Anderegg, *Sierra Hotel*, 73–74; Steve Davies, *Red Eagles: America's Secret MiGs* (Oxford, U.K.: Osprey, 2008), 10.

83. *Project Red Baron III*, 61, cited in Watts, *Six Decades*, 46. There were three Red Baron efforts. Project Red Baron I reported out in December 1966. Red Baron II and III did so in 1973 and 1974, respectively.

84. Michel, "Revolt," 211.

85. Laslie, "Red Flag," 51; Anderegg, *Sierra Hotel*, 51–52.

86. Michel, "Revolt," 196–97.

87. Ibid., 212–15.

88. Slife, "Creech Blue," 19.

89. The U.S. Pacific air forces initiated their own version of Red Flag, which they called "Cape Thunder," at Clark Air Base in the Philippines. The Canadian air forces started their version of Red Flag, named "Maple Flag," in 1978. Anderegg, *Sierra Hotel*, 97, 116; Lambeth, *Air Power*, 62.

90. Maj. Ronald L. Rusing, "Prepare the Fighter Force–Red Flag Composite Force," unpublished paper, U.S. Command and General Staff College, Fort Leavenworth, Kan., 1980, 24.

91. Michel, "Revolt," 239.

92. The assessment was conducted by members from the government, private industry, and academia. D. A. Paolucci, "Summary Report of the Long Range Research and Development Planning Program (Draft)," DARPA and Defense Nuclear Agency, February 7, 1975, iii, 1, 7–8, 45.

93. Testimony of William Perry to the U.S. Congress, Senate Committee on Armed Services, *Department of Defense Appropriations for FY77, Part 8: Research and Development*, February 28 and March 7, 9, 14, 16, 21, 1978, 76S181-68, 5598, cited in Van Atta et al., "Transformation and Transition," 18.

94. The term "Harvey" came from the motion picture of the same name, about a man whose friend is an invisible six-foot four-inch rabbit named Harvey.

95. Van Atta et al., "Transformation and Transition," 11–12.

96. Ibid.

97. Ibid., 13.

98. Ibid.; Ian A. Maddock, "DARPA's Stealth Revolution: Now You See Them . . .," DARPA, n.d., 152, https://www.hsdl.org/?abstract&did=805141.

99. Lockheed had not been invited to compete because DARPA was unaware of its work on the SR-71 aircraft. The Central Intelligence Agency allowed Lockheed to discuss its experience in stealth design with DARPA's director, George Heilmeier, who agreed to allow Lockheed to participate in the study under a one-dollar contract. Maddock, "DARPA's Stealth Revolution," 153.

100. Ibid., 153–54; Ben R. Rich and Leo Janos, *Skunk Works* (Boston: Little, Brown, 1994), 3–6.

101. Grissom, Lee, and Mueller, *Innovation*, 55; Van Atta et al., "Transformation and Transition," 11, 14; Maddock, "DARPA's Stealth Revolution," 154.

102. Watts, *Precision Strike*, 10.

103. Ibid., 196, 198.

104. Ibid., 194.

105. Ibid., 196–98. During the 1960s and most of the 1970s, the pilot in a squadron who could consistently drop his bombs most accurately in evaluations was accorded the highly sought status as the unit's "top gun."

106. United States Air Force, "Gen. Wilbur L. 'Bill' Creech: American Airmen, Breaking Barriers Since 1947: 1970–1980 Generation," accessed February 19, 2022, http://static.dma.mil/usaf/70/featuredHeros/GenWilburLCreech.html.

107. Slife, "Creech Blue," 39–40, 56.

108. Grissom, Lee, and Mueller, *Innovation*, 55.

109. Ibid., 28–29, 56.

110. Ibid., 30.

111. Ibid., 47.

112. Michel, "Revolt," 278–79.

113. Slife, "Creech Blue," 1.

114. United States Air Force, "Creech."

115. The reference is to the motion picture of the same name, in which the main character begins every day in the same circumstances as he did the day before.

116. Slife, "Creech Blue," 27–29; Grissom, Lee, and Mueller, *Innovation*, 56.

117. Slife, "Creech Blue," 29.

118. Laslie, "Red Flag," 101.

119. Grissom, Lee, and Mueller, *Innovation*, 57; Lambeth, *Air Power*, 63.

120. Slife, "Creech Blue," 52–53.

121. Grissom, Lee, and Mueller, *Innovation*, 57.

122. Slife, "Creech Blue," 10–11.

123. The Paveway II LGBs entered production in mid-1976. Their principal advantages over the Paveway I LGBs came in the form of folding fins that expanded the weapon's release envelope, along with their ability to be employed on a wide variety of U.S. and allied aircraft. Watts, *Precision Strike*, 190–91.

124. "Rockwell GBU-15(V)/B," *Directory of U.S. Military Rockets and Missiles*, accessed February 19, 2022, http://www.designation-systems.net/dusrm/m-112.html.

125. Gillespie, "Precision Guided Munitions," 198, 200–202. The GBU-27 is a GBU-24 adapted for use in the F-117 fighter.

126. GBU-27 production was eventually resumed for use with a hard-target kill warhead. Watts, *Precision Strike*, 190–91.

127. Slife, "Creech Blue," 54, 58.

128. Grissom, Lee, and Mueller, *Innovation*, 54; Slife, "Creech Blue," 57; Anderegg, *Sierra Hotel*, 99.

129. Grissom, Lee, and Mueller, *Innovation*, 53–55.

130. Slife, "Creech Blue," 57.

131. Stillion, *Air-to-Air Combat*, 19.

132. Ibid., 20.

133. Ibid., 22.

134. Slife, "Creech Blue," 32, 51.

135. According to General Joseph Ralston, who served as vice chairman of the Joint Chiefs of Staff and supreme allied commander of NATO, "LANTIRN would have died many times without Creech." Ibid., 32, 63; Watts, *Precision Strike*, 95.

136. Watts, *Precision Strike*, 192.

137. Michael Russell Rip and James M. Hasik, *The Precision Revolution: GPS and the Future of Aerial Warfare* (Annapolis, Md.: Naval Institute Press, 2002), 9, 66.

138. Ibid.; Watts, *Precision Strike*, 18.

139. Rip and Hasik, *Precision Revolution*, 12.

140. Ibid., 9. The Soviets deployed their Globalnaya Navigatsionaya Sputnikovaya Sistema (Global Navigation Satellite System, or GLONASS). The first GLONASS satellites were launched in October 1982. The system was not fully operational until 1995 but decayed soon after due to budget limitations. It was fully restored in 2011.

141. U.S. Air Force, "E-3 Sentry (AWACS)," September 22, 2015, https://www.af.mil/About-Us/Fact-Sheets/Display/Article/104504/e-3-sentry-awacs.

142. Lambeth, *Air Power*, 79.

143. The IFF system works by sending out a coded signal from an aircraft's radar. When a friendly aircraft equipped with an IFF system receives the signal, it responds with a coded signal of its own. If the challenged aircraft has the proper code in its system, it will be identified as "friend" and not "foe." Ideally, this enables friendly aircraft to avoid being attacked by friendly forces ("blue-on-blue" attacks or "friendly fire"). It also identifies enemy aircraft, as they will not respond properly. Unfortunately, a friendly

aircraft could also be identified as a foe if its IFF system were knocked out owing to battle damage or if it were simply out of order. The same would occur if the pilot inserted the wrong IFF code into the system.

144. Stillion, *Air-to-Air Combat*, 17.

145. Ibid., 17–18.

146. Although roughly half of the MiG kills claimed by Israeli fighters were achieved with Sparrow-equipped F-15s, the IAF insisted that its pilots "took no shots . . . from beyond visual range." Lambeth, *Air Power*, 93–94; Watts, *Precision Strike*, 142.

·147. Lambeth, *Air Power*, 92, 95.

148. Bernard Trainor, " '83 Strike on Lebanon: Hard Lessons for the U.S." *New York Times*, August 6, 1989, https://www.nytimes.com/1989/08/06/world/83-strike-on-lebanon-hard-lessons-for-us.html; Lambeth, *Air Power*, 96–98.

149. John Pike, "Operation El Dorado Canyon," GlobalSecurity.org, last modified May 7, 2011, https://www.globalsecurity.org/military/ops/el_dorado_canyon.htm; Lambeth, *Air Power*, 100–101.

150. Major Todd R. Phinney, "Airpower Versus Terrorism: Three Case Studies," unpublished paper, School of Advanced Air and Space Studies, June 2003, 19–20.

151. Other organizations that sought to further the DRM's objectives were Business Executives for National Security, the Military Reform Institute, and the Project on Military Procurement. Public-policy research institutes, such as the Center for Strategic and International Studies, the Heritage Foundation, and the Hudson Institute, were also involved in the movement. Peter W. Chiarelli and Raymond C. Gagnon, "The Politics of Military Reform," unpublished paper, U.S. Naval War College, June 1985, iv, http://www.dtic.mil/dtic/tr/fulltext/u2/a158220.pdf.

152. Gary Hart, "The Need for Military Reform," *Air University Review* 36 (September–October 1985): 43–44.

153. Slife, "Creech Blue," 69, 129–30.

154. Michel, "Revolt," 367–68.

155. Slife, "Creech Blue," 43, 46.

156. Warden's five rings held that the center, most crucial ring comprised the state's leaders. This ring was encompassed by the outer four rings. Moving out from the center, the second ring represented military production, including factories producing war matériel. The third ring comprised key infrastructure, including railroads and power grids. The population was included in the fourth ring. The fifth and outermost ring was the nation's armed forces. Warden argued that instead of attacking the enemy's forces, air power could be employed to attack the national leadership in the first ring, something he and his supporters called "inside-out warfare." Colonel Edward C. Mann III, *Thunder and Lightning: Desert Storm and the Airpower Debates* (Maxwell Air Force Base, Ala.: Air University Press, April 1995), 35–36.

157. Slife, "Creech Blue," 113–14; Grissom, Lee, and Mueller, *Innovation*, 63.

158. Slife, "Creech Blue," 113–14; Mann, *Thunder and Lightning,* 60–61, 63; Abraham Jackson, "America's Airman: David Deptula and the Airpower Moment," unpublished paper, School of Advanced Air and Space Studies, Air University, Maxwell Air Force Base, Ala., June 2011, 23.

159. Mann, *Thunder and Lightning,* 60–61.

160. Slife, "Creech Blue," 114–15.

161. Ibid.

162. Lambeth, *Air Power,* 110; Mann, *Thunder and Lightning,* 18.

163. Laslie, "Red Flag," 174–75.

164. Slife, "Creech Blue," 116; Grissom, Lee, and Mueller, *Innovation,* 67–68; Mann, *Thunder and Lightning,* 39, 46.

165. Watts, *Precision Strike,* 260.

166. Ibid., 152.

167. Lambeth, *Air Power,* 113.

168. Laslie, "Red Flag," 211–12; Slife, "Creech Blue," 129–30.

169. Mets, "Search for Surgical Strike," 37.

170. Watts, *Precision Strike,* 143.

171. Ibid., 145–46.

172. Ibid., 145–46, 188.

173. Stillion, *Air-to-Air Combat,* 26, 28.

174. Slife, "Creech Blue," 129–30.

175. Watts, *Precision Strike,* 8, 123.

176. Ibid., 144; Stillion, *Air-to-Air Combat,* 28–29. During 1965–73, of the 195 enemy aircraft downed by U.S. fighters, 56 (28.7 percent) were by AIM-7s. During Operation Desert Storm, coalition fighters scored 38 air-to-air kills, 26 (68.4 percent) with the AIM-7M.

177. Stillion, *Air-to-Air Combat,* 25, 28.

178. The growth in BVR engagements has enormous implications for air operations. As John Stillion notes,

> This transformation may be steadily reducing the utility of some attributes traditionally associated with fighter aircraft (e.g., extreme speed and maneuverability) while increasing the value of attributes not usually associated with fighter aircraft (e.g., sensor and weapon payload as well as range). Aircraft performance attributes essential for success in air-to-air combat during the gun and early missile eras such as high speed, good acceleration, and maneuverability are much less useful now that aircraft can be detected and engaged from dozens of miles away. At the same time, nontraditional attributes such as minimal radar and IR signature; space, payload, and cooling capacity; power for large-aperture long-range sensors; and very-long-range weapons seem to be of increased importance.

Ibid., iii; see also Watts, *Precision Strike,* 144–45.

179. Slife, "Creech Blue," 129–30.
180. Major General David A. Deptula, "Air Force Transformation: Past, Present, and Future," *Aerospace Power Journal* 15 (Fall 2001): 86.
181. Although the Gulf War Air Power Survey found that F-117 pilots hit their aim points 80 percent of the time, the U.S. Government Accounting Office argued that the F-117's hit rate may have been as low as 55 percent. The office arrived at the lower estimate based primarily on discounting pilot claims regarding hits and poor cockpit video quality. As Barry Watts notes, however, "even if the F-117's hit rate was *only* 55 percent, this lower hit rate would still appear to be more than sufficient to alter, fundamentally, the conduct of future air operations." Watts, *Precision Strike*, 8, 203–4. And, indeed, following the Gulf War, the Air Force began to shift away from "dumb" bombs to guided weapons in major air campaigns.
182. Mets, "Search for Surgical Strike," 36.
183. Lambeth, *Air Power*, 155–56.
184. The Air Force dropped roughly 93 percent of all guided weapons employed by U.S. air forces during the war, and approximately 80 percent of all guided weapons used by Coalition air forces. British Royal Air Force Tornado and Buccaneer aircraft, and French Air Force Jaguars also employed LGBs. The remaining guided weapons used were primarily the Maverick and the Hellfire missiles, as well as cruise missiles, anti-radiation missiles, and small numbers of special weapons. Hallion, "New Era of Warfare," 9.
185. Lambeth, *Air Power*, 160; Watts, *Precision Strike*, 8.
186. Lambeth, *Air Power*, 160; Gillespie, "Precision Guided Munitions," 203.
187. Watts, *Precision Strike*, 203.
188. Lambeth, *Air Power*, 125.
189. Slife, "Creech Blue," 129–30.
190. Ibid.
191. Lambeth, *Air Power*, 268.
192. That being said, 71 percent of all coalition fixed-wing aircraft lost or damaged in the First Gulf War were hit by AAA or short-range infrared SAMs. Ibid., 120. As noted earlier, however, the coalition's loss rate per sortie was more than an order of magnitude lower than the Vietnam War loss rate. The data also confirm Creech's vision of the need to develop an operational concept that would enable the Air Force to move beyond its "go-low" tactics.
193. Slife, "Creech Blue," 136.
194. Ibid., 138.
195. Michel, "Revolt," 398.
196. Gillespie, "Precision Guided Munitions," 196.
197. Soviet military leaders were also sensitive to what the First Gulf War implied for the military balance vis-à-vis the United States and sought to discount shortcomings in the Russian military equipment they had provided to the Iraqis. Among the Iraqi military deficiencies they cited were "the

lower level of training of command personnel, weak morale and psychological preparation of personnel, the unwieldy, poorly controllable, organization of strategic, operational, and tactical units, and the instability of control and communications systems and of combat and logistics support." Defense Intelligence Agency, "Soviet Analysis of Operation Desert Storm and Operation Desert Shield," October 28, 1991, 75, 77. Nevertheless, other Arab militaries, such as the Egyptian armed forces that exacted a fearful toll on Israeli aircraft in the Yom Kippur War and the Syrian IADS that downed several U.S. Navy aircraft during the December 1983 strike in Lebanon, performed well when confronted by advanced air forces employing outdated tactics and unimaginative operational concepts.

198. Both the JDAM and JSOW are initially guided by an inertial measurement unit that brings them very close to their aim point. They are also equipped with a relatively simple GPS receiver that receives updates as they are falling toward their target. Mets, "Search for Surgical Strike," 43. In 2009, the Air Force and Navy introduced the Joint Air-to-Surface Standoff Missile (JASSM), a stealthy 1,000-pound guided weapon that can be launched around 200 miles from its target. For guidance, the JASSM combines GPS cuing, inertial navigation, and a terminal IR seeker. An extended-range JASSM (JASSM-ER) is projected to have a range of over 500 miles. Gillespie, "Precision Guided Munitions," 59, 209–10.

199. Mets, "Search for Surgical Strike," 45, 113.

200. In 1991, the biggest obstacle to defeating Iraqi's mobile Scud launchers was not sensor-to-shooter cycle time per se but sensor limitations. Before the war, the Air Force flew F-111Fs and F-15Es in exercises against an actual Scud transporter-erector-launcher at night. The crews discovered that if the missile was not erected, they had little luck finding the transporter-erector-launcher using their onboard sensors, even when given the Scud's coordinates prior to takeoff. Operation Allied Force offers a better example of the challenge of compressing engagement cycle times. When the Air Force started going after Serbian ground equipment in Kosovo, the shortest time lags between sensing and ordnance release were a few hours. Still, this gave the Serbians enough time to relocate their equipment before U.S. strike aircraft arrived.

201. Douglas Jehl, "Digital Links Are Giving Old Weapons New Power," *New York Times*, April 7, 2003, 2.

202. Tom Bowman, "Strike Team Advances Precision, Pace of War," *Baltimore Sun*, April 20, 2003, 1A. Al-Majid earned his nickname for ordering poison-gas attacks against thousands of Kurds, including women and children, in 1988. Despite the relatively prompt strike, the general survived the attempt to kill him. He was finally captured in August 2003. According to U.S. Central Command Air Forces, U.S. aircraft conducted 156 missions against time-sensitive targets and 686 missions involving dynamic targeting. Moseley, "Operation Iraqi Freedom," 9.

Chapter Ten. Echoes of History

1. Lambert, *Fisher's Revolution*, 107.
2. Ibid., 92.
3. Von Seeckt, *Gedanken eines Soldaten*, 77, quoted in Citino, *Evolution of Blitzkrieg*, 72.
4. Heineman, "Armoured Forces," 40–41.
5. Reynolds, *Fast Carriers*, 1.
6. Trimble, *Moffett*, 228.
7. Slife, "Creech Blue," 30.
8. It bears noting that Vice Admiral Hyman Rickover, widely considered the father of the U.S. Navy's nuclear-powered submarine force, held his position as head of the Navy's Reactors Branch from 1949 to 1982.
9. Lord John Fisher to Lord Selborne, January 13, 1901, in *Fear God and Dread Nought*, vol. 1, 181. "Buggins's turn" was a promotion system based on seniority rather than on merit.
10. Ruddock F. Mackay, *Fisher of Kilverstone* (Oxford, U.K.: Clarendon, 1973), 297.
11. Massie, *Dreadnought*, 449–50.
12. Slife, "Creech Blue," 111.
13. Fairbanks, "Choosing Among Technologies," 128.
14. Heineman, "Armoured Forces," 40–41.
15. Watts, *Six Decades*, 20.
16. Friedman, "Aircraft Carrier," 39; Reynolds, *Towers*, 205.
17. The same tends to be true of transformation in other large, competitive organizations. John P. Kotter, "Leading Change: Why Transformation Efforts Fail," *Harvard Business Review* 73 (March–April 1995): 59–67. Kotter emphasizes the importance of creating "short-term wins." He notes, "Most people won't go on in the long march unless they see compelling evidence within 12 to 24 months that the [transformation] journey is producing expected results." Similarly, field exercises can do much to convince the officer corps that new warfare challenges are real and that there are innovative ways of dealing with them.
18. Lambert, *Fisher's Revolution*, 92.
19. The four classes were the *Grasshopper* (three ships), *Sharpshooter* (thirteen ships), *Alarm* (eleven ships), and *Dryad* (five ships), for a total of thirty-two dead-end ships.
20. Lambert, *Fisher's Revolution*, 246.
21. At the time of the Armistice, the Royal Navy had one carrier of the *Argus* class and three carriers in the *Glorious* class.
22. Some 153 divisions were involved in the campaign, of which 18 were either panzer or motorized divisions. "German Orders of Battle for the Campaign in the West, May 1940," *WW2-Weapons.com*, accessed February 19, 2022, https://ww2-weapons.com/german-orders-of-battle-for-the-campaign-in-the-west-may-1940.

23. The U.S. fleet at the time comprised 17 battleships, 7 carriers, 18 heavy cruisers, 19 light cruisers, 6 anti-aircraft cruisers, 171 destroyers, and 114 submarines. "U.S. Navy in Late 1941," *WW2-Weapons.com*, accessed February 14, 2022, https://ww2-weapons.com/us-navy-in-late-1941.

24. Dick Cheney, Secretary of Defense, *Annual Report to the President and the Congress* (Washington, D.C.: Department of Defense, February 1992), 138; Gillespie, "Precision Guided Munitions," 203; Lambeth, *Air Power*, 160; Hallion, "New Era of Warfare," 9.

25. P. G. Halpern, *A Naval History of World War I* (London: UCL Press, 1994), 7–20.

26. Doughty, *Breaking Point*, 247–49.

27. Alan Clark, *Barbarossa: The Russian-German Conflict, 1941–1945* (New York: Quill, 1965), 80–82.

28. Hughes, *Fleet Tactics*, 118.

29. Hone, Friedman, and Mandeles, *Aircraft Carrier Development*, 162.

30. Ibid., 125.

31. "BCG Matrix: Portfolio Analysis in Corporate Strategy," *Business-to-You*, accessed February 14, 2022, https://www.business-to-you.com/bcg-matrix.

32. Michael E. Porter, "The Competitive Advantage of Nations," *Harvard Business Review*, March–April 1990, 73.

33. George Stalk, Jr., "Time—The Next Source of Competitive Advantage," *Harvard Business Review*, July–August 1988, 41.

34. Kotter, "Leading Change," 63.

35. Bower and Christensen, "Disruptive Technologies," 47, 53.

36. Porter, "Competitive Advantage," 75.

37. Kotter, "Leading Change," 59.

38. Porter, "Competitive Advantage," 75.

39. Ibid.

40. Bower and Christensen, "Disruptive Technologies," 50.

41. Kotter, "Leading Change," 64.

42. Ibid., 60, 66.

43. Bower and Christensen, "Disruptive Technologies," 44, 50.

44. The term "pickle barrel accuracy" originated in the 1930s when the U.S. Army Air Corps developed the Norden Bombsight, which a pilot could use to "drop a bomb in a pickle barrel at 30,000 feet." As it turned out, during World War II, the combination of trained bombardier and bombsight failed to achieve anything close to the predicted results. Ironically, the bombsight was used in dropping the atomic bomb on the city of Hiroshima, Japan, in a situation where accuracy was of negligible importance. Christopher Kratzer, "The Enigma of the Norden Bombsight," Maxwell Air Force Base, January 20, 2012, https://www.maxwell.af.mil/News/Display/Article/420450/the-enigma-of-the-norden-bombsight.

45. Bower and Christensen, "Disruptive Technologies," 49.

Chapter Eleven. Where Do We Stand?

1. The reference here is to the National Defense Strategy summary document, which is unclassified. James Mattis, *Summary of the 2018 National Defense Strategy of the United States of America*, 2018, https://dod.defense.gov/Portals/1/Documents/pubs/2018-National-Defense-Strategy-Summary.pdf. The U.S. National Military Strategy is also silent on the subject. Joint Staff, *Description of the National Military Strategy*, 2018, https://www.jcs.mil/Portals/36/Documents/Publications/UNCLASS_2018_National_Military_Strategy_Description.pdf.

2. H. H. Gaffney, "Capabilities-Based Planning in the Coming Global Security Environment," CNA Center for Strategic Studies, September 2004. See also Colonel Michael W. Pietrucha, "Capability-Based Planning and the Death of Military Strategy," *U.S. Naval Institute News*, August 3, 2015, https://news.usni.org/2015/08/05/essay-capability-based-planning-and-the-death-of-military-strategy.

3. Secretary of Defense Les Aspin and General Colin Powell, "Department of Defense Bottom-Up Review," Department of Defense news conference, September 1, 1993, Pentagon, Washington, D.C., quoted in Andrew F. Krepinevich, Jr., *Operation Iraqi Freedom: A First-Blush Assessment* (Washington, D.C.: CSBA, 2003), 1.

4. Following the U.S. withdrawal from an active combat role in Indochina in 1973 and the fall of the Saigon regime in May 1975, the mood among Americans was for "no more Vietnams." This desire to avoid counterinsurgency warfare operations had bipartisan support, ranging from Defense Secretary Caspar Weinberger's "Six Tests" that should be satisfied before committing U.S. forces to such conflicts to the requirement for "exit strategies" that marked the debate over interventions in the developing world during the Clinton administration.

5. Andrew F. Krepinevich, Jr., *Why AirSea Battle?* (Washington, D.C.: CSBA, 2010); Jan van Tol, Mark Gunzinger, Andrew F. Krepinevich, and Jim Thomas, *AirSea Battle: A Point of Departure Operational Concept* (Washington, D.C.: CSBA, 2010).

6. As a member of the 1997 National Defense Panel, I was involved in the negotiations that led to Joint Forces Command being formed. From 2004 to 2011, I also served on its advisory board.

7. The process is described in Chairman of the Joint Chiefs of Staff Instruction 3010.02E, *Guidance for Developing and Implementing Joint Concepts* (Washington, D.C.: Chairman of the Joint Chiefs of Staff, August 17, 2016).

8. Air-Sea Battle Office, "Air-Sea Battle: Service Collaboration to Address Anti-Access and Area Denial Challenges," May 2013, i.

9. Sam LaGrone, "Pentagon Drops Air Sea Battle Name. Concept Lives On," *USNI News*, January 20, 2015, https://news.usni.org/2015/01/20/pentagon-drops-air-sea-battle-name-concept-lives-on.

10. Although the Summer Study lasts less than two weeks, a great deal of preparatory work is done prior to the event. A successful Summer Study finds the chairperson arriving with what amounts to a rough draft of the final outbrief, which is then subjected to rigorous scrutiny by the study members.

11. Andrew F. Krepinevich, Jr., "How to Deter China: The Case for Archipelagic Defense," *Foreign Affairs* 94 (March–April 2015): 78–86.

12. Andrew F. Krepinevich, Jr., *Archipelagic Defense: The Japan-U.S. Alliance and Preserving Peace and Stability in the Western Pacific* (Tokyo: Sasakawa Peace Foundation, 2017).

13. The Group of Five includes Australia, France, Great Britain, Japan, and the United States. India was invited to participate but declined.

14. Mattis, *National Defense Strategy*, 3.

15. National Defense Strategy Commission, "Providing for the Common Defense," U.S. Institute of Peace, x, 19. I served on the commission.

16. David E. Johnson, "Shared Problems: The Lessons of AirLand Battle and the 31 Initiatives for Multi-Domain Battle," *Rand Perspective*, August 2018, 6. In critiquing the Army's Multi-Domain Operations concept, one of the people involved in crafting the AirLand Battle doctrine, Brigadier General (Retired) Huba Wass de Czege, noted the absence of a "well-developed theory of the problem" (e.g., What adversary are we trying to deter or defeat, in what theater, and under what circumstances? What enemy advantages must be overcome? What enemy weaknesses can be exploited?). He went on to note the absence of a "theory of victory" (e.g., What is the operational concept intended to accomplish against the enemy that has been identified? In the case of AirLand Battle, the goal was to deter an attack on NATO by defeating Warsaw Pact armies, with emphasis on its front-line forces, whereas the Multi-Domain concept is focused on a "generic" threat). Wass de Czege also lamented the "use of vague language [that] confounds the reader's understanding of the concept. For example, the frequent use of ill-defined terms such as *standoff* and *domain* confuse the already thin logic of the concept." Huba Wass de Czege, *Commentary of the U.S. Army in Multi-Domain Operations in 2028* (Carlisle, Pa.: U.S. Army War College Strategic Studies Institute, April 2020), xix, xx, 16, 38–39.

17. Colin Clark, "Gen. Hyten on the New American War of War: All-Domain Operations," *Breaking Defense*, February 18, 2020, https://breakingdefense.com/2020/02/gen-hyten-on-the-new-american-way-of-war-all-domain-operations.

18. Theresa Hitchens, "JROC Struggles to Build 'Information Advantage' Requirement," *Breaking Defense*, September 17, 2020, https://breakingdefense.com/2020/09/jroc-struggles-to-build-information-advantage-requirement.

19. Thomas C. Greenwood and Patrick J. Savage, "Concept for Joint Warfighting," Institute for Defense Analysis, Spring 2021, https://www.ida.org/research-and-publications/publications/all/w/we/welch-award-2020-research-notes-spring-2021.

20. Admiral Philip Davidson, "Transforming the Joint Force: A Warfighting Concept for Great Power Competition," speech, San Diego, Calif., March 3, 2020, https://www.pacom.mil/Media/Speeches-Testimony/Article/2101115/transforming-the-joint-force-a-warfighting-concept-for-great-power-competition; Paul McLeary, "Indo-Pacom Presses All Domain Ops: Sends Plan to Hill Soon," *Breaking Defense*, March 24, 2020, https://breakingdefense.com/2020/03/indo-pacom-presses-all-domain-ops-sends-plan-to-hill-soon.

21. Theresa Hitchens, "The Joint Warfighting Concept Failed, Until It Focused on Space and Cyber," *Breaking Defense*, July 26, 2021, https://breakingdefense.com/2021/07/the-joint-warfighting-concept-failed-until-it-focused-on-space-and-cyber.

22. Ibid.

23. David Vergun, "DOD Focuses on Aspirational Challenges in Future Warfighting," *DOD News*, July 26, 2021, https://www.defense.gov/Explore/News/Article/Article/2707633/dod-focuses-on-aspirational-challenges-in-future-warfighting/source/GovDelivery; Jane Edwards, "Gen John Hyten Advances Joint Warfighting Concept with 4 Strategic Directives," *ExecutiveGov*, June 25, 2021, https://www.executivegov.com/2021/06/gen-john-hyten-advances-joint-warfighting-concept-with-4-strategic-directives.

24. Generally speaking, greater weapon range would enable a naval combatant to cover a greater area, offsetting the need for more ships armed with weapons of lesser range. Weapons of greater range could also boost the value of weapon speed as an MOE, especially when attacking mobile targets.

25. Tyler Rogoway, "You Have to Hear What Keeps the Head of U.S. Strategic Command Up at Night," *The War Zone*, September 22, 2017, https://www.thedrive.com/the-war-zone/14564/you-have-to-hear-what-keeps-the-head-of-u-s-strategic-command-up-at-night.

26. Among the systems that have been canceled over the past two decades are the Joint Tactical Radio System; the Army's Future Combat System, Crusader artillery system, Comanche helicopter, and Ground Combat Vehicle; the Navy's CG(X) Cruiser and DDG-21 Destroyer (after only three were produced as part of the Zumwalt class); the Air Force's Airborne Laser and Transformational Satellite Communications System; and the Marine Corps' Expeditionary Fighting Vehicle. Stephen Rodriguez, "Top 10 Failed Defense Programs of the RMA Era," *War on the Rocks*, December 2, 2014, https://warontherocks.com/2014/12/top-10-failed-defense-programs-of-the-rma-era; Robert S. Dudney, "The 75 Percent Force," *Air Force Magazine*, March 1, 2009, https://www.airforcemag.com/article/0309edit.

Index